A COMPANION
TO
GREEK TRAGEDY

BLACKWELL COMPANIONS TO THE ANCIENT WORLD

This series provides sophisticated and authoritative overviews of periods of ancient history, genres of classical literature, and the most important themes in ancient culture. Each volume comprises between twenty-five and forty concise essays written by individual scholars within their area of specialization. The essays are written in a clear, provocative, and lively manner, designed for an international audience of scholars, students, and general readers.

ANCIENT HISTORY

Published

A Companion to the Ancient Near East
Edited by Daniel C. Snell

A Companion to the Hellenistic World
Edited by Andrew Erskine

In preparation

A Companion to the Archaic Greek World
Edited by Kurt A. Raaflaub and Hans van Wees

A Companion to the Classical Greek World
Edited by Konrad H. Kinzl

A Companion to the Roman Republic
Edited by Nathan Rosenstein and Robert Morstein-Marx

A Companion to the Roman Empire
Edited by David Potter

A Companion to the Roman Army
Edited by Paul Erdkamp

A Companion to Byzantium
Edited by Elizabeth James

A Companion to Late Antiquity
Edited by Philip Rousseau

LITERATURE AND CULTURE

Published

A Companion to Ancient Epic
Edited by John Miles Foley

A Companion to Greek Tragedy
Edited by Justina Gregory

A Companion to Latin Literature
Edited by Stephen Harrison

In preparation

A Companion to Classical Mythology
Edited by Ken Dowden

A Companion to Greek and Roman Historiography
Edited by John Marincola

A Companion to Greek Religion
Edited by Daniel Ogden

A Companion to Greek Rhetoric
Edited by Ian Worthington

A Companion to Roman Rhetoric
Edited by William J. Dominik and Jonathan Hall

A Companion to the Classical Tradition
Edited by Craig Kallendorf

A Companion to Roman Religion
Edited by Jörg Rüpke

A COMPANION TO GREEK TRAGEDY

Edited by

Justina Gregory

Blackwell
Publishing

© 2005 by Blackwell Publishing Ltd

BLACKWELL PUBLISHING
350 Main Street, Malden, MA 02148-5020, USA
9600 Garsington Road, Oxford OX4 2DQ, UK
550 Swanston Street, Carlton, Victoria 3053, Australia

The right of Justina Gregory to be identified as the Author of the Editorial Material in this Work has been
asserted in accordance with the UK Copyright, Designs, and Patents Act 1988.

First published 2005 by Blackwell Publishing Ltd

Library of Congress Cataloging-in-Publication Data

A companion to Greek tragedy / edited by Justina Gregory.
    p. cm.—(Blackwell companions to the ancient world. Ancient history)
  Includes bibliographical references and index.
  ISBN-13: 978-1-4051-0770-9 (alk. paper)
  ISBN-10: 1-4051-0770-7 (alk. paper)

1. Greek drama (Tragedy)—History and criticism. I. Gregory, Justina.
II. Series.

PA3131.C56 2006
882'.0109—dc22   2004024920

A catalogue record for this title is available from the British Library.

Set in 10/12pt Galliard
by SPI Publisher Services, Pondicherry, India.
Printed and bound in India
by Replika Press

The publisher's policy is to use permanent paper from mills that operate a sustainable forestry policy, and
which has been manufactured from pulp processed using acid-free and elementary chlorine-free practices.
Furthermore, the publisher ensures that the text paper and cover board used have met acceptable
environmental accreditation standards.

For further information on
Blackwell Publishing, visit our website:
www.blackwellpublishing.com

Maenad and *aulos*-player. Attic red-figure pelike in the style of the earlier Mannerists. ca. 460 BCE. BPK Berlin, Antikensammlung, Staatliche Museen Zu Berlin. Photo: Johannes Laurentius.

Contents

Contents

Illustrations

Contributors

William Allan is McConnell Laing Fellow and Tutor in Classics at University College, Oxford. His publications include *The Andromache and Euripidean Tragedy* (Oxford, 2000; paperback, 2003), *Euripides: The Children of Heracles* (Aris and Phillips, 2001), and *Euripides: Medea* (Duckworth, 2002). He is currently writing a commentary on Euripides' *Helen* for the Cambridge Greek and Latin Classics series.

Herman Altena is a freelance academic and translator with a one-man business, Antiek Theater. He teaches ancient Greek drama and its reception in the Netherlands at the Department of Theater Studies of the University of Utrecht. He has translated several Greek tragedies for the Dutch professional theater and worked as a dramaturge. He is the Dutch representative in the European Network of Research and Documentation of Ancient Greek Drama.

Michael J. Anderson is an associate professor of Classics at Yale University. His principal research interests are archaic and classical Greek poetry and the Greek novels. His book *The Fall of Troy in Early Greek Poetry and Art* (Oxford,

1997) includes a study of treatments of the sack of Troy in Athenian tragedy.

Luigi Battezzato studied at the Scuola Normale Superiore, Pisa, at the University of California, Berkeley, and at University College London. He has written a book on monologues in Euripides, and several articles on Greek tragedy. His research interests include literary and social problems in ancient Greek texts. He has also published on textual criticism, and on ancient Greek language and meter. He teaches at the Università del Piemonte Orientale, Vercelli, Italy.

Douglas Cairns has taught at the universities of St. Andrews, Otago, Leeds, and Glasgow, and is now Professor of Classics in the University of Edinburgh. He is the author of *Aidôs: The Psychology and Ethics of Honour and Shame in Ancient Greek Literature* (1993) and editor of *Oxford Readings in Homer's Iliad* (2001) and (with R. A. Knox) of *Law, Rhetoric, and Comedy in Classical Athens* (2004).

Neil Croally assisted in the Royal Shakespeare Company's production of *The Thebans* in 1990–91. His doctorate was published as *Euripidean Polemic* by Cambridge University Press in 1994. Since 1990 he has taught Classics at Dulwich College in London. Teaching has left little time for theorizing; instead he has used his school's resources to stage a number of Greek plays in a variety of inauthentic ways. He thanks Jo, Mary, and Puss.

Martin Cropp is Professor of Greek and Roman Studies at the University of Calgary. He studied at Oxford and Toronto before moving to Calgary in 1974. His books include commentaries on Euripides' *Electra* (1988) and *Iphigenia in Tauris* (2000), contributions to *Euripides: Selected Fragmentary Plays* (Vol. 1: 1995; Vol. 2: 2004) with Christopher Collard, Kevin Lee, and John Gibert, and the edited volume *Euripides and Late Fifth Century Tragic Theatre* (*Illinois Classical Studies* 24/25, 1999–2000, with Kevin Lee, David Sansone, and others).

John Davidson holds the Chair of Classics at Victoria University of Wellington, New Zealand, where he has been since 1969 after completing a doctorate at London. T. B. L. Webster Fellow at the School of Advanced Studies in London in 2003, he has published extensively on various aspects of Greek drama, including theatrical production and the relationship between the Homeric texts and the tragedies of Sophocles and Euripides.

Paula Debnar, an associate professor of Classics at Mount Holyoke College, is the author of *Speaking the Same Language: Speech and Audience in Thucydides' Spartan Debates* (2001) and several articles on the rhetoric of Thucydidean speakers. She is currently at work on an article on the figure of Cassandra in Aeschylus' *Agamemnon* and a study of the Spartan general Brasidas.

Salvatore Di Maria is Professor of Italian at the University of Tennessee. His scholarly interests range from Dante and Ariosto (his annotated bibliography of Ariosto was published by the University of Missouri Press in 1984) to Machiavelli's theater and political writings. He recently published *The Italian Tragedy in the Renaissance* (Bucknell, 2002). At present he is working on the originality of imitation in the Renaissance theater.

Mary Ebbott is an assistant professor of Classics at the College of the Holy Cross in Worcester, Massachusetts, and an executive editor for the Center for Hellenic Studies in Washington, DC. She is the author of *Imagining Illegitimacy in Classical Greek Literature* (Lanham, Md., 2003). Her current work focuses on the language of physical pain and its limitations in Greek epic and tragedy.

Justina Gregory is Professor of Classical Languages and Literatures at Smith College. Her books include a translation of Aesop's *Fables* (1975, with Patrick Gregory), *Euripides and the Instruction of the Athenians* (1991), and a commentary on Euripides' *Hecuba* (1999). She is currently working on representations of education in Greek literature.

Mark Griffith is Professor of Classics, and of Theater, Dance, and Performance Studies, at the University of California, Berkeley. He has published editions of *Prometheus Bound* and *Antigone* in the Cambridge Greek and Latin Classics series, as well as a number of articles on Greek tragedy, poetry, and culture.

Michael R. Halleran is Professor of Classics and Divisional Dean of Arts and Humanities in the College of Arts and Sciences at the University of Washington. His primary area of scholarship is ancient Greek drama, and he has published widely on Greek literature and culture, including *Stagecraft in Euripides* (1985), *The Heracles of Euripides: Translated with Introduction, Notes, and Interpretative Essay* (1988), *Euripides: Hippolytus, with Translation and Commentary* (1995), and *Euripides' Hippolytus: Translated with Introduction, Notes, and Essay* (2001).

Stephen Halliwell is Professor of Greek at the University of St. Andrews. He is the author of seven books (including works on Aristophanes, Aristotle, and Plato), of which the most recent is *The Aesthetics of Mimesis: Ancient Texts and Modern Problems* (2002), and more than sixty articles on Greek literature, philosophy, rhetoric, and interdisciplinary cultural themes. He is currently working on *Greek Laughter: A Study in Cultural Psychology.* See further at www.st-andrews.ac.uk/classics/staff/ halliwell.shtml.

Albert Henrichs is Eliot Professor of Greek Literature at Harvard University. Born and educated in Germany, he received his Dr. phil. and his habilitation from the University of Cologne. He has written extensively on Greek literature, religion, and myth. His major areas of research include the Greek god Dionysus and his modern reception, the representation of ritual in literature and art, the religious self-awareness of the Greeks, and the history of classical scholarship since 1800. He is the author of *Die Götter Griechenlands: Ihr Bild im Wandel der Religionswissenschaft* (1987) and of *Warum soll ich denn tanzen? Dionysisches im Chor der griechischen Tragödie* (1996).

David Kovacs is Professor of Classics at the University of Virginia. He is the editor and translator of Euripides for the Loeb Classical Library. In addition to the six Loeb volumes he has written

three companion volumes discussing textual problems and setting out the ancient evidence for the life of Euripides. He is also the author of two monographs on Euripides and some thirty articles on tragic topics.

Ismene Lada-Richards is a lecturer in Classics at King's College London. She is the author of *Initiating Dionysus: Ritual and Theatre in Aristophanes' Frogs* (Oxford, 1999) and numerous articles on Greek drama in its ritual and performative context. Her current research interests range from post-hellenistic theater and Roman drama to aspects of the classical tradition and the cultural history of the European stage. She is completing a book on pantomime dancing in imperial and late antiquity.

Donald Mastronarde was educated at Amherst College, Oxford University, and the University of Toronto. Since 1973 he has taught at the University of California, Berkeley, where he is now Melpomene Distinguished Professor of Classical Languages and Literature. He has edited Euripides' *Phoenissae* in the Teubner series (1988), produced commentaries on Euripides' *Phoenissae* (Cambridge, 1994) and *Medea* (Cambridge, 2002), and published on other topics in ancient drama.

Judith Mossman is Professor of Classics at the University of Nottingham. She has published a book on Euripides' *Hecuba* and is currently preparing an edition of Euripides' *Medea*. She is also working on a book on women's speech in Greek tragedy.

Vassiliki Panoussi is an assistant professor of Classics at Williams College. Her research focuses on intertextuality, cultural anthropology, and the study of women and gender in antiquity. She is the author of articles on Vergil, Lucan, and Catullus, and is currently completing a book-length study of Vergil's *Aeneid* and its intertextual and ideological relationship to Greek tragedy.

Christopher Pelling has been Regius Professor of Greek at Oxford University since 2003; before that he was McConnell Laing Fellow and Praelector in Classics at University College, Oxford. His books include *Plutarch: Life of Antony* (Cambridge, 1988), *Literary Texts and the Greek Historian* (Routledge, 2000), and *Plutarch and History* (Duckworth and Classical Press of Wales, 2002); he also edited *Characterization and Individuality in Greek Literature* (Oxford, 1990) and *Greek Tragedy and the Historian* (Oxford, 1997).

Deborah H. Roberts is William R. Kenan Jr. Professor of Comparative Literature and Classics at Haverford College. She has published work on Greek tragedy, on Aristotle's *Poetics*, and on the reception and translation of ancient literature. She co-edited (with Don Fowler and Francis M. Dunn) *Classical Closure: Reading the End in Greek and Latin Literature* (Princeton, 1997); her translation of Euripides' *Ion* appeared in the Penn Greek Drama series, edited by David Slavitt and Palmer Bovie (Philadelphia, 1999).

Suzanne Saïd is Professor of Classics at Columbia University. She has written widely on Greek literature and mythology. Her books include *La Faute tragique* (1978), *Sophiste et Tyran ou le problème du Prométhée enchaîné* (1985), *Approches de la mythologie grecque* (1993), *Homère et l'Odyssée* (1998), and (with M. Trédé and A. Le Boulluec) *Histoire de la littérature grecque* (1997). She is the editor of *Hellenismos* (1989), on Greek identity, and co-editor (with D. Auger) of *Généalogies mythiques* (1998).

Ruth Scodel was educated at Berkeley and Harvard, and has been on the faculty at the University of Michigan since 1984. She is the author of *The Trojan Trilogy of Euripides* (1980), *Sophocles* (1984), *Credible Impossibilities: Conventions and Strategies of Verisimilitude in Homer and Greek Tragedy* (1999), *Listening to Homer* (2002), and articles on Greek literature.

Scott Scullion is Fellow of Worcester College and Faculty Lecturer in Classics, University of Oxford. A native of Toronto with a BA from the University of Toronto and a PhD from Harvard, he has published a book and a number of articles on Greek literature and on Greek religion. He is working on an introductory monograph on Euripides and, with Robert Parker and Simon Price, on a sourcebook of Greek religion.

Bernd Seidensticker is Professor of Greek at the Freie Universität Berlin. He is the author, co-author, or editor of books on Greek and Roman tragedy (*Palintonos Harmonia*, *Das Satyrspiel*, *Die Gesprächsverdichtung in den Tragödien Senecas*) and on the reception of antiquity in contemporary literature.

Jocelyn Penny Small is a Professor II in the Department of Art History at Rutgers University. She has written four books, of which the most recent is *The Parallel Worlds of Classical Art and Text* (2003). Her numerous articles are on a wide range of subjects, including iconography, Etruscan art, memory in antiquity, and database design. She is currently working on optics and illusionism in classical art.

Christiane Sourvinou-Inwood has been a Junior Research Fellow at

St. Hugh's College, Oxford, University Lecturer at Liverpool University, Senior Research Fellow at University College, Oxford, and Reader at Reading University. She has published many articles and the following books: *Theseus as Son and Stepson* (1979), *Studies in Girls' Transitions* (1988), *"Reading" Greek Culture* (1991), *"Reading" Greek Death* (1995; paperback, 1996), and *Tragedy and Athenian Religion* (2003).

Peter Wilson was born and educated in Sydney, Australia, and received his PhD at Cambridge. He held research and teaching posts in Cambridge, Oxford, and the University of Warwick before becoming a Fellow and Tutor in Classics in New College, Oxford, and University Lecturer. He is now Professor of Classics in the Department of Classics and Ancient History at the University of Sydney. His main research interests and publications are in the area of the Greek theater, especially its history and sociology; early Greek poetry and society more widely; and Greek music.

Paul Woodruff teaches philosophy and classics at the University of Texas at Austin. He has published translations of Euripides' *Bacchae*, and, with Peter Meineck, of Sophocles' Theban plays, as well as an abridged Thucydides translation and versions of several Platonic dialogues, two of them with Alexander Nehamas. He is, as well, the author of several plays and opera libretti. He has written a study of reverence as a classical virtue, and will publish a book on the ideas behind ancient democracy in 2005.

Preface and Acknowledgments

The Greek tragedians are very much alive in the twenty-first century, as is clear from the proliferation of new translations and new productions of the ancient plays. The study of Greek tragedy is also flourishing; two new sub-fields – performance studies and reception studies – have established themselves in the last twenty-five years, a period which has also seen a steady stream of new editions and scholarly studies. This volume aims to reflect the international scope, the variety of approaches, and the lively controversies that characterize the study of Greek tragedy today, even as it provides an orientation to the field. Each chapter is followed by suggestions for further reading, and the combined bibliography at the end of the volume provides additional guidance. In order to accommodate a range of readers, all Greek is transliterated and translated, and titles of plays and other ancient works are given in English, except in a few cases (such as *Eumenides* and *Bacchae*) where there is no satisfactory English equivalent.

This project owes much to many. The contributors not only entertained my suggestions but themselves proved a source of wise counsel; I am particularly grateful to Martin Cropp and Christopher Pelling. At Blackwell, Al Bertrand, Angela Cohen, and Sophie Gibson unfailingly provided advice and encouragement. Thanks to Mary Bellino's meticulousness, ingenuity, and expertise, a volume came into being from many separate files. My student Isabel Köster not only helped with preparing the manuscript, but also won her spurs as a translator. Finally, financial support was provided by the Smith College Committee on Faculty Compensation and Development and by the Loeb Classical Library Foundation.

Abbreviations and Editions

Addenda²	T. H. Carpenter. *Beazley Addenda: Additional References to ABV, ARV² and Paralipomena*. Second edition. Oxford: 1989.
ARV²	J. D. Beazley. *Attic Red-Figure Vase-Painters*. Second edition. 3 vols. Oxford: 1963.
CAH 5	D. M. Lewis, J. Boardman, J. K. Davies, and M. Ostwald, eds. *The Cambridge Ancient History*. Vol. 5: *The Fifth Century B.C.* Second edition. Cambridge: 1992.
DK	H. Diels, ed. *Die Fragmente der Vorsokratiker*. Rev. W. Kranz. Sixth edition. 3 vols. Berlin: 1951–52.
FrGHist	F. Jacoby, ed. *Die Fragmente der griechischen Historiker*. 15 vols. Berlin: 1923–58.
Gaisford	T. Gaisford, ed. *Scriptores Latini Rei Metricae*. Oxford: 1837.
HKGW	F. Nietzsche. *Historisch-kritische Gesamtausgabe: Werke*. Ed. H. J. Mette. 5 vols. Munich: 1933–42.
IG	*Inscriptiones Graecae*. Berlin: 1873–.
Kaibel	G. Kaibel, ed. *Comicorum Graecorum Fragmenta*. Berlin: 1899.
Keil	H. Keil, ed. *Grammatici Latini*. 8 vols. Leipzig: 1855–80. Repr. Hildesheim: 1961.
KGB	F. Nietzsche. *Briefwechsel. Kritische Gesamtausgabe*. Ed. G. Colli and M. Montinari. 3 vols. Berlin: 1975–.
KGW	F. Nietzsche. *Werke. Kritische Gesamtausgabe*. Ed. G. Colli and M. Montinari. 21 vols. Berlin: 1967–.
KSA	F. Nietzsche. *Sämtliche Werke. Kritische Studienausgabe in 15 Bänden*. Ed. G. Colli and M. Montinari. 15 vols. Munich: 1980.
LCL	Loeb Classical Library.
LIMC	*Lexicon Iconographicum Mythologiae Classicae*. Zurich: 1981–99.
M-L	R. Meiggs and D. Lewis, eds. *A Selection of Greek Historical Inscriptions*. Oxford: 1969.
OCD	S. Hornblower and A. Spawforth, eds. *The Oxford Classical Dictionary*. Third edition. Oxford: 1996.
Paralipomena	J. D. Beazley. *Paralipomena: Additions to Attic Black-Figure Vase-Painters and to Attic Red-Figure Vase-Painters*. Second edition. Oxford: 1971.

PCG	R. Kassel and C. Austin, eds. *Poetae Comici Graeci*. 8 vols. Berlin: 1983–.
PMG	D. L. Page, ed. *Poetae Melici Graeci*. Oxford: 1962.
P.Oxy	*Oxyrhynchus Papyri*. Oxford: 1898–.
Radermacher	L. Radermacher, ed. *Artium Scriptores (Reste der voraristotelischen Rhetorik)*. Vienna: 1951.
RE	*Realencyclopädie der classischen Altertumswissenschaft*. Munich: 1894–1978.
SEG	*Supplementum Epigraphicum Graecum*. Leiden: 1923–.
TRF	O. Ribbeck, ed. *Scenicae Romanorum Poesis Fragmenta*. Vol. 1: *Tragicorum Romanorum Fragmenta*. Third edition. Leipzig: 1897.

All references to fragments of Greek tragedy in this volume follow the numeration of *Tragicorum Graecorum Fragmenta* (Göttingen: 1971–2004):

Vol. 1. *Didascaliae Tragicae, Catalogi Tragicorum et Tragoediarum, Testimonia et Fragmenta Tragicorum Minorum*. Ed. B. Snell. 1971.
Vol. 2. *Fragmenta Adespota*. Ed. R. Kannicht and B. Snell. 1981.
Vol. 3. *Aeschylus*. Ed. S. Radt. 1985.
Vol. 4. *Sophocles*. Ed. S. Radt. 1977.
Vol. 5. *Euripides*. Ed. R. Kannicht. 2004.

Editions of Greek works not keyed to an abbreviation or a bibliography entry are those of the *Thesaurus Linguae Graecae Canon of Greek Authors and Works*, third edition, by Luci Berkowitz and Karl A. Squitier (New York and Oxford: 1990).

PART I

Contents

CHAPTER ONE

Fifth-Century Athenian History and Tragedy

Paula Debnar

Prologue: 431 BCE

Before dawn on the fourteenth day of Elaphebolion during the final months of the archonship of Pythodorus, residents of Athens and visitors alike made their way to the theater. The usual buzz and stir surrounded the celebration of the City Dionysia. Before the official opening of the festival, the tragic poet Euphorion had previewed his plays about the Titan Prometheus. Euripides, long overdue for a victory, would offer *Medea*, *Philoctetes*, and *Dictys*, followed by the satyr-play *Reapers*.

Not all of the excitement had to do with the festival. Two years earlier (433 BCE) the Athenians had accepted the Corcyraeans into alliance, and in so doing had embroiled themselves in a quarrel with Corinth, Corcyra's mother-city and a power-ful member of Sparta's alliance, the Peloponnesian League. The Athenians had hoped that by limiting themselves to a defensive agreement they could avoid direct contact with Corinthian forces, but their plan had misfired. In retaliation the Corinthians sent forces the following year to help the Potidaeans (colonists of theirs but members of Athens' alliance) secede. Then, with Potidaea besieged and their own forces trapped in the city, they had lobbied the Spartans to invade Attica. Early in the fall, a full synod of the Peloponnesian League had voted that the Thirty Years' Peace had been broken and that the league should go to war.

Despite the vote, war with Sparta and her allies was not yet certain. Members of both alliances continued to exchange heralds, and as the Greek world knew, despite their reputation as the world's finest hoplite force – or perhaps because of it – the Spartans were slow to go to war. If Potidaea were to fall soon, war might be avoided; at least the Corinthians could not argue that an invasion of Attica would help their colonists. The Dionysia brought a welcome break from rumors of war.

Euripides won only third prize at the Dionysia of 431; nevertheless, it is tempting to imagine that the crowd leaving the theater that evening spoke mostly of his *Medea*. The audience would have known the story, but most likely did not suspect the magnitude of the crime Medea would commit in Euripides' play. Even so, the poet had persuaded them to feel sympathy for his protagonist, much as Medea had persuaded the chorus of Corinthian women to keep secret her plan to protect her honor and avenge herself on Jason by murdering her own children. King Aegeus, Medea's friend and ally (*philos*), also succumbed to her persuasion and promised her refuge in Athens, provided she could get to the city on her own (723–24). The king's offer of sanctuary occasions a choral ode in praise of Athens that sits rather oddly in the mouths of the Corinthian women who comprise the chorus. Still, it must have pleased the Athenian spectators to hear their city praised as the birthplace of Harmony (830–34), where "sweet gentle winds breathe upon the land" (838–40).

Within two weeks of the festival, a small band of Thebans invaded Plataea, a Boeotian city allied with Athens. For Thucydides, the invasion marked the beginning of the Peloponnesian War. The historian, however, did not begin his account of the conflict with the attack on Plataea, but with the quarrel between Corinth and her colony Corcyra. This quarrel between *philoi*, cities related by blood, had escalated into a larger conflict between more powerful *philoi*, Athens and Sparta, cities tied by the customary obligations of a treaty of peace. Despite limiting themselves to a defensive alliance with the Corcyraeans, the Athenians had invited the quarrel between Corinth and Corcyra into their own city. As in Euripides' play, honor, revenge, and conflicting obligations – to friendship based on blood ties and friendship based on custom – would all figure prominently in Thucydides' account.

Tragedy and History

Both Thucydides and Euripides may have been present when Corinthians, Corcyraeans, and Athenians debated the proposed alliance. Both are likely to have known about the quarrel that prodded Corcyra, despite a long history of avoiding alliances, to seek Athens' help. And, as we have noted, there is a certain overlap of themes in *Medea* and the first book of Thucydides' history. Yet no one would argue that Thucydides modeled his account of the quarrel between Corinth and Corcyra on Euripides' tragedy or, conversely, that Euripides took inspiration from the quarrel between Corinth and Corcyra. The interrelationships between the two narratives are at once more subtle and more pervasive. To begin with, the questions they raise are not peculiar to them or to 431 BCE. In meetings of the assembly and in the law courts – in other tragedies as well – Athenians will have witnessed debates in which honor competed with expedience and conflicting obligations clashed. Moreover, although Euripides' tragedy ends with its protagonist about to flee from Corinth to Athens, the Corinth of *Medea* is not the Corinth of the fifth century, nor is Athens of the tragedy the Athens of Euripides' audience.

What *is* the relationship between tragedy's mythical past and the fifth-century Athenian audience's present? The goal of this chapter will be to lay the groundwork for answering this question. In order to suggest the range and direction of the movement between past and present in surviving tragedies, I will interleave with a brief overview of fifth-century Athenian history discussions of different facets of the interplay between tragedy and history. These subjects are, of course, more complex, and the scholarly debate much more nuanced, than I can convey in a short survey. Indeed, even the terms "tragedy" and "history" require some preliminary explication.

By "tragedy" I mean simply one of the thirty-two surviving dramas produced by Aeschylus, Sophocles, or Euripides and performed at the dramatic festivals, presumably in Athens (on lost tragedies see Cropp, chapter 17 in this volume). Not all of these tragedies, as it will turn out, lend themselves to a historical approach. "History" is more complicated. In one sense it refers to what Pelling calls "real-world events" (1997b, 213). But "history" does not consist of empirical facts to which poetry responds. Historians as well as tragic poets compose narratives. The narratives of Herodotus, Thucydides, and Xenophon provide the basis for our understanding of Athenian history of the fifth century (on sources see Rhodes 1992a, 62–63), but they also reflect their authors' purposes and bias and are colored by their historical circumstances (as is true of my own historical overview). Nonetheless, as products of the same culture as tragedies, ancient historical narratives are likely to "reflect its categories and concerns, whether psychological, social, or political" (Boedeker 2002, 116, on myth and history).

The tragedies under discussion fall into two broad categories. In the first, the poet alludes directly to fifth-century events or developments, but moves them back into the mythological past. In this category I place Aeschylus' *Persians* and *Oresteia*. Tragedies in the second group generally avoid overt references to fifth-century events or figures; paradoxically, they also draw the mythological past into the present (see Sourvinou-Inwood, chapter 18 in this volume). The bulk of the plays in this category are by Euripides. Strains of fifth-century Athenian rhetoric, sketches of political types, and reflections of Athens' institutions and society lend plays of this category a distinctly fifth-century Athenian flavor. The emphasis in Euripides' *Orestes* on political factions, for example, is directly relevant to the Athens of 408 BCE.

Sophocles contributes to both categories; indeed, one of his tragedies moves in both directions. Although Ajax's followers resemble fifth-century Athenian rowers more than heroic-age spearmen, the first half of Sophocles' *Ajax* draws the audience toward the epic past. Following the hero's suicide, however, the play's historical motion reverses direction. Sophocles' Agamemnon and Menelaus, with their meanness and flawed rhetoric, have more in common with what we know of politicians of the second half of the fifth century than with characters in epic or, for that matter, in any of Aeschylus' extant dramas. Questions raised by *Philoctetes* (409 BCE) concerning the relative power of *nomos* and *phusis* (roughly "nurture and nature") locate it squarely in the midst of a fifth-century sophistic debate. The suspicion of rhetoric *Philoctetes* generates, as well as the conflict in the play between appearance and reality, also project its mythic past into the world of Athenian politics of the final decade of the century.

Sophocles locates *Oedipus at Colonus* (406 BCE; his last tragedy) in the mythological past of Athens under King Theseus. The poet distances the action from contemporary Athens by shifting the setting from the heart of the polis to its outskirts at Colonus. This move, as we will see, allows the tragedy to gesture toward a future that bodes well for Athens.

Athens and the Sea

Of the more than nine hundred tragedies that could have been performed in the fifth century at the City Dionysia alone, only thirty-two have survived. Moreover, these do not span the entire fifth century, but were composed roughly between the end of the Persian Wars and Athens' defeat by Sparta and her allies (on the fourth-century *Rhesus* see Cropp, chapter 17 in this volume). When Vernant (1988a) speaks of tragedy's "historical moment" and tries to explain why Greek tragedy "is born, flourishes, and degenerates in Athens, and almost within the space of a hundred years" (25), he ignores the role that chance played in preserving the fewer than three dozen plays that have survived (see Kovacs, chapter 24 in this volume).

Tragedy did not end with Athens' defeat in 404, nor did it spring full grown from the head of Aeschylus in democratic Athens following the battles of Salamis and Plataea. The sixth-century tyrant Pisistratus and his sons may very well have set the stage for the political and cultural developments of fifth-century Athens. Nonetheless, the series of conflicts between Greeks and Persians culminating in Persia's defeat in 478 was a cultural as well as historical turning point. Recently discovered fragments of an elegy by Simonides on the battle of Plataea suggest that the feats performed by the Greeks against the Persians quickly became matter for poetry on a level with the heroic deeds of the Trojan War (Boedeker 2001; on Simonides' poem on Salamis see Plutarch, *Themistocles* 15). Tragedy, too, recognized the potential of this theme. An early failed experiment was Phrynichus' *Capture of Miletus* (Herodotus 6.21.2). Aeschylus was more successful with *Persians*, whose subject is the battle of Salamis.

Salamis was one of the final engagements of the Persian Wars, but, according to the boast of Athenian speakers in Thucydides (1.74.1), it was the first to show the extent to which "the affairs of the Greeks depended on their ships" – by which they mean Athenian ships. War with Aegina (around 505–491) is said to have forced the Athenians to become seamen (Herodotus 7.144). Athens' shift in military strategy from hoplites to a large state-owned fleet of triremes was unusual, at least for a Greek city. Given the manpower required by triremes (a full complement was 170 rowers per ship), a fleet of these warships was enormously expensive to maintain. Persia, of course, could finance its fleet with tribute from its subjects (Wallinga 1987).

Ancient writers characteristically attribute innovations to a single individual, and the Athenian fleet is no exception. Seven years after the Athenians helped to repel the first Persian assault on Hellas at Marathon, Themistocles advised the Athenians to use the profits of a newly discovered vein of silver at Laurium in southern Attica to expand their fleet for the war against Aegina. While Herodotus (7.144) says merely that the ships were never used against Aegina, Plutarch is more explicit: Themistocles' real motive was to prepare a defense against the Persians (*Themistocles* 4). A leader less shrewd than Themistocles could have anticipated a renewed Persian assault. Only the fortuitous destruction of Darius' ships off the Chalcidic coast (in 492) had saved Athens from the Persian navy. When Xerxes began the excavation of a canal through the peninsula of Mount Athos around 483 (Herodotus 7.22), he made clear his intention to take up where his father left off, to punish the Greeks who had assisted in the rebellion of the king's Ionian subjects (contra, Wallinga 1993, 160–61).

Soon after the final battle at Plataea (479), the Spartans abdicated leadership of the Greek alliance formed to repel the Persians. Thucydides says that the allies wanted the Athenians to assume leadership of the alliance and that the Spartans conceded, in part because they wanted to be done with the war against Persia, in part because they were still friendly toward Athens (1.95–96; cf. Aristotle, *Constitution of the Athenians* 23–24). The role that Athenian ships and soldiers played at Salamis and their willingness to pursue the enemy in the aftermath of that battle made them the likely candidates to assume leadership of an alliance of Greeks, primarily islanders, against Persian aggression.

In Thucydides' condensed (and tendentious) account of the approximately fifty years between the Persian and Peloponnesian Wars, the so-called Pentecontaetia (1.89–118), Athens methodically expands its power and control over its allies. Other sources tend to support Thucydides' picture. Immediately following the battle of Salamis, for example, Themistocles tried (in vain) to extort money from the island of Andros; he was more successful with Carystus and Paros (Herodotus 8.111–12). Around 476 the Athenians captured Eion and Scyros and sold their inhabitants (non-Greeks) into slavery. Nor was membership in the new alliance, the so-called Delian League, always voluntary. After the capture of Scyros, and not long before Aeschylus produced *Persians*, the Athenians forced the Greek city of Carystus on Euboea to join the league (around 474–72). Soon afterwards (around 471–65) they prevented Naxos from withdrawing from the alliance (Thucydides 1.98). Not all of the cities of Asia Minor may have been eager to exchange Persian for Athenian control (on Phaselis see Plutarch, *Cimon* 12).

The Persian threat may not have been dormant in the 460s. The forces the Athenians defeated at the Eurymedon could have represented an attempt by the Persians to reestablish themselves in the Aegean. Perhaps as late as 465 the Athenians routed Persians from the Chersonese, just before the revolt of another ally, Thasos (Thucydides 100.1–3). Diodorus (11.60) implies that Persian military activity was a response to Athenian aggression, although modern scholars are less certain (e.g., Meiggs 1972, 77–79). By the second half of the 470s, however, the line between offensive and defensive operations had been blurred. The war to save mainland Greeks from Persian aggression was increasingly presented as a war of liberation, protracted in order to extend freedom to the Greeks of Asia Minor (see, e.g., Raaflaub 2004, 58–65, 84–89). Regardless of whether the Athenians were justified in extending their power, by the time that Aeschylus produced *Persians* they had taken the initial moves to transform their alliance into empire.

Aeschylus' *Persians*

The relation of *Persians*, our earliest extant play (472), to history is, at first glance, the least problematic. It is the only surviving tragedy whose focus is a historical event, the defeat of the Persian king Xerxes at Salamis by the Greek fleet a mere eight years before the performance of the play. Aeschylus himself is thought to have been a veteran of Salamis (on the difficulties in extrapolating historical details from *Persians*, see Pelling 1997a). The tragedy is also unusual in that we can directly compare it with a fifth-century historical account of the same engagement (Herodotus 8.40–94). The exercise, however, is more complicated than it may seem. Although Herodotus does not agree with Aeschylus on all points, it is likely that he used *Persians* when composing his own account of Salamis (Saïd 2002b, 137–38). Conversely, although the historical referent of *Persians* is clear, modern scholars' interpretations of the poet's use of the event are shaped in large part by how far they believe the Athenians had moved toward empire by the end of the 470s. Both Herodotus and Thucydides play important roles in conditioning those beliefs.

Whereas Herodotus places Salamis within the context of a number of engagements between Greeks and Persians on land and at sea, Aeschylus conspicuously plays down the importance of land battles. The chorus, comprised of Xerxes' advisors, does refer to the Persian defeat at Marathon (244), but as the audience knows, they are wrong to overlook the importance of Athens' navy. Toward the end of the play the ghost of Darius predicts a Greek victory (on land) at Plataea (816–17), but the battle seems to be an appendage to the defeat of Persia's naval forces (e.g., Podlecki 1966a, 12). From a dramatic perspective, the diminution of the importance of land battles dissociates Darius from Marathon and allows the poet to portray him as an exemplary king, embodying the virtues of moderation and self-control in contrast to the rashness of Xerxes (Pelling 1997a, 10).

Saïd (2002b, 145) may be right to conclude that Herodotus' version of Salamis contains a warning to the Athenians about their own expansionism (more generally, Moles 2002). After all, Herodotus may have been composing his *Histories* well into the 420s or later (Fornara 1971), by which time Athens had firmly established its empire. Some have seen in *Persians* a similar warning (e.g., Rosenbloom 1995). The tragedy's emphasis on sea power seems to point out a parallel between Persia and Athens. The poet's reference to territories that once formed part of the Great King's domain, but which in 472 were part of Athens' alliance (864–906), would seem to highlight the Athenians' inheritance of Xerxes' position. At the very least, in 472 some Athenians – whether supporters or opponents of rule over the allies – may have been wary of the rapid pace and nature of the changes they were witnessing (Raaflaub 1998, 15–19).

The possibility that a reflection of Athens is to be seen in Aeschylus' Persian mirror could explain why the poet asks his audience to look at Salamis through Persian eyes and elicits great sympathy for the Persians, including Xerxes. Reminding us of the compassion that Achilles shows Priam in *Iliad* 24, Pelling (1997a) explains, "[Xerxes'] fate can still capture something of the human condition, and exemplify a human vulnerability which the audience can recognize as their own" (16).

Unlike Xerxes, however, Priam and the Trojans fought to defend their own city, not to conquer Greece. Nor did the Trojan king defy natural boundaries, as Aeschylus implies Xerxes does when he yokes the Hellespont (e.g., 65–71). Even without subscribing to a cultural stereotype of the barbarian East that had been crystallized by the Persian Wars (Hall 1989), many members of Aeschylus' audience had personal reasons to view the Persians with hostility: they would have witnessed the destruction that Xerxes wreaked on their city and lost friends and family in battles against Persian forces. Is it possible, then, that the sympathy the poet elicits for the Persians prompted his audience to imagine their city suffering a fate similar to that of Xerxes? To what extent does Aeschylus draw the recent past into the present – and extend it to a warning about the future?

Because modern readers know the ending of the story of Athenian imperialism and cannot "unread" the narratives of Herodotus or Thucydides, it is difficult to answer this question. There are, however, grounds for caution. That there is only a single passage alluding to Athens' alliance weakens the appeal of a minatory interpretation of the tragedy, as does the play's positive view of Greeks. The messenger reports that the gods saved the city (347). The song he hears at the beginning of the attack is noble: "Sons of Greeks, come, free your land; free your children and wives, and the temples of your ancestral gods and tombs of your forebears" (402–5). To the queen's question, "Does Athens remain unsacked?" (348), the messenger's response, "When [their] men live, [their] defense is secure" (349), echoes what seems to have become an Athenian commonplace after Salamis (e.g., Thucydides 1.74.3). By placing praise in the mouths of enemies, Aeschylus elevates the Athenians and would seem to agree with the boast of Thucydides' Pericles: "This city alone does not irritate the enemies who attack it, because of the kind of men they are at whose hands they suffer" (2.41.3).

Empire and Democracy

Fourteen years later, when Aeschylus produced his *Oresteia* trilogy, there could be no doubt about the nature of the Athenians' imperialist goals. Their ambitions came at a cost. Despite the Spartans' apparent acquiescence to the change in leadership of Greeks, they were far from content with the Athenians' growing strength and influence. Around 465 the Spartans promised to invade Attica if Thasos rebelled from the Delian League, but were prevented from putting this plan into action by an earthquake and the subsequent threat of a revolt of their helots, state-owned slaves (Thucydides 1.101). The transfer of the treasury of the league may have taken place around this time, given the degree of control Athens was exercising over the Aegean as early as 463: by then all of the islands of the Aegean except the Dorian colonies Thera and Melos were under Athens' control (e.g., Sealey 1976, 252–53; Robertson 1980, 112–19; contra, Rhodes 1992b, 51).

Growing tension between Athens and Sparta came to a head when the Spartans sent back Athenian forces they had requested to help with the siege of rebellious helots on Mount Ithome (around 462). Thucydides says the Spartans suspected the Athenians of meddling within the Peloponnese and mistrusted them because they were not "of the same tribe" – that is, the Athenians were of the Ionian rather than the Dorian Greek ethnos. According to Plutarch the Spartans thought the Athenians were "revolutionaries"(*Cimon* 17). Deeply insulted, the Athenians broke off the alliance still in effect from the Persian Wars and allied themselves with Sparta's enemy, Argos. Soon afterwards, Megara defected from the Peloponnesian League and the conflict known as the First Peloponnesian War began (around 462/61).

Plutarch's explanation for the dismissal of Athenian forces reminds us of the close connection between Athens' domestic and foreign policies (Rhodes 1992a, 73–75). The complaint about revolutionary tendencies most likely alludes to Ephialtes' reform of the Areopagus in 462/61 and its consequences. About Ephialtes we know very little (see Aristotle, *Constitution* 25–26; Plutarch, *Cimon* 10, 13, 15–16). His renown rests on his having successfully deprived the aristocratic council of the Areopagus of much of its power and shifted it from the elite to the Athenian people (Rhodes 1992a, 69–72). Soon after expressing his opposition to these reforms Cimon, who had urged the Athenians to cooperate with Sparta, was ostracized (Plutarch, *Cimon* 17). Quarrels triggered by the reforms are believed to have been responsible for the murder of Ephialtes in the following year. Athens, it would seem, was on the brink of civil war.

Extended military campaigns abroad concurrent with the war against the Peloponnesians may have exacerbated political discontent in Athens. In 460 the Athenians tried to increase their power at Persia's expense by sending a large fleet to help Egypt rebel from the Great King. The expedition dragged on for six years before its disastrous end: the Athenians and their allies lost 250 ships (Thucydides 1.109–10). Thucydides says that only a few men survived (1.110.1; cf. Diodorus 11.77). Based on epigraphic evidence (M-L 33; *SEG* xxxiv 45), Lewis estimates that Athenian casualties in 459 alone "ran well into four figures" (Lewis 1992a, 113 n. 57). In addition, in 458 the Athenians turned westward, forming an alliance with Egesta in Sicily (*IG* I³ 11; Rhodes 1992b, 53). At around the same time the Athenians began construction of the long walls. Once complete, the walls would transform Athens into a quasi-island, allowing the city to rely on its fleet to defend its harbor and guarantee the imports necessary to survive extended attacks by land. The Spartans and their Athenian sympathizers understood the implications of the project. According to Thucydides, "Some Athenians were secretly trying to bring in [Peloponnesian troops then in Boeotia] with the hope of checking the rule of the people and the building of the long walls" (1.107.4).

Aeschylus' *Oresteia*

The conflicts and resolution of the *Oresteia* are strongly colored by the difficulties the Athenians were facing in the 450s: clashes with the Persians, the First Peloponnesian War, and political upheavals within their own city. An outstanding feature of *Agamemnon* is the poet's use of naval power and protracted warfare conducted in distant lands as a metaphor for a perversion of natural order and a threat to the political stability in Argos. Unlike Homer's Agamemnon, Aeschylus' king is called "the elder leader of Achaean ships" (184–85) and "commander of ships" (1227). Agamemnon wonders how he can become "a deserter of the fleet" (212), and the chorus refers to the corrupt sacrifice of Iphigenia as the "preliminary sacrifice for ships" (227). The expedition acquires additional negative connotations when Ares, god of war, is called the "gold-changer of bodies" (438) and the long siege in distant Troy generates political problems at home (Rosenbloom 1995, 97–98, 105–11).

Eumenides finally brings an end to the ancient cycle of violence we see continued in *Agamemnon* and *Libation Bearers*. As the trilogy moves from Argos, in the first two plays, to Delphi and Athens in *Eumenides*, so too it moves historically from the earliest generations of the house of Atreus to the trial of Orestes on the Acropolis, where the mythical past borders on the audience's present. But the Acropolis is not the only backdrop shared by *Eumenides* and its fifth-century audience.

The extraordinary topicality of *Eumenides* is undisputed (e.g., Podlecki 1966a, 74–100); for example, despite differences in details, the alliance Orestes promises the Athenians (762–74) alludes to Athens' treaty with Argos in 462. It is equally certain that when Athena gives the jury of Athenian citizens the power to try cases of murder, the poet alludes to Ephialtes' reform of the Areopagus, which still retained this power in 458. In response to the Erinyes' threat to bring civil war in retaliation for Athena's decision to free Orestes, the goddess pleads with them not "to fix among my citizens war against kin, furious battle against one another" (862–63). She asks instead for war against external enemies (864). Once appeased the Erinyes – soon to be the Semnai ("Reverend Goddesses") – pray for the city to be free of civil war (976–87). Macleod cautions that "to pray for a city that it should be free of faction is natural and normal at any time" (1982, 130). Nonetheless, spectators who two or three years earlier had witnessed the factional conflicts sparked by Ephialtes' reforms were likely to be reminded of their own experience.

Athena successfully appeases the Erinyes by incorporating them into the new order: they will be installed in a cave beneath the Hill of Ares, where the cult of the Semnai will be established for them (see Pausanias 1.28.6). If given their due, the chthonic goddesses will guarantee the fecundity of the city. If dishonored, they will bring disease and its political analogue, civil war. Aeschylus' myth of the origins of the cult of the Semnai is yet another link to the world of fifth-century Athens, since it reflects contemporary Athenian religious practices.

Despite the play's topical references and its generally optimistic ending, Aeschylus deftly avoids wholesale endorsement of democratic policies (e.g., Pelling 2000, 171–77), in particular by avoiding exact correspondences with contemporary Athenian events or institutions. The terms of Orestes' alliance, for example, are not those of Athens' alliance in 462 (cf. Thucydides 1.102.4). Instead, as Macleod (1982) has shown, the Athens of *Eumenides* is the mirror image of the world of disorder in *Agamemnon* and *Libation Bearers*. Athena's decision reverses the confusion of gender relationships that led to Clytemnestra's murder of Agamemnon. The heir of the rightful king is returned to power over his own house and Argos. As Semnai, the chthonic Erinyes promise real fertility, in contrast to the rain of blood that Clytemnestra described as spurting from her husband's wounds (1388–92). It is equally important that *Eumenides* resolves the trilogy's conflicts by holding tensions in balance. Female is not utterly defeated by male. Despite the negative connotation of naval conflict in *Agamemnon* – or for that matter the negative picture of the king himself – Athena does not rule out war, but prays for war against external enemies. The Erinyes are incorporated into the new order, yet retain their former powers.

The real cessation of the cycle of violence in the *Oresteia* comes when Athena establishes the Areopagus as a court of law. It takes an Olympian to restore order, but she does so with the help of mortals. Aeschylus does not offer an idealized Athens, but he does lend authority to the origins of an Athenian institution by moving it into the past and associating with heroes and gods.

War and Peace

The conflict with Sparta that began in 461 may have encouraged the allies' renewed resistance to Athens' hegemony; irregular contributions recorded on the Athenian tribute lists may be evidence of unrest among Athens' allies in the 450s (Rhodes 1992b, 56–61). If so, it was settled by 449. Discontented cities perhaps thought the Athenians were too busy dealing with other conflicts to be able to respond to rebellion. Moreover, if Athens concluded a formal peace with the Persians around 450 (see Lewis 1992b, 121–27; in 460s, Badian 1993b), the allies would have had all the more reason to break with the alliance: after all, the raison d'être of the Delian League was to protect Greeks from the Persians. And in 446 Euboean cities and Megara (that is, cities close to home) rebelled; soon thereafter the Spartan king Plistoanax led forces of the Peloponnesian League to Attica's doorstep, only to turn back and allow the Athenians to subdue the Euboean revolt. The Spartans soon agreed to the Peace of 446 or Thirty Years' Peace.

According to the Peace, for the most part, each side was to keep what it had at the time of the treaty (Thucydides 1.40.2; however, 1.115.1; Ste. Croix 1972, 293–94). A defeat in Boeotia (late 447) convinced the Athenians to abandon attempts to expand their power on land. In effect, the Thirty Years' Peace agreed to divide leadership of Greeks between Athens, at the head of a naval hegemony, and Sparta, leader of a primarily hoplite-based alliance. Not until 431 would the Spartans and their allies openly challenge the arrangement.

Within Athens democracy had, by mid-century, firmly taken root. Although democracy was not entirely dependent on income from the empire, as is clear from the flourishing democratic system of the fourth century, the evolution of Athens' hegemony into empire helped to nourish its growth. By 454 the Athenians could use the league's treasury to pay their crews, primarily citizens of the lowest class, as well as to finance civic festivals and building projects like the Parthenon. Administration of the empire also brought allies into Athens' courts, stimulating the city's economy; pay for citizen-jurors came from allied tribute as well.

A recent argument by Eder (1998) that *real* democracy, in the sense of political power resting primarily in the hands of regular citizens, did not emerge until after the end of the Peloponnesian War, seems to go too far. But even Rhodes, who objects to such a view, agrees that "democratic leaders of the first generation were aristocrats" (Rhodes 1992a, 91). Sophocles' *Ajax*, traditionally dated to the period of the Peace, engages with the persistent tension in Athens between mass and elite.

Sophocles' *Ajax*

Although Sophocles adheres to the traditional outline of myth, he adds several new features (Rose 1995, 63–64). The audience is offered competing criteria for the army's decision to award the arms of Achilles to Odysseus: moderation, physical strength, obedience to laws. The poet also emphasizes Ajax's madness. The most pronounced departure from Homer's picture of Ajax is to put him in command of sailors – and not particularly brave ones at that – an innovation reminiscent of Aeschylus' treatment of Agamemnon. Repeated references to Salamis strengthen the connection to the navy (Rose 1995, 69–71).

As the tragedy moves from the indictment of Ajax to his defense, Sophocles gradually rehabilitates the warrior in anticipation of his final victory, the awarding of burial to his corpse. Whereas the prologue presents Ajax's madness as a moral flaw and punishment for immoderate behavior, by the end of the tragedy he seems a victim of the arbitrary exercise of divine power. Although Ajax is initially isolated from his society, his "insane isolation . . . is finally transformed into a stirring evocation of his unique lonely stance as defender" (Rose 1995, 69).

In the poet's attempts "to square the logic of the myth with the logic of [the] *apologia*" Rose identifies silences that point to contradictions in Athens itself. Sophocles' association of Ajax with "both the human rootedness of Hector and the absolutist isolation of Achilles" (64) draws the audience back toward the mythic world of Homer. At the same time, his command of sailors would have reminded the fifth-century audience of themselves and of the great aristocratic generals responsible for repelling the Persians and for the prosperity that the expansion of the empire brought their city. In the last third of the play, Sophocles blurs the tension between the *démos* and aristocracy by emphasizing the meanness and tyrannical behavior of the Atreidae in contrast to Ajax. "Big" men, such as Ajax, after all, are needed to protect the "little" (158–59) from the likes of Agamemnon and Menelaus. At the end of the play Ajax – or rather the idea of Ajax – inspires his illegitimate half-brother Teucer to imitate his behavior and defy the Atreidae. Thus Sophocles offers "a process of the democratization of an aristocratic ideal" (Rose 1995, 77).

The Early Years of the Peloponnesian War

When the war began most Greeks thought that it would last no more than three years and that the Athenians would quickly give in (Thucydides 5.14.3, 7.28.3). Instead it took four years for the fighting merely to reach its peak. By then the usual pattern was for the Spartans to invade Attica each spring, while the Athenians sent a fleet to harass the Peloponnese.

Frustrations grew as the war dragged on. In addition to watching the Spartans ravage their crops each year, soon after the war began the Athenians suffered repeated attacks of the plague; siege operations in Chalcidice were depleting their treasury. A rebellion of the cities on Lesbos (428), led by the Mytileneans, tried them further. The Athenians put down the revolt, but their initial decision to condemn all the Mytilenean men to death and sell the women and children into slavery reflects the seriousness of the rebellion's threat. But hostilities had yet to escalate to the point that the Athenians were blind to the savagery of their initial decision, which they quickly rescinded (Thucydides 3.49).

So, too, by the first Olympic festival of the war (428), the Peloponnesian League showed signs of strain. Although the allies who had convened at the festival agreed to a double invasion of Athens by land and sea, many of them failed to muster at the isthmus. Thucydides explains that they were "both in the middle of harvesting and tired of campaigning" (3.15.2). That the Spartans were willing to send a fleet to Lesbos to help with the rebellion the next spring further suggests that frustration – and perhaps fear of losing their grip on their alliance – was driving them toward more daring undertakings.

At around the same time, the Athenians began to act more aggressively. Before the outbreak of war Pericles asked the Athenians to think of themselves as islanders (Thucydides 1.143.5) and warned them not to try to acquire more or voluntarily undertake additional risks while they were waging war (1.144.1); he adhered to this advice even after the plague struck Athens (2.61.2). In 427, however, the Athenians captured the island of Minoa, off the coast of Megara. In the following year the general Demosthenes defeated troops consisting of Peloponnesians and their allies in Amphilochia and discredited the Spartans there by allowing important Peloponnesians to depart in secret, deserting the rest of the troops (3.109.2). The Spartans may have responded to increased pressure on their periphery by establishing a colony outside the Peloponnese, Heracleia Trachinia (Thucydides 3.92–93).

Euripides' *Children of Heracles*

More than half of our surviving tragedies were composed after the outbreak of the Peloponnesian War. A number of these plays have been mined for specific historical content – in my view with limited success. Zuntz (1955, 81–88), who dismisses most direct historical allusions in Euripides, is convinced that Eurystheus' promise at the end of the *Children of Heracles* to protect the Athenians' land from a future invasion by the children of Heracles (1032–36) can only allude to the Spartans' invasion in 430. Spartan kings were the putative descendants of Heracles, and in 430 the invasion led by King Archidamus spared a large part of Attica; afterwards he would show less restraint. Poole (1994, 6) is rightly skeptical; there is no reason to assume that the predicted invasion had yet taken place or that the play could not have been performed before the outbreak of war. Moreover, to sustain his argument, Zuntz must impart irony to the words of Heracles' friend Iolaus (82). After the Athenians have protected Heracles' children from the Argives, he advises them, "Never raise a hostile spear against [the Athenians'] land" (313). As we will see when we turn to *Suppliants*, if there are historical allusions in Euripidean tragedies, they are oblique; features such as anachronisms (Easterling 1985a), touches of sophistic rhetoric, and contemporary character types give the plays their topicality.

Pylos and the Peace

In the spring of 425 the Athenians tried to tighten a circle around their enemy by establishing an outpost on a deserted promontory at Pylos on the west coast of the Peloponnese (Thucydides 4.3–4). Initially Spartan leaders showed little concern, but when the king and his troops in Attica received news of the occupation, they quickly returned from their spring invasion and tried to dislodge the Athenians from their outpost. Due to the failure of the Spartan commanders to seal off Pylos' harbor, Athenian ships trapped 420 of their men on the island of Sphacteria (Thucydides 4.14.2, 38.5). A quick assessment of the situation convinced the Spartans to sue for peace – unilaterally.

The terms of Sparta's proposal were reasonable. In return for the men on the island, they offered peace and friendship. The Spartans expected the Athenians to be willing to make peace (2.59.2), since they had made an earlier offer, which the Spartans had rejected (Thucydides 4.21.1). In the meantime, however, the political environment in Athens had changed. Pericles, who had advised the Athenians to adopt a mostly defensive posture (1.143–44), was dead, and the Athenians had become increasingly aggressive. Demagogues like Cleon wanted more than a return to the conditions of 431, as the Spartans' proposal implied. By insisting on public negotiations, which would expose the degree to which the Spartans were willing to compromise their allies' interests, the Athenians, in effect, rejected the offer of peace.

Attacking Sphacteria proved to be a difficult task. Just as the Athenians were about to abandon their blockade, a strange series of events allowed them to launch a successful attack and surround the soldiers on the island. While admitting a degree of hyperbole, Thucydides likens the situation to the Spartans' stand against the Persians at Thermopylae (on numbers see Wilson 1979, 104–5). At Pylos, however, the Athenians held their fire long enough for the Spartans to consult with their commanders. To the astonishment of the Greek world, when instructed, "On your own decide what to do concerning yourselves, as long as you do not act disgracefully" (4.38.3), the Spartans on Sphacteria surrendered.

The consequences of the surrender were devastating for Sparta. Having already forfeited a significant number of ships, which the Athenians had refused to return following the failed negotiations, as well as the trust of their allies, they now lost both men and territory. The 292 men held prisoner by the Athenians (Thucydides 4.38.5) would effectively prevent the Peloponnesians from invading Attica. Pylos would provide a sanctuary for runaway slaves in the heart of the helots' homeland and an outpost from which to foment rebellion. Perhaps most important, the Spartans themselves lost their nerve and resolve.

The Athenians were clearly buoyed by their unexpected success. Soon afterwards they invaded Corinthian territory, secured the control of the entrance to the gulf of Corinth, captured the island of Cythera, off the south coast of the Peloponnese, and almost took Megara – all the while trying to secure a foothold in Sicily. During the same summer (424), they planned a daring double-pronged attack on Boeotia. But Athens would not enjoy its good fortune for long. The Spartan general Brasidas quickly forced the Athenians to withdraw from Megara. Then with an army of a thousand mercenaries and seven hundred helots (Thucydides 4.78.1, 80.5) he marched to the northeast, toward Thrace, to help the Macedonian king Perdiccas and the Athenian allies in Chalcidice, in rebellion from the earliest years of the war. Brasidas' daring campaign reversed Sparta's fortunes and pressured the Athenians into a negotiated peace.

Through a combination of military and diplomatic skills, Brasidas very nearly gained control of Chalcidice, an area rich in gold, silver, and timber for shipbuilding. He was also helped by the slow response of the Athenians. Not until they realized that Brasidas had control of the allied city of Acanthus and was threatening Amphipolis did they make a move. If the Athenians lost control of Amphipolis, the path would be open for their enemies to march to the Hellespont (Thucydides 4.108.1). As the final days of the war would demonstrate, if the Spartans could control the Hellespont they could starve Athens into submission.

Despite the successes in Boeotia and Chalcidice, the Spartans in power seem to have been more interested in retrieving the prisoners from Pylos and establishing peace than in defeating the Athenians. In the midst of Brasidas' campaign the two sides negotiated a truce. Brasidas, however, refused to return the town of Scione in accordance with the terms of the new agreement. At the instigation of Cleon, the Athenians voted to kill all the Scioneans, although they did not reduce the city for another two years. The harsh treatment that the Athenians inflicted on Scione reflected the fear that Brasidas' expedition had roused. As we have seen, on the occasion of the revolt in Lesbos, the Athenians had initially voted to kill all the men and sell the women and children into slavery, but on second thought recognized the savagery of their decision. By the eleventh year of the war, they were no longer so reasonable. When they finally took Scione in the summer of 421, they carried out the punishment that the Mytileneans so narrowly escaped (Thucydides 5.32.1). According to Ducrey (1968, 117–22), the fate of the Scioneans is the first sure example of such severe punishment inflicted by Athenians on a captured Greek city. (On the Thracian elements in *Hecuba* see Gregory 1999, xiii–xiv.)

Euripides' *Suppliants*

The campaign in Boeotia that distracted the Athenians from Brasidas' initiative in Chalcidice ended in their defeat at Delium. Bowie (1997) has revived the argument that the Thebans' refusal to return the Argive dead in Euripides' *Suppliants* (produced around 422) would have reminded his Athenian audience of this battle. Not all scholars agree (e.g., Mills 1997, 91–97). The return of the dead after battle was undoubtedly an important religious matter throughout antiquity. Aeschylus, in fact, seems to have treated the same subject in *Eleusinians* (Zuntz 1955, 4). Nonetheless, just as mention of civil war in *Eumenides* is likely to have reminded Aeschylus' audience of the political situation after Ephialtes' reforms, so in Euripides' play the refusal of the Thebans to allow burial of their foes could have reminded the Athenians of a similar incident involving Boeotians in the recent past. Bowie concedes that there are differences between the mythical and historical situations, and tries to show how the poet filters contemporary events to complicate the audience's response.

Equally important, as Bowie notes, is the cluster of features in the play that forcefully draw the mythical Athens of *Suppliants* toward its fifth-century counterpart. Although Theseus seems to have monarchical powers, he refers to his city as if it were democratic; he must consult the Athenian people before deciding to help recover the dead; he echoes the language of the assembly (438–39) and refers to magistracies (406–7). In her speech at 297–331 Aethra justifies intervening in the affairs of other states, as was Athens' wont in the fifth century, and speaks of the law of all Hellas (311), referred to as well by speakers in Thucydides (e.g., 4.97.2). The eulogies at the end of the play would have recalled Athenian funeral orations. The most glaring anachronisms are the references to "written laws" (433) and a tripod with an inscription (1201–4; on writing cf. Easterling 1985a, 3–6).

Bowie's article (52) also raises an important question about the limits assumed to have been imposed on tragedy after Phrynichus was fined for reminding the Athenians of "suffering close to home." Was Euripides treading on dangerous ground? Events in Euripides' tragedy turn out better than they did in real life, where the Athenians were twice defeated by the Boeotians. Nevertheless, by raising the audience's emotional investment, could the powerful contemporary resonances of this and other Euripidean plays have counted against the playwright when it came to awarding first prize at the City Dionysia?

Recoveries and Reversals

Thucydides contends that the treaty of 421 did not bring genuine peace (5.26.2). Powerful members of Sparta's alliance rejected it, and although the Spartans recovered the soldiers captured at Pylos, few of the other terms of the treaty were carried out. But the respite from battle offered both sides a chance to regroup. As early as 419 the impetuous Athenian aristocrat Alcibiades was stirring up trouble in the Peloponnese. The Spartans showed signs of their old selves when they defeated the Argive alliance in a hoplite battle at Mantinea. In 416 the Athenians captured the island of Melos, a Spartan colony, then put to death the adult males and sold the women and children into slavery (5.116.4). In the same year the Athenians voted to send a large expedition to Sicily under the command of Nicias, Alcibiades, and Lamachus. Technically the Peace still held; not until 414 would the Athenians openly break it by sending help to Argive allies under attack by the Spartans (6.105.1).

By 413 the Athenians seemed to be on the brink of defeat. By this time Alcibiades had fled to Sparta after being recalled to stand trial on charges of impiety in Athens (Thucydides 6.61.1) and for two years had been helping the enemy. The Spartans were at Athens' back door; the Attic deme of Decelea had been transformed into an outpost for the enemy and a haven for runaway slaves (7.27.3–5). The Athenians had suffered the total destruction of their forces in Sicily (7.87) and feared both a direct attack on the city and revolt among their allies. In response to the crisis the Athenians appointed a board of elders, including the poet Sophocles, to govern the city (8.1.3). The following year, Chios, one of the few allies still in possession of its navy, went over to the Spartans (8.14.2).

Over the final seven years of the war the Athenians showed remarkable resilience. Although consistently short of funds, they rebuilt their navy. With the help of Alcibiades, who had shifted his allegiance once again and had been elected general of the fleet stationed at Samos (Thucydides 8.81), the Athenians would go on to win a number of impressive victories in the east.

Alcibiades eventually returned to Athens (Xenophon, *Hellenica* 1.4), but his recall was a mixed blessing. He furthered the cause of oligarchs in Athens, who overturned the democracy in 411 (Thucydides 8.64–70). Their violent reign was unstable and short-lived. The fleet at Samos swore to remain democratic and to continue to fight the Peloponnesians (8.75). They went so far as to form an assembly and elect their own generals. In effect, they became an Athenian government in exile.

According to Thucydides, internal divisions were the real cause of Athens' defeat (2.65.11), and Xenophon's account of the final years of the war seem to bear him out. After winning naval victories at Cynosema and Cyzicus (Thucydides 8.104–7; Xenophon, *Hellenica* 1.1) and regaining control of much of the Hellespont (*Hellenica* 1.3), the Athenians failed to drive home their successes. Without tribute to fund the fleet, commanders had to extort pay for their rowers from cities in Asia Minor and the islands. During one such excursion to raise money, Alcibiades made the mistake of leaving his forces in the hands of a subordinate, who foolishly exposed the fleet to a successful attack by the Spartan commander Lysander (Xenophon, *Hellenica* 1.5). The Athenians, as Alcibiades well knew, were unlikely to accept his excuses. Rather than risk their wrath he fled to a stronghold he had prepared for himself in the Chersonese (*Hellenica* 1.5).

Despite a resounding naval victory, the Athenian generals at Arginusae (406) were less fortunate than Alcibiades. In the aftermath of battle, a storm prevented them from rescuing rowers who had been swept overboard. When they were brought to trial for neglecting their duty, they felt the full force of the Athenians' anger. Collectively (and therefore illegally) condemned, some fled the city, while others were put to death (Xenophon, *Hellenica* 1.6–7). Because of the trial the Athenians forfeited the services of some of their most capable commanders, including the younger Pericles (Jameson 1956, 222–24). They also rejected yet another Spartan offer of peace (Aristotle, *Constitution* 34).

Through jealousy, suspicion, or sheer incompetence, in the following year (405), Athenian commanders assigned to the fleet at the Hellespont failed to take to heart a warning from Alcibiades that their position at Aegospotami was vulnerable to attack by the Peloponnesian fleet. The details of the battle of Aegospotami are not clear, but the outcome is. Of the 180 ships in the Athenian fleet, only nine survived. The Athenian general Conon sailed with eight to Cyprus; one ship returned to Athens with the appalling news. Some Athenians escaped overland to Sestos; the rest, perhaps three to four thousand men, were captured and put to death (Xenophon, *Hellenica* 2.1). Lysander controlled the Hellespont and with it Athens' grain. By forcing all the Athenians he found in Asia to return to the city, he hastened the famine that eventually forced Athens to submit (*Hellenica* 2.2). By 404 the Athenians had torn down their walls, and with Sparta's blessing the city was ruled by a council of Athenian oligarchs, the so-called Thirty Tyrants.

Sophocles' *Philoctetes* and Euripides' *Orestes*

Soon after the overthrow of democracy in Athens in 411 Sophocles produced *Philoctetes* (409). Bowie (1997) has reexamined the parallels between the protagonist of this play and the historical Alcibiades and concluded that the similarities would have raised in Sophocles' audience religious as well as moral and political questions about Alcibiades' recall. In the play the Greeks need to retrieve Philoctetes to save their forces at Troy; Alcibiades was recalled to the Athenian fleet at Samos in 410 with the hope that his leadership could save Athens. Both figures are under a curse, Philoctetes because he was bitten by a sacred snake when he entered Chryses' grove, Alcibiades because of his role in the desecration of the herms and profanation of the mysteries prior to the Sicilian expedition (Thucydides 6.27–29, 53–61; Andocides, *On the Mysteries*; on the curse see Plutarch, *Alcibiades* 22).

The similarities, however, are outweighed by differences (Jameson 1956, Calder 1971). Philoctetes, in contrast to Alcibiades, is not a master of intrigue. Nor does Philoctetes want to return to Troy, as Alcibiades schemed to return to Athens. Even Bowie concedes that Odysseus as well as Neoptolemus exhibit Alcibiadian features (Jameson 1956); Odysseus, like Alcibiades (Plutarch, *Alcibiades* 23), possesses a chameleon-like ability to adapt and a belief in the power of words (Debnar 2001, 201–20; Podlecki 1966b).

Still, *Philoctetes* is without a doubt colored by contemporary concerns. For Rose (1976) the setting of the play and the introduction of Neoptolemus into the myth highlight the play's engagement with sophistic thought. Philoctetes' isolated life on Lemnos associates him with "primitive" stage in the Sophists' scheme of human progress. His joy at being able to communicate with fellow Greeks, the mutual sympathy felt by Philoctetes and Neoptolemus, and the bonds of friendship that they begin to form represent the second or "social compact" stage. The figure of Odysseus ushers in the Sophists' final stage, "contemporary society," with its developed political, economic, and social institutions.

In Rose's view, Sophocles challenges the Sophists' privileging of culture (*nomos*) over nature (*phusis*). The Sophists' attitude toward culture, education in particular, as Rose explains, was complicated. On the one hand, their value as teachers depended on the premise that "nature" could be changed, a potentially democratic view. Yet they could not dismiss "nature" altogether, since many of their patrons were aristocrats by birth. Instead, they claimed that training could bring out the best in nature, while a good nature could also be corrupted.

The young Neoptolemus has two instructors. Odysseus first convinces him to use deceit by claiming that the good of the Greek army justifies the base means they must use to lure Philoctetes to Troy. The argument of advantage, in other words, trumps that of justice in this play, as it often does in the debates in Thucydides (e.g., 1.32–43). Neoptolemus has learned his rhetoric lessons well: when asked by Philoctetes, "Child, do you not know who it is you look upon?" Neoptolemus artfully dodges the question: "How could I recognize a man I have never seen?" (249–50).

Philoctetes offers Neoptolemus competing lessons: claims of friendship and of favor in return for favor outweigh the pursuit of glory and gain. All that Philoctetes asks is to be returned to his family. After witnessing Philoctetes' suffering first-hand Neoptolemus' resolve wavers; he reveals his own duplicity in the hope that candor combined with persuasion can convince his new friend to help the Greeks take Troy. When Odysseus appears, seizes the bow, abandons Philoctetes, and orders Neoptolemus to depart, expedience and deceit seem to have won the day. But Neoptolemus soon returns in defiance, restores the bow to Philoctetes, and finally agrees to escort him home. In short, Rose argues, in the debate between nature and nurture, Sophocles comes down squarely on the side of nature by affirming the nobility of both Philoctetes and Neoptolemus.

In contrast, Calder (1971) contends that Neoptolemus is cleverly deceptive throughout the play. Goldhill (1990) also points out that the ending of the play complicates the picture. The sudden epiphany of the recently apotheosized Heracles sets the story back on its traditional trajectory: both Philoctetes and Neoptolemus are willing to go to Troy after all. At the same time, Heracles' warning to "be pious in matters concerning the gods" is likely to have reminded the audience that after the fall of Troy Neoptolemus murders Priam at his household altar and hurls Astyanax from the walls of Troy. Is nature really stronger than nurture? True, Philoctetes will win glory by killing Paris, but glory is a heroic value that he has forcefully repudiated throughout the play.

Rather than a specific debate about Alcibiades, it is much easier to see in the double-dealing and subterfuge of this play a more general reflection of Athens around the time of the oligarchic revolution of 411 (although the two are, of course, related; Calder 1971). When, for example, Philoctetes entrusts his bow to Neoptolemus, he shows himself unable to distinguish between friends and enemies. Thucydides offers a similar picture of Athens of 411. The authors of the oligarchic revolution promised the people that a council of five thousand would rule the city. No such council was ever formed. But when the Athenians finally resisted and decided to tear down a wall in the Piraeus that would have allowed the Spartans to enter their city, Thucydides says that rather than calling on the people for help, they called out to "whoever wanted the Five Thousand to rule instead of the Four Hundred" because they were afraid that this group might actually exist "and that in speaking to one of them they might make a dangerous mistake through ignorance" (Thucydides 8.92.11). At the same time, as Pelling (2000, 187–88) suggests, the questions raised by *Philoctetes* are far from one-dimensional. The Athenians were in danger of losing the war. Circumstances must have complicated their responses to Neoptolemus' disobedience to Odysseus and to Philoctetes' stubborn refusal to compromise, both of which put the safety of the entire Greek army at stake.

Euripides' *Orestes*, whose plot takes up where Aeschylus' *Libation Bearers* ends, is set in an even more troubling world of factions and wavering loyalties. One of the play's outstanding features is the sketches it offers of a wide range of political types. We first encounter members of a faction of young aristocrats, Orestes, Pylades, and Electra (as in Thucydides 8.65.2; Hall 1993, 269–71). Next we meet the noncommittal Menelaus, who pries from Orestes all the information he can get about which party has the upper hand in Argos; after promising to help his nephew (if only in words), he does not show up at the assembly where Orestes argues his case. The messenger who brings Electra news of Orestes' trial describes four speakers in addition to Orestes. Talthybius (formerly Agamemnon's herald, now "under the power of the strong") only "half-heartedly" praises Agamemnon, while reproaching Orestes for the bad precedent he has set concerning the treatment of parents (887–97). Diomedes receives a mixed response to his proposal that banishment be the punishment (898–902). An Argive of dubious citizenship (902–16) is said to bluster and to rely on outcries from the crowd (see Bers 1985). Orestes has one defender, a manly fellow (*andreios*) who warns that men will refuse to go off to war if they suspect their wives will be unfaithful (917–30). Perhaps recognizing the effect-iveness of this man's argument, Orestes adds (if his speech is not an interpolation) that if women like his mother go unpunished, men will be enslaved by their wives (931–42). The argument, however, is less effective coming from Orestes, and he and his friends are condemned to death. The entire trial, as these sketches suggest, is conducted in terms of advantage rather than justice or piety. There is no mention of Apollo's urging Orestes to murder Clytemnestra, although the god's role is men-tioned at the beginning of the play and Apollo himself will appear at its end.

The poet seems to have invited his audience to see a reflection of Athens in this play. As Easterling (1997b, 28–33) observes, *Orestes*' Argos is featureless. The lack of specific details about this setting allows the audience to project onto Argos the image of their own city. We can never know for certain how distorted or parodic this reflection may have seemed. In antiquity there were attempts to identify "real" Athenian politicians, like Cleophon or Theramenes, behind the cast of *Orestes* (on Orestes and Antiphon see Hall 1993, 267). As with *Philoctetes*, however, the vague-ness of the parallels makes it difficult to see more than types. The fifth-century Athenian audience may have perceived through these types many more men than the few individuals we know about from Thucydides and Xenophon (Pelling 2000, 166).

The striking differences between Euripides' *Orestes* and Aeschylus' *Oresteia* may also point to broad changes in the political world of Athens over the course of the fifty years between the two performances. At the very end of Euripides' play, for example, Apollo suddenly appears not only to order Orestes to go to Parrhasia and then to Athens (where he goes in Aeschylus' trilogy), but also to whisk Helen off to the heavens and to arrange marriages between Pylades and Electra as well as between Orestes and Hermione (whom Orestes has just threatened to kill). There is no divine authorization of the Argive council or of human law, as in Aeschylus' *Eumenides*, nor is there any sense of an old order being incorporated in the new. The torches of the procession that lead Aeschylus' Semnai to their new abode in *Orestes* become torches about to set fire to the palace (Hall 1993, 281). As in *Eumenides*, violence in *Orestes* is brought to an end, but not by the establishment of a court that will continue beyond the limits of the performance. Rather, it is ended by the delayed intervention of Apollo. Whether this god can be depended on for future help is left open. Several years before the *Oresteia*, Aeschylus' audience had survived one threat of civil war. Euripides' audience was just on the brink of another (see the nuanced discussion of Pelling 2000, 184–88).

Epilogue: 401 and Beyond

The rule of the Thirty Tyrants in Athens lasted only as long as Lysander retained influence in Sparta. In 403 the Spartan king Pausanias negotiated a peace between the democratic exiles, in control of the Piraeus, and the men in the city (Xenophon, *Hellenica* 2.4). The restoration of democracy and a general amnesty soon followed. The city's remarkable resilience may explain why Sophocles' *Oedipus at Colonus*, which celebrates Athens, could be produced five years after it was composed and three years after Athens' defeat. Kirkwood (1986; also Blundell 1993) points to another reason. The play is set, not in the city itself, the seat of bygone imperial power, but in the deme of Colonus, praised in the choral odes for its fertility and bounty. As Kirkwood observes, when Oedipus arrives at Colonus he first asks, "What land have we come to?" and the power Oedipus offers to Theseus in exchange for accepting him as suppliant in the grove of the Eumenides is chthonic power, power in the land itself (1986, 104–9).

The emphasis on the city as a collection of citizens instead of the city as *both* its land and people marked the beginning of Athens' naval hegemony and rise to imperial power. When the Athenians took to their ships under threat of a Persian invasion, they fought for a city that existed only in their "faintest hope" (Thucydides 1.74.4). On the final retreat from Syracuse the Athenian general Nicias tried to instill courage in his soldiers – the remnants of the rowers that manned the fleet – by telling them that men make the city, not walls or ships (7.77.7). When an oligarchy was established in Athens, the fleet in Samos became the democracy in exile (8.75).

At the end of his life Sophocles did not reject the city or its democracy. Rather he saw in Athens something more than the sum of its imperial power. In Theseus' treatment of the suppliant Oedipus we find the return of *epieikeia*, the prized sense of fairness and justice, which the Athenians had forfeited at Melos and Scione (Kirkwood 1986, 100–103). The poet's vision proved correct: the Peloponnesian War did not destroy Athens, or the Athenian democracy, or, for that matter, tragedy. All continued to flourish well into the fourth century.

FURTHER READING

On the relationship of tragedy to fifth-century history, two valuable collections of essays are Goff 1995a and Pelling 1997c. Goff's introduction (1995b) and Pelling's conclusion (1997b) are especially important. The care that Rose 1995 takes to articulate his theoretical assumptions and methodology is exemplary. Bowie 1997 offers a useful catalogue of candidates for historical tragedies (including fragments).

Pelling 2000 is a more broad-ranging study by a single author and complements the collections above, especially in its discussions of the reactions of the fifth-century Athenians to tragedy. Since we know so little about these reactions, much of what Pelling says is speculative, but he exposes many unspoken assumptions that modern readers bring to ancient texts. On a possible change in fifth-century audiences see Sommerstein 1997.

Interest in the ancient audience is connected to what scholars think tragic poets were doing (or thought they were doing) when they produced their plays. For an overview of different perceptions of tragedy's political and social roles see Conraidie (1981) and Saïd (1998). In response to Winkler and Zeitlin 1990 and to Sommerstein et al. 1993, see Griffin 1998. Meier 1993 assumes an essential tie between tragedy and democracy; Boedeker and Raaflaub 1998 question and explore this assumption.

The revised edition of the *Cambridge Ancient History* is addressed to a more advanced audience than the general public to which the earlier edition was directed. Contributors provide numerous references and draw attention to areas of disagreement. On sources and chronology see Rhodes 1992a and 1992b, and Lewis 1992a and 1992b. Gomme's section "Sources other than Thucydides" (1: 29–84) in his introduction to Gomme 1945–56 is still useful and should be read in conjunction with Hornblower 1996, 1–19: "General remarks; the relation of this commentary to *HCT*." For a quick list of sources, see the succinct notes at the end of each section in Sealey 1976. On the Athenian empire, see Meiggs 1972; for a more basic introduction, Rhodes 1985. On the chronology of the Pentecontaetia in addition to Rhodes (above) see Unz 1986 and Badian 1993c.

CHAPTER TWO

Tragedy and Religion: The Problem of Origins

Scott Scullion

This chapter deals with the origins of tragedy and, in that context, considers whether and to what extent tragic drama was a religious phenomenon. Opinion on these matters rests on painstaking interpretation of brief and often obscure ancient texts, and the scholarly literature is correspondingly vast and controversial. I here analyze much of the primary ancient evidence with a minimum of doxographical detail, referring to influential studies written or available in English where further bibliographical guidance can be found. We must evaluate as best we can what evidence we have for the origins of tragedy before hazarding any conclusions about its religious or ritual nature; this may seem obvious, but the assumption that tragedy is by origin a religious phenomenon is so common and ingrained that the question is often begged.

Aristotle on Origins

Modern discussion of the issue of origins is in large part an extended commentary on Aristotle's brief treatment in the *Poetics*. The key passages are these:

> Coming into being from an improvisational beginning – both it [tragedy] and comedy, the former from those leading the dithyramb, the latter from those leading the phallic songs, which even at the present day are still a customary practice in many cities – it was enhanced little by little as they developed each element of it that became manifest, and after passing through many changes tragedy ceased to change, since it had attained its own nature. Aeschylus first increased the number of actors from one to two, diminished the choral elements, and made speech play the leading role; Sophocles introduced three actors and scene-painting. And then, with respect to grandeur, because it changed from being satyric [*dia to ek saturikou metabalein*] it was late that tragedy left behind simple plots and humorous diction and became dignified. In addition its meter became the iambic trimeter instead of the trochaic tetrameter; at first they used the tetrameter because the poetry was satyric and more closely connected with dance . . . (1449a9–23)

> . . . As for the number of episodes and the other elements, how they are said to have been embellished, let us take all these things as read, for it would perhaps be a big task to go through them one by one. (1449a28–31)

...The changes in tragedy and those who made them have not been forgotten, but no attention was paid to comedy at first because no one took it seriously. It was, indeed, some time late in its development that the archon "granted a chorus" of comedians; until then they were volunteers. Memory of those called poets of comedy is preserved only from the period when it already had some formal features. Who introduced masks or prologues or numbers of actors, and all that sort of thing, is unknown. (1449a37–1449b5)

Most modern scholars have concluded that what Aristotle tells us, however sketchy it may be, must be sound. Lesky, who speaks of "according full authority to Aristotle's remarks," says that "the range and type of his sources on the question of tragedy can no longer be determined, but that does not mean they never existed" (1983, 5). Doubt about the evidentiary basis of Aristotle's statements has, however, deepened since Lesky's day. There are strong reasons for believing that no one in the fifth century or later had access to tragic texts, documents, or any kind of reliable information going back before 500 BCE. West has made the fundamental observation that the dates given in the tenth-century *Suda* lexicon for the earliest tragedians (Thespis, Choerilus, Phrynichus, Pratinas) are a product of schematization, the poets being arbitrarily located at intervals of three Olympiads in the chronological unknown (West 1989, 251; cf. Scullion 2002b, 81–82). Aristotle does not name any of these poets, which in the case of Thespis would seem a glaring omission, but he may be eschewing the sort of pseudo-knowledge preserved in the *Suda*. Beyond these names and dates and four probably inauthentic fragments of Thespis we have no precise information about sixth-century tragedy, and it is hard to understand why, if such information was available, none of it is preserved in Aristotle or our other sources.

That such history of sixth-century tragedy as was in circulation was a product of the familiar ancient techniques of synchronism and schematization is reflected in what Aristotle himself tells us. Since competitions were organized by the state, it can hardly have been individual playwrights who "introduced" additional actors, and Aristotle must be drawing inferences from the number of actors implied by whatever earlier tragic texts were available to him or combining inference from Aeschylus' two-actor plays with schematization of the next phase of tragic development as Sophoclean. So too Aristotle is clearly assuming that the lost history of comedy will have been precisely parallel to that of tragedy, with a series of individual poets introducing masks and prologues and adding actors. Yet even in the case of the tragic history Aristotle is very reticent – it would not, as he claimed, have been a "big task" briefly to mention the various innovations – and one wonders if that again reflects circumspection about the reliability of the information.

There is in fact more to Aristotle's statements than analogy between the history of tragedy and the lost history of comedy. In the first sentence quoted above Aristotle is using a developmental schema – a modest beginning developed and enhanced little by little – that occurs often, with verbal parallels, elsewhere in his work (for example, *Constitution of the Athenians* 3.3.11, *Politics* 1274a9–11; see Else 1957, 152–53). At *Sophistical Refutations* 183b22–34 he schematizes in the same way the "enhancement" of rhetoric, naming specific individuals who gradually developed it, and adds that such a scheme suits "practically all the other arts." Hence it is not just that he concludes on no evidence that comedy must have developed by the same process as tragedy, but that even in the case of tragedy he is applying a theoretical scheme of developmental process. Convinced that the scheme itself was sound, Aristotle was perhaps therefore the more inclined to be cautious about the details, and so only named those who introduced changes in tragedy when he was dealing with fifth-century developments and so felt some confidence. There is little to be said for the easy assumption that it was the other way round, that Aristotle's scheme of development was generated by his knowledge of the details, and that if he had chosen to lay out what he knew we would have a fairly full and reliable history (cf. Halliwell 1987, 79).

If Aristotle's account of the relatively recent history of drama is skimpy and schematic, what he says about the remotest origins of tragedy and comedy seems likely to be more schematic still (Pickard-Cambridge 1927, 121–31; Dale 1969, 176–77 n. 2; Else 1965, 12–22; Scullion 2002a, 102–10). His sketch of the earliest developments looks like another product of general considerations, which are not far to seek. The elements of Aristotle's scheme – tragedy, comedy, "the satyric" or satyr-play, dithyramb, and phallic songs – also occur together in the festivals of Dionysus at Athens, the context in which tragedy "attained its own nature."

It is typical of Aristotle, as his reconstruction of the history of rhetoric shows, to identify precursors that would lead comprehensibly to, or in other words are identified on the basis of, the developed "natural form" he knew. Thus he took the view that the art of rhetoric began in Sicily with Empedocles and was developed there by Corax and Tisias and by Gorgias, who transferred it to Athens, where it came to fulfillment (see A 5 Radermacher; Russell 1981, 117, 166). According to Cicero (*Brutus* 12, 46–48), Aristotle said that the first handbooks of rhetoric were composed when the Sicilian tyrants had fallen and judicial procedures for the recovery of private property began to be instituted; that is, when circumstances resembling those of democratic and litigious Athens came into being in Sicily. Aristotle's account is arbitrary and schematic and hence problematic. Gorgias is clearly the cardinal figure, and the generative notion is that the origins should point forward teleologically to the Athenian fulfillment, which is to say that the reconstruction was driven by the teleology.

Aristotle seems to have employed an analogous procedure in reconstructing the origins of drama, though in this case he had little or no factual flesh to put on the bones of his scheme. Tragedy, comedy, satyr-play, dithyramb, phallic song, and aspects of the relationships between them, are retrojected into the remote past as a scheme of development. Thus satyr-play, associated with tragedy in the festival context, is associated with it in the reconstruction. Very likely it is "the satyric" rather than "satyr-play" (*saturikon* might mean either) that Aristotle, with deliberate vagueness, says tragedy "changed out of" or ceased to be. The *Suda* states that satyr-play was introduced to Athens by Pratinas of Phlius around 500 BCE (*Suda* π 2230 Adler); vase-painters first depict satyrs with human feet and in spheres of myth and life other than their own about 520 to 510, and clearly theatrical satyrs make an appearance in the third decade of the fifth century (Brommer 1959). Whatever we may make of the *Suda*'s notice about Pratinas, it is consistent with the unmistakable evidence of the vases that satyr-play developed much later than tragedy and comedy (Burkert 1966, 89). Aristotle may have known this, and it would in any case be unlike him to derive tragedy from the developed form of satyr-play. On the model of organic growth that is typical of his thought the seeds of the satyric drama performed with tragedy in the fifth century must have been present in an undifferentiated satyro-tragic drama out of which tragedy and satyr-play developed – differently, but in institutional tandem. What "satyric" in that context may have meant to him is a question we will return to.

The descent of comedy from phallic songs is a straightforward concept and makes intuitive sense (though there are other, equally plausible, lines of descent). The role of dithyramb, however, remains to be explained. Aristotle says that tragedy "changed from being satyric," but he clearly regarded dithyramb as its proper "beginning" (*archê*), doubtless because tragedy shares with dithyramb choral song-and-dance as formal element and heroic myth as content. In the course of his discussion of origins it emerges that Aristotle considered epic the most important precursor of tragedy, since the two share significant common features of content, tone, and construction (1449b16–20; cf. Halliwell 1986, 253–59). Tragedy's inheritance from epic is vastly more important to him than that from dithyramb, but epic cannot account for tragedy's choral component. Dithyramb not only can do that, but can also anchor tragedy in the specific Athenian milieu in which it came to fruition.

Dithyramb

By the time of Pindar and Bacchylides at the latest, the content of dithyramb was what it remained in Aristotle's day, the whole body of Greek heroic myth. Although Aristotle neglects lyric poetry in the *Poetics*, he regards dithyramb as a mode of representation (*mimêsis*) similar to epic, tragedy, and comedy (1447a14), and treats examples drawn from Timotheus' dithyramb *Scylla* as equivalent to examples drawn from tragedy (1454a30–31 with Gudeman 1934, 276; 1461b30–32). This sort of conception and classification of dithyramb may go back to the fifth century and earlier.

Various sources, most but not all of them late, suggest that dithyramb and tragedy were seen as very close congeners. Some of this evidence has to do with the seventh-century citharode Arion of Methymna, described by Herodotus (1.23) as "the first man we know of to compose and name dithyramb and produce it at Corinth." According to the *Suda* (α 3886 Adler) Arion "is said also to have been the inventor of the tragic mode (*tragikou tropou*) and the first to make the chorus stationary and to sing dithyramb and to give a name to what was sung by the chorus, and to introduce satyrs speaking in verse." Proclus (*Chrestomathy* 12) attributes to Aristotle the view that Arion was the founder of dithyramb and "first led the circular chorus [*kuklios choros*]," the latter a well-established alternative name for dithyramb. In the commentary of John the Deacon on Hermogenes (Rabe 1908, 150) we are told that "Arion of Methymna introduced the first performance of tragedy [*tês de tragôidias prôton drama*], as Solon noted in his work entitled *Elegies*."

Other evidence has to do with choruses in honor of the Argive hero Adrastus. Herodotus (5.67) describes how Cleisthenes, tyrant of early sixth-century Sicyon, deprived Adrastus of honor: "besides worshipping Adrastus in other ways, the Sicyonians honored his sufferings with tragic choruses [*tragikoisi choroisi*], worshipping not Dionysus but Adrastus. Cleisthenes gave the choruses over to Dionysus and the balance of the rites to [the hero] Melanippus." It has been suggested that the *tragikoi choroi* of this passage are dithyrambs. As we have seen, dithyramb went by at least one other name, *kuklios choros*, which in the course of the fifth century became the more common term. If "tragic chorus" were an earlier equivalent of "circular chorus" as an alternative name for dithyramb, the evidence above would fall into place (cf. Burkert 1966, 96 n. 19). The "tragic mode" whose invention is attributed to Arion by the *Suda* is the tragic style in music under its technical name. Musical theory distinguished the tragic and dithyrambic modes, but confusion may have been caused by the difference between the dithyramb of Arion and the "new dithyramb" that arose later, by Aristotle's theory of the dithyrambic origin of tragedy, or by an equivalence of "tragic" and "dithyrambic" such as we are suggesting for Herodotus. John the Deacon's statement may then be a simple misinterpretation of some such statement by (or attributed to) Solon as that Arion introduced "tragic choruses." Herodotus' phrase is unlikely to be his own coinage, and "tragic" may already have been in use as a description of content, "treating heroic myth," as well as of form. The association of dithyramb with tragedy in the Athenian festivals would tend to reinforce such a use, as would the fact that dithyrambs like tragedies were given titles.[1]

The conception of dithyramb as "tragic" will have been the result of their common subject matter, heroic myth. Aristotle may then have had a terminological and conceptual prompt for his derivation of tragic drama from dithyramb that went beyond their association at the City Dionysia. He will also have been familiar with dithyrambs of the mimetic type represented for us by Bacchylides' *Theseus* (18), which consisted of lyric dialogue between a soloist or leader singing as a figure from myth and the chorus singing as some group; the parallel with the actor and chorus of tragedy is evident. From every point of view, then – content, choral nature, institutional setting, mimetic element, and terminology – Aristotle's association of dithyramb with tragedy was natural. Dithyramb was attested earlier than tragedy and, on his model of organic development, was its likeliest source.

A seventh-century testimony of dithyramb Aristotle must have known is a fragment of Archilochus (120 West): "I know how to lead off the fair song of lord Dionysus, the dithyramb, blitzed in my head with wine." This passage will have interested Aristotle for a number of reasons. First, it associates dithyramb with a festival of Dionysus and so provides historical precedent for its connection with the City Dionysia at which it was performed alongside tragedy. Secondly, the verb "lead off" (*exarxai*) is the one Aristotle uses when he speaks of the origin of tragedy "from those leading [*exarchontôn*] the dithyramb"; here is confirmation – or the source? – of Aristotle's explanation of the emergence of the actor. Thirdly, the leader's drunkenness implies an antic disposition, and finally the verse is trochaic tetrameter, the meter Aristotle says was characteristic of tragedy in its undignified, "satyric" phase. Is the passage itself a source – or the source – of his theory of "satyric" tragedy? We are speculating, but so it appears was Aristotle, and whether or not Archilochus' verses prompted his line of speculation about tragedy's ultimate origins, they will at least have seemed encouragingly congruent with it.

Satyr-Play

When Aristotle spoke of early tragedy as satyric, he probably had in mind that tragedy was at that stage improvisatory, antic, simple in plot, trochaic in meter, the adjective "satyric" referring to general mood and tone in much the same way as "tragic" could. One still encounters, however, the very different view that when he calls early tragedy "satyric" Aristotle means that those who performed it were costumed as satyrs. Lesky's final statement on these matters (1983, 1–24, 407–12) sums up the prevailing scholarly consensus down to and beyond his time. For him as for many other Aristotelian fundamentalists (as one might call them) the philosopher's *satur-ikon* must be an early form of satyr-play. The great virtue of Aristotle's explanation, on this view, is that it accounts for "the close bond between the satyr-play and tragedy, which is generic and points to genetic connections" (Lesky 1983, 7).

There is an interesting divergence of analysis here. Skeptics conclude that "the satyric" is a retrojection into the dim past of the mood and tone of the developed form, satyr-play, of which knowledge was readily accessible. Fundamentalists are by contrast attracted by the power of "the satyric" to resolve the great conundrum of the association of satyr-play with tragedy: it was ever thus. The latter view requires one to assume that Aristotle somehow had reliable knowledge of the remotest, improvisatory stage of tragedy. The skeptic makes what is in itself the far more plausible assumption that Aristotle's starting point was his knowledge of the developed form, which confronted him with the same conundrum. Those taking this approach may rest content with the evidence that satyr-play developed much later than tragedy. They may conclude that it was introduced to Athens by Pratinas or another and on the strength of its intrinsic appeal became a regular part of the dramatic competition, alongside tragedy, during the period preceding the introduction of comic competitions in 486. This skeptical position does not require us to explain away the clear evidence of the vases, as Pohlenz (1965) attempts to do with his lame suggestion that Pratinas was responsible only for a "Renaissance of the satyrs" (Lesky 1983, 10, who follows him).

To take Aristotle's *saturikon* as an early form of satyr-play is only to displace the conundrum of the genre's association with tragedy into the past. Those taking this approach support it with the argument that tragedy, *tragôidia*, means the "song of the goats," that is, of performers costumed as goat-like satyrs, a view dominant through most of the twentieth century (see Lesky 1983; Webster in Pickard-Cambridge 1962, 20, 96–98, 129) and still maintained by some scholars (for example, by Seaford 1994, 267–69 with nn. 147–48).

Etymology

Welcker suggested in 1826 that the *tragos* ("billy goat") element in the word *tragôidia* referred to goat-like satyrs and that satyrs of this type were the performers of Aristotle's *saturikon*, notions that were later widely accepted through the advocacy of Wilamowitz (Burkert 1966, 88 n. 2). Two pieces of evidence are cited. The first is from the *Etymologicum Magnum*, a Byzantine lexicon, which among other explanations of the term "tragedy" offers this: "Or because for the most part the choruses consisted of satyrs, which they called 'billy goats' mockingly, or because of the hairiness of their bodies, or because of their enthusiasm for things sexual, for that is the kind of creature they are" (764.5–9). The second is from the lexicographer Hesychius: " 'Billy goats': satyrs, because of having billy goats' ears" (τ 1237 Schmidt). Here "billy goats" and "satyrs" are in the accusative case, indicating that the first is a quotation which is being glossed by the second. The Hesychius passage reveals the background in ancient scholarly exegesis of the apparent attestation of satyr-choruses for tragedy that is found in the *Etymologicum Magnum*.

Three extant passages from satyr-play that connect satyrs with goats or goatskins exemplify the sort of literary text that prompted and guided the exegetical commentary. In Euripides' *Cyclops* (78–82) satyrs shepherding for Polyphemus wear goatskins, but these are garments typical of shepherds, not evidence for satyric costume. In Sophocles' *Trackers* (*Ichneutae*, fr. 314.367–68) a satyr is compared to a goat in point of beard and lust, and in a fragment of Aeschylus (fr. 207), though we lack the context, there is no reason to assume that the satyr is actually (as opposed to metaphorically) a billy goat (Pickard-Cambridge 1927, 153–55; Burkert 1966, 90 n. 5; Lesky 1983, 13–14). Hesychius is clearly glossing a comparable passage in which a group of satyrs were called "billy goats." The explanation of "tragedy" in the *Etymologicum Magnum* is just as clearly based on such passages rather than on a tradition that early tragedy was performed by goat-like satyrs. The author cites the fact that satyrs were "called 'billy goats' mockingly" to account for the notion of satyr-choruses in tragedy; in other words he is citing precisely the use of the term "billy goat" as simile or metaphor that we have seen in our passages from satyr-play. That is not evidence that satyrs *were* billy goats; on the contrary, it contradicts that claim. Nor does it suggest that the author has information about the remotest origins of tragedy, merely that he is familiar with classical satyr-drama. It is not then that the author has made a bad job of explaining the proposition that tragic choruses "for the most part" consisted of satyrs, but that the proposition is a guess based on, not information independent of, the metaphorical usage he was familiar with; the telling qualification "for the most part" betrays the not very confident guesswork. That is the full ancient evidence for tragedy as "the song of the goats = satyrs" and for the existence of goat-like satyrs in the classical period. Such creatures emerged in the Hellenistic period (and were perhaps known to the author of the passage glossed in Hesychius), but, as Furtwängler observed long ago, the satyrs of the classical period resembled not goats but horses (Pickard-Cambridge 1927, 149–54; Burkert 1966, 90 with n. 5).

A second fatal objection to the goat-satyrs theory is linguistic (Burkert 1966, 92–93 with n. 12). In determinative compounds of the type *tragôidos* ("tragedian," which, rather than *tragôidia*, "tragedy," is the primary form) the first component determines the second rather than vice versa; that is, the word does not mean "singing goat" or "goat that sings" but must denote a "singer" who sings about, or in some kind of connection with, a goat. "Singer for the goat-prize" is the only possibility that makes sense, and there is an excellent ancient parallel for it. Dionysius of Argos, in the fourth or third century BCE, said that *arnôidos* was an earlier term for *rhapsôidos*, "rhapsode," explaining the term on the basis of "a lamb [*arnos*] being appointed as the prize for the victors" (*FrGHist* 308 fr. 2).

There is abundant ancient evidence for *tragôidia* understood as "song for the prize goat." The best-known evidence is Horace, *Ars poetica* 220–24 ("he who with tragic song competed for a mere goat"); the earliest is the Parian Marble, a chronicle inscribed about 264/63 BCE, which records, under a date between 538 and 528 BCE: "Thespis the poet...first produced...and as prize was established the billy goat" (*FrGHist* 239A, epoch 43); the clearest is Eustathius 1769.45: "They called those competing 'tragedians' [*tragôidoi*], clearly because of the song over the billy goat [*epi tragôi...ôidên*]" (cf. Dioscorides, *Anthologia Palatina* 7.410.3–4; Diomedes 1: 488 Keil; Euanthius 13–14 Wessner 1902–5).

Convinced nevertheless that Aristotle thought the performers of the earliest tragic drama were got up as goat-like satyrs, most twentieth-century scholars went on to assume that this was a central issue in an ancient debate about the origins of tragedy (Lesky 1983, 1–24, is again representative). On their construction, Aristotle and his peripatetic successors consistently maintained his (that is, their) view of the name and original nature of tragedy against the opposition of those who interpreted the name as "song for the goat-prize" and regarded satyr-drama as a novelty of the late sixth century, introduced to Athens by Pratinas from Argive Phlius.

Rival Claims to Tragedy

There certainly was an ancient debate about tragedy's place of origin. The pseudo-Platonic dialogue *Minos* states the Athenian claim: "Tragedy is ancient here, not as people think begun by Thespis, nor by Phrynichus, but, if you want to consider the matter, you will discover that it is a very ancient discovery of this city" (321a). The *Minos* is countering the view that tragedy was by origin Peloponnesian, which clearly had partly to do with the traditions about Arion at Corinth and Epigenes of Sicyon discussed above, and which shifted the issue of origins to a period well before Thespis.

The Athenians' response to the Peloponnesian challenge was tendentious in inspiration and speculative in method. They produced an account not dissimilar to the Aristotelian theory, though with far more circumstantial detail (and correspondingly diminished credibility), but avoided a key vulnerability in it by steering clear of the dangerously Doric dithyramb. Putative ancient customs of the Attic countryside and strained etymologizing were enlisted to produce a primeval and purely Athenian tragedy.

Aristotle himself already knew of conflicting Athenian and Dorian claims to tragedy, and of etymological arguments supporting them:

> Hence, some say, they are called dramas [*dramata*], because they represent people acting [*drôntas*, stem *drá–*]. It is also for this reason that the Dorians make a counter-claim to tragedy and comedy (the Megarians to comedy... and some of those in the Peloponnese to tragedy), appealing to the names as evidence, for they say they call the outlying villages *kômai* while the Athenians call them *dêmoi*, the point being that comedians [*kômôidoi*] are so called not because of the verb "to revel" [*kômazein*] but because of their wandering through villages [*kômai*] when they were banned from the city [*astu*]. Also that their word for "act/do" is *drân*, the Athenians' *prattein*. (*Poetics* 1448a28–1448b2)

We must note parenthetically the remarkable fact that Aristotle does not mention the dispute over the meaning of *tragôidia* that many modern scholars regard as a central issue in the ancient debate. The most natural conclusion is that he fails to mention it because there was no such dispute, all the ancient writers, whether they favored an Athenian or a Peloponnesian origin for tragedy, taking it for granted that *tragôidia* referred to the billy-goat prize.

In point of fact *kômê* is Attic as well as Doric for "village"; furthermore, *astu* is the distinctively Attic word for "city"; Burkert rightly argues that the advocates of Peloponnesian origin Aristotle refers to must have been turning the tables on an argument originally offered by those favoring an Athenian origin (1966, 95). The certainly correct derivation of *kômôidoi* is from *kômos* "revel-band," but as the *kômos* was a panhellenic activity someone on the Athenian side must have located comedy's origin in rural Attica by the lame means of the derivation from *kômê*, which was vulnerable to the retort that the usual Attic term was *dêmos*. At the stage the debate was at in Aristotle's day only a minimalist narrative seems to have been generated to accompany the etymological argument: the comedians are placed in the villages by the simple expedient of having them banned from the city.

Hellenistic writers, however, would elaborate very fully the tale of tragedy's origin in the Attic countryside. A good example is Plutarch (*De proverbiis Alexandrinorum libellus ineditus*, Crusius IIIa, 30, heavily emended): "Nothing to do with Dionysus: they say that tragedy and comedy came into existence [?] from laughter. For at the time of the harvesting of the produce some people standing by the wine-vats and drinking the must [sweet new wine] were jesting and later wrote jesting poems, which because they were previously sung in the villages [*kômai*] were called comedy [*kômôi-dia*]. They went about the Attic villages [*kômai*] continuously and jested, with their faces chalked." Dioscorides connects the *kômê* theory with Thespis (*Anthologia Palatina* 7.410.1–4): "I am that Thespis who first molded tragic song, inventing new delights for the villagers [*kômêtai*], at the time Bacchus led the trieteric [?/ 'trugic'; see below] chorus, for which the billy goat [*tragos*] was the prize [?], and an Attic bushel of figs." Key points here are that the explanation of "nothing to do with Dionysus" (a proverb to which I shall return) claims that tragedy and comedy have a common origin, and that in both passages the location in the *kômê* is no longer a mere consequence of banishment from the city, but positively motivated as presence at the vintage or at a festival of Dionysus, that is at occasions associated with the patron god of tragedy at Athens.

An even more elaborate "village" version appears in the Atticist lexicographer Pausanias (α 161 Erbse): "*Askôlia*: Festival at Athens in which, honoring the discovery of wine, they invented singing and railing at their fellow-villagers [*kômêtai*], when also they set out as prize for the singing the goat [*aix*] that destroyed the vines, and the victors leapt on the [inflated] skin [*askos*], and this was 'to perform the *askôlia*' " (cf. Vergil, *Georgics* 2.380–84). This tradition casts a clear light on the ancient scholars' methods. Latte (1957) has demonstrated that *askôlia* really meant "jumping/standing on one foot" (from *ana*, "up," and *skelos*, "limb") and that it was applied to the sport (familiar from comedy) of dancing on an inflated skin via a false derivation from *askos*. This invention is then elaborated by the story that a goat's skin was used in order to punish the goat for gnawing Dionysus' vine, by the invention of an Athenian festival of the discovery of wine, *Askôlia*, which never existed, and by connecting the *kômê* theory of the origin of tragedy with that festival. This is not the heightening of a reliable tradition but free invention unchecked by established facts.

Another version of the Athenian-origins theory latched onto a parody word for "comedy" in fifth-century comic poetry, *trugôidia* or "the song for the prize of new wine" (for example, Aristophanes, *Acharnians* 499, 500). Here was impeccably Athenian ammunition for the etymological side of the battle, and it was brazenly claimed that *trugôidia* was the primeval name of both tragedy and comedy. Among the explanations of the name "tragedy" at *Etymologicum Magnum* 764.9–13 we find: "or from *trux* 'new wine' [it was called] *trugôidia*. This name was common also to comedy, since the two types of poetry were not yet distinguished. For this [*trugôidia*] there was a single prize, new wine. Afterwards tragedy had the common name. Comedy is so called because previously they said these things in the villages [*kômai*] at the festivals of Dionysus and Demeter." This fantastic tale is useful only as additional support for *tragôidia* as "song for the goat-prize," since *trugôidia*, "song for the new wine," was obviously coined on the model of that word (cf. Anonymous, *On Comedy* 1, p. 7 Kaibel; schol. Aristophanes, *Acharnians* 499).

Eventually the origins of drama in rural Attica came to be associated with a particular Attic deme: "The discovery of both comedy and tragedy in Icarion in Attica was the result of drunkenness, and at the very season of the vintage, whence comedy was at first called *trugôidia*" (Athenaeus 2.11.40a). By the early third century Icaria had been appointed hometown of primeval Attic drama. The Parian Marble (*FrGHist* 239A, epoch 39), under the date 561/60 BCE, says, "In Athens a chorus of comedians was established, the Icarians setting it up first, Susarion having invented it, and as first prize was established a bushel of dried figs and an amphora-measure of wine." Clement of Alexandria claims that "Thespis the Athenian [invented] tragedy, Susarion the Icarian comedy" (*Stromata* 1.79.1), and the *Suda* (θ 282 Adler) says Thespis was from Icaria.

Susarion's name rather suggests non-Athenian origins, and an alternative tradition made him a Megarian (Aspasius on Aristotle, *Nicomachean Ethics* 1123a20; Susarion fr. 1 *PCG*). West may be right to guess that Susarion was a Megarian writer of iambic poetry who was first put forward as inventor of comedy by the Peloponnesians and then transferred to Icaria by the Athenians (West 1974, 183–84). We hear a good deal more about Thespis, but we *know* no more about him than about Susarion; Aristotle mentions neither. There is every reason to reject the notion that both were citizens of the deme Icaria.

The first step in the creation of this tale was doubtless the derivation of *kômôidia* from *kômê*, not historical facts about Icaria. That the *kômê* should be identified as Icaria was a natural elaboration. Icaria, which had its own early theater and dramatic festival, is the most Dionysiac of Attic demes, its name connected with Icarius, who received the god there and learned from him to cultivate the vine and make wine. We have suggested that Aristotle's hypotheses about the development of tragedy were guided by the teleological endpoint of the dramatic Dionysia festivals in the city, and Icaria will likewise have been made the location of primeval village tragedy because of its preeminent association with the patron god of tragedy. Turning both Thespis and Susarion into citizens of Icaria was further reinforcement of this tendentious tale.

It seems likely that these various elaborations of the Attic-village version of the origin of tragedy were later than Aristotle, but not much later. The Parian Marble belongs to the second third of the third century, and a line preserved from Eratosthenes' third-century *Erigone* is generally held to be alluding to these tales: "Icaria, where they first danced about the billy goat" (fr. 22 Powell).

Since we possess only odd survivals of what was a much fuller scholarly tradition, there are of course quandaries about these traditions that cannot be resolved with confidence. An example is Plutarch, *Love of Money* 527d: "The ancestral festival of the

Dionysia was of old a popular and merry procession: there was an amphora of wine and a vine-branch, then someone dragged along a billy goat, someone else followed bringing a basket of dried figs, after everything else there was the phallus." The amphora of wine, billy goat, and basket of figs tally precisely with the prizes for tragedy and comedy mentioned by the Parian Marble and Dioscorides. The Plutarch passage has often been taken (as by Burkert 1966, 99–100) as a testimony to early Dionysiac ritual that is independent of, and can be used as a check on, the tradition we have been examining. It is at least as likely, however, that the prizes were turned into components of the primeval village ritual as a byproduct of the generation of purely Athenian origins for drama. Certainly it is clear, as we have seen, that the desire to generate such origins prompted many and various combinations and inventions. The invented festival *Askôlia* and the false etymology it was based on added inessential but useful circumstantial detail to the scholars' picture of the primeval Dionysiac ritual; amphora of wine, figs, and in particular billy goat were by contrast essential links in the continuity forged between primeval rites and developed dramatic festival.

Tragedy and Religion

The village-drama tradition, at bottom pure invention, brings us closer to the question in what sense tragedy was a religious phenomenon, and we have finally to take account of a set of ancient scholarly notices that bring us face to face with that question. These are a variety of exegeses of the phrase "nothing to do with Dionysus," which by the Hellenistic period had become a well-known proverbial saying. Similar accounts (with interesting variations) are given by Plutarch (*Sympotic Matters* 1.1.5, 615a), the *Suda* (o 806 Adler), and Zenobius, whom I quote:

> "Nothing to do with Dionysus": The adage is applied to those not saying the things appropriate to the subject. Because, the choruses from the beginning having been accustomed to sing dithyramb for Dionysus, the poets later abandoned this custom and set to work to write "Ajaxes" and "Centaurs"; hence the spectators jeering said "nothing to do with Dionysus." For this reason it later seemed to them best to introduce satyr-plays, that they might not seem to forget the god. (Zenobius 5.40, *Corpus Paroemiographorum Graecorum* I.137)

The explanation given is of course a guess at the origin of a preexisting phrase, which is far likelier to have been a straightforward observation about tragedy than a spontaneous and collective cry of protest (or an ironic question eliciting confident denial, as in the title of a collection of scholarly essays). We are unable to determine the source or original context of the observation, but since incomprehensible or idiosyncratic opinions do not become proverbial we can confidently conclude that the general view was that developed tragic drama had nothing to do with Dionysus. Everyone knew that tragedy was most commonly performed under the patronage of Dionysus, but that association must have been perceived as contingent, as it was clearly no obstacle to the view that there was nothing (essentially) Dionysiac about tragedy. The only recourse open to defenders of the Dionysiac essence of tragedy is the suggestion that the observation does not go back to Greeks of the classical period but to their Hellenistic descendants, who had lost a proper sense of the relationship between tragedy and Dionysus. There is the obvious possibility here that what Hellenistic Greeks lacked was not the classical understanding of tragedy but a modern understanding that owes far more to Romanticism and to Nietzsche (see Henrichs, chapter 28 in this volume) than to Aristotle or any other Greek.

It is the *contingent* link between Dionysus and tragedy that is important in Aristotle and the rest of the ancient tradition. The proverbial saying might be taken to imply that though tragedy had nothing to do with Dionysus it ought to have done, but that is not a necessary implication. The contingent association with Dionysus was manifest, and the proverb draws attention to the absence of any (concomitant but not necessary) essential association. Those generating stories of how the proverb originated posited a time when dithyramb or tragedy was all about Dionysus, but the observation that became proverbial has no such implication. The primeval Dionysiac tragedy in the ancient sources belongs to the neverland of aetiological conjecture, just as in modern scholarship the tragedy that undoubtedly has everything to do with Dionysus belongs to the neverland of reconstructed prehistory.

None of the ancient evidence we have quoted or cited attests a connection that goes beyond contingency between *developed* tragedy and Dionysus. Even Aristotle's conjectural proto-tragedy is not essentially Dionysiac, though modern scholars persist in reading their own assumptions into the *Poetics*. In his account of the prehistory of tragedy Aristotle says nothing of ritual, cult, or cultic myth, nor does he so much as mention the god Dionysus. He manifestly regards developed tragedy as a genre of poetry comparable to epic, and there is nothing to suggest that in this respect he saw its pre- and proto-forms any differently. His almost total lack of interest in the chorus, which for modern scholars is the cultic core of tragedy, has often been noted (for example, by Halliwell 1986, 250). At least as early as the first half of the fifth century, dithyramb itself had ceased to be distinctively Dionysiac; its subject matter was myth in general, and it was performed in Athens at festivals of Apollo, Athena, Prometheus, and Hephaestus as well as Dionysus (Scullion 2002a, 127–28). Aristotle was specifically interested in its role at the Dionysiac dramatic festivals, but there is no reason to believe that he conceived the dithyramb performed there as non-contingently Dionysiac or as distinguishable in principle from Apolline or Promethean dithyramb. So too in the case of tragedy, which was also performed as early as the fifth century in theaters and at festivals of gods other than Dionysus (Scullion 2002a, 112–14).

What do we mean by a purely contingent association between tragedy and Dionysus? This issue is related to a more general question. Even if tragedy was sometimes performed in connection with gods other than Dionysus, it does after all seem always to have been performed under "religious" auspices. Even if it was not or not always specifically Dionysiac, then, was not tragedy at any rate a religious phenomenon? The easy answer is yes, but much – indeed everything – depends on what we mean by "religious." We cannot go into this matter in anything like the detail it deserves, but it may be helpful to sketch a model of religious festivity that perhaps suits the dramatic festivals at Athens and other Greek festivals rather better than the model in general use today.

Tragôidia is sometimes figured on vases as a female follower of Dionysus – female not because tragedy is (say) inherently maenadic, but because *tragôidia* is a feminine noun. Greek tragedy was more often than not under the patronage of Dionysus, but in Delphi or Dion, for example, *Tragôidia* would just as naturally have been personified as a female follower of Apollo or Zeus. As an event common to the festivals of various gods, tragedy is comparable with other musical and athletic events. The prize-amphorae given to victors in contests at the Panathenaia festival in Athens depict Athena on one side and the particular event on the other. That does not mean that foot-racing or rhapsodic performance of Homer had a special or essential connection with the goddess Athena. Nor need it mean that they were experienced as "religious" phenomena in any strong or interesting sense.

A bit of amateur anthropology may not be out of place here. The *panéguri* "festival" in Greece today retains one of the names and perhaps also something of the spirit of ancient festivals. *Panéguria* routinely take place on "religious holidays" (as we must with etymological pleonasm put it) and sometimes in the vicinity of holy places, but the feasting, musical performance, and dancing that are their primary activities are practically and conceptually indistinguishable from the same activities on such other occasions as the *giorté staphidas*, "festival of the raisin-harvest," or *giorté krasiou*, "festival of wine," which are not religious holidays. The activities of the *panéguri* are traditional and are central to Hellenic identity, and so too is the orthodoxy that often provides the holiday occasion, but it is apparent that most people most of the time are wholly unaware of any distinction between feasting, music, and dance on orthodox holidays and on other occasions. If we were to speak of the whole complex as "religious" on the grounds that orthodoxy is a central component of the tradition and so cognate with the activities of the *panéguri*, we would need to acknowledge that "religious" in that sense covers much that has nothing to do with orthodoxy as such, and that a term such as "national" or "ethnic" would be more appropriate. It may well be that when Greek tragedy was performed on the occasion of religious holidays, in Athens as often elsewhere at festivals of Dionysus, it was no more Dionysiac or religious than the musical performances of the *panéguri* at the festival of the Dormition of the Virgin are religious or Marian – or than athletic events at the Olympian or Pythian festival were religious, whether Jovian or Apollonian. Under the aspect of Greek ethnic identity orthodoxy and the *panéguri* are cognate, but the association of the *panéguri* on 15 August with the dormition of the virgin is thoroughly contingent.

These observations raise issues that go beyond the religious aspect of the *origins* of tragedy, which is our topic here, but it is important for our purposes not to misjudge or judge arbitrarily the role of festivals of Dionysus in the speculations about the origins of tragedy of Aristotle and his successors. The occasion of a festival event need not have any particular significance for its nature. The role of the Dionysia festival in Aristotle's history of tragedy does not make tragedy Dionysiac in the modern sense any more than the role of Gorgias in Aristotle's history of rhetoric means that he regarded rhetoric as an essentially Sicilian art. So too the advocates of primeval Attic tragedy were inventing a history that culminated comprehensibly in the City Dionysia, not presenting tragedy as unthinkable apart from Dionysus. No ancient writer speaks of tragedy as Dionysiac in the strong sense employed by modern scholars.

Aristotle knew very little about the origins of tragedy, and his successors, though bold in invention, knew no more. We can analyze their methods and contextualize or deconstruct their claims, but cannot know any more than they did. There is every reason to accept as sound Aristotle's view that epic was the key influence on the development of tragedy. We ought not to father on him the view that tragedy is a manifestation of the Dionysiac spirit and inconceivable without it; that view is nowhere expressed or entailed in the ancient discussion of the origin of tragedy. Modern scholars offer various other grounds for regarding tragedy as Dionysiac, but these lose much of their force if one concludes that the standard modern view is not in, but has been read into, Aristotle. Tragedies were performed at festivals on holidays, which were by origin holy days and certainly retained cultic components but, to judge from some of the plays, were certainly not occasions for the suppression of religious controversy and doubt. The question in what sense, if in any, tragedy is a religious phenomenon ought to prompt examination and debate rather than assumption and assertion.

NOTE

1   Further evidence of such usage would be the statement of a scholiast on Aristophanes' *Frogs* (schol. V *Frogs* 320), "dithyrambics [*dithurambika*], that is Dionysiac dramas," and the *Suda*'s attribution (σ 439 Adler) to Simonides of *tragôidiai* but not of dithyrambs and to Pindar (π 1617) of "seventeen tragic dramas" as well as dithyrambs (see Sutton 1989, 33–34 on 16 T 2). If Herodotus' "tragic choruses" at Sicyon were dithyrambs we would also have an explanation of Themistius' attribution of the invention of tragedy to the Sicyonians (*Oration* 27, 337b) and of the doubt expressed in the *Suda* whether Thespis was the first tragic poet or the sixteenth (or possibly second) after Epigenes of Sicyon (θ 282 Adler s.v. "Thespis," cf. 1 806), whose status as *tragôidiopoios* might be referred to his composition of "tragic choruses."

FURTHER READING

The views argued in the present chapter are very far from representing a scholarly consensus; some of them are presented in greater detail in Scullion 2002a. Important earlier treatments along similar lines are Else 1965 (who is sometimes too uncritical of ancient scholarship, for example of the traditions about Thespis) and Herington 1985 (who does not question the origin of tragedy in Dionysiac cult, but sees its debt to Greek poetic tradition as much more fundamental). Rozik 2002 is a refreshing reconsideration by a specialist in modern theater of theories of the ritual origin of both ancient and modern drama.

The classic work in English is still Pickard-Cambridge 1927, a full, careful, and sober treatment that retains its value. Webster's 1962 revision of Pickard-Cambridge (which gives the Greek and Latin texts in English translation) is not on the whole an improvement; he adds useful information on vases, but interprets much of it over-confidently, and he revives a theory of Gilbert Murray's that now seems a mere curiosity of scholarship. Burkert 1966 is a classic article, fundamental on the ancient sources, but readers should beware his tendency to blur the distinction between the *prize* billy goat of most of the ancient evidence and the *sacrificial* billy goat that suits his own Dionysiac interpretation. Lesky 1983 on "The Problem of Origins" gives an excellent account of the dominant twentieth-century view and packs a great deal into a restricted compass; his chapter would make an ideal counterbalance to the account offered here, and contains fairly full bibliographical references. (Those able to read German will find Patzer 1962 a very thorough guide to the scholarly debate up to that time.)

Sourvinou-Inwood 2003 is a massive, learned, and provocative treatment of the relationship between tragedy and Athenian religion; it is based on assumptions and comes to conclusions that are radically different from those of the present chapter and more representative of recent scholarly trends; her reconstruction of ritual aspects of the dramatic festival is highly speculative.

CHAPTER THREE

Dithyramb, Comedy, and Satyr-Play

Bernd Seidensticker

During the classical period tragedy was performed at two of Athens' municipal festivals in honor of Dionysus, but tragedy was not the only poetic component of the festival program. At the Lenaea tragedy stood alongside – and in the shadow of – comedy (Pickard-Cambridge 1988, 25–40; Csapo and Slater 1995, 122–24, 132–37). At the City or Great Dionysia the final three days, with performances of three tragic tetralogies, were undoubtedly the high point; in addition to the tragedies and satyr-plays, however, there were also performances of dithyrambs and comedies (Pickard-Cambridge 1988, 57–101; Csapo and Slater 1995, 103–21). The four genres may well have come into being in the same or at least a similar cultic context, but they were apparently incorporated into the official festival program at different times (tragedy in 534/33 BCE, dithyramb and satyr-play at the end of the sixth century BCE, comedy in 486 BCE), and their developed literary forms are sharply distinct.

Dithyramb

The dithyramb or cult song in honor of Dionysus, out of which (according to Aristotle, *Poetics* 1449a10–11) tragedy developed, is fundamentally different from the three other Dionysiac genres because it is not (or only minimally) dramatic and mimetic, but rather lyric and narrative. Dithyrambic performances inaugurated the City Dionysia; as with tragedy and comedy, the dithyrambic program was organized as a competition. In contrast to tragedy and comedy, however, it was not individuals who competed for victory but the ten Athenian *phulai* (tribes), each of which contributed both a men's and a boys' chorus to the competition.

We possess only the most meager information regarding the performance and form of the dithyramb; it is known, however, that each chorus consisted of fifty men who sang and danced in a circle (or circles), while the *aulos*-player who provided the musical accompaniment stood in the middle. The members of the chorus wore neither masks nor costumes, as they did in performances of tragedy and comedy, but festive robes and wreaths. Their circular dance (*kuklios choros*, the technical term *turbasia* is also attested) was apparently full of animation (Pickard-Cambridge 1962, 32–35).

Given that thousands of dithyrambs were composed in the fifth and fourth centuries for the City Dionysia alone (Sutton 1989) and that dithyramb's popularity increased from the middle of the fifth century until it became to all intents and purposes the leading lyric genre, the state of transmission is especially regrettable. The few substantial fragments of Pindaric dithyrambs do not enable us to form a reliable judgment concerning the forms, style, and contents of the genre, any more than do the few and probably atypical dithyrambs of Bacchylides. While there is no lack of accounts of the so-called new dithyramb, they are either critical (e.g., Plato, *Republic* 397a–b2) or parodic (e.g., Pherecrates fr. 155 *PCG*; Aristophanes, *Birds* 904–57, 1372–1409); moreover, they concern themselves almost exclusively with style and music (Zimmermann 1992, 118–21). The surviving texts and the many attested titles of lost dithyrambs at least permit us to conclude that the narrative of a more or less substantial portion of a myth stood at the center of the classical dithyramb; this narrative was preceded by a personal introduction, in which poetic reflections and gnomic wisdom found room alongside the patron and the occasion (polis, festival, and god of the festival). A hymnic address to the god of the festival could serve as conclusion.

If we leave aside Bacchylides' dithyrambs, it appears that the dithyrambs composed for the festivals of Dionysus, at any rate, were clearly characterized as Dionysiac (Privitera 1970, 120–30). Later, according to ancient and modern critics alike (Pickard-Cambridge 1962, 39–58; Zimmermann 1992, 117–32), the new dithyramb brought an emphasis on metrical and stylistic experimentation and ever-bolder musical innovations (see Wilson, chapter 12 in this volume).

Comedy

Five comedies made up the program on the second day of the City Dionysia (Storey 2002). This genre is far better documented than the dithyramb; we possess no fewer than eleven plays by Aristophanes. In the case of comedy, too, however, the pattern of transmission poses considerable problems when it comes to reconstructing the genre and its development. In the first place, the extant plays from the years 426 (*Achar-nians*) to 388 (*Wealth*) document only a short period in the long and undoubtedly colorful history of Old Comedy, which was added to the official festival program of the City Dionysia in 486, but was surely being produced and exerting an influence far earlier. Secondly, all the extant comedies are the work of only one of the many playwrights whose names we know. On the other hand, the fragments of Aristopha-nes' predecessors and contemporaries display certain differences from Aristophanic comedy both in form and in content (Landfester 1979),[1] but there is also a strong family resemblance to the surviving comedies. We may conclude that even if we possessed not just fragments but entire plays by Eupolis or Cratinus, the two other major representatives of Old Comedy, the clear generic boundaries with tragedy (for which see Taplin 1986 and 1996) would not be blurred.

Plato emphasizes the separation between the two major dramatic genres at the end of the *Symposium*. Only with difficulty can Socrates compel his two interlocutors, Agathon and Aristophanes, to acknowledge that one and the same playwright would be capable of composing both tragedies and comedies (*Symposium* 223d1–7). The passage shows that up to now the clear separation of tragedy and comedy has been regarded as a matter of course by both successful practitioners of the two genres, and also that the separation is assumed by Plato to be universally valid. In fact, there is not a single documented case of a playwright who verified Socrates' thesis, and what is true for the composition of the plays also holds true for their performance. The first actor who is reliably attested to have performed in tragedies as well as comedies lived around 100 BCE (O'Connor 1908, no. 415).

To be sure, tragedy and comedy display similarities resulting from their shared dramatic mode, the common context of their origin and development, and their conditions of production. Both share the same theater, employ costumes and masks, and involve a chorus whose singing and dancing is accompanied by an *aulos*-player. On closer scrutiny, however, even these obvious similarities prove superficial. For example, the staging of tragedy and comedy alike is subject to the spatial and structural limitations of the Theater of Dionysus at the foot of the Acropolis, but tragedy and comedy accommodate these limitations in different ways. While in tragedy the one-story stage building normally represented a palace (and on occasion also a temple, tent, hut, or cave), in comedy it served, insofar as it is defined at all, as a visual sign of an urban ambience. When it comes to masks and costumes the difference is even more obvious. While the heroes and heroines of tragedy wore a long-sleeved garment, distinct from the everyday clothing of the audience, that reached to the feet and was adorned with rich geometric and figural decorations, the actors of Old Comedy were grotesquely fitted out. A tight flesh-colored leotard represented stage nudity; it was stuffed to emphasize the belly and the buttocks, and affixed to it was a huge phallus which was more emphasized than concealed by a skimpy shirt or coat (Pickard-Cambridge 1988, 180–90 [tragedy], 220–23 [comedy]). Complementing the outfit, the masks of comedy were grotesquely exaggerated, their most prominent feature being a gaping asymmetrical mouth. In contrast the masks of classical tragedy, as occasional representations on vases suggest, were naturalistic, and differentiated mainly with respect to gender and age (Pickard-Cambridge 1988, 190–96 [tragedy], 218–20 [comedy]). The choruses of tragedy and comedy, finally, not only differed in size (tragedy had twelve chorus members to begin with, raised to fifteen by Sophocles, whereas comedy had twenty-four), but had completely different dramatic functions. The dance and music, about which we are very poorly informed, must also have been sharply distinct (Taplin 1996, 191–94).

It is accordingly apparent that even the few elements which comedy and tragedy have in common (theater space, masks and costumes, chorus, dance, and music) serve more to differentiate than to link the two genres. Ancient theory also defines tragedy and comedy as polar opposites, diametrically opposed to each other in subject matter, characters, style, plot, and outcome, as well as in effect.

While tragedy draws its subject matter from the rich reservoir of Greek myth and only rarely and in its early period dramatized current historical events (see Cropp, chapter 17 in this volume), comedy invents its own stories. In so doing it adapts places, situations, topics, issues, and frequently also individuals from the immediate present. While tragedy transports the audience to times long past and (as a rule) to more or less distant places, Aristophanes' comedies as a rule take place within the walls of an Athens plagued by the Peloponnesian War and its consequences.

Of course, tragedy too uses the traditional stories in order to discuss the burning questions of the present (Meier 1993). The analyses of the French School associated with Vernant, Detienne, and Loraux, as well as numerous studies influenced by New Historicism, have revealed to what extent and by what means fifth-century tragedy participated in the social discourses of its time. Tragedy participates, however, in a way that is fundamentally different from comedy. Comedy addresses current problems directly and does not hesitate to name the individuals responsible and to mount personal attacks against them (*onomasti kômôidein*, "to make fun of by name"). Thus Aristophanic comedy discusses the war and its consequences, democracy and demagogy, the popular assembly and the judicial system, sophistry and education, rhetoric and literature – especially tragedy. It ridicules Socrates and Euripides and attacks the political heavyweights of the time – Nicias, Demosthenes, Pericles, Alcibiades, and (repeatedly) Cleon – either overtly or in transparent disguises.

Furthermore, the connection between stage and audience is closer in comedy than in tragedy because the boundary between play and reality remains entirely penetrable. The spectators are regularly addressed, and included in the play in ever new ways (Taplin 1986, 172–73). Tragedy, in contrast, remains in its own world (Bain 1977) and relies on the audience to supply the contemporary applications. More or less obvious anachronisms (Easterling 1985a), as well as the aetiologies that figure at the end of many plays and connect some fifth-century cult practice with the time of its origin, are the only textual markers that signal the contemporary relevance of the mythical material. It is up to the spectators to draw the lines linking the play to the present.

As a corollary to the difference in subject matter, tragedy and comedy also differ from each other with regard to the moral quality and social position of their characters. While tragedy presents heroes drawn from myth who are better and/or occupy a higher social position than the average, comedy entertains its audience with characters drawn from everyday life, who are just like or worse than the audience itself (Aristotle, *Poetics* 1448a16–18; b24–27). Moreover, the characters of tragedy are fairly homogeneous. Ordinary people appear only in supporting roles, and gods are for the most part confined to the beginning and ending of the plays. Comedy, however, brings on stage a colorful mélange of ordinary people and prominent politicians, gods and personifications of abstract concepts, and feels free to introduce all manner of animals (for example, birds or frogs), who speak or sing as a chorus.

The style of tragedy is serious and elevated, in conformance with its subject matter and its characters. Naturally each of the three great tragedians developed his own style; nevertheless tragic language, as compared to contemporary comedy, is fairly homogeneous both overall and within a single tragedy. Messengers, servants, and nurses speak the same language as kings and gods. Linguistic and stylistic differences serve only to mark off the different levels and components of tragedy: they differentiate spoken sections from those recited and sung, or messenger-speech from stichomythia, or monody from chorus.

The same differences are of course also found in comedy. In addition, however, the style of Aristophanic comedy is marked throughout by a colorful mix of heterogeneous stylistic elements and registers: pointed brevity and extravagant fullness, lofty poetic imagery and crude, direct obscenity, colloquial frankness and paratragic pathos. We also encounter borrowings from contemporary scientific and political discourse and from the most diverse literary genres, ranging from Homeric epic to the new dithyramb, as well as frequent dialect forms and barbarisms. All these combine – often in astonishing juxtaposition – into a richly textured idiom whose trademarks Silk rightly determined to be diversity, collision, and exuberance (Silk 2000, 120–59).

The plots and component parts of tragedy and comedy are also clearly different from each other. The basic dramatic rhythm of tragedy is shaped by a more or less regular alternation between episodes involving actors (which may extend over one or more scenes), and choral lyric (Taplin 1977, 49–60). The elements of comedy, such as the seven-part *parabasis* (the "stepping forth" of the chorus to address the audience) or the complex *agôn* (debate scene), are also worked out in rigorous detail; overall, however, the structure of Aristophanic plays is looser and more open than that of tragedy.

Aristotle never tires of emphasizing that the different parts of a tragic action should develop out of one another according to the rules of probability or necessity. In fact it is important for our sense of the tragic, as well as for Greek tragedy, that the disaster should follow as a natural and logical result of the actions and qualities of the characters. Tragedy depends on a certain proximity to real life, not only with respect to the internal logic of the dramatic development, but also with respect to the nature of the material and the individual situations and events, which should not be implausible (*apithanon*: *Poetics* 1460a27; 61b12), much less impossible (*adunaton*: 1451b17–19; 60b23–26; 61b9–12) or irrational (*alogon*: 1454b6–8; 61b4–8). The audience must not lose the feeling "that real persons in a real situation act and suffer in a real way" (Kitto 1961, 314). Otherwise the possibility of identifying oneself with the problems and sufferings of the heroes is lost, and without such identification the tragic effect is not possible. Old Comedy, on the other hand, draws its strength from fantastic and fabulously irrational ideas and actions which not infrequently shape the entire plot. One protagonist buys himself a thirty-year private peace in the shape of old wine (*Acharnians*); another flies up to Olympus on a giant dung beetle to bring back to earth the goddess of peace, who is being held captive by Ares (*Peace*); now women take over the state (*Women at the Assembly*), or by means of a sex strike force the men to end the war (*Lysistrata*); now two unhappy Athenians leave home and together with the birds establish a new state situated between heaven and earth (*Birds*); now the god of theater descends to the underworld and presides over a contest in which Aeschylus and Euripides compete over who is the best tragedian and will be allowed to return to Athens (*Frogs*). In this world probability and necessity do not rule, but rather arbitrary acts and pure chance, and the individual scenes of the plays are not infrequently linked up paratactically; they take place after one another (*meta tade*) rather than – as in tragedy – because of one another (*dia tade*; for the distinction see Aristotle, *Poetics* 1452a20–21).

An additional difference is that comedy constantly draws the audience's attention to its quality as fictional play (Taplin 1986). The tactics used extend from the direct and indirect involvement of the audience in the play to references to the festival and the competition in whose context the play is being performed. We encounter references to the author and his text and, finally, the text constantly alludes to its own theatricality. In tragedy self-referentiality was for a long time limited to statements made by the members of the chorus about their own singing and dancing (Henrichs 1994–95, 1996a, 1996c). Even when, with Euripides, this convention begins to change (Arnott 1973, 1978, 1982, Foley 1985, Segal 1982), the self-consciously theatrical remarks remain indirect, and the same is true for satyr-play (Kaimio et al. 2001). Comedy, in contrast, never misses an opportunity to present itself as theater.

Finally, tragic action is determined by extraordinary physical and/or mental suffering. As Aristotle recognized, the tragic effect is not achieved without a disastrous or painful event (*pathos*: *Poetics* 1452b9–13), either actual or imminent, that must be "incurable" (*anékeston*: 1453b35) or at least must be perceived as inevitable or unalterable for some extended period of time by those affected. In Greek tragedy this disaster does not necessarily form the end of the play. A glance at the Aeschylean *Oresteia* or the later plays of Sophocles shows us that tragic conflicts can be resolved, great dangers survived, and great suffering overcome. But even the trilogies and tragedies that end happily are with a very few exceptions shaped by agonizing and destructive events.

In contrast, Aristotle defines the ridiculous as "a fault and a mark of shame, but lacking in pain and destruction" (*Poetics* 1449a34–35, trans. Halliwell 1986). Although the protagonists of Old Comedy grumble and threaten, beat their adversaries up and chase them away, nobody is ever seriously harmed. At the end the hero has generally reached his goal and fulfilled his dream. The war is ended (*Lysistrata*), peace achieved (*Acharnians, Peace*), the hated politician driven out and the state as young and beautiful as in the good old days (*Knights*).

The quality of the characters, language and style, subject matter, structure of the action, and outcome: all these contribute to the emotional effect, which Aristotle describes as the "appropriate pleasure" (*Poetics* 1453b11) of both dramatic genres. Tragedy aims at the psychagogic shock of the spectator. It arouses his fear (*phobos*) for the characters who are threatened by suffering and death, as well as his fear for himself, to whom the same or something similar might happen; it also arouses his pity (*eleos*) for the individuals and their heartrending fate. Comedy, in contrast, aims to entertain and amuse. Like modern cabaret, Old Comedy tries to induce laughter even as it pursues serious pedagogic or political aims. In recent years Gomme's thesis (1938) that comedy disclaims seriousness even when it participates in contemporary intellectual and political discourse has found fresh support. The advocates of this view (Heath 1987c, Halliwell 1984a) have with considerable astuteness drawn attention to the difficulties that stand in the way of a consistent political interpretation of Aristophanic comedy; they emphasize above all its performative and artistic quality. Yet comedy's analysis of the political and social, intellectual, and moral questions of the time is hardly less profound than that of tragedy. In the *parabasis* of the first surviving comedy of Aristophanes the chorus claims for its playwright that "he will keep on saying what's just in his comedies" (*Acharnians* 655) and that he will give "the best instruction" (658) to the city and its citizens. Regardless of whether Aristophanes lived up to this claim (which is also the core criterion for the choice of best tragedian in *Frogs*), there can be no doubt that he was serious about the seriousness of his comedies (Reinhardt 1938, Taplin 1983b, Henderson 1990, Brockmann 2003; for a balanced assessment see Silk 2000, 300–49).

Satyr-Play

The creation and early phase of satyr-play is closely connected with the genesis of tragedy and is just as obscure and controversial (Lesky 1972, 17–48; Seidensticker 1999, 6–9). Around 520 or 510 Pratinas, who was regarded in antiquity as the inventor of the genre, probably gave literary form to the simple mimetic satyr dances and songs of his Peloponnesian homeland, dances and songs that apparently had parallels in the Attic cult of Dionysus (Seaford 1984, 11–14; Hedreen 1992, 165–66). Pratinas made satyr-plays so popular in Athens that they were eventually incorporated into the festival program of the City Dionysia (Pohlenz 1965). In contrast to comedy, which became part of the festival program some twenty years later, satyr-plays were not performed on their own for about 150 years, but were always connected to tragedy. From the end of the sixth century on each tragedian admitted to the tragedy competition had to produce not only three tragedies but also a satyr-play to serve as a cheerful epilogue. The tetralogy structure was only given up in the second half of the fourth century (*terminus ante quem* 340/39, cf. *IG* II^2 2319–23, 16 ff.).

Despite its lasting popularity satyr-play is far more poorly documented than tragedy or comedy. Of the three hundred satyr-plays that were performed at the City Dionysias in the fifth century, only one, Euripides' *Cyclops*, has survived. However, we also possess numerous fragments of many other plays (Krumeich, Pechstein, and Seidensticker 1999), substantial archaeological material (Krumeich 1999, 41–73), and literary attestations, so that the characteristics of the genre can be determined with some reliability despite the poor transmission.

Satyr-play, like tragedy, dramatizes mythical stories, and as in tragedy Dionysiac subjects are the exception rather than the rule (Seidensticker 2002). Generally the satyrs, who constitute the chorus, and their old father Silenus are integrated into mythical contexts in which they are not at home: Danae's arrival on the beach of the island of Seriphos (Aeschylus' *Net-Haulers*), Apollo's search for the cattle stolen by Hermes (Sophocles' *Trackers*), Odysseus' encounter with the Cyclops Polyphemus (Euripides' *Cyclops*).

In Aeschylean and Sophoclean satyr-plays the myth into which the satyrs have been integrated often serves merely as a framework for the antics of the satyrs. For example, the Perseus myth tells how Dictys, brother of the king of Seriphos, comes upon Danae and her baby on the shore of the island and takes them under his care; Aeschylus in *Net-Haulers*, however, confines Danae's arrival and reception to the beginning and end of his play, placing in the center the encounter of the satyr chorus and Silenus with the beautiful princess and her baby. Sophocles' *Trackers* shows a similar technique: Apollo and Hermes, the two protagonists of the Homeric Hymn from which Sophocles derived his subject matter, are banished to the beginning and end of the play. About two thirds of the dramatic action belongs to the satyrs: to their dog-like searching for the stolen cattle (from which the play derives its name) and to their encounters first with the mysterious strains of the lyre, then with the nymph Cyllene, and finally with Hermes himself, cattle-thief and the lyre's inventor.

François Lissarrague has formulated the recipe used by the tragedians for their satyric final course in one pithy phrase: "take one myth, add satyrs, observe the result" (Lissarrague 1990, 236). Aeschylus and Sophocles like to entrust the satyrs with a task which in the traditional story is of little importance: in *Net-Haulers* it is the drawing in of the fishing net, in *Trackers* the search for the missing cattle. The result is that a minor detail of the story develops its own momentum and becomes the main action. The satyr chorus, along with Silenus, take over the myth; they interrupt and modify the story, retard or advance the action into which they have been transplanted, and thus unexpectedly, but logically, become the protagonists. In Euripides' *Cyclops* their role is considerably smaller than in the satyr-plays of Aeschylus and Sophocles. Yet by virtue of their constant presence and their actions and reactions, songs and comments, gestures and dances, Silenus and the satyrs determine the tone and atmosphere of the play even in the parts dominated by Odysseus and Polyphemus.

Overall the satyr-play is shaped more strongly than tragedy by standardized patterns of action and generic topoi (Sutton 1980, 145–59; Seaford 1984, 33–44; Seidensticker 1999, 28–32); there is a special preference for stories in which the activity of violent fiends or monsters is curbed or thwarted.[2] Closely connected to this theme is the motif of imprisonment and rescue, as in Euripides' *Cyclops*, where first Silenus and his satyrs and then Odysseus and his crew find themselves at the mercy of the Cyclops, until Odysseus devises a plan of escape. The temporary enslavement of the satyrs was apparently a frequent although not an obligatory theme. The relationship of dependency is not always compulsory; sometimes the satyrs offer their services of their own free will, as in Sophocles' *Trackers*, where the satyrs undertake the search for Apollo's lost cattle in expectation of a reward. In any case they generally find themselves in an unaccustomed or uncongenial environment or situation. They constantly attempt, or are forced to attempt, activities for which they lack either the ability or the desire: we see them as fishermen and hunters, servants, herdsmen, and athletes, laborers in a vineyard, field, or forge, and they are freed from their hateful bondage only at the end of the play. They can be deprived of their beloved wine, or the women they are pursuing can be snatched from them at the last moment, but even under conditions of slavery there is no taking away their delight in music, song, and dance. The satyrs' thirst and their insatiable sexual appetite are recurrent topoi, as are swindles, ruses, and tricks, inventions and transformations, and the birth and upbringing of gods and heroes.

As Welcker (1826) pointed out, in satyr-play (as opposed to tragedy) it is not the dramatic events themselves that captivate the audience, but the effect the events produce on the minds of the satyrs. The special charm of the genre is due to the abrupt clash between two completely different worlds: the encounter with the satyrs takes place on their own territory. According to Vitruvius (5.6.9), the *scaena satyrica* was dominated by trees, caves, and mountains; indeed, satyr-plays evidently were not set before a palace (as is the case in most tragedies) nor in the city (which forms the background of most comedies), but rather in places where satyrs are at home: in mountain forests and deserts, in front of caves or on the seashore.

The clash between the two disparate worlds of satyr-play is visually highlighted by masks and costumes. The standard dress of the satyrs and their old father Silenus is known from many vase-paintings (Krumeich 1999, 53–55): whereas Silenus was fully covered by a costume of white-tufted fur (the *mallôtos chitôn*), the satyrs were bearded and snub-nosed, slightly balding, with the slim pointed ears associated with horses, mules, or donkeys. They cavorted around the *orchêstra* barefoot, naked except for a small loincloth to which was attached an abundant horsetail and a large erect phallus. In contrast, the other characters wore the long, richly embroidered robes of tragedy.

The contrast is particularly marked on the famous Pronomos vase (reproduced in Krumeich, Pechstein, and Seidensticker 1999, plates 8 and 9, and Csapo and Slater 1995, plate 8), which at the same time hints at a further aspect of difference: the contrast between the composed demeanor of the heroes and the dancing and jesting of the satyrs. The dances of the chorus doubtless left their mark on the character of the genre (Seidensticker 2003): accompanied by the Dionysiac *aulos*, they were lively and noisy and indeed often rather wild, full of swift jumps and agitated movement. While it appears that the choreography of tragedy was somewhat abstract (with some exceptions, such as the binding-song of the Furies at Aeschylus, *Eumenides* 308–96), vividly pantomimic dancing seems to have been characteristic of satyr-play.

Like the chorus in tragedy, the satyrs of satyr-play are generally in attendance on one of the protagonists of the myth into which they have been integrated. But unlike their tragic counterparts, Aeschylean and Sophoclean satyr choruses do not confine themselves to choral songs performed in the *orchêstra* and to short dialogues with the characters that are mediated by the chorus-leader. Unlike the regular chorus of tragedy they pursue their own goals (the possession of a beautiful woman, for example, or their own liberation from one of the many ogres of satyr-play), and unlike the tragic choruses they do not merely observe and comment on dramatic developments, but actively and continuously interfere with them. Their actions dominate large parts of the plays and determine their tone and atmosphere, and in the world of naked, ithyphallic, dancing satyrs it is the heroes who seem out of place – not only on account of their costume and demeanor, but also because of the things they do and say. In *Cyclops*, for example, Odysseus' opening words (96–98) sound a little too high-flown, and his plea to Polyphemus (286–312) also appears slightly absurd, because he forgets that he is speaking not to an equal as in tragedy, but to the ogre of satyr-play. Much of the genre's comic quality is derived from the tension between two worlds: the world of the satyrs and the world of the heroes into which these rascals have been transplanted.

Satyr-Play between Tragedy and Comedy

Demetrius' definition of satyr-play as *tragôidia paizousa* ("tragedy at play," *On Style* 169) neatly sums up the position of the genre between tragedy and comedy. The satyr-play is closely connected to tragedy not only structurally, as part of the tragic tetralogy, but in many other aspects as well. Authors, actors and chorus, costumes and props, language and meter, dramatic form and structure are either completely or to a great extent identical. Both tragedy and satyr-play, in contrast to comedy, take their subject matter from mythology. On the other hand, satyr-play is very far removed from the essence of tragedy. Its tone and atmosphere, happy ending, and emotional effect move it close to comedy, with which it also shares many stock characters and stories.[3]

Comedy and satyr-play also have in common the use of certain dramatic motifs and situations such as courtships and weddings, thefts and ruses, banquets and competitions. Sciron as pimp (Euripides' *Sciron*), Polyphemus as cook (Euripides' *Cyclops*),

Silenus as boastful *miles gloriosus* (Sophocles' *Trackers*, Euripides' *Cyclops*) and in particular, of course, the satyrs and Silenus in their stereotypical role as funny and crafty, impudent and cowardly, useless yet lovable slaves, who stand beside the hero and are later rewarded with freedom – all these figures have their analogues in comedy.

In both genres a happy ending is obligatory; in both poetic justice rules, whereas in tragedy a different principle, the incommensurability of guilt and punishment, holds sway. Both genres ultimately have the same aim: to get the audience to laugh. Yet the nature of the ridiculous, the methods whereby the common aim is achieved, and the quality of the intended laughter are fundamentally different.

Satyr-play shares with comedy a preference for the comic representation of commonplace situations, activities, desires, and anxieties; it does not, however, present these realistically in a way that mirrors the daily life of the audience, but at a mythical distance. The comic effect results in no small measure from the fact that great mythological figures are reduced to the petty roles of ordinary life: Heracles is shown as a slave (Euripides' *Eurystheus* or *Syleus*), Hermes as a thief (Sophocles' *Trackers*), Polyphemus as a cook (Euripides' *Cyclops*), Odysseus and Silenus at a typical symposium with the uncivilized Cyclops (*Cyclops* again).

As in comedy, the audience laughs about aesthetic and moral faults and shortcomings that are ultimately harmless: ugliness and physical defects, undependability and laziness, curiosity and cowardliness, impudence and lecherousness. The spectator recognizes the satyr in himself and in his neighbors. The mythical distancing, however, removes any sting of scorn or reproach from the representation of these faults and vices. The laughter is accordingly more relaxed and cheerful, less critical and bitter than in comedy.

The fact that direct and indirect attack on contemporaries – a striking feature of Old Comedy – is almost entirely foreign to satyr-play points in the same direction. Political attack, social satire, critical caricature are not the business of classical satyr-play. Its tone is not biting and hurtful but light-hearted and cheerful; mocking, but not derisive. The corollary is that the term "parody" should not be used in reference to satyr-play. As far as we can see, satyr-play does not aim at a distorting parody of familiar myth; rather, it selects cheerful or at least unproblematic subjects or dramatizes a happy episode from the life of one of the tragic heroes. From the Greeks returning from the Trojan War it selects Odysseus (Euripides' *Cyclops*) and Menelaus (Aeschylus' *Proteus*), not Agamemnon. From the life of Oedipus satyr-play chooses only the hero's victory over the Sphinx, from the career of Heracles only the triumphant successes. Satyr-play stages funny stories, but does not make fun of them.

Satyr-play no more parodies tragedy than it does myth. In this respect, too, it differs significantly from contemporary comedy, in which paratragedy looms large (Rau 1967). There is nothing in the surviving texts of satyr-plays that is equivalent to the Aristophanic parodies of Euripidean tragedy. Even in those tetralogies where there is a demonstrable connection (at the level of content or theme) between the three tragedies and the satyr-play, the satyr-play does not parody the tragedies that preceded it. Rather, the satyr-play presents a light-hearted aspect of the same problem (Aeschylus' *Amymone*) or a light-hearted episode from the myth (Aeschylus' *Sphinx* or *Net-Haulers*) without making fun of the tragic dilemma or the tragic hero.

Function of Satyr-Play

In all probability satyr-play owes its position next to tragedy at the City Dionysia to a desire to restore something of the original simple and jovial character of the rural Dionysia to the urban festival – an aim that gives the genre a meaningful cultic and social function. If we consider that comedy did not yet figure in the festival program at the time that satyr-play was introduced, this desire becomes even more understandable. The magistrates wanted to introduce an element that took into account both the light-hearted aspects of the cult and the spectators' need to amuse themselves after the harrowing experience of the tragedies.

The surviving evidence from ancient theory (Diomedes 1: 491 Keil; Marius Victorinus 2.4, p. 110 Gaisford; Photius s.v. *saturika dramata*) agrees in defining the aim of satyr-play as one of entertainment (*delectatio, diachusis*) and relaxation (*relaxatio*). Modern criticism since A. W. Schlegel (1966, 128–29 [1826]) has also emphasized the liberation and emotional relaxation that results from the light-hearted epilogue and has regarded comic relief as the most important function of the satyr-play within the tetralogy.

This relief is not, however, achieved because "by presenting as humorously incongruous and inappropriate what tragedy has just represented as serious and consequential, the satyr-play insinuates that the emperor has no clothes" (Sutton 1980, 165–66). Rather, after the tragic worldview, the satyr-play offers an uncomplicated, optimistic look at human life.[4] It chooses and creatively adapts to its purposes stories that allow the poets to present a philosophy of life that is not supposed to cancel or even weaken but rather to counterbalance the representation of death (or of death narrowly avoided) in the preceding tragedies. It is of course the satyrs who principally instantiate this philosophy, the satyrs with their amoral vitality, their exuberant singing and dancing, their craving for wine and women, and their ingenious avoidance of any serious or dangerous projects or actions. Against the tragic world with its eternal laws and strict ethical code, satyr-play juxtaposes its own vision of a brighter and less demanding life. It gives us *phusis* (nature) in place of *nomos* (culture), and the ethics of the countryside against the ethics of the polis (Lasserre 1973, Lissarrague 1990). This philosophy is presented in the framework of stories that lead from slavery to freedom, stories in which the hero – either by superior force or by his own wits – conquers and destroys the ogre. The hero's victory is the victory of life over death. To speak in the terms of Northrop Frye (1957, 163 and 206): after tragedy's myth of autumn, satyr-play presents the myth of spring.

According to Zenobius, Aristotle's pupil Chamaeleon offered the following explanation of the proverbial saying *ouden pros ton Dionuson* (*On Thespis*, fr. 38 Wehrli): "When *saturika* about Dionysus began to be replaced by tragedies on other themes, the audiences shouted: '[This has] nothing to do with Dionysus.' " This, Zenobius adds, led to the institutionalization of the satyr-play. Chamaeleon's explanation accords well with Aristotle's account of early tragedy and gains further credence when compared to similar developments in the Japanese and early English theater.[5]

Indeed, even if one is willing to endorse the results of recent studies that seek to show that the god of the theater plays a vital role, however indirectly and mysteriously, in many if not all tragedies (Bierl 1991, Seaford 1996a; see, however, Scullion 2002a and chapter 2 in this volume), there can be little doubt that satyr-play introduces Dionysus and his world in a much more direct and powerful way. The god himself seems to have appeared quite often on the satyric stage, whether as infant or adult; but it is, of course, mainly the stereotypical chorus of satyrs and their old father Silenus who impersonate and represent the Dionysiac world in all its facets: music and dance, wine and sexual license, as well as freedom or liberation from many different forms of physical and psychological bondage. At the moment when the naked, ithyphallic satyrs dance in the *orchêstra*, if not before, the festival god and his world once again move fully into the center of the theater. In this sense the satyr-play can rightfully be considered the high point of the tragic tetralogy performed in honor of Dionysus (Kaimio et al. 2001, 76–78).

Mutual Influences

A schematic overview of the three genres that together with tragedy formed the program of the City Dionysia has demonstrated that we have to do with four clearly differentiated literary forms. While dithyramb stands apart, as we have seen, insofar as it is not mimetic and dramatic but narrative and lyric, the three other genres share certain theatrical elements such as mask, costume, and chorus, but otherwise have little in common. As far as tragedy and comedy are concerned, Oliver Taplin in two complementary studies (1986, 1996) has documented in detail Bernard Knox's pithy formulation: "For the fifth-century Athenian tragedy was tragedy and comedy comedy, and never the twain should meet" (1979a, 251). Satyr-play was separated from tragedy by the obligatory chorus of satyrs, from comedy by its mythical material and the nature of its comic effect. Even if (as is probable) the three dramatic genres arose from the same or closely related cultural contexts, in their fully developed literary forms each has its separate identity.

On the other hand, since the three genres were produced for the same festival, there can be no doubt that the writers and choral directors, actors, members of the chorus, and musicians knew one another and not only followed the rehearsals and performances of their immediate competitors with great interest, but also kept an eye on the contiguous genres. It seems to me to go without saying that the great dramatists of the fifth century, who inhabited the same reasonably small space and competed against one another year after year, also discussed playwriting and production with one another. It comes as no surprise, therefore, that mutual influences can occasionally be detected.

Despite the sparse material available to us, certain interactions between dithyramb and the dramatic genres can already be determined in the first half of the fifth century. It appears that Aeschylus took inspiration from dithyramb in crafting the *parodos* of the *Agamemnon* (Fraenkel 1950, III p. 805); conversely, the dramatic character of some of Bacchylides' dithyrambs is hardly imaginable without the influence of tragedy (Zimmermann 1989, 64–116). In the second half of the century the dramatization of dithyramb was further reinforced by the introduction of monodies and mimetic interludes (Zimmermann 1989, 127–28). At the same time the new dithyramb strongly influenced tragedy and comedy, above all with its musical experiments but also with the stylistic innovations that accompanied them. Aristophanes playfully parodied these innovations (in *Birds*, for example) and caricatured representatives of the new dithyramb such as Cinesias (*Birds* 1372–1409), as well as their disciples such as the tragedian Agathon (*Women at the Thesmophoria* 101–29). It is an open question whether Euripides was on friendly terms with Timotheus, as the ancient biographies report; what is certain is that a number of his choral odes (Kranz 1933, 228–66), as well as the great aria of the Phrygian in *Orestes* (1369–1472), were inspired by new dithyramb.

For satyr-play, too, the scarcity of the evidence does not permit a detailed statement about possible reciprocal influences involving tragedy and comedy. Comparison of the larger fragments of Aeschylean and Sophoclean satyr-play with Euripides' *Cyclops* suggests, at any rate, that in the course of the fifth century the structure of satyr-play moved closer to that of tragedy. Taplin's statement that satyr-play (as compared to tragedy) shows a "loose and undefined structure that makes for a rambling continuity which does not really fall into parts" (1977, 58) applies to the fragments of Aeschylean and Sophoclean satyr-plays, but the dramatic form of *Cyclops*, composed at the end of the century, is essentially identical with the basic structure of tragedy.

In tone, too, *Cyclops* is clearly distinct from the surviving fragments of Aeschylus and Sophocles. The simplicity, naturalness, and joviality of early satyr-play commingle with the critical irony so typical for Euripidean tragedies and with varied forms of literary parody (Seidensticker 1979b, 222–24). Euripides not only parodies epic language (Kassel 1955) and the typical elements of literary and popular *kômos* (celebration) poetry (Rossi 1971a), but does not shrink from self-parody. Thus he puts into the mouth of the satyrs (179–86) and Polyphemus (280–81, 283–84) the criticism of the Trojan War – that it was fought for the sake of a whore – that runs through so many tragedies, and at 186–87 he has fun with Hippolytus' famous diatribe against women (*Hippolytus* 616–44) when he has the satyrs say, "Would that the race of women did not exist anywhere – except for my own private use." The great speech in which Polyphemus rejects Odysseus' demand for gratitude and guest-friendship (316–46) is crafted into a parody, as funny as it is biting, of the radical positions of contemporary sophistry – a parody that might have been inspired by comedy and its attack on issues and individuals of the day.

The intriguing interaction between tragedy and satyr-play is most clearly seen, of course, in *Alcestis*, which Euripides presented in 438 as the fourth play of the tetralogy, that is, as a satyr-play (Sutton 1973; Seidensticker 1982, 136–39). The clearest link of this singular tragedy to satyr-play is forged by Heracles, the premier hero of that genre. The role he is made to play in *Alcestis* is his traditional role in satyr-play: the strongman who must overpower the ogre. He is announced as such by Apollo (65–69), as such he appears on stage (476–77; undoubtedly he is equipped with lionskin and club) and introduces himself. It should come as no surprise that this hero of satyr-play is unable to understand the tragedy in which he has ended up. He continues to behave in the way he is accustomed to in satyr-play: he satisfies his vast appetite (753–55), carouses to his heart's content (756–59), sings loudly and out of tune (760), and preaches his philosophy of hedonistic materialism to the slave who serves him (773–802). Finally he wrestles the inevitable ogre to the ground and ushers in the obligatory happy ending. From his point of view the events at Pherae are no different from other satyr-play adventures (for example, his triumph over Syleus) – a recurrent sequence of arrival, banquet, victory over the ogre, happy ending, feast, and departure to new adventures. Grafted onto this pattern of action, characteristic of satyr-play and its most important hero, are additional dramatic and thematic motifs that seem to have been equally typical of the genre: deception, ruses, a symposium, a wrestling match. To be sure, these motifs of satyr-play are touched on only briefly, and even in the scenes involving Heracles the high-spirited tone of satyr-play does not dominate. All the same, there can be no ignoring the synthesis of tragedy and satyr-play by means of which Euripides has created a completely new form of tragedy.

Tragedy's significance for comedy is not limited to the fact that tragedy offered a welcome target for mockery. Aristophanes not only repeatedly parodied Euripides, but was also inspired by that restless innovator to undertake his own experiments. Tragedy "provides the essential perspective and point of reference against which Aristophanic comedy asks to be placed. It is arguable that only tragedy, sphere of the universal, could have provided the stimulus to construct a comic vision beyond the demotic and the everyday" (Silk 2000, 415; cf. 42–97).

Possible influences of comedy on tragedy are not easy to determine. Herington (1963; cf. Taplin and Wilson 1993) has indeed correctly drawn attention to the fact that the ending of the *Oresteia* (and also of the Danaid trilogy) bears a certain resemblance to the ending of some of Aristophanes' comedies. Whether we are entitled to conclude, however, that in these instances Aeschylus drew his inspiration from pre-Aristophanic comedy (which of course has not survived) is anything but certain. The same holds true for the freer treatment of time and space in Aeschylean tragedy (Taplin 1986, 165) and for comedic motifs that have occasionally been spotted in tragedy, such as a character's rapping at the door (*Libation Bearers* 653–56) or the entrance of two characters deep in conversation (Sophocles' *Philoctetes* 1222). Nor can the increasing significance of self-referential allusions be unhesitatingly ascribed to the influence of comedy. To be sure, it cannot be excluded that Euripides, the *poiêtês sophos* ("clever poet" – see Winnington-Ingram 1969), is indebted to Aristophanes for his self-referential play with the dramaturgical and thematic conventions of the theater and with the very genre of tragedy. But an increasing refinement and complexity of self-reference is a phenomenon frequently associated with the organic growth and development of a genre.

Particularly interesting for the question of the relationship between tragedy and comedy are the metamorphoses of old tragedy brought about by Euripides and observed and noted by Aristophanes. In the *agón* of *Frogs* Aristophanes' Aeschylus accuses Euripides of transforming the noble heroes he inherited from Aeschylean tragedy into pitiful, sorry creatures (1011, 1013–17); he adds that Euripides substituted banal chatter for the elevated thoughts and lofty language of Aeschylean tragedy (1058–62). Euripides defends himself by saying that as a good democrat he gave everybody a chance to speak (948–49), that he represented "ordinary matters that we're accustomed to and spend our lives with" (959), and that he put Aeschylus' swollen style on a diet (939–43). Exact observations lie behind the harsh accusations and bold exaggerations with which Aristophanes caricatures the innovator Euripides. Euripides did in fact, as his Aristophanic "I" claims, bring the world of the audience on stage. The representation of everyday objects and situations, anxieties and problems is one of the most noticeable characteristics of his "new" tragedy. The objects range from Alcestis' clothes-chest and Electra's water jug, to the broom with which Ion sweeps the courtyard of the temple of Apollo in Delphi, to Orestes' simple sickbed as depicted in the opening of *Orestes*, with a little stool placed at the side for his nurse Electra. The new anxieties range from Admetus' preoccupation, after

Alcestis' death, with the dusty floors in his palace, to the preparations for celebrating Ion's birthday, to Menelaus' unpleasant experience as a beggar in front of the Egyptian palace. Euripidean heroes discuss the education of children and the social position of women, questions of heredity and socialization as well as questions of military efficiency and political morale. As Knox (1979a) has shown, this demythologizing tendency, a realistic deheroization of situation and atmosphere that results in the creation of a completely new untragic tone, is particularly apparent in the first part of *Electra* and in *Ion*.

For all his mockery, Aristophanes hits upon the decisive point where tragedy changes with his critique of the stature and moral quality of the Euripidean hero. No longer better (or at least more powerful and more important) than the average but a human being like you or me, the tragic hero in Euripides moves into the unflattering light of mediocrity.

Euripides plays out the old stories anew with the people of his own time. He exploits the tension between myth and reality, between the elevated image of humanity presented in myth and high poetry and the historical actuality of human beings in all their weakness and wretchedness. The reduction of the Aeschylean and Sophoclean demigods to ordinary people stands out particularly sharply in the context of traditional tragic situations and dilemmas, with which Euripides' new-style heroes are also confronted. Against the background of the traditional portrait of the hero from Homer to Sophocles, Euripides' heroes present themselves as regular folk who distinguish themselves from the audience and its political leaders only insofar as they are not named Myrrhine and Callias, but Electra and Orestes; not Cleon and Alcibiades, but Eteocles and Polynices. Euripidean heroes are often too small for the large tragic roles they have to fill. The heroes' costumes, hanging loosely and pathetically around their all-too-small bodies, reveal their weaknesses more than they conceal them. It is only a small step, and often not even that, to the comic and ridiculous.

Sophocles is supposed to have said that he represented humans as better than they are, whereas Euripides represented them just as they are (Aristotle, *Poetics* 1460b33–34). How close the tragic hero may come to being average is not easy to determine; however, at the point when he forfeits his last vestige of the extraordinary, and (at the latest) when he sinks below the average moral and intellectual level of his audience, he readily becomes an object of contempt, derision, and mockery, of malicious pleasure and ridicule – an object more suitable for comedy or tragicomedy than tragedy.

Generally speaking, comic elements are not infrequent in Euripidean tragedy. Whereas Aeschylus and Sophocles limit their realistic and comic touches to minor supporting characters, Euripides repeatedly aims at comic effects. These extend from individual lines, such as Menelaus' inquiry as to whether Helen gained weight in Troy (*Trojan Women* 1050; cf., however, Gregory 1999–2000), to a few brief scenes, such as the dressing scene in *Bacchae* (925–44), to sequences such as the opening of *Electra* or *Ion*, and to whole plays such as *Helen*. With a few exceptions, however, the comic character of the numerous comic elements is as un-Aristophanic as is its function. As a rule Euripides is concerned with intensifying the tragic effect. So, for example, the labored joke about Helen's weight problem not only serves to ironically show up Menelaus but also sharpens the tragedy of Hecuba and the bitterness of the Trojans' fate. This Menelaus will not kill Helen; the guilty party will never have to pay.

In *Bacchae* too the comic features of the scene in which Dionysus dresses Pentheus as a bacchant only intensify the tragic effect; one of the funniest scenes in Greek tragedy is at the same time one of the most horrible and pitiful. And, finally, the seemingly light-hearted comedy about the rescue of the innocent Egyptian Helen is the true tragedy of the senselessness of the war. It is in particular the weakness of Euripides' heroes, the "dwindling and fading" (Reinhardt 1960, 239), which threatens to consign so many of them to the realm of the ridiculous, that is simultaneously sobering and frightening. The loss of intellectual and moral substance becomes a central tragic statement.

Time and again Euripides used whatever he may have learned from comedy (and satyr-play) to test the boundaries of tragedy, and surely time and again the Athenian audience was astonished, confused, and perhaps also angered by what Euripides offered up as tragedy. From our contemporary vantage point we can see that the restless, experimental innovator developed the basic forms of new genres such as tragicomedy or romantic comedy; with *Ion* he created the form of European comedy that was dominant from Menander to Oscar Wilde. Within the framework of the City Dionysia, however, tragedy's difference from comedy and satyr-play always remained apparent despite all experiments.

The most important of the Athenian festivals of Dionysus offered its audience a colorful program. In addition to processions and sacrifices, the community made poetic offerings of very different types to the god. At the center stood the two major dramatic genres, now far removed from their ritual origins and only rarely and sporadically linked (whether in theme or in content) with Dionysus. At the dithyrambic opening of the Dionysia and at the satyric close of each tragic tetralogy, however, the god stood fully at the center of his festival.

NOTES

Translated by Isabel Köster and Justina Gregory.

1 Since we unfortunately do not have any of the many parodies of myths which are attested for Old Comedy, we cannot determine whether and to what extent they differed from the surviving plays of Aristophanes. For Pherecrates and Crates, moreover, it is attested that – in contrast to the comic triad Cratinus, Eupolis, and Aristophanes – they avoided direct political attacks. Aristotle states in the *Poetics* (1449b7–9, translation here and subsequently by Halliwell) that Crates was the first to "compose generalized stories and plots."

2 The ogre, who can appear in ever-new variations as giant or evil king, highwayman or sorcerer, either encounters a stronger adversary (e.g., Heracles or Theseus) who answers violence with violence, or a clever trickster (e.g., Odysseus or Sisyphus), who achieves victory by means of wit and cunning.

3 Thus Epicharmus, the Sicilian comic writer of the fifth century, evidently shared with satyr-play a predilection for the strongman and glutton Heracles and the wily Odysseus, and in the (unfortunately only fragmentary) mythical travesties of Old and Middle Comedy we encounter Sisyphus, Daedalus, and Hephaestus as well as such monsters and sorcerers of satyr-play as Polyphemus, Cercyon, Amycus, Busiris, Sciron, Circe, and the Sphinx.

Moreover, satyrs are often the protagonists: comedies with the title *Satyroi* are attested for a number of authors (e.g., Cratinus).

4   This creates emotional relief without ridiculing the problems of the preceding tragedies. The opposite effect would in fact seem more likely. In Aeschylus' *Oresteia*, for example, the hilarious Egyptian adventure of Menelaus as represented in the satyr-play *Proteus* intensifies the tragic fate of his brother Agamemnon and his family; in Aeschylus' *Oedipodeia* the satyr-play's representation of Oedipus' greatest success, his victory over the Sphinx, deepens the effect of his fall. Conversely, the light-hearted world of the satyr-play appears that much brighter against the dark background of tragedy. The contrasting juxtaposition of tragic and comic results in a mutual intensification.

5   Seaford 1984, 12; Seaford has suggested that "unlike tragedy, satyric drama retained its Dionysiac content ... not only through retaining a chorus of satyrs, but also by virtue of its choice and adaptation of non-Dionysiac myths" (1984, 44). On this reading the most recurrent feature of satyr-play – the servitude and liberation of the satyrs – dramatizes (or rather recalls in ever-new variations) "a sacred story ... of the Dionysiac mysteries, in which the imprisonment and miraculous liberation of Dionysus (perhaps also of his followers), comparable to the Eleusinian loss and reappearance of Korê, was an important element" (1984, 43). Seaford further argues that the many marvelous inventions and creations and the recurrent *anodos* (ascent from the underworld) scenes presented in satyr-plays ultimately derive "from a pre-dramatic celebration by the Dionysiac *thiasos* of revelations associated with their cult" (1984, 42), and he tries to show that other important topoi of the genre (e.g., athletics, child-rearing, and marriage) may bear some relationship to specific features of the Anthesteria. This is a fascinating idea, although (like similar ritualistic explanations of the origin and early history of tragedy) it remains highly speculative, and does not suffice as an explanation of the nature and function of the fully developed literary form in its historical and cultural context.

FURTHER READING

For the City Dionysia and its program see Pickard-Cambridge 1988 and the influential article by Goldhill 1990. A short history of the dithyramb is presented by Zimmermann 1992. The differences between tragedy and comedy are treated by Taplin 1986 and 1996; see also Seidensticker 1982. The fragments of satyr-play are presented in Krumeich, Pechstein, and Seidensticker 1999; see also Sutton 1980 and Seidensticker 1999. For the new tragedy of Euripides see Knox 1979a, Burnett 1971, and Michelini 1987; and for comic elements in Greek tragedy see Seidensticker 1982 and Gregory 1999–2000.

CHAPTER FOUR

Tragedy's Teaching

Neil Croally

How does fifth-century tragedy relate to, reflect, and constitute the Athenian polis? One influential answer is offered by Vernant and Vidal-Naquet: "Tragedy could be said to be a manifestation of the city turning itself into theater, presenting itself on stage before its assembled citizens" (1988, 185). In the wake of Vernant and Vidal-Naquet, scholars have concerned themselves with (among other things) the festival context in which tragedy was performed; the constitution and *mentalité* of its audience; the representation of women, slaves, and foreigners; the importance of rhetoric within the plays and the relationship between tragic rhetoric and the Sophists; and the representation of gods and religious ritual. My primary concern is not to address the civic, political, or even democratic nature of tragedy in any of these ways (although all will be important). Instead, I intend to investigate the relationship between Athenian tragedy and the polis of fifth-century Athens by way of three questions: Was tragedy supposed to teach in fifth-century Athens? How did tragedy teach? And why is it important to acknowledge the educative function of tragedy?[1]

Was Tragedy Supposed to Teach?

The very way in which I have framed the question shows that I am interested not so much in the intentions of the tragedians as in the expectations of the audience. That is, I am more interested in the effects and the expected function of tragedy. I think that this needs to be said baldly and up front, as there are some scholars who have confused function with intention (Griffin 1998, 48–50; for thorough criticism, Goldhill 2000, 38–39; Gregory 2002; Seaford 2000), or are concerned to concentrate by contrast on intention. Malcolm Heath, for instance, argues that the sources do tell us about didactic uses made of tragedy, but that there is silence in those same sources about didactic intentions (Heath 1987b, 46–47, 88). He goes on to argue that, since didactic intentions are not necessary (to the production of the plays), they are unworthy of consideration. He adduces a comment from the author of the *Dissoi Logoi* to support this contention (DK 3.17: "Poets write their poems not for the sake of truth but to give men pleasure").

There are a number of difficulties with this position. First, relying on an argument from silence is rarely wise, and anyway one could argue that Aristophanes in *Frogs* does present us with tragedians talking at some length about didactic intentions (there will be more on this later). Second, the use of the *Dissoi Logoi* is unconvincing. Heath can only argue in the way he does if he holds that a didactic intention must be expressed as an intention to tell the truth: that is not necessarily the case. He has also overestimated the value of the *Dissoi Logoi* as evidence. The sort of playful and polarized sophistic arguments we find in the *Dissoi Logoi* should not be taken as having equal worth to the evidence of an author such as Aristophanes. The latter may be a comic poet, and we may have to use his evidence with proper care; he was also, however, chosen by elected political officers to stage his plays. In that sense, he is likely to be more representative of commonly held views than an unnamed Sophist.

In order to answer my first question, it is necessary to look at two different types of context. The first is the literary context: here I hope to show that poetry was generally regarded as having educative effects and that tragic poetry should not be seen as an exception. The second context is political. I should stress that we are looking at the contexts for the way the audience would have received the plays. I should also say that, in using the term "context," I am not saying that this context is somehow more important than the plays themselves. In some ways the context is prior to the performance of the plays; but the plays can also inform or change that context (here understood as the expectation of the audience). There is a flux, if you will, between plays and audience, with each affecting the other. In addition, we should not view the expectations of the audience as monolithic at any one time or as not changing over time.[2]

Throughout antiquity poets were seen as purveyors not only of entertainment but also of wisdom. It is important that the very first poet, Homer, should be seen in this way. One of our earliest pieces of evidence (Xenophanes, DK 10) makes clear that Homer was perceived as a teacher, even if Xenophanes wants to criticize that fact. If we move further forward to Plato, we find a philosopher who is trying to claim for philosophy the culturally and educationally prestigious position which had tradition-ally been occupied by poetry. More particularly, we find Plato's Socrates talking of Homer as the original master and guide of all the great tragic poets (*Republic* 595b10–c1), and as the educator of Greece in most people's opinion (*Republic* 606–7). An entire dialogue, *Ion*, is devoted to what Homer can teach you, although the view of teaching of and learning from Homer advanced by Ion is not very sophisticated. The *Hippias Minor*, however, depicts a very different educational experience. In this dialogue Socrates and Hippias engage in argument over the moral characters of the Homeric heroes and of their relationship to truth and falsehood. In another piece of early fourth-century evidence (Xenophon, *Symposium* 3.5) Niceratus explains how his father, concerned to see his son become a good person, compelled him to memorize all of Homer. The same direct connection between reading and learning Homer and the education of the young is made in the fourth century by Isocrates in his *Panegyricus* (159).

We can safely say, then, that the view that Homer was a teacher was commonly held. The same is true of other poets. A fragment of New Comedy (Alexis fr. 140 *PCG*) depicts a scene of Heracles being asked to choose from a number of poets (including Homer, Orpheus, Hesiod, and the tragedians) for his education.

A fragment of Heraclitus has the philosopher admitting that Hesiod is a teacher (DK 57; see Nussbaum 1986, 123). A later thinker, Protagoras, further stresses that we should see poets as teachers. In Plato's *Protagoras* (316d2–9) he states that, as a Sophist, he himself is a teacher (of *aretê*, or excellence), but Sophists are often viewed with suspicion (because of their teaching of, or association with, rhetoric). Interestingly, he then claims that poets (he mentions Homer, Hesiod, and Simonides) have taken the name of poet only to cover up their real nature as Sophists. If Sophists are teachers, and poets are really Sophists, then, according to Protagoras, poets are teachers.

Protagoras' claims appear in the eponymous Platonic dialogue, and in fact may more accurately represent Plato's views than those of Protagoras. Certainly (and I will be discussing this in more detail later), Plato is very concerned with the educative effects of poetry. At *Laws* 653–55 he discusses the role of arts generally, and poetry in particular, in education. In this section of the *Laws* (654a) Plato says that someone who is *achoreutos* is also *apaideutos*; that is, someone who has not been trained in the dance and to sing the tales of myth cannot count as educated. And in the *Republic* (608a–b) Socrates says that, because he has been brought up the way he has, he loves poetry, but also that he now knows that poetry has no claim to truth. This tells us both that a traditional education involved poetry, and that Socrates (and Plato) were competing aggressively with the poets to take over poetry's educational role (Detienne 1996).

Plato is also very well aware of the educational effects of symposia. Indeed, he spends some pages on this very thing in the *Laws* (645–50). He notes that symposia are a sort of playful examination of those present (649d10–e2). He also talks at some length about what happens at symposia, the role of music and so on, but we can find stronger, more direct evidence in Theognis, not only that symposia were important in educating young adults, but also that poetry played a crucial role in that education. Theognis often talks of how he intends to teach through his poetry, and there are many examples of advice (see, for example, 31–34, 61–66, 101–8, 1165–66; see also 415–18, 447–52, 1105–6, 1164; Levine 1985). But perhaps the clearest piece of evidence is at lines 27–30, where the poet addresses Cyrnus and says that he will pass on the good advice he received from good men (*agathoi*) himself when he was young. The specific advice is to the point: be sensible, and don't be too keen on honors, fame, and wealth, especially if they require shameful or unjust actions.

So far, then, we have seen that poets were viewed as teachers. The evidence is particularly compelling since it comes from a variety of different eras, places, and genres. But we still need to be surer about the teaching of tragedy. The evidence we have for this comes from Aristophanes' *Frogs*, and it is worth looking at in some detail, since it is explicit about tragedy's expected educative function.

It is in the debate between Aeschylus and Euripides that all the talk of tragedy's ability to teach occurs (Dover 1993b). For Aeschylus, tragedy – at least in Euripides' hands – is certainly capable of teaching bad things. These have mainly to do with sex: Aeschylus complains of unholy relationships in Euripides' plays (*Frogs* 850), of incest too (1081). By contrast there are no erotic women in Aeschylus' plays (1043–44). Aeschylus claims for himself that he has taught people to want to win (1025–26); that his teaching, like Homer's, has to do with war (1034–36). On a more general note he states that, while boys have teachers, men have poets (1054–55): poets, that is, provide adult education. Euripides, on the other hand, claims to offer a different, more intellectual sort of teaching. He has taught people to speak (954–55; Euripides is criticized for this by Aeschylus at 1069, and by the chorus at 1491–99), to reason clearly (971–75), and to ask questions (977–79).

Most telling, however, is the response that Euripides gives to Aeschylus' question about why poets should be respected: "For cleverness and advice, and because we make men in cities better [*beltious te poioumen tous anthrôpous en tais polesin*]" (1009–10). Euripides not only confirms that tragic poets are expected to be, and see themselves as, teachers; he makes clear as well that the teaching is in the broadest sense political. The language in which Euripides expresses the fact of tragic teaching is not unfamiliar. In Plato's *Protagoras* (318e–19a) Socrates asks Protagoras what he teaches. The Sophist's reply lists the proper management of one's own affairs, how best to run one's household, management of public affairs, and making an effective contribution to the affairs of the city in both word and action. Socrates summarizes by saying that Protagoras claims to teach the art of running a city and to make men good citizens. The Greek of this last point is very similar to Euripides' claim in the *Frogs*: both use the same verb for make (*poioumen, poiein*); both understand that it is citizens who are to be taught (men in cities: *tous anthrôpous en tais polesin*; citizens: *politas*); both see the aim of the education as moral improvement (better: *beltious*; good: *agathous*). We must remember that the debate between Aeschylus and Euripides is, after all, a contest in wisdom (*agôn sophias*, 882) between two wise men (*sophoin androin*, 896) about who is wiser (*sophôteros*, 780). Wisdom, as Dover (1993b) points out, is not necessarily something we would associate with artists, and the fact that the debate between the two poets is cast in these terms shows that Aristophanes and his Athenian audience did not respond to tragedy in a purely aesthetic way. It does not much matter to us here that it is Aeschylus rather than Euripides who wins the debate: what is important is that the winner is chosen for his wisdom. (Aeschylus at line 1485 is commended for the fact that he thinks well: *eu phronein*.) The final instruction given to Aeschylus by the chorus ("save our city," 1501) shows the political and educative nature of tragedy.

Now, while it is true that we have to be careful when using the evidence of a comic poet (comic poets tend to exaggerate if they are not inventing), it must be remembered that the one thing on which the two tragic poets agree during their debate in *Frogs* is that tragedy teaches. More than that, many of the jokes would not work unless that function were assumed. This sort of procedure is typical of Aristophanes. In *Knights*, for instance, he does not invent the function of the sovereign assembly (to pass laws and make important political decisions); and in *Wasps* he presumes that juries in law courts are there to come to a judgment. In both cases Aristophanes takes for granted the function of an institution (a function which anyway would have been obvious to the contemporary audience), and satirizes the way people behave within those institutions as they play their part in performing the appropriate function. I suggest that the same thing is happening in *Frogs*: the function of tragedy (to teach) is assumed; the stylistic and thematic peculiarities of Aeschylus and Euripides are used to provide the comic material. It is for all these reasons that I cannot agree with Malcolm Heath (1987b, 45) when he questions Aristophanes' evidence.

It may be true, however, that Aristophanes is parodying tragic teaching as unhelpfully vague, and that his real point is that for specific political advice one should turn to comedy rather than tragedy (Goldhill 1991, 201–22; Heiden 1991). Indeed, it is possible that Aristophanes was awarded a sacred olive crown for having, as his chorus puts it at 686–87, given good advice to the city (Sommerstein 1993). Still, the plot of *Frogs* has Dionysus descend to the underworld to find a *tragic* poet who can advise the Athenians in their hour of need. And even if Aristophanes is keen to assert the superiority of comic teaching, that still leaves untouched the fact that tragedy was expected to teach.

But we should perhaps not be surprised that the Athenians, and indeed other Greeks, accorded poetry and tragedy so much honor, for our sources from Homer through to the fifth and fourth centuries speak frequently of the power of words to achieve a variety of effects (Lain Entralgo 1970; de Romilly 1975; Walsh 1984). Words – and these are not only those used by poets, though they frequently are – can be deceptive and manipulative (Homer, *Odyssey* 13.294, 14.387, 19.203; Gorgias, *Encomium of Helen* 9, 11; Plato, *Cratylus* 408c, *Meno* 76e, *Republic* 382d); they can enslave those who listen to them, because they are irresistible (Gorgias, *Encomium of Helen* 8–9; Euripides, *Hecuba* 816; Plato, *Gorgias* 452e). More positively, like magic, they can enchant, producing pleasure even out of grief (Homer, *Odyssey* 4.113, 11.334, 18.282–83; Gorgias, *Encomium of Helen*; Plato, *Phaedrus* 261a ff., 271c, *Protagoras* 315a, 328d, *Republic* 413c4, 601b). Words can soothe (Hesiod, *Theogony* 98–103) and cure and, in Gorgias' famous analogy, work on the soul in the way that *pharmaka* (drugs) work on the body (Gorgias, *Encomium of Helen* 14; Plato, *Gorgias* 456b; see also Aeschylus, *Agamemnon* 16–17; Euripides, *Bacchae* 326–27, *Hippolytus* 478, *Trojan Women* 472–73). It is perhaps no accident that most of these references come from authors who are either Athenian or associated with fifth- or fourth-century Athens. For Athens was a *logopolis*, a "city of words" (see Goldhill 1986a, 57–78), and the Athenians were, according to the Thucydidean Cleon, *theatai tôn logôn* ("spectators of words," 3.38.4). Athens took a tradition that was already astonished by the powers of language and added to that a political system in which language, and more particularly rhetoric, was essential. Even Plato, in so many ways an anti-democrat, calls language a sort of instrument to organize reality (*Cratylus* 388b13): that was certainly what it was for the Athenian democracy.

The final way in which we can see that tragedy was expected to teach is to look briefly at the criticisms of the genre made by the two great philosophers, Plato and Aristotle. Plato wanted tragedy – along with most other forms of poetry – removed from his ideal state. This was because, firstly, tragedy, as a form of *mimêsis*, had too indirect a relationship with truth; in fact, Plato fairly frequently declares that tragedy lies. Secondly, the effects of tragedy were, in Plato's eyes, without exception pernicious. For Plato the tragedians and their audiences are too interested in pleasure and emotional reaction (Croally 1994, 23–26, gives all the Platonic references). What is absent for the philosopher from tragedy is any reflection about moral agency, which for him was the most important question (Halliwell 1996).[3] Also, the context of the performance before a mass audience meant that, for Plato, proper education was impossible (Plato, *Gorgias* 502b–e, *Republic* 604e, *Laws* 655e, 876b), because in his view education could only occur genuinely between one student and one teacher (Plato, *Laws* 666d–667a). However, one soon sees that Plato's problem with tragedy is not that it doesn't teach, but that precisely it is expected to. His complaint is that tragedy taught bad things badly, and his ambition was to take its place as the main source of a citizen's education. (It is interesting but perhaps not surprising that the dialogic form of Plato's writings owes as much to tragedy as to any other genre; see Sansone 1996, von Reden and Goldhill 1999.)

Aristotle's views on tragedy are considerably more difficult to pin down than Plato's. While Plato is perfectly aware of tragedy's educative function (though he criticizes it), Aristotle makes no overt mention of it. For Plato the relationship between tragedy and the polis, or the citizen, is paramount. Aristotle's *Poetics*, however, does not mention the polis at all (Hall 1996b). However, if we read the *Poetics* more carefully (and alongside other works of Aristotle), we can see that Aristotle has something valuable to say about the education that tragedy performs.

Plato, as we have seen, derides tragedy as a *mimêsis* that cannot attain or reflect the truth; for that reason, one cannot learn the truth from it. In Aristotle's more sophisticated view, *mimêsis* is directly connected to learning; indeed we start to learn through *mimêsis* (*Poetics* 1448b5–9). Not only that, Aristotle answers Plato's concerns about the pleasure the tragic audience felt when watching tragic *mimêsis* by arguing that pleasure, like *mimêsis*, is natural (for example, *Nicomachean Ethics* 1177a16–17, 1177b30–31). For Aristotle, in fact, pleasure and learning come together when the audience experiences a *mimêsis* (*Poetics* 1448b4–17). The emotions, which include not only pleasure, but fear and pity as well, do not exclude the possibility of thought, as they do in Plato (Lada 1993, 1996; Konstan 2001, 1–26). Emotions have an intellectual value in Aristotle (as they do in modern neurology): they can force people to deliberate (for example, fear at *Rhetoric* 1383a6–7), and they are related to an understanding of moral virtue (for example, *Nicomachean Ethics* 1104b11–12, 1179b24 ff.).

For Aristotle, tragedy – as a *mimêsis* which produces pleasure – can play an important part in educating the emotions, itself an important part of a moral education. It is true that Aristotle's pronouncement on *katharsis* – a key term in his analysis of the emotional effect of tragedy (*Poetics* 1449b24–28; Halliwell 1986, 89–90; Lear 1988) – remains a matter of argument, but whether we take *katharsis* to mean purgation of the emotions, intellectual clarification, or some sort of religious cleansing (Belfiore 1992, Nussbaum 1986, Nuttall 1996), it does not much matter: tragedy educates by educating the emotions, even more effectively because it deals in universals rather than particulars (*Poetics* 1451b5–11). As we have seen, Plato accepts the polis context of tragic teaching but also criticizes how and what tragedy teaches. Aristotle, by contrast, seems to have forgotten the polis but understands the beneficial emotional and intellectual effects tragedy can have.

So the answer to my first question is a firm "yes." Poets throughout antiquity and in various contexts were expected to teach: tragedians should not be seen as an exception. Furthermore, fifth-century tragedy arose from and reflected on the mixture of a poetic and philosophical tradition on the one hand and a new political system on the other, both of which championed and depended on the various powers of the word. Finally, our survey of fourth-century philosophical considerations of tragedy confirms that its expected function was educative. Yet it is not only because tragedy was poetry that it was supposed to teach. In fifth-century Athens tragedy enjoyed a very distinctive prominence on account of its political context.

During the fifth century tragedy was performed at the Theater of Dionysus. This theater lay below the Acropolis, where the city's main religious buildings were situated. It was also near the agora, the area that housed the five hundred councilors of the *boulé* (council), the law courts, and other religious and commercial activity, and was not far from the Pnyx, the hill where the assembly met. In a physical sense, then, tragedy has its place at the center of Athens (Croally 1994, 163–74; Wiles 1997, 63–86; Rehm 2002, 35–75).

This spatial aspect is important. The development of the polis could be said to be the development of civic space (Polignac 1984). Greeks everywhere seemed to have found the idea of the center important. Maps of the period – reconstructed from literary evidence – have the Greeks at the center of the world, with all the various barbarians at their edges (Dilke 1985, 22–31; Heidel 1937; Jacob 1988). Delphi is often thought of as the very center of the world (see, for example, Euripides, *Medea* 668, *Orestes* 333), and one of the early philosophers, Thales, thought that it would be better if Ionia (with its disparate Greek colonies) had one center (Herodotus 1.170). In Homer, one finds warriors striding *es meson*, toward the middle (for example, at *Iliad* 7.55), as well as the idea of putting things – ideas, spoils – into the middle so that they can be shared (as at *Iliad* 23.704). One can trace, especially in Herodotus but also in tragedy, how this idea of putting things into the middle, into the center, becomes politicized (Detienne 1965; 1996, 89–106).

In Herodotus we can see that the idea of putting things *es meson* becomes another way of expressing the idea of handing over at least some political functions to the people. For instance, in the famous debate between three Persians about the best form of government (a very Greek debate), Otanes' preference for something like democracy is expressed by the phrase *es meson* (3.80.2). When the tyrant of Samos, Maeandrius, argues for handing power (*tên archên*) over to the people, again *es meson* is used (3.142.3); similarly, an arbitrator from Mantineia reconstitutes Cyrene by putting things *es meson* for the people (*tôi dêmôi*; 4.161.3).[4] Turning to tragedy, we find that in Euripides' *Suppliants*, the king of Athens, Theseus, becomes involved in a debate with a Theban herald as to the best form of government. Theseus, though king, is a strident (and anachronistic) advocate of democracy. During his speech in the debate, he says: "That is freedom: 'Which man, having some good advice for the city, wishes to bring it into the middle [*es meson*]?' " (438–39). Theseus apes the technical language of the assembly here, but the important points for us are that democracy and *es meson* are combined in this one question.

Athens puts real weight on this idea of the center and its relationship to democracy. With its own center constituted by the Acropolis, the agora, the *koinê hestia* (public hearth), the Theater, and the Pnyx, Athens was also the center of the territory of Attica, and of an empire that grew during the fifth century; it became as well a center for both trade and intellectuals (Lévêque and Vidal-Naquet 1996, Osborne 1985; Ostwald 1992; Vernant 1982; 1983, 220–21). In contrast to the practice of most Greek states, Athenian religious processions such as the Panathenaic procession moved from margin to center (Polignac 1984). What happened at the center was crucial for the democracy: tragedy happened at the center. And what Athens put at its center was authority: tragedy shared that authority.

The immediate context in which tragedy was performed at the City Dionysia also shows the prominence given to tragedy in Athens. The sortitively selected five hundred councilors chose the judges of the dramatic contest through the system of the ten tribes established at the beginning of the democracy by Cleisthenes (Csapo and Slater 1995, 157–65). The sortitively selected eponymous archon selected the poets whose plays would be performed and the *chorêgoi* who would finance the choruses. (Griffin [1998, 54] has argued that there is nothing political about the archon's selection of poets, but this underestimates the fact that the decision is taken by a political officer in the first place.) The ceremonies which preceded the plays together demonstrate the political nature of the occasion (Connor 1989, Csapo and Slater 1995, Goldhill 1990, 2000; cf. Friedrich 1996). The generals, arguably the top ten officials of the polis, poured libations in the *orchêstra*; the tribute from the empire was displayed on the stage; civic crowns were awarded to those who had performed service to the state; orphans of war, educated at state expense in the absence of their fathers, processed through the theater. It would be difficult to imagine a more obviously political context for the performance of drama. In addition, events after the festival also demonstrate its political nature: it seems as though an assembly was held in the theater after the festival in order to discuss how the festival had been organized (Demosthenes 21.8–10).

Tragedy was not a commercial operation. Instead it was funded by the polis, either directly – through the fee paid to the authors – or indirectly, through a system of taxation called the liturgy. Liturgies, imposed on the rich, could be used to fund a variety of things, such as superintending games and gymnasia, upkeep of triremes and financial provision for dramatic choruses ([Xenophon], *Constitution of the Athenians* 1.13). To be chosen as a *chorêgos* (one who paid for a chorus) was something of an honor, although some tried their best to avoid the expense (Christ 1990, Wilson 1997, 2000a). The cost of a *chorêgia* almost matched that of the upkeep of a trireme (Csapo and Slater 1995, 147). Given Athens' dependence on her navy, this suggests that the Athenians literally valued the production of their tragedies (almost) as highly as their imperial ambitions and the defense of their homeland.

While the polis organized and financed the dramatic festival, the audience of the plays probably consisted of a large number of Athenian citizens, people with real power in what was a direct democracy. However, exactly how many people attended the City Dionysia is difficult to answer with any certainty. The only direct evidence we have is Plato's *Symposium* 175e, which states that the total size of the audience was 30,000. Aristophanes seems to indicate an audience of thousands (*Wasps* 1010), and the same author mentions the great throng in the auditorium (*Frogs* 676). But Greeks weren't very good with large numbers (hence the confusion perhaps with the numbers of the invading Persian forces in 480 BCE, and with the five thousand who were supposed to be entrusted with power by the oligarchic revolutionaries in 412–11 BCE). We can't be sure. Examination of the site of the Theater of Dionysus and its physical constraints suggests an audience of somewhere between 14,000 and 17,000 (Pickard-Cambridge 1988, 236; Goldhill 1997a, 57). Of that total, how many were Athenian citizens? We know that pride of place was given to some of those citizens: members of the *boulê* had reserved seats (Aristophanes, *Birds* 794 with scholion, *Peace* 887), as did some of the orphans (or ephebes) who had earlier processed (Aeschines 3.154). But we also know that there were certainly some foreigners there: the scholiast on Aristophanes' *Acharnians* 504 makes clear that the ambassadors who had brought the tribute to be displayed were present. It seems certain from later evidence that other foreigners were present (Theophrastus, *Characters* 9.5;

Aelian, *Varia Historia* 2.13). It also seems likely that a large number of metics (resident aliens) may have attended.

In a fascinating recent article Alan Sommerstein (1997) has challenged the current orthodoxy about the constitution of the audience. He tries to show that the theoric fund (the fund that subsidized theater attendance) was not in place in the fifth century, and that attending the plays was expensive. He concludes, first, that the proportion of Athenian citizens in the audience may have been as low as half; and, second, that as the fifth century progressed the political sympathies of the audience became increasingly "right-wing."

This argument, though interesting and enticing, has its problems. The evidence concerning the theoric fund is not good (Csapo and Slater 1995, 293–96), but it seems likely that all citizens received some form of subsidy during the fifth century (Demosthenes 10.38; Plutarch, *Pericles* 9). I believe that Sommerstein has anyway exaggerated the cost of attending. Also, it is difficult to agree with the view that the theater audience became increasingly right-wing. It is true that there may have been a decree restricting comic satire around 440 BCE, but, again, the evidence is not compelling (scholion at Aristophanes, *Acharnians* 67). And the fact that Aristophanes spends much of his time criticizing so-called demagogues such as Cleon does not on its own convince me that the audience was right-wing: we have too little evidence from comedies in the 440s and 430s with which to compare Aristophanes. I agree with Sommerstein that there was political disagreement and conflict in the Athenian democracy, but I think that that conflict occurred within the institutions of assembly and theater as much as between them. We have no record of "conservatives" not attending the assembly in the later years of the fifth century: quite the reverse in fact (note the case of Nicias). And, even if we accept Sommerstein's view that only half the audience was made up of Athenian citizens, that figure of 7,000–8,000 compares very favorably with our best estimates of how many attended the assembly (6,000: Hansen 1976) and how many were on the jury panels (up to 6,000: MacDowell 1978, 36–40). No one would say that either the assembly or the law courts were undemocratic because of the numbers attending. Tragedy had at least as many present, and perhaps more.

It is very likely that large numbers of Athenian citizens attended the performances at the City Dionysia, and that they almost certainly outnumbered foreigners. However, there may also have been a number of Athenian non-citizens in attendance: that is, women, slaves, and children. The evidence for this is far from conclusive. (For the evidence and various views, see Csapo and Slater 1995, 286–93; Goldhill 1994; Henderson 1991). My own view is that we cannot be certain: we are stuck between an understanding of a culture which restricted the access of women, slaves, and children to political occasions (and the City Dionysia was certainly one of those) and which by contrast encouraged at least women's participation in ritual events (and the City Dionysia was certainly one of those). As far as the presence of women goes, I agree that "whether women are to be thought of as a silenced presence on the map or an absent sign, the audience represents the body politic" (Goldhill, 1997a, 66).

Here is the key point: the audience – citizens, metics, foreigners, perhaps women, children, and slaves, but mainly citizens – represents the body politic. We began with the idea that tragedy is the city putting itself onto the stage. And the people who put it there, and who stand to gain from it, are the audience.

There is another way of expressing this idea about the audience, and that is to call it collective. Griffin 1998 has recently questioned this description for the following reasons: first, if the audience is collective and its expectation of the plays is importantly determined by that, then we should be able to say unambiguously that the plays reinforce social cohesion (cf. Griffith 1995; Pelling 1997b; 2000, 164–88); second, because the plays have as their collective voice the chorus, who are often different in gender, ethnic, and class terms from Athenian citizens, that collective voice cannot be that of the (mostly) Athenian audience; third, the audience comprises individuals responding individually to the plays. I cannot agree. The entire structure and fabric of democratic Athens was based on an expectation that Athenians citizens were citizens first, individuals second (see, for example, Pericles' Funeral Oration at Thucydides 2.36–46). Also, to assert that the collectivity of the audience is constituted by a desire to achieve social cohesion underestimates the fact that Athenian democracy institutionalized disagreement in the assembly, the law courts, and the theater (Connor 1994, Hansen 2003). That the chorus does not represent the collective voice of the polis because the chorus is often women or barbarians is something that other critics have argued (for example, Gould 1996). But Attic tragedy is almost entirely peopled by characters who were not Athenian citizens. As we shall see in a later section, the fact that tragedy gives voice to those who were "other" is part of the way that tragedy teaches. The chorus, however marginal, can represent a collective view (Goldhill 1996). Finally, the ancient evidence of Gorgias, Plato, and Aristotle (and we looked at some of it in the section dealing with the power of the word) depicts the emotional responses of the audience to words, to tragedy, precisely as collective (Seaford 2000, 32).

To this point we have seen that tragedy was performed in a central place – with all the political authority that entailed in fifth-century Athens – that it was organized, supported, and variously funded by the polis, and that it was watched by a mass of Athenian citizens, citizens who were burdened with direct political power and responsibility. In all these ways tragedy can be seen to have been a central discourse of the polis. As such it was expected to teach: this is the subject of the next section.

Tragedy, as part of the dramatic performances at the City Dionysia, was one of the main political institutions of the Athenian democracy, along with the assembly, the *boulê*, and the law courts. These institutions are variously associated in the evidence. Participation in all four is funded by the polis: there is the *ekklêsiastikon* for attendance at the assembly, the *dikastikon* for serving on juries; council members are paid throughout their year of service and have in addition reserved seats and a fund (the *bouleutikon*) to pay for their tickets to watch the plays. And there is, possibly at least, an analogous fund for attendance at the City Dionysia (the *theôrikon*). Plato links the audiences at assembly, law courts, and theater because they are all noisy (*Republic* 492b–e). And it is interesting to note that, outside Athens in the demes of Attica, the deme theater was often used for political and legal activity (Wiles 1997, 23–24). Tragedy – in its peculiar way – is the polis in action (Kolb 1979, 530), just as in their different ways are the assembly, the law courts, and war as well (Vernant 1980, 25: war is "the . . . city facing outwards").

The experience of watching – or rather hearing – tragedy would also have been familiar to the citizens in the audience. For the language of tragedy, though often stylized and poetic (Mastronarde 2002b, 81–96), is on other occasions strikingly similar to that used and heard in both the assembly and the law courts (Goldhill 1997b; Halliwell 1997). That is to say, tragedy incorporates the other political discourses of the city (Goff 1999–2000, 93). The plays often represent difficult decisions being made, often too in set-piece debates (*agónes*). Rhetoric, on which Athenian democracy so depended, is frequently examined.

There is an interesting piece of evidence in Plato's *Apology.* At one point in the speech Socrates starts to examine one of his accusers, Meletus (24e–25a). Socrates, keen to ridicule the charge of corrupting the youth made against him, asks Meletus what makes the young good. Meletus' first reply is that it is the laws (*nomoi*). Socrates continues by asking whether he means that the laws educate the young, making them better; the reply is "yes." Socrates then broadens his inquiry: do jurymen, members of the council and of the assembly also educate? Again, the answer is an emphatic "yes." Socrates clearly thinks that Meletus' answers are absurd, but there is no reason to think that many on the jury, and among the wider citizen body, would not have agreed with Meletus (Ober 1998, 170). It is true that here Socrates makes no mention of theater or tragedy, but elsewhere both Plato (in, for example, *Republic*, books 3 and 10, *Laws*, book 7) and Aristotle (*Politics*, book 8) are keen to investigate the educational effects of music (*mousikê*) and tragedy. Given this concern, we need not be alarmed at the absence of theater from Socrates' cross-examination. Elsewhere (*Laws* 701a), Plato connects theater with democracy when he complains that a sort of theatocracy had arisen in democratic Athens.

All the main institutions of the polis were presumed to have educative effects. Tragedy, not only as poetry but also as a political institution, was "a democratic *paideia*...in itself" (Arrowsmith 1963, 33). The position is nicely summed up by Paul Cartledge (1997, 19): "But in the first instance participation in the democratic process...was conceived primarily as an education for Athenian citizens....For such average citizens, tragic theater was an important part of their learning to be active participants in self-government by mass meeting and open debate between peers."

Tragedy filled a real need in fifth-century democratic Athens. On the one hand, there was no public system of formal education (Cartledge 1997, 19; Sinclair 1988, 51; Morgan 1998, 9–21); on the other, the Athenians were very interested in education (hence Meletus' remarks in the *Apology*) and also believed – along with Pericles in the Funeral Oration (Thucydides 2.40–41) – that their whole city could be an education, to themselves no doubt, but also to others. We should also remember the strange position that the Athenians in the fifth century found themselves in. Life during the period was "exuberant and disconcerting" (Meier 1993, 8) because the Athenians, starting with Cleisthenes' reforms in 508 BCE, were embarked on an unprecedented adventure. They had invented democracy and, lacking formal public education and what we would recognize as ordinary state apparatus, they needed perhaps as much help as they could get: decisions needed to be made. Of course, this does not mean that the teaching experience in the theater was the same as that in the assembly or law courts. There was no time, in the hurly-burly of the assembly, to engage in abstract discussion (Wilson 2000b, 100). What we find with tragedy is "a social body carrying out quite publicly the maintenance and development of [the citizen body's] mental infrastructure" (Meier 1993, 4).

An alternative view has it that the subject matter of the tragedies reflects an interest in the sorts of moral dilemmas encountered in Homer and other pre- and

non-democratic poets: "These terrible dilemmas and monstrous actions...are neither new in the democratic *polis* nor specific to it" (Griffin 1998, 59). Tragedy should
be seen, in fact, as "a uniquely vivid and piercingly pleasurable enactment of human
suffering, magnified in scale and dignity by the fact that the agents were famous
people of myth, and winged with every refinement of poetry and music" (Griffin
1998, 60). The second quotation, general as it is, is difficult to disagree with. The
first, however, underestimates the extent to which tragedy treated themes, such as the
refusal of burial and the problem of supplication, in a very different way from epic; it
also introduced subjects (incest, killing of kin) that make no appearance in Homer
(Seaford 2000, 36). The reason for these differences between tragedy and epic is that
tragedy was a political institution. The *Oresteia*, say, with its treatment of the themes
of justice and the social function of language, or Sophocles' *Antigone*, with its
examination of the nature of political authority, or Euripides' *Medea*, with its powerful portrayal of the relations between the sexes, or his *Trojan Women*, with its
examination of the effects of war, all demonstrate tragedy's sharp concern with
problems faced by Athenian citizens (and I have adduced only a few examples).
Finally, the evidence of Plutarch (*On the Glory of the Athenians* 348c, 350a) which
says that politicians are much more useful than the childish pastime of tragedy,
need not mean that tragedy was not political and did not teach. Plutarch may be
thinking of tragedy in his own time, but his evidence can anyway be interpreted
differently. What is interesting is that politicians and tragedians should be compared
at all: that, in my view, shows that, in their different ways, they occupied the same
political space.

Putting tragedy in both its literary and political contexts has demonstrated that
tragedy was expected to teach. But we are still left with the puzzling question: how
exactly did it teach?

How Did Tragedy Teach?

We have already seen that both Plato and Aristotle have much to say about the
(educative) effects of tragedy. But both, in their different ways, fail to say much
about what seems to be distinctive about tragic teaching. To begin with the obvious:
tragedy used stories from myth. These stories from the past – with their kings and
heroes and so on – don't at first sight seem to sit happily in the fifth-century
democratic context. However, the stories may be old but the treatment given them
is anything but: in the *Oresteia* Orestes' murder of his mother becomes part of an
examination of fifth-century conceptions of justice; the question of whether Philoctetes will return home or go to Troy in Sophocles' play of the same name is told
through an examination of the powers and abuses of rhetoric; Helen and Hecuba, in
Euripides' *Trojan Women*, debate as if they were fifth-century Sophists. No, it looks as
though the past is being used to talk about the present (Buxton 2002; Goldhill
1997b, 129–30; Hall 1997, 98; note Pelling 1997b, 217: "the interaction between
tragic and contemporary events [is] two-way"). In a similar way, tragedy is peopled
by characters "whose ethnicity, gender, or status would absolutely debar them from
public debate in democratic Athens" (Hall 1997, 123). Tragedy is full of barbarians,
slaves, kings, and women: we shall see that these "others" are important to the way
that tragic teaching worked.

Froma Zeitlin has argued in two powerful pieces that Attic tragedy used the Other to examine the self. In one article her emphasis is on Thebes as a sort of anti-city to Athens (Zeitlin 1990b; see also Vernant and Vidal-Naquet 1988, 334–38); in the second she analyzes the way women are used for the purposes of male self-examination (Zeitlin 1990a; see also Rehm 2002, 236–69). While Zeitlin can sometimes be overschematic (Thebes, for instance, is more variously portrayed than she allows), the argument is a useful starting point and, perhaps more importantly, gains credence from the fact that it is consistent with the polarizing habit of Greek thought generally (Lloyd 1966). Greeks – and this certainly includes Athenians – tended to define themselves against a range of others. So, for instance, an Athenian citizen would have understood himself as Greek because not barbarian, as male because not female, as human because not divine or animal, as free because not enslaved (Croally 1994, 70–119; DuBois 1982; Hall 1989). What we often encounter in tragedy is a questioning of the hierarchy of these polarities: thus a barbarian acts in a more Greek manner than Greeks, a slave appears to be freer than a free person, and so on (Buxton 2002, Ebbott, chapter 23 in this volume). Furthermore, this questioning is normally situated in another time (the past) and in another place (not Athens).

The self that tragedy examines is not something physical or a person (or persons) that the audience could identify in their contemporary world. Tragedy does not work like comedy. Rather, we should see the self as something more to do with the values and beliefs held by the audience, which, for reasons of economy, I prefer to call ideology. In an earlier work I defined this as the authorized self-definition of the dominant group, that is, the citizen body (Croally 1994, 259–66). I see no reason to change this definition (see also Ober 1989; 1994, 103; Pelling 1997b, 224–35; 2000, 177–84; Rose 1995, 62), but it should be said that in invoking the term I do not mean to say that there were no conflicts within Athenian ideology, nor that it stayed the same through the fifth century. We can still say, though, that tragedy taught by examining the self (ideology) in dramatic other worlds.

My point can perhaps best be seen if we look at a very small number of tragedies which do not present a dramatic other-world of the usual sort. We know of four exceptions to the rule that tragedy used stories from myth. Early in the fifth century Phrynichus produced two plays (*Phoenician Women, Capture of Miletus*) and Aeschylus one (*Persians*) that dealt with almost contemporary events. Very much later (417–16 BCE) Agathon produced the only known example of a purely fictional tragedy (Aristotle, *Poetics* 1451b21). This last seems to have been a one-time experiment, and we need not linger over it. But the earlier examples are interesting, partly because they came at a time when tragedy as a genre was young.

Unfortunately, we know little of the reaction to these plays, except in the case of Phrynichus' *Capture of Miletus* (probably 493/2 BCE). Herodotus (6.21) tells us of the distressed reaction of the Athenian audience to this play: the author was fined 1,000 drachmas for reminding them of a catastrophe – the actual fall of Miletus in 494 BCE – that affected them so deeply, and the play was never allowed to be reperformed (for discussion see Roisman 1988 and Rosenbloom 1993). This anecdote tells us that with this play the Athenians felt that they were seeing something too close to home, something not distant enough. The fact that there was possibly only one further attempt at contemporary subject matter – Aeschylus' *Persians* in 472 BCE

– seems to confirm that fact (Cartledge 1997, 25), even though Aeschylus' play told of Greek triumph rather than disaster. Distance between the world of the play and the world of the audience was important, at least for tragic representations. There was, for the Athenians, a certain value in the vagueness of the tragic world put before them: it enabled difficult questions to be asked without divisiveness or uniformity of interpretation (Easterling 1997b, 25), and without provoking the sorts of violent reactions demonstrated with the *Capture of Miletus*, a play that may have confronted too overtly the religious and political thinking of the day (Easterling 1997d, 172).

   In proposing this model of tragic teaching as a questioning of ideology, as an examination of the self through dramatic other places, I am not also saying that the definitions of self, the Other, ideology, and so on are all fixed. Athenian society changed in various ways through the fifth century; so too did the representations that tragedy put on the stage. As we have seen, there was at least some attempt to represent contemporary subject matter. And Athens – the home of the self – does appear in a number of tragedies (Aeschylus' *Eumenides*, Sophocles' *Oedipus at Colonus*, Euripides' *Suppliants* and *Children of Heracles*), often embodied by the mythical king Theseus (Mills 1997). There are varying degrees of more or less shocking anachronism (in Aeschylus' *Eumenides* Athens can daringly be represented as a city without a king, whereas in Euripides' *Suppliants* it is a king who launches a stout defense of democracy [Easterling 1984, 1985a]); of contemporary allusion (Croally 1994, 231–34; Roisman 1997); of naturalism, especially in Euripides (Michelini 1987, 1999–2000); of comedy, self-reference or metatheater and inter-textuality (Croally 1994, 235–48; Burian 1997; Goldhill 1986a; Gregory 1999–2000; Marshall 1999–2000; Mastronarde 1999–2000; Segal 1982; Zeitlin 1980). Debates about how tragedy developed, and even whether Euripides destroyed tragedy (an old Nietzschean point, this) go on. The point is: during the fifth century there was an evolution in what could be incorporated in the tragic world, and in what ways. Tragedy's method of teaching was not only to invent a fictional, make-believe world; it was to create one whose didactic effect depended to some extent on being different from the world of the audience. Tragedy, great ideological production itself, examined the ideology (the self) of the audience. This was its teaching.

Why is it Important to Acknowledge the Educative Function of Tragedy?

Attic tragedy of the fifth century was political; it was primarily a discourse of the polis. By understanding its educative function, we do not merely assert the political nature of tragedy; we give it substance. Tragedy is political because, in common with the other main institutions of fifth-century Athenian democracy, it teaches (though in its own distinctive way). That is, education was political, and the polis was educative. A purely aesthetic response to tragedy, as advanced for instance by Malcolm Heath (1987b), is of course permitted, but it cannot define for us what was distinctive about Attic tragedy of the fifth century. It cannot, for instance, clarify for us the ways in which this peculiarly Athenian literature is not Homer or, for that matter, Shakespeare. Responses to tragedy that make a significant use of an aesthetic or literary approach combined with a tendency to see morality or moral dilemmas (in contrast to ideology) as the true substance of tragedy miss first that, for the Athenian audience (peculiarly or not), morality and ideology were not separable (Green 1999, Griffin 1998). Such critics, by universalizing tragedy in the name of morality and art, may indeed capture the transhistorical appeal of Attic tragedy (although I suspect they are really interested in the tragic: nothing wrong with that), but again they miss the distinctiveness of tragedy and its historical moment.

We cannot say what the precise effects of tragic teaching were. We have no evidence, for instance, of an assembly vote or a decision in a law court affected directly by a tragedy (and we must remember anyway that it is unlikely that an audience of 14,000 or more responded in exactly the same way). However, on the basis of the evidence, we can still say that fifth-century Attic tragedy, in its distinctive way, was supposed to teach the citizens of fifth-century democratic Athens. There is another possible reward from this conclusion: we may not be in the same position as those democratic citizens of two and half thousand years ago; we may not learn the same things that they did from the plays. But tragedy can teach us that teaching and literature (or fiction, or art) are not mutually exclusive; that political literature is not some dull thing, without beauty or exhilaration; and that a reflective, communal response to the issues that most importantly affect us as human beings and citizens is something worth having.

NOTES

Many thanks to Angus Bowie, Pat Easterling, Simon Goldhill, and Justina Gregory for their helpful comments on earlier drafts.

1 I have discussed these questions elsewhere (Croally 1994, esp. 17–46), but some reviewers (Marshall 1995, Sansone 1995) were not convinced. That, along with a recent attempt to deny that tragedy had an educative function (Griffin 1998), has persuaded me to lay out the evidence again.

2 For a provocative article, which argues that "context" as used by Vernant et al. tends to limit the meaning of a text in a way analogous to the way invocations of the author (or authorial intention) limited meaning in earlier philological criticism, see Gellrich 1995. For a trenchant and perhaps surprising view of why we need authors (or context, perhaps), precisely so that we can limit meaning, see Foucault 1979.

3 Plato is wrong to say that there is no reflection about moral agency in tragedy. Medea, for instance, frequently considers the moral status and consequences of her intended actions. For an excellent dicussion of this issue of moral agency in tragedy (and epic), see Williams 1993.

4 For criticism of my use of *es meson*, see Rhodes 2003. I believe, however, that Rhodes underestimates the extent to which the term used by Herodotus was determined by the terms of political debate in democratic Athens. Rhodes also sees "Athenian drama as reflecting the *polis* in general rather than the democratic *polis* in particular" (2003, 119). Yet he himself says of the institutional setting of tragedy that it is "a democratic version" (2003, 113). It is very difficult to overestimate the importance of democracy in the Athenians' views of themselves and others.

FURTHER READING

On tragedy and teaching see Croally 1994 and Gregory 1991. On tragedy and the polis more generally, the first three chapters of Vernant and Vidal-Naquet 1988 remain essential. The best book-length introduction is Goldhill 1986a; a good article, from a different perspective, is Saïd 1998. The basic position of Meier 1993 – Athens was experimenting with democracy and needed all the help it could get – is attractive even if his particular readings of plays are less persuasive.

One fruitful way to approach tragic teaching specifically and tragedy's relation to the polis generally is through a consideration of civic and tragic space. For space in classical Athens, see Wiles 1997. Two recent and sophisticated books on tragic space are Rehm 2002 and Mendelsohn 2002. Zeitlin's articles on the Other on the tragic stage (women – 1990a; Thebes – 1990b) are a good starting point, although they can be too schematic. For a good, careful survey of tragedy's "peculiar blend of proximity and distance, in relation to time, space and ideology," see Buxton 2002, 188.

CHAPTER FIVE

Tragedy and the Early Greek Philosophical Tradition

William Allan

Poetry and Philosophy

Two of the most influential modern accounts of the relationship between tragedy and philosophy, those of Friedrich Nietzsche and Bruno Snell, present philosophy as, on the one hand, destroying tragedy through its insistent rationalism, or, on the other, as taking over tragedy's cultural and intellectual role and so rendering it obsolete (Nietzsche, *The Birth of Tragedy* [1872] secs. 10–15; Snell 1953, 90–112). In either case tragedy is seen as under threat from the encroaching claims of philosophy. By contrast, this chapter aims to present the relationship between tragedy and early Greek philosophy in a more positive manner. Not only did tragedy continue to flourish long after the foundation of the first major philosophical schools in the fourth century BCE, but during its most productive period (in fifth-century Athens) tragedy was deeply indebted to the early Greek philosophical tradition, and much more so than either Nietzsche's or Snell's model allows. Moreover, although our focus will be the influence of early Greek philosophical thought on tragedy, we might note at the outset that the impact of Greek tragedy on philosophy was no less important. Even contemporary philosophers, particularly those engaged in ethics, are returning ever more frequently to tragedy and Greek philosophy in order to support and develop their own arguments and ideas (for example, Nussbaum 1986).

To understand the influence of Greek philosophical thought on tragedy, we should first consider the scope of early Greek philosophy. The philosophical tradition before Plato and Aristotle is conventionally divided into two groups of thinkers, the Presocratics and the Sophists. It is often said of the Presocratics that their primary focus was the physical constitution of the world. A famous passage of Cicero claims that Socrates *primus philosophiam devocavit e caelo* ("was first to call philosophy down to earth from the heavens," *Tusculan Disputations* 5.4.10), rooting it in the fundamental problems of human society and behavior. Although it is true that many of the Presocratics were primarily interested in questions of "natural philosophy" and cosmology, they also reflected on ethics, politics, epistemology, and theology. The same can be said of the Sophists, whose human-centered interests show a remarkable affinity with the concerns of Socrates himself (despite Plato's determination to stress their differences). And these human-centered interests are also the domain of poetry. Although Plato sought to drive a wedge between philosophy and poetry (especially tragedy: see Halliwell, chapter 25 in this volume), poets from Homer and Hesiod onwards show an awareness of the widest range of "philosophical" (or perhaps better "intellectual") issues, from the justice of the gods to the origins of human society, so that, with respect to intellectual content, one cannot easily separate the poets from the philosophers. Even Aristotle, in the first detailed report on the Presocratics that we have (*Metaphysics* 983b–987a), allows that the question of first causes may originate with Homer (*Iliad* 14.201, 246) and Hesiod (*Theogony* 116–53).

Although Greek poetry from Homer to Euripides (and beyond) has an important philosophical dimension, there is a considerable difference between the methods of the poets and those of the philosophers. For the philosophical analysis offered by the Presocratics and the Sophists was unlike the explanations offered by such thinkers as Homer and Hesiod, whose "accounts of things (when they gave them) were primarily mythical rather than rational" (Curd 2002, 115–16). The distinction between philosophers or *phusiologoi* on the one hand, and *muthologoi* or poets on the other, is found already in Plato and is made even more explicit by Aristotle, as befits his tendency to classify and systematize (*Metaphysics* 983b27–84a3). Yet we should be cautious about articulating the distinction in terms of myth and reason. As Aristotle himself remarks, after saying that men began to philosophize out of wonder, "even the myth-lover is in a sense a philosopher, for myth is composed of wonders" (*Metaphysics* 982b18–20). Moreover, philosophers (especially Plato) continued to use myths, and numerous quotations from the poets, despite their hostility to them (Morgan 2000, 17). Thus, while the idea of "myth" as an untrue or unprovable story that was opposed to rational argument did gain currency among intellectuals in the fifth century (for example, Herodotus 2.23, Thucydides 1.22.4), the modern view of Greek culture as passing (in a logical and rational progression) from *muthos* to *logos* (classic statement in Nestle 1940) is too rigid: Protagoras, for example, is presented as asking his audience if they would like him to deliver his speech as a *muthos* or as a *logos* (Plato, *Protagoras* 320c; cf. *Gorgias* 523a).

Despite the common interests of philosophers and poets, the former were not averse to criticizing the latter: Heraclitus attacks Homer (DK 42), Hesiod (DK 40, 57, 67), Archilochus (DK 17, 42), and the "singers of the people" (DK 104), advertising his own philosophy as a superior source of wisdom and truth. And while poets might make appeals to truth (communicated to them by the Muses, whose knowledge transcends that of mortals: see *Iliad* 2.485–86; Hesiod, *Theogony* 26–28), the philosophers regarded only themselves as devoted to its rational pursuit. The Presocratics have, accordingly, long been recognized as the founders of a new style of logical and systematic thought. While they have also been described as healers, law-givers, and traveling mystics or shamans (see, for example, Kingsley 1995 on Empedocles and the Pythagoreans), their crucial role in the genesis of Western philosophy has never been in doubt.

The Sophists, by contrast, have only recently regained respectability as original and important thinkers in their own right. Their negative portrayal by Aristophanes, Xenophon, Plato, and Aristotle ensured that from the outset the word "sophist" carried "connotations of subversive irresponsibility" (Silk 2000, 12). Their rehabilitation began in the nineteenth century, when Hegel and Grote rejected such critical views, and since then the Sophists have gradually emerged as more than the spurious and superficial figures depicted by the tradition. In truth a Sophist like Protagoras (or a poet like Aeschylus) had as much right as any other Greek thinker to the title *philosophos* ("lover of wisdom").[1] Yet by appropriating the term "philosophy" for his own specialized discipline, and by forming it in opposition to the allegedly bogus wisdom of the Sophists (and poets), Plato ensured that the Sophists were seen as "lovers of cash" (cf. Barnes 1982, 449) rather than "lovers of wisdom." It is therefore important not only that we see the Sophists as a legitimate part of the early Greek philosophical tradition, but also that we seek to illustrate their relationship to tragedy, which was no less productive than that of the Presocratics.

The traditional (dismissive) view of the Sophists has led to many distortions: most strikingly, perhaps, it has obscured the continuities between their interests and those of the Presocratics. However, it is more illuminating to view the Sophists within the broad intellectual traditions of archaic and classical Greece, even if their emphasis on ethics and political philosophy emerged more strongly than that of the Presocratics. Like many of the Presocratics, the Sophists had diverse intellectual interests, from oratory and law to history, literature, and mathematics: they were not, *pace* Plato, simply interested in the profits of rhetoric and relativism.

Moreover, like the tragic dramatists themselves, who competed at the dramatic festivals of Athens and other cities, the philosophers, whether Presocratics or Sophists, presented their ideas in *performance* and in *competition* with other thinkers. Heraclitus speaks not of reading other people's books but of "those whose discourses I have heard" (DK 108), while the meters used by Xenophanes, Parmenides, and Empedocles (dactylic hexameter, elegiac couplet, and iambic trimeter) were the standard meters of public recitation. As with epic and later dramatic poets, the philosophers traveled from place to place performing their work before (they hoped) large audiences: Xenophanes describes his own ideas as having been "tossed throughout the land of Greece for sixty-seven years" (DK 8). As always in Greek culture, performance goes hand in hand with competition and vying for position. In a single remark Heraclitus disparages the wisdom of Hesiod, Pythagoras, Xenophanes, and Hecataeus (DK 40). That is, he targets a poet (Hesiod) and a mythographer (Hecataeus) as well as two of his fellow Presocratics. Pindar boasts that his *sophia* is superior to that of other poets (cf. *Olympian* 1.115b–17); similarly, the philosophers are rivals in the arena of intellectual excellence.

Fifth-century Athens saw not only the growth of tragedy into a massively popular genre with panhellenic appeal, but also the development of a complex and cosmopolitan intellectual culture, which is summed up by the Thucydidean Pericles' boast: "We love beauty without being extravagant and we have intellectual interests without being soft" (2.40.1). The opening scene of Plato's *Protagoras* vividly depicts the impact of their new ideas at Athens, as people flock to the house of Callias to hear the lectures of Protagoras, Hippias, and Prodicus. Comic dramatists were ready to mock Callias, who is said to have spent more on Sophists than anyone else in Athens (see MacDowell 1962, 11), but at the same time the Athenians were deeply proud of their city's reputation as the intellectual center of Greece. Both Sophocles and Euripides present choruses (one Athenian, one Corinthian) who praise Athens as a city of creativity and ideas (*Oedipus at Colonus* 691–93; *Medea* 824–45).

The blessings of intellectual inquiry are further extolled in a lost play of Euripides: "Blessed is he who has learned the art of inquiry, with no impulse to harm his fellow-citizens or engage in unjust actions, but who perceives from what origins and in what way the ageless order of immortal nature has been formed" (fr. 910). The passage may come from Euripides' *Antiope*, produced in the late 420s BCE.[2] The tragedy featured a debate between the twin brothers Amphion and Zethus over the best form of life to lead, the contemplative life of music, poetry, and philosophy, or the active life of politics and military service. The anapestic fragment would suit the choral ode following the brothers' dispute, but whatever its precise location, the passage attests to a keen awareness at Athens of the pleasures of intellectual investigation.

Any treatment of the relationship between tragedy and philosophy must confront the stereotypes (of Euripides in particular) presented by the ancient comic and biographical traditions. The picture of Euripides as the "philosopher of the stage" (Athenaeus 561a) is useful only insofar as it points to the tendency of his characters (more than those of Aeschylus and Sophocles) to express ideas of philosophical interest, often in a markedly argumentative manner. The comic poets respond to this aspect of Euripidean theater by alleging that Euripides wrote his plays in collaboration with Socrates (cf. Aristophanes fr. 392 *PCG*), while the biographers not only treat the plots of comedy as historical evidence, but also make Euripides the pupil of nearly every major philosopher of the fifth century (Kovacs 1994–2004, 1: 9–12). Most famously, Aristophanes' picture of Euripides the (Socratic) rationalist (*Frogs* 1491–99) inspired the vitriol of Nietzsche: "Even Euripides was in a certain sense only a mask: the deity which talked through him was neither Dionysus nor Apollo but a newly born daemon called *Socrates*" (*Birth of Tragedy* sec. 12; see Henrichs 1986).[3] In fact, all three tragedians, not just Euripides, had philosophical interests. As we will see, Aeschylus was an innovative and intellectually curious poet, who was ready to incorporate contemporary debates into his work. The depiction of Aeschylus in *Frogs* as an anti-intellectual conservative is no more reliable than the comedy's Socratic-sophistic Euripides.

Before we consider the plays and their ideas in detail, it may be helpful to say a few words on the issue of methodology. Various factors make it difficult to decide what constitutes a significant overlap with philosophical thought. The fragmentary nature of the Presocratics' and the Sophists' surviving work, and the oracular style of such figures as Heraclitus, make it far from easy to work out their meaning. And even if we do detect similarities of thought and argument, we must beware of wrenching the speaker's words from their dramatic context and so distorting them. In addition, we must not seek to construct a "philosophy" from a series of excerpts, nor attribute sentiments expressed by an individual character in a specific dramatic context to the dramatist himself. The importance of context becomes even clearer when we consider that intellectual statements are found in the mouths of both sympathetic and unsympathetic characters in tragedy (comedy is more decidedly anti-intellectual), so that "such details were apparently to be received by the audience in different ways in different contexts and not reflexively branded as suspect or immoral" (Mastronarde 2002a, 44 n. 73). In the following discussion I treat the interests of dramatists and philosophers in discrete thematic sections. Although the early Greek philosophers themselves had little or no conception of working within separate disciplines (ethics, epistemology, theology, etc.), such a format is useful as an expositional device and serves to remind us of the enormous range of these thinkers' intellectual interests.

Nature and the Cosmos

The speculations of the earliest Greek philosophers on the origins and structure of the universe took as their starting point the view of the world found in the poetry of Homer and Hesiod: "The so-called Presocratics were still embedded in the older traditions and were using them, at least as a kind of 'scaffolding'; their constructs were helped, though sometimes also somewhat twisted, by this pre-existing scaffolding" (Burkert 1999, 104). On this Homeric and Hesiodic model, which was itself deeply indebted to Near Eastern views of the world (cf. West 1997, 137–50), the cosmos was conceived as a flat, circular earth surrounded by Ocean, and covered by a dome-like sky containing sun, moon, and stars. Whereas the poets saw the origins of the universe in terms of anthropomorphic deities giving birth to other gods, the Presocratics sought to explain the universe in abstract, impersonal, and rational terms, as when Anaximander derives everything from the "infinite" (*apeiron*). The crucial difference between the mythological cosmogony of Hesiod and the philosophical cosmogonies of the Presocratics is well brought out by a later anecdote that purports to explain why Epicurus became a philosopher: having asked his schoolteacher where Hesiod's Chasm came from if it came first, the teacher replied that such questions were the domain of the philosophers, whereat Epicurus left school to study with them (Sextus Empiricus, *Against the Mathematicians* 10.18–19).

By seeking to explain the universe in a systematic and rational manner, the Presocratics revolutionized Greek views of the origin and nature of the world (Vernant 1982, 102–29). The tragedians responded to the new "natural philosophy" in various ways, yet the fact that the world of the plays remained the divinely governed universe of heroic myth imposed limits on their innovations. In Euripides' lost *Wise Melanippe*, the title character gives an account of the origins of the world that is still based in the anthropomorphic creationism of Hesiod: "This story is not mine, but from my mother. Heaven and Earth were once a single form; but when they were separated from one another, they bore all things and brought them into the light: trees, winged creatures, beasts nourished by the sea, and the human race" (fr. 484). Euripides' plays (of which only a fifth have survived complete) are likely to have contained more passages of this kind: the second hypothesis to *Rhesus* claims that "the [play's] preoccupation with celestial phenomena points to Euripides."

Reflection on such matters, however, was not confined to Euripides. The third play of Aeschylus' *Suppliants* trilogy, the *Danaids*, presents the "marriage" of Heaven and Earth as the cause of nature's growth (Aeschylus fr. 44). As in *Wise Melanippe*, the explanation is simultaneously anthropomorphic and cosmic. Aeschylus also adapts the Presocratic idea of a unified and ordered cosmos in his vision of a Zeus-centered universe: "Zeus is air, Zeus is earth, Zeus is heaven, Zeus is all things and whatever is beyond them" (fr. 70; cf. *Suppliants* 91–103, *Agamemnon* 160–66). Speculation on the causes of natural phenomena is found in all three tragedians, as, for example, on the source of the Nile (Aeschylus fr. 300, *Suppliants* 559–61; Sophocles fr. 882; Euripides, *Helen* 1–3) or the origin of snow (Aeschylus, *Suppliants* 792–93). There is even influence from contemporary medicine: Apollo's theory of the male's key role in human reproduction (Aeschylus, *Eumenides* 657–61; cf. Euripides, *Orestes* 552–53) draws on the ideas of *phusiologoi* like Anaxagoras (cf. Aristotle, *On the Generation of Animals* 763b31–3). These proto-scientific elements co-exist with the traditional view of a sentient natural world, to whom one can appeal in times of grief or despair (Sophocles, *Ajax* 412–27, *Philoctetes* 936–40; Aeschylus, *Prometheus Bound* 88–91). Sophocles in particular uses the world of nature metaphorically, stressing that all things are changed or destroyed by time (*Ajax* 670–75, *Oedipus at Colonus* 607–28).

Theology

There was a vigorous debate throughout antiquity on the nature and role of the gods (the absence of holy scripture and a priestly caste to regulate religious belief no doubt facilitated such debate). Despite their many differences of purpose and genre, no philosopher or tragedian could avoid *theologia* ("[giving] an account of the gods"). As one scholar has observed of the Presocratics, "Few words occur more frequently in their fragments than the term *god*" (Vlastos 1995, 3). Not surprisingly, given their attempts to describe the universe as an ordered and regular system, the Presocratics tended to depersonalize the gods and ascribe their traditional powers to nature, which they took to be both perceptible and rational. Such a view conflicted strongly with tragedy, where the gods of myth are presented as behaving in ways that defy human reason and comprehension.

The very origin of belief in the gods became an issue of debate for both the philosophers and the dramatists. In a fragment of a satyr-play by the Athenian Critias, an older cousin of Plato, a character claims that the gods are fictions, and that a clever man invented fear of the gods in order to curb human lawlessness (fr. 19). This fragment, which many scholars attribute to Euripides rather than Critias (see Pechstein 1999, 553–56), overlaps with Democritus' idea that the gods are a product of primitive man's fear of physical phenomena such as thunder, earthquakes, and eclipses (DK A75). The chorus of Euripides' *Electra* points to the role of fear in maintaining religious belief when they assert that "fearful stories benefit mortals by encouraging them to worship the gods" (743–44), while Polymestor in *Hecuba* claims that the gods throw mortals into confusion so that they will worship them "in ignorance" (956–60). A more positive, but equally skeptical, theory of the origins of established religion was propounded by Prodicus, who saw "a progressive evolution of deification" (Henrichs 1975, 112), which transformed "crops and everything else which is useful for life" into recipients of worship and cult (*Papyrus Herculanensis* 1428 fr. 19.12–19; cf. DK 5). Tiresias alludes to this conception of divinity in *Bacchae*, when he promotes the benefits of Demeter and Dionysus, givers of grain and wine (274–85).

The philosophers objected in various ways to the anthropomorphic gods of myth. The tragedians were aware of these ideas and incorporated them into their work. Xenophanes criticized Homer and Hesiod for presenting the gods as thieves, adulterers, and deceivers (DK 11; cf. Aeschylus fr. 350), and his ethical objections had a great influence on subsequent Greek thought. Euripides' Heracles asserts that he does not believe in gods who commit adultery or who bind or rule over each other: "a god, if he is truly a god, lacks nothing. These are the miserable tales of poets" (*Heracles* 1341–46). The hero's statement is clearly not true within the world of the play (Hera, after all, has destroyed Heracles' life because of Zeus' adultery; compare Hecuba's denial that the Judgment of Paris ever took place, *Trojan Women* 971–82), yet it has a dramatically explosive effect, as the audience is provoked to ask not only how far divine and human approaches to justice coincide, but also whether such deities deserve human worship at all. The philosophers' purer conception of divinity (cf. Xenophanes, DK 23–24, 26, A32; Heraclitus, DK 5, 32, 78; Empedocles, DK 134) not only stripped away the anthropomorphic failings of the gods, but also insisted that they be perfect moral exemplars for mankind (cf. Pendrick 2002, 257–59). As Ion says to Apollo, "Since you have power, pursue goodness!" (Euripides, *Ion* 439–40), while a character in one of Euripides' lost plays puts it most concisely: "if the gods do anything wicked, they are not gods" (*Bellerophon* fr. 292.7; cf. *Iphigenia among the Taurians* 380–91, *Heracles* 1307–8).

Both philosophers and tragedians reflect on the unknowability of the divine (cf. Euripides, *Trojan Women* 884–88, *Helen* 711–15). For Heraclitus a god cannot be straightforwardly known: "The lord whose oracle is at Delphi neither speaks nor conceals but gives a sign" (DK 93). Human inability to decipher oracles and prophecies generates much dramatic irony, especially in Sophocles (*Oedipus the King* 946–53). According to Xenophanes, no mortal knows the truth about the gods, but has only opinion (DK 34). Protagoras took such doubt to its logical conclusion and declared himself an agnostic about the very existence of the gods: "There are many obstacles to such knowledge, including the obscurity of the subject and the shortness of human life" (DK 4). The chorus of Euripides' *Helen* reacts to the undeserved suffering of the heroine, who is Zeus' daughter, by declaring, "I do not know what certain, what true word about the gods I can find among mortals" (1148–50). Yet although the chorus fastens on the baffling inscrutability of the gods, the audience is aware of the wider divine frame, the battle between Hera and Aphrodite to preserve their own reputations. Like other figures in tragedy, Helen is the (innocent) victim of a struggle between competing divinities. This notion of clashing divine personalities, basic to archaic and classical Greek thought, ensured that no simple and reassuring scheme of divine justice was possible. Humans might link the gods to the enforcement of universal standards of right and wrong (cf. Euripides, *Hecuba* 799–805), but Greek religious thought recognized that divine "justice" tolerated the suffering of the innocent and good (see, for example, Solon 13.31–32 West; Aeschylus, *Seven against Thebes* 602–8).

Knowledge and Reality

Already in Homer and other archaic poetry we find an emphasis on the gulf between gods and humans in the scope and quantity of their knowledge (for example, *Odyssey* 18.130–37; Semonides fr. 1.1–5 West). With the Presocratics comes the insight that true (or divine) knowledge differs in quality as well as quantity from human "knowledge," which is mere opinion. Compared to a god, says Heraclitus, a human being is an "ape in wisdom" (DK 83). Parmenides drew a crucial distinction between sense perception and reason: the senses are deluded by mere appearance, while reason grasps reality (DK 1.28–32, 6.4–9; for Greek conceptions of reason and rationality, see Frede 1996). To speak of "appearance versus reality" seems to us so familiar, indeed clichéd, as to make it difficult to appreciate the conceptual advance that underlies it. For Parmenides' audience the distinction between appearance and reality was a startling and revolutionary thought. Moreover, his argument that the phenomenal world is an illusion set Greek philosophy on a new and enduring course. Subsequent philosophers either sought to "save the appearances" (cf. Anaxagoras, DK 21a; Democritus, DK 125) or insisted upon the power of reason to reach beyond them to something more real.

The weakness of the senses is most powerfully expressed in tragedy by the blind Tiresias, who berates Oedipus' inability to see the reality of his situation (Sophocles, *Oedipus the King* 412–15). Oedipus, the most intellectually curious of all heroes (cf. *Oedipus the King* 120–21), does not even know who he is. Moreover, human senses are open to divine delusion (Sophocles, *Ajax* 84–86). Tragedy therefore abounds in deceptive appearances, from unawareness of one's real condition (as when the victorious Greeks of Euripides' *Trojan Women* do not know of their imminent destruction: 65–97) to the ignorance of identity dramatized in recognition scenes (such as Euripides' *Iphigenia among the Taurians* 467–901, *Ion* 1395–1548). The theme of epistemological fallibility is central to *Helen*, where the heroine's *eidôlon* (phantom) raises the issue of how one can tell the real from the unreal. Both Teucer and Menelaus meet the real Helen but are unable to grasp who she is (118, 160–61, 593). Like Gorgias' *On What Is Not* (DK 3), *Helen* combines playfulness with philosophical reflection on serious issues of language, knowledge, and reality.

Politics, Law, and Society

A central concern of early Greek philosophy was the study of human nature and society. The Sophists' inquiries into law, politics, and power find many parallels in the tragedians, especially Euripides. The Sophists also had a great impact outside literature on the political life of Athens, where their role as public intellectuals and educators brought them both success and notoriety: Aristophanes' *Clouds*, for example, parodies their new educational techniques, particularly in the domain of rhetorical training. (On the universally negative portrayal of the Sophists in Old Comedy, see Carey 2000.) Yet the interests of the Sophists ranged wider than day-to-day politics. As with the origins of religion, the Sophists speculated on the origins of human society, and the laws that (ought to) govern it (for these early "social contract theories," see Kahn 1981, 92–93). The development of human civilization from primitive beginnings was treated as a form of cultural progress, in contrast to the Hesiodic myth of human decline from a distant Golden Age (cf. Plato, *Protagoras* 320c8–322d5). A number of passages in tragedy share the Sophists' focus on the development of various skills (*technai*) and their capacity to improve human life (Aeschylus, *Prometheus Bound* 442–68, 478–506; Sophocles, *Antigone* 332–67; Euripides, *Suppliants* 201–18; cf. [Hippocrates], *On Ancient Medicine* 2–3; Cole 1990, 1–24). However, the dramatic context discourages any naive optimism about the human condition: suffering and death dominate the action of these plays (cf. Segal 2003, 30–31).

Athenians were aware not only of the distinctiveness of their mass participatory government (cf. Aeschylus, *Persians* 241–42; Euripides, *Suppliants* 403–8) but also of its openness to manipulation by clever speakers (Sophocles, *Philoctetes* 98–99). Just as it is wrong to regard the Sophists solely as rhetoricians, so it is misleading to see rhetoric itself as a fifth-century invention with no regard for truth (on Plato's key role in the development of such antisophistic ideas, see Cole 1991). Nevertheless, the peculiarly important role of rhetoric in Athenian politics and law ensured that it became an issue in tragedy, for in this arena (as elsewhere) the plays' heroic settings and characters address the concerns of contemporary Athenian society. Confronted by the Egyptian herald, the Argive king Pelasgus stresses his freedom of speech, which was a proud Athenian boast (Aeschylus, *Suppliants* 946–49).[4] Elsewhere characters deplore the power of rhetoric, which can be learned for a fee and deployed for unscrupulous ends (Euripides, *Hecuba* 255–57, 814–20, 1187–94). However, democratic rhetoric is also seen to have a positive impact, leading to social advancement for lower-class citizens who can master it (Euripides, *Suppliants* 423–25).

The Sophists were itinerant teachers, whose travels fostered the comparison of different communities and their respective *nomoi* (social, political, and ethical norms). As Herodotus noted, each community naturally thinks that its own *nomoi* are best (3.38). The debate over *nomos* (in its twin senses of "convention" and "law") and *phusis* ("nature") exercised all the major thinkers of the fifth century, including the tragedians. Champions of nature over convention ranged from those who equated "the good" or true/natural "justice" with pure self-interest (so Callicles and Thrasymachus: Plato, *Gorgias* 482d7–484b1, *Republic*, book 1) to those like Antiphon and Hippias who, although aware of the artificiality of the laws (Antiphon, DK 44a), also invoked the concept of universal human nature (cf. Sophocles fr. 591) to challenge popular stereotypes of "Greek" versus "barbarian" (Antiphon, DK 44b; Plato, *Protagoras* 337d–338b; cf. Euripides, *Andromache* 243–44, *Trojan Women* 764–65). In *Phoenician Women*, the debate over justice between Eteocles and Polynices is framed in terms of nature and power: Eteocles embraces absolute self-interest, "Tyranny, greatest of the gods" (506; compare also Thucydides 5.105.2 for the idea that both gods and men rule wherever they have the power to do so). In a reversal of the common link between "nature" and the "survival of the fittest" (cf. Hesiod, *Works and Days* 202–12), Eteocles' mother Jocasta appeals to the equality that is found in nature (541–48), but her plea fails and the brothers fight to the death.

By contrast, *nomos* was typically viewed by its defenders as "the foundation of all social life and the guarantee of justice" (Lanza 1963, 439). Although justice had long been seen as a peculiarly human institution (cf. Hesiod, *Works and Days* 274–80), Protagoras and Democritus explored in detail the importance of *nomoi* for the growth of human communities and the development of civil society. On this more positive view *nomoi* are essential for human societies to flourish – contrast the monstrous Cyclops, for whom laws are a nuisance (Euripides, *Cyclops* 338–40). Democratic Athens also boasted of its *isonomia* ("equality before the law": cf. Herodotus 3.80.6, Thucydides 2.37.1–3; for the right to an impartial trial, see Aeschylus, *Eumenides* 482–89; Euripides, *Hippolytus* 1055–56), and in Euripides' *Suppliants* the Athenian king Theseus insists on the role of *written* law in ensuring "equal justice" for all, rich and poor alike (433–37; cf. Thucydides 2.37). At the same time, however, there was an awareness of the fragility of law and the moral values it embodied: Thucydides depicts what could happen to a community when human nature is no longer restrained by *nomoi*, whether through the effects of plague (2.52–53) or civil war (3.82–83), and Euripides explores similar themes of demoralization in *The Children of Heracles* (961–1025; cf. Allan 1999–2000, 151–53).

Ethics

In recent years moral philosophers have turned with increasing frequency to Greek ethics as an alternative to Christian-based and Kantian moral theories. Indeed, one contemporary philosopher has even claimed that "the basic ethical ideas possessed by the Greeks were different from ours, and also in better condition" (Williams 1993, 4). Whether in the form of "virtue ethics" or in the analysis of shame (as opposed to guilt) as a sophisticated ethical concept, Greek ethics is seen to offer a liberation from traditional Christian-Kantian concerns, such as free will and duty, while at the same time encouraging the study of all moral codes within their particular historical and cultural contexts. Moreover, as is increasingly realized, Greek ethics is to be studied not only in the writings of the philosophers, but also in epic, tragedy, and historiography (compare the use of Herodotus and Thucydides by Williams 2002, 151–71), for these genres present related ethical debates in narrative and dramatic form: Is revenge justified? How can the emotions be controlled? How is one to live well? The exploration of these and other ethical issues in tragedy is particularly stimulating, since the variety of characters, attitudes, principles, and emotions presented in each play generates a moral universe which provokes, and challenges, the sympathies and moral judgments of the audience.

Despite its playful tone of daring myth-revision, Gorgias' *Encomium of Helen* has a serious premise, namely the fundamental moral and judicial idea that one cannot be blamed for something that one was forced to do. Questions of culpability were of particular interest to the Athenians, given the litigiousness of their society, and are canvassed by all three tragedians. In Sophocles' *Oedipus at Colonus*, Oedipus argues that he is both legally and morally innocent since his crimes (killing his father and sleeping with his mother) were unintentional (266–74, 521–23, 546–48, 976–77, 985–90): it was, he claims, the gods who led him to such suffering (964, 998). Of course, that his actions were "fated" in these terms does not stop them being *his* actions, and Oedipus must live with the consequences (pollution and exile). Similarly, Artemis tells Theseus "your ignorance frees your mistake of wickedness" (Euripides, *Hippolytus* 1334–35), but it still requires Hippolytus' personal pardon to cleanse Theseus of the pollution of his murder (1448–52). In Aeschylus the issue of responsibility frequently focuses on the tension between freedom and necessity, and specifically on the idea of parallel causation among gods and humans (cf. Patinella 1986, 69–95). Clytemnestra's claim that she merely embodies an *alastôr* ("spirit of revenge") stemming from the crime of Atreus does not, the chorus insists, absolve her of responsibility for the murder of Agamemnon (*Agamemnon* 1497–1508). Eteocles goes voluntarily to his death, even though the curse of Oedipus drives him on (*Seven against Thebes* 686–719). So too in Sophocles, curses do not negate autonomy (cf. *Oedipus at Colonus* 964–65, *Antigone* 582–603, *Electra* 504–15).

Another Greek idea that has enriched contemporary ethical theory is the concept of "moral luck," the insight that a good or happy life depends on a number of factors often outside our control (cf. Hurley 2003). Yet perhaps the most enduring insights of Greek ethics concern the issues of moral knowledge and lack of moral resolve (*akrasia*). Socrates famously claimed that no one knowingly does wrong, since if one knew the right thing to do, that knowledge would ensure that one did it, making weakness of the will (*akrasia*) impossible (cf. Plato, *Protagoras* 352b–358a). Both Medea and Phaedra contradict this position (Euripides, *Medea* 1078–80, *Hippolytus* 380–87), yet one need not see Euripides engaging in specifically anti-Socratic polemic, since a moral situation of knowing what is right but not doing it was relevant to all Athenians (Allan 2002, 90–92). Equally provocative was tragedy's exploration of the ethics of revenge (for example, Sophocles, *Ajax* 1318–73) and the idea that an individual's *aretê* (excellence) could be divorced from his or her social position (Euripides, *Electra* 380–85, *Andromache* 636–38; Sophocles fr. 667). Finally, the plays also reflect Protagorean moral relativism ("man is the measure of all things," DK 1: cf. Euripides, *Phoenician Women* 499–502) and the developing concept of an internal moral conscience (Sophocles, *Philoctetes* 902–3; Euripides, *Helen* 1002–3, *Orestes* 396; Democritus, DK 84, 174, 215, 244, 264).

In its dramatization of divine and heroic myths of conflict and suffering, tragedy addresses issues of knowledge, politics, religion, and ethics in ways that overlap with early Greek philosophy. Like the interlocutors of a philosophical dialogue, the characters of tragedy present various points of view on these complex issues (cf. Blondell 2002a, 1–52), yet each play, taken as a whole, does not lead the audience to a single definitive answer: rather than expound dogma, tragedy provokes further questions. Although no tragedian sought to elaborate a philosophical system, their works appropriated and explored various philosophical problems. This tendency is clearest in the plays of Euripides, since his characters are generally more analytical and outspoken, yet even here, as with Aeschylus and Sophocles, philosophical ideas are integrated into the drama, and do not stand out as extraneous intellectual display.

Much recent scholarship has insisted on the importance of tragedy's civic and political setting. It is equally crucial not to neglect its wider intellectual context (cf. Williams 1979, 16), nor reduce its interrogatory range to issues of collective ideology. Questions such as "Can I know anything?" and "How should one live?" are no less important to tragedy's intellectual depth, and underlie its continuing capacity to interest audiences throughout the world. Though it would be misleading to claim that tragedy "establishes theoretical thinking" (so Liuzzi 1992, 16), tragedy did develop the insights of early Greek philosophy over a wide range of intellectual issues. And just as a play may show a character undergoing a process of (painful) learning (Admetus in Euripides' *Alcestis*, for example), so the genre itself, through the presentation of conflicting arguments and values, may point the audience toward a more reflective appreciation of what it is to be human; of what it is to be, as Oedipus expresses it, "a child of Chance" (Sophocles, *Oedipus the King* 1080). The tragedians not only maintained the poet's traditional role as a figure of wisdom, but also contributed significantly to the development of Greek thought.

NOTES

1   "In classical Athens, the word 'philosophy' signified 'intellectual cultivation' in the broad sense. In other words, a wide array of intellectuals – *including* many poets – were described as practicing 'philosophy' " (Nightingale 1995, 60).

2 For a reconstruction of the play, see Webster 1967, 205–10; Kambitsis 1972, ix–xxxiv; for the date, see Cropp and Fick 1985, 74–76.
3 Such a view has led to numerous studies of Euripides' "intellectualism" (e.g., Nestle 1901, Reinhardt 1960, Assael 1993 and 2001).
4 Ironically, most Sophists were not Athenians, and so although they taught rhetoric, they did not themselves enjoy *parrhêsia* ("freedom of speech") or any other political rights in Athens: cf. Euripides, *Ion* 670–75.

FURTHER READING

The Presocratics and Sophists are discussed by Hussey 1972, Barnes 1982, and de Romilly 1992. For a collection of articles on all the major figures, with exhaustive bibliography, see Long 1999. The thought-world of Greek tragedy, especially its continuity with the literature of the archaic period, is best approached in the studies by Winnington-Ingram 1980 and Cairns 1993. An excellent starting point for the study of the philosophical (especially ethical) dimension of tragedy can be found in Blundell 1989, which has valuable remarks on all three tragedians. Nussbaum 1986 and Williams 1993 offer compelling arguments for tragedy's philosophical importance and set its insights within the context of modern philosophy. A more historical treatment of this topic (focusing in particular on tragedy's reception in German literature and philosophy) may be found in Schmidt 2001 and Szondi 2002, 7–48. Rösler 1970 and Poli-Palladini 2001b discuss the influence of philosophy on individual passages of Aeschylus. For Sophocles, see Winnington-Ingram 1980 and Blundell 1989, and for Euripides, see Conacher 1998 and Assael 2001, all with further bibliography.

CHAPTER SIX

Tragedy, Rhetoric, and Performance Culture

Christopher Pelling

Athens and Performance Culture

Athens performed. It was a city rich in festivals: to participate in those was to be a citizen. And, of course, the theatrical festivals of Dionysus were among the high spots of the citizen-year. Fifth-century Athens was also a city very aware of its own identity, and part of that self-imaging dwelt on the culture, the connoisseurship, the sophistication – or, more simply, the *sophia*, the skill and experience to recognize value and make distinctions where others would fall short. *Logos* was here a key concept: *logos* in the sense, as we would translate it, of "reason," the capacity to think things through; and particularly *logos* in our sense of "speech." This was a rhetorical culture, one in which listening to speeches – performances – in the assembly or the law-court was another central part of citizenly behavior. Listening required evaluation too, evaluation both of skill (that *sophia* again) and, much more important, of the substance of the case: is this speaker's proposal really the right thing to do, did things really happen the way he says, is he really as innocent as he claims? This is a city of words, of mouths, of ears – and of minds. And all this is to be a citizen: all these are roles which citizens perform.

Or so we are often told.[1] Perhaps, in fact, Athens was not so much more of a "performance culture" than many other cities. Spartan citizens had to perform too, though in very different ways; and was Athens really any more performance- or self-image-conscious than, say, Rome, with its spectacles, its elaborate religious ceremonial, its celebrity culture? (Probably not.) Than Nazi Germany? (Doubtful.) Or even than the political culture of Britain or America today, with television as the new medium and testing-ground of choice? (Probably, yes, but not by much.) What, anyway, is "performance," and where does it stop? Most of our behavior is ritualized in some way; most of it plays up to, or plays off, roles that are expected or constructed. It is all too easy for these categories to broaden in such a way that they are drained of interpretative value.

But that is indeed too easy a step, and we cannot ignore the insights that a stress on performance has brought – in Homeric studies, for instance, where the concentration on oral composition has been supplemented by more sophisticated reflection on the conditions of performance and on the audience expectations of oral discourse; in choral lyric, where performance and particularly reperformance enact the recognition of an achievement and secure its eternal fame; or in Athenian rhetoric in all its forms, where the elite politician and the citizen audience both have roles to play and expectations to fulfill. Analogous questions have purchase in tragedy too, whether one concentrates on the political – how far is it citizenly behavior to celebrate the city in the theatrical festival? How far is that celebration qualified by, and how far does it embrace, and even prescribe, a problematization of a citizen's duties? Or the social – how far is the construction of the free citizen male defined by reflection on the slave, the foreigner, the female? Or the religious – how far, and simply *how*, does the Dionysiac perspective of the festival interact with the themes of the plays themselves? How does the ritual go with the myth?[2] Not that those aspects are separate: the religious is the political, the political is the social. Nor, either, that we need apply a one-size-fits-all categorization to all tragedies. The festival context may affect the way we read Euripides' *Bacchae* in a way that it does not affect Sophocles' *Electra* or Aeschylus' *Persians*, just as it may affect Aristophanes' *Frogs* differently from his *Knights* or *Clouds*. But those are all good questions.

Here, however, the theme is tragedy, *rhetoric*, and performance, and that "and" is to be taken strongly, for I will concentrate on the way in which these three areas, rhetoric included, interact. In particular, Athenian pride in their rhetorical connoisseurship – this "city of words" (cf. Demosthenes 19.184; Goldhill 1986a, 57–78) – co-existed with a considerable readiness to feel distrust of rhetorical skill: a clever speaker was a suspected speaker (Dover 1974, 25–28; Ober 1989, 165–77; Hesk 1999 and 2000, 202–91). That links with "performance" in several ways. The audience's response to rhetoric on stage will draw on their extratextual experience of orators in real life, in those performances in the democratic polis where the roles of politician and citizen, speaker and evaluator, were so central: that is clear, for instance, in the description of the assembly in Euripides' *Orestes*, where a series of familiar oratorical types contributes to what becomes a travesty of a trial (852–956; Willink 1986, 223–25, 229–31; Pelling 2000, 165–67). In that case as in others, the form these suspicions may take is of sensing that speakers are affecting a role or an attitude: they are "putting on a performance" or "putting on an act." That last phrase may be even more apposite, for such a performance may have a hint of the metatheatrical, with someone acting a role – Clytemnestra acting as a faithful wife, or Orestes as a messenger bringing news of his own death, or the Creon of Sophocles' *Oedipus at Colonus* as a concerned relative; or manipulating others to play out the roles they have cast for them – Dionysus creating a part for Pentheus, or Odysseus staging and directing the plot of *Philoctetes* (Lada-Richards 1998). True, it is not clear that the audience would figure such cases as "theatrical" or "role-playing" quite as readily as we use those metaphors today,[3] but the analogies with the way the theater itself functions are still worth exploring.

"Rhetoric" too poses problems of definition, and there are again dangers of broadening the term so widely that it ceases to be illuminating. There is an important sense in which everything said is rhetorical: everything is cast to persuade, everyone tries to find the style most appropriate to its function. In that sense, Caesar's narrative is as rhetorical as Velleius', and Ajax's speech in *Iliad* 9 is as rhetorical as Aelius Aristides. But that is not the sense in which rhetoric aroused distrust, any more than the passionate outpourings of Achilles in the same book of the *Iliad* or of Philoctetes in Sophocles' play would excite any suspicion of disingenuousness. It is rhetoric in a narrower sense that is here in point: the rhetoric that shows signs of contrivance, artificiality, acquired technique, especially when articulated in formal and public speeches. There are adequate indications that such characteristics formed a recognizable cluster in fifth-century Athens: Cleon's dazzlingly rhetorical attack on dazzling rhetoric in Thucydides' Mytilenean debate is enough to show that (3.37 with Gomme 1945–56 ad loc; Yunis 1996, 90–92; Hesk 2000, 248–56); so is Aristophanes' *Clouds*, especially its confrontational debate between Right and Wrong (889–1112). And it is hardly coincidence that in each case a clever speaker, with a full range of rhetorical techniques in his repertoire, is negatively characterized.

It need not follow that every "rhetorical" speaker is felt as rhetorical in quite the same way, or has the same real-life resonance: those speakers in the debate of *Orestes* may not be seen as the same sort of rhetorical performers as the nurse in *Hippolytus*, and any real-life counterparts or models of those performers would be different too; and we will see cases below, especially *Ajax* and *Agamemnon*, where the rhetoric of a speech has less of the slickness of contemporary fashion, but is no less disquieting for it. Doubtless there are illuminating generalizations that can be made – that rhetoric tends to be uneasy because it strikes a public and political tone in contexts where the personal would be more appropriate (Halliwell 1997); that Euripides is less inhibited than Aeschylus or Sophocles in adopting contemporary mannerisms and formulations (Bers 1994, 181–82), and makes his characters more explicitly self-conscious about speechmaking (Lloyd 1992, 21); that confidence in the healing power of *peithô* (persuasion) on the whole diminishes as the fifth century goes on (Buxton 1982, 187); that Euripides becomes more flexible, fluent, and deft in his handling of rhetorical form in his later plays (Collard 1975b); that the engagement with rhetoric must be seen as part of a wider concern with the problematics of language and communication (Goldhill 1984, 1986a, 1997b). Those generalizations themselves point to the *variety* of effects which a sense of rhetoric can give: that, and the variety of "suspicions" too, will also be this chapter's theme.

For speech points in three directions at once, to the speaker, to the person addressed, to the features in the world it describes: and each of these directions can be felt as skewed. Sometimes the distortion is speaker-based in that people conceal what they know, feel, or want; sometimes it is hearer-based in that it misleads by its seductiveness – or possibly that it persuades *too little* rather than too much, that audiences have made up their minds already; sometimes it looks more to the features in the world which are mis-described or travestied. Some of our most interesting cases are where these different sorts of suspicion do not come together, where a speech makes claims that are unlikely to persuade but are nevertheless not clearly inaccurate, or where it says things which are clearly false but which the listener wants to hear, or things which are true but in ways that hearers, or even speaker, will misconstrue. Only a series of sample analyses can bring out the range of techniques which the tragic poets employ, as well as giving us a clearer idea of what markers point to different types of suspect speech.

Performance in *Electra*

Euripides' *Electra* brings out how closely "rhetoric" can intertwine with other aspects of performance. The play is full of roles to play, functions to perform, burdens to carry, persons to try to be. And nothing sits easily on anyone. One of those mismatches affects rhetoric, the way that speech itself misses its mark.

Other forms of performance come first, particularly those of ritual activity. Early in the play the chorus invites Electra to a festival of Hera – a significant deity, not merely as one who cared for Argos but as a goddess of marriage and the transition from virgin to wife (Zeitlin 1970). That transition has here gone amiss. Electra is wed, but to the farmer who has respected his social superior (no easy part for him to play either, then), and she is still a virgin. That leaves her with no role in that festival, no way to "perform." As a princess, she should lead the dance; yet her royal position is compromised, by husband and dwelling and the whole humiliation of her self and her house. Women, whether virgin or married, might have a role to play in a festival; married women seem to have had a particularly prominent role in the cult of Hera, as one would expect; but she is neither the one thing nor the other. The chorus try to persuade her, but they have no real understanding of the person or her predicament. Their choice of argument – if you haven't a thing to wear, borrow some of ours (190–93) – is in one way trivializing: there is more than clothing at stake in Electra's mindset. But in another way it emblematizes the predicament rather precisely. To borrow someone else's clothes would be to affect a role which was not her own; and just as there are no right clothes for such a person to wear, there are no right words for the chorus to say.

Ritual returns later in the play, in the messenger's report of Aegisthus' death. Orestes came upon him when he was sacrificing to the Nymphs. The earlier parts of the play have predisposed us to expect an Aegisthus who is a monster – the murderer, the adulterer, the person who urged Clytemnestra to kill her young children (25–28). Yet his behavior at the sacrifice is exemplary: here the disturbing thing is that he performs his role so well, not so badly. He invites the stranger to participate. As a "Thessalian," the visitor will of course know how to butcher a victim, so would he like to take the knife (815–18; Kraus 1992)? And so he does – but the victim turns out to be Aegisthus himself, though not without some missed cues (Arnott 1973, 55–56): Orestes does not take to his role very naturally. The theme of the perverted sacrifice (Zeitlin 1965) had been central to the Orestes myth since Aeschylus – a constant presence in this play – but here it takes an unnerving new form. Is the audience to suspect that all their previous impressions of Aegisthus were awry? That would not be out of keeping with a drama that so often plays on conflicting perceptions, and the difficulties of being sure about anything (Goldhill 1986a, 245–59, and 1986b). Once again, there may be no right thing left for a principal, in this case Orestes, to do; one can understand the growing unease at the role in which he is cast, the plot which Apollo is staging.

"Missed cues . . . his role . . . he is cast . . . the plot . . . staging": it is natural for us to use such theatrical phrasing. In most cases we should be cautious about extending such ideas of metatheater to fifth-century tragedy; true, explicit metatheater is frequent enough in comedy – but then comedy is often very different from tragedy, indeed may even define itself against it (Taplin 1986). Usually we should talk only of analogies with theatrical phenomena, without assuming that the audience would naturally or necessarily figure matters in those terms. *Electra* however may be different, not least when Electra cries "where are the messengers?" at a time when not merely real life but also dramatic convention leaves the audience clear about the expected next step (759: Arnott 1973, 50–51; Marshall 1999–2000; contra, Taplin 1986, 169). The roles cast for Orestes and Electra come from myth, and from previous drama, especially that omnipresent Aeschylus (self-conscious hints of the theater again): there is a sort of mythical and intertextual determinism about their actions. Yet time and again the discomfort of the characters is felt. They cannot even manage their essential, hackneyed recognition without outside help: it is the old man who recognizes Orestes, not his sister (558–76). The horrors of matricide are less easy to process when transposed into this more humdrum setting of empty larders and grimy cottages, and it is no surprise that the principals find them hard to process too: when it comes to the killing of Clytemnestra, they are barely able to carry it through.

Those mismatches concern actions. A further set concern words, and this is where "rhetoric" ties in with those other modes of performance. "I come from killing Aegisthus not in words but in deeds," says Orestes (893–94), and he has the corpse to prove it: he encourages Electra to maltreat that corpse. She is reluctant, and Orestes presses her for the reason: "say, sister, if you wish" (905). She does "say" – yet not "say" what she wants to do or why she is reluctant, which is the way Orestes' question would most naturally be taken (Kovacs 1987, 265–67, though he suspects textual corruption). Instead she delivers a long tirade against the dead man – that "killing Aegisthus in words" to correspond to Orestes' "deeds" (Mossman 2001, 377). "What shall I put first, what last?" she begins, echoing a trope of real-life speeches (907–8: cf. Andocides 1.8, Hyperides 6.6–9, and already Homer, *Odyssey* 9.14): but in fact her speech ranges less widely than one would expect. There is surprisingly little on the murder of Agamemnon, and almost all centers on the marriage with Clytemnestra: how silly to think she would be faithful to you (yet nothing else suggests that Clytemnestra was anything less, now, than a devoted wife to Aegisthus); how dreadful for a husband to be called a wife's belonging rather than the other way round (yet that is Aeschylus' weak Aegisthus rather than the one we see elsewhere in this play); as for his dealings with women – that is not appropriate for a virgin to speak of (yet this virgin seems peculiarly preoccupied with sexual matters).

This is a travesty of a funeral lament, and in several ways. This does not praise, it vilifies. But as invective it should be meant to hurt: yet its target is beyond hurting now. As funeral oratory, it should help some sort of closure – and so it does, with a swift move on to the next phase, Clytemnestra's killing: but where lament often energizes toward vengeance (Foley 1993), here the shaking of the siblings' resolve is almost immediate. As narrative of a marriage, it tells more about Electra's imaginings than about the reality: it celebrates justice, but the charges look anything but just.

A few minutes later, and we have a more elaborate rhetorical exchange. The next victim, Clytemnestra, gorgeously arrives in a chariot entry that matches that of Agamemnon in Aeschylus – indeed, probably outdoes it, for there may well be two chariots rather than one (998–99 with Cropp 1988 ad loc; Hammond 1984, 375 n. 6). Within a few lines mother and daughter are engaged in an *agón*: it is as if Clytemnestra is on trial – and yet Clytemnestra's fate is already sealed, her murderer Orestes is already waiting within the cottage. This is rather like Thucydides' Plataean debate (3.52–68), where the rights and wrongs may be difficult to establish, but anyway cannot affect anything, for the Spartan decision has already been reached.

Both speakers show a certain skill, as is usual with Euripides' *agôn*-participants (Lloyd 1992, esp. 55–70). In different ways, both may discomfit any of the audience who begin by thinking the moral issue an easy one. Yet both fail to make the most of the rhetorical possibilities. Clytemnestra of course dwells on the killing of Iphigenia, giving a nasty turn to the notion of Agamemnon as war-lord by using language appropriate to an enemy: Agamemnon "carried her away" to Aulis, he "slashed her cheeks" (1022–23). She also makes much of Agamemnon's return with Cassandra – a fair point in suggesting that the wrong was not all on one side, but spoilt by suggesting that this was the motive for Clytemnestra's own adultery, something that had evidently started long before. She then asks, very reasonably, why *her* daughter should have had to die for Menelaus' sake: but instead of asking (as her counterpart in Sophocles' *Electra* asks, 539–42) "why not Menelaus' own daughter," she goes into a fantastic set of unreal conditions – if Menelaus had been abducted, would I have been right to kill Orestes, and how would Agamemnon have reacted to that (1041–45)? Such hypothetical syllogisms again reflect a feature of real-life oratory (Lloyd 1992, 32–33), and she does have a point; but the comical twist – an abducted male hero – and the over-complication means that it strikes cold (Michelini 1987, 220).

Yet this is no monster of a Clytemnestra. She is quick to allow Electra the chance to speak out in return: that is another way in which the *agôn* seems odd, for this is not the demonized Clytemnestra we have seen in Electra's presentation earlier in the play (esp. 60–63, 264–65, 657–58). That demonizing continues in Electra's own speech, full of bitter invective. Clytemnestra had been beautifying herself for lovers as soon as Agamemnon left, and rejoicing at any bad news that came from Troy (1069–79): it may all be true, but by now we have lost confidence in any Electra narrative. She too turns to a fantastic, unreal picture at the end (1091–93) – why is Aegisthus not the one in exile rather than Orestes, why is he not dead instead of . . . me – as if Electra's living death was really on a par with the slaying of Iphigenia. If your killing was just, then it would be just for me and Orestes to kill you too (1093–96) – words with close application to the present, yet this "senseless chain of vengeance" argument would more naturally be deployed *against* the matricide rather than in its favor. Nor is it clear what the audience would make of Clytemnestra's swiftness to relent once the speech is over. At the point where an *agôn* would normally become an exchange of one-line insults (Kubo 1967, 27), she instead admits that she is not so very proud of what she has done (1105–6). "Some children prefer their fathers, some their mothers," she says – an uncomfortable casualizing of what is at stake, given extra point by memories of a culminating moment of the *Oresteia* (Athena's proclaiming that she is "wholly the father's" at *Eumenides* 738). Aeschylus is trivialized; the normal rhythm of an *agôn* is lost; the demonized queen is quite human after all; every direction the plot has taken has faltered – and yet the killing will happen anyway. Everything and everyone is out of kilter. And shortly we will see some divine characters too, the Dioscuri, who seem equally uncomfortable with the divine actions they have to explain.

So in this play – and *Orestes* is here similar (Zeitlin 1980) – "performance" of all sorts of roles and tasks is anything but morally straightforward. The audience's awareness of myth and of Aeschylus underlines the mismatch between those expectations and how it all now seems on stage; and the mismatch of the rhetoric to the situation goes closely with all those other mismatches.

Performance in *Hippolytus*

When the nurse in Euripides' *Hippolytus* first discovered the nature of Phaedra's love she was horrified: "Aphrodite is no mere god, but something more than a god," who is destroying us all (359–61). In the speech that will concern us (433–81) she puts that horror aside: yet the memory of it survives, with the suggestion that this, rather than the casualizing approach she now adopts, may be the more appropriate response, and perhaps the more sincere one, to so shattering a predicament. For *peithô* (persuasion) often has an erotic tinge (Buxton 1982), and here the nurse is a sort of vicarious seducer (Goff 1990, 48). Yet it is so evident that such talk, urging Phaedra to give in to her desire, has an altogether skewed relation to the realities of the situation. It is just not going to work, for Hippolytus himself is certain not to play.

Several features mark her speech as artful, contrived, over-clever – the attributes which cluster together, as with Cleon's speech in Thucydides' Mytilenean debate, and can reasonably be called "rhetorical" (Gould 1978, 56). That is partly a matter of style: the self-conscious beginning which contrasts the speech she is about to make to what she has said or thought before, just as Clytemnestra does in Aeschylus' *Agamemnon* at 1372–73 (discussed below), or as Cleon begins that Thucydidean speech with reflection on what "he has often thought before" (3.37.1; Macleod 1983, 92), or as an orator may start by comparing the tone he must strike now with his words or behavior on previous occasions (Antiphon 6.7–10; Lysias 22.1–4; Demosthenes 5.5–12, 15.1–4, 41.1–2, 48.2–4; Isaeus 3.3–4; Thucydides 1.68.2, 1.140.1; Aristophanes *Clouds* 1401–5; Fraenkel 1961).

Then the argument moves on in two-step, with a series of carefully balanced antitheses. Time and again the nurse makes a generalization about life – human life, divine life – and matches it to the current situation: yet a listener in the theater will surely suspect that the parallel does not work, or works in ways which are less cozy than she suggests.

> You are in love – what's strange about that – many people do it; will you then die for the sake of love? There's no benefit for those who love people near them, and those who will do so in future, if they must die for it. (*Hippolytus* 439–42)

Two lines there for love and death, but with a further internal contrast stressing that Phaedra is not alone in loving, phrased as a bullying, "epiplectic" (Mastronarde 1979, 13) rhetorical question. Then two further lines in which she and those "many people" are consolidated into a single "those," and love and death are brought together again, and absurdly. But *are* those lovers' predicaments all so similar? "People near them" (*tôn pelas*) is comfortably vague: but in this case the man is far too "near" for comfort. Others fall in love, that is true; but this is not just any love, but a desire for her òwn stepson, something close to incest.

> How many husbands do you think, if they are sensible, turn a blind eye to the sickness in their marriages? How many fathers help their sons to find a way of coping with their love-affairs when the boys have gone astray? This is a mark of sense among mortals, to let dishonorable things remain hidden. (462–66)

Yes, there may be complaisant husbands in the world, but who is the relevant husband here? Theseus. And who is the indulgent father? Again, Theseus. The nurse goes on, with an emphatic mix of metaphors:

> For neither should mortals toil too much over crafting their lives, nor would you spend time on perfecting the roof of a house. Falling into fortune like yours, how do you think you could swim away? (467–69)

Again, the close antithetical structure, putting together two points as if they are evidently and comfortingly equivalent, is anything but comforting. Athenian listeners, like modern, would probably prefer their house-roof to be the object of *some* concern, for otherwise one gets very wet when it rains. And the house-imagery, so frequent in this play, marks exactly why this is so wrong. It is the house which is so threatened, to its foundations as well as to its roof.

Other features too mark the unease. The gods too behave badly: why should you be different? That is a style of argument we find elsewhere. It was there already in *Eumenides*, where the Erinyes "resort to mythologized mudslinging" (Lebeck 1971, 135) against Apollo (640–51); it is used by Helen in her exchange with Hecuba in *Trojan Women* (948–50); Theseus adopts it in his attempt to argue Heracles out of suicide in *Heracles* (1313–19), in a way that Heracles himself in famous lines finds morally unacceptable (1341–46). Aristophanes makes it one of the disreputable arguments in the mouth of "Wrong" in *Clouds*:

> If by chance you are taken in adultery, this is what you will reply to the husband, that you have done nothing wrong. Then transfer the responsibility to Zeus, saying that even he is a slave to love and women, and how can you, a mortal, be stronger than a god? (1079–82)

So – a pretty clear marker of suspicious rhetoric. But notice too how the nurse even outdoes the exaggeration of Aristophanes' parody. Not merely is resistance hopeless (*Clouds*), it is actually *hubris* even to try – "for this is nothing other than *hubris*, to want to be superior to the gods [*kreissô daimonôn einai thelein*]" (475–76). The bullying tone is clear, but also again the slipperiness of the argument, helped by the breadth of the word *kreissô*, "more powerful" as well as "better."

The slipperiness continues in the end of the speech (Mills 2002, 63). *Tolma d' erôsa*, says the nurse: "Bear up under your love," as Barrett translates it (1964, 246) – or is it rather "Be bold in your love," pointing to a "daring" which will be more a question of action, seizing the initiative rather than simply submitting? Then the nurse talks vaguely of ways it can be coped with: there are charms and spells, and some *pharmakon* for this disease will be found...(478–81). Charms, spells, cures (Goff 1990, 48–53; McClure 1999, 140–41) – but for what? For Phaedra, to treat and heal her love? Or for Hippolytus, to instill love rather than repress it?

So the "rhetorical" cast of this speech – its antithetical smoothness, its concatenation of different analogies and metaphors, its carefully modulated rhythm as it builds to its final appeal – goes with the "sophistic" nature of the case it makes (Knox 1952a 10–12; Gregory 1991, 68–70), casualizing what is not to be casualized, using arguments which are transparently inadequate. What does this contribute to the play? This is not a case that maps straightforwardly onto contemporary life: the corrupt speakers of *Orestes* might have reminded an audience of politicians they had heard, but they are unlikely to have much acquaintance with smooth-speaking and sophistically adept household servants. The psychology of the speaker matters (we need to know that the nurse is not reflecting her deepest or at least her initial feelings), but that cannot be as important as it might be with Electra's tortured imaginings: the nurse is not sufficiently important a figure for that, and her suffering, however real, is only tangential to the downfall of the house. There may well be some suggestion again of a travesty of role-playing: the nurse has to serve as confidante and aide, just as Orestes is cast as avenger or Clytemnestra as villain, but all those roles sit uncomfortably on the needs of the situation: this aspiring go-between has nowhere realistic to go. We will get a similar, and even more elaborate, travesty of roles later in the play, when Theseus and Hippolytus confront one another in what is effectively a trial scene, with many touches of forensic rhetoric (Barrett 1964, 348; Lloyd 1992, 34, 47–51; Hesk 2000, 276–77, 286–89). It is there chilling that father and son should have to indulge in public rhetoric at all: family members should be talking to one another as intimates, not as if at public meetings (Halliwell 1997), and here Theseus' refusal to communicate is particularly clear (Mastronarde 1979, 78). It is even more chilling that, even as a trial, it is a false trial: Theseus has given his verdict before the start, Hippolytus is doomed because of Aphrodite, because of his oath, because of his lack of contact with his father. The unspeaking, solid testimony of the tablet is eventually more persuasive than anything artful speech can achieve (Zeitlin 1985) – and no less misleading. This is a play about failed communication, and rhetoric that misfires is central to it.

But rhetoric may misfire in one way but not in another. In this case the direction of the speaker is skewed, for the nurse does not believe her own arguments; the direction to the situation is skewed, because it travesties the issue; but the direction to the hearer is all too well judged. Phaedra says:

> This is what destroys fine cities of mortals, and their houses too – over-fine words: for one should not say what's pleasant to hear, but what will make one respected. (486–89)

"Over-fine words"? Our audience connoisseurs would not have found the nurse's case so impressive. "Pleasant to hear"? Not, presumably, just because of the beautiful turns of the language, more because Phaedra at some level *wants* to believe the nurse. There will soon be more talk of *pharmaka*, still ambiguous, but with an ever-clearer hint that the charms will be love-philters, things to "weld together one joy from two people." Phaedra suspects as much, suspects even that the nurse may be planning to approach Hippolytus himself (520: "the child of Theseus," she calls him there, stressing that near-incestuous element that the nurse is eliding). But she does not stop her. Perhaps she is simply overborne, sick, confused, and exhausted as she is, by the stronger character's bullying (Michelini 1987, 303–4); but there is no need to shy from that psychological dimension of what she really desires (Mills 2002, 55, 59–60; Griffin 1990). After all, Phaedra does not shy from it herself:

> I am so worked over by desire, and if you speak such foul things fairly I shall be caught and spent on doing the very thing I am trying to avoid. (504–5)

So psychology matters here, but more the psychology of the character who is listening and persuaded than the character of the person who speaks. Such cases are not rare where "rhetoric" is in point: the rhetorical power of Philoctetes is interesting for its effect on Neoptolemus; that of Theseus in *Heracles* is interesting for the way it plays on Heracles rather than for anything it tells us about Theseus.

Here rhetoric misses the mark in not being true to the world, to what it describes; but it hits the mark completely in its gauging of the person to whom it is addressed. It is that mismatch which makes it so important to the play.

Rhetorical Complications

So if her rhetoric is viewed one way the nurse gets it exactly right; yet she is profoundly wrong when it is viewed in another. Such a catastrophic mixture of fire and misfire is found again and again, especially when the notion of formal speech is most prominent. In Euripides' *Suppliants* Theseus must strike an Athenian audience as fundamentally right in defending democracy, and the Theban herald as wrong in attacking it; and yet the herald's picture is the one that would more often strike an uncomfortable chord in its acute pointers to contemporary realities (Collard 1975a, 211–12; Pelling 1997b, 233). In the debate in *Phoenician Women* (446–637) Eteocles is very honest about his own thoughts on tyranny: he is not going to give it up, whatever was agreed (499–525). Yet the effect is to make this formal exchange, so carefully set up by the worried Jocasta, thoroughly useless: it should be to air the rights and wrongs, yet one party refuses to play; the idea was to reconcile, yet one party wants no reconciliation; rhetoric should be to persuade, yet Eteocles' words are likely to persuade no one; and it all does not matter anyway, with the armies poised for action. However rightly Eteocles' speech reflects his mindset, its inappropriateness brings out the wrongness of all the dynamics of the encounter. So then do Jocasta's platitudes (528–85), in a different way: they are far more ethically right, and yet have no purchase on the situation at all.

Matters are no less complicated in Aeschylus and Sophocles – indeed, they are often even more interestingly complicated. In the early scenes of *Seven against Thebes* Eteocles is surely right to stem the flood of fearful female emotion, and his language is appropriately powerful; yet he also stands up to the fears of the chorus once it is clear that it is his brother he will have to fight (686–719), and it is their case there, based though it is on emotion, that has more *logos* on its side. The Creon of *Oedipus at Colonus* pleads with Oedipus to return to Thebes, and says all sorts of things that a right-minded Theban ought to think and say (728–60); but the audience knows enough to be clear that he does not mean them at all, all is disingenuous, and Oedipus is right to reject him so magnificently. Yet a little later right and wrong are harder to disentangle, when Polynices belies expectations and says many things that sound more attractive (1252–1446). His repentance may strike the right note, and may well seem to the audience to be sincere. But it will not be enough for Oedipus: even if the audience discriminates the two sorts of appeal, he does not, and no words could be the right ones to persuade him (Buxton 1982, 137–45; cf. Easterling 1967; Blundell 1989, 241–48). As so often, a failure of rhetoric marks a terminally dysfunctional family, and once again it is the onstage listener's mindset that is illuminated – but by the flatness of the rejection rather than, as in Phaedra's case, by the willingness to accept.

All those cases (and many more) invite more detailed analysis, but let us take two cases, those of Sophocles' Ajax and Aeschylus' Clytemnestra, where the mix of over-whelming rhetorical power and deeply dangerous performance is particularly inter-esting. In each case what makes the performance so sinister is that the speakers' themes and images cohere so closely with other aspects of the play: the speakers may, in different ways, be saying things at odds with their own natures, but there is a deeper reality and truth which speaks through their words. There is *logos* there, but not as the speakers know it, or at least not in ways that they can wholly accept. If their speech has a quizzical relation to reality and to their own natures, it also has a distorted impact on those to whom they speak: communication itself is what speech is for, but is here travestied, distorted, sinister, and simply *wrong*.

Rhetoric in *Ajax*

First, the great speech of Ajax (646–92), "perhaps the most rhetorical speech in Sophocles" (Fraenkel 1977, 20), full of stunningly honed *gnomai* (maxims) – and of their antithetical juxtaposition with the catastrophic particularities. No viewer of this play could doubt that this is a critical moment. Ajax dominates the stage. His thoughts and his language have an intensity that, even in a play of extreme suffering and passion, is unmatched. Part of the point is indeed the contrast with the pettiness of the formal speech that follows, with the contemptible rectitudes of Agamemnon and Menelaus as they confront Teucer (Reinhardt 1979, 31–32; cf. Knox 1961, 2, 28). There is no more genuine contact between two speakers in those *agônes* than there is in the self-absorbed language of Ajax, and the world is by then a smaller place.

Interpretation is of course deeply controversial (the debate is summarized by, for example, Winnington-Ingram 1980, 46 n. 107; Segal 1981, 432–33 n. 9; Garvie 1998, 184–86; Hesk 2003, 74–103). Yet the nature of that scholarly dispute is itself suggestive, for so many of the problems come from the fact that this is *logos*, deeply powerful, articulated, thoughtful *logos* – but it is rhetoric with a difference, for it is barely *communication*. Indeed, what sort of performance is Ajax putting on – is it a performance at all? Is it a "deception speech," as it has so often been called? "Deception" implies an intended effect on a hearer: but it is not clear that Ajax is thinking of his hearers at all. It indeed has many of the marks of a soliloquy (Knox, 1961, 12–14); yet that is not clearly right either, as by the end he addresses Tecmessa ("You, wife, go in," 683–86) and the chorus ("And you, my comrades," 687); even at the beginning he is aware of Tecmessa's presence ("this woman here," 652). Fraenkel 1967, 82–83, and Battezzato 1995, 92–104, compare and contrast similar mixes of "soliloquy" and awareness of audience – a "quasi-monologue," as Fraenkel puts it. Yet this is still a very strange form of communication, if it is communication at all. He muses rather than informs. Even if in some way he responds to Tecmessa's earlier arguments (Gill 1996, 204–16), even as he acknowledges her presence, he does not seem to be talking *to* her at all.

> I, who then bore so much, like iron in the dipping, have been unmanned in what I say [and also "in the edge of my resolve," for *stoma* is ambiguous] by this woman here: I feel pity at leaving her a widow, and my child an orphan, among my enemies. (650–53)

Only "in what I say," and "unmanned" dismisses this new register even as he adopts it; and the language also leaves it unclear if his "pity" is leading him to relent or not. Language is as slippery and ambiguous as it was with the nurse, but with a very different effect. We knew that the nurse was aiming her rhetoric at Phaedra and to have a particular effect, but we are much less clear about Ajax. If his language is riddling, is that because of any concern for his listeners, or indeed because of anything in his own mind at all? Or are there wider forces at play, toying with him and his language just as they toy with Oedipus' riddling speech at *Oedipus the King* 216–75?

Scholars also debate (or used to) a more fundamental question of his psychology too: has he changed his mind about suicide (so, for example, Bowra 1944, 39–40)? But, as so much discussion of tragic psychology, these debates have centered too much on *motives and intentions*. From *Seven against Thebes* and *Libation Bearers* onwards, much of the most interesting tragic psychology centers on what a person *knows and understands*, and the same is true here. Not unlike the Achilles of the *Iliad*, Ajax may have been led by his sufferings to a deeper understanding of the human condition – but what that understanding implies for *what he is to do* is a different question.

It is a question, though, that matters not just to scholars but to people in the play, above all to Tecmessa and the chorus. The audience in the theater may or may not wonder if Ajax intends to deceive; if they do, they are unlikely to be able to give a confident answer. But they are certainly aware that those listeners *are* deceived, that they get their man wrong. Ajax asks rhetorical questions: "How shall we not learn the lesson to be sensible (*sôphronein*)?" (677: Knox 1961, 16–17). Earlier, "And so [*toigar*] in future [or "for the rest"] we will learn to yield to the gods, and revere the Atreids. They are the leaders, so we must yield to them. What else?" (666–67).[4] But what are the answers? The reason why we call such questions "rhetorical" is that they are for effect on a listener, who can immediately supply the answer: but here we have already seen that communication is skewed, and the speaker of such a rhetorical tour-de-force seems almost unaware that an audience is there. And is the answer to those questions so clear? The listeners in the play, Tecmessa and the chorus, take him as implying that he will live on, and are indeed deceived: that is the reason for their joy and relief (683–718, esp. 693, 716–18; 743–44, 787–88, 807). Yet the listeners in the theater, the audience, are surely not so taken in. The ironies and double meanings of the speech may initially be genuinely puzzling, and the audience may not be clear how to take them (though they will surely notice that the double meanings are there); that may help the audience to understand that the onstage listeners can be so misled. But already at 667, quoted above, the verbs are reversed, so that "revere," a word more naturally used of the gods, is applied to the Atreids (as the scholiast remarks: Knox 1961, 16); when used of mortals, it should encompass "admiration of authority which one regards as legitimate; it responds to the value of the powerful person, not simply to the fact of his power" (Cairns 1993, 207). That makes it even harder to think that Ajax might ever be willing to bow to these men of power whom he despises – unless that single act of "yielding" is by taking his own life. The emphatic *toigar* at the beginning of that sentence – "a strong logical force" (Denniston 1954, 565), i.e., "of course it follows that . . . " – tells the same way: *does* the need for submission really follow so clearly, any more than with Medea's angry "And so [*toigar*] you have made me the envy of many Greek women in return for this" (Euripides, *Medea* 509–10)? By the end of the speech the implications are clear enough. Ajax instructs Tecmessa to pray for "what my heart desires" (686; cf. 967–68); "I will go where I must make my way" (690). The audience knows what that journey must be; Tecmessa and the chorus do not. They care too much to understand. Skewed communication, indeed.

So one of our three directions, to the listener, is certainly out of kilter; another, to the speaker's own mindset, is enigmatically thought-provoking. Yet in our third direction it points to so many things that are right, and truths of which even Ajax is now convinced. It is indeed rhetoric that maps closely onto something in the play. This talk of change reflects the reality of the world all too closely: changes in seasons and changes in life such that even the greatest must bow to them. The imagery too – of hard and soft, of iron, honor, light and dark, cold and warm, storm and calm, sleep and waking, trusty havens – again echoes motifs that cut through the whole play, recurring in speaker after speaker.[5] Like the nurse in *Hippolytus* (446–50) and like real-life speakers (for example, Demosthenes 9.69, 18.194, 19.136; [Demades] 1.1, 1.54), Ajax develops analogies with the natural world; the difference is that the nurse's analogies seem false, yet these appear all so true. "He utters not a single word of actual falsehood" (Segal 1981, 114; cf. Dale 1969, 155). Ajax has indeed been brought low from a great height; that this could happen to anyone is an insight that Odysseus shares in the play, and in Odysseus' case fundamentally shapes the way he responds to the predicament (esp. 118–26, 1332–73). If Ajax sees a world of change but cannot live in it or persuade himself to answer "yes" to those rhetorical questions, that relation of words to speaker's mentality illuminates his psychology in ways which cut much deeper than any question of whether he "intends" to deceive.

Clytemnestra and Rhetoric

With Aeschylus' Clytemnestra some things are strangely similar. Once again the rhetoric is immensely powerful; it, and she, dominate the stage. Once again much of that power comes from the uncanny closeness of what she says to the truth (Neustadt 1929, 254–61; Thalmann 1985, 226). She sees the way the world is; she deceives, but she rarely lies – indeed, much of the uncanniness lies in how closely she represents the truth, but in chilling ways that her onstage hearers cannot grasp. Once again communication is skewed and once again her listeners may be overpersuaded, but here their response is clearly in line with what she intends. If Ajax's speech conveys control, it is only intellectual control of the way he now sees the world to be; the issue lies in the gap between that and his inability to control that world and his place in it more directly. Clytemnestra's speech is so unnerving because she controls a good deal more. Her intellectual control is matched by her control of her listeners' response, and the control over events that this gives her. (Contrast Cassandra, whose grasp of events is at odds with her inability to persuade or dominate.) And once again this is Clytemnestra's performance, playing the part of the faithful and welcoming wife, even if this role-playing is not figured as metatheatrically as it is in Euripides' *Electra*. Hers is not the only force at play: but for most of *Agamemnon* she is so powerful because she is at one with those other forces, even comes close to embodying them, so that it is uncertain whether she is "unforgetting Child-avenging Wrath" incarnate (*mnamôn Mênis teknopoinos*, 155, with the differing views of Fraenkel 1950 and Denniston and Page 1957 ad loc). All the more telling, then, that toward the end of the play her rhetoric is no longer so controlling, and the dynamic of encounters starts to be different.

The chorus's first address to the Queen marks their respect for her "power" (*kratos*), "for it is right to honor the wife of one's leader when the throne is left empty of the male" (or "when the male throne is left empty"; *Agamemnon* 258–60). No doubt in their mind, then, about where power should lie when the male is present. We soon see a control that cuts much deeper. When she explains how she knows that Troy has fallen, the "beacons speech" (281–316; Goldhill 1984, 38–39) is suggestive not merely for the disquieting places and names the signal has visited on its path – Lemnos, Cithaeron, the "Arachnaean heights": as so often in the *Oresteia*, the imagery touches a truth deeper still, the sense in which the flames of Troy are indeed licking toward Argos where they will engulf a second royal house. She can see and her language can convey the scenes of destruction at Troy; she knows the dangers too, that the conquerors may disrespect the gods, and dangers may strike before they can return home. In prosily realistic terms, she cannot *know* this. All she can infer from the signal is that the Greeks have taken the city. Yet the power of her description persuades the chorus, at least until they pull themselves up 120 lines later (475–87); and the audience in the theater knows it *is* true, even before the herald in the next scene confirms so much (including the devastation of the altars, 527). That audience already senses too the deadly double-speak. Clytemnestra wants the army to get home safely: "if the army comes without transgressing against the gods, the suffering of the dead may still be wakeful" (345–47). Which dead? Not merely those at Troy, though those as well. There is another among the dead whose suffering makes demands, and that is Iphigenia. Tragic rhetoric is often unnerving because it fails to persuade, or because it makes people believe things that are false. Yet here we have no lies and no failure of persuasiveness – only a closeness to truth in a form that goes beyond anything normal or comfortable or safe.

Agamemnon is expected: Clytemnestra sends the herald back to him with a message.

> Report this to my husband, that he should come as quickly as he can, a darling to the city: when he comes may he find in the house a faithful wife just as he left her, a good guard-dog for him and an enemy to those who are hostile; and one who is the same in all other ways too, one who has broken no seal in all those years: I know no pleasure, nor any slanderous talk from any other man, any more than the dipping of bronze. (604–12)

Not all that is as "heavy with truth" (613) as she claims, but it again *grazes* the truth (Thalmann 1985, 226). The wish – "may he find" – is one which has different purchase in Clytemnestra's mindset from the way Agamemnon might take it: she is indeed the woman of the sort he left, a guard-dog of the house – with a hint there of her half-sister Helen, so frequently denouncing herself in Homer as "dog-faced," and Clytemnestra is no more chaste a wife than she (Goldhill 1984, 56); yet she is "faithful" in a different sense, to those whose claims are higher than her husband's; now she will indeed be an enemy to those who are hostile; the "seal" she has not broken through the long years may be less to do with chastity, more with the commitment to vengeance she has in store.

But most unnerving of all is the extremity of her language, now and when Agamemnon returns: "a darling to the city" (not to herself, we notice) here leads on to similar extravagance of phrasing in Agamemnon's presence:

> If he had suffered as many wounds as the story channeled back to us, he would have more holes in him than a net; if he had been killed as often as the stories multiplied, he would have been a second three-bodied Geryon boasting of a triple cloak of earth, dying once in each form...In my dreams I would be woken by the gentle breezes of a trumpeting gnat, seeing more sufferings than could happen in the time I slept. (866–72, 891–94)

Her imagery again chimes closely with that of the trilogy as a whole (cf. Gould 1978, 59–61). There is a sense in which Agamemnon *has* been wounded more than he knows by the fighting at Troy, that this all *is* like a net that enfolds more than he (or even she, yet) may sense, that there are three waves of killing at stake. Thus she has dreamed – and was that in fear, or in hope? And did those dreams come from within, or from a deity who knows future as well as past (as dreams so often come from deities, and will come later in the *Oresteia*)? Still, that time has now passed:

> Now, after bearing all that, with ungrieving heart I would describe this man as the watchdog of the halls, the forestay cable that saves the ship, the firm-fixed column of the lofty house, the only child to a father, the spring-stream for a thirsty traveler, the land that appears to a despairing sailor, the fairest day to see after storm. (895–903)

Not all is false: she is indeed glad that he has returned, and would not have wished him to die by others' hands; and as in *Hippolytus* the imagery of house is all too pertinent, and the stability of the *oikos* does depend on him. And still she is "performing" (McClure 1999, 72–92, esp. 78–79); this is the role of the faithful wife. Yet she is performing too well, and the hyperbolic language strikes chill.

That is partly because it is performative in a fuller sense. "Let envy [*phthonos*] be absent," she goes on (904): for envy, both human and divine, can so easily be stirred by god-like language like that, and the words can in themselves cause the result which she desires. This is the prelude to the tapestry-scene, when in Agamemnon's own deeds as well as in Clytemnestra's words he will run those risks. There may be a further way too that the language here prepares for that scene. Scholars have detected an "oriental" tinge to Clytemnestra's phrasing (Fraenkel 1950, 410; Hall 1989, 204–6; Steiner 1994, 170): can this be the right way to address a Greek king, hot from the defeat of the Eastern foe? Perhaps it can; we have already followed in the first stasimon a train of thought suggesting that what had been true of Troy may turn out true of Argos too; a moment later, and Clytemnestra will be shrewdly asking, "what would Priam have done, if he had achieved what you had?" as a way of enticing Agamemnon to tread those silks (935). What is happening in that tense interchange is much discussed and disputed, especially the question of why Agamemnon is persuaded so easily. (For discussion of this most powerful and enigmatic of all tragic scenes see especially Fraenkel 1950, 441–42; Denniston and Page 1957, 151–52; Lloyd-Jones 1962; Easterling 1973; Taplin 1977, 308–16; Buxton 1982, 106–8; Goldhill 1984, 75–78; McClure 1999, 80–92.) Perhaps the force of Clytemnestra's own personality is important, and Agamemnon is bullied; perhaps the audience again senses forces at play that go beyond Clytemnestra herself, but with which she meshes perfectly (something that is reinforced by the way her language picks up themes and images that are much more pervasive in the play); certainly, again, her own command of argument is important too, here articulated not in continuous logic but in bewildering switches of point of attack. But we need not rule out psychology *as well*, and as in *Hippolytus* it is the psychology of the hearer rather than the speaker that is in point. As with Phaedra the arguments that persuade are transparently weak, and as with Phaedra this makes them all the more revealing. This may indeed be the way to speak to Agamemnon; that is partly because it chimes in with the dynamic of other irresistible forces, but his own mentality may also be not so far from an Eastern king's. There are multiple reasons why what happened at Troy should be living on, and about to happen again in Argos.

For the moment, Clytemnestra's control is total, and Agamemnon is as good as dead already. But then things falter. She cannot dominate Cassandra: controlling men with words is one thing, but Cassandra is female and silent (see Mossman, chapter 22 in this volume). Soon Clytemnestra has no more need to perform. Like the nurse in *Hippolytus*, she can revel in her change of tack – "I have said much before to suit the moment; now I shall not be ashamed to say the opposite" (1372–73) – but unlike the nurse Clytemnestra is now, not then, speaking straight. Her language is now shocking in a different way, with explicit sexual imagery – extraordinary in tragedy – as she celebrates her orgasm of delighted triumph:

> As he breathed out the sharp slaughter of his blood he struck me with a dark shower of his deathly dew, and I responded with pleasure no less than at the god-given refreshment that brings the bud to birth...(1389–82)

Yet the chorus refuses to be cowed, and as the scene goes on Clytemnestra's tone changes too. She moves from iambics to anapests, chiming in more closely (though not completely) with the chorus's lyrics. Instead of vaunting her own part in this, she now talks of the *daimôn* who afflicts the house: you may say it is my deed, but...

> it was the old, piercing avenging spirit that took the form of the dead man's wife and brought this sacrifice of a grown man to join the young, in vengeance for the dread feasting of Atreus. (1500–1503)

Once again this is not false, indeed it is all too true – but it is not the same tone as before. Soon she is pleading with this *daimôn* to go away and assault another house, not this: she is content with a small part of her possessions, if only she can free the halls of this madness (1566–76).

True, Aegisthus now appears, and her domination of onstage males can be momentarily reasserted. It remains telling that her language has come to control events less decisively just as its grasp of their true significance has become greater. The next wave of destruction is beginning, and in *Libation Bearers* others will have their roles to perform and pretences to enact. She has become more like Ajax, with *intellectual* control, an understanding of her place within the rhythm of events, coupled with an insight that she will not be able to control those events as she wishes. But whereas in Ajax's case – or in that of Herodotus' Xerxes at the Hellespont (7.44–52) with his acquiescence in the dangerous role that history has given him – the rhetoric is no less impressive for being calmer, Clytemnestra's words falter rather than drive. The psychology they illuminate is no longer her victim's, it is her own.

Conclusions

Peter Wilson has explored the way in which the tragic is treated in oratory. Tragedy can certainly be a source of edifying examples, but also tragic coloring or imagery can often evoke an air of strong censure: that tends to focus on spectacularly dysfunctional families, but there is also a sense that "tragic" behavior in public life may suggest "putting on a performance," and doing so transgressively – too much violent bluster and not enough substance, a failure to demarcate adequately what belongs in literature from what should be the case in reality. (See Wilson 1991, 182–86; 1996; 1997, 81–85; and 2000a, 148–51; cf. Ober and Strauss 1990, 257–58; Hall 1995, 54–55; the most explicit cases are Andocides 1.129, [Andocides] 4.20–23, Antiphon 1.17, Demosthenes 21.149). This chapter has investigated the mirroring phenomenon of the rhetorical in tragedy, and the types of suspicion aroused there are not wholly different, again pointing to too much of a misleading or disturbing performance. That disquiet may point in any of our three directions, illuminating the speaker, the audience, or the distance of it all from reality.

None of these themes is surprising in the intellectual world of fifth-century Athens. Thucydides too presents us with speakers who persuade so easily because the audience is so ready to be persuaded (Alcibiades at 6.16–18, and ironically Nicias too at 6.20–23) and with speakers who have no chance because the affair is already prejudged (the Plataeans at 3.53–59); speakers who strike the right note for the occasion but whose words raise questions about their relation to the truth (Nicias urging the Athenians that all is not hopeless at 7.61–64, and in a different way even Pericles' funeral speech at 2.35–46); debates with a dynamic that illuminates a political scene (the Mytilenean debate at 3.36–49, the debate at Syracuse at 6.32–41); speeches that raise questions about the speaker's sincerity (Alcibiades at Sparta, 6.89–92); speeches that make claims which may be thought-provoking in ways deeper than the speakers or listeners know (Cleon's claim that democracy cannot rule an empire at 3.37.1, or Alcibiades' that his fame and Athens' will be inextricably connected at 6.16); speeches that are most illuminating for arguing in unexpected ways (Euphemus at Camarina, 6.82–87); speeches that explore broader themes of human nature, vindictiveness, and empire (Diodotus in book 3, Hermocrates in book 4, the Melian Dialogue in book 5). There as here, it is the *variety* of uses to which rhetoric can be put that is striking; all are thought-provoking, few are reassuring, and all require the speeches to be set against their context, the "situation" in which they sit.

Indeed, A. M. Dale famously talked of speeches as illuminating that "rhetoric of the situation" more than the character of the speaker (1954, xxv, xxvii; cf. Dale 1969, 139–55 and 272–80) – an overstatement, as several scholars (especially Conacher 1981; cf. Blundell 1989, 16–25; Halliwell 1997, 123 n. 10) have thoughtfully brought out, even if it was one which contributed in a timely way to the current of scholarly debate. Dale thought of the playwright as "a kind of *logographos* [speech-writer] who promises to do his best for each of his clients in turn as the situations change and succeed one another" (1954, xxviii; cf. for example Gould 1978, 57–58; Buxton 1982, 153; Heath 1987b, 131–32; Mossman 1995, 94–137); yet we so often see characters *not* making the best of their cases – Euripides' Electra and Clytemnestra, for instance – and it is precisely the ways that the rhetoric misfires which make it most interesting. And even where rhetorical moves do suit "the situation," speakers were left choices and those choices were illuminating. Haemon need not have argued *like that* to his father, displacing matters of right and wrong on to questions of prudence before popular opinion (Sophocles, *Antigone* 682–723, "a masterpiece of obliquity and implication," Bers 1994, 188); Medea did not need to have mentioned childbirth in a play where so much will center on a parent's love for children (Euripides, *Medea* 250–51). And those choices can be as illuminating of the hearer's mindset, or at least the speaker's reading of it (Haemon), as of the speaker's. Plato in *Gorgias* and *Phaedrus* and Aristotle in book 2 of the *Rhetoric* agreed that a knowledge of psychology was inextricably connected with the art of rhetoric, as speakers had to gauge their audience and judge the strategies which would suit their temper and extract the desired result. How accurately speakers do gauge their listeners, and particularly the distinctive mix of insight and misunderstanding that so often typifies the personal exchanges of tragedy, even or especially when speaker and listener are closely linked by friendship or by blood – all these have emerged as crucial themes. In fact we do best if we turn Dale's formulation on its head: if rhetoric is conditioned by "the situation," it is therefore most illuminating for what it tells us about the dynamics of that situation, and in particular how they are amiss.

Thucydides' Cleon attacked his audience for taking too much delight in second-guessing speakers, swifter and keener to anticipate what would be said than what would result in the world of action (3.38.4–7). In the theater that second-guessing can take several forms, as the audience works out what else a speaker might have said if he or she had chosen to be more honest, or managed to be more effective, or gauged reality better. Familiarity with real-life rhetorical performances can sensitize an audience to what is particularly off-key as well as what is particularly accomplished – even or especially when the same passage is both. And that is so often what helps an audience to anticipate and understand the catastrophic consequences that will swiftly unfurl on stage.

NOTES

1   Goldhill and Osborne 1999 is a very useful collection, especially the introductory overview of Goldhill 1999. See also now Mackie 2004, and the works listed in n. 2.

2 On Homer, e.g., Martin 1989, Bakker 1997. On Pindar and lyric poetry, e.g., Herington 1985, Gentili 1988, Krummen 1990, Stehle 1997, Currie 2004. On the relation of Dionysiac festival setting to the plays itself, cf. esp. the papers in Winkler and Zeitlin 1990, esp. Goldhill 1990, and Carpenter and Faraone 1993, Seaford 1994, Sourvinou-Inwood 1994 and 2003, Easterling 1997f; for a skeptical counterblast, Scullion 2002a and chapter 2 in this volume.

3 Many analogies can be found between theater and courtroom performances, but these analogies are rarely reflected in the application of theatrical metaphors to forensic phenomena. Thus Hall 1995 collects material on this isomorphism and illuminatingly arranges it under theatrical headings – "stagecraft," "protagonists," "the cast," etc. – but those figures are largely her own (and none the worse for that), not (except for *hupokrisis*, "delivery") explicit in the way the texts themselves usually conceptualize oratory. The exceptions where tragic figuring is indeed used (Hall 1995, 54–55, and, e.g., Goldhill 1997b, 127; Easterling 1999, 161, 164) are also significant for tragedy itself, suggesting by analogy that it is not illegitimate to see metatheatricality in extreme instances even though we should not do so casually or without textual prompts. When such figuring is used in oratory, it usually characterizes negatively, and is applied to the life an opponent lives more often than the way he speaks in court: see my concluding section. All this also goes for the material treated by Ober and Strauss 1990, esp. 255–58 on Andocides 1.

4 Punctuation is here difficult. The *ti mên* (Linwood: *ti mê* codd., cf. Fraenkel on Aeschylus, *Agamemnon* 672) is of course a question, building closely on what goes before: but it can build on it in different ways, either strongly affirming the preceding statement (as Denniston 1954, 333, counts this case) or, more unusually, following the rejection of a supposition (Denniston 1954, 333). Hence the phrasing suggests, but does not make it quite clear, that the previous postulate – the necessity of yielding – is for the moment accepted. That postulate, "They are the leaders, so we must yield to them," could itself be printed as a question. However they are punctuated, we should anyway see these sentences in terms of Ajax musing on the implications. On this mode of introverted self-dialogue see esp. Gill 1996 (the book's subtitle is "The Self in Dialogue").

5 Hard and soft: 594, 926, 1119, 1361. Iron: 147, 325, 584, 820. Light and dark: 85, 147, 195, 217, 223, 257, 285–86, 394–95, 708–9, 856–59, 929, 1088, etc. Cold and warm: 478, 1411. Storm and calm: 207, 257–58, 351–53, 558–59, 889, 1081–83, 1143–50. Sleep and waking: 291. Trusty havens: this links with the recurrent motifs of sea and shore (Segal 1981, 121–24).

FURTHER READING

The bibliography on many of the issues touched in this chapter is overwhelming. Bers 1994, Halliwell 1997, and Wilson 1991 and 1996 are good chapter-length studies of the relation between tragedy and oratory; Buxton 1982 investigates tragic "persuasion" more generally. A good introduction to the questions raised by Athenian "performance culture" is the collection of Goldhill and Osborne 1999; Goldhill's sweeping introduction to that volume is especially thought-provoking. Hesk 2000 is interesting on the suspicions that can be aroused within Athenian culture itself when a "performance" is too transparent. Some recent work on oratory in the city has stressed the performative analogies with drama, especially Hall 1995; Ober and Strauss 1990, developing the ideas of mass and elite role-playing implicit in Ober 1989 (esp. 152–55). Among general studies of language and rhetoric within the plays, Goldhill 1984, 1986a, and 1997b have been particularly influential. On the formal *agôn* see Lloyd 1992; on rhetorical narratives, de Jong 1991 (like Lloyd, concentrating on Euripides but with implications for all three tragedians); on women's speech, McClure 1999, Mossman 2001 and chapter 22 in this volume; on rhetoric and characterization, Dale 1969, 139–55 and 272–80; Gould 1978; Conacher 1981; and Mossman 1995, 94–137. As for the four plays treated in detail in this chapter, Mills 2002 and Hesk 2003 give useful and thoughtful surveys of recent scholarship on, respectively, *Hippolytus* and *Ajax*. The best introductions to Aeschylus' *Agamemnon* and Euripides' *Electra* are still the standard commentaries: Fraenkel 1950 and Denniston and Page 1957 (*Agamemnon*), Denniston 1939 and Cropp 1988 (*Electra*).

CHAPTER SEVEN

Pictures of Tragedy?

Jocelyn Penny Small

What does it mean to illustrate text? Must the pictures physically accompany the text? Do the pictures, whether they are together with or apart from the text, have to agree with the story? What does such agreement entail? Do pictures agree, if they add details not in the story? Conversely, what about if they omit certain details? Are they still illustrating the text if they contain elements that contradict what the text says? What role does literacy play? Can an illiterate artist illustrate a text? What about the nature of the tools available? Does it matter that for most of antiquity the dominant form for long texts was a roll and not a codex? If texts are used to understand pictures, can pictures be used to reconstruct texts? Does the relationship between text and picture change over time? These are basic questions, some of which have been considered from the beginning of modern art history, others of which have seldom been treated. Yet all are necessary for understanding how pictures and text work together and apart in classical antiquity.

Of the questions just asked it is strange that one of them is rarely posed. With the exception of a handful of scrappy, incomplete literary papyri and a similar handful of fragmentary technical treatises, no illustrations from antiquity are joined physically to any text. Even those scrappy, incomplete papyri are relatively late, since the earliest technical papyri date from the second century BCE and the earliest extant illustrated literary papyri from the second century CE (Small 2003, 121–23 and 138–41). It is not just that the pictures do not physically accompany texts. The pictures were created independently of the texts. While today illustrations are sometimes created long after texts were first written, such as for new editions of Mark Twain, in antiquity, until the Hellenistic period, the common practice was for text and pictures to be made and sold independently of each other as totally distinct entities. In other words, no physical evidence, including statements in classical texts, indicates that the pictures we have are illustrations of texts. Even for the Hellenistic period and later the evidence remains sparse. Objects like the Hellenistic relief bowls and the Iliac Tablets do combine text and pictures, but the sizes of the objects limit the amount of text to quotations (Small 2003, 86–90 and 93–96).

Although Greek art and literature often shared the same subjects, as is only to be expected, the correspondence between the two media for choice of subject is far from exact. Even where they do overlap and tell the same story, the renderings differ. Most frequently scholars have interpreted this situation as a gap in the knowledge of the texts by either us or the artist. Paradoxically, we are both more and less likely to know texts than they: more, because we know all sorts of obscure variants preserved for us by later ancient scholars, which are more easily retrievable today; less, because we often miss knowing the obvious that never made it into a written text or was merely not preserved. Our very dependence, however, on preserved texts has led to an over-emphasis on texts for art, not just in our need for the literary sources to help us identify and interpret scenes, but also in the very way that we approach art. *We assume that, because we need the texts, classical artists must have also needed them.* The idea rarely occurs that artists might depend more on other artists than on texts for their sources. Even less often considered is the idea that artists do not depend on texts at all or, at best, only indirectly.

Before beginning the discussion of pictures of Greek tragedies, it is useful to distinguish an "illustration" from a "representation." I use "illustration" only for pictures that match (or should match) the text in the way that Sir John Tenniel's engravings fit Lewis Carroll's *Alice in Wonderland*. A representation has only a loose connection with the text. The covers of cheap paperback editions of mysteries may contain the elements of the story, but put together not quite in the way they are in the story. Three synonyms for representation are depiction, image, and picture. There is no uncontested representation of an extant tragedy on Attic vases, and the situation is not much better for South Italian vases. Methodologically this is an extremely important point, because the scenes on the vases are often used to reconstruct lost Greek tragedies. *If we do not have both parts of the equation – the picture and the play – we cannot tell how painters "used" tragedy. And not just one such pairing is necessary, but multiple pairings, for a single example may be anomalous.* Otherwise, we are totally in the realm of speculation about how artists used texts. Please note that I distinguish between influence of a text on how a picture represents a story from how actors acted and might have influenced gestures of figures on vases. An actor and a figure on a vase, for example, might use the same physical gesture to express horror without sharing the same text or story.

The View from Statistics

First consider the statistics for just the three great Athenian tragedians from the fifth century BCE. Aeschylus wrote between seventy and ninety plays, of which only seven survive; Sophocles 123 plays, of which we also have only seven; and Euripides approximately ninety plays, of which we have nineteen (assuming *Rhesus* is authentic). In the fourth century BCE Carcinus, for example, was credited with 160 plays and Astydamas with about 240 plays, not one of which has survived. The output for each playwright, even a laggard like Aeschylus, is remarkable by today's standards. So, without even calculating what all the other playwrights wrote, we have a grand total of thirty-three plays out of a possible 303, or approximately 11 percent of the total output of the three great tragedians. That is a tremendous amount of missing information. In other words, even if these three playwrights had more than a proportionate influence over what artists depicted, we still do not have most of what they wrote.

Nor do our scholarly woes stop here, for the playwrights sometimes wrote more than one play about the same figure. Aeschylus is credited with at least three plays about Prometheus, of which only *Prometheus Bound* has survived. Furthermore, the playwrights sometimes wrote plays that contradict each other, such as Euripides' *Telephus* (in which Telephus is separated from his mother at birth) and *Auge* (in which the infant Telephus and his mother are set afloat in a chest). Certain subjects were treated by a number of different playwrights, like the plays on the house of Atreus. Yet scholars assume that a representation of a particular subject must depend on a particular text. Furthermore, if more than one playwright wrote on a particular topic, it is often assumed that the object depends on the play written by the most famous playwright in the list. If the object is from the archaic period, then Homer and epic are cited; if the object is from the fifth century BCE and later, then it must go back to a dramatic source, even though the major epics are still in wide, if not wider, circulation than in the archaic period. The argumentation is circular:

1 The scene on the vase has names for characters that appeared in this or that play according to literary sources.
2 Therefore the scene must represent that play, the one by the playwright best known to us.
3 Hence we can add to our knowledge of what happened in that play from the information on this vase.

Two Examples: *Andromeda* and *Medea*

With this background in mind, let us turn to the representations themselves. Richard Green (1991, 42) believes that: "The clearest and most convincing example of depictions derived from the theatre is the series which seems to relate to Sophocles' *Andromeda*." He considers five Attic red-figure vases dating from just after the mid-fifth century and later. On them appear different moments drawn from the exposure of Andromeda as an offering to appease the sea monster (*kêtos*), who has been terrorizing her land. Each vase chooses one segment of the action. A hydria in London (No. 1; see List of Objects at the end of this chapter) shows Andromeda held by two youths, as the stakes are planted in the ground on the right. A pelike in Boston (No. 2) chooses the next moment with Andromeda's right hand already attached to one of the stakes (plate 7.1). A third vase (No. 3), a white-ground calyx-krater in Agrigento, has the end moment with Andromeda fully attached and exposed, as her rescuer, Perseus, contemplates her on the left. Green argues that the vases form a coherent group dated roughly to the 440s and, significantly, are from different workshops, hence likely to have been created independently of each other (Green 1991, 43).

Yet the motif of tying a person to stakes occurs at least as early as the sixth century BCE and therefore before Sophocles wrote his play. Similarly, Persian dress for Andromeda in the second half of the fifth century BCE need not go back to a staged performance, because before the time of Sophocles it had already become part of the wardrobe of the wealthy (Miller 1997, 164). Showing successive moments in the

Plate 7.1 Andromeda. Attic red-figure pelike attributed to the Kensington Painter and Kensington Class. ca. 450–440 BCE. Boston, Museum of Fine Arts 63.2663. Photograph: Courtesy, Museum of Fine Arts, Boston. Reproduced with permission. © 2004 Museum of Fine Arts, Boston. All rights reserved.

tying of Andromeda to the stakes likewise does not require a theatrical source, for an even greater variety of moments is shown in Theseus' fight with the Minotaur, which would not have appeared on stage (Brommer 1982, plates). All of which brings us to the major problem: the play by Sophocles has survived only in snippets quoted by other classical authors. As a result, it is disputed what parts of Andromeda's story Sophocles used, especially since the literary tradition about Perseus and Andromeda goes back to the sixth century BCE (Phillips 1968, 1–2). Finally, the two alternate traditions for the exposure of Andromeda – tied to stakes or to a cliff – co-exist. More importantly, the Darius Painter (No. 4), one of the more notable and more "learned" of Apulian vase-painters, uses *both* motifs. In conclusion, I think that neither a text nor a particular performance can be cited as the source for these vases in the current state of our knowledge.

Oliver Taplin (1993, 22–23) takes an intermediate position on the dependency of artists on texts. He examines one of the rare examples where we have both text and pictures: *Medea* by Euripides with its possible representations on South Italian vases. Consider an early Lucanian calyx-krater (No. 5), now in Cleveland and dating to around 400 BCE, with Medea flying off in her dragon-drawn chariot after having killed her children. Medea and her chariot are enclosed by a rayed nimbus, a symbol of her grandfather Helios (plate 7.2). Below on the right lie her two slain sons draped over an altar, as their white-haired nurse stands in mourning, pulling at her hair. Just behind her stands a tutor. Jason appears on the left and holds a staff. Seated on the upper left and right are matching female demons, probably the Erinyes. No stage is portrayed. Taplin (1993, 22) makes the connection to Euripides on the basis of the depiction of Jason as helpless, "since this is where the whole emphasis lies in Euripides' closing scene." Taplin readily admits that the story predates Euripides' *Medea*, produced in 431 BCE, but notes that the extant visual representations date to after the play. At least seven other playwrights, all later than Euripides, wrote about Medea, yet Taplin ignores the possibility of a lesser playwright inspiring a painter. He proceeds with his analysis and gives six differences from Euripides' *Medea*:

1   Jason is naked or half-naked.
2   The children are on the altar and not in the chariot.
3   Dragons drawing the chariot are not mentioned by Euripides.
4   The nurse has been added.

Plate 7.2   Medea. Lucanian red-figure calyx-krater attributed to near the Policoro Painter. ca. 400 BCE. Cleveland, Museum of Art 91.1. Photograph © The Cleveland Museum of Art, 2004, Leonard C. Hanna Jr., Fund, 1991.1.

5   The tutor has been added.
6   The Erinyes are alluded to by Jason (*Medea* 1389–90), but are not present in this
    scene.

The question is whether these differences are plausible additions or contradictions
of the action. Taplin suggests that some of the discrepancies are due to artistic
reasons. Actors always appeared dressed on stage, but figures in art were often in
heroic nudity. Hence each medium follows its own conventions. Nonetheless, I am
not sure that one should consider heroic nudity irrelevant in judging whether a
particular picture reflects a particular play, because phlyax vases and three Sicilian
vases with indisputable stages have dressed figures (Small 2003, 52–61). The other
differences are more complicated. Although Euripides does not bring the Erinyes on
stage, it is, of course, possible that they were part of the overall story, if not the
Euripidean version. And that is the crux of the problem. When does the depiction
depend on the "general" tradition, and when does it derive from a specific literary
rendition?

Taplin maintains that he has a decisive answer that is also an advance in our
ways of dealing with such material. He asks, "Does the image 'call for acquaintance'
with a text or performance of a text?" And he responds, "The most important
point is that the viewer's pleasure would have been enhanced by an observant
recollection of the play, and yet not offended or diminished by substantial departures
from any particular scene" (Taplin 1993, 22–23). I find this reasoning very slippery.
I can think of few cases in which more knowledge does not enhance one's appreciation of either a work of art or a text. As one notes the divergences, one thinks
that this or that is a nice touch or wonders why in the world the artist or writer
put such and such into the scene. And this is not just a modern reaction on my
part. Pausanias compares what Polygnotus has painted in his *Iliupersis* in the
Lesche of the Cnidians at Delphi with what Homer has said. For example
(Pausanias 10.25.4, trans. Jones 1935): "These names too are different from those
given by Homer in the *Iliad*, where he tells of Helen going to the wall with her
slave women." Here Pausanias' knowledge of Homer definitely enriches his view of
the painting.

Furthermore, Taplin's suggestion lacks any critical standard for accepting or rejecting a particular artistic rendering as dependent on a text. He basically says that
differences between picture and play do not matter, which is true only if you are
not trying to figure out how the two media work both together and separately. If you
want only to enjoy either the play or the picture or both, Taplin's approach is
admirable and, actually, would strike a classical person as eminently reasonable. Taplin
believes the crucial feature is the "helplessness" of Jason, since that is the crux of the
end of Euripides' play. In contrast, I am particularly disturbed by the fact that the
artist of the Cleveland vase has focused visually not on Jason, who is off to the side,
but on Medea first and the children next. Even more striking to me is the element of
the children on the altar with Medea flying away without them. To me, Euripides
focuses not on Jason's helplessness, but on Medea's not allowing Jason to touch or
bury his sons. She is taking them with her. Euripides does not say whether the
children are visible during the final scene. The text can be read either way. Nor

does he mention an altar, nor whether Jason has a sword, much less whether he waves it at Medea.

In conclusion, I certainly agree that this vase shows Medea and Jason. I agree with the interpretation that Jason is ineffectual. I find that a number of the differences from Euripides' version are plausible. Yet the vase portrays a different outcome. Medea clearly abandons her children, and Jason gets to bury them. This element violates the story line that Euripides has set up. It implies compassion for Jason and gives him what he pleaded for most of all in the Euripidean version. Finally, my argument about the central importance of plot finds support in Aristotle (*Poetics* 1450a38–39, trans. Halliwell 1986), for he says: "The plot-structure [*muthos*] is the first principle and, so to speak, the soul of tragedy, while characterization [*ta êthê*] is the element of secondary importance." As a result, the "call for acquaintance" argument must be discarded for the following reasons: it does not follow the logic of the plot, which makes it un-Greek in concept, and it specifically does not work for Taplin's best-case example.

Theatrical Representations on South Italian Vases

Since the production of plays was prodigious in fifth-century Athens, it is significant that contemporary Attic vase-painters did not base their representations on the plays. Not until the following century in South Italy are there depictions of scenes taking place on actual stages. Complicating the scholar's task in finding pictures to fit tragedies is the scarcity of representations of stage settings for subjects drawn from tragedy. Most such scenes are comic, and, even in those cases, they generally lack secure attribution to specific plays. Only one vase (No. 6), a fragmentary Sicilian calyx-krater, has been related to an extant tragedy (plate 7.3). The participants stand on a wooden platform supported by beams, whose edges can be seen just below the floor. Though without inscriptions, it preserves enough of its figures for an identification as Oedipus and his family, when they learn the news that he has married his mother, the subject of *Oedipus the King* by Sophocles. The figures are elaborately dressed and have quite expressive faces that resemble caricatures. On the left, a white-haired messenger stares directly out at the viewer, as he gives his message to Oedipus. His daughters stand on either side of him with Jocasta, his wife and mother, on the right. Behind her a female attendant completes the scene, which takes place in front of four columns. Yet neither Ismene nor Antigone was present in this scene in Sophocles' play.

There are three possibilities: (1) the painter has conflated two scenes; (2) he depicts a different play; or (3) he shows his own or some other version of the story. We do not have enough information to decide. What may be most interesting about this vase, however, is the lack of action on the part of the figures in contrast to what is normally seen on South Italian vases with scenes drawn from myth. The figures really do appear like a cast delivering and receiving lines. The messenger faces us the viewers, while the two adults stand still listening. In short, since the depiction of the stage definitely indicates a play, some scenes rely on the theater. The question then becomes whether the pictorial scene depends on the artist's memory of an actual performance or on his reading of a text.

Plate 7.3 Oedipus. Sicilian calyx-krater by the Capodarso Painter. ca. 350–325 BCE. Syracuse, Museo Archeologico Regionale "Paolo Orsi" 66557, from Syracuse, Necropoli dell' Ospedale Civile. Photograph © Museo Archeologico.

The Importance of the Salient Detail and Telephus

An Apulian red-figure bell-krater (No. 7) with a simple two-figured scene is the best candidate for a pictorial scene dependent on a play (plate 7.4). Both figures wear grotesque masks with open mouths and are dressed like women in long garments, although the figure on the right has short hair like a man. That figure kneels on an altar, whose sides are splattered with blood. He holds a sword upright in his right hand and a rather odd object, which wears two shoes, in his left. A slightly hunched-over woman, carrying a large skyphos or krater with both hands, approaches him from the left. Between them a mirror, seen in profile, hangs on the wall. The clue to the meaning of the scene rests on the right figure and the object he holds. Taking refuge at an altar occurs in several stories, but only one tale focuses on someone simultaneously taking a hostage – Telephus threatening Orestes.

In one of the encounters before the Greeks reach Troy, Telephus, the leader of the Mysians, manages to best the attacking Greeks, but is himself wounded in the thigh by Achilles. Telephus learns from an oracle that only the one who wounded him can cure him. Since the Greeks are unlikely to help Telephus voluntarily, he enters Argos

Plate 7.4 "Telephus" threatening "Orestes." Apulian bell-krater by the Schiller Painter. ca. 370 BCE. Würzburg, Martin von Wagner Museum H 5697. Photograph © Martin von Wagner Museum, Universität Würzburg. Photographer: K. Oehrlein.

dressed as a beggar, hoping to trick them into healing him. When his disguise is penetrated, he flees for sanctuary to an altar with the baby Orestes, whom he threatens to kill if Agamemnon, the father, does not help him. We know of at least seven Attic tragedies and five parodies involving Telephus. From summaries and fragments it is believed that Euripides introduced the motif of Telephus as a beggar sneaking into Argos for his play *Telephus*, performed in 438 BCE.

Now our plot thickens. Aristophanes in 411 BCE parodied the scene of Telephus threatening Orestes in his *Women at the Thesmophoria* (704–56). We know it must be a parody of Euripides and not Aeschylus or Sophocles, who also wrote plays about Telephus, because Euripides is one of the characters in the play. Aristophanes gives Euripides an elderly relative, Mnesilochus, who disguises himself as a woman in order to penetrate the exclusively female festival of the Thesmophoria. The women are plotting against Euripides because of Euripides' nasty characterizations of them in his tragedies, and Mnesilochus' task is to find out what they are up to. He succeeds quite admirably until he makes the mistake of defending Euripides, at which point the women become suspicious. Mnesilochus flees to the altar, stopping only to grab one of the women's children as a hostage. Mnesilochus threatens to kill the child, but, as he unwraps it from its swaddling, it slowly dawns on him that he is holding not a baby, but a wineskin wearing Persian booties – in short, the scene on the Apulian vase.

The play explains other details of the vase. The woman, who rushes forward with a bowl to catch the "blood" (actually wine) from the sacrifice about to be performed, must be the mother of the "child" (*Women at the Thesmophoria* 752–56). She is meant to be an "equivalent" of Clytemnestra, the mother of Orestes, who also is supposed to have appeared in Euripides' play and certainly is present in some pictorial representations of the story. As Taplin (1993, 38) rightly points out, the scene is not intelligible without knowledge of the play. Up to this point there is universal agreement about the vase and its source. Whether the vase belongs to the category of phlyax scenes or directly illustrates Attic comedy does not matter for this discussion. What does is whether the vase depends on a text, an actual performance of the play, visual prototypes, or a combination thereof.

In support of the independence of the visual scene are the vases with straightforward scenes of Telephus threatening Orestes. The earliest example occurs on an Attic red-figure pelike (No. 8) where Agamemnon approaches Telephus, who is seated on an altar holding a diminutive Orestes hostage. Because of its date of around 450 BCE, the absence of Clytemnestra, and the fact that Telephus is holding a spear upright in a non-threatening manner, this version has been associated with Aeschylus' lost play. The type with Clytemnestra, combined with Telephus threatening Orestes with a sword, does not appear until around 400 BCE on a red-figure calyx-krater (No. 9). The subject also appears on the other side of the Cleveland calyx-krater with Medea, which dates to the same period (No. 10; plate 7.5). It is this version that the Würzburg vase spoofs. It is immaterial for the interpretation of the Würzburg vase whether this visual type depends on Euripides' play of approximately forty years earlier, because the Würzburg vase need depend only on Aristophanes and other visual prototypes, even though Aristophanes *must* depend on Euripides. In other words, there are two traditions, the visual and the literary. It is also disputed whether Euripides staged the scene of Telephus threatening Orestes or had his threats reported in a messenger's speech. (Gould 1973, 101–3, argues for the messenger speech; Heath 1989, 275–76, argues against it.) In the latter case, the visual tradition cannot depend on what went on during a performance, but must rely on the artists' imaginations to create the visual scene, even if the story itself was created by Euripides.

In conclusion, I think that the Würzburg vase is one of the rare examples of a scene that may truly illustrate a text, or if not a text directly, then a performance of a text. The wineskin with booties, along with the action and the details, makes the meaning clear, especially since this salient detail appears uniquely in this story. Although I accept a direct connection to Aristophanes, nonetheless, it is not possible to ascertain from the extant evidence whether the artist saw the play performed on stage, read the text, or knew only the story *and* the visual tradition associated with Telephus taking Orestes hostage, *or*, indeed, any combination thereof. In any case, the visual difference between the spoof and the "original" is not that great. Finally, it is important to note that the Würzburg vase depicts a two-figured scene. Artists have little trouble in matching picture to text in simple scenes, but generally stray from the text in more complex ones (Small 2003, 143–53).

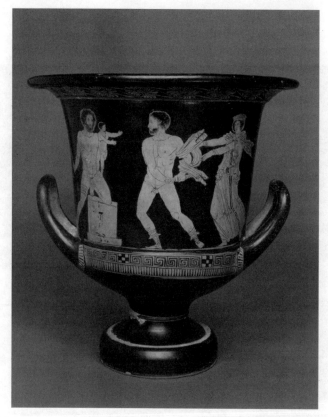

Plate 7.5   Telephus threatening Orestes with Clytemnestra. Lucanian red-figure calyx-krater attributed to near the Policoro Painter. ca. 400 BCE. Cleveland, Museum of Art 91.1. Photograph © The Cleveland Museum of Art, 2004, Leonard C. Hanna Jr., Fund, 1991.1.

Iphigenia among the Taurians

Roman wall paintings with "settings" are commonly interpreted as *scaenarum frontes* (stage fronts), such as the painting from the House of Pinarius Cerialis with Orestes and Pylades among the Taurians (No. 11; plate 7.6). Euripides' *Iphigenia among the Taurians* opens after Orestes has killed his mother, Clytemnestra, and has been ordered by Apollo to retrieve the statue of Artemis from her sanctuary in the land of the Taurians. Thoas, the king of the Taurians, has the unfortunate habit of putting all foreigners to death as a sacrifice to Artemis. Now comes the Euripidean twist. The priestess of Artemis is none other than Iphigenia, Orestes' sister, who was miraculously saved by Artemis from sacrifice at Aulis. Orestes and Pylades, his inseparable childhood friend, are captured, bound as prisoners, and taken to Iphigenia. Iphigenia questions them before they are to be sacrificed and offers to save Pylades' life by sacrificing only his companion, if Pylades will deliver a letter to her brother. Before handing the letter to Pylades, she tells them what it says (760–65). At this point Orestes recognizes Iphigenia and she, in turn, learns who they are. Together the three

Plate 7.6 Orestes, Pylades, and Iphigenia among the Taurians. Roman wall painting. 62–79 CE. Pompeii, Regio III 4, 4, cubiculum a, north wall. Photograph © Alinari 43169/Art Resource, NY.

plot to escape with the statue from the clutches of Thoas. Iphigenia secretes Orestes and Pylades in the temple. Then she sets up Thoas by telling him the two captured Greeks must be cleansed in the sea before they can be sacrificed to Artemis. She has Thoas order the Taurians to stay indoors, and gets him to purify the interior of the temple, while she takes the prisoners to the sea – supposedly for purification, but in fact for an escape by boat.

Now let us look at the painting. The figures are set within an architectural framework divided into three parts with the center and most important one jutting forward with an elaborate entrance, framed by columns, a pediment, and acroteria. At the top of its steps stands a three-figure group of Iphigenia flanked by two attendants. She holds a branch in her lowered right hand and the statue of Artemis in her left, resting it against her left shoulder. On the ground level, on the right, stand Orestes and Pylades with their hands bound behind their backs. On the left sits King Thoas with an attendant standing behind him. The painting unites the main characters in one visual scene, though they do not appear together in this way in the play. Nothing in the text indicates that Thoas is seated when he talks with Iphigenia (to the contrary, cf. 1159). It is true that he begins their conversation by inquiring about the statue, which in the play, as in the painting, Iphigenia holds in plain view (1157–58). Yet Euripides' Thoas never sees Orestes and Pylades. According to the play, Iphigenia tells Thoas to "shield your eyes with your *peplos* [garment]" when the two appear from within the temple (1218). Even if Thoas peeked, the two "prisoners" themselves were essentially "blindfolded" with "their heads covered with their *peploi*" (1207). Yet the painting shows the two in heroic nudity – remember actors were always dressed – with artistically arranged mantles and bared heads. Moreover, they are standing on the right, waiting and not leaving the temple – the only time when they would be in the presence, if not the sight, of Thoas.

The painting is neither depicting a performance nor trying to illustrate the text of Euripides. What it is doing is showing key elements in the story told by Euripides within a single visual frame. The distinction is important. It is not just that art has a different vocabulary or way of telling the same story. It is that this artist was not even thinking of illustrating the text, because he could have made a number of easy adjustments to avoid the contradictions in the action. He could have shown Orestes and Pylades with their heads covered or, conversely, Thoas avoiding looking at them. Thoas could have been standing. The painting by its backdrop misleads us into thinking that it represents a performance of the actual play. One is, thus, left wondering whether the background is meant to be a *scaenae frons* or some other building, such as a temple. In fact, the very versatility of such *scaenarum frontes* makes it difficult to tell when it is a real *scaenae frons*, such as one sees in permanent Roman theaters. I pass over the fact that real buildings shared similar façades, as do, for example, the library and theater at Ephesus.

A Brief Aside on Some Omissions

Three additional classes of objects possibly fall within the purview of representations of Greek tragedy: Attic vases with choruses, Hellenistic relief bowls, and Roman sarcophagi. Of these the first and third groups are the easiest to deal with. Simply put, there are no extant representations of tragic actors on Attic vases from the fifth century BCE (Green 1991, 41). The choruses are either from unknown tragedies or comedies. The actors are from comedies or satyr-plays, of which the Pronomos vase (No. 12) is perhaps the best-known Attic representation. On the other hand, Roman sarcophagi do not differ in the problems they present from the vases or Roman paintings and hence for the sake of brevity I have omitted them. Hellenistic relief bowls claim a close connection between text and picture, sometimes including quotations. Even here, however, there are divergences from the text. For instance, two sets of relief bowls (No. 13) state that they show the "Iphigenia of Euripides," but in both cases there are divergences from the text. Electra is added to the family group in Aulis, while the scenes on the other set do not follow in Euripides' order (Small 2003, 82, 86–90).

In my survey of a few of the best cases for classical illustrations of Greek tragedy, one general principle has been used to judge the fidelity between picture and text. If the action in the image contradicts the plot of the text, then the artist was not portraying that particular text. A second principle is fundamental. Artists' use of texts can only be established through an analysis of multiple paired examples of picture and text. Unfortunately, very few such sets have survived. Nonetheless, some patterns can be discerned. To state the obvious: art is never static, especially over a period of approximately a millennium. The choice of subjects changes. The way those subjects are represented changes. The objects that carry those representations change. The one variable that changes the least has been the focus of this study: the relationship between the artist and text, even though artists become increasingly literate. With the major exception of the Apulian vase with Telephus threatening a wineskin, no object before the Hellenistic period can be indisputably tied to a text. Even in this case, it is not possible to tell whether it is the text of Aristophanes' play or a performance that lies behind the scene. This major exception, however, means that other pictures *may* depend on text, although that number must be low or we would have more such pairings despite the erratic survival of text and objects. In any case, artists who paid attention to particular texts must have been the exception and not the rule.

Never, ever forget that, unlike manuscript illuminations and books today, the so-called classical illustrations *never* accompanied full texts. The most coordinated texts and pictures consist only of a few quotations and an accompanying picture – a phenomenon that began in the Hellenistic period, as preserved on the relief bowls, and appeared only spasmodically thereafter. Instead, the dominant pattern is one of artists and writers pursuing independent and parallel paths with only occasional intersections. Pausanias in his description of the *Iliupersis* of Polygnotus cites five different authors, as well as oral tradition, as sources for Polygnotus (10.25–27). Hence the idea of a single literary source for a single picture is plain wrong. Artists selected what they wanted from any available author, oral telling, visual rendering, or their own imagination. They are depicting stories, not illustrating texts. In fact, their use of myth resembles that of classical writers (see Anderson, chapter 8 in this volume). Just as we expect the tragedians to manipulate myth – or why else would we want to see or read their plays? – so we should expect artists to create their own independent, but plausible, interpretations.

Not until the Hellenistic period, when the Library was established at Alexandria, does a class of objects, the relief bowls, appear that comes even close to illustrating, not merely representing, texts. The Roman material continues the loose connection between story and picture. If the picture is simple – limited to a figure or two – the correspondence between text and picture is good. As soon as the picture becomes more complex, divergences between text and picture creep in. Scenes from the Late Antique Vatican Vergil (No. 14) show that the approach to illustrations had not changed significantly some five hundred years or so after the relief bowls and several centuries after the invention of the codex (Small 2003, 143–55). Writers and artists persisted in pursuing their separate ways, even when joined together on the same page, as they had when separated by appearances in different places on different objects. In short, in a world that depends primarily on oral transmission, the variant is king and there is no original!

List of Objects

1   Hydria. London, British Museum 1843.11–3.24 (E 169). *ARV*^{2} 1062 = Workshop of the Coghill Painter. *LIMC* 1, 776 Andromeda No. 3, with pl. 623.

2   Pelike. Boston, Museum of Fine Arts 63.2663. Not in *ARV*^{2}. *Paralipomena* 448 = Kensington Painter and Kensington Class. *LIMC* 1, 776 Andromeda No. 2, with pl. 622.

3   White-ground calyx-krater. Agrigento, Museo Civico AG 7, from Agrigento. *ARV*^{2} 1017 No. 53 = Phiale Painter. *LIMC* 1, 776 Andromeda No. 5, with pl. 623.

4   Moret 1975, 263–64. The vases he cites are as follows, with the first two using stakes and the third a cliff. (1) Calyx-krater; Matera, Museo Ridola 12538, from Irsina. *LIMC* 1, 781–82 Andromeda No. 64, with pl. 633. (2) Loutrophoros; Naples H 3225, from Canosa. *LIMC* 1, 777 Andromeda No. 13, with pl. 626. (3) Amphora fragments; Halle, Albertinum 214, from Ruvo. *LIMC* 1, 777 Andromeda No. 12.

5   Cleveland, Museum of Art 91.1. Attributed to "near to the Policoro Painter." *LIMC* 6, p. 391–92 No. 36 Medeia, with pl. 199.

6   Syracuse 66557, from Syracuse, Necropoli dell'Ospedale Civile. *LIMC* 1, Antigone No. 1 with pl. 659. *LIMC* 7, 9 Oidipous No. 83, with pl. 14. *LIMC* 5, Iokaste No. 5.

7   Apulian bell-krater by the Schiller Painter, dated to ca. 370 BCE. Würzburg, Martin von Wagner Museum H 5697. *LIMC* 7, 868 Telephos No. 81, with pl. 601.

8   London, British Museum E 382. Attic red-figure pelike, Near the Chicago Painter. *ARV*^{2} 632. *Addenda*^{2} 272. *LIMC* 1, 260 Agamemnon No. 11, with pl. 192.

9   Attic red-figure calyx-krater. Berlin, Staatliche Museen V.I. 3974. Unattributed. *LIMC* 1, 260 Agamemnon No. 260, with pl. 192. *LIMC* 7, 866 Telephos No. 55, with pl. 599.

10 Cleveland, Museum of Art 91.1. *LIMC* 7, 866 Telephos No. 59, with pl. 600. Compare No. 5 above.

11   Pompeii, Regio III 4, 4, cubiculum a, north wall. Ling 1991, 129 fig. 131 = 62–
      79 CE. *LIMC* 5, 722 Iphigeneia No. 58.
12   Name vase of the Pronomos Painter. Naples 81673 (H 3240), from Ruvo.
      *ARV*² 1336 No. 1 where the play is identified as a "Hesione."
13   The first set of three bowls, all of which have the same scenes, are dated to the
      first half of the second century BCE according to the *LIMC* entries. (1) Berlin,
      Staatliche Museen 3161 q, from Athedon. *LIMC* 5, 711–12 Iphigeneia No. 8,
      with fig. on 712. (2) Athens, National Museum 2114, from Boeotia. *LIMC* 5,
      712 Iphigeneia No. 9, with fig. on 713. (3) Brussels, Royal Museum A 893.
      LIMC 5, 712 Iphigeneia No. 10.
         The second set of three bowls is similarly dated. (1) New York, Metropolitan
      Museum of Art 31.11.2, from Greece. *LIMC* 5, 711 Iphigeneia No. 6, with
      drawing on p. 711 and pls. 466–67 (photographs of details). (2) Athens,
      National Museum 22633, from the Piraeus. *LIMC* 5, 711 Iphigeneia No. 7.
      (3) Volos, Museum DP 71–34, 86, from the Anaktoron at Demetrias. Men-
      tioned in *LIMC* without entry number at the end of No. 10 on p. 712.
14   The Vatican Vergil (Vatican Library, Cod. lat. 3225). Wright 1993.

NOTE

This essay is based on my book, *Parallel Worlds of Classical Art and Text* (Cambridge, 2003). It
should be consulted for full discussions, references, and pictures.

FURTHER READING

Woodford 2003 is an excellent introduction to the interpretation of classical pictures, and
    Carpenter 1991 is a copiously illustrated, reasonably priced handbook. Shapiro 1994 pre-
    sents a well-illustrated survey from a non-skeptical point of view. J. R. Green 1994 offers an
    introduction to all major aspects of the Greek theater, again from a non-skeptical point of
    view; Green 1995 is an excellent bibliographical essay. Green and Handley 1995 give a good
    survey along with color photographs. Taplin 1993 represents the non-skeptical classicist's
    view. Trendall and Webster 1971 take an old-fashioned approach to vases, but include many
    illustrations arranged by putative play. Small 2003 sets out the case for the skeptics from
    archaic art through Late Antique. Moret 1975 is a skeptic like me, but he focuses on South
    Italian vases.

PART II

Elements

CHAPTER EIGHT

Myth

Michael J. Anderson

Myths of violent conflict and turbulent crisis among the heroes of the distant past constituted a chief element of the collective cultural heritage in ancient Greece, and Athenian tragedy was one among several specialized art forms through which these myths were articulated and transmitted. In dramatizing stories of Orestes, Oedipus, and other familiar heroes, the tragedians blended tradition with contemporary innovation. They borrowed heavily from preceding poetry, particularly from the vast corpus of epic, but they also customarily reshaped inherited myths by modifying plots, introducing new characters, and even creating new episodes. The license to invent was not unlimited – with few exceptions the characters of drama remained located in the legendary world of the past and closely linked with established myths – but a Greek tragedy was never merely a dramatic transcription of a preexisting narrative.

Origins and Functions of Greek Myth

The development of the corpus of Greek myths was a complex process of accumulation and synthesis. Many myths originated as dim reflections of the Mycenaean world, and epic characters like Ajax may in fact be survivals from Bronze Age poetic traditions. Other myths reflect the conditions of Greece in later periods, as for example the adventures of Jason and Odysseus reflect the influence of exploration and colonization in the centuries following the dark ages. Near Eastern tales of gods and heroes provided another rich source of inspiration for Greek myths, including some of the canonical myths of Zeus, Heracles, and Achilles. Herodotus credited Homer and Hesiod with the codification of the Greek pantheon (2.53), and epic poetry also offers the earliest evidence for the codification of heroic exploits – detailed genealogies connecting the various gods and heroes, as well as a rough chronological arrangement of Theban, Trojan, and other myth cycles. While the monumentality of the surviving Homeric and Hesiodic poems gives the impression that this tradition had become fixed by the seventh century – and most of the major myth cycles were established within the system by this time – the process of development did not come to a complete halt with any single poet or poem. Many tales of Theseus, for example, began to take shape only late in the sixth century, when Athenians reformed him into a legendary embodiment of their developing civic identity. And adaptive mythmaking continued throughout the fifth century in Athenian tragedy.

For the communities that preserved and transmitted them, myths provided a revered form of validation for cultural institutions, practices, and beliefs. They recorded the foundation of cities and sanctuaries, explained the origins of religious rituals, conveyed beliefs about the gods, mapped out social relations and hierarchies, exemplified positive and negative behavior, and reflected generally upon the cycle of human life, exploring its most intense joys and its deepest sorrows. The frequent public presentation of myths in conjunction with religious and civic ceremonies provides abundant evidence of their authoritative status in ancient Greek society. Images of gods and heroes adorned sacred precincts, and religious festivals often featured the recitation of heroic epic and hymns recounting the births and exploits of the gods. The victory odes of Pindar and Bacchylides publicly celebrated successful contemporary athletes and their home cities by recalling the paradigmatic achievements of legendary heroes like Pelops, Heracles, and Perseus. Simonides' elegiac memorial to the warriors who fought at Plataea monumentalized the contemporary battle by invoking the precedent of the Trojan War (frs. 10–18 West). Tragedy too, performed in competition at festivals that honored the god Dionysus and celebrated Athens, was a highly authoritative, culturally relevant, and publicly endorsed articulation of myth.

The *Oresteia* as Exemplar

Aeschylus' *Oresteia* provides illustrations of several characteristic features of tragic myth. First, the trilogy exemplifies tragedy's general practice of inspiring reflection upon fundamental cultural values by dramatizing moments of violent conflict and crisis. In the first play Clytemnestra murders her husband Agamemnon and defends her act as retribution for the murder of their daughter. In the second Orestes is obligated to honor his dead father by murdering his mother and her accomplice. And in the third play Orestes stands trial against the Furies on charges of matricide. Together these three depictions of conflict examine failed kinship relations, competing claims of maternal and paternal authority, differing conceptions of justice, and the community's power to intervene in private disputes.

Secondly, the characters and plot of the *Oresteia*, as of Greek tragedy in general, are partly traditional and partly invented. The *Odyssey* repeatedly invokes Agamemnon's homecoming and Orestes' vengeance as potential models for Odysseus' return and Telemachus' maturity to manhood, thus recognizing these stories as already firmly established several centuries before the production of the *Oresteia*. Fragments of the epic *Returns* (see Proclus' plot summary, in West 2003) and the Hesiodic *Catalogue of Women* (fr. 23a.27–30 Merkelbach and West) also preserve references to Orestes, and in the early sixth century Stesichorus composed an extended lyric account of Orestes' matricide and subsequent confrontation with the Furies (fr. 219 Page). Aeschylus adopted from these earlier poets not only a basic plot outline, but also specific narrative details. A prototype of the watchman who opens *Agamemnon* appears already in *Odyssey* 4 (524–28), and Stesichorus' poem provided a model for

Clytemnestra's prophetic dream in *Libation Bearers*. Aeschylus' own contributions to the mythic tradition, on the other hand, include major plot innovations such as the reunion of brother and sister at the tomb of Agamemnon, possibly the introduction of Electra herself, and the resolution of Orestes' conflict with the Furies in an Athenian court of law.

Third, the myth treated in the *Oresteia* is culturally authoritative and prestigious not simply because it had been recounted by preceding poets, but because of the wider cultural significance of its subjects. Tragedy is populated by characters of greater than normal social stature, characters whose ancestry, political power, and personal achievements commanded respect. The Greeks regarded many of these figures not as fictional poetic creations, but as semidivine heroes of the distant past. And while not all of them merited emulation, many were judged worthy of veneration through sacrifice and other ritual observances. Herodotus records that the Spartans, acting on advice from the Delphic oracle, retrieved the bones of Orestes from Tegean territory as a prerequisite to their conquest of this enemy in the middle of the sixth century (1.68). This tale implies the existence of an Orestes cult at Sparta and reflects the belief that after death the heroes exercised a talismanic power to protect and to harm. Aeschylus' drama accords Orestes a similarly privileged cultural status. Apollo's patronage and Athena's intervention alone identify him as an extraordinary mortal, but Orestes' promise to punish from the grave any Argive who raises arms against Athens and to bless those who support Athens (*Eumenides* 767–74) boldly antici- pates his eventual status as a cult hero with power to harm and to help. Agamemnon too, incidentally, enjoys a form of hero-worship in *Libation Bearers*, when son and daughter honor their father at his tomb and seek his aid in their struggle against Clytemnestra. Moreover, the drama regards Orestes' confrontation with the Eume- nides as paradigmatic and foundational, serving to establish both the Athenian court of the Areopagus (482–88, 570–74, 681–710) and the shrine of the Eumenides (804–7, 927–29). Similarly, a myth first attested in Euripides' *Iphigenia among the Taurians* explains the practice of drinking from individual rather than shared vessels at the Athenian Anthesteria festival as ritual commemoration of Orestes' visit to Athens (947–60), when the pollution of his matricide barred him from participating in communal activities.

Finally, tragedy represents a contemporary, predominantly Athenian appropriation and reconfiguration of myth. The *Oresteia* celebrates the city of Athens as a distinctive site of conflict resolution, a city that tames violence with persuasion and transforms the weaknesses of other states into its own strengths. Aeschylus' choice of the Areopagus as the setting for conflict resolution alludes conspicuously to recent political controversy over the functions appropriate to this ancient court (see Debnar, chapter 1 in this volume). While conservative aristocratic forces had advocated wider powers for the largely aristocratic institution, progressive democratic forces wished to restrict the court's jurisdiction – a dispute evoked by Athena's establishment of the Areopagus court and by the Furies' initial rejection of its authority. More generally, the contrast between the austere older Furies and the innovative younger gods (778– 79) recalls the continual political opposition of conservative and progressive elements in fifth-century Athens, and the ultimately peaceful resolution of the mythic dispute to the satisfaction of all involved suggests a hope that present-day Athens too can peacefully accommodate the differing political views of its inhabitants. In addition,

Orestes' pledge of continued friendship with Athens (762–74) provided mythic confirmation of a contemporary military alliance between Athens and Argos. While not all dramas praise Athens or mirror Athenian affairs so overtly, most view myth from a distinctly fifth-century perspective, and democratic institutions and Athenian values, though not always part of the plot machinery, are frequently invoked.

Functions of Myth in Tragedy

Greek myths in general embody and explore fundamental social institutions and the beliefs and values associated with them. Greek tragedy in particular examines these institutions and values by dramatizing moments of extreme crisis, violent conflict, and emotional distress, moments in which traditional values are threatened and social bonds break down. Greek poets, including tragedians, sometimes employed myth for overtly didactic purposes by presenting heroic characters as decidedly positive or negative models, inspiring emulation or deserving censure. Pindar in his victory odes, for example, celebrates athletic champions by recounting the similarly praise-worthy achievements of mythic heroes, and conversely he cautions against human excesses by recalling legendary offences like Tantalus' misuse of nectar and ambrosia (*Olympian* 1.59–64), Ixion's attempt to rape Hera (*Pythian* 2.21–48), and Bellero-phon's attempt to scale Olympus (*Olympian* 8.84–92, *Isthmian* 7.44–47). The *Odyssey* exhibits clear moral inclinations in rewarding its hero's exemplary conduct with a successful homecoming while punishing the overweening suitors and their accomplices with dishonorable deaths. Some tragedies share this moralistic view of a just universe in which the virtuous are rewarded and the wicked punished. The villains in these plays are often unquestionably villainous, and the concluding scenes appear to validate the actions of some characters while condemning the errors of others. Few spectators of *Iphigenia among the Taurians*, for example, could condone the barbar-ian practice of sacrificing strangers to Artemis, even if Athena did not intervene visibly at the play's conclusion and sternly reprimand the barbarian king. More commonly, however, the tragedians eschew simplistic illustrations of moral codes in their myths and instead inspire a more complex debate, presenting ethical dilemmas without assigning unqualified approval or condemnation. Such dramas are often more closely aligned with the *Iliad*, which is concerned less with Achilles' ethical choices than with the depth of the hero's suffering and the extremes of behavior that this suffering provokes. Thus Oedipus in Sophocles' *Oedipus the King* exemplifies not reprehen-sible conduct or poor judgment so much as the inscrutability of human fortune and the fallibility of human intent. And the chorus's hollow attempts to find fault with his behavior only emphasize the failure of popular morality to explain extreme personal suffering. The trial in Aeschylus' *Eumenides*, with its balance of votes for acquittal and condemnation, offers a productive political resolution but not an objective ethical judgment of Orestes' matricide. Instead of sanctioning an individual act of homicide, the play venerates an institution that reconciles deadly differences peaceably.

By far the most widespread instances of crisis and conflict in tragedy are those that threaten the institution of the family. Not only did the tragedians frequently drama-tize disputes between family members – between sisters in *Antigone*, between hus-band and wife in *Medea*, for example – they repeatedly drew upon myths in which one family member kills or nearly kills another, thus dramatizing the most transgressive violations of the most fundamental human bonds. The frequency and variety of such violations are astonishing. They include the killing of one's own offspring (*Iphigenia at Aulis, Medea, Hippolytus, Heracles, Ion, Bacchae,* recalled in *Agamemnon*; compare Oedipus' curse in *Oedipus at Colonus*), of a husband (*Agamemnon, Women of Trachis*) or a wife (*Heracles*), of a mother (*Libation Bearers,* Sophocles' *Electra,* Euripides' *Electra, Ion*), of a father (recalled in combination with incest in *Oedipus the King,* figuratively of Polynices in *Oedipus at Colonus*), and of siblings (*Seven against Thebes, Phoenician Women, Iphigenia among the Taurians*). Related instances of kinship conflict include the debates over the relative values of family members' lives in *Alcestis* and Orestes' near murder of and subsequent betrothal to Hermione in *Orestes.* In addition to these many instances of strife within the family, tragic conflict also frequently arises from attempts to honor kin or preserve kinship bonds against external threats. Antigone insists on performing burial rites for her brother despite Creon's prohibitions. In *Hecuba* the former queen blinds Polymestor in retaliation for the murder of her son Polydorus. Menelaus attempts to preserve his marriage against Theoclymenus in *Helen,* and in *Andromache* he intervenes violently in Phthian affairs in support of his daughter. The revenge killings in the *Oresteia* and the Electra plays combine these two categories of family-based conflict, as retribution exacted on behalf of one family member entails the killing of another.

Family crisis in Greek tragedy frequently centers upon a character's transition from youth to adulthood. In ancient Greek communities, as in contemporary societies, arrival at physical and sexual maturity entailed a considerable reconfiguration of kinship and other social relationships, as young women left their birth families to assume the roles of wife and mother, and young men gained some measure of independence from paternal authority and entered the ranks of the citizenry. Heroic myth is rich in reflections of the passage into adulthood and its attendant rituals, and Greek tragedy in particular explores several instances of incomplete or otherwise irregular transitions. An extreme example is Euripides' *Hippolytus.* Heroes like Perseus, Jason, and Theseus typically mark their entry into adulthood with a hunting exploit, the slaying of a beast or monster, and then proceed to secure wives by surpassing rival suitors or successfully challenging the bride's father. In the case of Hippolytus, however, the hunting rite and the marital rite are systematically inverted. Though on the threshold of adulthood physically, Hippolytus emphatically shuns the rites of Aphrodite and instead declares perpetual devotion to the virgin huntress Artemis. Refusing to assume an active sexual role, to pursue a wife, he becomes instead the passive object of his stepmother's incestuous desires. And when she paradoxically accuses him of rape, Hippolytus' alleged wooing catapults him into conflict not with a bride's father, but with his own. Finally, instead of confirming his manhood by slaying a monster, the perpetual adolescent himself falls victim to the monstrous bull of Poseidon. A similarly perverted passage into adulthood lies behind Sophocles' *Oedipus the King.* Conforming to the heroic model, Oedipus has slain a monster and thereby secured a wife, but his present investigations reveal that, as the oracle of Apollo predicted and despite his contrary intentions, he has married his mother and slain his own father. Instead of directing adolescent aggression and sexual desire outwards and maturing beyond the kinship ties of his youth, he has in fact directed these impulses against his own family, violating the closest of kinship bonds through incest and parricide.

Sophocles' *Antigone* and Euripides' *Iphigenia at Aulis* provide notable examples of female characters who fail to reach adulthood. Instead of leaving her father's house and forming a new family with Haemon, Antigone devotes herself completely to her brothers and ultimately joins them in death (see in particular the disputed lines 904–20). Sophocles underscores the contrast between her tragic death and the marriage she might have enjoyed by characterizing the subterranean enclosure in which she dies as a kind of perverted bridal chamber (891; compare 806–16). Euripides engineers a similar opposition between marriage and premature death in *Iphigenia at Aulis*. Although led to Aulis with the promise of marriage to Achilles (another hero, incidentally, often characterized by failure to enter fully into adulthood), the virgin daughter of Agamemnon will instead be sacrificed to the virgin goddess Artemis and never attain maturity. Several scenes of the drama feature disturbing juxtapositions of marital and sacrificial motifs, as for example when Clytemnestra anxiously inquires about the wedding preparations and Agamemnon's equivocal responses anticipate instead the imminent sacrifice (716–41). And the chorus paints a vivid contrast between the joyful festivities that once accompanied Thetis' marriage to Peleus and the bloody ritual killing of Iphigenia soon to be performed (1036–97). In both of these plays attention to marriage as the traditional rite of passage for young women may be understood as emphasizing the perversity of the execution or sacrifice. Insofar as Antigone and Iphigenia embrace their deaths, however, the juxtaposition with marriage also distinguishes these heroines as extraordinary figures and monumentalizes their sacrifice.

In contrast to these premature deaths, Sophocles' *Women of Trachis* concludes with a successful but decidedly unconventional entry into adulthood. Heracles' deathbed instructions to his son Hyllus – to light his funeral pyre while he still lives and to marry his concubine Iole – carry troubling undertones of parricide and incest. Yet these near violations of kinship bonds serve to salvage the remains of a family in turmoil. By burning his father's body Hyllus releases him from the torments of Deianira's poisoned robe, and the paternally sanctioned marriage between Iole and Hyllus neatly replaces the disastrous extramarital relationship between Iole and Heracles. A less ambiguously successful coming-of-age myth is dramatized in Sophocles' *Philoctetes*. Here Neoptolemus, whose assumption of Achilles' role at Troy was traditionally symbolized by the inheritance of his father's armor (see Proclus' summary of the *Little Iliad* in West 2003, and compare *Philoctetes* 62–63), aligns himself with Achilles also in ethical terms. Though at first tempted to adopt Odysseus' stratagem of deception, he instead joins the recalcitrant Philoctetes in resistance to the entire Achaean army, thereby adopting a stance of indignation and defiance commonly associated with his father. Other dramas that address entry into adulthood include Aeschylus' *Suppliants* and the many plays featuring Orestes and Electra.

Another typical concern of tragic myth is conflict between an individual or family and a larger community, specifically a polis or an army. Myths of the Trojan War, in particular, highlight disagreements between individual warriors and the wider contingent of Greeks. Aeschylus' lost *Myrmidons* was modeled on the hero's withdrawal from the fighting as previously narrated in the *Iliad*. And Achilles is again featured acting upon his individual convictions and preserving his own honor in *Iphigenia at Aulis*, where he alone among the leaders contests the decision to sacrifice Iphigenia.

Conflict arises in Sophocles' *Ajax* when the hero's assessment of his value as a warrior differs from the assessment rendered by the army's leaders. And abandonment on the island of Lemnos has left the title hero of Sophocles' *Philoctetes* bitter and enraged against the Greek army at Troy. Examples of discord between individuals and citizen communities are also abundant. The Argive citizenry condemns Orestes and Electra to death in Euripides' *Orestes*. In *Oedipus the King* Oedipus banishes the murderer of Laius from Thebes, thereby unknowingly banishing himself, in order to rescue the community from a plague. Creon in *Antigone*, claiming to speak for the community, condemns the heroine's resistance as an affront to the state. And in *Oedipus at Colonus* Oedipus declares allegiance to Athens while adamantly renouncing his former ties to Thebes. In addition, tragedies occasionally depict, or rather recount, military confrontation between communities, but such hostilities are viewed primarily through the lens of personal enmity or private suffering. Thus the war in Aeschylus' *Seven against Thebes* centers upon a feud between two brothers. Euripides' *Suppliants*, while recalling the war of the Seven and recounting a subsequent engagement of Athens and Thebes, foregrounds instead the burial of the fallen Argive warriors. And rather than focusing on ambushes and battles during the night of Troy's capture, *Trojan Women* displays the lamentations of Hecuba and her fellow captives in the immediate aftermath of the city's fall.

Several tragedies examine relationships between individuals and communities by dramatizing an act of supplication. The suppliant, in seeking refuge at an altar, cult statue, or other hallowed place, technically invokes the protection of the gods, but it is incumbent upon those who control the sacred precinct to grant the suppliant's request and thereby preserve the sanctity of the location. Although some tragic instances of supplication serve as a focal point for conflict within or between families (*Andromache* and *Ion*), the convergence of suppliant, pursuers, and community representatives upon a sanctuary provides several dramas with an ideal setting for political conflict and debate over communal values. When, for example, Orestes takes refuge at a statue of Athena in Aeschylus' *Eumenides*, the goddess appoints an august body of Athenian citizens to settle the dispute by trial (470–88). The act of supplication thus precipitates a radical redefinition of the conflict, as justice is left neither in the hands of individuals (Orestes and Clytemnestra) nor in the realm of the divine (Apollo and the Furies), but entrusted instead to representatives of the Athenian community. In assuming this authority, the community risks incurring upon its entire populace strife originally centered solely upon an individual (476–79, 719–20, 780–87). But this risk is far outweighed by the city's ultimate gains, Orestes' pledge of a perpetual alliance between Athens and Argos (762–77), and the promises of the rehabilitated Eumenides to protect the city, safeguard its internal peace, and ensure its prosperity (916–1020). Acts of supplication prompt states to intervene in foreign or private disputes also in Aeschylus' *Suppliants*, Sophocles' *Oedipus at Colonus*, and Euripides' *Suppliants* and *Children of Heracles*. The choice to support the suppliant in these plays again endangers the community with the threat of military conflict, but intervention simultaneously offers substantial potential benefits. In both *Oedipus at Colonus* and *Children of Heracles* the establishment of hero cults promises Athens future protection against enemy states: against Thebes in the former play (607–28), while in the latter, paradoxically, the hostile pursuer Eurystheus is entombed in Athens as a talisman against future Heraclid aggression (1026–36). In Euripides'

Suppliants the bones of the Argive heroes are returned to Argos for burial, but the substitute burial in Athens of a sacrificial knife provides the city with protective powers analogous to those of hero shrines (1183–1212).

A third general category of conflict witnessed in tragedy pits a mortal character against a divine antagonist. Oedipus' self-discovery in *Oedipus the King* is the climax of a long and unsuccessful struggle against Apollo's oracle. Euripides' *Andromache* recalls that Neoptolemus challenged Apollo at Delphi (49–55, and compare 1085–1165). In *Prometheus Bound* a Titan with pronounced mortal sympathies suffers for opposing the will of Zeus, while Io suffers as an object of Zeus' lust and Hera's jealousy. Artemis confronts Agamemnon with a painful dilemma in *Iphigenia at Aulis* and in the *parodos* of *Agamemnon*. This category of opposition is also easily recognizable in *Eumenides, Ajax, Hippolytus, Heracles,* and *Bacchae,* where adversarial divinities actually appear on stage. While Orestes prevails in *Eumenides* with the assistance of other divinities, the typical confrontation between mortal and god instead highlights the supremacy of the latter and the limitations of the former. With the exceptions of Dionysus, Demeter, and some lesser divinities, the immortals of Greek myth existed largely above the reach of the deepest mortal suffering. Although Artemis, for example, can feel sorrow over Hippolytus' misfortune (*Hippolytus* 1338–40), she cannot defile herself by witnessing his death (1437–38). Thus the gods were never, it seems, chosen as the principal subjects of tragedy without some accompanying involvement of mortals. The experiences of these greater-than-human beings simply could not generate in an audience the pity and fear that Aristotle judged essential to tragedy.

Insofar as it explores institutions common to all or most societies, tragedy can lay claim to near universal cultural significance. But Athenian tragedy developed out of a specific cultural tradition and within a specific cultural environment, and many of the institutions it explores and the forms they assume are particular to ancient Greece. One element that frequently advertises tragedy's local significance is the inclusion of an aetiology – an interpretation of the play's action as the foundation story for a contemporary cultural institution – at the close of the play. In this, tragedy continues a long tradition of poetic mythmaking that grounded religious practices in the distant past. So, for example, the myth of Prometheus' duplicitous sacrifice at Mecone, as narrated in Hesiod's *Theogony* (535–60), explains why the Greeks customarily offered to the gods the less valuable portions of sacrificial animals. And the *Homeric Hymn to Demeter* records the foundation of the sanctuary at Eleusis and implicitly characterizes the Eleusinian mysteries as a commemorative reenactment of the goddess' sojourn there. Several tragedies end with divinities announcing the establishment of religious institutions in Attica, thereby setting a seal upon the action of the drama with the promise of perpetual ritual commemoration. Examples include the worship of the "kindly goddesses" instituted in the *Eumenides*, of Oedipus in *Oedipus at Colonus*, of Hippolytus at Troezen in *Hippolytus*, and cults of Artemis at Halae and Brauron in *Iphigenia at Aulis*. Tragedy also provides aetiologies for a variety of other social institutions. *Eumenides* offers a foundation myth for the court of the Areopagus, together with the custom of counting a tie vote as an acquittal (741–42, 752–53; compare Euripides' *Electra* 1266–69, *Iphigenia among the Taurians* 1469–72). Thetis in *Andromache* announces the continuation of her own, Peleus', and Andromache's lineage in the succession of Molossian kings, thereby celebrating a contemporary dynasty (1243–49). Aeschylus' lost *Women of Aetna* dramatized the foundation of the city of Aetna. *Ion* identifies its hero as the eponymous ancestor of all the Ionians and proclaims Athens the ancestral origin of Ionians, Dorians, and Achaeans (1571–94).

Aeschylus' *Persians*, with its detailed account of the naval victory at Salamis, is anomalous in its attention to specific events of the recent past (compare Herodotus 6.21 on Phrynichus' *Capture of Miletus*), but several plays reflect more generally upon the politics and history of fifth-century Athens. Sophocles in his *Oedipus at Colonus* and Euripides in his *Suppliants* portray Theseus as a prototypic democratic ruler, a king who shares political authority with the populace (compare the Argive Pelasgus in Aeschylus' *Suppliants*). Creon's adamant disavowal of tyrannical ambitions in *Oedipus the King* (583–602) and the chorus's moralizing dictum, "insolence breeds the tyrant" (873), suggest democratic unease over concentrating political power in the hands of a single individual. Conspicuously anachronistic is Menelaus' characterization of his brother in *Iphigenia in Aulis* as a politician who curries favor with all when canvassing for votes but grows aloof once in office (337–48). Courts of law do not appear regularly in tragedy outside the *Oresteia* and *Orestes*, but the extended formal debates, or *agónes*, common in Euripides' plays, attest interest or at least familiarity with the judicial system. Several plays allude to current Athenian foreign policy: alliance with Argos in the *Oresteia* and Euripides' *Suppliants*, hostility toward Thebes in *Oedipus at Colonus* and toward Sparta in *Andromache*. Athens' reputation as a dependable sanctuary for suppliants in tragedy also finds parallels in contemporary history. Herodotus records that the alliance between Athens and Plataea began with an act of supplication in the Athenian agora (6.108). Euripides' *Trojan Women* is often read in conjunction with the Athenian destruction of Melos in 416 BCE (see Thucydides 5.84–116), although chronological considerations argue against a clear causal relationship between the historical event and the drama (see van Erp Taalman Kip 1987). It is also tempting to believe that the plague in *Oedipus the King* was inspired by the plague that devastated Athens at the beginning of the Peloponnesian War (see Thucydides 2.47–54).

While thus deeply embedded in its particular cultural context, tragic myth nevertheless preserves neither an exact nor a comprehensive account of Athenian society and history. Although, for example, Athens was a highly successful mercantile state, tragedy lacks crisis centered upon manufacture and trade. This avoidance is due in part to the inherited traditions of Greek myth, whose heroes are warriors and kings of illustrious lineage, not merchants or industrial entrepreneurs, and in part to the limited cultural esteem of these occupations in contemporary Athens, where they were pursued not by Athenian citizens, but predominantly by foreign residents and visitors. The images of the contemporary world in tragedy's mythical past are selective and often oblique, emblematic rather than descriptive. Historians must turn instead to Athenian comedy to find a more inclusive and more direct fictional engagement with contemporary society.

Bringing Myth to the Stage

Although Aristotle records that both the characters and the plot of Agathon's *Antheus* were wholly invented (*Poetics* 1451b21–23), such independence from established myth was uncommon among the tragedians. In referring to his dramas as "slices from the banquet of Homer" (Athenaeus 347e), Aeschylus reverently acknowledged the debt the tragedians owed to heroic epic, and a brief survey of the surviving plays reveals repeated borrowing from canonical traditions. Eight plays, approximately one fourth of the corpus, are based on familiar myths of the Trojan War, and the fragments record a similarly high percentage of Trojan plays overall. The popularity of this material among the dramatists stems partly from the monumental status of the *Iliad* and the *Odyssey* in the Greek poetic tradition and partly from the sheer number and variety of well-known myths surrounding the war against Troy. The surviving plays include three stories of discord within the Greek army (*Ajax, Philoctetes, Iphigenia at Aulis*), one account of a night raid on the Trojan camp (*Rhesus*), three accounts of the suffering of the Trojan captives (*Hecuba, Trojan Women, Andromache*), and one account of the reunion of Helen and Menelaus in Egypt after the war (*Helen*). Another seven of the surviving tragedies draw upon well-known traditions of the family of Agamemnon (eight if *Iphigenia at Aulis* is included here instead of with the Trojan material). While the Trojan War figures in the background of these myths, their appeal to the tragedians lies primarily in the violent family conflicts they record. An interest in kinship strife also repeatedly attracted the dramatists to Theban legend. Six plays treat Oedipus and his fratricidal sons, and *Bacchae* reaches its conclusion with the dismemberment of Pentheus at the hands of his mother and her sisters.

Tragic innovations upon the banquet of heroic tradition assumed many forms. In a handful of works the dramatists adhered to tradition with little noticeable alteration of plot or character, and exercised artistic license instead by emphasizing particular characters or dramatic perspectives over others. The Euripidean *Rhesus*, for example, preserves the basic elements of the myth found in *Iliad* 10. In both works Hector sends Dolon to spy on the Achaeans, but Odysseus and Diomedes intercept him and subsequently slaughter the newly arrived Rhesus. As in the epic, so too in the tragedy Dolon is promised the horses of Achilles as his reward, but Odysseus and Diomedes thwart Dolon's expectations and make off with Rhesus' horses instead. The circumstances surrounding the raid are also the same in both epic and drama: Achilles has withdrawn from the fighting and in his absence Hector anticipates Trojan victory. Apart from brief appearances of Athena and Paris, in fact, the play introduces little substantive alteration of the inherited myth. The tragic dramatization does, however, differ from the epic in its greater development of characters in the Trojan camp. Whereas in the *Iliad* we glimpse Rhesus only when sleeping or dead, the drama casts him in an active role, boasting that he will rid Troy of its enemies in a single day (443–50). And the dramatist offers a more intimate perspective on the catastrophe by introducing both Rhesus' charioteer, who delivers a grim report of the hero's death and accuses Hector of the murder (756–855), and Rhesus' mother, who arrives at the play's close to lament and retrieve the corpse.

Trojan Women, despite its unconventional tripartite structure, is constructed around several traditional plot elements attested in the fragments of the epics *Little Iliad* and the *Sack of Troy*: Helen's reunion with Menelaus, the sacrifice of Polyxena at Achilles' tomb, the allotment of Cassandra to Agamemnon and of Andromache to Neoptolemus, and the murder of Astyanax. The drama's originality lies not in any significant departure from this tradition, but in the dramatic configuration of these elements into a series of encounters with the Trojan queen Hecuba – her painful farewells to Cassandra and Andromache followed by her bitter parting quarrel with Helen. This final encounter, staged as a debate over whether or not Menelaus should execute his adulterous wife, replays in agonistic form the epic tradition that Menelaus initially intended to kill Helen upon discovering her at Troy but dropped his sword at the sight of her beauty (*Little Iliad* fr. 28, West 2003).

Tragedians occasionally altered mythic traditions more substantially by introducing a new principal character into an established plot, as is the case with Neoptolemus in Sophocles' *Philoctetes*. In contrast to earlier versions of the myth, in which Diomedes (as in the epic *Cypria*), Odysseus (in Aeschylus' *Philoctetes*), or both men in combination (in Euripides' *Philoctetes*) retrieve Philoctetes and his bow from Lemnos, Sophocles' play introduces Neoptolemus as a potential protégé of the duplicitous Odysseus. Epic attests at least two other occasions on which Neoptolemus and Odysseus cooperate. The *Little Iliad* credits Odysseus with bringing Neoptolemus to Troy and giving him the arms of his father Achilles (see Proclus' summary in West 2003). And the *Odyssey*, recalling Neoptolemus' inclusion among the warriors under Odysseus' command in the wooden horse, contrasts his youthful eagerness with the patience of the more experienced leader (11.523–32). But in Sophocles' newly fashioned expedition Neoptolemus' distaste for deception and his sympathy for the ailing Philoctetes soon dissolve his partnership with Odysseus, and his resolution to return to Greece threatens a radical departure from traditions that record his participation in Troy's capture. The divine intervention of Heracles at the play's close, with prophetic instructions for Philoctetes and Neoptolemus to rejoin the campaign, reconciles the action of this play with established myth, but the obvious artificiality of this intervention underscores the disparity between Sophocles' portrayal of an idealistic Neoptolemus and the murderous youth we find depicted elsewhere.

The participation of Electra in the murders of Aegisthus and Clytemnestra, also unattested in literary sources before the fifth century, may be another tragic interpolation. The surviving plays chart her development from a subsidiary to a central figure and simultaneously attest to the variety of treatments possible for a single character in a single myth. In Aeschylus' *Libation Bearers* Electra remains secondary to Orestes in importance, adamantly opposed to Clytemnestra but lacking the initiative or power to oppose her alone. She joins Orestes in a moving lament for their father, and her hatred for Clytemnestra stimulates her brother's anger; but Aeschylus clearly distances her from the murders, assigning her no role in preparing Orestes' trap, and she remains silent throughout the second half of the play. Sophocles and Euripides, in contrast, diminish the role of Orestes and organize their dramas instead around Electra, who but for a few brief absences remains onstage for the duration of both plays. In Sophocles' play she aggressively opposes Aegisthus and Clytemnestra by confronting her mother directly, plotting to murder Aegisthus herself (954–57 and 1019–20), and chiding her timid sister (probably another Sophoclean invention) for failing to assist. In Euripides' play a humiliating marriage to a peasant exacerbates her bitterness, and she rivals Orestes' involvement in the murders by actively luring her mother into the house where she will meet death – a deed reminiscent of Clytemnestra's sinister past (compare the carpet scene in *Agamemnon*). It is most unlikely that she played a similarly aggressive role in earlier works of which no record survives.

Another common form of substantial innovation is the insertion of new episodes into established narrative frameworks. According to early epic fragments, after his madness and suicide Ajax's body was buried in a coffin as a mark of dishonor, a divergence from the normal epic practice of cremation (*Little Iliad* fr. 3, West 2003). Sophocles' *Ajax* expands this detail into a potentially deadly conflict between advocates and opponents of proper burial and ultimately contradicts the epic record of dishonor. The three other dramas that include lengthy verbal disputes over burial – *Antigone, Oedipus at Colonus*, and Euripides' *Suppliants* – are similarly suggestive of tragic extrapolation. Such verbal conflict may also be viewed more broadly as a tragic analogue to the epic motifs of battling over, mutilating, and ransoming corpses.

Remarkable in the case of both *Andromache* and *Iphigenia among the Taurians* is the extent to which Euripides duplicates motifs traditionally associated with these characters elsewhere to construct new plots. In Phthia Andromache essentially relives her past suffering at Troy. The fickle Hermione now fills the role played formerly by her mother Helen, while the hostile Menelaus replaces the menacing Greek army. The death of Neoptolemus parallels the death of Hector, and the threats to Andromache's son recall the murder of Astyanax. Euripides invokes these Trojan paradigms, however, only to overturn them by saving Andromache's Phthian son from the fate of his Trojan counterpart. While the death of Astyanax definitively marked the extinction of Priam's family, Thetis promises Peleus that his descendants will flourish for generations. In *Iphigenia among the Taurians* the dramatist again generates suspense by threatening his protagonists with a repetition of their grim past. In nearly sacrificing her brother to Artemis, Iphigenia mimics her own sacrifice at the hands of Agamemnon, which she herself has recounted in the prologue. But instead of continuing the cycle of kinship murders, the siblings discover one another's identity in an elaborate and joyful scene of recognition, reminiscent of the reunion Orestes previously shared with Electra. Dramatic reenactments thus neatly link the newly extrapolated episode to preceding chapters of the legend. Moreover, by uniting the legends of Orestes and Iphigenia, Euripides fashions this new episode into a comprehensive cathartic resolution to the entire cycle of family conflict, rivaling and superseding the resolution previously offered by Aeschylus' *Oresteia*. Whereas the *Oresteia* apparently accepts the tradition that Iphigenia simply died as a sacrifice to Artemis, Euripides' play instead reports that Artemis rescued her from the altar and paradoxically established her as a priestess among the barbarian Taurians, where she must participate in the ritual sacrifice of foreigners (1–41; compare Proclus' summary of the epic *Cypria* in West 2003). And whereas according to Aeschylus' *Eumenides* Apollo simply administered purification rites to Orestes at Delphi (40–45 and 578), in Euripides' play Orestes can escape the lingering stain of matricide and the accompanying madness only by delivering the cult statue of Artemis from the Taurians (939–82). The ruse by which the siblings launch their escape, the claim that the matricide and the statue must be purified in the sea (1028–51 and 1153–1233), ironically epitomizes the polluted condition of both hero and goddess and underscores the hitherto incomplete state of both the Orestes and the Iphigenia traditions. Euripides finally perfects their legends by enshrining in Athenian cult Orestes' escape from the Furies and Artemis' former association with human sacrifice (1446–67).

The preceding examples of old paradigms recycled into new plots exemplify the general tragic practice of enhancing dramatizations of individual episodes with allusions to related events in the broader mythic cycle. Homeric epic had previously employed the device extensively and for varying effect: the *Iliad* ominously antici- pates the death of Achilles and the capture of Troy beyond the poem's narrative boundary, and characters in the *Odyssey* share numerous stories of the war and their journeys home. Such allusions were particularly suitable to works that conventionally dramatized portions of a larger whole, "slices from the banquet of Homer." In several dramas a synopsis of preceding events in the prologue or the closing proph- ecies of a *deus ex machina* neatly locate the present action and its principal thematic concerns within the wider mythic context. The exchange between Poseidon and Athena in the prologue of Euripides' *Trojan Women* simultaneously recalls the sacrilegious atrocities that accompanied Troy's recent capture and predicts the con- sequent destruction that awaits the Greek fleet after the drama's close. The prologue thereby invokes the traditional association of Troy's fall with divine retribution, although it offers cold comfort to the powerless captives featured in the subsequent scenes. Allusions to the past pervade *Oedipus the King*, where the hero's discovery of his true identity entails a comprehensive reassessment of his entire life, from the oracle predicting that his birth would result in Laius' death to his present incestuous union with Jocasta. In *Oedipus at Colonus* the incest and patricide committed long ago remain fundamental components of the aging hero's character. In addition to includ- ing abundant verbal debate over these transgressions, Sophocles invokes them visually at the play's opening when Oedipus trespasses into the grove of the Eumenides, thereby symbolically retracing his blind and accidental kinship transgressions. The capture of Troy, the abduction of Helen, and the murder of Thyestes' children all cast shadows over *Agamemnon*, but none so pervasive as the sacrifice of Iphigenia. The chorus laments the horrific events at Aulis in their first song, Agamemnon unwit- tingly replicates the sacrifice in symbolic form when he tramples the costly tapestries (905–65), Clytemnestra invokes Iphigenia's sacrifice as justification for murder (1432 and 1523–29), and she repeats the sacrilege by staging Agamemnon's death as a sacrifice (1384–87 and 1432–33).

Finally, a unique form of mythic innovation in tragedy is the blending of multiple traditions in *Prometheus Bound*, which fuses the previously independent myths of Prometheus and Io. It is not unusual for a play to contain allusions to myths outside the narrative cycle to which it belongs, particularly in choral odes (the parallels for imprisonment cited at *Antigone* 944–87 and the account of Demeter's grief at *Helen* 1301–52, for example), but the mixing of distinct traditions in a dramatic plot is uncommonly bold. The logic of the novel pairing of Titan and mortal in the *Prometheus Bound* lies in their common status as victims of Zeus' tyranny. Pro- metheus' punishment and Io's wandering place them both at the extremities of the world, far removed from civilization, and Io's intense suffering confirms Prometheus' dim view of Zeus' rule. In addition, the dramatist discovers a weak narrative link between the two figures: Prometheus' prediction that Io's distant descendant Hera- cles will prove instrumental in securing his release (771–74, 871–73, and compare

Hesiod *Theogony* 526–34) anticipates the tidy resolution of Prometheus' conflict with Zeus in the companion play, *Prometheus Unbound*. Not content with combining just two traditions, however, the dramatist incorporates one more innovation, Prometheus' prophecy that some unspecified child of Zeus will overthrow him (755–70 and 946–47), presumably an allusion to the offspring of Thetis. According to a myth first clearly attested in Pindar but already indirectly acknowledged in the *Iliad*, Zeus and Poseidon pursued the goddess Thetis, but upon learning that she was destined to bear a child greater than its father, the gods forced her to marry a mortal in order to prevent cosmic unrest (*Isthmian* 8.27–46; compare Metis in Hesiod's *Theogony*, 886–900). Though not previously associated with Prometheus, this third myth again accords neatly with the dramatic context. The threat of deposition is plausible at this early stage of Zeus' rule, not long after he himself has overthrown his father Cronus. Furthermore, Zeus' fear of begetting a successor may restrain his sexual aggression and could even hinder his pursuit of Io. Prometheus' knowledge of the prophecy thus provides him with considerable leverage in his present struggle. Finally, like the Prometheus tradition, the myths of Thetis explore a complex linkage between the mortal world and the divine. Forced to marry a mortal husband and give birth to a mortal child for the sake of the divine hierarchy, the goddess experiences directly and personally the anguish of mortality. Gods join mortals in celebrating her wedding, but for the bride the ultimate consequences of this celebration are the Trojan War and the death of her beloved son Achilles. Thetis' divided experience thus complements the transgressive roles of both Prometheus, the divine patron who suffers to alleviate the suffering of mankind, and Io's descendant Heracles, the suffering hero who comes closer than any other to crossing the boundary between mortality and divinity.

NOTE

I thank Justina Gregory and Victor Bers for helpful comments on earlier drafts of this chapter.

FURTHER READING

Graf 1993 provides an excellent introduction to the study of Greek myth, and the contributions in Bremmer 1987 and Edmunds 1990 exemplify various scholarly approaches. For discussion of myths in their cultural context see Buxton 1994; on gender issues in the study of myth see Doherty 2001. Gantz 1993 provides an encyclopedic study of the sources of early Greek myth, for which *LIMC* and Frazer 1921 are also very useful. West 2003 makes available in English translation the fragments of early Greek epic. In addition, the mythic traditions treated by the tragedians are customarily well documented in the introductions to philological commentaries on individual dramas; for example, Garvie 1986 on *Libation Bearers*, Sommerstein 1989 on *Eumenides*, and Cropp 2000 on *Iphigenia among the Taurians*. On Antigone's failure to marry see Seaford 1990, and for paradigms of initiation ritual in Sophocles' *Philoctetes* see Vidal-Naquet 1988. Burian 1974 examines Oedipus' supplication in *Oedipus at Colonus* with attention to parallels in other plays, and Slatkin 1986 explores the relationship between Oedipus and the Athenian community. See Anderson 1997, chs. 7–9, for the treatment of traditions of Troy's capture in the *Oresteia, Trojan Women,* and *Andromache.* And on the relevance of myths of Thetis to *Prometheus Bound* see Garner 1990, 40–46.

CHAPTER NINE

Beginnings and Endings

Deborah H. Roberts

[Comedy] differs from tragedy in its matter, in that tragedy is tranquil and conducive to wonder at the beginning, but foul and conducive to horror at the end, or catastrophe.... And for this reason some writers have the custom of saying in their salutations, by way of greeting, "a tragic beginning and a comic ending to you."

Dante, letter to Can Grande della Scala (Haller 1973, 100)

Of all literary genres, tragedy and comedy have come to be most identified with particular sorts of endings, the comic ending emblematized in the cultural imagination by united or reunited couples and the tragic by a body-littered stage. The expectation that the tragic ending will involve some kind of overturn further suggests (as in the passage from Dante above) that the beginning of a tragedy should be marked by serene good fortune. In fact, however, whatever the later development of the genre and of our conceptions of the tragic, Greek tragedy reveals a considerable variety of modes of ending and of beginning. A number of plays (for example, Aeschylus' *Eumenides*, Sophocles' *Philoctetes*, Euripides' *Iphigenia among the Taurians* and *Alcestis*) end with deliverance, reunion, or reconciliation, even if these are qualified by what came before or will come after. And many tragedies that end with disaster begin not with happiness but with deep distress, among them Aeschylus' *Persians*, Sophocles' *Women of Trachis*, and Euripides' *Medea*. It is in Aristotle's *Poetics* (written some decades after the heyday of tragedy in fifth-century Athens) that we first find articulated the view that an unhappy ending, with a change from prosperity to misfortune, is, if not definitive of the genre, at least a mark of those plays that are best constructed and most essentially tragic.

Aristotle also identifies beginnings and endings as elements in a connected narrative sequence and as points of demarcation required by any plot that is a well-structured whole, and it is in this connection that he defines them:

A beginning is that which does not come necessarily after something else, but after which it is natural for another thing to exist or come to be. An end, on the contrary, is that which naturally comes after something else, either as its necessary sequel or as its usual sequel, but itself has nothing after it. (*Poetics* 1450b27–30, tr. Hutton 1982)

The appearance of obviousness is (as often for Aristotle) deceptive. The problem of creating beginnings and endings in the continuous flow of events confronts all writers, but presents particular complexities for ancient authors, given that virtually all their stories are taken from longer myths familiar in general if not in detail to the audience. Aristotle here anticipates the interest of modern narratology in the workings of beginnings and endings as such (Richardson 2002). How does a beginning deal with what (inevitably) came before, so that it feels like an acceptable beginning? How does it prepare us for what follows? How does an ending complete the action of the play, and how does it deal with what (inevitably) comes after? How does it create what has come to be called closure, the sense of finality or conclusiveness at the end of a work (Kermode 1967/2000, Smith 1968, Fowler 1989, 1997)?

If beginnings and endings in Greek tragedy do not define the genre by a predictable trajectory from happiness to misery, they remain definitive in other respects. Beginnings have a programmatic authority in drawing the audience's attention to the tragedy's characters, choice of story, approach, and relationship to the genre (Dunn 1992, Segal 1992); endings have, or appear to have, an interpretative authority, since the point of closure may also be seen as the point at which the audience can finally look back at a completed action and read it fully, in a version of what Barbara Herrnstein Smith has called retrospective patterning (Smith 1968, 10–14, 212, 218). The ancient tragedians both enlist these modes of authority and undercut or complicate them, offering us at times obscure or misleading beginnings and open or disconcerting endings.

In what follows, I consider some of the varieties of tragic beginning and ending, drawing on examples from the three surviving Greek tragedians to explore some of the functions and effects of these parts of the drama, the development of conventions of beginning and ending, and the ways in which writers create, meet, or undercut audience expectations.

A tragedy may begin with the *parodos* (entry and first song of the chorus), but this is most often preceded by a prologue of some kind: a long opening speech, a dialogue scene, or a combination of the two (usually speech followed by dialogue). Some tragedies also include a monody (solo song by a single character) before the *parodos*, or a *kommos* (duet between the chorus and a character) in its place.

In the plays that have come down to us, Aeschylus' beginnings are formally the most varied, perhaps in part because some of his plays (*Eumenides, Libation Bearers, Seven against Thebes*) form the second or third part of a trilogy and thus have a kind of secondary status as beginnings, but also perhaps because set conventions for the prologue develop gradually in the course of the fifth century. Of the plays that we know either begin a trilogy or stand alone, both *Persians* (perhaps our earliest extant tragedy) and *Suppliants* begin with the entrance of the chorus; *Agamemnon* begins with a monologue followed by a particularly long and complex choral sequence.[1] In all three, however, the chorus dominates the opening moments of the play as it relates past events and expresses the emotional valence of these events, evoking a mood of shared apprehension.

All but one of Sophocles' extant tragedies begin with a dialogue scene in which two characters speak, sometimes joined by a third (the exception is *Women of Trachis*, in which monologue is followed by dialogue). In all our extant plays the first two characters are joined by some sort of affective tie, such as patronage, friendship, or kinship: we see (for example) Athena and her favorite mortal, Odysseus (*Ajax*), Antigone and her sister Ismene (*Antigone*), Oedipus and the priest who speaks for Oedipus' trusting subjects (*Oedipus the King*). But in spite of these modes of alliance the perspective evoked is inevitably double, not single, and tensions and differences characteristically emerge as the story begins to unfold.

Euripides begins almost all his plays with a monologue, of a type so marked that Aristophanes makes fun of it in his *Frogs* for its stock narrative of past events. The speaker may be the play's central character (Helen in her name-play), a secondary character (Heracles' old father Amphitryon in *Heracles*), a minor character (the nurse in *Medea*), or a god (Aphrodite in *Hippolytus*), and the speeches vary accordingly. But what distinguishes these Euripidean monologues in general from others is their relative detachment from the action and the thoroughness and directness (unmotivated by the story) with which they provide information. Consider, by way of contrast, the opening monologue of Aeschylus' *Agamemnon* (1–39). The watchman, asking the gods for a respite, tells us where and who he is as part of a complaint about the task he has been forced to undertake, years of watching from the palace roof in Argos for the signal fires that will mark a Greek victory in Troy. He alludes to the circumstances, breaks off to announce that he has sighted the beacons, and concludes with some ominous and enigmatic words about conditions in Argos. This speech is part prayer, part soliloquy, and part news report. But Euripidean prologues, though they may reflect the circumstances and feelings of the speaker (the nurse in *Medea*, for example, narrates the chain of events that led to her mistress's current predicament in the form of a wish that none of it had ever happened) are never really a part of the action. The lack of any clear motivation for the detailed account the speaker gives of the past and the absence (in many instances) of an obvious addressee gives the impression not of a soliloquy but of speech directed to the audience, one that self-consciously fulfills the function of a prologue in providing necessary information. This impression is particularly strong in the plays in which a god speaks the prologue and never reappears: the combination of apparent authority over the play's events and absence from these events makes these figures seem almost an approximation of a narrator.

All beginnings must of course provide a certain amount of information, however they do so. Athenian playwrights had an opportunity at the *proagón* (preliminary presentation of the playwrights and their casts) to give some kind of advance notice of their subject matter, but it may not have been extensive, and prologues generally seem to take pains to let the spectators know who the characters are, where the characters are, and what has happened by the time the story begins. To some extent, the last of these follows from the first, given tragedy's repeated use of well-known myths; in a fragment from the fourth-century BCE comic playwright Antiphanes (fr. 189 *PCG*) the speaker complains that his job is much harder than that of the tragedian, who need only introduce a character named Oedipus for the audience to be acquainted with both background and plot. But many figures in myth are associated with enough different stories, or long enough stories, to make many tragedies, and many of these stories exist in variant forms; furthermore, even if we can deduce story from character, we still need to know exactly where we are in the story and what has happened up to this point. (This is to some extent true even in a trilogy, since any amount of time may have passed between one play and the next.)

Compare two plays in which Oedipus is the central character. The beginning of Sophocles' *Oedipus the King* shows us Oedipus as a ruler in conversation with his people, identified as the descendants of Cadmus (1); he refers to himself as "Oedipus, whose fame is known to all" (8). The spectators know, then, not only who is speaking, but where and when. We are in Thebes, and Oedipus is king; the riddle of the Sphinx, the killing of Oedipus' father, and the marriage with his mother are all in the past, but not yet discovered; fame has not yet turned to infamy. But in Sophocles' later *Oedipus at Colonus*, the opening words here (again spoken by the title character) situate the speaker at quite a different point in his story:

> Child of the blind old man, Antigone,
> what place have we come to, what people's city is this?
> Who will receive the wandering Oedipus
> today with scanty gifts...? (1–4)

Oedipus' address to his daughter serves also as a self-identification, and tells us that this play takes place after his fall, in changed circumstances, and in a new setting. But there is a further difference. The earlier play evokes a story and a setting found in the tradition as far back as Homer's *Odyssey* (11.271–80); once the audience knows where and when we are, they know what the play must reveal. But the plot of *Oedipus at Colonus* seems to have been in part Sophocles' own invention; the opening questions thus not only provide the audience with information, but also point to their own lack of knowledge and to the mystery of the particular significance of this setting (Dunn 1992, 2–3).

The beginning, then, may supplement or confirm the audience's partial knowledge to clarify the point at which we enter the story; it may also limit clarification, and it may exploit that partial knowledge by playing with the audience's expectations. In Aeschylus' *Prometheus Bound*, at the end of the opening monody, Prometheus expresses alarm at the sound of approaching wings (124–25). The audience will presumably wonder whether this is the vulture, come to tear out his liver, but as it turns out, that is far in the future; what he hears now is the friendly chorus of the daughters of Ocean in their winged chariot.

Euripides' prologues may also play with the spectators' expectations in spite of their apparent straightforwardness in identifying the speaker (who generally names himself or herself without the dramatic pretext offered by the other two tragedians) and circumstances. In some plays (such as *Ion*, *Helen*, and *Electra*) he makes use of less well-known stories or variants an audience will be slow to recognize. Why, in the prologue of *Helen*, is Helen in Egypt and not in Troy or Greece? (She turns out to have spent the war there while the Greeks fought for a phantom.) Why is an unnamed farmer speaking the prologue in *Electra*? (It turns out that Aegisthus has married Electra to this man so that her children cannot be a threat to him.) In others, the very directness and completeness of the information may keep the audience guessing for some time exactly where this play will start. In *Phoenician Women*, for example,

Jocasta gives us a detailed history and genealogy of the house of Laius; an audience familiar with the tradition that she killed herself after discovering her marriage to her son will be surprised to learn that that discovery is far in the past and that she is a helpless spectator of the battle between the sons she bore to Oedipus.

As this last example suggests, the opening scene or song of a tragedy typically acquaints the audience with at least some of the events that have led up to this beginning. How this is done not only affects what version of events the audience presupposes and how much it knows from the outset, but also the perspective from which these events are viewed.

In *Agamemnon*, the watchman lets us know that the war in Troy is over, but that matters here at home are not as they should be. As he leaves the stage, the old men of the chorus enter, chanting in lyric anapests; with their opening words ("It is now the tenth year since Priam's great adversary, the lord Menelaus, and Agamemnon...," 40–42) they take us back to the origins of the war and to its outset. Menelaus and Agamemnon are pictured as justly taking vengeance, with divine support, for Helen's abduction by Paris. But Helen herself ("a woman of many men," 62) is a dubious reason for the suffering on both sides. Nor has the suffering been limited to death in battle. As they move into song the old men go back in memory to a troubling portent that ultimately (and somewhat mysteriously) led to the sacrifice of Agamemnon's daughter Iphigenia to gain a fair wind for the fleet. The singers omit the actual moment of sacrifice ("what came next I neither saw nor speak of," 248), but even as they hope that everything will turn out well they do not conceal their fears or the words of the prophet Calchas about "child-avenging Anger" (155).

Aeschylus has not yet given us the whole of the relevant past. At later moments in the play other speakers (Cassandra, Aegisthus) will reveal the terrible earlier history of the house of Atreus and its connection with present events. But the chorus has already set before us not only past events themselves but the complex and unexpected connections of these events. One thing leads to another in unforeseen ways; no story is complete in itself; no end can be relied on. The trilogy will bear out these conclusions.

The beginning of Sophocles' *Antigone* tells the story of what came before first through a conversation between Antigone and her sister Ismene, and then in the voice of the chorus. Because the past is initially presented through dialogue it is made known only gradually and piecemeal. Antigone speaks of the suffering that has come from their father and that dishonors the family, and wonders whether Ismene has heard the latest news; Ismene replies that she knows of their two brothers' death, but no more than that. Antigone then tells her sister of Creon's decree that Eteocles alone will receive funeral honors, while Polynices remains unburied, and proposes that the two of them bury their brother. In her reply, Ismene reminds her sister of their father's self-blinding and death and of their mother's suicide.

This way of introducing the past not only allows it to emerge with a certain naturalness but also presents it as the differentiated experience of individual characters. Antigone sees the past in terms of family dishonor, and will not allow any additional dishonor; Ismene, in contrast, sees the family history as one of death and destruction, and hopes that she and her sister can escape with their lives. When the chorus enters, we are given yet another perspective; in describing the battle just ended, and hailing the Theban victory rather than lamenting the dead brothers, these citizens tell the history of a royal family that posed a danger to the city and its inhabitants (Roberts 1989, 163–64).

If the beginning of *Agamemnon* adumbrates a past of linked and overlapping stories, and the beginning of *Antigone* constructs a past that is a different story for different characters, the beginnings of certain Euripidean tragedies suggest – in different ways – the existence of several possible pasts, only one of which the poet has chosen to write. *Medea* begins with a narration of the past as something that ought never to have occurred but did. In *Helen*, the title character relates a past that departs from the usual version of her story. The prologue of *Orestes*, like that of *Phoenician Women*, gives such an extensive retelling – going back to the distant past of the house of Atreus, and including almost every character associated with the myth – that it gives an impression of inclusiveness and authority. But the prologue ends with an unexpected twist: Orestes has indeed killed his mother, but instead of escaping the Erinyes by the judgment of an Athenian court (the version in the *Oresteia*) faces the prospect of being condemned to death by an Argive court – unless Menelaus rescues him.

Unless Menelaus rescues him. The beginning of a tragedy does not simply include or allude to the past; it generally looks ahead to what is to follow as well. If audience knowledge precludes major surprises it leaves room for both minor surprises and suspense (when and how will the expected ending come about?). It also fosters the use of foreshadowing, since the sorts of clues that in invented plots are accessible only the second time through may in traditional, myth-based tragedy be noticed at the initial presentation. Sometimes the beginning of a play anticipates the future only by the ordinary expectations and fears of characters: the Electra of Euripides' *Orestes* hopes Menelaus will rescue her brother; the chorus in Aeschylus' *Persians* dreads bad news of Xerxes' army, long since gone to Greece; Sophocles' King Oedipus promises to do all he can to find out what has caused the plague in his city. But a play may also begin with a prophecy known to one or more characters. The opening chorus of *Agamemnon* includes the prophecies of Calchas about the sacrifice of Iphigenia, already fulfilled except for certain ominous words about secret anger and the child that is to be avenged. Four of Sophocles' prologue scenes (in *Oedipus at Colonus*, *Women of Trachis*, *Electra*, and *Philoctetes*) include or refer to the words of oracles.

The famous ambiguity of oracles finds an analogue in the allusive language of foreshadowing or prolepsis, a mode of anticipation particularly prominent in Aeschylus (Lebeck 1971). The opening lines of *Persians* speak of "the Persians gone to the land of Greece" (1) but the word translated as "gone" can also have the meaning of "dead" or "ruined," and thus anticipates both the outcome the audience knows must follow and the play's gradual shift from uninformed anxiety to mourning. The opening passages of *Agamemnon* are still more densely proleptic. The images of fire, the images of birds and their young, and the patterns of three evoked by the chorus all anticipate subsequent developments in the trilogy.

As in so many other respects, Euripidean prologues are distinctive in the mode of anticipation they sometimes exhibit. In five plays in which a god speaks the prologue (*Alcestis*, *Hippolytus*, *Trojan Women*, *Ion*, and *Bacchae*) that god not only sums up the past but also predicts the future. These predictions are not like ordinary prophecies:

they are apparently straightforward declarations of the god's plans and they are available only to the audience (Hamilton 1978). But their apparent straightforward-ness – as with other aspects of Euripidean prologues – is misleading: in at least one of these (*Ion*) and some would say in two others (*Bacchae* and *Hippolytus*), although the god's will is ultimately fulfilled, the details of its fulfillment are not quite as stated, and in one case (*Ion*) the god's plan goes seriously astray and the mortals behave in unpredictable but not surprising ways. In the beginning of *Ion*, Hermes tells how Apollo raped Creusa, the princess of Athens, how she abandoned the child out of shame, and how that child (now named Ion) was raised in Delphi. He also anticipates the eventual happy reunion, through Apollo's machinations, of Creusa and her son. As the play proceeds, however, mortal resentment, longing, and disappointment (all natural and understandable) cause Apollo's projected plot to go off-track; another divinity, Athena, must be introduced at the close of the play to return things to their proper course.

This brings us to the endings of tragedies. These have received more critical attention than beginnings, for several reasons: the traditional association of tragedy with a particular type of ending, the sense that it is the end that confirms or enables interpretation of the drama as a whole, the general interest in issues of closure in literary studies in the past few decades, and the existence of certain particularly problematic endings.

With tragic endings as with tragic beginnings we see somewhat more formal variety in Aeschylus than in his successors, but the chorus plays a prominent role in all of his endings (often as a partner in a concluding exchange, spoken, chanted, or sung) and has the last word in all but two. In Sophocles and Euripides the choral role in the ending is diminished but formalized; dialogue exchange or long speech and response dominate their final scenes, but in all of their extant plays (with one possible and debated exception, Sophocles' *Women of Trachis*)[2] the chorus still speaks the last words in what seems to have gradually evolved into a conventional coda, a few lines of verse, usually anapestic, that mark (in a curtainless theater) the ending of the play. This coda is (not surprisingly) most formulaic in Euripides: two of his choral tags, whose sentiments are broadly applicable, are repeated with little or no variation in several plays. In other respects, too, Euripidean endings are most likely to make use of conventional features that in one way or another underscore closure (Dunn 1996); the most prominent of these is the *deus ex machina*, the god who appears above the action, sometimes suspended by the *mêchanê* or crane, sometimes on the top of the stage building.

As I noted above, the endings of Greek tragedies are not necessarily unhappy, although they are generally fairly solemn (a word that better conveys the sense of the adjective *tragikos*, "tragic," in the fifth century). Aeschylus' *Oresteia* ends with the acquittal of Orestes on the charge of matricide and the reconciliation of the Erinyes with the city of Athens; Sophocles' *Philoctetes* ends with the return of Philoctetes from pain and isolation to companionship, victory, and healing; and in a set of endings that have tempted critics to look for a different generic term (tragicomedy, romance, or melodrama) Euripides has his characters reunite (*Helen, Ion, Iphigenia among the Taurians*), escape from danger (*Helen, Iphigenia among the Taurians, Orestes*), or even return from the dead (*Alcestis*).

Both these endings and the endings that fit the preferred Aristotelian model of a change of fortune from good to bad contribute to our sense of closure by resolving questions raised in the play and bringing the play's action somehow to a successful conclusion. Different modes of dramatic closure may be associated with recurrent plot patterns or motifs: vengeance completed (Aeschylus' *Oresteia*, Euripides' *Medea* and *Hecuba*, the *Electra*s of both Sophocles and Euripides), mysteries solved (Sophocles' *Oedipus the King*, Euripides' *Ion*), lost relations found (Euripides' *Alcestis*, *Ion*, *Iphigenia among the Taurians*), danger escaped (Aeschylus' *Suppliants*, Euripides' *Iphigenia among the Taurians* and *Helen*), disaster realized (Euripides' *Trojan Women*), prophecy fulfilled (Sophocles' *Oedipus the King*, *Ajax*, and *Women of Trachis*), arrogance or strength brought down (Aeschylus' *Persians*, Sophocles' *Ajax*, and Euripides' *Bacchae*).

Many of these types of endings reinforce closure not only by meeting expectations raised in the course of the play but also by evoking natural or cultural markers of closure in human lives: departure, reunion or reconciliation, solution or fulfillment, death, and ritual (Smith 1968, 101–2, 172–82). Not surprisingly, mourning is the most common of concluding rituals; of twenty-three plays that end in one way or another with death, nineteen end with some form of or reference to burial or mourning ritual. We find other rituals less often, but *Eumenides*, the last play in the *Oresteia*, ends with a celebratory procession to install the Erinyes – now become kindly – in their new home, and some Euripidean endings allude to a form of ritual that is to be established in the future. In *Hippolytus*, for example, Artemis declares that in the future young Athenian girls will offer up their hair in Hippolytus' honor before their wedding day.

Such markers may, however, also be used in such a way as to interfere with closure. In several plays the ritual of burial is deprived of some of its effect by the exclusion of a would-be participant (Roberts 1993). In Euripides' *Medea*, for example, Medea forbids Jason any part in his children's burial – which she alone, their murderer, will carry out; a couple united only in their grief for their dead children will remain divided in the ritual expression of that grief.

Division and uncertainty undercut or qualify closure at the end of a number of tragedies. The effect is perhaps most striking in those Aeschylean plays whose endings are only provisional, since they come first or second in a trilogy: *Agamemnon* ends with a quarrel, *Libation Bearers* ends with a series of questions (including, tellingly, "where is the end?" 1075), and *Suppliants* ends with the emergence of a division of opinion between two parts of the chorus (or two choruses; scholars differ on this point). But plays that have no sequel may also incorporate in their endings such anti-closural topoi as division, disbelief, and uncertainty. Orestes and Electra are separated forever at the end of Euripides' *Electra*, as are Agave and her father Cadmus at the end of his *Bacchae*. At the end of Euripides' *Orestes*, Apollo's concluding arrangements meet with an acceptance strongly tinged with skepticism from the characters involved. At the end of *Oedipus the King*, a scene explored by a number of scholars in recent decades (Taplin 1983a, Kitzinger 1993), we do not have any clear sense of the outcome that is to follow the play's dreadful discoveries. Will Oedipus be exiled, as he requests? Will Creon force him to linger on in Thebes? The presence of this uncertainty is particularly striking in a play that in other senses exhibits such strong closure, revealing the fulfillment of all the story's oracles and with them fulfilling the audience's expectations.

So far I have been speaking of the audience's expectations as aroused and fulfilled by the events of the plot, and as confirmed or disrupted by the author's use of various closural modes. With endings as with beginnings, however, audience expectations in Greek tragedy are conditioned not only by the unfolding events of the plot, but also by their knowledge of the myth from which that plot is taken. To some extent, this knowledge may further reinforce closure: we expect in *Oedipus the King* that Oedipus will prove to have killed his father and married his mother not only because the prophecies in the play predict this outcome, but also because the traditional story demands it. When Agamemnon's corpse is revealed at the end of Aeschylus' play, his death is not only overdetermined by a variety of causes the drama has set before us (Clytemnestra's anger at Iphigenia's death, her love for Aegisthus, Aegisthus' own desire for vengeance, the curse on the house of Atreus, Agamemnon's actions at Troy); it is also the expected end of a very old and very familiar story, already a part of the tradition in Homer's *Odyssey* (1.35–36, 3.193–94, 4.519–35, 11.404–434, 24.20–22, 96–97, 199–202).

In some plays, however, the traditional ending is made to conflict with the direction the play has been taking; it thus seems to enforce (rather than reinforce) closure and to some extent to disrupt the audience's expectations. In Sophocles' *Philoctetes*, Odysseus has brought Achilles' son Neoptolemus to a deserted island so that he may trick Philoctetes (marooned there years before) into rejoining the Greeks and helping them take Troy. As the play draws to an end, Neoptolemus has abandoned deception for friendly persuasion but has failed to overcome Philoctetes' rage at the Greeks who abandoned him. Philoctetes reminds Neoptolemus of his earlier (false) promise to take him home, and Neoptolemus prepares to make this promise good; the two of them set off together. It appears, and this impression is reinforced by stylistic elements of the scene (Hoppin 1990), that the play is going to depart quite radically from tradition; if these two men simply return home, the Greek expedition will fail. At this point, however, Heracles appears, and commands them to embark for Troy and capture the city; the myth is back on track.

Readings of what some have called the two endings of the *Philoctetes* vary, but it is at least arguable that the ending the myth requires is the right ending in other respects and does no violence to the drama (Schein 2001). Philoctetes, who suffers from a hideous wound, will be healed, and will regain his rightful place. Furthermore, his final conversation with Neoptolemus has suggested that he would like to do as the younger man asks, but cannot bring himself to let go of his anger. The *deus ex machina* may be read as enabling such a letting go. In Euripides's *Orestes*, however, we find the tension between mythical outcome and plot pushed to an incomprehensible extreme. In the final scene of a play that derails the traditional story even as it echoes every earlier version (Wolff 1968, Zeitlin 1980), Orestes and Pylades (condemned to death for matricide along with Electra and disappointed of Menelaus' help) have tried to kill Helen and have kidnapped Hermione, the daughter of Helen and Menelaus. Orestes, confronting Menelaus, stands on the roof with his sword at Hermione's throat and prepares to set fire to the palace. At this point Apollo – whose oracle has been thoroughly discredited in the course of the play for commanding matricide – arrives as *deus ex machina* and commands an outcome appropriate to the traditional story, with more or less happy endings for all, including a marriage between Orestes and his erstwhile hostage Hermione. This disjunction between the direction of the plot and the imposed (if traditional) conclusion makes the ending one of the most disconcerting in all of Greek tragedy, and it is hard not to see it in part as a comment on the struggle between the inherited myth and the natural direction in which the playwright wishes to take the play.[3]

A myth known to an audience can also qualify closure by leading the audience to think of what lies beyond the end of the play. We know that the death of Agamemnon at Clytemnestra's hands, traditional though it is, cannot really be the end of Aeschylus' play, since the same tradition includes Orestes' vengeance for his father's death. Here the open-endedness (created not only by audience knowledge but also by various forms of prolepsis in the drama itself) simply looks forward to the rest of the trilogy. But there are also single plays in which audience knowledge of the myth qualifies or complicates closure. At the end of *Philoctetes*, for example, Heracles promises Philoctetes and Neoptolemus victory at Troy, but warns them that when they sack the city they must respect the temples of the gods. An audience that knows the tradition knows that the Greeks in general will disregard this command and that Neoptolemus – who in this play has been an almost entirely sympathetic, if at first misguided, character – will commit a striking act of sacrilege in killing Priam at his household altar.

This type of ending, in which a subtle allusion to a familiar story opens up a future beyond and even at odds with the mood of the play's conclusion, seems to be particularly characteristic of Sophocles (Roberts 1988). Euripidean endings, in contrast, often seem to be trying to avoid such openness by including (almost enclosing) the future in a speech by a *deus ex machina*. Most of these concluding speeches prophesy the future of the surviving characters, often in such detail as to appear to leave little to the audience's imagination. Apollo's speech at the end of *Orestes* tells us that Helen will become a star; that Menelaus will remarry; that Orestes will be exiled for a year, will be acquitted at Athens, and will marry Hermione; that Neoptolemus, who expects to marry Hermione, will be killed at Delphi; that Electra and Pylades will marry; that Menelaus will rule in Mycenae and Orestes in Argos. This speech thus includes not only elements traditional in the inherited myth or familiar from its treatment by others (Orestes' marriage with Hermione, the trial at Athens) but bits of other, tangential stories (Neoptolemus' death) and unusual elements (Menelaus' remarriage). It seems designed to give the audience everything it could expect and more, so that what is outside the drama (*exo tou dramatos*, in Aristotle's phrase, *Poetics* 1453b32, 1454b3) is actually contained within it, and constitutes no sort of distraction or opening-up.

In other respects too Euripides appears to make regular use of certain conventions, "closing gestures" in Francis Dunn's term (Dunn 1996), to effect or reinforce closure. The authority of the *deus ex machina*, the prophecy that contains the future, the regular use of the *aition*, or aetiology (an explanation of some later institution or monument known to the audience in terms of the play's events) – all of these to some extent have the effect of confirming the end, in part by inducing a kind of stasis. The god's authority declares the proper end, the prophecy prevents us from wondering about the future, and the *aition* displaces the movement of historical narrative with the stasis of contemporaneous presence or repeated practice. His choral codas too, by their generality of application and their stock morals, seem to cut short speculation in favor of a simplified understanding of the events.

But as Dunn has argued, "this blaze of clarity leaves the process of closure all the more uncertain" (Dunn 1996, 7). Euripides' devices are by their very nature subversive, since they may be said to draw attention to themselves as conventions, as self-conscious rhetorical gestures. But they also lend themselves to particular modes of subversion in individual plays. The god who appears (or whose authority is evoked) at the end may already have had that authority compromised. Apollo fares particularly badly in this respect, both in Euripides' *Orestes*, where earlier criticisms of the matricide he commanded linger to taint the resolution he brings, and in *Ion*, where he avoids facing any criticism of his behavior and sends Athena in his place. When Artemis appears at the end of *Hippolytus*, her promise that Aphrodite too will suffer the death of a favorite seems trivial next to the picture of human suffering and reconciliation provided by Theseus and his son. The prophecy that appears to present a settled (and generally familiar) future may frame that future in such a way as to make it seem problematic: at the end of Euripides' *Electra*, Castor and Pollux predict for Orestes the familiar Aeschylean sequence of pursuit by the Erinyes and ultimate acquittal in Athens; Electra, as expected, will marry Pylades. But this resolution is deprived of any evident justice by the accompanying declaration that what Apollo did was wrong, and likewise of any redemptive force by the exile and separation imposed on the wretched and remorseful siblings. Euripidean aetiologies, as Francis Dunn has argued, include puzzling ambivalences and discontinuities (Dunn 1996, 45–63, 94–96, 136–37; Dunn 2000). The rite Artemis establishes at the end of *Hippolytus* in compensation for the hero's sufferings is also said to commemorate Phaedra's love, a central cause of that suffering; when at the end of *Helen* the Dioscuri (brothers of the heroine and *dei ex machina*) announce that mortals will in the future call by Helen's name the island where she stopped on her way to Egypt, the insignificance of the link between plot and later fact seems merely to trivialize the aetiological gesture. And Euripides' choral codas, especially the ones that recur at the ends of several plays, have seemed so abrupt and simplistic as to provoke readerly resistance and scholarly claims of spuriousness. We encounter the following at the end of five very different tragedies (*Alcestis, Andromache, Helen, Bacchae*, and with a different first line, *Medea*):

> Many are the shapes divinities take,
> Much that's unanticipated the gods accomplish,
> What we expect goes unfulfilled,
> And the god finds a way for the unexpected.
> Such was the outcome of this matter.

A number of the plays to which I have already alluded end in ways that challenge any simple reading. When Heracles makes Philoctetes abandon his resistance and rejoin the other Greeks, should we see this as a redemptive move that reintegrates him into a society exemplified by the honest and sympathetic young Neoptolemus, or the betrayal of a principled hatred for a treacherous enemy exemplified by the opportunistic Odysseus? When Apollo returns the plot of *Orestes* to its traditional outcome in a manner quite at odds with the preceding action, should we see this as an ironic critique of the god, as a reflection on the mess that mortals make of things when they act without divine guidance, or as a metatheatrical comment on tragedies and how they end?

One of the most controversial endings is that of Sophocles' *Electra*. This play tells essentially the same story as Aeschylus' *Libation Bearers*: Orestes returns from exile in disguise, and with his sister Electra's help takes vengeance on Clytemnestra and her lover Aegisthus. Electra, not Orestes, is the central character here, and there are other significant departures from the Aeschylean version, but the most striking comes at the end. Orestes (spurred on by Electra) has killed Clytemnestra first, in a reversal of the Aeschylean order, and now forces Aegisthus into the house to meet his death. The chorus, left behind on stage with Electra, chants a short coda, celebrating the success and freedom of the family of Atreus, and the play ends. The reversal of the deaths allows Sophocles' play to end with the less problematic of the two killings; the chorus's words suggest that we should regard this as a happy outcome; and, most striking of all, the Erinyes neither appear (as in Aeschylus' play) nor are mentioned at the end (as in Euripides' version). On the other hand, the chorus's words, like many choral codas, seem inadequate to what preceded; Aegisthus has made an ominous reference to the future evils of the house, and the Erinyes have been mentioned in a general way earlier in the play (112, 276, 491, 1079). What are we to make of this? In particular, given that the audience knows the events of the Aeschylean ending, should we take their omission by Sophocles to signal that we should assume that ending (the Erinyes will pursue Orestes), or that ending plus its resolution in *Eumenides* (the Erinyes will pursue Orestes but will eventually be reconciled to his acquittal), or neither of the above (the Erinyes will never bother this Orestes)? Alternatively, should we simply assume that since this is Electra's play we are not meant to be concerned with an ending that features Orestes? And how will each of these choices affect our reading of the play as a whole?

The endings I have mentioned so far are debated in the sense that there is not clear agreement on how to read them, but they are all at least accepted as the work of the playwright. Several Greek tragedies present us with endings whose authenticity has at some time or another been questioned, most notably the final scenes of *Seven against Thebes* and *Iphigenia at Aulis* and the closing lines of *Oedipus the King* and *Phoenician Women* (which partially replicate each other).

I will not enter into these debates here, but will just note that the claim of spuriousness itself points to the way in which individual tragedies were read as part of a continuing myth and in relation to previous tragic versions of that myth, since each instance involves a supposed interpolation of material from another version or a continuation of the story, sometimes one familiar from a well-known tragedy. The ongoing debate about these endings also reflects our own lack of certainty (and our occasional presumptuousness) about ancient closural convention. It is a similar lack of certainty that has led scholars to be suspicious of the codas at the end of Sophocles' and Euripides' tragedies. But though we may have particular reasons to reject some of these, a general rejection is uncalled for. These endings are formulaic, and rarely shed any particular light on the tragedies they conclude, but they mark in several ways the boundary between the world of the play and the various worlds to which it is tangential: the world of continuing myth, the larger world of discourse, the world outside the theater (Roberts 1987; Dunn 1996, 13–25).

Debated endings should remind us that just as the endings of Greek tragedies may confound our sense of the tragic, they may also confound our sense of endings. They should also remind us of the role played by the spectator or reader in the creation of closure. Our interpretation of particular tragedies thus calls for an understanding of the general conventions and strategies of tragic beginnings and endings and for a certain self-consciousness in our own assumptions about what it means for a tragic plot to have Aristotle's required beginning and end. (I leave the middles to others in this volume.)

NOTES

1 I have omitted *Prometheus Bound* here both because some scholars doubt that it is by Aeschylus and because we cannot be absolutely sure of its place in a trilogy, if indeed it was part of a trilogy. (My own feeling is that it is Aeschylean, that it is the first play in its trilogy, and that it shows its lateness in the Aeschylean corpus in part by its use of a dialogue scene as prologue.)
2 Some of the manuscripts of *Women of Trachis* ascribe lines 1275–78 to the chorus, others to Heracles' son Hyllus.
3 Aristotle criticizes such uses of the *deus ex machina*, since he holds that the resolution should properly arise from the plot (*Poetics* 1454a37–1454b6). Euripides – in many respects a critic as well as a practitioner of tragedy – may also be commenting critically on the practice he exemplifies here.

FURTHER READING

In the last few decades of the twentieth century, partly because of the dominance of narratology in literary studies, beginnings and endings emerged as a frequent subject of critical and theoretical interest, with a particular emphasis on what came to be called closure. Brian Richardson's edited collection *Narrative Dynamics: Essays on Time, Plot, Closure, and Frames* (Richardson 2002) contains a helpful section on beginnings and endings (Part IV, chs. 18–23), including a chapter by Edward Said, excerpted from his influential book *Beginnings: Intention and Method* (Said 1975). For a good collection of essays on beginnings specifically in Greek and Latin literature readers can then turn to Dunn and Cole 1992, and in particular to Charles Segal's essay in that volume (Segal 1992). Readers interested in the study of closure should begin with two seminal works that are still of interest: Kermode 1967, now available also in a second edition with an epilogue (2000), which draws our attention to the fictive nature of endings not only in literature but also in our histories and in our lives, and Smith 1968, which combines detailed close reading of poems with the application of insights drawn from cognitive psychology. They should then have a look at Fowler 1989 and Fowler 1997; these discuss the issue of closure in classical literature and classical scholarship and also consider closure as a theoretical construct. Both are reprinted in Fowler's collection of essays, Fowler 2000; the second first appeared in *Classical Closure: Reading the End in Greek and Latin Literature* (Roberts, Dunn, and Fowler 1997), which includes twelve essays on endings in different genres in ancient literature and a fairly comprehensive bibliography of work to date in the field. Among works cited there I would particularly recommend Dunn 1996 not only for its treatment of Euripidean endings but also for its general insights into issues of closure.

CHAPTER TEN

Lyric

Luigi Battezzato

Song and dance are traditional features of the tragic genre. Song is a special mode of delivery; it is a "marked" term (Nagy 1990, 5) that stands in opposition to the normal way of declaiming verse, just as "dance" is opposed to normal movements. In tragedy, actors or choruses do not mention the fact that they deliver iambic trimeters; they refer to their recited lines as speech (Hall 2002, 7). They often comment, however, on their singing and/or dancing. In fact, "singing" often comes close to meaning "speaking as a poet" (cf. Nagy 1990, 33–40). Song and dance perform-ances become a theme that is commented on in the play (Szondi 1987). They are often presented as a spontaneous reaction to the events on stage:

> Nonetheless the dirge without a lyre
> is chanted,
> the dirge of the Erinys is chanted by my mind, self-taught
> within me [*autodidaktos esôthen*], altogether lacking
> the cherished confidence of hope.
> And my inward parts do not speak vainly...
> (Aeschylus, *Agamemnon* 990–96; trans. Lloyd-Jones 1970)

The chorus here alludes to a crucial passage of the *Odyssey*, where the singer Phemius explains the origins of his skill: "I have learned by myself [*autodidaktos eimi*] [the art of singing]; god made grow [*enephusen*] all sorts of ways [for song] into my mind" (22.347–48). Divine help is difficult to prove or rule out, but choral lyric in tragedy is certainly anything but spontaneous. In tragedy, whoever sings locates himself or herself in a literary tradition – a tradition that in fact often postdates the mythical events portrayed on stage. The lyric meters of tragedy follow the literary tradition of archaic choral song, the tradition of Pindar and Bacchylides. Its language has a Doric patina; Homeric words and phrases are more apt to occur; prayers, hymns, and other subgenres of non-dramatic lyric are taken up by tragic choruses and characters (Herington 1985). Not surprisingly, song is the best place in tragedy for metaliterary comments.

The tension between spontaneity and tradition contributes to the ambiguity of the choral voice, which can be taken either as the voice of the author or the judgment of an "ideal spectator." Metaliterary allusions (Euripides, *Heracles* 673–95) or bold general reflections that affirm the originality of the speaking voice (Aeschylus, *Agamemnon* 757–81) used to be understood as personal statements of the author. On the other hand, cautious, non-committal comments on the events on stage or reactions of horror to the atrocities perpetrated by the characters could be taken as a projection of the way a spectator should react to the play.

The very structure of tragedy betrays the subterfuge of spontaneity. Song is expected at some specific points in the play, and of some characters only. Comedy tells the spectators the names of its parts; for example, Aristophanes mentions the terms "*parabasis*" and "anapest" (*Peace* 735). Tragedy is less explicit (see, however, Lloyd 1992, 4–5, on the quasi-metaliterary use of *agón*, "contest [of words]"). Sophocles may have composed a prose manual entitled *On the Chorus*, but that is now lost (*Suda* σ 815 Adler; cf. Rossi 1971b, 77–78). For naming the parts of tragedy, we have to consult Aristophanes and Aristotle's *Poetics*. We also gain information from the commentaries on the plays, mostly anonymous, that are transmitted in the medieval manuscripts. These commentaries (called scholia; the singular is scholion) are part of a continuous scholarly tradition extending from the third century BCE to the fourteenth century CE.

The explicit labels of the scholarly tradition are not always a perfect fit for the rules implicit in tragic texts; these labels have, however, become standard in modern scholarship, and accordingly will be defined in the first five sections of this chapter. The next four sections deal with some of the unwritten rules of the tragic genre: the form of lyric dialogues, the choice of speakers and singers, the organization of dramatic time and choral narrative. The evolution of lyric structures from the allegedly ritual origins of tragedy to the late plays of Sophocles and Euripides is the subject of the last five sections.

Lyric, Song, *Parakatalogê*

The term "lyric" refers to lines accompanied by music. The word literally means "accompanied by the lyre." It will be accepted here, even though it does not correspond to ancient practice. Tragic lyric was sung to the accompaniment of the *aulos*, a wind instrument; the lyre was rarely used in tragedy (Pickard-Cambridge 1988, 165–67; West 1992, 351; see Wilson, chapter 12 in this volume). Choral songs were regularly accompanied by dance, both in tragedy and in other performance contexts. As Plato observed, "the choric art [*choreia*] as a whole consists of dance [*orchêsis*] and song [*ôdê*]" (*Laws* 654b3–4, trans. Barker 1984–89, 1: 141; cf. also 665a3; Herington 1985, 20–31; Pickard-Cambridge 1988, 246–57).

Our manuscripts do not specify which sections of the plays were sung; we can recognize lyric passages by certain linguistic peculiarities and by their meter (Mastronarde 2002b, 83 and 103–7). Actors sang one at a time. Some modern scholars believe that in a few instances (the hymn to Artemis in Euripides' *Hippolytus* 61–71, and the call for Helen's murder in Euripides' *Orestes* 1302–10), the actor accompanied the chorus, singing to the same text and music.

It is likely that music accompanied some passages that were not sung. This type of accompanied delivery is often called *parakataloge* (Barker 1984–89, 1: 191 and 234; Hall 1999a, 107; Pickard-Cambridge 1988, 156–64). We do not know whether *parakataloge* implied some special sort of chanted delivery. It is generally admitted that the *aulos* accompanied non-lyric anapests, trochaic tetrameters, and some iambic lines within lyric sections. Lyric anapests are differentiated from non-lyric or recitative anapests by certain metrical characteristics. (On these meters see West 1982, 91–95, 121–24.)

Parodos and Stasimon

According to Aristotle's *Poetics* (1452b22–24), "*Parodos* is the whole first utterance of the chorus, Stasimon is choral song [*melos*] proper, i.e., it contains no [recitative] anapests or trochaics" (translation and discussion in Dale 1969, 35). *Parodos*, literally "entrance" (plural *parodoi*), is the section delivered by the chorus while entering the stage. As Aristotle's definition implies, *parodoi* did not necessarily involve singing. In extant tragedy a *parodos* without singing occurs only in Euripides' *Hecuba*, where the chorus arrives on stage delivering recitative anapests. Stasimon (plural stasima) stands in opposition to *parodos*; literally, the term means "something that stays in place, stationary, stable," in reference to the fact that the chorus members took their position in the *orchêstra* and "stayed there" while singing (cf. Henrichs 1994–95, 62 and 93 n. 21).

Parodoi and stasima are generally preceded by the exit of one or more actors, and followed by the entrance of one or more actors: entrances and exits define the division of the tragedy into episodes (Taplin 1977, 49–60). (For a list of *parodoi* and stasima see Kranz 1933, 124–27; Rode 1971, 87–88.) In five extant tragedies, the chorus leaves the stage in the middle of a tragedy. The choral section delivered or sung on reentering on stage is called *epiparodos*, "*parodos* that is added over, second *parodos*" (for a discussion of the *epiparodos*, see Taplin 1977, 379–80). In a few plays, a secondary chorus appears and sings short lyric sections (for example, Euripides' *Suppliants*, 1123–64: Taplin 1977, 230–38).

Strophic Structure

All stasima and very many lyric passages exhibit a strophic structure whereby a strophe (*strophê*, plural *strophai*) is followed by an antistrophe (*hê antistrophê* or *hê antistrophos ôdê*). The antistrophe repeats the series of metrical units (not the words) of the strophe. Strophe refers to the "turning" (of the chorus), or "twists" of the music; the antistrophe is the "corresponding turn" or the "turning back" of the chorus. When a strophe is divided between different speakers, the antistrophe is normally divided at the same points. The speakers may change from strophe to antistrophe.

In tragedy, the metrical sequence of each strophe is repeated only once, in the antistrophe that follows it. This metrical correspondence, regulated by complex and (sometimes) debated metrical laws, is called responsion. In tragedy the strophe and antistrophe may be followed by a single odd stanza called the epode (*hê epôdos* [*ôdê*]: "the ode that comes after the ode"). Non-tragic lyric poets, on the other hand, had the option of repeating the metrical sequence of a strophe more than once in the same poem. A few short strophic types (the Sapphic strophe, for example) were repeated not only throughout a poem, but in different poems as well.

Aeschylus is known for the length and complexity of his lyric passages. The longest lyric passage in tragedy is the lament in *Libation Bearers* (306–478). The chorus, Orestes, and Electra sing eleven strophic pairs; the lament also includes some sections in anapests delivered by the chorus. Its structure is unusual and particularly complex (strophe 1, strophe 2, antistrophe 1, anapests, strophe 3, antistrophe 2, antistrophe 3, etc.). The average length of lyric structures is shorter; the *parodos* of *Agamemnon* is composed of six strophic pairs plus anapestic introduction and epode. The lyric sections of Sophocles and Euripides are never longer than three strophic pairs plus epode.

Less common types of stanza in tragic lyric include the proode, mesode, and ephymnion. The proode (*hê prôdos* [*ôdê*]: "the ode that precedes the ode") is a single stanza preceding the strophic structure (for example, in Euripides' *Bacchae* 64–72). The mesode (*hê mesôdos* [*ôdê*]: "the ode that occurs in the middle of an ode") is a lyric section that occurs between strophe and antistrophe, and is not repeated (for example, in Aeschylus' *Libation Bearers* 807–11). The mesode seems to be an innovation by Aeschylus, taken up in late plays of Euripides (Münscher 1927). The ephymnion ("what is sung afterwards; refrain") is a lyric refrain that recurs after a lyric section (for example, in Aeschylus' *Suppliants* 118–21 = 129–32).

In some instances a strophe occurs in the middle of an episode, and the responding antistrophe is sung later, after a long scene in trimeters or even after an intervening choral song or stasimon; for example, in Sophocles' *Philoctetes*, 391–402 responds with 507–18 (West 1982, 80). The chorus may occasionally sing a single astrophic lyric section in the middle of an episode (Euripides' *Electra* 585–95: see Taplin 1977, 208–9). If a lyric piece does not have a responding section, it is called astrophic, from the Greek *astrophon* ("which does not turn around"). Astrophic pieces were apparently common in late fifth-century non-tragic lyric, and this practice had an influence on late fifth-century tragedy, especially Euripides (Aristotle, *Problems* 19.15; Barker 1984–89, 1: 192–93 and 249–55). In tragedy, however, astrophic passages are much less common than strophic songs (Rode 1971, 85–86).

Dialogue and Song: *Kommos, Amoibaion, Epirrhêma*

The structure of actors' songs is much less rigid than that of choral lyric passages; the terminology used to define them is quite varied. Aristotle singled out *kommoi* ("lamentations") as an example of songs involving actors and chorus (*Poetics* 1452b24), but the term does not take account of the fact that many songs involving actors express joy. Some scholars refer to the *amoibaion* (plural *amoibaia*), i.e., dialogic section (Popp 1971). This is preferable as a general term. It refers to sung dialogues as well as to dialogues that mix sung and recited sections. *Epirrhêma* ("words added afterwards"; plural *epirrhêmata*) or "epirrhematic dialogue" is used when a spoken section follows upon song, or when sung and spoken sections are mixed together. In this chapter, I will use "*epirrhêma*" or "epirrhematic dialogue" when a lyric section includes spoken verses, and "lyric dialogue" when all the lines are sung.

The epirrhematic dialogues in Aeschylus often follow a strict symmetrical plan: the number of spoken lines following each strophe or antistrophe is the same (for an example see Aeschylus' *Seven against Thebes* 202–44). Sophocles and especially Euripides abandoned this rigid symmetry in favor of freer forms, and also wrote astrophic *epirrhêmata*. In epirrhematic dialogues, a character may complete a non-lyric line (typically the beginning of an iambic trimeter) initiated by someone else, and turn the ending into a lyric line. For instance, in Euripides' *Heracles* 1185–87, Theseus is cool and rational in the face of disaster, but the anguished Amphitryon completes Theseus' lines with song. In some cases, the same speaker changes type of delivery within the same sentence, moving from spoken iambic trimeters into sung lines or vice versa (for examples, see Aeschylus, *Agamemnon* 1147–48; Euripides, *Phoenician Women* 145–46). In those cases, it is obvious that the recited passages were accompanied by music. It is often tricky to decide whether or not a line was sung. The decision rests on the meter and on the presence of key linguistic characteristics (such as Doric alpha) which tend to be confused in manuscripts; moreover, these characteristics are present only in certain words, which may or may not occur in the lines under consideration.

Monodies

Aristophanes already used the term *monôdiai* to indicate lyric sections sung by the actors in opposition to *melê*, "songs" of the chorus (*Frogs* 849, 944, 1329–30). He did not consider lyric and epirrhematic dialogues, which made the problem of classifying forms much simpler. Monodies probably developed out of *amoibaia*, when the section sung by one actor was expanded. The borderline between *amoibaion* and monody is at times difficult to draw.

In Aeschylus and Sophocles we do not find any self-contained section where a single actor sings alone. In *Agamemnon* Cassandra sings a long lyric passage, but as part of a dialogue with the chorus (Cassandra and the chorus are also given some spoken lines). In the prologue of *Prometheus Bound* the protagonist alternates spoken and sung sections (88–127). Later in the play, when the character Io arrives on stage, she recites some anapests and then sings a long lyric section (561–608). She is interrupted by four iambic trimeters recited by Prometheus (589–93).[1]

For lyric monodies by a single actor we have to wait for the *Hippolytus* of Euripides (428 BCE), where Phaedra sings 669–79 (this passage is the long-postponed antistrophe to the choral song of lines 362–72), and Hippolytus has a long lyric astrophic passage (1347–88). (See also *Andromache* 103–16, sung by Andromache, *Trojan Women* 308–341, sung by Cassandra, and *Ion* 859–922, sung by Creusa.) Other monodies are either interrupted by short recited sections (Euripides, *Suppliants* 990–1030), by passages in other meters accompanied by music, such as hexameters (see Sophocles, *Women of Trachis* 1004–43), or by a lyric dialogue (Euripides, *Phoenician Women* 1485–1582). Monodies may be immediately preceded or followed by other lyric sections (Euripides, *Electra* 112–66).

The Social and Poetic Status of the Chorus:
Otherness, Authority, and Integration

The chorus is often marginal to the action of the play, and to the community of the heroes who act on stage. This remoteness affects the relationship of chorus and actors and is registered in the structure of their lyric dialogues. The tragic chorus's marginality is also central to some theories about its status and function.

The tragic chorus was extremely important to nineteenth-century Romantic theories of Greek theater. Schiller argued that the chorus creates a distance from the tragic action, contributing to the general object of art, which is to make the spectator "free" and removed from the material "by means of ideas." A. W. Schlegel maintained that the chorus is "the ideal spectator" ("ideal" in Schiller's sense), because "it mitigates the impression of a heart-rending or moving story while it conveys to the actual spectator a lyrical and musical expression of his own emotions, and elevates him to the region of contemplation" (trans. Carlson 1993, 179). Coleridge argued that choruses are created "as ideal representatives of the real audience, and of the poet himself in his own character, assuming the supposed impressions made by the drama, in order to direct and rule them" (quoted in Booth 1961, 99).

Schlegel's approach proved especially influential, but it is in some ways misleading: in fact the chorus members do guide the audience, even when they express wrong judgments on the tragic action. We can accept a modified version of Schlegel, however, if in place of the Romantic concept of the "ideal" spectator we substitute modern theories of the reader/spectator. Literary theory distinguishes an "implied" reader (the reader the text itself envisages), a "model" reader (an abstract entity, a reader "supposedly able to deal interpretatively with the expressions in the same way as the author deals generatively with them," according to Umberto Eco [1979, 7]), and an "empirical reader," that is, each reader (or spectator) who approaches a text. (For an overview, with references, see Rabinowitz 1995; also Carlson 1993, 520.)

The members of the chorus offer a response to part of the text that is itself part of the text. Thus they are "empirical readers/spectators" located within the text. Several views of the play are possible; the men or women who comprise the chorus offer one plausible reaction, in accordance with their social status, national characterization, and sex. The tragic chorus may split into two half-choruses, especially on the occasion of their entrance on stage, and each semichorus may have different information or different views on the action (see, for example, Euripides' *Suppliants* 598–633), but they are always homogeneous with respect to social status and sex. (Comedy follows a different convention, as evidenced by Aristophanes' *Lysistrata* 254–349, where a half-chorus of old men opposes a half-chorus of old women.)

The chorus members "read" the action, but they offer an empirical, not an ideal, reaction to it. In fact their reaction is both less correct and more profound than that of an ideal spectator. Choruses often make crucial mistakes of judgment: for instance, in *Ajax* they do not see through the deceptive speech delivered by the protagonist before his suicide, as the audience is meant to do; in *Oedipus the King* they fail to understand the identity of Oedipus. In this way they offer the audience the chance to see the action from a radically different point of view; the audience feels both more perceptive and more involved in the action than the chorus. On the other hand, choral passages offer some of the more complex and elusive general reflections in tragedy. In some cases, the social pressure put on the chorus members pushes them to eschew direct statements and speak in abstract, quasi-philosophical terms. In Aeschylus' *Agamemnon* the old men of the chorus deliver complex meditations on social structure and the mechanisms of guilt (40–257, 355–487, 681–781), even as they avoid any harsh confrontation with Clytemnestra and Agamemnon. The chorus of *Antigone* meditates on the fate of humankind (332–75, 582–625), but their reflections may imply criticism of the king (see also 509). The chorus often leaves indeterminate the relationship of such passages to the details of the action, thus forcing ancient and modern audiences to explore radically different interpretations of the events presented on stage.

Tragic choruses present a plausible reaction to the events. They do not act in bad faith and do not lie, except to dangerous tyrants (Euripides, *Iphigenia among the Taurians* 1056–77 and 1293–1310). On the other hand, the marginality of the chorus members frees them from the dignified stance that is expected of male citizens, and allows them to react in a way that would be considered too wild and "feminine" in everyday life. (On the problematic moral stance of acting see Plato's critique at *Republic* 395d–e and Lada-Richards, chapter 29 in this volume.)

The marginality of the chorus is what allowed choral passages to be taken as "the voice of the poet" (scholion to Euripides, *Medea* 823; Wilamowitz-Moellendorff 1959, 2: 132–33; 3: 149). This was especially the case for general reflections voiced by the chorus. Since the chorus is for the most part not directly involved in the action, their reflections are not swayed by self-interest; the poet is not imitating a character. Earlier critics therefore assumed that general reflections voiced by the chorus reproduced the author's "view" of the play. This approach has now been abandoned, but it is worth noting that the authority of the chorus is textualized in its namelessness. The scholarly consensus that chose "chorus" as a manuscript siglum, rather than assigning specific names appropriate to each tragedy ("slave women," "women of Corinth," "old men of Argos," and so forth), encourages readers to apprehend the choral pronouncements as possessing a collective character, voiced by an impersonal entity free from social conditioning.

A more radical and less personalized version of the "voice of the poet" approach is the theory that considers the chorus "the mouthpiece of the city" (Vernant and Vidal-Naquet 1988, 311). On this reading, the marginality of the chorus is a source of authority; by *not* being involved in the tragic action, the chorus is less swayed by the immediate circumstances and can give a reliable interpretation of the play. In opposition to Vernant and Vidal-Naquet, John Gould has recently stressed the fact that "the tragic chorus is characteristically composed of old men, women, slaves, and foreigners (the last often non-Greek as well as non-Athenians)," arguing that these groups are "marginal or simply excluded from the controlling voice of 'the people' " (2001, 383). This perspective would limit the importance of the chorus in guiding audience response to the tragic events, and stand in the way of an interpretation of the chorus as "the citizen body."

The typology of tragic choruses is more varied than Gould allows. Gould curiously excludes old men from the "citizen body," by assimilating them to the very broad category of the Other. Old men are certainly viewed as weak and frail in tragedy, but there is a significant strand in Greek culture that regarded old men as particularly wise and authoritative in matters of politics (the starting point is *Iliad* 9.60). The old men of the chorus are often called "citizens" (Aeschylus, *Agamemnon* 855; Sophocles, *Antigone* 806, *Oedipus the King* 512, *Oedipus at Colonus* 1579). Indeed, "it is tempting to describe them as super-citizens, since they were privileged in the assembly (where it was their right to speak first) and in the council" (Vernant and Vidal-Naquet 1988, 312). In two plays by Sophocles, *Ajax* and *Philoctetes*, the chorus is composed of adult citizens (soldiers). Sophocles apparently shows a preference for male choruses (twenty-four against fifteen), when we can be certain about their identity. The opposite tendency is evident in Aeschylus (fourteen male, twenty female) and Euripides (fifteen male, twenty-six female: Mastronarde 1998, 62–63; see also Foley 2003, 13 and 25–27). A similar trend can be observed in the choice of singing characters, to which I now turn.

The Social Status of Singing Characters

With the exception of the Phrygian slave in Euripides' *Orestes* (Maas 1962, 53–54), slaves and characters of low social standing are not important enough to be given a lyric section. They deliver anapests and hexameters, but they are not exalted enough to be given proper singing parts (on the delivery of hexameters in tragedy see Pretagostini 1995). On the other hand, song is generally not sufficiently dignified for male Greek heroes. Since song expresses uncontrolled emotion, it is more appropriate for the female sex, or for barbarians such as Xerxes in Aeschylus' *Persians*, Polymestor in Euripides' *Hecuba*, and the Phrygian slave in Euripides' *Orestes*. As a rule, male heroes in their prime do not sing. In Euripides, boys, young adults, and old men often have lyric parts. In order of age, we can mention the young children of Alcestis (*Alcestis*) and Andromache (*Andromache*), the title characters of *Ion* and *Hippolytus* (young adults), and the old men Peleus (*Andromache*) and Oedipus (*Phoenician Women*; see Hall 1999a, 112). Theseus briefly laments the death of Phaedra in *Hippolytus*, and Menelaus sings a few lines in a lyric dialogue with his wife in *Helen*; Adrastus laments the death of the heroes fallen at Thebes in a lyric dialogue with their mothers (*Suppliants*); Orestes repents the killing of his mother in a dialogue with his sister and accomplice Electra (*Electra*). These characters are swayed to a display of lyric emotionalism either by their wives or by other women.

Sophocles is the important exception to this rule. His male heroes sing on stage, and they engage in lyric dialogues with male choruses or companions. This happens especially when they are overtaken by extreme physical suffering (Oedipus in *Oedipus the King*, Heracles in *Women of Trachis*) or psychological anguish (Ajax and Philoctetes in their name-plays, Creon in *Antigone*). This reversal is rather surprising. Aristophanes mocks Euripides with some justice for discussing everyday subjects in his monodies (*Frogs* 1329–63) and for presenting kings in rags (*Acharnians* 412–34, *Frogs* 842, 1063); but Euripides does not go as far as Sophocles in giving his male heroes a large lyric presence. Euripides is more of an innovator in the visual presentation of the play, whereas Sophocles explores the range of expressive possibilities in assigning lyric sections to his male protagonists. *Hippolytus* is the most important Euripidean experiment in this direction, with two monodies for the two male protagonists, Theseus and Hippolytus; this innovation might reflect the influence of Sophocles.

Sophocles' choices struck some ancient critics as provocative. Cicero criticized Sophocles for his portrayal of the suffering Heracles in *Women of Trachis*, as well as Aeschylus for his portrait of Prometheus (*Tusculan Disputations* 2.19–25); some of the passages he objects to are in lyric meters. Cicero praised the Roman tragedians, who showed male characters bearing physical suffering with "stoic" patience and without abject lamentation (*Tusculan Disputations* 2.38–39, 48–50).

Lyric Forms of Contrast and Contact from Aeschylus to Euripides

The extent of the chorus's "otherness" or social integration affects the form of lyric sections, especially lyric dialogues. Contrast is one of the most important functions of epirrhematic or lyric dialogue in Aeschylus. The distance between chorus and protagonist is obvious in most cases: the Egyptian herald (or secondary chorus) wants to drag away the chorus of suppliants (*Suppliants* 825–910); a chorus of righteous old men opposes Agamemnon's murderer (*Agamemnon* 1406–1576); the chorus of Furies argues fiercely against Athena and her city (*Eumenides* 778–880; see also the section on lament in this chapter). Persuasion (*Suppliants* 348–447) and reaction to dramatic news (*Persians* 256–89) are some of the other functions of epirrhematic scenes. In *Libation Bearers* the chorus, composed of slave women, supports Orestes and Electra in their decision to punish Clytemnestra and urges them to take action. The faithful slaves side with the royal children against their wicked and illegitimate masters.

The affinity between protagonist and chorus is important in the *Prometheus* trilogy. Prometheus is the child of Iapetus, one of the Titans, and (according to Hesiod, *Theogony* 510) of one of the daughters of Ocean. The daughters of Ocean form the chorus of *Prometheus Bound*; that of the lost *Prometheus Unbound* consisted of Titans. The dialogic *parodos* is one of the elements that situates the dramatic technique of *Prometheus Bound* between the late works of Aeschylus and the early works of Euripides. *Prometheus Unbound* may have had a dialogic *parodos* (see frs. 190 and 192).

The dialogic *parodos* occurs in three of the complete plays by Sophocles and in eight by Euripides. The protagonist is on stage before the chorus arrives, and the *parodos* consists of a lyric or epirrhematic dialogue between them. In several plays the chorus members not only sympathize with the protagonist, but also share his or her fate. It may happen that both chorus and protagonist are enslaved: they are either freed (*Helen, Iphigenia among the Taurians*) or deported together at the end of the play (*Hecuba, Trojan Women*). In other plays the initial empathy fades away as the action evolves, as in *Medea*.

In the plays that stage the myth of Orestes (Aeschylus, *Libation Bearers*; Sophocles, *Electra*; Euripides, *Electra* and *Orestes*), the relationship between chorus and protagonists is one of basic sympathy; Sophocles and Euripides heighten the intimacy by making the chorus consist of freeborn women from Argos or the vicinity.

In his early *Ajax*, Sophocles already has a lyric dialogue between the chorus and Tecmessa (201–56) following immediately after the *parodos*. The dialogic *parodos* proper makes its appearance only in his late plays: *Electra, Philoctetes*, and *Oedipus at Colonus*. *Oedipus at Colonus* presents a variation on the normal pattern of dialogic *parodoi*. In the strophic section the chorus, after some initial perplexity, shows compassionate sympathy for the unknown wanderer, and gives careful instructions for him to reach a spot from which "no one will ever move you away against your will" (176–77). Their attitude changes in the epode (208–53), when Oedipus reveals his identity. The chorus members are horrified and, taking back their promise, urge him to leave the place immediately (233–36). The astrophic structure of the epode is well suited to the lively and irregular dialogue, whereas the promise of safety occupies the symmetrical strophic section. Antigone concludes the epode with a long, monodic section in which she supplicates the chorus (237–53).

Euripides develops a characteristic form of epirrhematic dialogue, mostly astrophic. In this form, an actor receives new information and expresses his or her dramatic reaction to it (see Popp 1971, 260–66). Many of these lyric sections make use of the dochmiac, a meter characteristic of tragedy and very often associated with situations of fear or extreme emotion (Dale 1968, 104–19; West 1982, 108–14). The Greek word *dochmiakon* means "which runs askew," and the basic rhythm is "asymmetrical" (five syllables: ∪--∪-). This pattern is subject to a number of variations and "resolutions" (substitution of two short syllables for one long, in certain positions). In the Euripidean epirrhematic dialogues, desperation is the usual reaction, as typified by the dochmiac meter (for example, *Hecuba* 684–720, *Heracles* 1178–1213, *Trojan Women* 239–91, *Ion* 763–99). However, dochmiacs can also be associated with feelings of joy, especially in late Euripides. In the recognition scene in *Iphigenia among the Taurians* (827–99), joy at the siblings' reunion is mixed with fear for the future; joy and sorrow commingle in the mother–son recognition at *Ion* 1439–1509 and the husband–wife reunion at *Helen* 627–97. In such scenes it is female characters who sing the emotional lyric sections; an exception is *Heracles* 1178–1213, where the lyric section is given to Amphitryon. Male characters may occasionally sing part of a line, or a very short section; more often they initiate an iambic utterance, shorter than a trimeter, which is then continued into song by the other character.

Time and Narrative Technique

Time is another important structural aspect of choral songs. Time is notoriously subject to complicated manipulations in archaic lyric, for instance in Alcman and Pindar (Pfeijffer 1999, D'Alessio 2004). This precedent may have played a role in the handling of time in tragic lyrics, especially if one considers the links between archaic lyric and tragic lyric with respect to meter, language, and genre.

In non-dramatic genres performance time and the time of the events narrated are normally distinct. When they coincide, even if the coincidence is not complete or entirely consistent, the poems are called "mimetic" (Fantuzzi 1993). "Mimetic" lyric sections are also common in tragedy; an example is the *parodos* of Aeschylus' *Seven against Thebes*. Time passes roughly at the same speed on stage as for the audience, when the actors are speaking.

During *parodoi* and stasima, however, time has the chance to move faster. Characters often leave before choral songs, and arrive after them – and in the meantime they take decisive action. During the short span of a choral song, people may travel a long way (Aeschylus, *Agamemnon* 355–487, 493); political assemblies debate and decide on important matters (Aeschylus, *Suppliants* 524–99; Euripides, *Orestes* 807–43);

battles are fought (Aeschylus, *Seven against Thebes* 720–91; Euripides, *Suppliants* 598–633; Sophocles, *Oedipus at Colonus* 1044–95).

Ancient commentators noticed that choral songs fill a temporal gap, a space that would be otherwise empty of events. A complicated lapse of time is assumed in *Agamemnon*, although the text does its best to divert attention from it. Clytemnestra announces that Troy is taken "today" (320); a choral song covers the time it takes the herald to travel from Troy to Argos. As an ancient scholar noted, "some criticize the poet because he represents the Greeks as coming back from Troy in a single day" (scholion on line 503; Taplin 1977, 290–94; Meijering 1987, 171).

The other, more mimetic lyric passages (lyric dialogues and monodies) do not seem to possess the magic of making time run faster (slowing down the action is much easier: nothing seems to happen, for example, during the *epirrhêma* of Euripides' *Orestes* 1394–1502). One should however note that time on stage is very different from clock time, and that distortions of various sorts occur even in dialogic scenes (Di Benedetto and Medda 1997, 302–12).

In some of Euripides' plays the choral sections are linked by the narration of a series of correlated events: the fate of Troy (*Hecuba, Trojan Women*), the story of Cadmus and Thebes (*Phoenician Women*). The narration is cut up into discrete sections, and the chronological order is often altered. In *Phoenician Women* the chorus begins with Cadmus and the foundation of Thebes (first stasimon), then recounts his marriage with the goddess Harmonia and the construction of the city walls (second stasimon), and finally sings of the Sphinx (third stasimon). The impending battle is a recurrent topic (*parodos*; second and fourth stasimon), and the second stasimon mentions Oedipus and Mount Cithaeron. In *Trojan Women*, the fall of Troy is the subject of the first stasimon; the second stasimon goes back to the story of Laomedon, an ancient king of Troy, and of his son Ganymede, loved by Zeus; the third stasimon returns to the fall of Troy, and concludes by cursing Menelaus. This linkage creates a sense of unity, and provides a frame for the extended narratives that are characteristic of Euripides' late style. The order of choral narrative is at times calculated to create a thematic counterpoint to the dramatic action. In *Phoenician Women* the narrative of the Sphinx (1018–46) comes after a scene with the prophet Tiresias; in *Trojan Women* the story of Laomedon and Ganymede (1060–1117) serves to juxtapose Zeus' previous concern with Troy to his present disregard, evident in the failure of Hecuba's prayer to him (884–88). Aeschylus employed a similar unifying technique in his trilogies: the second stasimon of the *Seven against Thebes* takes up the subject matter of the previous plays in the trilogy, *Laius* and *Oedipus* (Hutchinson 1985, xxiii–xxx).

Literature and Ritual: Dithyramb, Paean, Lament, *Humenaios*

Who sings in everyday life, and why? And who sings and why in a play? Choruses generally have a reason for coming on stage: for instance, they respond to a plague that affects the city (*Oedipus the King*), or to the cries of a distraught woman (*Medea*). They often choose speech genres that could involve song in real life, such as songs for the gods, laments, or marriage songs.

Ritual songs generally involved *choral* singing, and Aristotle explained the presence of the chorus in tragedy by stating that the genre started "from the leaders of the dithyramb" (*Poetics* 1449a10–11). "Dithyramb," an epithet of Dionysus, of uncertain meaning, designated a genre of choral lyric in honor of that god. In Athens, dithyrambs were performed as part of Dionysiac festivals, along with plays. Whether tragedy started from the leaders of the dithyramb is incapable of proof. Some scholars argue for a strong Dionysiac influence on the origins of tragedy, whereas others are skeptical (Pickard-Cambridge 1962, 89–97; Scullion 2002a, 102–10, with references). The genre of dithyramb underwent great changes in the fifth century (Pickard-Cambridge 1962, 1–59; Harvey 1955, 173; Zimmermann 1992; Ieranò 1997).

Paean, "Healer," is an epithet of Apollo, and refers to a song performed by "men, often young men of military age," and is associated with "the safety of the polis, with healing, and with controlled celebration" (Rutherford 2001, 6–7), as can be demonstrated in the extensive remains of Pindar's paeans. Real-life performances of the paean took place on the battlefield and in the symposium. (For paeans in tragedy see the section on *Seven against Thebes*.)

The lament for the dead is often presented as a spontaneous reaction of the mourners (for example, at Euripides' *Hecuba* 685, with references to Dionysiac loss of control). The lament was a formalized literary genre in archaic and classical Greece, practiced by Pindar and Simonides among others, and was at times performed as a civic ritual (Euripides, *Suppliants* 1114–64). The spontaneous lament is often called *goos*, in opposition to the formalized *thrênos*, but the distinction is not absolute. The oscillation between spontaneity and formalized lament is already evident in the *Iliad* (see 19.301–2 and 24.720–76; on lament see Alexiou 1974; Battezzato 1995, 137–81; Foley 2001, 19–55 and 145–71).

Another ritual genre that is taken up in tragedy is the wedding-song, or *humenaios*. There are few occasions for real, joyous celebration in tragedy, and the *humenaios* often makes a paradoxical appearance, either because the bride or bridegroom dies or because they are denied a proper wedding. In particular, the motif of "marriage to death" emerges as a frequent tragic theme (see Rehm 1994 and Panoussi, chapter 26 in this volume).

Patterns of Evolution: Critics Ancient and Modern

The evaluation of lyric structures has been crucial in creating the history of Greek tragedy. Aristotle did not consider the chorus a necessary element of tragedy; therefore, its presence in drama had to be justified. On the other hand, Aristotle argued that tragedy originated not just in dithyramb but also in epirrhematic dialogues between chorus and actors (*Poetics* 1449a11). Aristotle is thus able to describe the history of tragic structures as a struggle between the irrational heritage of tradition, involving the overwhelming presence of the chorus, and the artistic urge to create an organic whole in which all elements are indispensable.

The chorus has a large role in Aeschylus; in the lyric sections, it sings between 35 percent (*Libation Bearers*) and 55 percent (*Suppliants*) of the lines. *Prometheus Bound* is exceptionally sparing in choral lyric sections (13 percent). This is close to some of the figures for Sophocles (*Electra*: 11 percent) and Euripides (*Medea*: 19 percent; see Griffith 1977, 123). In Euripides' later plays the proportion of song to speech does not change much overall: actors' songs make up for the diminished role of choral lyric (Csapo 1999–2000, 410–12, with figures).

Aeschylus' tragic predecessors were evidently even more lavish in their use of choral lyric. According to Aristotle, Aeschylus "reduced the choral sections and gave the most important role to speech" – that is, to the recited lines of the actors (Aristotle, *Poetics* 1449a17–18). The process of "naturalization" of choral parts continued in Sophocles, but in a different way. According to Aristotle, Sophocles integrates the chorus in the action, treating it as "one of the actors," whereas Euripides is less successful in this respect (*Poetics* 1456a25–27). Some authors of the late fifth century composed choral sections that have no relevance to the action; Aristotle calls them *embolima*, "something added in, intercalated" (*Poetics* 1456a29). These embolima parallel a development in fourth-century comedy, whereby choral sections become completely immaterial to the plot. Manuscripts do not give the text of these choral sections, but simply insert the indication "a song of the chorus" (*chorou* [*melos*] or similar phrases) where a choral lyric was required (Hunter 1979). Papyri of some late tragic texts seem to present the same phenomenon (West 1982, 80 n. 10).

Aristotle gives us a neat pattern: Aeschylus and Sophocles struggle in different ways to solve the problem of the chorus; Euripides is less successful, and some other late fifth-century authors attempt a wrong solution: they marginalize it by making the chorus sing decorative lyric pieces. In the nineteenth and twentieth centuries many scholars, especially in Germany, studied the evolution of tragic forms in detail. They accepted Aristotle's assumptions and combined them with the Platonic critique of the so-called New Music, an innovative musical and poetical style that became popular in the last twenty years of the fifth century (see Csapo 1999–2000 and Wilson, chapter 12 in this volume). It has been argued that the style of late Euripidean lyrics is in some ways "decadent," "decorative," or "empty"; the lyrics become some sort of libretto for an artificial style of music, aimed at showing off the virtuoso qualities of the singers. Similarly, the non-lyric dialogues in late works by Euripides supposedly became more schematic and rigid (Schadewaldt 1926, 104–8), in contrast to Sophocles, who attuned his dialogic forms to the needs of the action.

Some of these assumptions are dubious, and the idea of a linear progression is untenable. A radical revision is needed. As we will see, Aeschylus and Sophocles were not less bold than Euripides in manipulating the conventions they inherited from non-dramatic choral genres. Aristophanes describes Euripides as an innovator and Aeschylus as an old-fashioned classic, and his view strongly influenced the scholarly tradition, both ancient and modern. Aristophanes' point, however, does not imply that Aeschylus was simply reproducing "reality" or "tradition," nor that Euripides was an isolated avant-garde artist.

Lament from Aeschylus to Euripides

Aeschylus' portrayal of ritual is no more "primitive" or "original" than is Euripides' (or, for that matter, Sophocles'). The Persian evocation of the dead in *Persians*, or the lament that concludes the play, is no more evidence of a genuine Persian ritual than the lament in *Iphigenia among the Taurians* is a reproduction of rituals indigenous to the Black Sea. Both are fifth-century Athenian recreations of a fictional world. Considering Aeschylus traditional and Euripides innovative is a question of false perspective. Since we can compare the laments of Euripides to those of Aeschylus, and we can see that their form has changed, we assume that it changed because the poet has changed the form. Because the laments in Aeschylus cannot be compared to anything else before them in tragedy, they seem the original tragic representation of a lament. The strong orientalizing touch that Aeschylus chose to add to some of his laments (*Persians* 120 and 908–1077, *Libation Bearers* 423) is taken up in later authors (Euripides, *Iphigenia among the Taurians* 180, for example), but Aeschylus also put on stage non-orientalizing forms of *thrênos* in *Seven against Thebes*.

Euripides modifies the structure of the lament, reversing the relationship between the chorus and their leader, and assigning to men rather than to women the duty of performing the mourning ritual. This modification is particularly clear in *Andromache*, where Peleus starts the lament (1172–96), and in *Suppliants*, where Adrastus takes up the role of *exarchos*, leader of the female chorus (798–814); both Peleus and Adrastus end up their laments in a subordinate position, responding to the chorus who has taken up a leading role (*Andromache* 1197–1225), or facing criticism from the chorus members, who direct the lament by themselves (*Suppliants* 819, 824–36; Battezzato 1995, 144–52).

Failed Paean and Interrupted Ritual: Aeschylus' *Seven against Thebes*

Expectations about the genres of choral poetry are crucial in *Seven against Thebes*. This play stages a struggle between the desire of the chorus to sing and the attempts of Eteocles to silence or control them. The choral songs take two forms: fear and lament. The chorus members present fear and lament as spontaneous reactions, and oppose the order of Eteocles to channel their song into a different ritual, the paean, defined as "a beneficial sacred cry [*ololugmon*]" (268). The paean is "the male equivalent of *ololugê*," the female ritual cry in sacrifices and celebrations and in requests for help (Hutchinson 1985, 87; cf. Käppel 1992, 81).

The chorus is composed not of male citizens but of Theban women, and their behavior is the opposite of the way male citizens should act, as Eteocles emphasizes. Whenever Eteocles is not on stage, the women of the chorus cannot control their fear (see 287 and 720). When news arrives that the battle is won, the chorus is faced with a dilemma: should they "rejoice and cry out" [*apololuxô*]" for the victory (825) or "weep [*klausô*] for the wretched and ill-fated army leaders" (828)? Crying aloud for victory would mean obeying the order of Eteocles at long last, after his death in the battle. Ultimately, however, the delayed paean is abandoned in favor of lament. The chorus is under the influence of a Dionysiac urge to mourn: "I prepared a song for the tomb, manic as a bacchant [*thuias*]" (835–36). They evoke the image of Charon's boat, "on which Paean [or Apollo, according to different editors] does not set foot" (858). The play ends with one of the longest examples of antiphonal lament in tragedy. The chorus splits into two half-choruses; one leads the lament and the other responds, taking up the same words ("unhappy," 877; "unhappy indeed," 879; see 931–32). In the final section (961–1004) the antiphonal sections become shorter and shorter; they diminish to a single line, or even single words, giving the sense of a final acceleration before the ending. Lament (*goos*) is presented by the women of the chorus as a self-referential speech act (*autostonos*, "lamenting for one self/coinciding with wailing"), and as a spontaneous, uncontrollable reaction to their sorrows (*autopêmôn*, "for one's own woes": 915–16).

The relationship between community and chorus becomes clear only in the end. In spite of the initial disapproval of Eteocles, the chorus members do not represent a negative female model. In the course of the play their insight into the future and their ability to understand the predicament of Eteocles proves in some ways superior to that of Eteocles himself (see esp. 686–708). Women were possibly present in the audience, and they could have legitimately identified with the chorus. The chorus is *not* the citizen body, but the chorus members do speak up for the city, and they guide the spectators in their perception of the play. The lyric forms chosen by the chorus legitimize their position within the drama and the city. The initial *epirrhēma* presents them as subject to the leadership of the actor, and they accept their subordinate role; they remain silent during most of the drama. The chorus takes up the important role of concluding the play precisely because they fall into a speech genre, the lament for the dead, that is normally reserved to the female sex. The fight between paean and lament is decided by sexual appropriateness: gender determines genre. The female chorus members cannot force themselves to sing the male paean, and prefer the "spontaneous" lament.

The New Music and Generic Consistency in Euripides

Plato is responsible for a complex and aggressive critique of the decadence of *mousikē* (song) and *choreia* (dance): he accuses some composers of being "instigators of unmusical law-breaking" who, "though by nature skilled at composition, were ignorant of what is right and lawful in music. In a Bacchic frenzy, and enthralled beyond what is right by pleasure, they mixed lamentations with hymns and paeans with dithyrambs" (*Laws* 700d, trans. Barker 1984–89, 1: 156–57). This comment is generally associated with the bad practice of the New Music of the late fifth century; the late plays of Euripides are often considered to exemplify this trend. The *kommos* of Aeschylus' *Libation Bearers*, however, starts as an invocation of the dead (315–71); it turns into a prayer to Zeus (380, 394–409); it continues into a reperformance of the orientalizing lament, through the evocation of a repressed *thrēnos* and of a prevented funeral (423–34); and it ends with a prayer to the gods (462). In Sophocles, the female chorus of *Women of Trachis* mixes the male paean (210) and the dithyramb (219) in the same song (205–24: Rutherford 1994–95, 120). The paradoxical "paean of the dead" (that is, lament) already appears in Aeschylus (*Libation Bearers* 151; see *Agamemnon* 645; Euripides, *Helen* 177; Käppel 1992, 48; Rutherford 2001, 118–20). In short, the different genres of archaic lyric are mixed in the lyric sections of tragedy from Aeschylus onward, and in fact Plato argued that the hybridizing of Greek lyric genres started after the Persian Wars, in connection with democratic reforms in Athens (699d; Harvey 1955, 165).

Some of the most rigorous examples of generic consistency occur in late Euripides. In *Ion*, the protagonist sings a paean for Apollo (112–43), and he does not stray from the theme of praising Apollo, the laurel, and the service to his temple; even the meter used in the refrain to Paean (the molossus: - - -) recalls archaic invocations to the gods (West 1982, 55; Rutherford 2001, 111–12). The twist lies in the everyday nature of the occasion, the very fault that Aristophanes criticized in *Frogs* 1343–63: as he sings, Ion describes his task of sweeping the floor of Apollo's temple. The *parodos* of *Bacchae* is a transposition to the stage of a cult song, the arrival of a chorus celebrating

Dionysus: "The Chorus themselves emphasize the point: they use a formula which must be designed to give the illusion of a religious procession (68–70), and announce that they are about to sing 'the traditional things in honour of Dionysus' (71). The hymn is written mainly in a traditional cult meter [. . .]; it introduces ritual cries" (Dodds 1960, 71–72). The meter is ionics *a minore* (general metrical pattern: UU--). This meter is used elsewhere in orientalizing (Aeschylus, *Persians* 65–114) and Dionysiac (Aristophanes, *Frogs* 323–53; Dale 1968, 124–28; West 1982, 124) contexts.

Another instance of Euripidean generic consistency occurs in some late stasima, which contain little else but narrative of mythical events (Panagl 1971). These stasima have been considered a transposition for the tragic stage of a type of fifth-century dithyramb, which included long mythic sections (Plato, *Republic* 394c; Harvey 1955, 173; Barker 1984–89, 1: 215 n. 76). In the second stasimon of *Helen* the chorus narrates the story of Demeter, identified with the Mother of the Gods, and of her daughter Persephone (1301–68). The ode ends by stressing the links between the cult of the Mother of the Gods and the cult of Dionysus (a possible allusion to the dithyrambic genre), and criticizing Helen for not having given enough attention to the Mother of the Gods. The thematic connections with the action of the play are left implicit. The false news of the death of Menelaus has just been announced. The life that awaits mortals after their descent to Hades is the theme of the stasimon, a theme linked to the immortality promised in the mystery cults of the Mother of the Gods and of Dionysus. This and other similar narrative stasima have often been compared to the embolima mentioned by Aristotle, but even if the links are not made explicit, the songs have a clear connection with the plot, and present some of the finest examples of tragic lyric narrative.

Aeschylus, Sophocles, and Euripides often took care to provide explicit links between the mythic narrative in stasima and the action on stage. These passages have been grouped into a category with a special name: the stasima that feature a "mythological example" (for example, Aeschylus, *Libation Bearers* 602–38; Sophocles, *Antigone* 944–87; Euripides, *Medea* 1282–92; see list and discussion in Oehler 1925). "Mythological examples" are shorter than "dithyrambic" narratives, and have more explicit connections with the plot. A tradition of criticism that placed aesthetic value on explicit coherence and dramatic effectiveness gave bad marks to the "dithyrambic" evolution of the late Euripides. Although the lyric forms of tragedy do not follow a linear pattern of change, it is true that the late plays of Euripides display an array of lyric forms, both mimetic and narrative, choral and epirrhematic, dialogic and monodic, that has no equal in Aeschylus and Sophocles. The protean quality of Euripides' song-writing skills yields such diverse results as the loosely connected second stasimon of *Helen* and the imitation of cultic song performance of *Bacchae*.

In discussing the lyric sections of tragedy, many critics have adopted Platonic, Aristotelian, or Romantic assumptions, often all at the same time. We might now be tempted to revise them all. It would be easy to read generic inconsistency as a bold literary revolution, anticipating the Hellenistic "crossing of genres"; to praise dithyrambic stasima because they open up meaning and break away from the constraints of dramatic context; to recognize in choral passages not the voice of the "author" or that of an "ideal spectator" but the marginalized speech of slaves and women. Such revisions do not yield a completely satisfactory critical formula, precisely because no such formula exists. In fact, tragic choruses adopt the authority of public genres even when their members are foreigners or slaves and insist on giving us authoritative (if not authorial) views about good and evil. They may even question the appropriateness of their own *choreia* (Sophocles, *Oedipus the King* 895–99; Henrichs 1994–95, 65–73). Actors' songs are split equally between spontaneous expression of emotion and self-conscious generic experimentation. Lyric structures give form to contact and conflict; in interpreting them we must learn to recognize the literary choices made by the authors (song versus recitative, paean versus lament, spontaneity versus convention, lyric dialogue versus *epirrhêma*), and the gender roles, social implications, and metaliterary allusions that these choices presuppose or challenge.

NOTE

1   *Prometheus Bound* is attributed to Aeschylus by our manuscripts and by ancient sources. Many influential scholars now argue that it is not by Aeschylus, and that it was written after Aeschylus' death: Griffith 1977, West 1990a, Bees 1993. The play's authenticity is defended by other critics: Herington 1970, Saïd 1985, Pattoni 1987. See also Battezzato 2001, 15–16. The style, form, and ideology of the play present strong similarities to the other plays attributed to Aeschylus, even if there are significant differences of (especially) meter and language. It is likely to have been written in the period between Aeschylus' *Oresteia* and Euripides' *Medea*.

FURTHER READING

Meter, language, and performance: On Greek meter, West 1982 is concise, informative, and very clear. Martinelli 1997 and Gentili and Lomiento 2003 offer different approaches on some questions and updated bibliographies. Dale 1968 offers a perceptive and readable discussion of lyric meters in tragedy, with detailed analysis of several passages for each type of meter. Her metrical analyses of all tragic lyric (Dale 1971–83), published posthumously, are useful. For Aeschylus, one should consult the metrical appendix in West 1990a. Breitenbach 1934 analyzes the language of the lyric sections in Euripides, listing the influences of Homer and lyric poetry. Pickard-Cambridge 1988 presents all the evidence on the performance of lyric sections, with thorough discussion. For translation and discussion of the most important ancient sources on music and theater see the excellent collections of Barker 1984–89 and Csapo and Slater 1995.

Forms: Kranz 1933 is an excellent discussion of choral songs. The chapters by Barner, Popp, and Rode in Jens 1971 classify and discuss monodies, *amoibaia*, and choral songs. Taplin 1977 is essential reading on the structural elements of tragedy. On the use of non-dramatic lyric genres in tragedy see Herington 1985 (general overview), Alexiou 1974 (lament), Rutherford 1994–95 and 2001, 108–21 (paean), Panagl 1971, and Csapo 1999–2000 (dithyramb). Henrichs 1994–95 is excellent on the Dionysiac aspects of tragic lyric. On the authority and otherness of the chorus see Gould 2001, 378–404, and Mastronarde 1998, with their bibliographic references. On singing actors see Hall 1999a and 2002. Carlson 1993 surveys theories of the theater from antiquity to the end of the twentieth century, including discussions of the chorus. There are book-length studies of the lyric/ choral sections of each tragedian: Scott 1984 (Aeschylus), Burton 1980 (Sophocles), Hose 1990–91 (Euripides, with abundant bibliography). Two journals have published special issues on the chorus, with papers by leading scholars: *Dioniso* 55 (1984–85) and *Arion* 3rd series, 3.1 (1994–95) and 4.1 (1996–97).

CHAPTER ELEVEN

Episodes

Michael R. Halleran

Definitions

Writing nearly a century after the acme of Attic tragedy, Aristotle defined an "episode" (*epeisodion*) as the "complete part of tragedy between full choral songs" (*Poetics* 1452b20–21).[1] With this short phrase, Aristotle identified the two defining elements of Greek drama – choral song and what comes in between. The dynamic of all Greek drama lies in the alternation of the song of the chorus and the in-between speech of the actors. This alternation provides the rich and varied texture of tragedy (and comedy): song, with its complex patterns and bolder images, emphasized speculation, imagination, and reflection, while speech, with its repeated and steady rhythms, lent itself to exposition, declaration, and debate.

Greek theater history contains murky and conflicting stories about the genre's origins. Most accounts suggest that tragedy developed over several stages from a purely choral phenomenon associated with a ritual in honor of Dionysus, and one pivotal step in this development was the addition of an actor. This innovation is often attributed to Thespis, who is said to have added a prologue and speech to what had previously been exclusively a choral performance. Whatever the truth behind this particular story – and however tragedy developed from purely song to its fifth-century instantiation – it reflects the dyadic nature of Greek drama: song and speech.

Another ancient anecdote of theater history relates that Aeschylus increased the number of actors from one to two, and Sophocles introduced a third (Aristotle, *Poetics* 1449a16–19). Here, it seems, the number of actors remained. By actor (*hupokritês*) was meant one with a speaking part, as other figures without speaking parts (attendants, children, servants, etc.) appeared regularly in these plays. In addition, the chorus-leader could have a speaking part and engage in dialogue with the play's characters. The fact that a tragic dramatist had only three actors with speaking parts had several important consequences. First, the stage tended to be significantly less populated, and the interactions were often between just two individuals or even one individual and the chorus (or chorus-leader). Second, actors typically played multiple roles in a given drama, taking advantage of the full-face masks worn by all participants. As a third consequence, and the one most relevant to this discussion, the comings and goings of actors clustered around the choral songs, so much so that the standard pattern of Greek tragedy was actor's exit, followed by song, followed by actor's entrance (Taplin 1972 and 1977, 49–60, and passim). An episode, then, was defined not only by being "in between" full choral songs but also by the movement of actors into and away from the acting space in conjunction with the choral songs.

Over time the number of characters in plays increased significantly. *Persians*, for example, had only four characters and *Seven against Thebes* perhaps as few as two, while some of the later plays of Euripides had as many as ten (*Orestes*) or eleven (*Phoenician Women*). Having more characters allowed for greater variety of perspectives, additional plot complications, and more dynamic dramatic movement. On a formal basis, the increase in the number of characters also made it easier to multiply the number of scenes within an episode.

Structures

It is not possible to provide a simple (or even complex) taxonomy of episodes; they present too many variations and too few patterns. In length, they could vary from fewer than forty lines (*Alcestis* 935–61) to over six hundred (*Iphigenia among the Taurians* 467–1088). But these were extremes. The vast majority of episodes were between one hundred and three hundred lines in length, with the average about two hundred. Among the three tragedians, there is not a great difference in the average length of an episode, although in general the later plays of Euripides, expansive in many ways, tended to be longer. These plays featured not more episodes but longer ones, segmented by the arrivals and departures of actors. The arrival of another character and the departure of the first or other character(s) would also be common but not required. A fifth-century Greek tragedy was not very long by the standards of later European theater. All of Aeschylus' plays, with the exception of *Agamemnon*, spanned fewer than 1,100 verses, and Euripides' and Sophocles' plays tended to have no more than 1,500 lines (*Oedipus at Colonus*, *Phoenician Women*, and *Helen* are exceptional in this regard). The scope and pace of the action was accordingly tight and quick. Each episode needed to be focused and purposeful.

The most common way to break up an episode into smaller parts was through exit and entrance of characters, dividing an episode into what we might call discrete scenes. At the far end of the spectrum, Euripides' *Helen* has an unusually long episode (528–1106) that is broken up into six smaller scenes by arrivals and departures of characters. In *Libation Bearers*, for example, even a relatively short episode (653–782) is broken up into four scenes by the entrances and exits. The almost frenetic pace of this section of the play reflects the intensity of the action (Orestes is moving toward matricide) and stands in sharp contrast to the static, ritual-filled first half of the drama.

Longer episodes could also be punctuated by a brief choral song that was not a stasimon (a "full choral song" in Aristotle's language). Euripides' *Hippolytus*, for example, has a very long episode (170–524) that is broken into two smaller units by a short choral song (362–72). This break occurs at a critical moment – the nurse has just learned that Phaedra's illness and delirium are caused by her passion for her stepson – and in the following section of the episode, Phaedra will explain her intention of committing suicide, while the nurse will argue fiercely to save her life. The episode does not feature any arrivals but is given variation and new movement by this brief song.

While the dyadic interchange of speech (actors) and song (chorus) serves as a useful definition, it is not fully accurate. Not only did the chorus-leader have a regular, if typically short, speaking part, but actors, too, found lyric expression in song. These songs (on which see Battezzato, chapter 10 in this volume) could help to articulate a longer scene. For example, Creusa's monody (858–922) punctuates the third episode (725–1047) in *Ion*, and Polymestor's song of pain (1056–1106) breaks up the *exodos* in *Hecuba*.

In his definitions, Aristotle characteristically distinguished episodes (the "between the full choral songs" parts of the drama) from those parts which preceded and followed choral songs, namely the *prologos* and *exodos* (*Poetics* 1452b19–22). The prologue preceded the arrival of the chorus and tended to be much shorter than other episodes (for variations among prologues, see Roberts, chapter 9 in this volume). Both prologue and *exodos* were in the same meter as the episodes, could include the arrival and/or departure of characters (more common in the prologue than in the *exodos*), and connect with the following or preceding episodes in meaningful ways.

In its later history, ancient drama developed a "five-act rule" – each drama had five (and only five) distinct episodes, as seen in the New Comedy of Menander and the Roman dramatists Plautus and Terence. For fifth-century tragedy, however, such a rule had not evolved. In fact, only six of the extant plays conform to the supposedly pure form of prologue, *parodos* (first choral song), and then five episodes followed in each case by a stasimon (full choral song subsequent to the *parodos*), with a concluding *exodos*.

If an episode was one of the constituent parts of tragedy, what were *its* own constituent parts? Individual speeches and dialogue. By the standards of contemporary cinema or even modern drama, Greek tragedy might seem rigid in its formal presentation of human speech. In addition to following the generic conventions by which they speak in verse and do not stammer or slur their words, characters also do not interrupt each other, even when angry or making dire threats. They frequently deliver longish speeches, often highly rhetorical in nature. Even when characters engage in heated stichomythia (alternating one-line dialogue), they remain within the structure of the verse, with the syntax of one line at times dependent on a preceding one. Stichomythia allowed for the economical, if stylized, progression of argument, information, and revelation. Euripides was especially fond of this and in his later plays has scenes with more than a hundred consecutive lines of stichomythic dialogue (see, for example, *Ion* 262–368). Dialogue could also progress in units of two verses (called *distichomythia*).

Antilabê is a line shared between two speakers, often at the conclusion of a long section of stichomythia. Repeated lines of *antilabê* are used to great effect in the painfully crisp exchange between Oedipus and the herdsman, as Oedipus solves the final clues to his identity (Sophocles, *Oedipus the King* 1173–76). Euripides, often the dramatist to push conventions to extremes, has a very extended and nearly comical run of *antilabê* in *Ion* (530–62), when Ion meets Xuthus, who believes (erroneously) that he is the young man's father.

A *rhêsis* was an extended speech. It might be very long (upwards of a hundred lines) or much shorter (fewer than ten). It was the vehicle for characters to make arguments (typically highly rhetorical), provide information, or deliberate. These speeches could be delivered to other characters on stage or to oneself (soliloquy). Just as dramatists alternated song and speech, they also were careful to modulate the speech within episodes, using both *rhêsis* in differing lengths and dialogue of different sorts (including stichomythia).

After some trial and error, tragedy found its proper voice with the iambic trimeter (Aristotle, *Poetics* 1449a22–28). Well over 90 percent of all the spoken verse in extant tragedy consists of iambic trimeter. Between the production of Aeschylus' *Oresteia* trilogy in 458 and Euripides' *Trojan Women* in 415, there is no uncontested example of trochaic tetrameter, the older verse form, in surviving tragedy.[2] Euripides seems to have reintroduced this verse form into his later plays but even so he employed it sparingly, relying on iambic trimeter as the regular mode of spoken verse. The nature of the iambic trimeter also developed over time. A feature of iambic trimeter was that two short syllables could replace a long syllable at certain places in the verse, often called "resolution." The plays of Aeschylus and Sophocles show relatively little resolution in their iambic verses, while Euripides demonstrated a remarkable progression in the use of resolution, from about 7 percent in his early plays to over 40 percent in his later ones (see Cropp and Fick 1985, 5). This increase in resolution accommodated a wider range of vocabulary and gave the impression of greater naturalism in speech.

Junctures

Tragedy's structural alternation of speech and song framed by exits before and entrances after the song had a significant consequence: the junctures of exit/song and song/entrance provided fertile opportunities for suggestive juxtapositions, important oppositions, and playful and painful ironies. These junctures could be used both to indicate the drama's movement and to comment on its action; the juxtaposition could underscore a point or paint a sharp contrast. A few striking examples will suffice to show the potential effect of such juxtapositions. Agamemnon's arrival (810) in Aeschylus' play of that name receives elaborate preparation, as the overall shape of the drama is the *nostos* (homecoming). Immediately before his entrance, the choral stasimon (681–782) draws evocative yet pointed connections between Troy's destruction and Argos. Just as a lion cub turns on its human hosts, Helen has brought ruin to Troy, sing the Argive elders, and just as one act of violence (*hubris*) begets further violence, now this ruin comes to Argos – in the form of Agamemnon, whom the chorus announces immediately at the conclusion of this song. His death at Clytemnestra's hands becomes an illustration of the choral reflections on violence and a continuation of the ruin brought by the Trojan War.

Sophocles' *Oedipus the King* is, at one level, a tightly crafted detective story, revealing slowly and painfully the identity of Laius' murderer. In the scene immediately before Oedipus unravels the final part of the riddle and learns that he is Laius' murderer (and his own mother's husband), the chorus (1086–1109) imagines that the "orphan" Oedipus may have a divine birth – perhaps Pan is his father. As is signaled repeatedly throughout the play, Oedipus is the opposite of what he thinks he is – he is not the result of a divine union but the offspring of ill-fated mortals. The ensuing scene juxtaposes his imagined lofty origins with his true and pain-filled heritage.

Euripides' structurally bold *Heracles* presents a tour de force with the mid-play appearance on high of Iris and Lyssa ("Madness" personified). The play's first half has shown Heracles' just-in-time rescue of his family from death at the hands of the new tyrant in Thebes, Lycus. No sooner has the hero dispatched this evil man than the chorus sings a celebratory hymn (734–814), announcing the divine justice seen in Heracles' triumph. This declaration of a theodicy is premature: immediately after this song, the chorus screams in horror at the arrival of Iris and Lyssa, who have come to madden Heracles into murdering his own children, sending the play in a drastically different direction.

The juxtaposition of song and entrance could also take on a more gentle form. The young, female, and Asiatic maenads who comprise the chorus in Euripides' *Bacchae* conclude their *parodos* with the image of a bacchant compared to a swiftly leaping foal (165–69). Arriving immediately on stage is Tiresias – old, male, and Greek, but, remarkably enough, wearing the bacchant's costume. In his ensuing exchange with Cadmus, he explains that he feels young in the service of the god Dionysus, but his ludicrous appearance stands in sharp contrast to the bacchants, a contrast heightened by the juxtaposition of song and entrance. Episodes, then, display not only their own internal arrangement but also purposeful connections with the nexus of exit, song, and entrance that define them.

Epic narrative, to which all of Greek literature was much indebted, could move easily from scene to scene. Drama did not have this narrative elasticity and had to rely on fewer characters to tell its tale. Another contrasting factor is tragedy's static scenic space. By convention, the action in a Greek tragedy occurred outdoors (there was no "missing fourth wall") and only very rarely did a tragedy change its location in mid-play (*Eumenides* and *Ajax* are the sole examples from extant tragedy). Another "static" feature was the constant presence of the members of the chorus (their departure during a play was likewise highly unusual), with whom entering characters would commonly engage in dialogue.

Prometheus Bound and Sophocles' *Oedipus at Colonus* presented striking structural choices and challenges. At the opening of *Prometheus*, Prometheus is bound to a rock at the ends of the earth, and there he remains. Since he cannot leave the scene, all the action must come to him, and the play consists of dialogue between the bound Prometheus and the chorus of Oceanids and conversations with other visitors. At the start of his *Oedipus at Colonus*, Sophocles has Oedipus take refuge at the shrine of the Erinyes. This decision has a vital thematic point – the importance of the physical connection of Oedipus to Athens, of which Colonus was a suburb – and designates the aged exile as the literal focus of this long drama, with all characters coming to him. These bold dramaturgical choices of *Prometheus* and *Oedipus at Colonus* are extreme versions of the more common "suppliant play" pattern. In plays such as Aeschylus' *Suppliants* and Euripides' *Suppliants*, *Helen*, *Heracles*, and *Children of Heracles*, a character takes refuge at a sacred space but remains in that position only until a rescuer arrives.

Although no simple set of categories encompasses the variety of episodes in Greek tragedy, I group together three prominent types: those involving all three actors with speaking parts; those that contain a messenger scene; and those that comprise an *agón* (verbal contest). These three types will provide a framework for exploring episodes' dramatic possibilities. Following this survey of scenes, I discuss Euripides' *Medea* in greater detail to present the overall structure built from episodes, their intersections with choral song, and their contributions to the play's architectonics and dramatic meaning.

Three-Actor Scenes

As we have seen, at any given time there could be only three actors with speaking parts on stage. More often than not scenes in Greek tragedy did not use all three actors, as the playwrights preferred to work with one or two in most scenes. It is instructive to consider Aeschylus' *Persians*, our earliest extant drama (produced in 472), in this regard. Not only are there no scenes with three actors with speaking parts but there are only two scenes featuring two actors, and even here one senses a degree of stiffness in the flow of dialogue.[3] Later plays of Aeschylus and those of Sophocles and Euripides show smoother handling of the interactions between and among the actors, but three-actor scenes remain less common, and even in such scenes the dialogue tends to unfold between pairs in sequential combination.

Nevertheless, all three tragedians exploited the possibilities of scenes with three actors. It is not until halfway through *Agamemnon* that Aeschylus takes advantage of three actors, and he does so in a surprising way. After ten years away fighting at Troy – and after more than eight hundred verses filled with foreboding about his homecoming and Clytemnestra's usurpation of his power – Agamemnon arrives on stage in a chariot (810), a seemingly triumphant victor. In a masterful stroke of dramaturgy, Aeschylus has Clytemnestra persuade her husband to enter the palace by walking on the house's delicate tapestries. With misgivings, the king does so, and the two enter the house. Everything in the play thus far leads the audience to expect death-cries from within. But after the following choral song (975–1034), Clytemnestra reappears and attempts to lead into the house Cassandra, the young captive who accompanied Agamemnon back from Troy. Although silent in the previous scene, Cassandra was visible to the audience, who could readily infer her identity. But it is not until after Clytemnestra's unsuccessful attempt to lure her indoors that Cassandra speaks. Her impassioned, initially incomprehensible cries (1072, 1076) come as a surprise. Aeschylus does not have all three actors engage each other in the same scene, but it is only the use of the third actor that makes this sequence possible.

Aeschylus uses a third actor as a surprise in the second play of the *Oresteia* trilogy, *Libation Bearers*. Pylades, Orestes' dear friend who has accompanied him on his return home from exile, has been silent throughout the play. But at the critical moment when Orestes, intent on avenging his mother's murder of his father, is faced with his mother's plea for mercy, he wavers. Turning to Pylades, he asks what he should do, and his companion does speak, urging action ("Make all mankind your enemy rather than the gods," 902). The impasse between husband-murdering mother and soon-to-be mother-murdering son is broken by the surprising utterance of this hitherto silent character.

In two consecutive episodes of *Oedipus the King*, Sophocles makes shrewd theatrical use of three-actor scenes. This play's impressively tight structure initially revolves around one question – who is the murderer of the former king Laius, the murderer whose exile will free Thebes from its present blight? All of the play's energy until this moment has been focused on this search, with the disturbing possibility that Oedipus, the current king, might be Laius' murderer. It is the unexpected arrival of a character from *outside* of Thebes that moves the play in a different direction. A messenger from Corinth (924) reports that King Polybus is dead and that Oedipus, his (putative) son, will now become king. Jocasta was on stage at the start of the episode when the messenger arrived and Oedipus soon joins them – it takes all three characters to drive the play to its first conclusion. First, the messenger speaks with Jocasta; then Jocasta, having sent for Oedipus, speaks with her husband, who then engages with the messenger. Oedipus addresses to Jocasta his fear that he might still fulfill the second half of the prophecy by marrying his mother. At this point, the messenger intervenes with the information that Oedipus is not in fact the son of Polybus and Merope but a foster child. In dialogue (primarily stichomythia), Oedipus questions the messenger about how he came to Corinth. When the messenger explains that he himself took a foundling Oedipus from a shepherd from Laius' house, Oedipus turns to Jocasta, silent for the preceding sixty or so lines, and questions her. Jocasta, who has come to realize that Oedipus is both her son and husband, tries to dissuade him from his pursuit of his identity but, failing in this, she leaves the scene with ominous words (1071–72).

At this point, Jocasta (and the audience) knows the full truth, but Oedipus does not. In the following scene another forceful manipulation of all three actors brings the full and painful truth home to Oedipus. The shepherd from Laius' household, having been summoned in the previous episode, arrives (1123) and is questioned by Oedipus. When he seems to be making no progress in his questions, the messenger intervenes to confront the shepherd about their encounter years before. This shepherd is now addressed by Oedipus, and in a fierce stichomythic exchange Oedipus learns that he is the son of Laius, the murderer of his father the king, and the most wretched man alive. A taut sequence of two-way exchanges among the three parties has allowed the truth to come forth.

In the three examples just discussed, the third actor was on stage from the beginning of the scene. *Helen* shows how the arrival of a third actor can radically move the course of the drama. Menelaus, returning from ten years of fighting at Troy to reclaim his wife, is startled to find her in Egypt, where his storm-driven ship has landed. He cannot believe that this woman with Helen's features and physique can possibly be his wife, whom he has left behind on his ship, and he starts to return to the shore, only to be thwarted by the arrival (597) of a third actor, a messenger from the ships who explains that the Helen Menelaus left on his ship was only a phantom. That phantom has now escaped into the sky, revealing that the real Helen never went to Troy at all but lived in Egypt. At this point, the reunion between faithful wife and warrior husband, almost achieved in the previous scene, unfolds in lyric delight (625–97).

Messenger Scenes

One common shape of an episode was created by the arrival of a character who would report offstage events; this is commonly called a messenger scene, although the character relays not a message but information. Such scenes, of which the preceding one in *Helen* is a truncated version, provide important news to which the characters on stage react and expand the scope of the drama as events not visible to the audience could be revealed. These reported incidents could come from another continent, another city, the neighboring countryside, or even from within the palace represented by the scene building (*skênê*). It is also well known that Greek tragedy avoided displays of onstage violence (Ajax's suicide in Sophocles' play is a notable exception to this practice), and so these scenes could depict, often in graphic detail, the brutal acts that were essential elements of the drama's story.

A strong majority of the surviving plays include a messenger scene, and some even have two (*Bacchae* and *Phoenician Women*). No two scenes are identical in form, but we can identify some common characteristics. Typically the messenger arrives, usually immediately after a choral song; he communicates with the chorus-leader or another character already on stage and announces in brief the substance of his report. Before or after this initial report, another character may arrive. The messenger then delivers a long speech in which he describes in detail the events he has announced. A short dialogue between the messenger and the chorus-leader or other character follows; the messenger then exits, and the episode either concludes at this point or after a brief dialogue. The content of messenger speeches is vivid and often graphic: they contain descriptions of horrific suffering, battles, and even miraculous events. They are typically very long, often the longest *rhêsis* in a play. In many instances, the messenger scene fills an entire episode, while in others it constitutes only one scene within the larger act.

From a literary perspective, messenger speeches resemble epic narrative in several ways. The leisurely pace of the narrative echoes Homeric technique. The effective use of direct speech also corresponds to epic practice, and the more frequent use of epithets resonates with epic formulas. The greater abundance of the imperfective verbal aspect (for a contemporary equivalent, we might think of a video clip rather than a still photo) is also reminiscent of epic. Formally, messenger speeches, while still fundamentally composed in the Attic dialect of the rest of the spoken sections of tragedy, contain a higher number of Homeric forms, which add to the epic flavor of these reports.

The identity of the messenger can vary. Most commonly, he has no particular connection to the drama's action, but on occasion he is an important character in the play. Rarely does the messenger have any name. No messenger is more memorable than the guard in *Antigone*. While he functions as a messenger does in many other plays – he delivers critical information from outside the acting area – he is exceptional in at least three respects. First, he has two scenes (he returns with Antigone in the next episode). Second, unlike most "messengers," who are given little personality, delivering information and departing the theatrical space as quickly as they arrive, this guard is memorable for his hesitation to report his news and for his frank concern for his own lot. Third, the sudden nature of his appearance is underscored by the lack of an entrance announcement. (By convention, a character arriving on stage *within* an episode, rather than at its beginning, is announced when there are at least two persons on stage.)

Variations on the common pattern of messenger scenes could be highly effective. In *Women of Trachis*, Sophocles introduces a messenger (180), who reports (very briefly) on Heracles' whereabouts, the subject of his wife Deianira's and the chorus's deep anxiety up to that point in the play. Then a second messenger, Lichas, arrives (229) with the further news of the hero's imminent homecoming, and he delivers a more substantial and typical messenger speech (248–90). Lichas, however, lies. He conceals the fact that Heracles has fallen in love with Iole, the princess of Oechalia and one of the captives who have accompanied Lichas on stage. It is only when the first messenger takes Deianira aside and informs her of these lies that she can confront Lichas and learn the full truth of Heracles' passion and her own profoundly changed situation. This discovery sets in motion the play's plot and tragic outcome.

Aeschylus' *Seven against Thebes* makes the most remarkable use of messenger speeches, structuring its centerpiece around them. At 369–74, a scout/messenger and Eteocles are simultaneously introduced, each arriving from one of the two *eisodoi* (entrance ramps). Over three hundred lines are then taken up by seven reports from the scout/messenger about each of seven enemy soldiers placed at one of Thebes' seven gates with Eteocles responding to each report with the designation of an Argive defender. The climax is reached when Eteocles learns that at the seventh gate stands his brother Polynices. He determines that he himself will go out to meet him, even though he is well aware of the fate awaiting him – dying at the hands of the brother he is about to kill.

While most messenger scenes bring someone from outside with information from the countryside, the port, or another land, some scenes carry a message from within the *skênê*, representing in most cases the royal palace. The name *exangelos* (as opposed to *angelos*) is sometimes given to the messenger reporting events from within, but there is no formal distinction between the two types. Messenger scenes bringing news from within (for instance, of the suicide of Jocasta and self-blinding of Oedipus at *Oedipus the King* 1223–96) conform to the same basic patterns as those bringing news from abroad, although they tend to be shorter in length.

Messenger scenes not only convey information not readily presented otherwise and enlarge the scope of the plays, they also serve as a bridge to a subsequent visual display. In many cases, the messenger's narration of events is all the audience learns of them, but frequently the consequences of the events depicted vividly *in words* in the messenger's report are soon revealed before the audience's eyes in the following scene or episode. In *Hippolytus*, the mysterious bull from the sea and its gruesome destruction of Hippolytus and his chariot could not be shown on stage, but the young man, on the point of death and pained with every step he takes, dominates the following scene. Perhaps the most affecting use of a messenger scene as a bridge is in *Bacchae*, in which the (second) messenger's report of Pentheus' dismemberment at the hands of his mother and her fellow crazed maenads is followed in the next episode with Agave rejoicing in the murder of her son, whose head she brandishes (in all probability the actor held the mask earlier worn by the actor playing Pentheus), in the deluded belief that she has killed a lion. Cadmus then arrives with attendants carrying back Pentheus' dismembered corpse and gradually guides Agave toward realizing her infanticide.

Agôn

From the law-courts to the marketplace, from the Sophists to the politicians, Athens was a city of words. It is unsurprising, then, that one form that episodes took was the *agón* – a contest of words. The basic form of an *agón* was a formalized debate between two parties. As is the case in many areas, such episodes were more formalized and frequent in Euripides than in Aeschylus and Sophocles, occurring in almost every play. While the *agón* could be flexible in its structure, its most commonly recurring elements were: introductory exchange between the two parties, one of whom has typically just arrived on stage; set speeches of roughly equal length by each party in which he or she lays out the particulars of the argument; a choral "buffer" – a few, often banal, lines that serve mainly as a break between the two longish set speeches; and a concluding exchange between the two parties (see Duchemin 1968, 156–66, on the flexibility of this form; and Lloyd 1992 on *agónes* in Euripides). A third actor, if present, could play the role of judge and issue a verdict. As was the case in the Athenian law-courts, the first party to speak was generally the character in the role of prosecutor, with the second one playing the role of defendant. Neither party, even when one of the arguments was much stronger, ever persuaded the other; the conflict only deepened. The speeches were retrospective and did not directly advance the plot.

Greek tragedy's only actual courtroom scene is found in Aeschylus' *Eumenides*. In this scene, the court of the Areopagus is established as the site of all future homicide trials, but the scene does not take the form of an *agón*. It lacks the characteristic set speeches and does not have the formalized structure that we find in many later plays. What defines an *agón*, then, is not its resemblance to Athenian legal procedures or language, but rather its structure foregrounding two opposing, nearly equal speeches.

Each of the two opposing speeches was highly rhetorical and tightly structured, with forcefully marshaled arguments and (often) with clear enumeration ("first," "and next," etc.). On numerous occasions, a participant expressly acknowledges that she or he is engaged in a "contest of words." Reflecting contemporary rhetorical and forensic practice, characters often adduced arguments from probability to make their point. The second speech of the pair was responsive to the first, sometimes engaging the previous arguments point by point, at other times simply making a strong counter-argument without point-by-point refutation.

Although the *agón* became a regular part of Euripidean drama and reflected the Athenians' keen interest in legal debate, it never became so formalized as to lose its dramatic relevance. These scenes always were connected to issues within the drama, albeit with varying degrees of tightness. No scene could be more integral to a drama than the *agón* in Euripides' *Hippolytus* between father and son over the allegation that Hippolytus had raped his father's wife (902–1101). Theseus' stinging denunciation of his son's seemingly hypocritical life of virtue is met unsuccessfully by Hippolytus' assertions of virtue and arguments from probability. The stakes are high – Hippolytus is trying to persuade his father to rescind his proclamation of exile – and Theseus effectively functions as judge as well as prosecutor. Phaedra's corpse, present throughout the entire scene, serves as a most damning witness (972). The formalism of an *agón* might seem contrived to a modern audience, but this example demonstrates how effectively it can juxtapose Theseus' implacable anger and Hippolytus' futile defense. In some other plays, the *agón* might not be so integrally related to the dramatic action, but in every instance, the *agón* scene provides a well recognized and appreciated forum for the crisp articulation of vital issues.

An *agón* with two participants and a third party as judge is well represented by the third episode of *Trojan Women*, a scene that also illustrates the rhetorical possibilities of this form. Demonstrating the innocence of Helen, condemned in Greek myth as the cause of the Trojan War, became a challenge for fifth-century rhetoricians, who claimed they could make the weaker argument prevail over the stronger one. The contemporary Sicilian rhetorician Gorgias' *Encomium of Helen* presented an artful, if at times gloriously specious, defense of Helen, and in this play Euripides brings Helen and Hecuba into debate, with Menelaus, her betrayed yet still smitten husband, as judge. Atypically for the "defendant," Helen speaks first, and begins with an explicit reference to a debate in which she will match Hecuba point for point (916–18). She argues that, whatever her role, other factors, including the (in)action of Paris' parents, led to the Trojan War; that, in any case, her marriage to Paris was good for Greece, since a different outcome of the Judgment of Paris would have led to Greece's subjugation; that Aphrodite accompanied Paris to Sparta and as a god was not to be withstood; that she did in fact try to escape from Troy after Paris' death; and, finally, that she should not be put to death for being forced into a marriage and made subject to the gods.

Hecuba responds point for point, disagreeing with Helen's account of the Judgment of Paris as being insulting to the gods involved; asserting that *aphrosuné* (lack of good judgment) and not Aphrodite was responsible for Helen's running off with Paris; challenging Helen's claim that she was abducted by Paris; disputing her story that she tried to escape once at Troy; criticizing Helen for decking herself out for Menelaus' benefit; and concluding with an appeal to Menelaus that he execute Helen for her adultery. This detailed refutation of Helen's arguments seems to persuade Menelaus, and in his capacity as judge he announces that she will be punished by death. But he was husband as well as judge, and, as was well known in the mythological tradition, he did not execute Helen. Overwhelmed by her beauty, he spared her and they resumed their life together in Sparta. Hecuba's apparent victory is undercut by Menelaus' equivocation (e.g., 1057) and the force of tradition.

Sophocles did not develop the *agôn* scene as fully as did Euripides. The debate between Clytemnestra and Electra in *Electra* about the former's murder of Agamemnon (516–633) comes closest to the Euripidean norm, with set speeches of substantial length and clearly delineated arguments. But even in this instance he does not follow the Euripidean practice of concluding the debate with an exit by one of the participants in the *agôn* (Lloyd 1992, 11). Mother and daughter remain on stage, and the play moves forward with the arrival of the pedagogue (660) bringing news of Orestes' supposed death.

Medea

Unlike Sophocles, who opened most of his plays with two characters in dialogue, Euripides preferred a single opening monologue. Euripides' prologues have been compared to playbills in a modern theater: they provide necessary background information for the drama. This is true, but they do much more, as they emphasize certain elements, establish themes, contain (at times) misleading information, and display a character's *éthos* (Dunn 1996). In her opening speech (1–48), the nurse explains from her very sympathetic perspective Medea's history and current plight – Jason is in love with the king's daughter and has abandoned Medea, who had forsaken family and homeland for him. In her narration, the nurse also expresses her concern that Medea may harm her children, at which point she announces their arrival.

After learning from the tutor of Creon's plan to exile Medea, the nurse sends the children into the house, again expressing her fear for their safety (90–95). The prologue seems to have run its course and one would expect the arrival of the chorus with their opening song. But Euripides plays against this expectation and introduces Medea from off-stage. First, we hear Medea's cries of woe delivered in lyric anapests (a rhythm between the spoken iambics of the preceding scene and the full lyric of the following *parodos*). The nurse, who remains on stage, also changes her delivery to anapestic verse, but of a slightly different variety that does not express the same emotional valence as the lyric anapests uttered by Medea. When the chorus of Corinthian women sing their entry song, they begin with anapests, picking up the nurse's and Medea's rhythm, and then move into aeolic verse for the strophic part of the song. Interspersed throughout this song, but metrically distinct from it, are the continued anapestic cries of Medea and fears and reflections of the nurse.

The first episode (214–409) is tightly structured. It opens with Medea giving what amounts to a second prologue, matching in length the nurse's opening speech. The nurse has told Medea's story, and now Medea gives her own perspective in a *rhêsis* addressed to the Corinthian women who comprise the chorus. She cleverly frames her speech around the difficult plight of women, a bond she shares with her audience of Corinthian women (her speech's first words are the polite and pointed "women of Corinth"). Having connected with her fellow women, Medea explains her plan to punish Jason for his betrayal and is able to win a promise of silence from the chorus. Medea's speech both balances the nurse's prologue and contrasts with her own earlier cries from within. Those cries of pain and anger have yielded to the subtle and effective rhetoric of her *rhêsis*.

Creon's arrival (271) poses a threat to Medea's intended vengeance as he commands that she go into exile immediately. Medea, however, uses supplication (325–51) to win from Creon a one-day reprieve. As a suppliant, she places herself at the king's mercy by grasping his hands and knees. This physical act of supplication occurs almost at the center of the episode, in the second of its three scenes, and it is pivotal to the plot, as Creon's stay of exile allows Medea the time to exact her vengeance and implicates Creon in the ensuing violence. After the king leaves, the episode concludes with Medea expanding her plan for vengeance. The episode forms a triptych: Medea with chorus (214–70); Medea with Creon (271–356); and Medea with chorus (357–409). And in the course of these three panels, Medea, having duped Creon, moves from an intention to punish Jason to an explicit declaration that she will kill Jason, Creon, and Glauce, if only she can find a means of escape.

The sanctity of oaths and a sense of what is right have vanished from Greece, the women of Corinth sing in the concluding stanza of their first stasimon (410–45), and immediately Jason, the living proof of these assertions, arrives (446). This is the first of three episodes between Jason and Medea, and collectively these three scenes provide much of the play's architecture. Here, the two engage in a typical *agôn*. After Jason's arrival and his opening remarks, Medea delivers her attack on her husband in clear and neatly articulated arguments (465–519). Following a short introduction, she says she'll deal with first things first (475) and then marshals her case: she saved Jason's life, gave up everything for him, and he swore oaths of fidelity to her, which he has now violated by his new marriage, while she, having abandoned all for him, is left with nothing. Jason's reply (522–75), almost identical in length, seeks to rebut her argument point for point: Aphrodite is responsible for his salvation, Medea has benefited by being rescued from a barbarian land, his marriage is motivated not by passion but by political advantage, and Medea, like all women, is too easily distressed by matters of passion and sex. There is no "judge" to declare a victor in this debate, although the chorus-leader voices her opinion that Jason has unjustly betrayed his wife (576–78). The two principals then continue their assaults in dialogue. As is typically the case, the conflict, now fully articulated, has only deepened, and Jason departs with Medea's ominous words at his back ("perhaps you will regret this marriage of yours," 625–26).

The following song (627–62) looks both backwards and forwards. By singing of the great power of excessive passion, it clearly connects to the preceding episode and contains a precise verbal link to the final line of the episode. That line, framed by the word for marriage (*gameis...gamon*, 626), is echoed in the song's emphatic anaphoric opening of *erôtes... erôtes* ("passion ... passion"). Less commonly recognized is the subtle yet strong link between the song and the following episode. In their concluding stanza (654–62), the chorus, summarizing Medea's situation, emphasizes the importance of friends, repeating the word *philos* three times. Aegeus immediately arrives on stage, greeting Medea and proclaiming them to be friends (*philoi*), 663–64. Aegeus' appearance has long been found wanting in motivation (Aristotle called it "improbable," *Poetics* 1461b19–21). It is true that nothing *explicitly* prepares for it and his reason for showing up in Corinth is weak; his arrival is a surprise. But the situation that has developed requires such an appearance. Medea has expressed her intentions of killing king, princess, and husband, if she can find a means to escape, and we have just witnessed her verbal *agón* with Jason. Something must resolve the impasse of a lack of escape; otherwise the play sputters. So Aegeus' appearance has been prepared for by the situation, and the verbal link between song and episode creates an unobtrusive connection.

Aegeus, sympathetic to Medea's plight, promises her sanctuary in his home city of Athens but will not be involved in rescuing her from Corinth. His departure and the following brief anapestic choral "send-off" (759–63) breaks off this section of the episode, just as similar anapests marked the conclusion of the scene between Medea and Creon (358–63). With a place of sanctuary assured, Medea advances her intended vengeance even further: she now will kill her own children, which she sees as the best way to sting her husband (817). The chorus responds to this episode with an encomium of Athens. They also wonder how this city (of all cities) could receive a child-murderer.

Like the second episode, the fourth one begins with Jason's arrival and its shape is what one might think of as an anti-*agón*. After Jason's brief remarks on arrival, Medea addresses her husband (her first word is "Jason," whereas in the previous episode between them her first word was "most vile one" and nowhere in that episode did she call him by name), acknowledges her mistakes, and says that Jason's actions are sensible. In her words, she echoes many of Jason's claims about her behavior in the previous episode (see Mastronarde 2002b, 312–13). She then calls out their children in an effort to persuade their father of her plans. As in the first scene, Jason's speech responds, albeit not so closely, to hers, and these two speeches are followed by dialogue. The previous episode showed the two in hostile combat; this one shows a supposedly chastened Medea and an understanding Jason. In the previous episode, Medea rejected Jason's offer of financial support for the children; in this one, Jason accepts a gift from Medea. This encounter, like the previous one, ends, as it began, with Jason's departure, but this time accompanied by his children. In the *agôn*, Medea was unsuccessful, but in this anti-*agôn*, she persuades Jason and thereby accomplishes the first stage of her revenge. Just as this episode echoes the previous one between husband and wife, it is also the third episode in which we witness Medea winning a critical concession from a male character. First, she wins a one-day reprieve from Creon, then a promise of refuge in Athens from Aegeus, and now an agreement from Jason to have their children present his new bride with a wedding gift.

Underscoring Jason's naiveté, the Corinthian women sing about the inevitable consequences of his accepting this gift: the children will no longer live once Glauce puts on and is destroyed by these wedding offerings of robe and crown. This song is very brief (976–1001), as the plot drives forward. The tutor returns with the children, announcing the princess's happy acceptance of the gifts and the end of the strife between Medea and Jason. He soon repairs into the *skênê* and Medea is left on stage, with her children, to deliver a soliloquy (1019–80). Faced with the enormity of her intended actions, she hesitates, going back and forth between her decision to kill her children and a desire to escape with them. Few speeches in Greek tragedy are as affecting or powerful as this one. Its power is achieved primarily through the remarkable psychological display of Medea's thinking and it is enhanced structurally by the intense focus it receives. This scene is very brief, framed by a full choral song and by choral anapests (1081–1115) reflecting on the sorrows that children cause parents. Although this fifth episode is not formally closed off by a choral song, the lengthy run of chanted anapests serves functionally as an act-dividing song, and the messenger scene that follows constitutes the sixth episode. The spotlight, as it were, falls on Medea in her moment of anguished deliberation.

The sixth episode (1121–1250) conforms closely to the conventions of messenger scenes. The messenger arrives, gives in dialogue a summary of events, and delivers a full and rich narrative, detailing how Glauce received the gift from the children and then died piteously along with her father, who came to her aid. One small variation on the common pattern underscores the unusual situation: upon arrival, the messenger's opening words are for Medea to flee (1121–23). Medea, who at the end of the preceding episode had resolved to kill her children, now leaves the stage (1250), after announcing that she must do this as quickly as possible and steeling herself for the act of infanticide.

Is this Medea's first exit in the play? Most likely, yes. It is possible that she exited with the children at 1080 and reemerged after the choral interlude to announce the messenger.[4] Her lines announcing the messenger (1116–20), however, suggest that she has been on stage throughout the song and has not just returned. And it would be dramatically less effective if she were to enter the house to kill her children, return (with no comment) to interact with the messenger, and then enter the house once again to carry out the murder. Rather, Medea, who has been on stage for over a thousand lines (one of the longest continuous stage presences in tragedy), and who has dominated the dramatic focus, successfully manipulating three men, and finally resolving to perform this grim and painful murder, leaves only when she is in fact going to finally carry it out. This play could have been produced with only two actors with speaking parts; no scene requires three such actors. Medea's domination of the action is underscored by the consistent and intense focus the play puts on her.

A full choral song follows Medea's exit (1251–92), but it is broken up by cries from within. After an initial pair of stanzas invoking Earth and the Sun to behold this crime and claiming the futility of rearing children, from within the *skêné* we hear the cries of the children as they seek to avoid their mother's murderous hands. This bold stroke echoes an earlier scene. Medea's first appearance was preceded by her cries from within the *skêné*, embedded (in part) within the opening choral song, while her final appearance is preceded by her children's cries from within the *skêné*, embedded within the play's final choral song.

Jason's third and final encounter with Medea forms the *exodos* of this play. In the previous two scenes with Medea, Jason arrived with Medea already on stage. Here, she is not present but seemingly within the house. Jason learns from the chorus-leader that his children are dead, but in a vain attempt to rescue them, he commands his attendants to force open the doors. At this moment, Medea appears on high, triumphant in the chariot of the Sun (her grandfather), with the children's corpses safely on board. The contrast between Medea and Jason could not be greater. Medea is now fully in command, literally on high, in control of the children, and about to depart for Athens. She has exacted her vengeance, and Jason is reduced to idle words and feeble threats. The first two scenes between them are verbal contests – the first a conventional *agón*, the second a type of anti-*agón*. In the third scene, however, their verbal exchange takes on a new character. Medea has entered a different realm, from which she is invulnerable to Jason's power or threats. She no longer needs to argue but to proclaim. Like a god at the end of many Euripidean plays, she confidently predicts what will happen to the children and what awaits Jason himself. And she denies Jason what at this point, deprived of his new wife and their intended offspring, he wants most of all, his children, and departs for Athens victorious.

NOTES

1   For the purposes of this essay, I accept, with modification, Aristotle's definition. The definitions in this section of the *Poetics*, however, are not without problems. For a concise survey of the key issues, see Taplin 1977, 470–76.

2   Sophocles' *Oedipus the King*, the date of which is unknown but commonly thought to be from the early 420s, concludes with lines of trochaic tetrameter (1515–30), but the authenticity of these lines has been debated; see Dawe 1982 and Lloyd-Jones and Wilson 1990.

3   See Michelini 1982, 27–40. Even if one concedes the point about the stiffness of the play's dialogue, it is possible that this does not reflect its early date but the playwright's design.

4   It has also been suggested that Medea exited initially at 823 to apply poison to the gifts, but the text gives no reason to infer this, and such realism (that is, the consideration that Medea has to apply poison to the gifts at this point) is not likely to have concerned an ancient playwright. On the timing of Medea's exit, see Mastronarde 2002b, 304 and 346.

FURTHER READING

Suggestive raw data about Greek episodes can be found in Aichele 1971. On the *agón*,
Duchemin's 1968 study remains the most comprehensive and is strong on structural
elements. Lloyd 1992, devoted to this form in Euripides, offers valuable commentary on
individual scenes and their function in the plays. Messenger scenes, like *agón* scenes, are most
common in Euripides. The best treatment of them, from a narratological perspective, is de
Jong 1991. On the general structure and architectonics of Greek tragedy, Taplin 1978 (in
addition to his thorough and very scholarly *The Stagecraft of Aeschylus* [1977]) is also very
valuable. Focusing on three plays of each of the tragedians, it explores the ways in which
dramatic structure creates meanings. Halleran 1985 considers various structural elements in
Euripides, with a special focus on *Heracles*, *Trojan Women*, and *Ion*. Donald Mastronarde's
recent edition of *Medea* (Mastronarde 2002b) contains much useful commentary on structural aspects of the drama.

CHAPTER TWELVE

Music

Peter Wilson

Stopped on his way to the tragic competitions of the City Dionysia and asked where he was headed, the average classical Athenian in the street would very probably have replied, "*es chorous*" ("to the choruses") or perhaps "*es tragôidous*" ("to the *tragos*-singers"). If he was quizzed further as to just how he would categorize this activity so beloved of his city, the term *mousikê* (the "craft of the Muses" and the origin of our "music") would have very soon entered the conversation. For the Athenians, tragedy was – fundamentally, predominantly, and persistently – a *musical* event.

Fundamentally, since – at least until the middle of the fifth century – tragedy was oriented around its singing-and-dancing heart, the chorus (*choros*), and (to dip our toes in the dangerous waters of origins) it was probably in the bifurcation of a single lead singer from a choral group that the distinctive double form of tragedy, with its individual actors and singing-dancing chorus, arose.

Predominantly, because the chorus, with its highly choreographed dance-songs performed by some twelve or fifteen elaborately costumed and masked men in the wide open space of the orchestra, must have been the dominant physical and aesthetic presence in tragedy, one that, unlike the actors, virtually never left the space that they entered at or near the start of a play. And even as the quantitative contribution of the chorus progressively declined over the course of the classical period, as though to counterbalance this musical loss, the actors began to sing more and more from the stage.

And *persistently*, because even centuries after the end of the most creative period of classical tragedy, audiences from Syracuse to Abdera and beyond clamored for the *songs* of Euripides as much as the speeches, to the extent that the craze could be deemed a national epidemic (see the fascinating story told by Lucian, *How to Write History* 1; cf. Axionicus fr. 3 *PCG*).

The musical orientation of Greek tragedy was not lost on those sixteenth-century Florentine pioneers of opera who conceived of their new cultural project as basically a regeneration of Greek tragedy for a new age (see Blom 1954, 6: 194–200). But the modern era has been more forgetful. One reason for this is the simple loss of virtually all the material that might help us understand tragedy in its fully musical dimension.

But another important factor is the huge influence exerted by the Aristotelian conception of drama on all modern criticism. In his *Poetics*, Aristotle promulgated a formalist approach to the genre that largely edited out its performative dimension. Action (*praxis*), plot (*muthos*), and moral disposition (*êthos*) were the controlling interests of this approach; the least important of the elements that went to make up tragedy were spectacle (*opsis*) and song (*melos*). Indeed, song was little more than a sweetener, a kind of pleasing spice to the serious business of action, word, and thought (*Poetics*, esp. 1449b2–1450b20, but see the Further Reading section for a new and very different interpretation from Sifakis). According to Aristotle, it was not even necessary to see – or to *hear* – tragedy in order to experience "the tragic" (*Poetics*, esp. 1450b18–20, 1453b4, 1462a12).

In sharp contrast, many other ancient scholars devoted special studies to the music of tragedy – the greatest musicologist of antiquity, Aristoxenus of Tarentum (born around 370 BCE), among them. He wrote works entitled *On Tragic Poets, On Tragic Dancing*, and *On Aulos-Players*, but with the total loss of these works, combined with the enormous prestige of Aristotle's authority, not to mention Plato's more aggressive and generalized condemnation of the genre, it is little wonder that the music of tragedy has remained a rather abstruse special interest within dramatic studies. As a result of three factors, however – the recent burgeoning of performance studies, the application of this approach to Greek tragedy, and the widespread, indeed global, increase in the restaging and multimedia reworking of ancient tragedy – this situation is rapidly changing.

The Place of Music in Tragedy

The chorus very often chanted and marched in unison as it entered the stage at or near the start of the drama (this was known as a *parodos*, or entrance-song), and as it departed at the end (the *exodos*), though in both cases their delivery may have been fully sung; there were usually at least three or four major choral dance-songs (known as *stasima*) that interwove the episodes throughout the drama and gave the form its distinctive pattern. The chorus could also engage in sung exchange with actors, known as *kommos*. This term means "dirge" (and is close to the other common term for lament in tragedy, *thrênos*), which is the activity usually, though not always, involved in such tragic sung exchange: the mighty *kommos* of Aeschylus' *Libation Bearers* 306–478 is the finest example and is effectively the dramatic, emotional, ritual, and musical core of the play. On the other hand, actors could sing solo songs, and less often duets, from the stage: for instance, the blinded Polymestor sings in Euripides' *Hecuba* (1056–1108), and Polyxena and Hecuba sing to each other in the same play (177–215). And there is the unforgettable, shocking song (where we might have expected a messenger speech) by the Phrygian eunuch slave in Euripides' *Orestes* (1369–1502). Actors could also be required to deliver lines (usually in anapestic meter) in a kind of recitative: in fact, there may have been a number of different modes of delivery for actors between full song and plain speech (see Hall 1999a, esp. 106–7). The sound of such semi-sung anapests is often a marker of movement, physical and emotional, as with the frenzied entry and exit of Io in Aeschylus' *Prometheus Bound* (561–65, 877–86). And we should remember that by "plain speech" is meant the lines in the iambic trimeter which, though a spoken meter close to the cadences of ordinary speech (Aristotle, *Rhetoric* 1404a31–35), was much more highly rhythmical and ordered than plain speech. There was, finally, limited use of purely instrumental interludes – perhaps nothing more than brief flourishes between the stanzas of choral odes (known as *mesaulia* or *diaulia*: Psellus [?], *On Tragedy* 9, Perusino 1993).

Resources

Virtually all our evidence (images on vases, inscriptions relating to the theater, and literary texts) points in the same direction: the instrument of tragedy was the *aulos* or pipe – or rather a pair of *auloi* played together, as was normal tragic practice. As one ancient scholar comments: "the choruses of tragedy used to sing their entrance-songs (*parodoi*) to the accompaniment of the *aulos* with great energy, and the finest *aulos*-players executed the accompanying music" (Psellus [?], *On Tragedy* 12, Perusino 1993). The sound made by these double pipes, each of which had a double reed, a bit like an oboe or the medieval shawm, was penetrating and strident, and well suited as a result to outdoor use. It was a sound associated in the Greek mind with madness, possession, drunkenness, orgiastic frenzy, and satyrs – in other words, with "bacchic activity and all movement of that sort," as Aristotle put it (*Politics* 1342b). There may have been a special variety of the *aulos* designed for use in tragedy (see Athenaeus 182c–d with Wilson 2002, 44). It is at any rate certain that over the course of the fifth century the technology of the instrument developed rapidly, allowing for all sorts of musical innovation. By the last decades of the century, for instance, the player was able to move between different musical "modes" (see below) as he played, by means of sliding metal sleeves attached to the pipes; previously, he had had to switch between a different set of *auloi* for each separate mode.

The *aulos* was in any case an enormously adaptable instrument. Ancient sources refer to it as highly mimetic or "polyphonic" (for example, Pindar, *Olympian* 7.12, *Isthmian* 5.27; Plato, *Republic* 399d), and this musical flexibility, and its power to imitate the manifold voices – and sounds – of others, made it essential to tragedy's broader evocation of the Other. For instance, outside tragedy the *aulos* is frequently associated with the sound of lamentation and many of its formal musical expressions, in particular, with lament as voiced by *females* (for example, Pindar, *Pythian* 12, esp. 19–22). The musical and tonal power of the *aulos* to evoke such registers beneath the singing of the all-male tragic chorus will have been vital in a genre where the music of lament is a dominant form. Later in the fifth century the technical innovations on the instrument that I have mentioned meant that inanimate, even mechanical, noises, as well as the sounds of wild nature, could be reproduced on the *aulos*: we hear of storms, the noises of axles, ropes, and pulleys, and the cries of women in labor (Plato, *Republic* 396b, *Laws* 669c–d; Aristotle, *Poetics* 1461b30).

There is some debate as to whether the other most widespread instrumental resource available to the Greeks – namely, the two common varieties of stringed instrument (lyre and kithara) – were used in tragedy. It is at least clear that they were not the "standard" accompaniment (and so, strictly speaking, the term "tragic *lyric*" is something of a misnomer; we would be well advised to use "melic" instead). The poet almost certainly used a lyre when composing – and directing – the music of his tragedies: at the most basic practical level, he would need a "free mouth" for both these activities. The stringed instruments seem to have made appearances on the tragic stage under rather special circumstances: when the mythic plot demanded it, for instance, as in the case of Sophocles' popular (but lost) work called *Thamyras*, a tragedy about the musical *hubris* of the Thracian singer-musician who dared to compete with the Muses themselves. (If it is not identical to *Thamyras*, Sophocles' play *The Muses* is another likely candidate for lyre-playing on stage, perhaps even by a chorus of Muses.) Euripides' *Antiope* is another case (see Wilson 1999–2000): this play featured an extended *agón* between the twins Amphion and Zethus that debated the virtues of the "quiet life" of music (Amphion) as opposed to the life of military action (Zethus). Amphion certainly played his lyre on stage in this tragedy, and the quarrel between the brothers was to some extent resolved by an order from on high that Amphion should use his lyre-music to build the walls of the city of Thebes. In thus combining their skills, the brothers overcame the opposition between the practical and the "musical" worldviews.

While clearly special cases, these tragic lyres command our interest for a number of reasons. In the first place, they remind us of the fact that a significant body of specifically musical myth found a home on the tragic stage. In other words, *mousikê* was an area of such cultural and dramatic importance in Athens that it demanded the treatment of the genre best suited to probing the most difficult issues of social life. Secondly, it is revealing that the stringed instruments appear on stage in the hands of high-status, heroic figures, a fact that is in keeping with contemporary educational debates in Athenian society as to who should learn the art of lyre-playing, traditionally the preserve of the moneyed elite. These debates arose at a time when the traditional cultural formation was being significantly challenged by the arts of rhetoric, which offered new sectors of society access to political power.

The pipe-players (*aulêtai* in the plural, singular *aulêtês*) of tragedy are very much the genre's unsung heroes: they helped lead in the chorus at its first entry and off again at the end. (See the frontispiece for an illustration of an *aulêtês*.) Present throughout, they provided, in addition to their specifically instrumental contribution, direction and support for the smooth running of the choral parts, perhaps even serving to support the leader of the chorus as an onstage director of dance and musical timing. Their technical skills, physical stamina (the *aulos* required a formidable supply of air under high pressure), and musical contribution must have been vital to the overall success of any dramatic performance (compare Demosthenes' anecdote [21.17] about how the *aulêtês* Telephanes saved his choral performance when his poet-trainer had been corrupted by a rival). And yet we cannot with confidence name a single pipe-player who performed at an original production of Aeschylus, Sophocles, or Euripides. This anonymity is in part attributable to their status. These introducers of alterity, as we might call them, were themselves somewhat "other" in Athenian civic terms – almost always lower-class and non-Athenian (and so sharply distinguished from the citizen-choristers with whom they worked most closely); associated with the more technical, and so banausic, aspect of musical performance (cf. Aristotle, *Politics* 1339a11–1342b26).

In terms of melodic structures, timbre, performance styles, and even rhythms, the music of tragedy is a largely lost world. Perhaps the single most important building-block of all Greek music was the mode (in the earlier period usually termed *harmonia*, later sometimes also called a *tonos* or *tropos*). Basically a mode is a kind of scale, a set of notes of fixed intervals to which an instrument would be tuned. Although our knowledge of the (complex) system of modes in use in the classical period is far from full, it is clear that each different mode carried very powerful associations, based on the contexts in which it was regularly used. The modes bore (approximately) ethnic names – Dorian, Lydian, Ionian, Phrygian, and so on – reflecting an at least imagined origin for these different musical patterns in distinct geographical and ethnic regions. But crucially, the modes were above all understood in highly *moral* or ethical terms (to use "ethical" in its Aristotelian sense of relating to moral disposition). Plato, a severe critic of Athenian musical as well as poetic practice, wanted to have most of the modes banned from public usage, including nearly all of those used in tragedy. Particular targets included the Mixed Lydian and High-Pitched Lydian modes – because, in his view, they were too closely linked to excessive mourning, and to women. He was also keen to eliminate the modes that were termed "soft" (a descriptive term with both musical and ethical meanings), such as the Ionian mode, commonly found in "Eastern" sympotic contexts, and some other Lydian modes, the implication being that listening or singing to such music would induce indolence and pathic homosexuality (see Plato, *Republic* 397–98). The Dorian mode, by contrast, the only one that could be associated closely with the Hellenic heartland (and conservative Sparta in particular), was regarded as making its hearers courageous, more manly, even more just. The basic notion behind this thinking – that music makes the man, that different tunes, scales, and instruments actively shape the moral and physical disposition of their players and hearers – was not some bizarre theory conjured up by a few philosophers, but was extremely widespread in Greek culture. And it helps us understand one important way in which the Athenians saw the musical medium of tragedy as having a formative, broadly educational force: if we peel off the polemical parti pris of Plato, we might say that tragedy's complex combination of musical styles "formed" those complex, adaptable citizens who constituted the Periclean ideal (see Thucydides 2.41.1).

We hear of a range of modes being used in tragedy, and, as with all technical matters, the situation certainly changed over time. But the fact that multiple modes were used at all made of tragedy an extraordinary new phenomenon, a musically, as well as metrically, complex medium; and correspondingly, a morally complex experience for its performers and audience alike. The Dorian was a staple, perhaps regularly associated with male choruses, and linked in Plato's mind with such scenarios as soldiers facing adversity with strength and courage. The Mixed Lydian and the Phrygian were also used in tragedy, and were associated with the strong emotions of grief and ecstasy – the former said on good authority to have been borrowed by the tragic poets from Sappho (Aristoxenus fr. 81 Wehrli), the latter supposedly introduced by Sophocles (*Life of Sophocles* 23).

Were we able to advance our understanding of these important musical structures, we would certainly gain a more nuanced and profound appreciation of the emotions and psychology, as well as the sound, of tragedy. And this would go some way toward helping us break down the unhelpful dichotomy that still persists (see, for example, Griffin 1998) between views of tragedy as, on the one hand, preeminently an emotional experience, a matter of enjoyment and entertainment, however harrowing, and, on the other, as a medium for intellectual reflection more concerned with matters of state and society. For the Greeks, the emotions generated by and reflected in musical media were intimately related to matters moral and political. Indeed, one highly influential fifth-century Athenian musical theorist and politician, Damon, formulated the position that "the modes [*tropoi*] of music are never changed without changing the most important laws [*nomoi*] of the city" (quoted by Socrates in Plato, *Republic* 424c; see Wallace 2004).

When we extend our survey of tragedy's music beyond the issue of its specifically instrumental and melodic resources to encompass other musical elements, the un- usually absorbent and polymorphic nature of the genre again comes to the fore. The chorus of tragedy has long been something of a problem for modern sensibilities. Its collective identity, and its habit of shifting suddenly from something like an active participant in the action to a fully fledged operatic and balletic group that seems to suspend the very time of dramatic narrative, unsettles modern notions of theater, even of identity. Recent work on this fascinating and flexible component of drama has however shown how effective its layering of identities and shifting of time-frames can be. As well as being a particular, characterized group – for instance, of Salaminian sailors, following their heroic leader and interacting with him, as in Sophocles' *Ajax* – the chorus of tragedy remains a chorus in the wider Greek religious and social sense of a group constituted to sing and dance for the gods, and to express the most important moments in a society's individual and collective life (marriage, death, victory, making the transition to adulthood, and so on). The tragic chorus can take on the activities of any number of such real-life choruses: it can sing and dance what looks very much like elements of the victory-song (*epinikion*) commissioned by aristocratic winners in the panhellenic athletic games, as the chorus of old men in Euripides' *Heracles* somewhat incongruously do at 348–450. It can sing a wedding-song (*humenaios*), or a paean (*paian*), the song of thanksgiving or call for aid usually addressed to Apollo (the entrance-song of the chorus of old men in Sophocles' *Antigone*, at 100–161, has marked paeanic elements). It can perform any number of more or less formal choral dirges, often in exchange with actors. And when, as in Euripides' *Bacchae*, it is in character as a choral *thiasos* for Dionysus, it can even sing and dance the god's characteristic hymn, a dithyramb (the entrance-song of *Bacchae*, at 64–169, is in effect a dithyramb taking place on the tragic stage). At the same time, *all* of these song-dances are also, at a further level, devoted to Dionysus from Eleutherae, as the patron and recipient of tragedy itself. With such a vast array of preexisting musical and social forms upon which it can draw, tragedy's power to shape expectations, to control tone and mood, is virtually boundless. Sophocles is famous for the way he produces a mood of fragile optimism before the disaster, and much of the depth and irony of that effect was registered at the musical level: in *Women of Trachis*, for instance, the chorus of Trachinian women – as is fitting for their status as adult women – anticipate singing a wedding-song to celebrate what amounts to a remarriage of Deianira and Heracles after the latter's long absence (cf. 205–7). Yet the audience knows that a wedding-song will in fact be more appropriate to the actual marriage Heracles is planning with his new young spear-won bride, Iole – the plan which, when she learns of it, sets Deianira on the disastrous course of action that ends with Heracles' death.

There are many such cases of performative, musical irony in the tragedians. Euripides is particularly adept at shifting between musical forms to produce jarring emotional effects. In his *Ion*, for instance, at 452–71 the chorus of female attendants on Creusa (played, we must always remind ourselves, by males) pray for the fertility of their royal mistress in an echo of the traditional wedding-song, just as the female relatives and friends of a woman might do outside the theater. Since Creusa is of course a married woman, their song already has something of a metaphorical quality to it. But further layers of irony soon open up, since the audience is well aware that Creusa has long since given birth, even though she herself is ignorant that she is now face to face with her child.

At the heart of Euripides' *Ion*, Creusa sings an immensely powerful, long monody (859–922) – "the emotional and structural centre of the play" (Lee 1997, 257). Quite apart from its own poetic, emotional and (doubtless) musical brilliance, this monody further demonstrates Euripides' skill in redeploying musical forms in highly challenging ways. Near the midpoint of this story of her life, Creusa rebukes the god who raped her, Apollo himself, for "screeching paeans" (905–6) to himself on his golden kithara while ignoring the misery of an abandoned mother forced to abandon her child. A monodic paean is odd enough (it was usually a choral form), but to accuse its glorious recipient, Apollo, of having to sing it to himself is to use powerful musical and religious means to express her feelings of utter misery, of the disordered relations between gods and men (whereas song should normally be a prime means of establishing *order* and communication).

There is much scope for further exploration of the ways in which tragedy "stages" all other kinds of musical performance in its uniquely rich and challenging format. Such restaging poses some major questions: does the sort of dangerous music alleged by Creusa imply a failure of musical forms in Athenian society at a broader level, beyond the confines of the theater? Does the very imitation of such forms in unreal dramatic contexts threaten to undermine their operation in life, as Plato seemed to fear? Or, on the other hand, does this shake-up of musical forms under the auspices of Dionysus leave its audience with a renewed sense of the need to maintain and safeguard the musical foundations of their religious and civic life?

Perhaps the most challenging "staging" of musical form and meaning in extant tragedy are those moments in Euripides where characters imagine (and usually sing about) forms of musical expression – and therefore of social organization – that do not (yet) exist. Most strikingly, it is forms of women's song that are imagined in this way. Again, *Ion* provides an extraordinary example: not long after they have heard Creusa's song of her suffering, the women of the chorus respond musically, with a visionary choral generalization:

> Look, you who in songs of ill repute slanderously sing of our sexual affairs and our impious unlawful unions, look how superior in piety we are to the unjust crop of men! Let song rebound against them, a cacophonous muse concerning their sexual affairs! (*Ion* 1090–98)

The chorus of Corinthian women in *Medea* are even more shockingly prophetic. What is more, their words are given a touch of social realism (at 424–26 they say, in effect, "women don't receive a musical education") that must have made its musical polarization of the genders seem all the more radical, and chilling, to some:

> Honor is coming to the female race: no more will woman be maligned by cacophonous rumor. The music of ancient bards will cease to hymn our faithlessness. Phoebus, leader

of song, never endowed our minds with the glorious strains of the lyre. Else I would have
sounded a hymn in reply to the male sex. (*Medea* 414–28, trans. Kovacs 1994–2004,
adapted)

Musical Revolution

Our understanding of the music of Greek tragedy is further complicated by the fact
that in the last thirty or so years of the fifth century – the period of Euripides' greatest
productivity and notoriety, as well as of social and intellectual turmoil in his city –
Athens was the center for what has been dubbed a musical revolution. So radical was
the perceived impact of the constant and varied experimentation and change that
some conservative critics like Plato saw something approaching the End of Civilization as he knew it, the overturning of all moral and social hierarchies. History is
dotted with such outraged response to musical change, and when we probe more
closely into the precise nature of the innovations introduced by these so-called New
Musicians (a modern term), we find that, to modern eyes (and ears), they appear
rather tame – the extension of one syllable of song over more than one note, for
instance; or the abandonment of the repeated metrical patterns in tragic choral
stanzas (known as "strophic responsion") in favor of a freer, less regular metrical
pattern.

These developments arose in the neighboring performance categories of the dithyramb (dithyrambic contests, in two categories, men and boys, were a major choral
event at the City Dionysia that took place alongside tragedy and comedy) and the
kitharoidic *nomos*, a solo concert performance in which kithara-players sang long arias
to their own accompaniment. But they soon spread to tragedy, a genre always avid for
innovation, and the later works of Euripides (especially *Trojan Women*, performed in
415, and subsequent tragedies) show clear signs of their influence. Euripides was in
fact said to have befriended, even collaborated with, the most radical of all these
musical innovators, the fiery Timotheus of Miletus, composer of a kitharoidic *nomos*
called *The Persians*, of which a lengthy fragment survives.

The style and structure, as well as the content, of tragic music were very significantly affected by the musical revolution; so too was the economic and social basis of
the theater itself (see the excellent study of Csapo 2004). It is in this period that
individual actors' monodies start to grow as the collective form of song, the chorus,
shrinks. New music demanded new levels of virtuosity that a group of amateur
citizens could not easily reproduce. We should thus also mark this age as seeing the
birth of the diva, for the most famous tragic actor-singers now became international
stars, commanding huge fees and audiences around the Greek world. It is in this
context too that the potential of the *aulos* for all manner of mimetic effects came into
its own. The *aulos*-player himself, for so long inconspicuous in the record, achieved
star status in this period; and the line between instrumental musician and actor
blurred a little, as *aulos*-players added facial and bodily forms of *mimêsis* to the
acoustic. If the commemorative vase made in Athens and named (by modern
scholars) after him is anything to go by, the most famous *aulos*-player of the ancient
world, Pronomos of Thebes, stole the show when he played for the tragic poet
Demetrius and his team late in the fifth century (for the vase see Csapo and Slater
1995, plate 8).

Survival

By a very lucky chance, one of the handful of transcriptions of ancient music that we possess is from a choral song in Euripides' *Orestes*, and, even though it is only some seven lines long (338–44), it demonstrates a couple of the characteristics of the new musical style, and so nicely corroborates our other evidence for them. For instance, in the last phrase, the monosyllabic word *en* ("in") is given two different notes, rather than one, as would be musically traditional. It is even written *e-en* in the papyrus to make this rhythmic point entirely clear. This raises the intriguing question of whether these fragments of musical scoring are the very music Euripides himself composed for the work; and more generally, it makes us wonder how long and under what conditions the music of tragedy survived. In other words, the questions of transmission investigated for so many centuries in connection with the *literary* texts of tragedy need also to be asked of their music.

There can be no doubt that the music of Aeschylus survived at least until the end of the classical period, and very probably much longer. In Aristophanes' comedy *Frogs* (405), a significant segment of the contest in the underworld between Aeschylus and Euripides assumes not only that the audience will be able to follow what is to us a fairly technical discussion of *ta melê*, the "musical parts" (see, for example, *Frogs* 1248, 1255, 1261–62), but that it will also recognize (at least a rough caricature of) Aeschylean musical style. Elsewhere in comedy the older generation of around 420 is imagined as still liking to sing snatches of Aeschylus or even of his somewhat older contemporary, Phrynichus (active around 500 BCE). It is most likely that the music of this early generation of tragedians was transmitted primarily or entirely by oral means. At any given time, there would have been a pool of chorus members who over the years had gone through rigorous training under the guiding eye of the poets themselves. Since a musical formation was basic to any Greek upbringing – to varying degrees of complexity according to class and local culture – it seems likely that the music of tragedy was preserved mnemonically in living form, according to a kind of pyramidal structure. The poet, actors, and chorus members who had learned it for months (not to forget the *aulos*-player) represented the tip of the memory pyramid, and were able to transmit their knowledge for further performances; less engaged audience members at the base of the pyramid perhaps picked up the simple melodic structure of choral songs that had struck them with special force. So much is clear from the famous story told about the Athenian soldiers taken captive in Sicily around 413 who supposedly saved their own lives by singing songs of Euripides to their captors (Plutarch, *Nicias* 29). We should remember that at the City Dionysia in Athens alone there were some 1,165 citizens involved in the tragic, comic, and dithyrambic choruses *each year*. Over the decades this would represent a very significant pool of choral competence and musical memory.

The *Orestes* musical papyrus is dated to around 280 at the very earliest. What of the century or more that separates it from the death of the poet? Here we must also stress the role of reperformance. Although we are quite rightly encouraged to conceive of the Athenian festival theater as nothing like a modern repertory theater, free to (re)produce plays at more or less any time or place, we are starting to see more clearly just how much reperformance there in fact was in and outside Athens, and from how early a date. We can be fairly sure, for instance, that after Aeschylus died in 456 "anyone who wished to" could "ask the archon for a chorus" to produce his work (*Life of Aeschylus* 12; cf. Aristophanes, *Frogs* 868, *Acharnians* 9–12). This seems to reflect a political decision of the Athenian people as a whole, and demonstrates the cultural and political importance of Aeschylus to the city. And so it is unimaginable that any chorus granted by the archon in this way would have performed tunes and dance-steps other than those of the master himself. Over a century later, around 330 (and thus much closer to the date of our musical fragment of *Orestes*), the Athenian statesman Lycurgus legislated to have the texts of Aeschylus, Sophocles, and Euripides transcribed and deposited in the state archive and required that actors follow them without deviation. It is hard to imagine that so evident a desire to preserve the works of the three canonical tragic poets would not have extended to such an important component as their music, and so it may well be that knowledge of the music of the great tragedians was transmitted to Alexandria along with their texts. The Alexandrian edition, then – the ultimate source of our manuscript tradition – may have had notation, and it may also have set out the melic parts in such a way as to reflect the musical phraseology of the original. If so – and even though their notation is lost – it may in fact be possible, as some scholars believe (see Fleming 1999), to deduce something more of the rhythmic patterning of their music from the way the later copyists reproduced the phraseology of the Alexandrian edition.

The complexity of tragedy's music demands an approach on many levels, using as wide a range of methodologies as we have available to us: an approach that incorporates the strictly musical and metrical technicalities, insofar as we can reconstruct and understand them, along with the cultural, historical, and ethical associations they bring, and that takes stock of the sociology of theater music, the status and perception of its players and their instruments. Finally, our approach should fully integrate an understanding of tragedy's Dionysian restaging of musical culture, and its own supple discourse on music – its penetrating, prismatic reflection on its own broad medium, its functions, its emotions, its power; the somewhat uncanny sense of "anti-music" it creates with its constant talk (and song) of the "lyreless muse," with the threnodic exploration of musical loss. And in all of this we must also keep a sharp eye on the diachronic, historical dimension, for musical developments were for the Greeks among the clearest markers of profound cultural and social change.

FURTHER READING

The best assemblage of sources relating to Greek music in general is that of Barker (1984–89; 2 volumes), who also provides excellent guiding commentary on all of the major points of dispute; West 1992 and Landels 1999 are the most thorough synthetic studies, and provide the best discussion of all technical matters, including the musical papyri. On the latter see also Pöhlmann and West 2001. The material specifically relating to the theater is presented in the original Greek in Pickard-Cambridge 1988, 257–62, and in English in Csapo and Slater 1995, 331–48; 331–34 of the latter give an excellent introduction to the material in its historical context. Winnington-Ingram 1968 is a fundamental study of the difficult topic of the musical modes. For further reading on the way the Athenians conceived of tragedy as a "choral" event, see Wilson 2000a. A valuable introduction to Aristotle on tragedy is provided by Halliwell 1986. Hall 1996b gives a good account of the possible reasons behind the extreme formalism of Aristotle's approach. Sifakis 2001, chapter 4 ("The function and significance of music in tragedy"), offers a challenging new interpretation, arguing that Aristotle recognized a far greater role than is normally thought for music in tragedy as a means of ethical and emotional imitation and persuasion.

Sociological study of Greek music is a relatively underdeveloped area. Stephanis 1988 is a scholarly prosopography of theatrical and musical performers and will be an invaluable resource for such work. Csapo 2004 is the first major sociological study of the momentous fracture in Greek music and social practice known as the New Music. Wilson 1999 and 2002 study the *aulos* and its players from a largely sociological perspective. Hall 1999a and 2002 are important studies of the rise of the actor-singer virtuoso, the relationship between song types, gender, and status in tragedy, and much else. Some of the contributions to Cassio, Musti, and Rossi 2000 are in a similar vein.

Much of interest has been written recently on the chorus, and on tragedy's staging of musical traditions by means of the chorus (and otherwise): see Henrichs 1994–95, as well as the other contributors to the *Arion* volume in which this appears, Gould 1996, Goldhill 1996, Calame 1999, Stehle 2004, and Wilson and Taplin 1993 on the *Oresteia*. The related topic of tragedy's own formulation of a specifically tragic sense of *mousikê* is well discussed by Segal 1993 and Loraux 2002; see also Wilson 1999–2000 on Euripides.

For the reperformance and spread of tragedy outside Athens see Easterling 1994, Le Guen 1995, Taplin 1999b and Allan 2001a. On the question of musical transmission, see the interesting work of Fleming 1999.

CHAPTER THIRTEEN

Theatrical Production

John Davidson

It is not so very long ago that Greek tragedies, at least in the context of Western classical scholarship, were primarily regarded as literary texts for translation and philological analysis. Over the course of the last three decades in particular, however, many new and exciting approaches to the plays have opened up, one of which relates to the question of how they might have been originally produced and performed at Athens. The production side of things had not, of course, been entirely neglected, but it had often been regarded as a side-issue, confined to cursory notes in editions and literary monographs, with ad hoc bursts of interest occasioned by the actual staging of a play, especially one using the original Greek language, in a modern theater.

A more active interest in the production and performance aspect of Greek tragedy had naturally been an ongoing feature of the work of theater practitioners, but their focus was more on modern realizations of the text than on any reconstruction of the terms of the original performance. Indeed, there was quite a significant gulf between the approaches taken to Greek tragedy by classical scholars and theater practitioners. This situation has been radically changed with the development of performance and theater studies as an academic discipline and its cross-fertilization with more traditional classical scholarship. The result has been an intellectual environment in which a study such as *The Play of Space* (Rehm 2002) fits comfortably, the author being a trained classicist but also a member of a university theater studies department and theater practitioner, and accordingly able to extend the parameters of discussion beyond the relatively uncomplicated notion of "staging" to include more sophisticated dimensions such as modern theories of space.

In the context of classical scholarship in the English-speaking world itself, a turning point is often seen in the publication of *The Stagecraft of Aeschylus* (Taplin 1977), which followed soon after the German monograph *Das Theater der Tragödie* (Melchinger 1974). This chronology is slightly misleading, because important studies by classical scholars had already been appearing, even if at irregular intervals, one such example being *Greek Theatre Production* (Webster 1970a), first published in 1956. It was Taplin's book, however, that had the greatest impact on a greater number of scholars working in the classical field, coming as it did at a time when a wider interest in theater studies in general was developing. Since the 1970s, indeed, there has been a sensational increase in the amount of published academic material on the subject.

The Evidence

The main obstacle hindering the recovery of the original production practices of Greek tragic plays is scanty evidence. The most important testimony, of course, resides in the text of the plays themselves. As these plays were composed for a first performance in the Theater of Dionysus, it is that first performance in that particular theater in the fifth century BCE that has become the focus of investigation. And this approach seems justified, even if the texts that we possess today may, to a limited extent, reflect changes made for a subsequent performance in the same theater or indeed in another theater. It appears that the basic layout of the theater throughout the Greek world remained more or less the same during the course of several centuries. There would, of course, have been local variations of a minor nature, and no two performances of a given play would ever be exactly the same, even in the Theater of Dionysus. However, the texts as we have them must be seen primarily as evidence for that very first production, and this will be the working assumption followed here.

We must at the same time acknowledge the ongoing debate over the extent and accuracy of any picture of the original performance which may be reconstructed when the text is used as the primary evidence. On the one hand, it has been argued that all "significant" actions in a Greek tragedy are embedded in the words (Taplin 1978, 17). On the other hand, it has been maintained that the text itself carries no sign of entire dimensions of important action, much of which can actually be recovered through consideration of other factors such as performance space (Wiles 1997, 15–21 and passim). There is clearly cause for considerable caution, especially since the very methodology of so-called performance criticism has been challenged (Goldhill 1986a, 276–86; 1997c, 336–40).

Closely connected with the evidence of the texts is the evidence provided by the archaeological remains of the Theater of Dionysus in Athens. The obstacles here, however, are formidable, since by and large the surviving remains date to later periods. Moreover, there have been varying interpretations of the earlier archaeo-logical layers, with the result that crucial details about the exact configuration of the performance space at different stages in the fifth and fourth centuries BCE remain a matter of controversy. Nevertheless, the essential relationship between the texts and the original performance area seems clear enough.

The third type of evidence comes from vase-painting. Here again, however, there are significant problems of interpretation (see Small, chapter 7 in this volume). It is difficult to be sure of the extent to which a more or less contemporary painting actually reflects a particular performance, or performance in general, rather than the imaginative creativity of the artist. Moreover, as has been convincingly argued (J. R. Green 1994), the convention for depicting a tragic subject differed from that relating to comedy because the figures were not shown as actors in their masks and theatrical costumes, but as characters from the myth that supplied the subject matter of a play. Nevertheless, there are sometimes hints of a theatrical context, although these too must be treated with caution since they often do not relate specifically to the Theater of Dionysus.

Serious problems also surround the fourth main type of evidence, namely material found in other ancient written sources, such as observations made by the scholiasts (ancient commentators). In many cases their comments about original performances refer to the situation in their own day, often several centuries after the fifth century. We must now consider what kind of tentative picture can be built up, drawing on these different types of evidence, concentrating on the texts of the plays and the archaeological remains of the theater.

The General Context

We need to be reminded that Greek tragedy represents a radical development in the history of Western theater (Rehm 2003, 9). Tragedies began to be performed as part of the City Dionysia (sometimes called the Great Dionysia), an Athenian festival celebrated at the beginning of spring in honor of the god Dionysus, at some time in the latter half of the sixth century BCE. Little is known for certain about the early stages of tragic production, and the first performances may in fact have taken place in the agora (civic center). However, by the time we reach the period some decades into the fifth century for which firmer evidence exists, we find a system whereby each year three tragic playwrights took part in a dramatic competition held in the specially developed Theater of Dionysus, producing three tragedies and a satyr-play each, which in all cases employed the two basic components of a chorus and actors. Tragedies were also performed to a more limited extent at the winter festival of the Lenaea, whose main emphasis was actually comedy, but it is on the City Dionysia that we will be focusing here.

The "production" of a tragedy effectively began from the day, some time in August, when the annually elected magistrate who gave his name to the year (the eponymous archon) chose the three playwrights who were to perform at the festival to be held in about six months' time (Pickard-Cambridge 1988, 58). Details of the rehearsal process are almost entirely unknown, and what there is relates to the chorus for whose training the *chorêgos* (financial sponsor) might offer a large room in his own house or hire a gymnasium (Wilson 2000a, 71–86). Nothing at all is known about dress rehearsals, and it has even been denied that these would have taken place in the theater itself (Arnott 1989, 23–24). This seems highly unlikely, however, given all the complicated movements and technicalities of production that would need to be worked out (Rehm 2002, 42). A few days before the performances there took place the *proagôn*, at which the playwrights and casts were publicly presented. Exactly what happened here, however, is again unclear. On the first day of performance, various ceremonies were carried out beforehand, ceremonies that have been seen as crucial in setting the civic context for the plays themselves (Goldhill 1990). Once the preliminaries were over, the plays themselves became "the thing."

The Performance Space

The complex known as the Theater of Dionysus is situated on the southern slope of the Acropolis at Athens, and it was here that the original performance of the plays for which texts survive will have taken place, adjacent to the actual sanctuary of the god. As is the case for most other Greek theaters, tiered seating set in the hillside (the *cavea* or *theatron*) looks down on a level open area known as the *orchêstra* (dancing area). As its name indicates, this large space was especially associated with the chorus, which early in the fifth century numbered twelve and was subsequently increased to fifteen. The *orchêstra* was easily large enough to accommodate the choreographed movements of a group of fifteen performers who were accompanied by a single *aulos*-(pipe-) player. The same space, after all, could accommodate a chorus of twenty-four for comic plays and fifty for performances of the dithyramb or "circular choruses" (see Seidensticker, chapter 3 in this volume). Two side-entrances (*parodoi* or *eisodoi*) led into the *orchêstra*. These could be used by actors, as well as being the normal means of entrance for the chorus and the exit at the conclusion of a play.

There is debate over the shape of the *orchêstra*. It used to be taken more or less for granted that it was circular, this arrangement being projected back to the Theater of Dionysus from that found in our best-preserved example, the fourth-century theater at Epidaurus. The notion of circularity is still an important conceptual basis for some reconstructions of the theater space (Wiles 1997, 23–50). There is today, however, also a strong body of opinion that argues that what archaeological evidence there is, taken in conjunction with the shape of the *orchêstra* in other Attic theaters, points to an original rectilineal shape for the *orchêstra* of the Theater of Dionysus (Rehm 1992, 33; 2002, 39–41; Moretti 1999–2000). Certainty on this point is unobtainable, although one plausible argument for the traditional view is the fact that a circular *orchêstra* would have better suited the regular performance of dithyrambic choruses.

Controversy also surrounds the question of where exactly the actors, the other main component of the cast of a tragedy, would have been positioned in the performance space. Given the use of a raised stage in the later Greco-Roman theater, it has often been assumed that some kind of stage would have been used in the fifth century too, even if it was relatively low; such a stage would mark the actors' territory as opposed to the *orchêstra*, which would be the home of the chorus (Webster 1970a, 7; Arnott 1962, 6–41). Vase-paintings showing a stage with wooden steps leading up to it have been taken as confirmation of such an arrangement (Arnott 1962, 16). The vase-paintings in question, however, normally relate to dramatic performances in Greek cities of southern Italy, so this is by no means conclusive. Some scholars today, in fact, arguing that no surviving tragedy actually needs a raised stage for the actors, either express skepticism (Taplin 1977, 441–42) or reject the idea outright (Rehm 1992, 34–36). An arrangement by which all performers were basically operating on the same level would certainly have facilitated the close relationship between actors and chorus that is reflected in the texts.

Just as the actors had a close relationship with the chorus and thus with the space occupied by the chorus, so they were also closely related to the structure standing immediately behind the performance area. This structure was called the *skênê*, which literally means "tent," the name presumably going back to the earliest period of dramatic performance when a tent-like arrangement sufficed as the place for the actors to dress and emerge from. The *skênê* of the postclassical period became increasingly elaborate, developing by Roman times into a significant piece of multi-storied architecture. In the fifth century, however, it seems to have been a relatively simple one-story wooden structure erected specifically for the dramatic festivals and dismantled at their conclusion. Wings projecting from either end of the *skênê* façade (*paraskênia*), attested for later periods, may have already been a feature of the fifth-century theater.

The *skênê* became an important feature of the fictional world that the audience was required to imagine as the setting for any given play. It often represents a palace, as, for example, in Sophocles' *Oedipus the King* and *Antigone*, where it stands for the royal palace of Thebes. Characters arriving by one of the side-entrances may greet the *skênê*, or rather the building that it is supposed to represent. An example of this is Euripides' *Heracles* 523: the hero returns from the underworld and begins, "Greetings, dwelling and entrance to my hearth," before noticing the perilous situation of his family. It is interesting to note that the word used here for "dwelling," *melathron*, can also be applied metatheatrically to the rock containing a cave which the *skênê* represents in Sophocles' *Philoctetes* (147).

There is debate as to how many doors would have opened from the *skênê* onto the performance area. For most tragedies, at any rate, one central door would have been sufficient, and this central door would have been a focal point for the audience's attention. Through this door actors would make many of the entrances and exits, and it marked the point of transition between the "seen" and "unseen" in terms of both the fictional world of the play and the real world of the theater complex. In a play such as Aeschylus' *Agamemnon*, the door will have played a significant role in the central scene where Clytemnestra entices her husband, via the tapestries, into the palace where she will murder him.

Frequently, too, the *skênê* could be made to represent something other than a palace. Thus in Sophocles' *Ajax*, for example, it initially represents the hero's tent or hut, part of the Greek encampment during the siege of Troy. Then again, in Sophocles' *Philoctetes*, as we have seen, it represents the cave where the hero has been living since his abandonment by the Greeks on their way to Troy many years before. There is a slight puzzle associated with Philoctetes' dwelling. The cave is described early on as having two entrances, and reference is made to this feature later in the play. The orthodox view today is that the door in the *skênê* will have served as the only entrance visible to the audience, the other one requiring to be imagined at the rear of the *skênê*, out of sight of the audience. There are some difficulties associated with this solution, attractive and dramatically economical though it is, and it is just possible that some ad hoc arrangement was made in this case, for example a screen placed in front of the door, the two cave entrances being at either end.

Euripides' plays too show flexibility in the characterization of the *skênê*. In *Iphigenia at Aulis*, for example, it represents the tent or hut of Agamemnon in the encampment where the Greek army is waiting to set sail for Troy, while in *Hecuba* it functions as the quarters of the captured and enslaved Trojan women. In a number of plays it represents a temple, that of Apollo at Delphi in *Ion*, for example. In *Electra*, on the other hand, it becomes a peasant's hut, this relocation of the action away from the palace context of the equivalent play by his predecessor Aeschylus being an important aspect of Euripides' strategy to reinterpret the myth.

Sometimes the *skênê* may have moved in and out of focus, as it were, or even changed its identity during the course of a play. In Euripides' *Trojan Women* it serves specifically as the quarters of the captured women of Troy at the start of the play, but perhaps comes by the end of the play to represent more generally the walls of the city of Troy, which is supposedly going up in flames. In Aeschylus' *Libation Bearers*, it seems that during the first part of the play, set in the vicinity of Agamemnon's tomb, the *skênê* is not brought into focus as the façade of the royal palace; this only becomes the case later, when Orestes seeks entry incognito in order to carry out his vengeance. The fact that "in real life" a king's tomb would not be close to the front door of his palace is simply unimportant (Garvie 1986, xli–xliii).

In some plays, too, there seems to be a significant change of setting. Thus for Sophocles' *Ajax* it is generally accepted that the scene shifts from the hero's hut or tent to a grove near the seashore where he will commit suicide by falling on his sword (although this has been denied by Scullion 1994, 109–16). In this case the *skênê* as a structure may have moved out of focus. Change of scene is also a feature of Aeschylus' *Eumenides*. Here the *skênê* initially represents the temple of Apollo at Delphi, but later in the play must become a backdrop to the trial of Orestes on the Areopagus at Athens. It is extremely difficult to recreate the original staging of a series of features of this play, as modern discussions well illustrate (Taplin 1977, 362–415; Podlecki 1989, 11–17). Another interesting case is Sophocles' last play, *Oedipus at Colonus*, set at the grove of the Eumenides near Colonus. Here it is not entirely clear what role, if any, the *skênê* will have played as part of the grove environment.

The setting of the earliest surviving tragedy, Aeschylus' *Persians*, is left somewhat vague. The chorus of Persian elders appears at different times to be outside their council chamber, inside it, at the tomb of Darius for a ghost-raising, and more generally somewhere in the Persian capital of Susa. Perhaps it is easiest to think in terms of scene change through refocusing without specific verbal indicators, although this has been denied by Hall 1996a, 118–19. As there is nothing at all to indicate the proximity of the door of a building façade, the suggestion that this play was performed at a time when the *skênê* had not yet become a regular feature of the performance space seems plausible. Indeed, lack of reference to a building façade for the setting of both *Suppliants* and *Seven against Thebes* suggests that the Oresteian trilogy of 456 BCE may be our first surviving plays reflecting composition for a performance space with *skênê* backdrop (Taplin 1977, 103–7, 452–59). On the other hand, it has been argued (Rehm 2002, 239) that the *skênê* roof would have been ideal for an unexpected appearance of the ghost of Darius in the *Persians* and that, in general, all of Aeschylus' early plays would have been enhanced by presentation against a *skênê* backdrop (Walton 1984, 48). The weight of probability, however, does seem to be against this proposal, even if, on the Taplin hypothesis, Aeschylus must be credited with an almost immediate masterful exploitation of the *skênê* innovation in general, and at the same time with a stunning use of the "special effect" of the *ekkuklêma*.

The case of *Prometheus Bound* is special. A strong body of opinion today holds that this play is not by Aeschylus but belongs to later in the fifth century (Griffith 1977; West 1990b). If this is so – if, that is, the play was performed at a time when the *skênê* was a well-established feature of the theater – then the *skênê* may have done service as the Caucasus Mountains to which the hero is nailed at the start of the play. If, on the other hand, the Prometheus figure was impaled in the center of the *orchêstra*, as appears possible, the *skênê* may simply have been used to provide the more distant rocky background.

We have mentioned the importance of the *skênê*'s central doorway for the action of the plays. Another part of the structure that seems to have served an extremely important purpose from time to time was its (presumably) flat roof. The first play of Aeschylus' Oresteian trilogy, *Agamemnon*, begins with a short monologue delivered by a watchman placed, as he says, on the roof of the royal palace to watch for the signal indicating the capture of Troy. If, as just suggested, the trilogy dates from the early years of the *skênê*, this appearance of the watchman on its roof would still be part of an exciting new development in the history of Greek theater.

Another use of the *skênê* roof is found in Euripides' *Phoenician Women*. In one of the early scenes, the young Antigone is taken up by a servant onto the walls of Thebes, so that she can gaze out over the encampment of the attacking Argive army. Technically known as a *teichoskopia* ("watching from the walls"), this scene has its origin in the third book of the *Iliad*, where Helen converses with Priam, king of Troy, as she identifies figures from the attacking Greek army. Euripides' use of a *teichoskopia* in his play, then, represents, so to speak, a concrete realization of a literary motif.

Perhaps the most innovative and exciting use of the *skênê* roof is made by Euripides in his late play *Orestes*. At the climax, Orestes, along with his friend and companion Pylades, appears on the roof with his cousin Hermione, whom he is holding hostage; he threatens to kill her and burn down the palace. Meanwhile Menelaus, the father of Hermione, blusters helplessly below. The *skênê* roof can thus be used as a way of establishing an impossible physical gulf between characters that at the same time can also symbolize a spiritual, emotional, and communicative gulf. In the same play, as the scholiast suggests, the Phrygian slave may have leaped down from the roof in his attempt to escape from the mayhem caused inside the palace by Orestes and Pylades (West 1987, 275–76). We shall consider in a moment the possible use made of the roof by divine characters.

The performance space (whether just the *orchêstra*, or the *orchêstra* plus low stage) and the *skênê*, then, were the main features of the Theater of Dionysus, apart, of course, from the seating for the spectators. Because the theater was an open-air one, there was no question of lighting. Both performers and spectators would be dealing with natural light and would also be exposed to the elements. There also seems to have been relatively little in the way of scenery or major stage props, although there are some indications of these in the texts. Thus, for example, characters may address deities in ways that strongly suggest that statues of such deities were present in front of the *skênê*. This is clear in the case of Euripides' *Hippolytus*, where the hero greets his patron goddess Artemis, while ignoring her rival Aphrodite. In Sophocles' *Oedipus the King* too, it is clear that Jocasta makes offerings before an image of the god Apollo whom she addresses as "nearest." Such an arrangement will have reflected the normal Greek practice of placing statues in front of houses.

The question of altars is a somewhat vexed one. In the past, scholars have often thought in terms of a permanent structure dedicated to Dionysus, the *thumelê*, in the center of the *orchêstra* and additional ad hoc stage altars, especially when a low stage was assumed (Arnott 1962, 43–45). There are certainly many occasions when altars and tombs must have been used, as the texts indicate, especially in the case of suppliant scenes. Even if such scenes (as seems more likely) took place in a central position in the *orchêstra*, rather than up against the *skênê* on a low stage, we need not assume the presence of a permanent altar there (Rehm 2002, 41). A suitable structure could be brought in when needed for any given play. In Euripides' *Heracles*, for example, the hero's family are "discovered," as the play opens, seated at an altar in front of the palace, having taken refuge there in an attempt to escape the murderous intentions of the usurper Lycus. In the same playwright's *Andromache*, the play's name character has taken refuge at the shrine of Thetis, while in his *Children of Heracles*, the persecuted family of the now dead Heracles have again sought sanctuary at the altar in front of the temple of Zeus at Marathon. There are surviving plays called *Suppliants* by both Aeschylus and Euripides in which a similar scenario is the basis for the dramatic action.

We turn now to two features that provided the fifth-century theater with "special effects." The first of these is the *ekkuklêma*. This appears to have been a trolley that could be rolled out of the *skênê* door, often containing a tableau representing a scene resulting from an action "performed" in the *skênê* out of the audience's sight. The classic usage was to display the bodies of characters that had been killed. Thus, at the appropriate moment in *Agamemnon*, the bodies of the king and Cassandra are displayed together, being pushed out on the *ekkuklêma* via the same door through which they had previously stepped individually into the palace. This is echoed in the second play of the Oresteian trilogy, *Libation Bearers*, when the bodies of Clytemnestra and Aegisthus are produced from the palace. In Sophocles' *Electra* there is an ironic twist, since Clytemnestra's covered body is produced for the benefit of Aegisthus, who mistakes it for the body of Orestes.

There is considerable debate about the possible use of the *ekkuklêma* for other purposes. In Sophocles' *Ajax* it does seem likely that when the hero is revealed sitting in despair among the animals he has slaughtered in mistake for the generals of the Greek army, this tableau would have been displayed by means of the *ekkuklêma*. More controversial is the question of whether the device was used in some way for the staging of the hero's suicide. We shall return to this question later.

One suggestion in connection with Sophocles' *Philoctetes* is that the *ekkuklêma* was pushed out at the beginning of the play and remained as a fixed feature throughout, providing the "extra height" that makes the hero's "threat to throw himself off the cliff more convincing" (Webster 1970b, 8). This seems highly unlikely, since such an attempt at "naturalism" to give an impression of height would have been pointless from the perspective of spectators seated above the performance area. The *ekkuklêma* has also, on occasion, been thought to have been rolled out at the beginning of *Prometheus Bound*, and used as the place where the hero is nailed to his rock. We shall consider this possibility again below.

The second important part of the theater's technology was the *mêchanê* or crane (a counterbalanced swing-beam). Quite apart from the implications found in some of the tragic texts themselves, compelling evidence for the existence of this piece of machinery is found in the text of the tragedians' comic contemporary Aristophanes. The use of the device is clearly parodied by the comic poet, and the crane operator can be metatheatrically addressed, as in his *Peace* (174). It seems that the *mêchanê* was primarily used to present the aerial arrival of supernatural beings (Mastronarde 1990). It is sometimes difficult to be as certain, however, when deities appearing "on high" would have been on the *mêchanê* rather than on the roof of the *skênê*. A clear case for the *mêchanê* is provided by Euripides' *Orestes*. The hero and his sidekick Pylades were already, as we noted earlier, on the *skênê* roof. The god Apollo, however, then makes an appearance to resolve the situation. He must surely have appeared at above roof level, on the *mêchanê*. Such a scenario seems quite in keeping with the theatrically flamboyant Euripides.

In the surviving plays of Euripides in particular, the appearance of one or more deities to prevent some threatened action, throw light on a situation, or resolve an impasse becomes almost a commonplace, and it seems likely that the *mêchanê* was used for this. Preparation for the appearance of the deity can on occasion be detected in the text, as when the chorus of *Andromache* says in effect, "Look! What deity do I see flying here?" (1226–30), clearly drawing the audience's attention to the new focus of interest. In *Trojan Women* there is a variation on this formula, as Hecuba remarks on the flames taking hold of the walls of Troy, almost as though to draw attention to the fact that on this occasion the gods are conspicuous by their absence (1295–97).

Deities also figure in the prologue of a number of Euripides' plays, but it is not clear whether they appeared on the *mêchanê*, on the roof of the *skênê*, or at ground level. The prologue of *Trojan Women*, for example, features Poseidon and Athena in conversation; *Alcestis* uses the same technique, the speakers being Apollo and Thanatos (Death). *Hippolytus* begins with a prologue speech delivered by Aphrodite, balancing the epilogue appearance of Artemis. *Bacchae* presents an unusual case, since Dionysus appears in the prologue having assumed mortal disguise, so that one might suppose that here he appeared on ground level, marking a significant distinction from his divine epiphany at the conclusion of the play when he would presumably have appeared "on high." An interesting variation can be found in *Heracles*: Iris and Lyssa (Madness) appear not at the beginning or end, but midway through the play, yet another example of Euripides' willingness to adapt a theatrical convention.

It seems too that Euripides could use the *mêchanê* to carry human characters on occasion. The parody of *Andromeda* found in Aristophanes' *Women at the Thesmophoria* implies that in Euripides' lost tragedy the flying hero will have arrived on the *mêchanê* to rescue the damsel in distress. Use of the *mêchanê* is also possible for Bellerophon in at least one of the lost tragedies that dealt with his story. An especially interesting case is encountered in *Medea*, where the title character is made to appear in the chariot of the Sun along with the bodies of the sons she has just murdered. Whether this appearance was on the *mêchanê* (Mastronarde 2002b, 39) or on the roof of the *skênê*, it is another example of Euripides' instinct for the theatrical coup. During the play Medea has been a human character, with no hint of supernatural powers, yet she appears at the end transformed, as it were, having entered a "higher" dimension. Moreover, when Jason comes running in search of his children and shouts for the door to be unbarred, the audience will have perhaps expected the *ekkuklêma* to be brought into play. Instead, the door remains closed and the audience's focus is suddenly redirected to the area above the *skênê*.

There is less evidence for the use of the *mêchanê* in the plays of Sophocles and Aeschylus. At the start of Sophocles' *Ajax*, Athena appears, apparently out of sight of Odysseus, who, however, can hear her voice. This perhaps implies that the goddess was on the *skênê* roof. Apart from that, the only appearance of a deity in the surviving Sophoclean plays occurs in the late *Philoctetes*. This is Heracles, who, one supposes, must have appeared at least on the roof, if not on the *mêchanê*. The surviving plays of Aeschylus do not appear to contain a *mêchanê* appearance, and it looks as though this was more of a development in the second half of the fifth century, perhaps associated primarily with Euripides, from whom Sophocles perhaps borrowed the technique in the latter part of his long career.

One further aspect of the *skênê* remains to be discussed, namely the question of *skênographia* (scene painting). It is not clear, however, exactly what the term (as used by Aristotle, *Poetics* 1449a) refers to. Suggestions range from painting of the *skênê* façade itself to painted panels hung in front of the *skênê*. The idea of removable painted panels is perhaps more attractive, since it must be remembered that, on any given day, the *skênê* would be the backdrop for three tragedies plus a satyr-play. It would have been awkward to say the least if the façade itself were painted in some way to enhance its appearance as a palace for one play, when a subsequent play required it to look like a cliff face or even a peasant's hut. If one thinks in terms of painted panels, then it would have been relatively easy to fix them in position between plays, to provide whatever backdrop was appropriate at any given time.

The issue is, however, complicated, because the notion of perspective has been associated with *skênographia*. If, as seems most likely, the *skênê* in the fifth century was a temporary structure, it will not have had anything of the elaborate architectural features that will have been part of the later, permanent stone building. A well-known fragment of a mid-fourth-century calyx-krater from Tarentum in southern Italy, now in the Martin von Wagner Museum in Würzburg, Germany (see Csapo and Slater 1995, plate 3B), shows a building with an elaborate façade, part of what must be a theatrical scene; it includes a portico with pillars at one end, with a matching portico at the other end perhaps to be supplied for the missing part of the picture. One theory is that the portico is, in fact, painted in perspective on the façade (Simon 1982, 22–25). If this is so – if, that is, this technique was available for use in the fifth century – it could have important implications. The possibility of any kind of scenery for the Greek theater beyond simple panels, however, has met with skepticism (Green 1990, 283–84), and the use of perspective painting for the fifth-century theater has been categorically denied (Rehm 2002, 18, with 306 n. 104).

The Performers

We have seen that the two basic components of the cast of any Greek tragedy were the chorus and the actors. They never directly address the audience as they do at times in comedy, so that the "tone" of their contact with the audience is different (Easterling 1997d, 167). According to the testimony of Aristotle, there was originally only one speaking actor who was also the playwright. It was Aeschylus, Aristotle states (*Poetics* 1449a), who introduced a second actor, while Sophocles went one better and added a third. Three appears to have been the maximum number used, although Sophocles' last play, *Oedipus at Colonus*, can only work with three actors if one of the roles is shared among all three to cover different scenes of the play. Apart from the speaking actors, there were also, as the texts make clear, a variable number of non-speaking supernumeraries, such actors taking the part of attendants, soldiers, and so on.

The limit on the number of speaking actors had implications for the way in which the text was composed. Thus characters sometimes exit to commit suicide, appropriate in itself for the tragic context, but also necessary in practical terms since the actor will be required to change mask and costume and return in another role. It is not certain why the number of speaking actors was limited in this way. Suggestions range from the question of expense to the idea that the limit would ensure that the three competing playwrights would be operating on the same terms. Perhaps the key rather lies in the nature of masked theater (Easterling 1997d, 153). Even with three actors available, it is interesting to see that Greek tragedy makes very little use of three-way interaction among the actors. The basis of most plays is confrontation or debate between two characters, and this may simply stem from the fact that it would have been difficult for an audience, the majority of whom were seated at a considerable distance from the acting area, to be sure which masked character was speaking at any given time if there had been verbal interaction among four or five characters.

   All the performers were male. They were also all masked, as we have seen, with the natural exception of the *aulos*-player. The mask, in fact, is one of the most significant characterizing features of Greek tragedy, indeed Greek theater in general. The audience never saw the face of the performers, and so facial expression as an enhancement of performance was out of the question. The masks, which were apparently made of stiffened linen and which covered the whole head, created representative human beings rather than individuals with facial idiosyncrasies. In any case, given that many of the spectators were seated so far above the performance space, they could not have seen facial movements even if masks had not been worn.

   The use of masks facilitated the convention already mentioned by which the speaking actors were often required to play a number of roles within the same play. An analysis of the texts to determine how the roles were divided reveals some interesting information. In *Philoctetes*, for example, the Odysseus actor must not only play the part of the pseudo-merchant who is the onstage agent of Odysseus' behind-the-scenes machinations, but also, ironically, the part of the deified Heracles who resolves the impasse. Then again, in *Women of Trachis*, it appears that the actor who played Deianira (the wife of Heracles) in the first part of the play would have played the dying Heracles in the second part. This raises the question of whether particular actors specialized in different types of roles. The Deianira/Heracles example would, at first sight, seem to suggest that there was no female or male role specialization. On the other hand, it is interesting to note that the dying Heracles describes himself as "crying like a girl" (1071–72), so there may in fact be a close connection between the roles. Unfortunately, we do not know if actors with voices of particular pitch played female roles, or if the "femaleness" was adequately conveyed by the mask alone. What we do know is that individual actors were increasingly turned into "stars" in the fourth century (Easterling 2002).

   It seems likely that, on some occasions, there will have been a mask change for an actor even when he was not changing roles. An example of this would be in *Oedipus the King*, when a mask in some way indicating bloodied, sightless eyes will presumably have been put on by the Oedipus actor before he reemerges from the *skênê* after the self-blinding. An especially effective, and gruesome, use of the mask may well have been made in Euripides' *Bacchae*, for which it seems reasonable to suppose that the mask was used as the severed head of King Pentheus, brought on stage by his mother, who, in a maddened state, has killed him unwittingly (on this scene see Lada-Richards, chapter 29 in this volume).

   As far as costume in general is concerned, vase-paintings appear to give some idea of what the performers wore – formal robes befitting royal contexts, at least for the central characters in many of the plays. Euripides, however, poses something of a problem here. Aristophanes makes fun of him for lowering the dignity of tragedy by introducing a series of heroes in rags. Many of the plays referred to in this connection in the comedy *Acharnians* (lines 410–34) are now lost. However, we can see the phenomenon at work in a play like *Helen*, where Menelaus, who repeatedly emphasizes his status as the conqueror of Troy, is introduced as the ragged and disheveled survivor of a shipwreck. Then again, the Electra of Euripides' play of that name is made to draw attention to the wretched state of her own dress. Exactly how the actors were costumed in such plays is not known. It has, in fact, sometimes been supposed that there would have been a relatively constant "dress standard" for all tragedies, irrespective of a particular setting or the situation of individual characters, and that such things as "rags for robes" would have simply been left up to the audience to imagine. It does seem unlikely, however, that the cave-dweller Philoctetes, for example, would have been dressed much the same as the king Oedipus, or that soldiers in the field, as we find in *Ajax*, would have looked like their counterparts in a civic context. When one considers the chorus too, the differences between old men, sailors, and young girls would seem to demand corresponding and marked differences in costume. As far as torn clothing goes, the earliest surviving tragedy, Aeschylus' *Persians*, features the climactic entrance of King Xerxes in garments that he says he has rent in despair after the destruction of his army and fleet. Again, it seems reasonable to suppose that this situation will have been visually reflected. Caution is needed, however. Our expectations, based as they are on experience of different kinds of theatrical conventions, may not be so readily transferable to ancient Greek dramatic practice.

In general, it is assumed, with good reason, that the style of performance in Greek tragedy must in no sense have been naturalistic. The universal use of masks, for a start, throws increased emphasis on both gesture and verbal enunciation. One imagines expressions of grief and jubilation to have been accompanied by appropriate gestures on a grand scale. The language of Greek tragedy, moreover, does not use everyday speech but the "high" register of poetry, even if, as Aristotle notes (*Poetics* 1449a), the iambic trimeter, which came to be the normal meter for dialogue, emerged as most appropriate for the very reason that, of the available poetic meters, it was the one closest to the rhythm of natural speech.

The most common pattern for a Greek tragedy features scenes of spoken dialogue involving the actors, interspersed with songs sung and danced by the chorus. It is impossible to recapture anything like the full effect of the chorus's contribution, since our knowledge of their words as transmitted in the texts is not matched by knowledge of the accompanying music and dance. The complicated meters of the choral songs do, however, show responsion. That is to say, a stanza is normally complemented by another stanza in exactly the same meter. The names "strophe" and "antistrophe" applied to this phenomenon suggest that the repeated meter will at least sometimes have been accompanied by complementarity of music and dance movement. Vase-paintings showing choral performers may well give some idea of particular choral steps caught, as it were, in freeze-frame. Indeed, it has been argued that identity of choreography between strophe and antistrophe must have been an absolute rule (Wiles 1997, 97–113). Almost nothing is known for certain about the accompanying music, although the texts have been closely studied in an attempt to demonstrate what general musicality the metrical patterns reveal (Scott 1984 and 1996). Some-times references are made to music in the fictional world of the play that will have directly corresponded with the sounds made by the *aulos*-player, for example during Io's initial frenzied monody in *Prometheus Bound* (Griffith 1983, 196). Although the notes, so to speak, are largely lost to us, there is considerable evidence about musical development during the course of the fifth century, especially the so-called New Music by which Euripides seems to have been influenced (Csapo 1999–2000).

Euripides' plays, in fact, show increased emphasis on sung monodies or "arias," whose virtuoso flavor became an obvious target for Aristophanes' comic criticism. At some point in the fifth century an actors' competition was introduced at the City Dionysia, running parallel with the existing competition among the three play-wrights. It was restricted, however, to the three protagonists or leading actors, who clearly needed to be high-class singers as well as actors as such (Hall 2002). Indeed, the significant musical content of Greek tragedy, which included laments shared between the chorus and an actor, must have brought the plays close to the form of modern opera or musical theater.

Apart from speech and song, there appears to have been a mode of delivery in between, somewhat similar to recitative. This could be employed by both actors and chorus, especially as an introduction to a choral song. An example of this is the *parodos* or entrance-song of the chorus in Sophocles' *Ajax*, where the lyrics are preceded by a preamble of thirty-eight lines in the anapestic meter that is often associated with entrances. It is not known whether such anapestic passages were delivered by the whole chorus or by the chorus leader alone. In addition to these various modes of delivery, one also has to take account of expressions of grief and pain that often stand in the text. Famous instances of pain occur in *Women of Trachis*, when Heracles is brought in dying, wracked with agony, and in *Philoctetes*, when the hero has an attack associated with his wounded foot.

At the other extreme, Greek tragedy makes good use of dramatic silences. This is a technique of Aeschylus', which is touched on in the underworld debate between Aeschylus and Euripides in Aristophanes' *Frogs*. This comedy was produced at the end of the fifth century, shortly after the death of Euripides, Aeschylus by this time being long dead and clearly regarded as the "classic" tragic playwright. Aeschylus' play *Niobe*, now lost, evidently contained a long sequence in which the heroine, grieving for her slain children, maintained silence. Of course, we do not know how the audience of *Niobe* reacted to this ploy. We can, however, see it exploited brilliantly in *Agamemnon*, when Cassandra's long silence constitutes a significant victory over Clytemnestra, who endeavors unsuccessfully to elicit some spoken response from her (on this scene see Mossman, chapter 22 in this volume).

Yet another effective use of silence, through the very breaking of it, seems to have been employed by Aeschylus in *Libation Bearers*. When Orestes balks at the imminent prospect of killing his mother, Pylades, played by an otherwise mute actor or super-numerary, unexpectedly interjects to remind him of Apollo's command. The very fact of the three-speaking-actor convention, of course, leads directly to situations that appear tailor-made for dramatic silences. In *Women of Trachis*, for example, the woman Heracles has captured as his concubine is sent on ahead with a group of fellow captives, in a scenario that in some respects recalls the Cassandra episode in *Agamemnon*. The structure of *Women of Trachis* does not allow for Iole to have a speaking part. Her very silence, however, as Heracles' wife asks about her before she enters the house in an ominously symbolic action, greatly enhances the dramatic effect of the scene. The silent presence of children, as in Euripides' *Medea*, must also have been exploited with telling dramatic effect.

The exploitation of one further dramatic convention is especially interesting. Having once entered the *orchêstra*, the chorus did not then normally leave it until the end of the play. Interesting consequences of this can be seen in *Agamemnon*. The king's death cries are heard from inside the *skênê*, whereupon the chorus engages in a lengthy discussion as to whether or not they should go in and help. If, as suggested above, this play was performed if not at the very beginning, then at least near the beginning of the period when the *skênê* was added to the performance space, there could as yet be no convention by which the chorus qua chorus was unable to leave the *orchêstra* and enter the building. However, it might have been assumed to be out of keeping with the tragic genre to make the chorus scramble inside. Moreover, the effect of the subsequent action, when the door opens and Clytemnestra emerges with the bodies, would have been entirely lost. Thus purely practical considerations might have been behind the non-intervention of the chorus. Something similar occurs in Euripides' *Medea*, staged more than twenty years later, by which time conventions concerning the *skênê* and the chorus's relationship with it may well have developed. Again, however, intrusion of the chorus into the *skênê*, clumsy in itself, would have spoiled Euripides' later strategy, so again the chorus is made to debate whether or not to go in and help the children whose death cries are heard from within.

The debate in both cases means at least that the chorus is not left to stand around unresponsive to what is supposedly going on inside the *skênê*. This raises another question. What was the chorus doing during the extended scenes involving the actors alone? Some have imagined that the chorus will have responded mimetically when they are not given words. Others have felt that this would be too distracting and have thought in terms of a seated chorus, at least for some of the long passages in which they were not involved. Certainty is impossible. The constant presence of fifteen old men or young women must undoubtedly have been imprinted on a playwright's mind as he was creating his text. Thus on a number of occasions we find attention being drawn to their presence, for example in situations where a plan is being concocted, and one of the characters needs to be reassured that the group of people hovering round are friends who will not give the game away.

This question of the chorus's presence and the spatial limits within which they are allowed to operate has other manifestations too, especially in Euripides. For example, in *Hippolytus* Phaedra is listening at the door of the *skênê* to a conversation supposedly taking place inside, and she asks the chorus to join her. They, however, decline the invitation, pointing out that it is her role to relay news from the house, a response "in character" that at the same time appears to show Euripides drawing attention to a convention by which the chorus would not normally approach the *skênê* door too closely. In *Helen*, however, we actually find Euripides making the chorus enter the *skênê*. This is an unusual case that allows the entrance of Menelaus into an empty performance space where he delivers what is in effect a second prologue. If there was a convention about choral non-entry into the *skênê* from the *orchêstra*, Euripides is certainly breaking it here. In two other surviving plays the chorus is made to leave the *orchêstra* during the course of the action, to return later, but both of these instances require departure down an *eisodos*, not into the *skênê*. The plays in question are Euripides' *Alcestis*, in which the stage needs to be cleared for the entrance of the drunken Heracles, and Sophocles' *Ajax*, where the hero will need to be alone for his suicide scene.

The Audience

We should not overlook the importance, as one of the key components of any performance of a Greek tragedy, of the audience, whose experience must have been richly aural as well as visual (Hall 2002, 4). The Theater of Dionysus perhaps held up to 15,000 spectators, so that the atmosphere at a play would have been very different from what prevails in most modern theatrical situations. The tragedies presented must have posed a significant intellectual and emotional challenge to an audience, and there must have been some discomfort involved in sitting in fairly cramped conditions for lengthy periods. Even though the audience did not directly judge the competition, their reaction to the plays they watched must surely have influenced the appointed panel of judges. We lack clear evidence, however, about the audience's precise responses. One story, found in Plutarch's *Cimon* (8.7–9) about an incident that happened near the end of Aeschylus' career and the beginning of Sophocles', suggests that factionalism may have played a role, with different sections of the audience backing a different playwright. Plutarch's story (admittedly written down more than 500 years after the event) tells how the archon on this occasion refused to choose the judges by lot, as was the usual practice, but obliged the ten *stratêgoi* (generals) to act instead, on account of the increased prestige which these men would bring to the judging, in a situation of divided audience partisanship.

The exact composition of the audience is unknown, the debate focusing on whether women were allowed to attend, or whether tragedy was basically an occasion for citizens (freeborn male adults). The evidence is inconclusive, although it appears unlikely that women, who were surely participants in the Festival of Dionysus in general, would have been excluded from the theatrical part as such. Stories dating from a later period, however, like the one in the anonymous *Life of Aeschylus* telling how the chorus of Furies in *Eumenides* were so terrifying that they caused children to faint and women to have miscarriages, cannot be used as reliable evidence on this question.

In a theater without much in the way of scenery, smaller stage props would have been used with telling effect. We can assume that significant items – the tapestries Clytemnestra lays out as the deceptive and seductive welcome mat for Agamemnon, Ajax's whip, shield, and sword, Philoctetes' bow, the urn supposedly containing Orestes' ashes in Sophocles' *Electra*, even chariots on occasion – would have been represented by real objects in the theatrical performance. This, however, raises an interesting question of interpretation. It is sometimes difficult to decide whether some given object or phenomenon is referred to or described in the text because it was visible to the audience, or for the very reason that it was not, and that the playwright is therefore inviting his audience to imagine it.

To illustrate the point, we can mention cases where the audience must simply have been invited to use their imagination. When one character refers to another as having tears running down his or her face or looking triumphant, it is clear that the audience members were the ones to supply, as it were, the visualized emotion, since the mask of an actor was unable to display it (the actor could, however, express the required emotion through voice, stance, and gesture). The same applies, of course, to contexts where characters verbally set the scene of the locale to be imagined for the fictional world of a given play. When, for example, at the beginning of *Philoctetes*, Odysseus announces, "This is the shore of the island of Lemnos surrounded by sea," the audience obviously saw no waves. Interestingly, though, when characters point out landmarks such as buildings, the audience could see equivalent buildings around them from their seats in the theater, even though they could not see the buildings of the fictional world of the play. Similarly, references to the sky and the sun become instantly transferable to the natural environment of the audience.

There are, however, many problematic contexts. For example, when the chorus of Euripides' *Ion* arrive in Delphi, they slip into the role of tourists, describing the sculptural decorations of the temple of Apollo. It is not easy to be sure whether the *skênê* was decorated with at least some figures, even if not precisely those described, or whether the audience is being invited to imagine them. In that play too, the playwright could not have guaranteed that birds would be flying overhead at the precise moment that the hero shoos them away, even if he was holding in his hand the bow with which he was threatening to shoot them. There is a teasing point in *Orestes* when the hero asks for a bow with which to ward off the Furies assailing him. Given that he is temporarily mad and his Furies only imaginary, it has to be asked whether Electra hands him an actual bow (on this scene see Gregory, chapter 16 in this volume). The locus classicus for this issue, however, is seen in *Bacchae*, where the chorus describes an earthquake that shakes Pentheus' palace. Controversy rages as to whether anything concrete took place in the theater or whether the earthquake was simply conveyed by the reaction of the chorus. Given that this is a play much concerned with illusion, the latter seems more likely, especially since characters entering subsequently make no reference to any damage.

Some Problem Cases

A number of the surviving plays present particular problems. One such is *Prometheus Bound*. On the assumption that a *skênê* was available to the author, whether this was Aeschylus or not, many scholars have imagined that the nailing of Prometheus to his rock must have occurred up against the stage building. Because Prometheus first hears the chorus of Oceanids rather than sees them and because they say they have flown to the spot, it is assumed that they appeared first on the *skênê* roof. It makes more practical sense, however, to imagine Prometheus being "nailed" to some ad hoc structure in the center of the *orchêstra* and the chorus entering, behind and unseen by him, either on some kind of wheeled carriage or with their flying indicated by the accompanying choreography. Oceanus, who subsequently tells his audience that he has flown in on a griffin, may, in fact, have been similarly earth-bound, or have possibly used the *mêchanê*. How the earthquake and swallowing of Prometheus into the earth could have been staged is another difficult problem. A neat solution would be to imagine Prometheus, fixed all along on the *ekkuklêma*, being withdrawn through the *skênê* door at the end of the play. However, we have no way of judging the extent of realism felt appropriate in such situations. Thus a Prometheus in a central position in the *orchêstra* could just as easily have been surrounded and obscured by the chorus, whose choreographed movements could suggest engulfment, their own included.

The suicide of Ajax is another talking point, the problem being that the actor who as Ajax falls on his sword will have been required shortly afterwards to appear as Teucer and lament over the body. This question is tied up with the further question of a change of scene, normally assumed, from Ajax's tent to a grove near the seashore. The use of different ends of the *skênê* for the two sites is one suggestion (Pöhlmann 1986, 28). With regard to the suicide, a number of solutions have been offered, such as the idea that the Ajax actor may have fallen in death through the *skênê* door (Arnott 1962, 131–32), the body thereafter being represented by a dummy, or that a suitably adapted *ekkuklêma* was used (Webster 1970a, 17–18). Suicide entirely out of sight of the audience has been presented as the other option (Pöhlmann 1986, 27), even with no change of scene involved (Scullion 1994, 89–128). Certainty in such cases is impossible.

When we consider the texts of Greek tragedy for the light they may shed on the original performances, a whole world of living theater opens up. Yet it may be, in a sense, an idealized theatrical world. Theater does not necessarily run smoothly, and things can go wrong in any kind of performance context. While there are few records of such things associated with the performance of tragedy in ancient times, the evidence that we do have serves to remind us that Greek tragedies too were vulnerable to mishap. Perhaps the most famous case involves the actor, mercilessly twitted by Aristophanes and other comic poets, who unwittingly undercut the seriousness of a dramatic moment in Euripides' *Orestes* by mispronouncing a key word: Orestes misspoke and said, not that he saw "calm" after his storm of madness, but that he saw a "pussycat." And there is an enigmatic reference in Aristotle's *Poetics* 1455a to a mistake made by the fourth-century tragedian Carcinus, who seems to have made one of his characters appear from a totally unsuitable or illogical direction, which aroused the ire of the audience and led to Carcinus' spectacular failure in the competition. Stories such as these bring us close to Greek tragedy as living theater working through fallible human agents. At the same time, it leads to significant frustration that our knowledge is so limited and that so much about the subject remains in the realm of speculation. But what if we *could* travel back in time and attend the premiere of *Oedipus the King*? Let us conclude with the sobering reflection of one sensitive scholar (Dale 1968, 214) who suggests that perhaps if we did, "we should first have to...acquire new idioms of music and orchestic and stagecraft no easier than the language itself; perhaps harder, if the prejudices of our modern aesthetic should prove to be too deeply wrought into our consciousness."

FURTHER READING

There are many useful general introductions to the ancient Greek (and Roman) theater (often dealing with comedy as well as tragedy) that contain discussions of theatrical production. Among the best are Rehm 1992, which succinctly sets out the general social and theatrical background before considering a number of tragedies in the light of this background, and Simon 1982, which draws extensively on the evidence of vase-painting. Walton 1984 includes brief discussions of all the surviving tragedies, and Walton 1980 applies general principles to the staging of Aeschylus' *Libation Bearers* and the two *Electra* plays. Useful books for the generalist are Arnott 1989, Wiles 1997, and Wiles 2000, although Wiles tends to stray at times beyond scholarly safety and should be treated with a degree of caution. The polemical approach of Ashby 1999 is refreshing but contains errors of fact and again needs to be treated with care. A recent and most convenient summary of the archaeological evidence for the Theater of Dionysus can be found in Moretti 1999–2000.

Useful books with a production slant geared to individual tragic playwrights include Halleran 1985 (dealing with Euripides), Seale 1982 (a more detailed consideration of Sophocles), and Taplin 1977 (an extremely detailed and rigorous study of Aeschylus). J. R. Green 1994 is essential reading for the evidence provided by surviving material objects such as vases, relief sculptures, mosaics, and terracotta figurines; it covers the whole period of Greek and Roman theater. Pickard-Cambridge 1988 is a mine of information about all aspects of theatrical production. Indispensable as a record of both relevant artifacts and written sources in English translation is Csapo and Slater 1995. Recent specialized studies in English that greatly broaden our knowledge of important areas include Wilson 2000a, which considers the arrangement by which performances such as tragedy were sponsored by wealthy citizens, and Easterling and Hall 2002, which covers actors and acting in the ancient world. Rehm 2002 is the best recent specialized work in English focusing on production.

PART III

Approaches

CHAPTER FOURTEEN

Aeschylean Tragedy

Suzanne Saïd

Less than fifty years after his death, Aeschylus was portrayed in Aristophanes' comedies as a symbol of archaic grandeur beloved by old men such as Dicaeopolis and Strepsiades, the heroes of *Acharnians* and *Clouds*, whereas the young cared only for Euripides and his "new" tragedy. In Aristophanes' *Frogs* Aeschylus' style is depicted as "noble" (*semnos*, 1004). His heroes are "half-gods" (1060), "with the spirit of a lion" (1041), and his thoughts are "great" (1058). His style is commensurately heroic, full of "words with flashing helmets" (818) and "horse-riding sayings" (821). This poet of manic inspiration (816) and wild temper (994, 1066) is assimilated to unbridled natural forces such as hurricanes (848) and raging fire (859), or fierce animals such as the bull (804, 822). He is said to "amaze" (962) the audience and play on their emotions by creating uncivilized and monstrous creatures. But he is also a political advisor who aims at the preservation of the city by giving good advice to his fellow citizens and who claims to teach them regard for hierarchy and martial virtues. This complex portrayal became very influential. Nineteenth-century scholars opted for the primitive Aeschylus, opposing him to the mature Sophocles and the decadent Euripides. Contemporary scholars tend to put more emphasis on the political character of the genre he illustrated or, better, created.

In fact, so little is known about Athenian tragedy before Aeschylus that Gilbert Murray had good reasons to entitle the book he devoted to the first extant tragic poet *Aeschylus, the Creator of Tragedy* (1940). Aeschylus, who competed with Choerilus, Pratinas, Phrynichus, and, at the end of his life, Sophocles, produced his first play in 498 and won his first victory in 484. He was both productive (the number of plays attributed to him by our sources varies between seventy-three and ninety) and successful: he won thirteen victories during his life and not a few after his death (a circumstance which may explain the figure of twenty-eight victories given by the *Suda*).

Only seven plays, as well as many fragments, survive. Moreover, only four are truly complete. *Persians* (472), a single play with no link to the (lost) plays produced with it, is the only surviving tragedy whose subject matter is taken from contemporary history; it stages the defeat of the Persians and the return of Xerxes. The *Oresteia* (458) is the only surviving trilogy – in all probability a form invented by Aeschylus.

It comprises three connected tragedies: *Agamemnon*, on the return of the victorious King Agamemnon and his murder by his wife Clytemnestra; *Libation Bearers*, on the revenge of his son Orestes and the murder of Clytemnestra and Aegisthus; and *Eumenides*, on the trial and acquittal of Orestes at Athens.

Seven against Thebes (467) is the conclusion of a trilogy that covered the fate of the Labdacids; the two plays that preceded it (*Laius* and *Oedipus*) are lost, but may be reconstructed from the second stasimon of the surviving tragedy. The first play focused on Laius and his death in consequence of his disobedience to Apollo. The second was devoted to Oedipus' discovery of his parricide and incestuous marriage and its consequences: Oedipus' self-blinding and his curse upon his sons. The third, surviving, tragedy begins with the siege of Thebes, defended by Eteocles, by an Argive army led by Polynices, and ends with mutual fratricide and the defeat of the Argives.

Suppliants, produced in competition with Sophocles – that is, no earlier than the 460s, as revealed by a scrap of papyrus published in 1952 (P.Oxy 2256.3) – was either the first or the second play of a trilogy devoted to the story of Danaus and his fifty daughters. It deals with the arrival in Argos of the Danaids, pursued by their cousins the sons of Aegyptus, and the Argives' decision to grant the fugitives asylum. All we know of *Egyptians* is the title, which explains why it has been considered either as the first play focusing on the pursuit of the Danaids by their cousins and ending with their flight (Del Grande 1947, 90–92; Sommerstein 1996, 143–46), or as the second (a view accepted today by most scholars, e.g., Winnington-Ingram 1961; Garvie 1969, 185–86; Herington 1986, 101), beginning with the surrender of the Danaids to the sons of Aegyptus after an Argive defeat and ending with the murder of the sons of Aegyptus by their cousins on the wedding night. The third play, *Danaids*, is better known: it began with the discovery of the corpses and was devoted to the trial of Hypermestra, the only Danaid who disobeyed her father and spared her husband, her vindication by Aphrodite, and the eventual reconciliation of her sisters to marriage.

The authorship of *Prometheus Bound*, which portrays the punishment of the rebel Titan by Zeus, has been discussed with particular heat in recent years. Following Schmid (1929), Griffith (1977) and West (1979) strongly deny its authenticity, relying mainly on stylistic and metrical arguments. Saïd (1985) and Herington (1986), in contrast, who point out that the major themes of the play are entirely consistent with the themes observable elsewhere in Aeschylus' plays, tend to accept the ancient – and unanimous – attribution of *Prometheus Bound* to Aeschylus. This play, the only surviving part of a trilogy, was followed by *Prometheus Unbound*, devoted to the loosing of Prometheus by Heracles, who killed the eagle and released the Titan from his bonds. The content of *Prometheus the Fire Carrier* is not clear: according to some, it was the first play of the trilogy and staged the bringing of the fire to men, but many think that it concluded the trilogy with the establishment of a cult of Prometheus at Athens and its associated torch race.

The Man in His Time

The *Life of Aeschylus*, which depends on anecdotes collected by Ion of Chios, a contemporary of Sophocles, and the caricatures of the comic poets, contains few reliable facts. It is valuable, however, as a piece of literary criticism, since the stories about the tragic poets usually derived from impressions about their style and from representative verses of their poetry. Aeschylus' aristocratic origin may be a translation into biographical terms of his striving for "a grand style" and his bestowing "heroic dignity" on his characters (*Life* 5).

It is the Athens in which Aeschylus grew up, however, that provides the most reliable guide to his tragedies. For Aeschylus belongs to the glorious generation of those who fought at Marathon. Significantly enough, the epitaph preserved in his life commemorates him not as a poet but as a warrior:

> Of his noble courage the sacred field of Marathon can tell,
> and the long haired Mede, who had good cause to know. (*Life* 10)

He is also said to have taken part in the battles of Salamis and Plataea, and the legend gave him as brothers Cynegirus, who died heroically at Marathon in the rush to seize the Persian ships (Herodotus 6.114), and Ameinias, who was the best warrior at Salamis (Diodorus 11.27.2). Indeed, war features prominently in all his surviving plays. *Persians* is a "Salamis symphony" (Adams 1952), displaying the magnitude of a disaster that is first adumbrated by the dream and the omen of the queen mother, then narrated by a messenger who is an eyewitness of the battle, and lastly demonstrated with the arrival on stage of Xerxes in rags. The action of *Seven against Thebes* coincides with the siege of Thebes, and the chorus envisages the destruction of the city in vivid details that owe much to the sack and burning of the Acropolis by Xerxes' troops. In *Suppliants* it is Argos that is under threat, and the play ends with the prospect of war against the Egyptians. The *Oresteia* is framed by two wars, the Trojan War just won by Agamemnon and the glorious contests to be waged in the future by the Athenians, for it was during the lifetime of Aeschylus that Athens became a major power and the head of a naval league that was soon to be transformed into a tribute-paying empire.

Aeschylus also witnessed the transition from tyranny to radical democracy: he saw the abrupt end of the Pisistratid tyranny, the constitution of Cleisthenes that granted the citizens limited political participation, and the reforms of Ephialtes that stripped the aristocratic council of the Areopagus of almost all its political powers and devolved them to the assembly and the popular Council of Five Hundred. It is no accident that *Suppliants* is the first text to explicitly refer to "the ruling hand of the people" (*dêmou kratousa cheir*, 604; cf. our "democracy"), and to portray a city-state where the king behaves like a contemporary Athenian magistrate: he refuses to commit the polis to the support of the suppliants without the approval of the *dêmos* (365–69, 398–401) and subjects his proposal to the vote of the people in the assembly. *Eumenides* contains various topical allusions to the Argive alliance (289–91, 669–73, 762–74) and also alludes to the expedition of 459, when Athenian ships were sent to Egypt to help an Egyptian revolt against Persia (see Debnar, chapter 1 in this volume). It also gives an account of the foundation of the homicide court that is clearly the charter myth for the post-Ephialtean Areopagus. The play thus directly addresses a highly controversial political event.

The Stagecraft of Aeschylus

Aeschylus, who "raised standards far above his predecessors in writing and staging, in the splendor of his choral productions, in his actors' costumes and in the serious content of his choral songs" (*Life* 2), was also, to a greater degree than his successors, a complete man of the theater: playwright, composer, director, and actor. As a director, he made the best of the minimal stage resources existing in his time and introduced startling innovations. With the exception of the *Oresteia*, all his surviving tragedies are set in the open. The building where the old councilors are supposed to sit in *Persians* was left to the spectators' imagination. *Seven against Thebes* takes place on an Acropolis decorated with the statues of the gods. In *Suppliants*, the Danaids are advised by their father to sit as suppliants at the *pagos* (mound, rock) that belongs to the assembled gods (189). In *Prometheus Bound*, there is also a rock to which the hero is nailed at the beginning of the play. It has been suggested by Hammond (1972) that this mound was in fact a natural outcrop of rock that existed at the time of Aeschylus and then disappeared, whereas others (such as Rehm 1988) have identified it with the altar of Dionysus located in the center of the *orchêstra*. In the *Oresteia* there is a major change as the *skênê* is integrated into the scenic space: this building is successively identified as the palace of the Atreids in *Agamemnon* and *Libation Bearers*, and the temple of Apollo at Delphi and the temple of Athena at Athens in *Eumenides*. The door plays a major role, with Clytemnestra, "the watchdog of the house" (*Agamemnon* 607), forestalling any entry into the palace by another person in *Agamemnon*, and Orestes preventing Clytemnestra from entering the palace in *Libation Bearers* (Sommerstein 1996, 220–21). And the roof is put to use by the watchman of *Agamemnon*, who speaks the prologue from it.

Aeschylus also broke new ground in the *Oresteia* by shifting the spatial focus in the middle of the play: the first part of *Libation Bearers* takes place around the grave of Agamemnon, whereas the second part is centered around the gateway of Agamemnon's palace. In *Eumenides* the change is even more drastic: along with Orestes and the Furies, the action moves from Delphi to Athens at line 235. According to Pollux, who wrote in the second century CE, Aeschylus was the first to put to use the *mêchanê* (crane) to bring on stage the corpse of Memnon in his *Psychostasia* (4.130), and it is believed by many scholars (though denied by the author of the best study of Aeschylean stagecraft, Taplin 1977, 432–33) that a crane was used in *Eumenides* for the entrance of Athena and in *Prometheus Bound* for the entrance of Oceanus. It is tempting to believe that the *ekkuklêma* – a trolley with wheels that was rolled out to reveal interior scenes – was used to display Clytemnestra standing over the corpses of Agamemnon and Cassandra at the end of *Agamemnon*, and Orestes standing over the dead bodies of Aegisthus and Clytemnestra at the end of *Libation Bearers*.

According to Aristotle, Aeschylus invented the second actor (*Poetics* 1449a15–16), "a vitally important step in the development of drama" (Garvie 1969, 125). He used him first and foremost as a messenger who brings fresh news from the outside. In *Persians*, the second actor generally addresses the chorus; there are only two short dialogues between the two actors. In *Seven against Thebes*, the second actor reports to the king what is happening on the battlefield. In *Suppliants*, when Danaus faces the king of Argos together with his daughters, he is totally eclipsed by the chorus and his part is limited to ten lines. But at the end of the play the interaction between the two actors, the Argive king and the Egyptian herald, amounts to a real *agôn*, a confrontation between two hostile characters. In the *Oresteia*, similarly, there is a dramatic *agôn* between Clytemnestra and Agamemnon (*Agamemnon*) and Clytemnestra and Orestes (*Libation Bearers*), as well as dialogues between two actors. In *Prometheus*

Bound the handling of the second actor is even more developed, with long exchanges between Cratos and Hephaestus, Oceanus and Prometheus, Prometheus and Io, and Hermes and Prometheus.

Once Sophocles had introduced the third actor, Aeschylus put the innovation to use in the *Oresteia*. In the two first parts of the trilogy he used it sparingly. Cassandra in *Agamemnon* is a mute character who bursts into a torrent of song and speech only after the two other actors have left the stage. Pylades in *Libation Bearers* speaks only three lines when he becomes Apollo's spokesman. But in *Eumenides* the trial scene (566–777) makes effective use of the three actors (Athena, Apollo, and Orestes). Aeschylus may have adopted another Sophoclean innovation, the increase in the number of chorus members from twelve to fifteen. Hammond (1972, 419 n. 58) and Taplin (1977, 323 n. 3) both argue for a chorus of fifteen in *Agamemnon*, adducing lines 1344–71, where the first three lines can be assigned to three members of the chorus and followed by twelve couplets.

By comparison with his predecessors, Aeschylus "diminished the part of the chorus and gave the leading role to speech" (Aristotle, *Poetics* 1449a17–18). But compared to his successors, he gave the chorus and the lyrics extraordinary prominence. In *Suppliants* the chorus of Danaids is the leading character; this has been interpreted either as a return to archaic technique (Taplin 1977, 206–7) or as a bold experiment (Garvie 1969, 106–20). In *Eumenides* the chorus of the Furies is a deuteragonist, if not a protagonist: they play the role of the prosecution pitted against the defender Apollo, and the action revolves as much around their honors as around Orestes' acquittal. The chorus also plays an active role in *Libation Bearers* by asking the nurse to summon Aegisthus without his bodyguards, thus facilitating his murder, and in *Persians* by advising the queen mother to pray and make sacrifices and joining her in invoking the ghost of Darius. In *Prometheus Bound* the chorus of Ocean's daughters shares the ultimate fate of the hero, disappearing with him into a chasm. For the most part, however, "the chorus cares, but cannot act" ([Aristotle], *Problems* 19.48): the chorus's attempt to intervene physically in *Agamemnon*, first by giving help to the king and then by opposing the tyranny of Aegisthus, comes to nothing. In *Persians* and *Seven against Thebes* the choruses (of old councilors and Theban women, respectively) have an important emotional stake in the action, since in each case their fate is linked to the result of the battle. The chorus is also a mediating principle between the heroes and the audience and often communicates directly with the audience. As narrator, the chorus comments on what has already occurred or sets the mood for the events to come. As enunciator of wisdom speaking in a higher style than the characters, the choral voice carries authority and may appear as the mouthpiece of the poet.

Aeschylus' plots are usually simple. According to the *Life* (5), "they do not abound in peripeteiai [reversals] and complexities like those of the later poets." But Aeschylus is a master of reversal (Herington 1986, 161). In *Persians* there is a striking contrast between the initial description of the might of the Persian army on its way to Greece and the final return of its leader, alone and in torn robes. In *Agamemnon* the return of the victorious king (which is announced twice, by the beacon signal and the speeches of the herald) is followed by his murder. In contrast, Orestes' return and successful revenge in *Libation Bearers* is a reversal from negative to positive.

The same is true for *Suppliants* and *Eumenides*. In *Suppliants* the daughters of Danaus are granted asylum by the Argives. In *Eumenides* Orestes, who entered the stage as a hunted fugitive, is acquitted, and returns home with his patrimony restored. Meanwhile the Furies, who appeared first as figures of unspeakable horror, are transformed into tutelary goddesses who watch over the fertility of the land and the fecundity of its women. In *Seven against Thebes*, the reversal takes place in the middle of the play. Initially Eteocles is identified with the city; his use of the first-person plural tends to associate him with his fellow citizens (4, 194, 516). In contrast to the panic-stricken chorus, he behaves like the calm and responsible leader of a threatened city-state; he is the exact opposite of his brother, who brought an alien army to ravage his fatherland. But when Eteocles is told that Polynices will be posted at the seventh gate and decides to fight against him (he is his perfect match: "chief against chief, brother against brother, enemy against enemy," 674–75), he becomes filled with a mad lust for his brother's blood, and it is the chorus that tries in vain to restrain his rage and to prevent him from emulating his brother's temper (677–78). From this moment on, the two brothers become one: they are equally characterized as "men of many quarrels" (*poluneikeis*, 830) and associated by the use of dual or plural. If we assume the spuriousness of 1005–78 (a view shared by many scholars, including Winnington-Ingram 1977, 4; Herington 1986, 92; Sommerstein 1996, 130–34), the play closes with the arrival of their two bodies and a choral lament over both.

The plot of *Prometheus Bound* is even simpler, since there is no reversal: the punishment of the benefactor of mankind, which begins in the prologue with the pinning of the Titan to a lofty rock, ends with his engulfment in the rock without breaking his resistance.

The decision that forms the core of the plot and provokes the reversal is often taken or carried out on stage. In *Seven against Thebes* the audience sees Eteocles, who had already announced that he would post seven champions, himself included, to the seven gates (282), fulfilling his duty as king and deciding to fight at the seventh gate against his own brother. In *Suppliants* the audience listens to the king of Argos when he agrees to ask his citizens to grant asylum to Danaus' daughters. In the *Oresteia* Agamemnon is persuaded on stage to walk the purple path prepared by Clytemnestra. It is also in full view of the audience that Orestes puts an end to his hesitation and embarks on the matricide, and that Athena, asked to choose between the competing claims of her suppliant, Orestes, and the Furies, decides to entrust the case to a court of Athenian citizens presided over by her and casts her vote for him. Accordingly many critics, beginning with Snell 1928, have opposed Aeschylus to Sophocles in these terms: whereas Sophocles focuses on the moment when the heroes (such as Ajax or Oedipus) become aware of what they did before the beginning of the play, Aeschylus puts the decision and "the deed" (in Greek: *drama*) at the center of his tragedies.

Tragedy, Myth, and History

The usual material of Attic tragedy consists of the complex of heroic myths that represented for the Greeks the stories of their distant past, to be reinterpreted time and time again and made credible for a contemporary audience. Aeschylus is said to have called his plays "slices from the great banquets of Homer" (Athenaeus 347e); "Homer" here refers to the entire corpus of archaic epic narrative, not only to the author of the *Iliad* and the *Odyssey*. Why does Aeschylus prefer the distant past to the recent one? Undoubtedly because it was more glamorous, but also because it allowed the dramatist to address contemporary issues without running the risk of being fined, like the tragic poet Phrynichus, for "reminding the Athenians of their own woes" (Herodotus 6.21.2) when he staged *The Capture of Miletus*. Last but not least, Aeschylus preferred the past because myth was still a highly flexible medium, as the murder of Agamemnon illustrates. In the *Odyssey*, Aegisthus both plotted and carried out the murder of Agamemnon, which took place in his own house (4.512–37), whereas in Aeschylus the murder takes place in the house of the Atreids, Aegisthus is only "the one who plotted death against him but did not dare to do the deed with [his] own hand" (*Agamemnon* 1634–35), and it is Clytemnestra who strikes the actual blow (1384–87).

Persians is an exception: the only extant Attic tragedy (and among the very few we know of) that takes its subject matter from recent history. In this play Aeschylus presented to the Athenians the defeat of their foes at Salamis eight years earlier. But proximity in time is compensated by distance in space: the play takes place at the court of the king of Persia, in Susa. It opens with a triumphant litany of the wealth and majesty of the Persian army by the chorus of Persian elders, followed by the expression of their anxiety for the departed host. The entrance of the queen mother brings more doubts, with her narrative of divine signs (a dream followed by an omen) that portend a defeat. These signs come true when a messenger enters and gives the news of Salamis to the queen and the chorus. Then the ghost of Darius, wearing the full regalia of a Persian king and evoked from his tomb by the queen's offerings and the dance and song of the chorus, announces the disaster to come at Plataea. In contrast to the messenger and the queen, who attributed Xerxes' disaster to the cruelty of a fickle god, the ghost accounts for it in light of the moral order upheld by Zeus: For "*Hubris* (Arrogance) ripening bears its crop, the wheat-ear of *Atê* (Infatuation), and reaps a harvest of tears" (821–22). The narrative turns into spectacle with the entrance of Xerxes, the first example of a king in rags in extant Greek tragedy, followed by members of the chorus who tear to shreds their magnificent robes.

Given the theme, it is easy to imagine a partisan play gratifying the pride of the victors at the expense of the defeated. Aeschylus does nothing of the kind. It has even been suggested that the play should be read as a warning to the young Athenian democracy and its imperialist policy (Rosenbloom 1995). In Aeschylus' portrayal the defeat of Xerxes becomes an exemplary reversal that demonstrates the limits set by the gods to human happiness and the danger of infatuation induced by enduring prosperity. Numbers, used at the beginning to evoke Persian manpower and the multitude of their ships, signify the magnitude of the disaster in the wake of Salamis. The vast wealth and luxury that become visible to the audience with the splendid entrance of the queen, "radiant as the eyes of gods" (150–51) and seated in a chariot with her many attendants, has vanished by the time she reenters, unattended and without her chariot. Similes too change their meaning: the young king launched his attack on the Greeks with an army as irresistible as the ocean tide (90), but at Salamis an ocean of disaster breaks on Persia (433, 599–600). The impressive catalogue of the Persian army that opens the play (16–58) is matched first by the catalogue of the eighteen commanders who have perished at Salamis (302–30) and second by the list of all the fighters who did not return with Xerxes (957–1003).

This catastrophe came about because of Xerxes alone – his youth and his "over-proud rashness" (831) – since his decision to invade Greece is totally at odds with the policy of his predecessors, as is demonstrated by the long historical excursus of Darius (765–81). Unlike these wise kings, Xerxes violated a natural order guaranteed by the gods by "devising a means to yoke the strait of Helle, so as to have a passage across" (722); he "yoked to his chariot" (190–91) Europe and Asia, which were meant to remain separate, and "put the yoke of slavery" (50) on the Greeks, a people who should be free according to the will of Zeus. But nature turned against him by killing with famine those exceedingly numerous (794) and by setting as a trap a bridge of ice that melted at the first rays of the sun (495–507). He was also guilty of sacrilege, since the Persians "did not scruple to plunder the images of the gods and to burn their temples" (809–10).

Individual and Group

Persians, which closely associates the individual catastrophe with the collective disaster, best exemplifies a theater concerned with human beings in a polis. Aeschylus' next surviving tragedy, *Seven against Thebes*, is also a political play, as suggested in the first place by the vocabulary: the occurrences of *polis* (74) far outnumber the occurrences of the words signifying "house" or "family" (*oikos* occurs six times, *domos* thirteen, and *dôma* five). The staging is also significant: there is no royal house in the background, and all the movement is to and from the city walls. Moreover, the characters on stage as well as the chorus are all Theban. From the outset the play, which opens with a public speech of the ruler addressing his fellow citizens, focuses on the city-state threatened by an Argive army and surrounded by enemies. Accordingly, the hero, Eteocles, is defined only by his relationship to the polis: he is "the helmsman in control of the tiller" (3) who prays for the safety of the city and acts on its behalf. In *Suppliants* and the *Oresteia* as well, the characters – including the gods, such as Athena – are concerned with the city-state, and their actions always have serious consequences for the citizens. At the beginning of *Suppliants* the king of Argos does his best to avoid shedding the blood of his fellow citizens for the sake of women. In *Agamemnon* the hero is criticized for causing the death of countless Argives by launching a bloody war for the sake of "a woman of many men" (62); Paris, "convicted of rapine and theft," is condemned for having "brought down in utter destruction the house of his fathers along with his land" (534–36). In *Libation Bearers* Orestes' private vengeance also has political motives: as he says right from the beginning, he acts for the sake of the people, since he does not want them to be "subjects to a pair of women" (301–4). In fact, at the end of the play he exults in having liberated the whole city of Argos by killing "the two tyrants of the land" (973). In *Eumenides* the Athenians even play an active part: their best representatives are to judge the issue between Orestes and the Furies. By the time the trial is over it is the fate of the Athenian community, threatened by the Furies and saved only by the persuasion of Athena, that has become the major issue.

Aeschylean heroes also belong to a family, and the trilogy form that covers the fate of a great royal house over two generations (Agamemnon and his son Orestes) or even three (Laius, Oedipus, and his sons Eteocles and Polynices) illuminates the close link between the individual and his *genos*. Eteocles in *Seven against Thebes* is not only "the lord of the Cadmeans" (39), he is also "the son of Oedipus" (203). His fate, as well as the whole action of the Theban trilogy, is determined by Laius' disobedience: "Overmastered by the ill counsels of his near ones" (750), the king disregarded the oracle of Apollo, who told him three times "to die without issue if he would save the city" (748–49). As a consequence his family, which should never have come into being, is characterized by perverted relationships among its members: first a father (Laius) is killed by the son he had exposed, then a father (Oedipus) curses his sons because he was angry at their *trophê* (either "origin" or "nurture"), and lastly two brothers alike in wrath fight over their patrimony, and do not stop at the pollution of fratricide. In the end, the city is saved only because the family collapses from inside: with the help of an Erinys (Fury) "that ruins the house" (720) and "destroys the race" (1054), the brothers who die "without offspring" (828) have achieved the sacking of their own house. This positive outcome is possible because right from the beginning of *Seven against Thebes*, Aeschylus has carefully separated the polis, the city of Cadmus and its inhabitants, the Cadmeans, from the royal family, which has no connection whatsoever with Cadmus. This separation, which amounts to the negation of any family ties between the citizens and their leaders, explains why the Cadmeans are spared by the gods, who were only angry at a maddened race.

In much the same way, in *Agamemnon* "the impious act begets more after it, like the stock from which they come" (758–60). The sacrifice of Iphigenia by her own father duplicates the killing of the children of Thyestes by their uncle, Atreus, Agamemnon's father. This sacrifice, in turn, is avenged by Clytemnestra, aided by Aegisthus who seeks revenge for the murder of his brothers. Therefore, Agamemnon pays both "for what he began" (1529) and for "the old crimes of the house" (1197). Then, in *Libation Bearers*, the murderers are killed by Orestes, who used deceit just as they did. The acquittal of Orestes in *Eumenides* not only stops this endless process of repetition and retaliation, it also coincides with the creation of a political and religious order that integrates as metics the deities traditionally in charge of watching over family ties. Settled in Athens, the Furies will ward off internecine wars opposing members of the same tribe (862–63) and "birds of the same nest" (866) in the city as they did in the family.

Men and Gods

Aeschylean tragedy, which never disentangles the individual from the group, also shows a direct and constant involvement of divine forces in human action. With Aeschylus gods appear on stage not only to frame the plot by delivering the prologue or bring the action to closure as *dei ex machina*, as in Sophocles and Euripides, but to play a major role in between. Their physical presence and active participation form the very heart of the action in *Eumenides* and *Prometheus Bound*. Human figures, in contrast, are passive: in *Eumenides* Orestes has practically a token role in a trial that opposes Apollo and the Furies. In *Prometheus Bound* human beings are either the targets of Zeus' wrath or the helpless recipients of Prometheus' gifts, and their only representative on stage, Io, "the girl with horns" (588), is the victim of Zeus' lust and Hera's resentment.

In both plays the young Olympians and the ancient gods come into conflict because of human beings, for the consideration shown to men leads to an encroachment upon divine privileges. But from *Eumenides* to *Prometheus Bound* benefaction and guilt change sides. In *Eumenides* it is the "young" god Apollo, spokesman (*prophêtês*, 19) and expounder (cf. *exêgeito*, 595, and *exêgou*, 609) of his father Zeus, who protects Orestes (64, 90) and promises to deliver him from his pains (83). But by showing consideration to a matricide, he behaves like a "thief" (149, 153) and wrongs the old female deities, the Furies, whose privilege and prerogative is to drive such criminals from their homes (210). In *Prometheus Bound* it is the "old" Titan son of Gaia/Themis (not, as in Hesiod's *Theogony,* her grandson), who is philanthropy incarnate (11, 28; also 123, 385, 446). But in order to save men and prevent them from going crushed to Hades (236), he had to "steal" (8, 946) the fire that was Hephaestus' privilege (30) and challenge Zeus' apportionment of honors to the gods.

In the *Oresteia* the conflict is preceded by cooperation and ended by a new settlement. In *Agamemnon* Zeus, the Fury, and Night joined forces: "Zeus sends on the transgressors her who brings punishment, though late, the Fury" (58–59); together, Zeus the king and kindly Night have cast the net of all-capturing destruction upon the towers of Troy (355–60). Similar alliances figure in *Libation Bearers.* Apollo threatens Orestes with the attacks of the Furies (238–84), the chorus invokes the Fates and Zeus together to punish Agamemnon's murderers (306–7), and Electra appeals both to Zeus and the powers below in her prayer (394–99). It is only in *Eumenides* that the conflict breaks out. The first movement of the play, at Delphi, demonstrates that the old deities cannot be overcome by violence and Apollo's golden bow. It is only at Athens that they yield to Athena's gentle persuasion and the power of Zeus *agoraios* (973), the god associated with "assembly" (*agora*) and speech-making, when they are offered an honored home in the city. To be sure, there is also an allusion to the other side of Zeus' power, the brute force of his thunder (826–28), but it is mentioned only to be excluded. This integration of the Furies into the new order does not come as a complete surprise, since the Furies embody values, such as fear and reverence for justice (516–25), that are indispensable to social life.

In *Prometheus Bound*, similarly, Prometheus helped Zeus against Cronus and the Titans before opposing him. In *Prometheus Bound* the "new" master of the gods, whose representatives' names are, significantly, the Greek words for "strength" and "violence," and who rules by laws of his own invention (403) without constitutional authority (151), attempts, like the Apollo of *Eumenides*, to impose his will by sheer force. In the prologue he chains Prometheus to the rocks, and in the epilogue he threatens to entomb him underground and send an eagle to feast upon his liver when he reemerges into the light. Zeus cannot overcome Prometheus' resistance and the conflict between brute force and cleverness reaches an impasse. But by piecing together the prophecies of the hero in *Prometheus Bound* and what we know about *Prometheus Unbound*, we have reason to believe that eventually a compromise was reached between Zeus and the Titan. Taught by time, the new god will assume a different character in the future: Io will be released from her wanderings and hailed as "the glorious wife of Zeus" (834), her descendant Heracles, who is also the son of Zeus, will put a stop to Prometheus' tortures (872–73), and Zeus himself will achieve harmony and friendship with Prometheus (191–92). This change will be mirrored by a parallel advance in the human world. Men were given technical knowledge and skills by Prometheus, but they are still lacking the virtues that belong to Zeus and make possible the existence of human communities; these virtues, in the words of Plato's *Protagoras* (322c), are *diké* and *aidôs* (justice and restraint).

Even when they are not physically present on stage, gods play a major role in Aeschylean drama. Their statues are visible in the *orchêstra* in *Seven against Thebes* and *Suppliants*. Their messages arrive in the form of omens, oracles, dreams, and prophecies given by inspired interpreters. In the *Oresteia* the Atreids are dispatched to Troy by an omen (two birds of Zeus feasting upon a hare) interpreted by Calchas. The cursed prophetess Cassandra foretells on stage the murders to come. By Apollo's threatening oracle, Orestes is sent home and commanded to avenge his father's death. Clytemnestra has a terrifying dream, which according to the palace prophets signifies the wrath of those below the earth against the killers. Moreover, the gods preside over the development of the plot in a mysterious way, for "the desire of Zeus is hard to hunt" (*Suppliants* 87).

In *Seven against Thebes* the quarrel between the two brothers and the duel that follows are clearly the result of both human and supernatural agencies. On the one hand, there is the desire of the two brothers to have sole control of Thebes and of Oedipus' property. On the other, there is the wrath of Apollo, who avenged the disobedience of Laius on the race of Oedipus (800–802) and the role of the Fury that embodies the curse of Oedipus (70, 699–700, 720–75, 790–91, 886–87, 976–77, 986–88, 1054–56).

Gods also share a joint responsibility for every crucial event of the *Oresteia*, as is emphasized by such compound forms of the word *aitios* (responsible) as *metaitios* (five occurrences), *sunaitios* (one occurrence), or *paraitios* (one occurrence). Human and divine causation are so entwined that an expression such as "the ever again arising guileful keeper of the house, the unforgetting child-avenging wrath" (*Agamemnon* 154–55) can be interpreted as a direct reference either to the human agent, Clytemnestra, or to the *daimón* of the house. In *Agamemnon* Aeschylus presents the Trojan War as occurring through the will of Zeus and also of Agamemnon, for the kidnapping of Helen was an outrage against the house of the Atreids and a violation of Zeus' law of hospitality (401–2); the sacrifice of Iphigenia, demanded by Artemis (150–51), was also passionately desired by Agamemnon (215–17); and Troy was "uprooted" by Agamemnon "with the help of the mattock of Zeus, who does justice" (525–26). The murder of Agamemnon was the work of Clytemnestra, who avenged both her daughter's death and Agamemnon's infidelities, and of Aegisthus, who punished the son for the crimes of his father, but it was also the work of the gods who punish the killers of many (*Agamemnon* 461–62), of "Zeus cause of all, doer of all" (1486), and of "the *daimón* that fell upon the house and the descent of Tantalus" (1468–69). Cassandra was killed by Clytemnestra with the help of Apollo the destroyer, who avenged Cassandra's deception on him (1080–82, 1202–8, 1275–76). In *Eumenides* Orestes' acquittal was made possible by the cooperation of the Athenian jurors and of Athena, who cast the last vote.

This cooperation of gods with men is not only to be read a posteriori in the outcome of events. It is also visible beforehand in human decision-making (for example, in the deliberations of Agamemnon or Orestes in the *Oresteia*). Much ink has been spilled over Agamemnon's dilemma. According to Denniston and Page (1957) or Lloyd-Jones (1962), the king had no choice but to do what he does, on account of the curse. For Fraenkel (1950), on the contrary, "Aeschylus ... makes it

clear that all the evil ... has its first origin in [Agamemnon's] own voluntary decision"
(2: 99). But the best analyses remain those of Lesky (1966), Rivier (1968), and
Vernant (1972b), which do not try to simplify Aeschylean thought by eliminating
either the king's "passionate desire" (215–16) for war (and for the sacrifice which is
its necessary preamble) or "the evil counsels of merciless infatuation" (222–23) that
suggest a divine agency. The comparison with Euripides' *Iphigenia at Aulis* is quite
illuminating. In that play Agamemnon pretends to be a mere victim of fate and
complains that he has "fallen under the yoke of necessity" (443). Aeschylus' description is more ambiguous: his Agamemnon has himself "slipped his neck through the
strap of compulsion's yoke" (218). In *Libation Bearers*, Orestes' presentation of his
own motives for avenging the death of his father similarly juxtaposes divine and
human causation: on the one hand the mighty oracle of Apollo (269–97), and on
the other grief for his father, the loss of his inheritance, and the desire to liberate the
Argives from their tyrants (298–304).

Past, Present, and Future

Aeschylus' tragedies, which do not sever the individual from the community or from
the gods, do not separate the future from the most remote past. In *Persians*, the
evocation of the past serves only as a foil for the present: the ghost of Darius,
appearing at the very center of the play, goes back to the beginnings of Persia's
history to contrast its unbroken record of successes with the defeat of Xerxes, before
prophesying other disasters to follow in the near future, according to certain oracles
once given to him (739–41). In *Prometheus Bound* the hero, who has inherited the
prophetic skill of his mother Gaia/Themis, is able to tell of the past wanderings of Io
as well as the future of her descendants, from Epaphus to Heracles.

In *Agamemnon*, Cassandra's visions not only juxtapose but also connect the past
atrocities – the adultery of Thyestes and the feast at which he was served the flesh of
his own children – and those now impending – her own murder and the revenge to
come. Indeed, as long as justice is synonymous with retaliation, the past determines
the future and the punishment rigorously mirrors the crime: "*a woman* shall die,"
says Cassandra, "in return for me, *a woman*, and *a man* for *a man* unfortunate in his
wife" (*Agamemnon* 1318–19). Furthermore, "the murderers, who by *cunning* slew
an honored hero, are to be taken by *cunning*, perishing in the same snare" (*Libation
Bearers* 556–58), and the wife who "killed whom [she] should not" has to "suffer
what [she] should not" (*Libation Bearers* 930).

In *Eumenides* Orestes' acquittal coincides with the end of retaliation. But there is
no radical break with the past. The new court remains closely associated with the old
deities and is given the same covenant (*thesmos*): they were in charge of "the ruin of
households, when violence nurtured in the home strikes a dear one down" (354–56).
The Areopagus, their mortal counterpart, is entrusted with restraining the citizens
from internecine war and from unjust action by fear. Moreover, at least half of its
members (if the number of jurors is even, as is argued by many scholars from Müller
1833 to Podlecki 1989) – or perhaps the majority of them (if there is an odd number
of human jurors, as other scholars from Hermann 1799 to Sommerstein 1989 have
argued) – side with the Furies. In any event Athena is responsible for Orestes'
acquittal, whether she decrees that Orestes is the winner if the votes prove equal

(741) or whether by casting her vote for Orestes she first creates a tie (735–40) and then announces that the tie will be in favor of Orestes (741). She gives her support to Orestes because "There is no mother who bore me; / and I approve the male in all things, short of accepting marriage, / with all my heart, and I am wholly on the side of the father" (736–38) – thus echoing Apollo's argument that the son is closer to his father than to his mother, since the father alone is the begetter, whereas the mother is only a "nurse" (658–61). This reasoning has shocked modern readers, but it is only "the statement, in physical terms, of a principle thought necessary for moral and social order" (Macleod 1982, 143) and the translation into biological terms of an existing cultural fact. In Athens the legitimate child had to be acknowledged as such by his father and integrated by him into the family, when he was given his name at the festival of the Amphidromia, and subsequently into the city, when he was registered by him as a member of his phratry.

By and large, the conclusion of the *Oresteia*, by incorporating the old into the new cosmic and political order, demonstrates that a new order, if it is to last, has to make room for parts of the old order – a lesson that comes straight from Hesiod. According to the *Theogony*, the new ruler Zeus assigned to Aphrodite (203–6) and Hecate (421–25) the spheres they had ruled from the beginning. He confirmed and even increased the privileges of the Styx (399), married venerable deities such as Themis (901–6), Mnemosyne (915–17), and Leto (918–20), and became the father of the Fates (904–6). Such a conclusion is adumbrated by the prayer of the Pythia that opens *Eumenides*. Contrary to the dominant tradition, according to which Apollo took possession of Delphi by force from a chthonic power, Aeschylus invents a peaceful transfer of the oracle possessed first by Earth, and next by her daughters Themis and Phoebe, who gave it to Apollo as "a birthday gift" (7). This version, which may well be an Aeschylean invention, foreshadows the later reconciliation of Olympian and chthonic powers at Athens, where the young goddess Athena will give a dwelling near her temple and a cult to the old daughters of Night. The comparison with the Prometheus trilogy, where the two generations of gods were also reconciled at the end, suggests some kind of confidence in progress and the healing power of time.

The Art of Aeschylus

The Aeschylean "theater of ideas" – this label, applied by Arrowsmith (1963) to Euripides, would also suit his predecessor – is extraordinarily concrete: it conveys the essence of a character or the meaning of a situation through sights, words, similes, or myths.

Aeschylus was justly famous as a "Regisseur" (to borrow the expression of Karl Reinhardt 1949), and his stagecraft has been the topic of an authoritative book by Oliver Taplin (1977). His plays are full of special stage effects, "used more to frighten and astound than to trick his audience" (*Life* 5), such as the raising of the dead Darius, the apparition of the ghost of Clytemnestra, and the entrance of the maddened Io. They often turn "image into action" (Lebeck 1971, 74) and tend to move "from verbal to visual" (Herington 1986, 67). The destruction of Persian power and wealth is first conveyed through the words of the messenger, who gives a lengthy description of the battle of Salamis, its coda, Psyttaleia, and the retreat of the main force from Greece; and then through Darius' prophecy of the disaster of Plataea. All of this destruction is made visible with the arrival, in the *exodos*, of the king dressed in rags. This scene was anticipated first by the dream of Atossa, in which she saw her son tearing his robe (199), then in the form of a simile, by the omen in which the eagle's head is plucked by the hawk's claws (208–9), and finally by the narrative of the messenger telling how the king "tore his robe" (468) when he saw the slaughter at Psyttaleia.

In *Suppliants*, the audience, after hearing of the "outrageous" behavior (*hubristês*, 30; *hubris*, 81, 104, 426, 487, 528, 817) and "impious minds" (*dusagnois phresin*, 751) of the Egyptians who want to marry their cousins against their will and without the consent of their father Danaus, sees this impious behavior on stage with the entrance of the Egyptian herald, who, in "one of those climactic epiphanies that are so characteristic of [the] poet's dramaturgy" (Herington 1986, 100), attempts to drag them off by force (812, 821, 831, 863) from the shrine where they have fled in panic.

In the *Oresteia* the concept of the "lawsuit" begins as a metaphor for "a retribution which strikes not only the offender but his whole city" (Macleod 1982, 134), with the Atreids as "powerful adversary at law" (*Agamemnon* 41), Paris "accused of rapine and theft" (534) as defendant, and the gods as jurors who, after hearing the parties' pleas by no spoken word, put in the urn of blood their votes for the death of men and ruin of Ilion (812–17). But in *Eumenides* the metaphor becomes actual, with the establishment of the Areopagus council and the trial of Orestes. The carpet scene in *Agamemnon* and the change of the Furies from mere illusions into real beings in *Eumenides* (Brown 1983) are also a case in point: "When Agamemnon walks upon the carpet, he performs a symbolic act. Throughout the trilogy 'trampling with the foot' is a metaphor which describes the crime of sacrilege" (Lebeck 1971, 74). In *Agamemnon* the Furies are very much there (59, 463, 645, 749, 992, 1119, 1433, 1580), but are seen and heard only by the visionary Cassandra (1186–93). At the end of *Libation Bearers* they also become visible to Orestes, as is shown by the use of the demonstrative: "*Here* are ghastly women, like Gorgons, with dark raiments and thick-clustered snakes for tresses" (1048–50). But for the chorus and the audience alike they are still mere "fancies" (1051), hallucinations created by Orestes' frenzied imagination. At the beginning of *Eumenides* they first appear to the Pythia (though not to the audience) and so terrify her that she makes her entrance crawling on hands and knees. It is therefore highly probable that both Orestes and the Furies become visible to the audience at 64, although the Furies are still asleep. The ghost of Clytemnestra urges them to awake at 94, but it is only at 143 that they all wake up and begin to sing and dance as a chorus.

In Aeschylean drama appearances never deceive. In *Suppliants*, the dark masks of the Danaids, in contrast to the usual pale masks worn by female characters, are not only realistic and appropriate to the "swarthy" (154) complexion of Egyptian women, but also signify the true nature of these virile maidens who blackmail the king, threaten to pollute the city, and will end up by killing their husbands. In *Prometheus Bound* Cratos' harsh speech is matched by his ugly look (cf. 78). In *Eumenides* "the whole manner of [their] form suggests" (192–93) the brutality of the Furies, and their "fearsome faces" (990), which "so frightened the audience that children fainted and unborn infants were aborted" (*Life* 7), convey their ferocious character.

Gestures have a symbolic value. When Clytemnestra, in *Libation Bearers*, bares the breast that fed Orestes and appeals to her son's pity (896–98), she is meant to remind the audience of the appalling character of matricide, and this meaning is reinforced by two verbal echoes inside and outside the play – inside, since it resonates with the dream in which the serpent at her breast sucked out a clot of blood, and outside, since it echoes the famous moment in the *Iliad* (22.79–89) where Hecuba bared her breast in an appeal to her son not to confront Achilles.

Staging is significant. In *Prometheus Bound*, knowledge is powerless; Prometheus is fastened with immovable bands of bronze. The punishment duplicates the crime: the final scene of *Libation Bearers*, with Orestes standing beside the corpses of Clytemnestra and Aegisthus, obviously parallels the scene in *Agamemnon* where Clytemnestra triumphs over the bodies of Agamemnon and Cassandra. In *Eumenides*, the change of costume of the Furies conveys their change of status: on top of their black dresses they don the purple robe (1028) that symbolizes their new status as metics (resident aliens; at the festival of the Panathenaea metics marched in the procession wearing purple robes).

The tragic reversal may be illustrated by the changed use of a single word. In *Persians*, "number" (*plêthos*), which in the beginning refers to the number of Egyptian sailors (40) and the magnitude of the Persian wealth (166), is used to emphasize the number of corpses and wrecks that fill the shores of Salamis and the sea (432; cf. 272, 420–21) and the magnitude of the woes and calamities that fell upon the Persians (477). When it alludes to the number of Persian ships at Salamis (413) or the mass of elite troops left at Plataea (803), the word *plêthos* shows how this huge number of ships jammed into narrow straits becomes the major cause of the Persian defeat, or how the worst suffering is in store for them. Conversely, in the *Oresteia* words hitherto negative are turned into positive. The *ololugê*, the ritual cry that accompanies a sacrifice or celebrates good news, changes its meaning over the course of the trilogy. In *Agamemnon* it initially celebrates the announcement of the victory over Troy (28) and accompanies the celebratory sacrifices (595), before changing into the negative cry raised by the Furies over "the sacrifice that stoning must avenge" (1118) – the murder of Agamemnon. In *Libation Bearers*, it is answered by the cry that the chorus wants to raise over the corpses of Clytemnestra and Aegisthus (386) and their loud celebration of the escape of the palace from evil (942). But in *Eumenides* the *ololugê* becomes again the glad cry accompanying the sacrifices to the Furies, who have been transformed into tutelary goddesses (1043, 1047).

Repetitions are a highly significant means of conveying resistance to threat or persuasion. In *Prometheus Bound*, the stubborn resistance of the heroes from the beginning to the end is expressed by the parallel between 989–91 and 175–77 – lines that are only a variation on the same theme. As long as the Furies, in *Eumenides*, remain impervious to Athena's persuasion, they answer her in the same words (778–92 = 808–22, 837–47 = 870–80). Conversely, the possibility of a reconciliation between Athena and the Furies is suggested by the parallelism between the song of the Furies and what has been called the charter of the Areopagus: both acknowledge the necessity of fear that checks injustice (517–19 and 690–92), and both warn against anarchy and despotism (526–28 and 696–97) in nearly the same words.

A simile may communicate, better than any abstract expression, the monstrousness of a crime against nature. Clytemnestra gloats over her husband's death:

> So did he fall and quickly breathed away his life,
> and spouting out a sharp jet of blood
> he struck me with a dark shower of gory dew,
> while I rejoiced no less than the crop rejoices
> in the Zeus-given moisture at the birth of the bud.
>   (*Agamemnon* 1388–92)

In "a perversion of the primaeval myth of the mating of Heaven and Earth in the spring rains . . . [she] seems to have cast Agamemnon in the role of Heaven and herself in the role of Earth, while the spurt of blood stood for the gentle falling of the rain/semen; she transformed the ancient world's supreme symbol of love between the sexes into her own supreme symbol of hatred" (Herington 1986, 123–24). The impact of this speech is reinforced by a series of biological metaphors assimilating the proliferation of evil to procreation ("the impious act *begets* more after it, like the stock whence they come," 758–60); the coming of the punishment is described as "the child of ancient murders" (*Libation Bearers* 648–49), and semen is transformed into embryo by curdling: "because of the blood drunk up by the nurturing earth, the avenging gore congeals and does not flow away" (*Libation Bearers* 66–67).

Recurrent similes are often used by way of demonstration. In the third stasimon of *Agamemnon*, Aeschylus introduces the parable of the lion's cub (cf. Knox 1952b; Lebeck 1971, 47–51):

> In the beginnings of its life
> gentle, dear to children
> and a delight to the aged . . .
> But in time it showed the temper
> it had from his parents; for returning
> kindness of those that reared it
> with horrid slaughter of their cattle
> it made a feast unbidden,
> and the house was befouled with blood
> woe irresistible for the servants
> a vast havoc of much slaughter. (720–34)

The allusion is in the first instance to Helen maintained by the Trojans: *en biotou proteleiois*, which may be translated "in the beginnings of its life," refers, strictly speaking, to the sacrifices preliminary to the marriage. But the image extends its significance to the action of the entire trilogy. It applies to the Greek army at Troy, compared to "a ravening lion leaping over the wall and licking his fill of the blood of kings" (827–28), but also to Agamemnon, the "noble lion" (1259) who killed his daughter as a "preliminary sacrifice for the sailing of his ships" (*proteleia naôn*, 227); and to his murderers, Aegisthus "the strengthless lion" (1224) and Clytemnestra "the two-footed lioness" (1258). In *Libation Bearers*, it refers also to his avengers, Orestes and Pylades, "the double lion" (938). It appears again in *Eumenides* with reference to the Furies: according to Apollo their fit dwelling place is "the den of a blood-supping lion" (193–94).

As many critics have pointed out (e.g., Zeitlin 1965, Vidal-Naquet 1972a), the recurrent imagery of hunting and sacrifice best exemplifies the tragic reversal in the

Oresteia. Agamemnon, who led his troop of "huntsmen" (694) on the track of Helen and, with the help of Zeus and Night, cast an all-embracing net over Troy (357–59), is caught in the net put out by Clytemnestra (1115–17, 1382–83; *Libation Bearers* 492–3) and displayed by Orestes at the end of *Libation Bearers* (997–1000). The man who dared to become the sacrificer of his daughter (*Agamemnon* 224–25) became in his turn the victim of a sacrifice (*Agamemnon* 1409).

Myth replaces theory. By transforming the Furies, who according to Hesiod's *Theogony* were born from Earth and the blood gushing out from Ouranos (183–85), into the daughters of Night in *Eumenides*, Aeschylus associates them closely with darkness. They are "black" not only outside, because of their dresses, but also inside, because of their temper as bitter as black gall (832).They dwell in evil darkness (71–72) in the lower depths of Tartarus. They are worshipped by night (108–9). Moreover, because they have only a mother and no father, they are wholly on the side of the female, as opposed to the Olympian gods, Apollo and Athena, who belong to a male-dominated world and are exclusively defined by their link to their father Zeus: Apollo is introduced as "the spokesman of his father Zeus" (19), and Athena, who "was never nurtured in the darkness of the womb" (665), is a partisan of the male in every way and, because of her origin, "wholly on the side of the father" (737–38).

The convergence between spectacle, verbal imagery, and mythical genealogy is such that it is often impossible to separate them. The most tangible aspects of a character's appearance invariably possess some symbolic value. The fearsome faces or masks (in Greek *prosópa*, singular *prosópon*) of the Furies with their hair entwined with snakes (*Libation Bearers* 1049–50; cf. *Eumenides* 128) resemble the snake-haired Gorgons (*Prometheus Bound* 799) to whom they are often compared (*Libation Bearers* 1048; *Eumenides* 48–49). This imagery also associates them with the murderers, the viper Clytemnestra (*Agamemnon* 1233; *Libation Bearers* 249, 994, 1047) and the serpent Orestes (*Libation Bearers* 527, 549). The blood that drips from their eyes (*Eumenides* 54) reminds the audience of all the blood shed earlier in the trilogy. This powerful coincidence of the visual and the verbal explains the lasting impact of Aeschylus' plays. According to the *Life*, their heroic grandeur impressed the Athenians so profoundly that "they voted after his death to award a chorus to whoever was willing to put on one of his dramas" (11).

FURTHER READING

The major commentaries on the plays include Fraenkel 1950 (*Agamemnon*), Sommerstein 1989 (*Eumenides*), Podlecki 1989 (*Eumenides*), Friis Johansen and Whittle 1980 (*Suppliants*), Griffith 1983 (*Prometheus Bound*), and Garvie 1986 (*Libation Bearers*). See also, on *Persians*, Broadhead 1960 and Podlecki 1991; and on *Seven against Thebes* Lupaş and Petre 1981 and Hutchinson 1985.

The best general introductions to Aeschylus are (concise) Herington 1986 and (more developed) Sommerstein 1996. See also Solmsen 1949, di Benedetto 1978, and Rosenmeyer 1982. Winnington-Ingram 1983, a collection of his papers on Aeschylus, is also valuable. On stagecraft, Taplin 1977 is indispensable. On similes, the best study is (in German) Petrounias

Suzanne Saïd

1976; on style, see Stanford 1942. On Aeschylus and politics, see Podlecki 1966a and Gagarin 1976. There are also good studies on various plays: on the *Oresteia* see Lebeck 1971 and Goldhill 1992; on *Eumenides*, Meier 1993, 108–16; on *Persians*, Michelini 1982; on *Seven against Thebes*, Thalmann 1978 and Zeitlin 1982; on *Suppliants*, Garvie 1969; on *Prometheus Bound*, Saïd 1985.

CHAPTER FIFTEEN

Sophoclean Tragedy

Ruth Scodel

Sophocles the Difficult

Sophocles has suffered two great misfortunes in his reception. First, he became canonical too easily and blandly. Only a few months after his death in 405 BCE, Aristophanes' *Frogs* dramatized a contest in Hades between the noble but primitive Aeschylus and the clever but decadent Euripides. The play excludes Sophocles completely; he is too "good-tempered" to want to leave the underworld (82) and has too much respect for Aeschylus to claim the honor of being the best tragedian (788–90). The play was very influential, defining Sophocles as a nice guy and a great tragedian, but not controversial. Furthermore, Sophocles had a long life and a distinguished public career. He served as a treasurer for the Athenian alliance in 443/42, and was elected general, Athens' highest office. An anecdote told by the contemporary poet Ion of Chios has him joking that his skill in amatory affairs disproved Pericles' criticism of his strategic inability. The biography also describes him as very pious; he gave hospitality to the god Asclepius when the cult was introduced in Athens. So Sophocles quickly became a symbol of Athens and its most perfect cultural product in its greatest period. The poet's genial character was transferred into the texts he had left. When Aristotle in the *Poetics* made *Oedipus the King* his favorite source of examples, Sophocles was doomed to be a classic, too perfect to be really interesting. Ever since, Sophocles has stood for moderation, neither too archaic nor too innovative. Inevitably, the voice of the middle is worthy, but not so exciting.

The surviving selection of his works is also unfortunate, because the three plays about Thebes give a false impression of his range. The scholar Aristophanes of Byzantium (around 200 BCE) referred to 130 plays, of which seventeen were spurious (another source says there were 123), and the biographies list twenty or twenty-four victories. We can see from the fragments that his favorite subject matter was the Trojan War, not Thebes, though the surviving titles and quotations cover a broad range. Papyri have yielded extensive fragments from *Trackers*, a satyr-play about the birth of Hermes, and some of a Trojan play, *Eurypylus* (on *Trackers* see Seidensticker, chapter 3 in this volume). He first produced in 468, but none of his surviving plays is likely to be early. *Ajax* and *Antigone* probably belong to the 440s. *Women of Trachis* shows the influence of Aeschylus' *Oresteia* (458) and Euripides (first production 455), while it may have influenced Bacchylides, who probably died at the end of the 450s. *Philoctetes* was produced in 409, and *Oedipus at Colonus* was posthumously produced; *Electra* is not too long before *Philoctetes*. *Oedipus the King* is usually put in the 420s, but this is a guess (Reinhardt 1979, 1–8).

Almost all translations of Sophocles present the "Theban plays" together, as if they were a trilogy, although they were probably composed over a space of almost forty years. It is not easy for the nonspecialist to realize that the man who composed *Antigone* could hardly know that he would write *Oedipus the King*, and that when he wrote *Oedipus the King* he is very unlikely to have already planned *Oedipus at Colonus*. Indeed, we should not immediately assume that the first audience of *Oedipus at Colonus* would have understood allusions to earlier and later Theban legend as references to Sophocles' earlier tragedies. There were many other versions, including, for example, Euripides' *Antigone* (in which Antigone and Haemon had a son).

Still, the surviving plays are wonderfully diverse. The single character Odysseus is evaluated quite differently in different plays. In *Ajax*, Odysseus, because he is able to adapt to changing situations, refuses to continue his enmity with Ajax after Ajax's death. His flexibility is admirable. In *Philoctetes*, Odysseus is so willing to adapt to any situation that he has no principles at all except utility (Nussbaum 1976), and the character is loathsome. Or consider Sophocles' treatment of women and sexuality. *Antigone* and *Electra* are about virgins who assume heroic roles and are criticized for exceeding female boundaries. Haemon in *Antigone* is in love, but Antigone is not. *Women of Trachis* is a tragedy of *erôs*, about a woman who is in love with her husband. *Philoctetes* has no women at all. Among Sophocles' lost plays we know of two about Tyro, who bore twin sons to Poseidon. She exposed her children, and was persecuted by her stepmother, but ultimately reunited with her children (see Cropp, chapter 17 in this volume). In *Hermione* the heroine, married to Orestes during the Trojan War, was taken away from him and given to Neoptolemus in accordance with a promise her father Menelaus had made. Neoptolemus was killed at Delphi, and Hermione went back to Orestes. In *Eriphyle* Sophocles dramatized the story of the woman who was bribed to convince her husband, the prophet Amphiareus, to take part in the expedition of the Seven, although he knew he would die.

There is no one kind of Sophoclean drama. *Oedipus the King*, *Electra*, and *Philoctetes* have tight plots. In *Electra*, there are two precipitating events: Orestes decides to seek his revenge by stealth, without communicating with his sister, and Clytemnestra has an ominous dream. Everything else is the seemingly inevitable response and counter-response of the characters. *Oedipus the King* begins with what Alfred Hitchcock called a MacGuffin: the plague at Thebes initiates the action, but the oracle transforms the problem into the search for Laius' killer, and the plague is ignored once its job is done. Through the arrival of the messenger from Corinth (the one flaw in the tight construction), this search becomes joined with the search for Oedipus' origins. Because the same slave who is summoned as a witness of Laius' death also saved the infant Oedipus, when he arrives Oedipus interrogates him only about his birth. Once he proves that Oedipus is Laius' son, the murder is regarded as solved, and the play avoids any anticlimactic fixing of details. In *Philoctetes*, the prophecy of Helenus requiring that Philoctetes come to Troy "willingly," along with Odysseus' awareness that he will not be willing to come, causes everything. Yet the action almost concludes the "wrong" way, so that Heracles must appear as the god from the machine. Other dramas divide into two parts. In *Ajax* and *Women of Trachis*, the most important character dies halfway through. The second part of *Ajax* is a protracted dispute about his burial, dominated by the body of the dead hero, while *Women of Trachis* shifts its attention to Heracles. The last part of *Antigone* focuses on Creon. *Oedipus at Colonus* keeps its attention on the title character throughout, but the action is episodic, as different threats to the divinely sanctioned outcome arise and are removed.

We must be careful of demanding too quickly that Sophocles be what we want him to be. Much Sophoclean criticism of the second half of the twentieth century engaged in a debate between "hero-worshippers" and "pietists" (these widely used terms come from Winnington-Ingram 1980, 13): those who admire the stubborn, self-directed protagonists and those who claim that we should perhaps pity, but clearly recognize the folly of, characters who ignore their proper limits and defy the gods. This debate is not worth continuing. The responses of critics are heavily influenced by their own attitudes to authority, convention, and religion. Each side has to ignore something. Hero-worshippers tend to dismiss choral moralizing as ethically trivial, mere conventionality. Pietists tend to ignore the plays' emotional weight and moral complexity, finding trite judgments where the spectator open to the drama is carried away by sympathy or deeply troubled. The extreme differences of opinion show just how tricky this author is.

Still, the argument makes salient some central issues. The tragedies explore situations in which women's loyalties to their families conflict with their appropriate social roles; in which the boundaries between the will of the gods and human attempts to achieve their ends are unclear; in which the central characters are in various ways isolated or displaced. Ajax has attacked the leaders of the Greek army, but has a chorus of loyal Salaminians, a devoted concubine, and a loyal brother; Philoctetes has been abandoned by those who should have been his friends; *Oedipus the King* plays almost as much with the ambiguities of the protagonist's relationship to Thebes – savior and destroyer, native and immigrant – as with those of incest; Deianira is far from her native city and family and her husband is absent, while the chorus members are sympathetic but too young to be wise; Electra is isolated within her family but has a friendly chorus.

We would be foolish to ignore the biographical information. An interpretation that denied Sophocles' Athenian patriotism or his support of civic religion would be absurd. *Oedipus at Colonus* not only idealizes Athens, but refers to specifics of cult with obvious affection. That does not mean that we know his political or religious opinions: the plays emphasize leadership more than democracy (Szlezák 1994), mysterious more than helpful gods. Of the great tragedians, Sophocles holds most strictly to purely dramatic laws. Once he has created a particular situation, with all its theological or political implications, he has his characters act in accordance with the demands of the situation and with the traits that he has assigned them. Unlike his rival Euripides, he does not frame passages of special contemporary relevance or draw audience attention to his own manipulations. On the one occasion his characters have a formal debate, in *Electra*, it concerns mostly the sacrifice of Iphigenia and the killing of Agamemnon, and it concentrates on specifics rather than generalities. Certainly

Sophocles was interested in intellectual developments. For example, in the second half of the fifth century teachers of rhetoric developed the argument from probability; Creon in *Oedipus the King* argues this way (584–602), claiming that he would not have plotted against Oedipus because his position as the king's brother-in-law is preferable to being king.[1]

Style

Despite the clumsiness of trying to describe style in a foreign language, it is worth starting there, because Sophocles' Greek, ferociously energetic and sometimes eccentric, warns us not to make him bland. The ancient critic Longinus describes Sophocles as "sometimes burning everything in his impulsive drive, but often losing all fire absurdly and failing completely" (33). Plutarch tells us that Sophocles divided his own style into three periods: first he imitated the weighty grandeur of Aeschylus, then he used a style that was harsh and contrived, but at last developed a style that was "most revealing of character and best" (*Progress in Virtue* 7.79). Probably all his surviving plays belong to the last period, but there is still plenty of weight and harshness. Jebb translates the first line of *Antigone* "Ismene, my sister, my own dear sister," Lloyd-Jones, "My own sister Ismene, linked to myself." The verse begins *ô*, in Greek a marker of direct address in ordinary speech, then *koinon*, "shared," a common Greek word, but poetic when it refers to the shared blood of relatives. The second is *autadelphon*, a distinctly poetic compound meaning "true brother/sister" or "full brother/sister." Then the genitive of Ismene's name, and *kara*, "head." Everyday speech used "dear head" as an affectionate mode of address, but *kara* is not the regular word but a special, poetic form. Heads are not what relatives are normally said to share. Using a full line of verse for a direct address is in itself a poetic, formal mode. The phrase conveys Antigone's love for Ismene, but also how for Antigone her feelings for her sister are not separable from their shared origin. *Autadelphon* may remind the audience that the sisters are the children of incest, even more closely related than sisters should be. The Greek hearing the line in performance would immediately have understood it as affectionate address emphasizing family ties; but there would be no time to unpack its strangeness.

Sophocles' style, even in songs, is only occasionally pretty. His lyrics have an astonishing power to convey both thought and emotional nuance, and to work for both their singers and the playwright who sings through them. In *Ajax*, the Salaminian sailors sing "Famous Salamis, you, surely, dwell sea-beaten, happy, to everyone conspicuous forever" (596–99). The singers idealize their home and its glory in contrast to the now tarnished fame of Ajax and their own misery in Troy, where they expect to come to "Hades who-makes-invisible" (with a wordplay – *aïdêlon Haidan* – the name "Hades" means "invisible"). The poet invites the audience to remember the glory of their victory at Salamis. Especially the particle *pou*, which I have translated "surely," conveys the depth of the chorus's homesickness. It literally means "somewhere," but is often used to express vagueness or lack of certainty. Here it conveys the chorus's difficulty in even imagining adequately the very place they belong.

In spoken verse, he drives one verse into the next without a break more fiercely than any other Greek poet (known as Sophoclean enjambment). He revels in antithesis and in contrasts both subtle and overt, but his parallelism is often untidy. Sometimes he composes lines in which parallelism itself becomes harsh. When Antigone says to Ismene, *su men gar heilou zên, ego de katthanein* ("you chose to live, I to die," 555), the infinitives almost rhyme, and the echo accentuates the break in the middle of the line, where Greek iambic trimeters are not supposed to break. His speeches sometimes have a simple, rolling grandeur, in which related ideas come one after the other with a careful balance between plain language and metaphor, while his dialogue is often staccato.

Sophocles' difficulty goes beyond such basics of style. His language often carries multiple levels of irony, and signifies differently for speakers, internal audiences, and the external audience. The Ode on Man in *Antigone* (332–75) announces "Many things are awesome, but nothing more awesome than a human being [*anthrôpos*, unmarked for gender]." Following contemporary speculation, the song enumerates the achievements of "this thing," humanity: seafaring, agriculture, subduing animals, civic life. In the middle, it uses *anêr*, "man." In its last stanza, it expresses the fear that human contrivance leads to evil if a man ignores "the laws of the land and justice sworn in the name of the gods"; "no city has he who, for his rashness, lives with wrong." (Is he cityless because he is driven out, or because he destroys the city?) The elders have in mind the clever but lawless man who has buried Polynices. The audience may think of Creon (Crane 1989). The song subtly develops the gender issues that are overt elsewhere in the play.

In the prologue of *Ajax*, Athena displays Ajax to Odysseus. When Ajax went out at night to kill his enemies, the sons of Atreus and Odysseus, she drove him mad and led him to attack cattle instead; the mad Ajax thinks Athena is his friend. When Ajax has gone back into his tent, she uses him as an instance of divine power. Inviting Odysseus to compare the man he has just seen to the man he knew, she asks, "Would anyone have been found who had more forethought, or was better at doing what was appropriate [*ta kairia*]?" Odysseus seems to agree with the assessment. This fits the situation in one way. In driving Ajax mad, the goddess has not taken away his physical strength, but his ability to use it appropriately. Yet it is a curious description of Ajax, whether the traditional character or the Ajax this play will reveal. The great heroic qualities of Homer's Ajax are his courage and loyalty. While there is no reason to think that he is less intelligent than others, he is not one of the orators of the Greek army: his speeches are brief, and mostly rally or rebuke other warriors. He is not a strategist. The association of *ta kairia* (the right things to do in a particular situation) with Ajax is surprising, because he stands for values that do not change. The hero noted for "foresight" and being able to do what changing circumstances require is Odysseus himself, Ajax's enemy and opposite. The scene concludes with Athena's warning, "the gods love the *sôphrones* and hate the *kakoi*" (133). To be *sôphrôn* is, literally, to be sane, to be aware of one's limits and social obligations, and to respect the claims of others. It is easy to see that Odysseus is *sôphrôn* and Ajax is not. To be *kakos* most often means to be "bad" in ways defined by aristocratic values, to be cowardly or base. Most of Sophocles' contemporaries might well have agreed if Socrates had asked them whether all those who are not *sôphrôn* are *kakos*. Yet applying *kakos* to Ajax does not seem right, because the tradition has always treated him as a great hero. He was the recipient of cult in Athens as one of the heroes after whom the political divisions of the citizens were named. His appearance so far has been repellent. Yet how could someone who excelled at forethought and doing what was fitting be among the *kakoi* the gods hate? Normally one would associate *sôphrosunê* with foresightedness, since those who anticipate the consequences of their actions avoid excess. Everything Odysseus and Athena say here corresponds to traditional Greek morality, and it is delivered as if it were to be the moral of the play. So pietists interpret the play as a lesson in *sôphrosunê*, and hero-worshippers insist that these clichés are too hackneyed to mean much. But the real problem seems to be that the categories do not entirely fit Ajax. They fit other characters. Odysseus behaves well at the end of the play, arguing that Ajax, though his enemy, should be buried, since he, like Ajax, will someday need others to bury him. It is the most attractive side of the morality Athena has preached. Equally, Menelaus has shown his own folly, when he insists that it is his turn to be arrogant as Ajax was arrogant once (1087–88). In invoking Ajax's lack of *sôphrosunê*, he reveals his own. These men are *sôphrôn* or *kakos*. Ajax is neither.

Myth, Story, and Time

Tragedies were based on traditional stories that were embedded in a broader mythical history, and many tales existed in many variants. In the epic, Haemon was killed by the Sphinx before Antigone was born; in the poet Mimnermus (and on some vase-paintings) Ismene was the lover of one of the attackers of Thebes, and was killed by Tydeus on the order of Athena; in a dithyramb by Sophocles' contemporary Ion, Antigone and Ismene were burned to death in the temple of Hera by Eteocles' son. Aeschylus had already dramatized a story that the Thebans forbade the Seven against Thebes to be buried, but were convinced by Athens. Sophocles may have invented the story of Antigone's burial of her brother; but even if he did not, his original audience would have found little to take for granted in his version.

The poet could invent within the main outlines of the inherited stories, and was free to select focal characters and distribute sympathy exactly as he liked. It is likely that Oedipus the dedicated investigator into the murder of Laius was Sophocles' idea. Earlier versions of the story of Philoctetes had Odysseus approach the hero directly (in Euripides he was disguised by Athena). Sophocles had him bring Neoptolemus as an intermediary, and thereby introduced a new element in the plot, the conflict within the son of Achilles, and a new theme, that of moral education. Sophocles may have taken an Athenian story that connected Oedipus with the Dread Goddesses of the Areopagus and transferred it to the grove at Colonus. *Electra* follows the basic outline of a familiar story, but Sophocles himself probably thought of having Electra herself be deceived by Orestes' false story of his own death.

Selecting an episode from an ongoing but varying story presents special narrative difficulties and opportunities. Aeschylus composed trilogies, where the later plays could build on what the audience had already seen. In *Agamemnon*, which is the first play in its trilogy, the playwright provides extended and authoritative accounts of earlier events – though he also complicates audience response by introducing some parts of the backstory late in the play. Euripides typically has a prologue that locates the present action precisely, and his conclusions often specify exactly what will happen next. In contrast, it is striking how indefinite Sophocles can be about events outside the drama. In *Ajax*, for example, it is clear that the Judgment of the Arms, a story with many variants, was decided by some kind of panel of judges (1136); Teucer claims Menelaus somehow manipulated the vote (1135, 1137). We do not find out what the procedure was, or whether Teucer is right. In *Electra*, Clytemnestra and Electra tell very different stories about the sacrifice of Iphigenia (516–609). Of the murder of Agamemnon there is no account at all. In *Antigone*, Ismene specifies that Jocasta hanged herself, and that Oedipus, having blinded himself, perished "hated and ill-famed because of crimes made manifest" (50–51). The *Iliad* refers to Oedipus' funeral games (that is, an honorable burial at Thebes), while *Oedipus at Colonus* has him die in exile; *Antigone*'s version seems to be different from any other that we know, but the allusion is too brief to be expanded into a real story. Creon's opening speech gives the impression that he has never held political power before, but in the Tiresias-scene he implies that he has had occasion to take Tiresias' wise advice in matters of state before. *Oedipus the King* provides no information about the reasons or occasion for the oracle that told Laius he would be killed by his own son. It just "came" (711). In *Women of Trachis*, the tangle of lies and truth in Lichas' two versions of the events leading to the sack of Oechalia cannot entirely be resolved. In *Philoctetes*, we never learn the true story of Achilles' arms. At 442–45, Philoctetes asks Neoptolemus whether Thersites is still alive; Neoptolemus answers that he has heard that Thersites lived. In epic, Achilles killed Thersites and was purified by Odysseus. Is Neoptolemus lying, in order to make Philoctetes as desperate as possible, or should we assume, since his other responses have followed traditional "truth," that Sophocles has changed this story, removing an instance of cooperation between Achilles and Odysseus?

Sophocles can be even more evasive about what will happen after the drama ends. In *Oedipus the King*, Creon insists on consulting the Delphic oracle again before deciding what to do with Oedipus. Since Tiresias has predicted that he will be a blind beggar (454–56), so that the audience thinks it knows where the play is going, this is curiously frustrating. In *Women of Trachis*, Heracles demands that his son Hyllus marry Iole, his own concubine, and insists on being placed, alive, on a pyre on Mount Oeta, though he agrees that Hyllus need not light the fire (traditionally, Philoctetes did). Hyllus and Iole were the ancestors of the kings of Sparta, and Heracles, at least in later mythology, ascended to an eternally blessed life on Olympus from the pyre. Yet we do not exactly have a happy ending. When Heracles insists that his son perform what seem to be utterly impious actions, the strangeness invites the audience to suspect that a divine plan is at work, and so to remember the rest of the story. Yet these hints do not go far enough to specify what will happen (cf. Stinton 1986). After all, in the *Iliad*, Heracles is said to have died like other men (18.117–18). To what extent would having glorious progeny mitigate the horror of a sexual relationship with a woman who had been a father's concubine and the cause of a mother's death?

While he can be vague about specifics from outside the play, Sophocles often gives the impression that the action the audience actually sees is a recapitulation of earlier events. In *Ajax*, we do not find out exactly what happened in the Judgment of the Arms, but when Agamemnon and Menelaus try to prevent Teucer from burying Ajax, they again seek to deprive the hero of honor he deserves. It does not matter exactly what happened before, since we see just what all these characters are like here and now. Deianira opens *Women of Trachis* by claiming that, despite the old advice to judge no life until it is over, she is already certain that hers had been bad. She then narrates how, in her life, a threatening situation has appeared to have a happy ending (Achelous wanted to marry her, but Heracles defeated him). Her life with Heracles, however, has been a life of endless loneliness and worry. The pattern of the drama is much the same. Apparent good news (Heracles is safe and victorious) becomes bad news (Heracles has made war for a woman, whom he has sent home). A possible solution to this crisis (the love-potion) turns out to be calamitous (it poisons Heracles).

Sophocles can also imply that the action on stage is a foreshadowing of what will happen. This is clearest in *Oedipus at Colonus*. Oedipus predicts that someday, when Thebes and Athens are at war, the Thebans will be defeated near his burial-place, through his power. (Sophocles must refer here to a skirmish during the Peloponnesian War, but the event is not certain.) Theseus is perplexed, since he is on good terms with Thebes, and Oedipus delivers a moving speech about time and change (607–15). Yet within the play itself, Creon has his Theban troops kidnap Antigone and Ismene, and Theseus leads the Athenian cavalry to recover them. The transformation takes place within the play, as an image of what will someday happen. Similarly, in *Ajax*, during the argument with Agamemnon, Tecmessa and Eurysaces arrange themselves as if they were suppliants of the dead hero. The tableau prefigures the contemporary cult of Ajax as one of the protective heroes of Athens (Henrichs 1993b). Each Sophoclean drama displays an exemplary section of a life that displays larger patterns, so that past and future show themselves in the present of the action.

Characterization

If at some levels Sophocles is difficult, at others he is eminently approachable. The frequent ambiguity and complexity of language in details make it difficult to judge his great characters precisely, but there is no ambiguity in their outlines. Sophocles is famous for his use of contrasts in characterization. Antigone is set against Ismene, Electra against Chrysothemis. Contrast goes far beyond these obvious pairings. The guard's concern for his own safety in Antigone helps define not only Antigone but Ismene, whose motives for not helping her sister go beyond simple cowardice. The chorus may often sympathize with a character while trying to persuade her to act very differently. Antigone, lamenting how she will be immured in rock, neither living nor dead, compares herself to Niobe, who wept until she became stone. The chorus tries to make the comparison a consolation, since Niobe was descended from gods. Antigone thinks they are laughing at her (839–40). Clearly, they are genuinely trying to console her, but the inability of either side to communicate with the other, even in lament, is telling.

Sophocles' characters do not have complex personalities in a modern, novelistic sense. There is no reason to attribute unconscious motives to them; Oedipus has no Oedipal desires. They are not, however, flat. They have specific, intense, vivid traits, and these are usually extremely consistent. Oedipus in *Oedipus the King* is the conscientious ruler of a city gripped by plague, confident in his ability to solve problems through energy and intelligence. Oedipus shows an obvious concern for his people, and the early scenes win him sympathy as he asks for advice (always a sign of wisdom), and then turns out to have already done what he is advised. As the play continues, this energy turns out to have a darker side. Oedipus is impatient, hot-tempered, prone to jump to conclusions. When he speaks about his past, it is evident that the same qualities of character governed his actions: he killed Laius and his followers with the same anger he displays toward Creon and Tiresias. After the revelation, he vigorously defends his self-blinding to the chorus and unsuccessfully tries to convince Creon that he should be expelled from Theban territory; he still thinks he knows best what to do.

That the characters do not have complex personalities does not mean that they lack inner conflict. Deianira is determined not to be angry with her husband for taking Iole as a concubine. It is impossible not to hear resentment when she speaks of how "Heracles, called the faithful and noble, has sent such a payment for my long time of keeping his house" (540–42). At the same time, she insists that she is not angry. The conflict is easy to understand: she wants to be a perfect wife and a wise mortal, who understands human limits; she is also in anguish about being displaced. Sophoclean characters regularly face choices that seem to them impossible. Neoptolemus cries out in frustration at his inability to solve his dilemma at *Philoctetes* 969–70, and Philoctetes is even more distressed at 1348–57. Ajax runs through and rejects all alternatives except suicide at 457–80 (Fowler 1987 suggests that Sophocles first developed the tragic "desperation speech.") The nearest Sophocles comes to a formula is the phrase *oimoi, ti drasô*, "Alas, what should I do?"

Sophocles' characters, then, are relatively uncomplicated characters who must act in complex situations. The opening scene of *Antigone*, for example, represents the single-minded determination of one sister and the helpless goodwill of the other, beginning the action with a dramatic tension that is sustained throughout. At the same time, it evokes an impressive array of moral categories and cultural stereotypes. Antigone sees her family as noble, while Ismene speaks of its history of incest and fratricide: how are we to place the Labdacids? Ismene insists that as women, she and her sister should not naturally fight with men, while Antigone's eagerness to die nobly evokes traditional male battlefield heroism: does Antigone's willingness to ignore female limits make her better than other women, or dangerously transgressive? The culture could see women who undertook male roles either way. Ismene criticizes Antigone for trying to do the impossible, a familiar theme of Greek morality. Antigone succeeds in burying Polynices, so perhaps her success shows that Ismene's rebuke is wrong; but she is caught by Creon and cannot hope to protect the corpse from scavenger animals, so maybe Ismene is right. There is no simple rule to define what is ritually or socially adequate as a burial. Later, the chorus will suggest that Antigone's fierceness is inherited from her father (471–72), but is this true, and what does it mean if it is? The elders will also raise the possibility that divine hatred for the family has affected Antigone. She herself seems to accept the suggestion that she "repay[s] an ancestral ordeal" (856). Yet when the chorus in this context sings of her as deluded, in accordance with a traditional scheme of archaic Greek morality – because the gods hate her family, they help lead its members to self-destructive acts (615–25) – the audience may wonder whether it is not Creon who is truly deluded. Both the underlying causes of her being as she is, and the correct judgment of her, are in doubt. Ambiguity often gives a sense of depth to Sophoclean characters: they seem more real because we do not fully understand them (Easterling 1977).

Similarly, Electra's basic qualities of loyalty to her father, intense hatred for his killers, and complete dedication to an aristocratic ethos are not at all complicated in themselves. They are put in a complex context, however. Electra admits that her behavior, governed by one set of norms that she accepts, conflicts with the norms of proper female behavior, which she also accepts. (Unlike Antigone, she expresses embarrassment at 616–21.) Furthermore, Electra's violations of female norms may make her resemble her mother, whom she detests. Chrysothemis raises the additional question of whether Electra's resistance to those in power will have any useful practical effect. If Electra's struggle does not harm her enemies, but only brings her more suffering, the audience's very sympathy for Electra may distance them from her. Electra, however, sees value in her making her enemies uneasy (355–56), even if she can do no more. In *Oedipus at Colonus*, there can be no question that Oedipus takes the audience's sympathy from the start, and keeps it. Subordinate characters – Antigone, Ismene, Theseus, the chorus – direct the audience to pity him and respect him. Oedipus is pathetic but dignified. Furthermore, the play makes Oedipus a permanent part of a sacred landscape whose details the play evokes with exceptional feeling. Yet this pathetic Oedipus, despite the claims his physical weakness makes on the audience, is immensely powerful in his power to bless and curse, a power he uses with terrifying ferocity. The same subordinate characters whose feelings for him guide those of the audience also distance the spectator from him by their greater humanity. When Oedipus curses his son, Polynices may deserve no less, but the audience sees Antigone's suffering in her brother's doom. The character is not complicated, but the response of an audience to him may be.

An extremely consistent character may offer a very rich set of moods. Ajax initially appears in despair. When Tecmessa tries to convince him to live, he is brusque and harsh. Yet in his famous Deception Speech (646–92), as he describes the cycles of nature as a model for the importance of "yielding" in human life, he sounds both wise and eloquent. Although there are distinct notes of bitterness in the speech, it is calm and resolved. Tecmessa and the chorus are reassured as much by the tone of the speech as its content, since the resignation it expresses seems to indicate that Ajax, now so rational, will not kill himself. (Realistically, many suicides appear calm and not unhappy once they have decided to die.) In his final soliloquy before he kills himself, he begins with a quiet detachment: he seeks to demonstrate how perfect a situation for his death this is. He goes in quick succession from cursing his enemies to speaking a moving and dignified farewell to the natural world.

Like the other tragedians, Sophocles tends to explore different aspects of a character and a situation in separate speeches and songs. In the first part of *Antigone*, Antigone shows no fear of death, and even insists that the miseries of her life make death desirable (461–64), but before her final exit she delivers a protracted lament that emphasizes her failure to marry or have children (806–82). It is entirely reasonable that a young woman in her position should feel that death is desirable; it is also reasonable that any young woman would lament a death that deprived her of the usual goals of a maiden's life. The play has Antigone show no fear of death when she argues with Ismene, since she is trying to persuade her sister to risk her life, or when she confronts Creon, since by doing so she denies him any power to harm her. If the audience is to feel the pathos of her death, however, somebody has to express it. Sophocles mitigates the change in Antigone in three ways. First, Haemon is introduced only after the passages in which she expresses eagerness to die, so that the horror of her family history can have its full effect in motivating her wish to die before her best possible reason to want to live appears. Second, Creon says that everyone would lament interminably before dying, if it were possible (883–84), and although Creon is not sympathetic, the audience may recognize his statement as true. Third, Antigone is not condemned to die by stoning, as Creon's original decree announced. Instead, she is immured in a rock tomb. The change is thematically rich in making Antigone, like Polynices, anomalous (he is dead but not buried, while she is buried without being dead). It marks difficulties in Creon's position (he is concerned about pollution, despite his denials, and he perhaps worries that a public and participatory execution would not go well). But it also helps explain Antigone's reluctance to die both practically and thematically, for it deprives her of the sense of clearly belonging to the dead. That her transition from life to death is distorted resonates with her loss of the transition from maiden to wife: she laments being trapped in in-betweenness. Her lament, however, is also a continuing argument with the chorus. If the elders are to understand her position (as they never do), they must be brought to sympathize with her suffering, and she tries the power of song.

Sophoclean characters, then, do not exactly develop, but they show different aspects of themselves as their situations change, and they can surprise an audience. Oedipus at the opening of *Oedipus at Colonus* describes himself as having learned from suffering, time, and his nobility to be satisfied with the "less than little" that he receives as a beggar (58), but he is furious when provoked. There is no real contradiction in being gracious in response to small kindnesses and furious in reaction to injuries, but the angry Oedipus is not predictable from the long-suffering Oedipus, either. He is also only in some ways predictable from the myth. The Oedipus of *Oedipus the King* also had a hot temper, for the killing of Laius implies it; it is essential to the story. However, when the Oedipus of *Oedipus at Colonus* responds to the pleas of Antigone and Theseus to see his son Polynices (1205), he is quite unlike the earlier Oedipus who yielded to Jocasta and the chorus ("For I pity your pathetic speech, not his – he will be hated wherever he is," *Oedipus the King* 671–72). Oedipus of *Oedipus at Colonus* is fearful (113–16, 651–56, and 1206–7), as the earlier Oedipus never is. The two dramas move the protagonist in opposite directions: the first Oedipus goes from utter self-confidence to pathetic gratitude for Creon's common humanity, though he still trusts his own understanding (1517–19); the anxious later Oedipus makes his last exit confidently leading Theseus and his entourage.

Characters have a particular nature, but external pressures may keep them from following it. The timid Deianira, with the encouragement of the chorus, decides in her desperation to see whether a love-potion will win Heracles back to her. Neoptolemus goes against his nature in agreeing to deceive Philoctetes (though he does it very well). When *Ajax* begins, Ajax has already violated his nature, which rejects trickery of all kinds, in attacking his enemies at night; he does so again in tricking them in order to find an opportunity to kill himself. The bitter resignation of the Deception Speech, in which he acknowledges that all things change, seems to express his own frustration that he himself is implicated in change.

We have access only to the voices and actions of the characters, and Sophocles is a master of simultaneous clarity and ambiguity. When Antigone later refuses Ismene's attempt to say that she joined in the burial, and says to Ismene, "You chose to live, I to die" (555), we simply do not know whether she is trying to save her sister, and cares about her, or whether she has rejected Ismene's affection. Haemon in *Antigone* argues that he defends Antigone out of concern for his father, not because he is in love with her; but Creon insists that sexual desire is Haemon's only motivation. The chorus appears to agree with Creon. The messenger speech describes how Haemon, finding Antigone dead, first attempted to kill his father, then stabbed himself. Evidently, he is passionately in love with Antigone. Yet that does not mean that he is hypocritical when he approaches his father. Sophocles is fascinated by the dynamic of conflict and of rhetoric itself.

In *Ajax*, Teucer and Menelaus loathe each other from the start. Menelaus is rude from his first word. Still, their debate becomes more vulgar as it continues, reaching the generic limits of tragic decorum. They conclude their argument by hurling pseudo-fables at each other as if each thought the other beneath real argument. In their growing anger, they show less and less control. In other vehement exchanges, characters often put themselves into extreme positions, and in long speeches, like Achilles in the *Iliad*, they sometimes seem to be carried away by the passion of their own language. This can complicate our judgment of them, since it is impossible to be certain when characters express convictions that they fully endorse and when they are, like real people, drifting into hyperbole or worse. Hyllus in *Women of Trachis* curses his mother in his anger, only to lament when he realizes the truth (808–20, 932–35). When Antigone insists that she, and Polynices, will hate Ismene for her refusal to help in the burial, does this mean that her later claim to be of a nature to "join in love rather than hatred" (523) is false? Perhaps not. When Creon invites scavenger birds to carry bits of Polynices' corpse to the throne of Zeus (1040–41), he would surely not speak this way if he were not enraged. Yet the belief that mortals cannot pollute the gods is serious.

Argument from probability was only one aspect of the fifth century's fascination with clever argument. Critics usually associate paradoxical argument with Euripides, but it is there in Sophocles, too. In Sophocles, however, it flows so smoothly from and into intense feeling that it does not stand out as argument. In *Oedipus the King*, after Oedipus sings a lament with the chorus, the chorus-leader comments, in spoken verse, that he cannot agree that Oedipus has planned well, since suicide would be preferable to blindness. Oedipus, in response, catalogues those he would prefer not to see (his parents, his children, Thebes), then says that he would prefer not to be able to hear, either, and addresses Cithaeron, asking why he was not allowed to die. Then he begs to be killed or driven out (1367–1415). The paradoxical cleverness of the argument is almost invisible. Ajax's great speech before his death begins by noting that someone with leisure to calculate would see that the sword is ideal for killing: a gift of his enemy Hector, fixed in hostile soil, carefully positioned (815–23). In *Oedipus at Colonus*, Oedipus argues that not only was he justified in killing his father unknowingly, since he was attacked first, but that he would have been justified had he known that his victim was his father (270–72) – a stunningly bold argument. Most surprisingly, Antigone gives a final argument for the wisdom of her actions just before her death, claiming that she would not have defied the citizens for a husband or child, but did so for her brother because her brother was irreplaceable (904–15). The argument is borrowed from Herodotus (3.119), where it makes better sense, since the woman who speaks it is explaining which member of her family she will have saved from death. It seems ill-suited to the earlier breadth of Antigone's claims about the unwritten laws. Antigone, however, has not yet succeeded in persuading the chorus using more general arguments, so she tries to make them understand why she had to act as she did in this particular case.

Dramatic Technique

Sophocles contrasts not only characters but points of view, and these tend to place the characters in a richer light. The plays often begin with sharp contrasts of perspective, both literal and figurative. Sophoclean tragedies are nearly always concerned with what realities the characters can and cannot see and know, and they constantly play seen against hidden, speech against silence, true speech against falsehood, specific gods against unspecified divine forces (Budelmann 2000, 139–87). The prologues both set different characters in sharp relief and present the instabilities that will drive the action. In *Ajax*, the opening action is a conflict between Athena and Odysseus about her desire to display the mad Ajax to the reluctant Odysseus. As if this were the end of a tragedy rather than the beginning, a god directs a horrifying spectacle. The audience is placed almost, but not exactly, in the position of Odysseus (since we see him along with the others), and in seeing the characters see Ajax we are drawn into the play's play with point of view. When the chorus enters, we hear a new viewpoint; then Tecmessa describes the events of the prologue as they appeared to her, inside the house. Later, the messenger reports prophecies of Calchas that motivate Athena's anger against Ajax, and offer a new frame for the entire action: the prophecy demands that the story begin with Ajax's departure from Troy.

The beginning of *Philoctetes* is similar. Odysseus must persuade Neoptolemus to follow his strategy for dealing with Philoctetes. The opening scene introduces one of the main dramatic tensions in the play, Neoptolemus' struggle between his inherited nature and the needs of the situation as Odysseus has explained them. At the same time, it places the audience in the position of Neoptolemus as he hears about Philoctetes from Odysseus and explores Philoctetes' cave: Philoctetes is the mystery whose reality the play will reveal. In *Oedipus at Colonus* the initial contrast lies between the young Antigone and her old, blind father. Yet it quickly becomes clear that in this play, the location is as much a character as the people. In all these plays, one character sees what another literally does not. In *Electra* the very beginning of the play stresses that Orestes is now seeing what he had always longed to see, his home in Argos. The prologue then prepares the outline of the intrigue to come. At its conclusion, Orestes hears Electra's lament, but the Pedagogue convinces him not to stay to listen to it. We are thus prepared for the exciting action that will dominate the last part of the play, but the main dramatic tension is also opened, between Orestes' ability to act and Electra's frustrated waiting for him, his decision not to meet her and her ignorance of his presence.

Typically, Sophocles looks for dramatic effect rather than worrying too much about how the story would actually work if all the details needed to be included. Antigone knows of Creon's edict, and the play begins as she asks for help in disobeying it. After she exits, the chorus enters, greeting the just-risen sun and singing about how the enemy has fled. Then Creon appears to deliver his edict. We do not find out how Antigone knows about it in advance, for what matters is that even before Creon makes his decision public, the audience knows that opposition will come where Creon does not expect it. It is relatively easy to find inconsistencies and

minor difficulties in Sophocles' plots, but they are not salient in the speed and
emotion of performance. The trickiest plot is that of *Oedipus the King*, because the
poet has chosen to define Oedipus as extraordinarily intelligent while not allowing
him to see the truth for a long time. His tendency to concentrate on one fact at a time
is important in delaying the recognition; once Jocasta mentions the place "where
three wagon-roads meet" (716) he clearly pays no attention to what she says about
her lost child, in his worry that he killed Laius. Also critical is the survivor's lie that
Laius was attacked by several bandits rather than one man. The lie is both naturalistic
(who would be eager to admit that a single wanderer killed a king and his attendants?)
and thematically rich (since the claim at 845 that "one could not equal many" turns
out to be false in the person of Oedipus).

Lying, and more generally control of speech, is at the center of Sophoclean drama.
Women who exit to kill themselves are conspicuously silent (Jocasta at *Oedipus the
King* 1074–75, Deianira at *Women of Trachis* 813–14). Ajax deceives Tecmessa and
the chorus in order to go to the seashore by himself to die. To Deianira, Lichas denies
knowing anything about the captives he brings, but he has already told the true story
to a large crowd, and one of his hearers reveals the truth to Deianira, hoping for a
reward. In both *Philoctetes* and *Electra* the main plot is an intrigue that deceives the
main character. Only in *Antigone* and *Oedipus at Colonus* is deception not an engine
of the action. Even in *Oedipus at Colonus*, the chorus accuses Oedipus of tricking
them (229–33), and Oedipus accuses the elders of fearing a "name" instead of a
reality. In *Antigone*, Creon initially assumes that whoever buried Polynices did so for
political reasons, and the chorus too sees the deed as political. It is this misapprehension that makes Antigone's entrance with the guard at 376 such a powerful moment.

The oracles and prophecies that are so important in Sophoclean drama are closely
related to lies, even though they follow the dramatic rule that they always come true.
In *Oedipus the King*, for example, Oedipus' crimes and his discovery of them both
result from a combination of his own character, the lies of others (his adoptive
parents, the survivor of the attack on Laius), and the oracle's withholding of the
truth. The truth of the oracle is overtly thematized. Oedipus has been accused by
Tiresias and becomes convinced there is a conspiracy against him. Jocasta comforts
Oedipus by describing how she exposed her only child, so that the oracle that
predicted Laius would be killed by his son was certainly false. The chorus follows
her argument that it is best to ignore prophecies with a song about *hubris* (863–910).
The singers are deeply distressed about the evidence of political strife in Thebes. They
pray for purity for themselves in all matters governed by divine law, and curse the one
who does not fear Justice or revere the gods. In the last stanza, they warn the gods
that they will not visit the famous shrines again unless the oracles are proven true:
"The divine," they sing, "is disappearing." In yet another of Sophocles' surprising
entries, Jocasta comes with offerings for Apollo. Her lack of faith in oracles, then,
does not mean that she does not believe in the gods, but only that mortals lack access
to divine knowledge. The oracle is true, but it is not clear that Jocasta's recommendation is wrong.

The spectator's knowledge that oracles must be true, along with prior familiarity
with the basic stories, is only one aspect of the audience's superior knowledge.
Sophocles manipulates what the audience knows and the characters do not to create
complex effects. In *Ajax* a god actually appears, but even here, Athena does not

address the audience, as a Euripidean prologue-god does. Because Odysseus apparently does not see her, but only hears her voice, while Ajax, who is mad, sees her but not Odysseus, the scene places the spectator in an uneasy relationship to his own theatrical experience. The audience sees more than any character. We are aware that Athena is in complete control. However, we learn very little about her own motives or broader purposes, since she is so carefully manipulating the human characters. Later, we hear of a prophecy by Calchas that explains her motives for punishing Ajax (he had refused her help). Calchas says that her anger will not go beyond this one day, if only Ajax survives it, so he must be kept in his tent. This message seems straightforward, but it is mysterious. Ajax has already left his tent: did the goddess arrange for this knowledge to arrive too late? In any case, why would he be safe from her anger as long as he remained inside? The audience knows that he has gone to the seashore to kill himself, but earlier in the play it seemed likely that he would commit suicide inside.

Different spectators may have different responses in balancing their own privileged knowledge and their sympathy with the characters on stage. In *Electra* the speech describing Orestes' death at the Pythian Games is so long that some critics have thought the audience should forget that they know the hero is alive (680–763). Yet the story has the power, as stories do, to move even the hearer who knows it is a fiction. The spectator, though, also sees two very different auditors hearing the story: Clytemnestra is both relieved and distressed, while Electra is devastated. In the following scene, Orestes watches as Electra mourns over the urn she thinks contains his ashes. Even though the scene invites a metatheatrical reading, in which Orestes makes the audience aware of itself as audience, here as elsewhere the pathos of the action forbids too detached a response from the spectator in the theater.

Ethics

For all the moral complexity of the Sophoclean world, certain values recur with great clarity. In *Oedipus at Colonus*, Theseus is surely right to accept Oedipus, and the chorus wrong in their initial horror of his pollution. The play directs the audience to feel contempt for the Thebans' plan to keep Oedipus and his grave under their control while not admitting his pollution to their territory. Yet Oedipus himself restrains his impulse to kiss Theseus (1130–31), not wishing to touch one who is so uncontaminated. Although he insists on his innocence, Oedipus sends Ismene to perform a ritual of atonement for his trespass on the goddesses' sacred grove. He remarks that one person "of good will" could suffice to repay for vast numbers (498–99). At the same time, he inquires carefully about the exact requirements of the ritual. So there is a positive piety of respect for the divine and for local customs, but no endorsement of ritual anxieties.

In *Antigone* Creon (the rationalist) insists that the gods cannot care about Polynices, who wanted to destroy their shrines, and denies Tiresias' assertion that the pollution of the exposed corpse has interfered with communication between gods and mortals. Mortals, he insists, cannot pollute the gods. At the same time, he has had Antigone immured, to die of starvation, in order to avoid the pollution of a violent death. For Tiresias, this compounds the initial crime, since it is a second violation of the proper separation of living and dead. The attempt to avoid pollution can make pollution worse when it is not guided by a deeper sense of the world's order. Whether mortals can pollute the gods is not the point. Both *Oedipus at Colonus* and *Antigone* show a dislike of legalistic attitudes toward religion.

Ajax, too, is much concerned with the hero's burial, but in this play pollution is not a concern at all, though Odysseus refers to the right of burial as "the laws of the gods" (1343). The issue lies almost entirely within human ethics: maltreating corpses goes beyond a proper limit for enmity. Odysseus says that he urges that Ajax be buried because he himself will someday need burial. Agamemnon expresses frustration at the universality of self-interest, for he does not really understand Odysseus' point. Athena has used the example of Ajax to warn Odysseus not to be arrogant toward the gods, but Odysseus changes the emphasis of the lesson slightly, so that it is directed at recognizing how vulnerable human beings are. Similarly, Theseus explains that his sympathy for Oedipus is based on his own experience of wandering and exile.

Sophocles is consistently concerned with this aspect of the traditional virtue of *sôphrosunê*. Those who recognize that all human beings are vulnerable to calamity will show compassion to the suffering of others. Theseus is willing to fight on Oedipus' behalf, and Odysseus in *Ajax* spends his own political capital on behalf of Ajax, even though he hated him in life. Deianira pities Iole and the other captives, even though they represent her husband's triumph. Neoptolemus, though tormented by his pity for Philoctetes, still takes a long time to act on his feeling, probably because he is too young to recognize Philoctetes' fate as one that could happen to him.

The plays are equally concerned with the effects of profound suffering. There is no single reaction: Oedipus is not Ajax. Sophocles is interested especially in pro-longed anguish. Learning that Iole is Heracles' concubine has the effect it has on Deianira because Deianira has waited so long, because Heracles has betrayed her so often, and because she depends on him so completely. Oedipus in *Oedipus at Colonus* has learned patience in material things through his wanderings, but the ferocity of his anger surely is in part the result of his years of deprivation. Philoctetes and Electra are both difficult and harsh. Neoptolemus complains that Philoctetes has "become savage," yet the audience has to be impressed by his endurance – how could anyone expect him to give up years of resentment in a moment? Electra's attempt to persuade her sister that they try to kill Aegisthus themselves represents a particular heroism of despair, when the news of Orestes' death follows her endless waiting. These characters test the limits of the audience's ability to imagine such experience, to try to understand it, and to feel appropriately.

So when the chorus of *Oedipus the King* sings about the vulnerability of all mortals in response to the disaster that has befallen Oedipus, the conventionality of their reaction should not make us dismiss it. Oedipus was the savior of Thebes, the most capable man in the world, yet he has met with calamity. The chorus does not sing about anything Oedipus did to deserve his fate, nor do they offer an explicit warning against human self-confidence. Even *Antigone*, where Creon's final lines acknowledge his error, is not a cheap lesson. Even if the moral seems familiar, it is not easy.

At the end of *Philoctetes*, Heracles appears to proclaim the will of Zeus. Heracles says that he has won "an immortal glory for my excellence [*athanaton aretên*], as you can see," and he promises Philoctetes similar fame (1419–22). The speech thus elides the apotheosis of Heracles and the eternal fame of Philoctetes, even though these are ordinarily quite distinct. At the end of the speech, when he warns the heroes to revere the gods' shrines when taking Troy, he says that "Zeus regards all other things as second: piety does not die with mortals; it does not perish, among the living and the dead" (1442–44). If these lines imply that Zeus rewards piety more than anything, they elide the distinction between heroic action and piety just as the speech earlier confused eternal fame and apotheosis. The crucial terms are unstable.

Philoctetes' action arises from a prophecy, Helenus' statement that Troy will fall only when Philoctetes comes willingly to Troy with his bow. That is at least one version of the prophecy, which is quoted in different forms. Neoptolemus and Odysseus try all three possible ways to bring Philoctetes along: deception, force, and persuasion. None is successful, and throughout it is not entirely clear what "willing" means or whether it is an essential condition. Indeed, some passages suggest that the bow alone would suffice to enable the Greeks to win. At the end, when Heracles persuades Philoctetes, not only is the prophecy fulfilled in its strongest interpretation, but that interpretation turns out to be the only humanly satisfying one. It is wrong to deceive or force one's friends, or to deprive a hero of the honor he deserves, and the bow itself is a numinous object that should be respected. Piety in a broad sense includes all these concerns. So the elision of piety and heroic deeds is no accident, but lies at the center of Sophocles' view of the human condition.

NOTE

1   Other examples: Philoctetes' life on the island is influenced by anthropological speculation (Rose 1976), as is the famous Ode on Man in *Antigone* (332–75). Oedipus in *Oedipus at Colonus* compares his children to Egyptians in a passage obviously based on Herodotus (337–41).

FURTHER READING

For the pietist/hero-worshipper debate, the English-speaking reader can most easily hear the pietist side from Bowra 1944, the heroic from Whitman 1951. Another famous study of the Sophoclean hero is that of Knox 1964; he is also the author of a very rich close reading of *Oedipus the King* (Knox 1957). Segal 1981 sees Sophocles as examining the place of human culture between the constant danger of becoming less than human and the desire to become more; it is full of interesting close readings. Winnington-Ingram 1980 is not a single interpretation but a set of lively studies of individual plays and issues. All these are concerned, at bottom, with the ethical meanings of the dramatic action and with the role of the gods. An especially good study of a single ethical question is Blundell 1989, which looks at Sophocles' treatment of themes of revenge and reciprocity.

On dramatic technique, von Wilamowitz-Moellendorff 1996 [1917] aggressively argues that Sophocles is full of inconsistencies that prove he was interested in the theatrical effect of individual scenes more than in the unity of the whole; the reader without German can get a sense of his work from Lloyd-Jones 1990c. For dramatic technique more generally, Kirkwood 1958 is very helpful. For stagecraft, an especially fine essay is Taplin 1971. More recent work has, not surprisingly, shown the variety of approaches typical of literary studies generally. Foley 2001 is especially helpful for Antigone and Electra. Ormand 1999 looks at women as objects used in negotiations among men. Many studies treat Sophocles politically; a hostile but useful guide to these is Griffin 1999a.

CHAPTER SIXTEEN

Euripidean Tragedy

Justina Gregory

Why was Euripides a favorite target of Aristophanic humor? Was it because he was a well-known and respected playwright, or a notorious and scandalous one? Either conclusion is possible from the evidence. Euripides is a central figure in *Acharnians* and *Women at the Thesmophoria* and the butt of scattered jokes in other plays. In 405 BCE, the year after Euripides' death, Aristophanes won first prize at the festival of the Lenaea with his *Frogs*. As the play begins the god Dionysus has descended to Hades with the aim of bringing Euripides back with him to Athens. Once arrived in the underworld Dionysus adjudicates a debate between Aeschylus, the current occupant of the throne of tragedy, and the recently deceased Euripides, who has wasted no time in lodging a rival claim. Since Sophocles too is now dead, this "great event among the dead, and terrific conflict" (759–60) might have taken shape as a three-way contest; Sophocles, however, has graciously withdrawn from the competition. The contest mingles disparate criteria from different realms (see Halliwell, chapter 25 in this volume), all exploited for maximum comic effect. Dionysus' choice remains in doubt until the last possible moment. In the end he reverses his original intention and opts to rescue Aeschylus, the playwright most likely to "give useful advice to the city" (1420–21).

Both the contest and its outcome draw attention to their own arbitrariness. By excluding Sophocles Aristophanes is able to caricature Euripides as the anti-Aeschylus, sharpening the "grand antithesis" (Halliwell 2003, 105) that drives his plot but obscuring the complex relationships that actually prevailed among the three tragedians. Dionysus' decision provides a political resolution to the context, but hardly a literary one (Willi 2002). Nevertheless, Aristophanes' comic portrayal became the basis for serious nineteenth-century characterizations of Euripides (Silk and Stern 1981, 36–37) as a decadent rationalist who subverted the tragic genre – a view that with modifications is still widely held today.

In the twenty-first century, Euripides remains a contested figure. The sharpest disagreements concern his relationship to Aeschylus and Sophocles, and, indeed, to the genre of tragedy as a whole. Many critics broadly adhere to the nineteenth-century assessment, even though it depends on a prescriptive rather than a descriptive definition of Greek tragedy. Others maintain that Euripides' differences from the other tragedians are a matter of degree rather than of kind, that Euripides developed rather than destroyed the tragic genre, and that there is more that unites the three dramatists than sets them apart (for the debate see Mitchell-Boyask 2002, xii). Readers should be forewarned that the following account of Euripidean drama reflects the revisionist point of view (more traditional assessments can be found in the essays of Roberts and Seidensticker, chapters 9 and 3 in this volume). I begin with a brief and selective survey of Euripides' reputation from the fifth century to the modern era, and then address some aspects of continuity and innovation in his plays.

Euripides in the Fifth and Fourth Centuries

Our sense of how Euripides was viewed in his own time was long conditioned by the ancient biographical accounts, which portray a man disappointed in his public and humiliated in his private life, the last heir of an exhausted genre. Lefkowitz (1979) has demonstrated, however, the unreliability of the biographical information, much of which falls into three categories. First, there are details originating in the comedies of Aristophanes. The story retailed in the ancient *Life* (1) that his mother was an herb seller – implausible in view of his level of education and contradicted by the fourth-century historian Philochorus (Kovacs 1994, 11) – is based on a joke, impenetrable to modern readers, that Aristophanes liked well enough to repeat five times (*Acharnians* 478, *Knights* 19, *Women at the Thesmophoria* 387 and 456, *Frogs* 840). Second, there are details transferred from Euripides' own tragedies. For example, the statement in the ancient *Life* (24) that Euripides' wives were both unfaithful is in all likelihood inspired by mythical Euripidean heroines such as Phaedra and Sthenoboea, again as filtered through Aristophanes (cf. *Frogs* 1043–44). Finally, there are anecdotes reflecting traditional lore about poets and their destiny. The statement that Euripides was born on the day of the victory of Salamis (8) tallies with the reports that Aeschylus fought in the battle (*Life of Aeschylus* 10) and that Sophocles danced in a boys' chorus to celebrate the victory (*Life of Sophocles* 3). When taken together, as they often are, these stories imply that the torch of tragedy passed from Aeschylus to Sophocles and finally to Euripides, but in reality the tragedians' chronological and professional relationships were intertwined. Euripides, who is variously reported to have been born in 484 or 480, first competed in 455, only three years after Aeschylus produced his *Oresteia*; Sophocles' career overlapped with both Aeschylus' and Euripides'; Aeschylus' plays continued to be produced after his death, at the same time that Sophocles and Euripides were producing their mature work; and Sophocles outlived Euripides. Nor did the genre die with Euripides, since new tragedies were still being produced in the fourth century.

Although a residue of credible biographical information remains after such dubious anecdotes have been discounted, there is no consensus on its interpretation. It is known from the production records that of Euripides' surviving plays only *Hippolytus* belonged to a tetralogy that won first prize at the City Dionysia. Indeed, his entries garnered first prize only four times in his lifetime, although he competed twenty-two or twenty-three times. When compared to Sophocles' eighteen (or more) victories in about thirty attempts, this record might seem to support the implication of the ancient *Life* (34) that Euripides was fundamentally at odds with his public.

It is not obvious, however, that first prize in the tragic competition should be considered the principal criterion of success. Sophocles' record was clearly exceptional; not even Aeschylus fared as well. Moreover, the system for selecting judges did nothing to ensure either an informed or a representative verdict (see Pickard-Cambridge 1988, 96–97). Finally, plays that did not receive first prize seem nonetheless to have registered strongly on the popular consciousness. Aristophanes could parody Euripides' *Telephus* thirteen years after the play's production, in his *Acharnians* of 425, and again fourteen years later in his *Women at the Thesmophoria* of 411, and both times count on the audience to recognize his source.[1] Produced in the same tetralogy as *Telephus* was *Alcestis*, which so impressed Plato that he alludes to it twice in the *Symposium* (179b, 208d) – yet this tetralogy was awarded only second place in 438.

Half a century ago P. T. Stevens made the case that the true measure of success was not winning first prize in the competition, but being chosen to compete at the Dionysia by the eponymous archon; this honor, after all, committed the city to providing a public venue for a playwright's productions and arranging financial backing. Stevens concludes with the rhetorical question (1956, 92), "If we think of [Euripides'] career as one in which he could practically count upon production, in which on three occasions at least and probably many more he won the second prize, and on four occasions won the first prize, should we regard this as a failure?"

Euripides' removal to Macedon in old age is given a psychological spin by the ancient *Life* (35), which implies that he left Athens a disappointed and rejected playwright. Yet there is a more straightforward explanation for his departure. The last decade of the fifth century saw an intellectual exodus from Athens, as King Archelaus of Macedon, in a bid to enhance the prestige of his own court with celebrities drawn from the Athenian cultural establishment, persuaded not only Euripides but also the younger tragedian Agathon, the composer Timotheus, Choerilus the epic poet, and Zeuxis the sculptor to take up residence in Macedon (Aelian, *Varia Historia* 14.13). Moreover, Euripides' removal to Macedon is indicative of tragedy's undiminished popularity and increasing geographical diffusion – a trend that would accelerate in the fourth century (Easterling 1994).

Although Euripides did not enjoy Aeschylus' iconic status or Sophocles' universal esteem, he clearly commanded both official and popular recognition in his own lifetime. The fourth century saw a shift: Aeschylus moved out of fashion, Sophocles maintained his reputation, and Euripides became the most admired of the three. The plays of all three dramatists were copied for preservation in the Athenian state archives (see Kovacs, chapter 24 in this volume), but when orators like Aeschines, Demosthenes, and Lycurgus wanted dramatic excerpts read into the legal record in support of some political or moral point, it was Sophoclean and Euripidean tragedy to which they turned (Wilson 1996, 312–15). New Comedy drew heavily on Euripides both for its plot elements and its rhetorical flavor – an additional testimony to his influence. As Porter remarks: "Menander's comedies attest the ultimate triumph of Euripides' art: one can argue that they reflect a period when 'tragedy,' for the popular audiences that attended Menander's plays in Athens and elsewhere, was in many ways fundamentally *Euripidean* tragedy" (1999–2000, 172).

Aristotle's treatment of Euripides rounds out the picture of his fourth-century status. Everybody knows that Sophocles' *Oedipus the King* was Aristotle's favorite tragedy, but it is also worth remembering that in the same chapter of the *Poetics* where

Aristotle celebrates plays with unhappy endings and singles out *Oedipus* for praise, he calls Euripides "the most tragic of the poets" (1453a29–30). In the next chapter, moreover, Aristotle proceeds to extol plays with happy endings and singles out Euripides' *Iphigenia among the Taurians* for praise. As White explains, Aristotle's criteria for excellence turn on the protagonist's response to misfortune, regardless of the ultimate issue of events (1992, 236–37). Aristotle recognized what the surviving work of all three playwrights makes plain: a happy ending is not incompatible with tragedy (see Roberts, chapter 9 in this volume).

Postclassical Developments

To move beyond the classical era is to recognize that accidents of transmission have played no small role in shaping Euripides' reputation. The extraordinary variety of Euripides' work is often discussed as if it were a consequence of the poet's restless temperament (e.g., Whitman 1974, v). But our perception of this variety is due at least in part to the circumstance that eighteen of Euripides' plays have come down to us in their entirety, as opposed to seven for Aeschylus (six, if we discount *Prometheus Bound*) and seven for Sophocles. The numerical discrepancy is the result of pure chance. In addition to the ten tragedies selected from Euripides' complete works (as edited by the scholars of Alexandria) during the Roman period,[2] an additional cache survived, which was rediscovered, copied, and edited by the fourteenth-century Byzantine savant Demetrius Triclinius (Reynolds and Wilson 1991, 76–77). These are the so-called alphabetic plays: eight tragedies plus a satyr-play, *Cyclops*, whose Greek titles begin with epsilon, eta, iota, or kappa. (For discussion of *Cyclops* see Seidensticker, chapter 3 in this volume.)

It is not the case that the alphabetic plays alone are responsible for Euripides' reputation as a restless experimenter. The problematic *Orestes*, for example, was part of the canonical selection; conversely, *Heracles* and *Iphigenia at Aulis*, tragedies by any measure, are alphabetic plays. Still, many of the plays that have seemed to pose challenges to the tragic genre as prescriptively defined belong to the alphabetic group: the "romantic tragedies" (Conacher 1967, 15), *Iphigenia among the Taurians*, *Helen*, and *Ion*; the patriotic and political dramas, *Children of Heracles* and *Suppliants*; and *Electra*, which engages so pointedly – to some critics, so antitragically – with other versions of the myth.

The good fortune that allowed so many plays of Euripides to survive has also worked against him. If more plays of Aeschylus and Sophocles were extant, they would in all likelihood display a range of mythical subject matter, characterization, and theatrical effects comparable to Euripides', and we would recognize that Euripides' productions were not unique in their variety. For example, the fragments of Sophocles' *Tereus* and of his two *Tyro* plays reveal that filicidal mothers and seduced and abandoned heroines were a feature of Sophoclean as well as Euripidean drama. We know that Aeschylus' *Lycurgeia* trilogy prefigured Euripides' *Bacchae* in portraying an effeminate Dionysus (cf. fr. 61.1). And it is probable that Sophocles' *Polyxena*, like Euripides' *Hecuba*, opened sensationally with a prologue spoken by a ghost (cf. fr. 523; on the fragmentary plays see Cropp, chapter 17 in this volume).

Although Byzantine scholars played an important role in preserving Euripidean tragedy, their appreciation of its qualities remained "superficial in the extreme"

(N. G. Wilson 1983, 179). Michael Psellus, for example, saw fit to compare Euripides' iambics to those of George the Pisidian, a seventh-century Byzantine author (N. G. Wilson 1983, 178), while Thomas Magister's summary biography commends Euripides' skillful use of rhetoric and his plentiful aphorisms (Kovacs 1994, 13). In the thirteenth century a further winnowing took place to select titles for the school syllabus, resulting in the production of hundreds of copies of three chosen plays. The tragedies in question (known as the Byzantine triad) are *Hecuba, Orestes,* and *Phoenician Women* – a salutary reminder of the different literary estimations of different historical eras. (The triads chosen for Aeschylus – *Persians, Seven against Thebes, Prometheus Bound* – and Sophocles – *Ajax, Electra, Oedipus the King* – are equally surprising from a modern point of view.)

The aesthetics of a tragedy such as *Hecuba* struck a responsive chord with sixteenth-century critics who appreciated the play's complex structure, horrific subject matter, and (implicit) moral instruction (Heath 1987a, 43–48). In the seventeenth century Racine reserved his greatest admiration for Sophocles but was most influenced by Euripides (Philippo 2003, 22): he used *Iphigenia at Aulis* and *Hippolytus* as direct models for two plays (*Iphigénie* and *Phèdre*), while drawing on Euripidean material for others.

Euripides in the Nineteenth and Twentieth Centuries

It was only in the nineteenth century that invidious distinctions began to be drawn between Euripides and the two other tragedians. In the evolutionary assessments of the brothers Schlegel, Aeschylus represented the dawn of tragedy, Sophocles the zenith, and Euripides the decline. In this schema Euripides was not so much the anti-Aeschylus as the anti-Sophocles, disorganized where Sophocles was harmonious and self-indulgent where Sophocles was disciplined (Behler 1986, 350–51). Nietzsche carried this account even further. Following the lead of Aristophanes (*Frogs* 1491–92), he linked Euripides to Socrates and ascribed to both a rationalism and an optimism inimical to tragedy (see Henrichs, chapter 28 in this volume). As noted, these attitudes took root in twentieth-century Euripidean criticism.

Euripides also found his champions. Wilamowitz's sympathy for the playwright rested in part on an idiosyncratic identification with the Euripidean heroes Hippolytus and Heracles and even with the poet himself (Calder 1986, 417–19), but also on a lucid appreciation of the difference between ancient and modern understandings of tragedy: "A [Greek] tragedy does not have to end 'tragically' or be 'tragic.' The only requirement is a serious treatment" (Wilamowitz-Moellendorff 1959, 1: 113).

In the English-speaking world Gilbert Murray played a crucial role in popularizing Euripides through his translations and through his *Euripides and His Age*, first published in 1913 in that idealistic venture in popular education, the Home University Library, and repeatedly reprinted thereafter. Murray's account of the playwright, like Wilamowitz's, was skewed by identification – in his case a tendency to conflate his "own stance on social and political issues and the picture he draws of Euripides" (Easterling 1997c, 118). A lifelong pacifist, Murray interpreted *Trojan Women* as making a statement about the hollowness of military glory (1946, 83); but while the play (like Homer's *Iliad*) unsparingly conveys war's horrors, it never proposes an end or an alternative to war, and indeed (in another Homeric reminiscence) finds consolation in the thought that the Trojan conflict will be a theme of song for later generations (*Trojan Women* 1245, cf. *Iliad* 6.357–58). Furthermore, Murray had a tendency to identify certain aspects of Euripides' era with his own. Murray opens his book by cautioning, "It is fatal to fly straight at [Euripides] with modern ready-made analogies" (5–6). Yet a page later he comments, "The Victorian Age had, amid enormous differences, a certain similarity with the Periclean in its lack of self-examination, its rush and chivalry and optimism, its unconscious hypocrisy, its failure to think out its problems to the bitter end.... Euripides, like ourselves, comes in an age of criticism following upon an age of movement and action."

The analogy is misleading, not only because of the chronological distortion involved in consigning Euripides to the post-Periclean world, but also because it fails to recognize that throughout the fifth century the Athenians designated an official time, set aside a civic space, and allocated financial resources to an institution that – precisely – encouraged them to "think out...problems to the bitter end" by subjecting their values and assumptions to intense examination. Meier argues that tragedy provided the spectators with a "platform for an utterly unique form of institutionalized 'discussion'" (1993, 42). By addressing political and ethical issues of the day (not specifically and directly as in the assembly and legislature, but more generally and at a mythical remove), the tragedians helped the spectators find their bearings in an era of rapid and unprecedented political and intellectual change. Halliwell and Croally (chapters 25 and 4 in this volume) remind us that poets were traditionally viewed as teachers, and that the playwrights too were expected to instruct. If these scholars are correct, then the ethical complexity and the persistent questioning that characterize Euripides' plays are not only not at odds with the tragic enterprise but fundamental to it.

In the second half of the twentieth century Euripides was still being defined as the anti-Sophocles – the Sophocles of the strong, steadfast hero (Knox 1964, 8–11, 45–50) and the smooth, "organic" style (Michelini 1987, 60). With critical understandings of Sophocles now shifting (see Scodel, chapter 15 in this volume), it is time to reevaluate Euripides as well. In the following section I offer a selective sketch of Euripides' relationship with his tradition under the headings of language, style, and meter; structure and design; consistency and realism in characterization; age classes; shared characteristics; genre and humor; and theatrical and literary references. Euripidean drama is no less tragic, I will suggest, for distinctively combining innovation with tradition.

Language, Style, Meter

Tragic language distinguishes itself from everyday speech and from literary prose not only by its meter but also by its stylistic elevation: rarified vocabulary, fullness of expression, complex word order, and ornamental figures. Tragic speakers may have different outlooks and preoccupations depending on their age, gender, class, or ethnicity, but by and large all employ the same high-style diction. The language of Euripidean tragedy is not fundamentally different from Aeschylus' and Sophocles' (Mastronarde 2002b, 81–82 and 92–96). The existence of a monograph entitled *Colloquial Expressions in Euripides* (Stevens 1976) might give the impression that the dramatist makes lavish use of the vernacular; in fact the spoken portions of Euripidean tragedy are couched in supple, straightforward but formal Greek with only rare colloquialisms, as Stevens himself makes clear (2–5, 64–5; see also Silk 1996b, 459 with n. 6). Both Euripides and Sophocles show themselves receptive to the new vocabulary, in particular the abstract nouns that are a feature of fifth-century intellectual prose (Long 1968, 73 n. 37 and passim). Although Euripides does not elevate metaphors into leitmotifs in the manner of Aeschylus (see Saïd, chapter 14 in this volume), he does repeat images for effective emphasis and contrast. Thus the touch of hands is evoked throughout *Medea*, signifying now a sacred pledge, now tender intimacy, and now death and destruction (Flory 1978). Again, Heracles on his return from the underworld speaks of his children as "boats in tow" (*epholkidas, Heracles* 631), dependent on him for their protection; at the end of the play, having been humbled by madness, he describes himself trailing after his friend Theseus like "a wretched boat in tow" (*panóleis epholkides*, 1424).

Euripides' language can be vividly and succinctly pictorial, as when Medea's nurse speaks of her mistress's baleful, "bull-like gaze" (*omma tauroumenén, Medea* 92). He has a flair for pithy formulations, often incorporating a paradox. For example, after Phaedra's nurse has first sworn Hippolytus to secrecy and then revealed Phaedra's guilty passion, Hippolytus in his first shock threatens to contravene his oath (a threat he will never in fact translate into action), and tells the nurse, "My tongue swore, but my mind remains unsworn" (*Hippolytus* 612). This statement became proverbial (cf. Aristophanes, *Frogs* 101–2 and 1471; Plato, *Symposium* 199a); quoted out of context, it could be mistaken as representing the viewpoint of the poet himself.[3]

Euripides' metrical practice is eclectic. His handling of the iambic trimeter grows ever freer over time, and this pattern is of the utmost importance in establishing the relative chronology of his undated plays. His trimeters show a continuous increase in "resolution" from the early plays to the late – that is, an increase in the rate at which two short syllables are substituted for a long syllable in certain positions. The trimeters also display increasing rhythmic variety as they admit differently shaped words. Nine of Euripides' plays are datable from external indications,[4] and the evidence of trimeter resolution can be used to situate the undated plays relative to the dated ones (see the table in Cropp and Fick 1985, 5).

Euripides does not invariably move, however, in the direction of metrical freedom. The trochaic tetrameter, associated by Aristotle with early tragedy (*Poetics* 1449a21), is increasingly at home in his late plays (Drew-Bear 1968, 386), where it is used to mark the excitement that accompanies quickened dramatic action. Archaizing effects are also on occasion discernible in his lyrics: he uses meters traditionally associated with cult songs in Ion's paean to Apollo (*Ion* 112–43) and in the hymn to Dionysus which comprises the *parodos* of *Bacchae*. He thus has at his disposal an extraordinary range of metrical associations and effects.

The lyric portions of tragedy are ornate and highly figured. Euripidean lyric is no exception; it abounds in antitheses, oxymoronic expressions, *polyptoton* (the juxtaposition within the same sentence of different forms of the same word, or of cognate words), and emotional repetition (Breitenbach 1934, 291). Less obscure than Aeschylus' and less condensed than Sophocles', Euripides' lyric passages often feature precise, evocative detail and striking effects of color and light, and display a finely calibrated sense of contrast. Thus the third stasimon of *Hecuba* describes the fall of

Troy by focusing on a single individual, a Trojan woman who late at night, after the singing, sacrifices, and dancing that celebrated the end of the siege, is preparing for bed and "gazing into the gleaming depths of a golden mirror" (925). It is at this tranquil, reflective moment that she hears the shouts of the victorious Greeks from the citadel.

Euripides' later lyric style bears the imprint of the musical innovations associated with the name of Timotheus (see Wilson and Battezzato, chapters 12 and 10 in this volume). In Euripidean as (to a lesser extent) in Sophoclean drama the individual singer gains prominence, his virtuosity displayed in free-form monodies and duets. The increase in the actors' singing roles is reversed, however, in the two plays produced posthumously, *Bacchae* and *Iphigenia at Aulis* (Csapo 1999–2000, 412) – not, presumably, because the playwright suddenly saw the error of his ways, but because at every stage of his career and in all aspects of his art he moved back and forth between new ways and old.

Equally characteristic of Euripides' later style are elaborate mythical choral odes of the type labeled "dithyrambic" by Kranz (1933, 235–41). The name implies that these choral odes are self-contained and unconnected to the dramatic action, in this resembling the mythic narratives of Bacchylidean dithyramb, but close study often reveals otherwise. Thus the third stasimon of *Iphigenia among the Taurians* recounts the life and deeds of Apollo. After giving birth to Apollo on Delos, Leto brings him to Delphi. While still an infant Apollo kills the oracle's resident dragon, expels Themis from the site, and with the help of Zeus defeats Themis' mother Gaia, who had dispatched dream-apparitions to give mortals a rival version of "events first, after, and to come" (1264–65). Not only have misleading dreams and the reliability of Apollo's oracular directives to Orestes figured in the play thus far, but "the triumph of Olympian Apollo over Earth and her offspring (dragon, dreams) implies Orestes' ultimate escape from the Furies and his success in bringing Artemis and Iphigenia from the barbarian to the Hellenic realm" (Cropp 2000 on 1234–83).

Structure and Design

Euripides introduces new structures but also revives old ones. In 438, in an apparent innovation, he produced *Alcestis* instead of the satyr-play that would normally have come fourth. We do not know whether the omission of a satyr-play was a unique experiment, nor how the fourth-place position affected the audience's response to the play. Nor is there any scholarly consensus on its genre: some scholars (e.g., Seiden-sticker, chapter 3 in this volume) describe the play as combining tragic and satyric elements, while others (e.g., Gregory 1979) regard its exploration of the place of death in human life as fundamentally serious. While Euripides' preference was for free-standing tragedies, in 415 he seems to have produced a set of plays reminiscent of an Aeschylean connected trilogy: *Alexander, Palamedes,* and *Trojan Women* all concern the Trojan War, and are linked by recurring characters, themes, and imagery (Scodel 1980, 105).

Material is drawn from the entire range of myth (on the implications for tragic plots see Mastronarde 1999–2000, 28–29). Plot-lines are varied. Some tragedies (*Medea, Hippolytus, Trojan Women, Ion, Bacchae*) proceed in linear fashion from beginning to end in the continuous structure associated with the extant plays of Sophocles. Others involve an unforeseen development in the middle (*Heracles, Andromache, Hecuba, Suppliants, Orestes*), and still others feature an unexpected twist at the end (*Alcestis, Iphigenia among the Taurians, Helen, Children of Heracles, Electra*). In the case of *Iphigenia at Aulis* and *Phoenician Women*, extensive interpolation has obscured the original structure.

While Euripides' tragedies vary considerably in design, some distinctive tendencies can be described. Typically they open with a lengthy monologue delivered by either a divinity or a human character who, speaking directly to the audience, sets forth essential background information in an orderly fashion and affords the spectators a partial glimpse of developments to follow. Sophocles, more naturalistically, arranges for background information to emerge through dialogue. The Euripidean monologue often includes genealogical information that Euripides, like the other tragedians, shapes to suit his artistic purposes (cf. Saïd, chapter 14 this volume, on the genealogy of Prometheus and of the Furies). Thus in *Hecuba*, a tragedy set in the Thracian Chersonese, he gives Hecuba a familial connection to the locale by making her the daughter of Cisseus, a Thracian king mentioned in the *Iliad* (Gregory 1995).

Both Euripides and Sophocles make regular use of the *agón* (debate) to structure their episodes. The Euripidean *agón* is generally more detached from the action (see Halleran, chapter 11 in this volume) and has been condemned as "self-indulgent digression for the sake of rhetorical display" (Collard 1975b, 59). The paired speeches are rhetorical in the sense that they are rigorously structured with beginning, ending, and internal transitions clearly marked (Lloyd 1992, 3–5) and also in the sense that they tend to clarify entrenched positions rather than resolve or alter the situation at hand (Lloyd 1992, 15). They are not, however, rhetorical in the sense of being frigid display pieces (see Collard 1975b for a defense of their relevance). In *Medea*, for example, the debate between Medea and Jason (465–575) makes a vital contribution to the play's characterization and dominant themes. Medea's capacity for rage and Jason's unshakable complacency are both on view; Medea adverts to Jason's broken pledges and Jason to Medea's barbarian background; ominously, each parent uses the children as a means to berate the other.

Euripides deploys established dramatic techniques to bring a speech, an episode, or an entire play to a formal resolution, but does so without necessarily closing off the emotional, ethical, or political implications of what has come before. This technique can be interpreted either as an intellectually stimulating overrun, or as problematizing the very idea of an ending (so Roberts, chapter 9 in this volume). General reflections are endemic to tragedy, but Euripides is particularly apt to give them a summarizing function (Friis Johansen 1959, 151–60). Euripidean characters are known for their critical reproaches to the gods, which they tend to level "just before going off at a climax of the action" (Dale 1969, 182). Since eight of Euripides' extant tragedies conclude with a *deus ex machina*, we tend to regard the device as distinctively Euripidean. Sophocles' *Philoctetes* ends the same way, however, and by the fourth century (possibly, to be sure, through Euripides' influence) it was viewed as tragedy's general stock in trade: Antiphanes grumbles that a tragedian at his wits' end can always bring on a *deus ex machina*, a recourse unavailable to comic playwrights (fr. 189.13–17 *PCG*).

Since tragedy unfolds in two time-frames (see Debnar and Sourvinou-Inwood, chapters 1 and 18 in this volume), the aetiology is early recognized as an effective means of bridging the temporal gap. Aeschylus uses aetiology for this purpose at the end of *Eumenides*, when Athena establishes the Areopagus council, familiar to his fifth-century audience as the Athenian homicide court; in *Ajax* Sophocles hints at the cultic honors received by the hero (Henrichs 1993b). Euripides appropriates the device, introducing his own aetiologies generally (though not invariably) at the close of tragedies. Thus at the end of *Andromache* Thetis gives directions for Neoptolemus to be buried at Delphi, in a tomb that would presumably be known to many in the audience (see, however, Dunn 1996, 45–57 and passim, Dunn 2000, and Scullion 1999–2000 for the possibility that Euripides may have invented at least some of his aetiologies).

Consistency and Realism in Characterization

It was standard practice for tragedians to alter not just the genealogy but also the characterization of mythical figures from play to play. Thus the Odysseus of Sophocles' *Ajax* is honorable and compassionate, while the Odysseus of *Philoctetes* is devious and manipulative. Similarly, the cautious Orestes of Euripides' *Electra* is slow to reveal himself to his sister Electra; the trustful Orestes of *Iphigenia among the Taurians* is quick to reveal himself to his sister Iphigenia; the psychotic Orestes of *Orestes* takes Electra for one of his Furies. Such variations spark renewed audience interest in well-known mythological figures even as they further specific dramatic aims.

What about consistency of characterization within the plays? Aristotle finds fault with the Iphigenia of *Iphigenia at Aulis* for first supplicating Agamemnon for her life and subsequently affirming her death (*Poetics* 1454a31–33). Iphigenia herself maintains, however, that she has changed her mind on the basis of insight and reflection (Gibert 1995, 224), and critics must concede that she supplies reasons for her decision, whether or not they agree with them. The contrast drawn by Knox (1966, 213–15) between the inflexible heroes of Aeschylus and Sophocles and the volatile protagonists of Euripidean drama does not stand up to critical scrutiny (Gibert 1995, 255–62). Instead (as might be expected) all three tragedians use doubt and uncertainty to create suspense. In the most spectacular example in all of Greek tragedy, Aeschylus' Orestes hesitates before he kills his mother (*Libation Bearers* 899). At the end of *Antigone* the chorus-leader advises Creon to release Antigone and arrange burial for Polynices (1100–1101); Creon wavers and then capitulates, though his change of course comes too late to save Antigone's life. But whereas Aeschylus and Sophocles pass rapidly over such moments of indecision, Euripides is inclined to draw them out. Medea agonizes over her decision to kill her sons, and as she contemplates the children's bright faces (*omma phaidron teknôn*, 1043) her diction – incoherent exclamations, the plaintive question, "What shall I do?" and the repeated cry, "Farewell, plans!" – reflects her torment. Stagecraft can be enlisted for the same purpose. In *Hecuba* Euripides makes use of a prolonged aside to represent Hecuba's uncertainty about appealing to Agamemnon: she turns her back on the king (who, unaccustomed to being ignored, manifests increasing bewilderment and impatience) to carry on a debate with herself (736–51; for other aspects of Euripidean stagecraft see Davidson, chapter 13 in this volume).

Euripides does not linger over such moments, I believe, in the interests of verisimilitude, but because they make for effective theater. Critics who regard him as aiming at psychological realism can appeal to Sophocles' remark that he himself portrayed men as they should be, whereas Euripides portrayed men as they are (Aristotle, *Poetics* 1460b33–34). Sophocles' own characterizations are less idealized, however, than this remark suggests – the Odysseus of *Philoctetes*, for instance, has much in common with the corrupt fifth-century politicians who are also a target of Euripides, and Deianira in *Women of Trachis* could be any unfaithful husband's fearful and conflicted wife. Furthermore, Euripides is more concerned, as we shall see, to illuminate aspects of human nature than to delineate specific individuals. It is true, as Seidensticker (chapter 3 in this volume) points out, that Euripides' incorporation of the homely concerns of everyday life imparts an overlay of realism, as when Admetus imagines the "unswept floor" of his neglected house (*Alcestis* 947), or the shipwrecked Menelaus is mortified by his near-nakedness (*Helen* 415–24). Yet such details may well evoke the literary tradition rather than (or along with) everyday life. Similar concerns already figure in the *Odyssey*, where the point is made that housekeeping deteriorates in the master's absence (*Odyssey* 17.320–21), and the shipwrecked Odysseus is troubled and embarrassed by his own nakedness (6.135–48). Domestic details even find a place in the *Iliad*, when Phoenix speaks of his care for the small Achilles' physical needs (9.485–95) – a motif reworked by Aeschylus in *Libation Bearers* (755–60).

That realism is not a primary aim is made clear by moments when the characters themselves, presumably mirroring within the play an aspect of the dramatist's own technique, draw attention to the expressive or performative value of their own actions or speech (see Scodel 1999–2000 and Pelling, chapter 6 in this volume). Thus Electra, humiliated at having been married to a farmer and relegated to a cottage in the country, observes that she fetches her own water "not from necessity, but to display Aegisthus' outrageousness to the gods" (*Electra* 58; cf. *Trojan Women* 472–73). The playwright's preference for illustrative exposition over psychological realism is even more strikingly exemplified by scenes in which a heroine in extremis hallucinates in lyrics, only to follow up with a lucid trimeter exposition of her case. Thus Alcestis on her deathbed, after reacting with terror to her vision of Charon in his boat, calmly explains her rationale for dying on Admetus' behalf and demands a concession from her husband in return (*Alcestis* 252–325; for a similar sequence in Aeschylus see *Agamemnon* 1072–1197, and in Sophocles, *Antigone* 806–928). The abrupt shift of mood is psychologically implausible, but Euripides is in pursuit of a larger insight: he aims to set forth the two modes, emotional and rational, with which human beings confront their own mortality (cf. Dale 1954 on *Alcestis* 280 ff.).

Age Classes

In view of this purposeful stylization it seems more fruitful to discuss Euripidean characters in terms of classes – age classes in particular – than in terms of individuals. Euripidean characters are sharply demarcated by age, even more so than by gender or social status. The other tragedians seem readier to let the masks convey this category. Aeschylus' Xerxes, for example, is described as young and headstrong (cf. *Persians* 744), but when he finally appears on stage his stylized lamentations convey little sense that he is a youthful character; Sophocles' aged Oedipus says that age and suffering have taught him tolerance (*Oedipus at Colonus* 7–8), but his responses throughout the play do not bear out this claim. Pathos and vulnerability are dominant notes in Euripides' characterizations of young people; he tends to view the middle-aged and the old with a colder eye.

Euripides was not the only dramatist to exploit the dramatic potential of children – Sophocles brings Eurysaces on stage (*Ajax* 545–95) in a scene that alludes to the meeting of Hector, Andromache, and Astyanax in *Iliad* 6 – but he may well have been the first to give them singing parts. The children do not have lengthy roles, presumably on account of the challenges of staging such scenes: perhaps the lyrics were sung by inexperienced boy actors, perhaps the boy actors mimed the appropriate emotions while an adult actor sang their lyrics (for the possibilities see Sifakis 1979, 73).

The brief songs function to enhance the pathos inherent in the children's small stature and youthful masks, and to underscore their situations of loss or danger. Alcestis' son and daughter are on stage as their mother breathes her last, and the boy then bewails their orphaned state; in *Andromache* Molossus mourns his impending death at the hands of Menelaus; in *Suppliants* the sons of the seven dead Argive heroes participate in the funeral lamentation. And in a traditional representation of murder by means of shouts within (a convention first attested in Aeschylus' *Agamemnon*), Medea's two boys cry out (not in lyrics, but in trimeters) from inside the *skênê*.

Euripides' adolescents are often high-minded and idealistic – particularly those who embrace a sacrificial death for the sake either of their community (Heracles' daughter in *Children of Heracles*, Menoeceus in *Phoenician Women*, Iphigenia in *Iphigenia at Aulis*) or of their own honor (Polyxena in *Hecuba*). The nobility displayed by these young people makes their deaths all the more affecting. A less attractive aspect of youth, to which Euripides is equally attentive, is its arrogance and intransigence. Conspicuous examples are Hippolytus in his name-play and Pentheus in *Bacchae*. Hippolytus' fate is already sealed as the play begins, and he pays with his life for his rejection of Aphrodite; Pentheus receives repeated warnings and is given the chance to change his ways, but he too is destroyed in the end for his resistance to Dionysus. The gods use their fates to point a lesson (*Hippolytus* 5–6, *Bacchae* 1345), but what stays with the audience is a sense of divine vindictiveness and of the waste of young lives.

Characters in the prime of life have left youthful idealism behind them. Some few (such as Lycus in *Heracles*) are evil through and through, with no explanation provided for how they got that way. More typically Euripides' adult characters are flawed but uncomfortably aware of their shortcomings, at once conflicted and apologetic. Thus Agamemnon in *Hecuba* explains that he pities Hecuba, understands the justice of her cause, and would like nothing more than to come to her aid, if only helping her did not endanger his standing with the Greek army (*Hecuba* 850–63). Clytemnestra in *Electra* comes to visit her daughter when summoned, allows Electra to pour out her grievances, and admits that she herself "does not rejoice too much at what [she] has done" (1105–6).

Euripides' older characters tend to be survivors whom the passage of time has hardly ennobled. Cadmus in *Bacchae* advises his grandson Pentheus that even if Dionysus is not divine, he should "say that he is and tell a lie in a good cause, so that Semele will seem to have given birth to a god, and honor will accrue to our whole family" (334–36). The aged Alcmene of *Children of Heracles* gloats over her captured enemy Eurystheus, then insists on having him put to death in defiance of the normal Athenian policy for prisoners of war. Euripides, like the other tragedians, makes much of the feebleness of old age (de Romilly 1968, 143–66); in fact, as we will see, their debility becomes the occasion for humor.

Shared Characteristics

Certain qualities transcend both age and gender. Men and women alike display a passionate, protective love for their children; this universal characteristic, implicit in the words of Aeschylean and Sophoclean characters (e.g., *Agamemnon* 1417–18; *Oedipus at Colonus* 1617–19), is both recognized (e.g., *Heracles* 633–36) and acted on by Euripidean speakers. Amphitryon in *Heracles* and Cadmus in *Bacchae* tenderly and cautiously guide their deranged offspring back to sanity; Andromache and Hecuba in their name-plays are willing to give up their own lives to save their children. Precisely because parental love is universal and predictable it is subject to manipulation, as when Medea convinces Creon to postpone sending her into exile by appealing to his fellow feeling as a parent, and subsequently recognizes that murdering her and Jason's two sons will constitute her most effective revenge.

A distinctive intellectualism of response also characterizes Euripidean characters of various ages and both genders. In all of Greek tragedy, characters and choruses relate specific events to general patterns by appealing either to mythical paradigms or gnomic wisdom (on the complementarity of the two modes see Gould 1999). In an updated variation on this response, Euripidean speakers attempt to locate their situation in a broader context through allusion to intellectual topics of the day. Such interests (which are not in fact unique to Euripidean characters; see Allan, chapter 5 in this volume) led Euripides to be commended as the "philosopher of the stage" by Athenaeus (561a) and condemned for irrelevant philosophizing by Friedrich Schlegel (1979, 61 [1794]).

Schlegel's censure depends on the anachronistic assumption that poetry and philosophy have nothing in common. The question is not whether the plays include passages that strike a philosophical note, but whether such passages detract from the action. When, for example, Adrastus in *Suppliants* asks Theseus to help the Argives recover their war dead, the king prefaces his rejection by passing in review the stages by which human beings have advanced, always with divine aid, from savagery to civilization (201–13). The idea of progress is a topos of both the Sophists and tragedy (see Collard 1975a ad loc), but by stressing the role of divinity Theseus reinforces his main point: Adrastus has tried to be "wiser than the gods" (218), has ignored warning oracles, and accordingly bears responsibility for his own misfortunes. When Phaedra explains that she has devoted many nights to pondering why human beings know and recognize what is good but cannot put their understanding into practice (*Hippolytus* 375–80), the topic is recognizably Socratic (Irwin 1983), but there is nothing gratuitous about its introduction here, in a play where all the human characters mean well but make ruinous choices. After Hecuba in her name-play has learned of her daughter Polyxena's noble death, she ponders the relative roles of nature and education in forming character – another topic of debate in fifth-century intellectual circles. Although Hecuba herself dismisses her musings as "arrows shot in vain" (603), they are relevant to a play in which two of the principals, Polyxena and

Polymestor, exemplify natures inherently good and inherently evil. Euripides is able, in short, to "contribute to theoretical disputes without taking time off from being a dramatist" (Irwin 1983, 197).

Euripides' characters are more inclined than Aeschylus' or Sophocles' to challenge the order of things, and this critical attitude extends to the gods. Some few protest the Olympians' cruelty: thus Cadmus acknowledges that his family deserved punishment for resisting Dionysus, but adds that the god has "gone too far" (*Bacchae* 1346). More commonly it is divine indifference that elicits bewilderment or reproach. The spectacle of the erstwhile queen of Troy prostrate on the ground prompts Talthybius to wonder whether the gods watch over mortals or whether chance is operative in human affairs (*Hecuba* 488–91). The female captives who comprise the chorus of *Trojan Women* address themselves to Zeus as they contemplate the ruined city of Troy, asking "whether you have any thought for this, as you sit on your heavenly throne" (1077–78).

Accusations of divine cruelty or carelessness serve less to indict the gods – often they cast light on the ignorance or naiveté of the accusers, as Mastronarde (chapter 20 this volume) observes – than to point to the human community as the place where help should be sought and found. The importance of friendship, especially in dark times, is a recurrent Euripidean theme. The exile Polynices notes bitterly that friendship counts for nothing once someone has encountered misfortune (*Phoenician Women* 403). And in a concluding gnomic statement, Amphitryon advises that "whoever wishes to acquire wealth or power rather than friends does not reason well" (*Heracles* 1425–27; cf. *Orestes* 804–6, 1155–57).

Euripidean speakers also turn their scrutiny on human institutions. That the playwright incorporates references to Athenian democracy into plays set in the mythical past would not have surprised the spectators; Aeschylus had done the same in his *Suppliants* and *Eumenides*. Euripides' allusions are less obvious but also more controversial, for Euripidean speakers express a range of opinions about the democracy. Thus Theseus in *Suppliants* extols the rule of the *dêmos* (common people), the authority of written law, and the opportunity for free debate (403–8, 429–41). But he is speaking in the context of an *agôn* where the Theban herald has just taken the opposite view, stressing the vulnerability of the *dêmos* to manipulation by glib politicians (409–25). One such politician is the "agile-minded, sweet-talking, *dêmos*-pleasing" Odysseus of *Hecuba* (131–32). Another is Agamemnon, whose trawling for popular favor as he campaigned for leadership of the Trojan expedition is recalled with contempt by his brother Menelaus (*Iphigenia at Aulis* 337–45). No more than the other tragedians does Euripides make overt references to current events. Nevertheless, it is hard to miss the contemporary resonance of such descriptions: Agamemnon resembles the demagogues who came after Pericles and who, as Thucydides describes it (2.65.7–10), catered disastrously to the *dêmos* in furthering their own ambitions.

Social issues, a recurrent concern of tragedy, are canvassed most pointedly by Euripidean characters. Aeschylean and Sophoclean speakers observe that slaves in name are not necessarily slaves in mind, but Euripidean speakers go further, suggesting that where there is a discrepancy between an individual's physical and mental condition, the latter is the true index of worth (Gregory 2002, 153–55). Women are prominent in Euripidean drama as in all of Greek tragedy – in fact more prominent, to judge by the number of plays with female choruses (Mastronarde 1998, 63). Euripides may appear unique in developing a theoretical analysis of women's situation, but here as elsewhere he remains within the literary tradition. As part of her bid to win over the female chorus, Medea describes the hardships and restrictions of women's lot (*Medea* 230–51). The rhetorical device whereby a child-murderess forges bonds of sympathy with other women by speaking of "our" plight, as well as the critique of virilocal marriage and of the dowry-system, has parallels in Procne's speech from Sophocles' *Tereus* (fr. 583). A speaker in *Wise Melanippe* protests the prejudice against women in terms that simultaneously evoke the reflexive misogyny of Athenian culture and recall Agamemnon's remarks in the *Odyssey* on Clytemnestra's damaging legacy: "The hatred for women is very harmful. Women who have stumbled are a reproach to those who have not; the wicked ones share the blame with the good" (fr. 493.1–4; cf. *Odyssey* 12.430–34 and 24.199–202). Aeschylus had already complicated the stereotypical contrast between noble Greeks and savage barbarians in *Persians* (see Ebbott, chapter 23 in this volume), but Euripides provocatively inverts it, as when Andromache, upon learning that the Greeks intend to cast her little son Astyanax to his death from the walls of Troy, denounces the "Greeks who have devised barbarian atrocities" (*Trojan Women* 764).

Related to the critique of institutions and attitudes is the utopian desire that the conditions of life might be altered for the better. A recurrent wish is for transparency in human beings, so that exterior and interior, appearance and reality, words and deeds could be clearly differentiated (cf. Scodel, chapter 15 in this volume, on deceptive speech in Sophocles; and contrast Saïd, chapter 14 in this volume, on how "appearances never deceive" in Aeschylean drama). Thus Medea regrets that there is no visible stamp (*charactêr*, 519; she employs the imagery of coinage) on human beings that can distinguish the good from the bad. Misogynist characters would prefer that propagation could take place without women: Hippolytus wishes that men could go to the temples, lay down an amount of bronze, iron, or gold, and purchase a child commensurate to their economic status (*Hippolytus* 618–24; cf. *Medea* 573–75).

Euripidean choruses express the same desire for different conditions to apply, often responding to the anguish of the protagonist's situation with a wistful wish to be somewhere or something else; their impulse is not irrelevant to the action but "a reassertion of the themes and problems of the play in a different and distant context" (Padel 1974, 227). Thus after Pentheus' angry confrontation with Tiresias and Cadmus the chorus of Asian bacchants wish themselves in Cyprus – sacred to Aphrodite, whose connection with Dionysus is central to the play – or Pieria, seat of the Muses, who like Dionysus are patrons of the arts (*Bacchae* 402–16; for similar wishes cf. *Hippolytus* 732–34, *Helen* 1478–86).

Genre and Humor

Euripides has been described as writing plays that are akin to comedies (Knox 1979a, 250). As we have seen, however, a happy ending is not indicative of genre. Moreover, the fact that plays such as *Iphigenia among the Taurians*, *Ion*, and *Helen* feature motifs (of intrigue, recognition of long-lost kin, rescue, escape) that became staples of New Comedy does not mean that in the fifth or fourth centuries these plays were apprehended as comic, or as falling between the genres. The years of solitude and misery experienced by Iphigenia, Creusa, and Helen alike continue to shape their responses to subsequent events; despite their light moments and happy endings, these are "plays of suffering, misapprehension, struggle and barely won victory" (Whitman 1974, 104).

The issue of genre is closely connected to the issue of humor. Since tragedy concerns serious individuals and is an imitation of a serious action (*Poetics* 1448a2, 1449b24), humor might seem to possess a destabilizing potential, threatening to turn tragedy into something other than tragedy. Yet humorous episodes are found in all three tragedians; in Aeschylus and Sophocles they feature lower-class characters (the nurse in *Libation Bearers*, the guard in *Antigone*), whereas in Euripides they tend to center on old men (Iolaus in *Children of Heracles*, Cadmus in *Bacchae*). The scholar who has made the most extensive study of comic effects in tragedy maintains that these effects exist in a fruitful tension with their context that enhances the tragic resonance of the whole (Seidensticker 1982, 244). The validity of this interpretation will emerge if we consider one episode as a test case. (For the doubtful humor of isolated Euripidean lines see Gregory 1999–2000.)

An episode widely and rightly regarded as comic is the arming of Iolaus in Euripides' *Children of Heracles*. Whereas other versions of the myth associate him with Heracles' generation, Euripides' Iolaus is the same age as Alcmene. He is therefore well on in years, and his physical debility receives considerable emphasis at the beginning of the play. When Eurystheus' herald arrives to demand that the Athenians hand back the fugitives, he sneers at the old man's "useless strength" (58) and reviles him as a "tomb" and a "nothing" (167). After Heracles' daughter has been led away as a human sacrifice, Iolaus collapses (602–3). Weakened by grief and age, he fails to recognize Hyllus' servant when that familiar figure arrives to report his master's return at the head of an army (638). Yet this news brings about a decisive shift in Iolaus' mood. He energetically questions the servant about the impending battle between the Athenians and the Argives, then announces that he intends to participate in the fighting (680).

The desire of a superannuated warrior to take up arms is not inherently humorous. Homer uses the motif to set the seal on a victory: at the end of the *Odyssey* Laertes fights valiantly alongside his son and grandson, and Athena gives him the strength to kill his man (24.496–99, 520–25). Later Vergil uses it to enhance the pathos of a lost cause: on Troy's last night both Priam and Anchises express the desire (though both are ultimately dissuaded) to meet their deaths fighting against the Greeks (*Aeneid* 2.509–25, 645–49).

In *Children of Heracles*, however, the motif of the superannuated warrior is deployed with unmistakable humor. To the servant's skeptical questions Iolaus returns absurdly over-confident answers. Finally the servant asks the old man (694) how he can function as a warrior when he has no armor, and Iolaus orders him to borrow the dedicatory weapons that have been deposited inside the temple. It is difficult not to detect a deflating, anti-epic wit in this solution: rather than pin his hopes on armor manufactured by Hephaestus, Iolaus devises a practical, low-cost expedient. The servant has scarcely gone inside than the chorus-leader reproves Iolaus for his unrealistic attitude, telling him flatly, "It is impossible for you to get your youth back again" (707–8). Alcmene also weighs in to reproach Iolaus for abandoning her and the children. When the servant returns with a borrowed panoply the audience is treated to an aborted arming scene whose farcical quality would only be enhanced in performance.

The sequel, however, defies expectations. In a messenger speech the audience and Alcmene are told that a miracle has occurred: Iolaus has been rejuvenated with the help of Zeus, Heracles, and Hebe, the goddess of youth who is Heracles' divine consort. Regaining his youthful strength for a single day, Iolaus has succeeded in capturing Eurystheus, whom he sends back to Alcmene to punish as she likes.

The miracle demonstrates that the audience, the servant, the chorus-leader, and Alcmene were all mistaken in assuming that Iolaus lacked the strength to be effective in battle, whereas the much-maligned Iolaus was in the right. If rejuvenation was a traditional feature of the Iolaus myth (see Allan 2001b, 27), knowledgeable spectators could guess, even as the arming scene took its humorous course, that Iolaus would be vindicated. But even if Iolaus' rejuvenation was invented by Euripides, the spectators would not be confused by the scene's humor. Whether witnessed in the characters or demanded of themselves, the revision of a previous assumption in the light of subsequent events would serve as a generic prompt, for it is nothing other than the late recognition or learning from experience that is a recurrent theme of tragedy (cf. *Agamemnon* 176–83; *Antigone* 1270–72; *Bacchae* 1345; and Silk 1996b, 469). The arming scene becomes the catalyst for a fully tragic response – a response that must be mobilized once more at the end of the play, when Eurystheus proves less and Alcmene more antipathetic than might have been anticipated (for the element of surprise in *Children of Heracles* see Allan 2001b, 185). The humor of the arming scene thus ultimately enhances rather than subverts the tragic tone of the play.

Theatrical and Literary References

Allusions to the chorus and actors as inhabiting the world of the theater, or to the audience as spectators of a play, are now acknowledged to have a place in tragedy as well as comedy (Easterling 1991, Marshall 1999–2000; for the opposite view see Taplin 1986). These allusions include choral references to their own singing and dancing (Henrichs 1994–95) and direct address to the audience (see Sommerstein 1989 on *Eumenides* 1039 and 1047). There are also fleeting remarks that could be taken either way, as when Sophocles' Electra appears to allude to the unchanging expression of her tragic mask (*Electra* 1309–11). Euripides appears to be unique, however, in incorporating critical comments on another playwright's treatment of the same myth into his plays. In *Phoenician Women* (751–52) Eteocles criticizes as ill-timed the description of the shields that forms the centerpiece of Aeschylus' *Seven against Thebes*, and in *Electra* (524–44) Electra finds fault with the tokens that figure in the recognition scene of Aeschylus' *Libation Bearers*.

From the perspective of the playwright, these references are another manifestation of the pervasive intertextuality of tragedy. All the tragedians are in constant dialogue with the literary tradition, above all with epic, and they regularly evoke that tradition in a spirit that can be either laudatory or critical. It is only to be expected that they should also enter into dialogue with their fellow tragedians. In the scenes from *Phoenician Women* and *Electra*, Euripides makes explicit the implicit critique that is involved in rewriting a scene handled differently by another poet.

From the perspective of the audience, references to the theatrical context "need not be in any way disruptive of a play's serious atmosphere" (Easterling 1991, 56). It is a requirement of successful theatrical viewing that the spectators experience a play on several levels simultaneously; they cannot be so immersed in the action unfolding before them that they forget they are watching a play, nor so detached that they fail to be moved by what is taking place on stage (see Lada 1996 and Marshall 1999–2000, 330 and 340–41). There is no reason why a theatrical reference – oblique or overt, fleeting or developed – should disrupt the dramatic illusion, for that illusion was not total to begin with. Members of the audience who caught Euripides' references on the wing could presumably enjoy them with no sacrifice of emotional involvement.[5]

What happens when a play becomes a tissue of literary allusions? Such is the case with *Orestes*. One scholar has argued influentially that in *Orestes* Euripides reaches "a new level of self-consciousness and authorial extravagance that does not seem to have existed before" and that with its reminiscences of Stesichorus, Aeschylus, Sophocles, Homer, and Euripides himself the play conveys a "self-conscious awareness of a tradition which has reached the end of its organic development" (Zeitlin 1980, 51). While intertextuality is indeed a prominent strain in *Orestes*, it is possible to put another construction on it. Euripides invokes the tradition as a foil to his own serious and coherent exploration of Orestes' madness, as the allusions to Stesichorus and Aeschylus will serve to demonstrate.

When Orestes in an access of madness asks Electra to hand him "the horn bow, Loxias' gift, with which Apollo told me to ward off the [dread] goddesses" (268–69), the scholiast tells us that Euripides here follows Stesichorus, who in his own version of the myth had Apollo give Orestes a bow, and adds that actors of his own day played the scene without a bow. It seems to me probable that the actor in Euripides' day did the same, and that Euripides is making the point that for his Orestes, as opposed to Stesichorus', the bow is imaginary (for other views see Porter 1994, 301 n. 13).

Euripides plays off the Aeschylean tradition of Orestes' madness to make a similar point. The Aeschylean Orestes was driven mad by his fear of real, objective Furies (*Libation Bearers* 1448–50). For Euripides' Orestes, however, the Furies are imaginary; as Electra tells him, "You see none of the things you think you're so clear about" (259). Orestes himself believes that he has been driven mad by the "consciousness" of his crime (*sunesis*, 396), but the chorus describes Orestes' murder of his mother as itself an act of madness, "the delusion of wrong-thinking men" (*kakophronón ... andrón paranoia*, 824). Indeed, delusion has long been Orestes' companion: he admits to uncertainty that it was Apollo who ordered the matricide, as opposed to one of his own (private) demons (1668–69).

Not for the first time, Euripides' interpretation of a myth has been influenced by contemporary thought. The Hippocratics denied that illnesses such as epilepsy were divinely caused (*On the Sacred Disease* 1), and in *Orestes* Euripides experiments with a similar explanation for his hero's madness. Despite this striking innovation, the play remains faithful to the literary tradition in one crucial respect. It keeps returning to a fundamental aspect of Orestes' situation that was already articulated in *Libation Bearers* (930, 1016–17): the fact that killing his mother was at once right and wrong (*Orestes* 194, 546–47, 819, 824). Driven by his demons, Orestes wanders so far from his mythical destiny that Apollo must intervene to bring him back.

It does not follow, however, that Euripides is out to demonstrate the bankruptcy of the tradition.

Throughout the fifth century tragedy was a "living and changing genre" (Mastronarde 1999–2000, 27). Phrynichus, Aeschylus, and Sophocles introduced major changes (plays on historical subjects, the addition of the second actor, the addition of the third actor); Euripides made innovations on a smaller scale that have impressed some critics as cumulatively leading to a radical change of direction. This view does not, however, factor in the playwright's reputation up to the nineteenth century, the distortions produced by relying on Aristophanes, the range of Aeschylean and Sophoclean tragedy as suggested by their fragments, and the conservative aspects of Euripides' own work. The account I have sketched of Euripidean drama suggests a playwright who did not hesitate to introduce contemporary topics into his plays and to make variations on theatrical conventions, but who never ceased to respect and cherish the tragic tradition that he inherited and also did so much to shape. We would be well advised to follow the lead of Euripides' own contemporaries, including Aristophanes, and to take all three dramatists into account when defining the range of Attic tragedy – a genre that is characterized (as Wilamowitz knew) by its fundamental seriousness, and that is sturdy and flexible enough to accommodate Aeschylus' *Eumenides* and Euripides' *Orestes* as well as Sophocles' *Oedipus the King*.

NOTES

Many thanks to Martin Cropp, Paula Debnar, and Donald Mastronarde for their comments on earlier versions of this chapter.

1 For the parodies see Collard, Cropp, and Lee 1995, 18–19. The visual evidence for the play's popularity is more difficult to assess, since vase-paintings referring to the Telephus myth do not necessarily allude to tragic versions of that myth (see Small, chapter 7 in this volume).

2 The ten tragedies are *Alcestis, Medea, Hippolytus, Andromache, Hecuba, Trojan Women, Orestes, Phoenician Women, Bacchae,* and the spurious *Rhesus,* which is discussed by Cropp, chapter 17 in this volume.

3 Thus Aristotle recounts what Euripides said to Hygiaenon, who "accused him of impiety because of his line advocating perjury, 'My tongue swore, but my mind was unsworn.' Euripides replied that [Hygiaenon] did wrong to bring into the law courts trials from the Dionysiac contest" (*Rhetoric* 1416a29).

4 They are: *Alcestis* (438), *Medea* (431), *Hippolytus* (428), *Trojan Women* (415), *Helen* (412), *Phoenician Women* (409), *Orestes* (408), *Bacchae* (ca. 407; produced posthumously), and *Iphigenia at Aulis* (ca. 407; produced posthumously).

5 This notion can perhaps be illustrated by an analogy from opera. Few, I think, would deny that *Don Giovanni* is the darkest opera Mozart ever wrote, or would describe it as a work that signals the exhaustion of the operatic genre. Yet in the finale of Act II Mozart sees fit to indulge in a sly in-joke at the expense of himself as well as his contemporaries. Don Giovanni has invited the marble statue of the Commandante to dinner, and as he begins his meal the musicians strike up three tunes. First Mozart quotes passages from two minor

composers of his own time, and then he quotes from his own *Marriage of Figaro*, at which point Leporello comments, "That's a tune I've heard once too often!" Anyone who caught the joke must have cherished it as a pungent counterpoint to the tragic denouement. I thank Professor Peter Bloom of the Smith College Music Department for drawing this example to my attention.

FURTHER READING

The standard Greek edition of Euripides is J. Diggle's Oxford Classical Text (three volumes, 1984–94). D. Kovacs' six-volume bilingual edition and translation of Euripides (1994–2004) provides ready access to the plays. Kovacs' text is attentive to Diggle's but not dependent on it, and the translation is both readable and reliable.

There is no comprehensive, up-to-date book that can serve as an introduction to Euripides; the best approach, accordingly, is through articles. Seventeen classic essays, some translated into English for the first time, are assembled in Mossman 2003. The best overview of contemporary perspectives on the playwright is *Euripides and Tragic Theatre in the Late Fifth Century* (Cropp, Lee, and Sansone 1999–2000). Traditional, revisionist, and intermediate viewpoints are represented in the volume's twenty-five essays, and the bibliography is generous and wide-ranging. In addition to the standard commentaries, notable book-length studies of individual plays are Winnington-Ingram 1997 (*Bacchae*), Croally 1994 (*Trojan Women*), Mossman 1995 (*Hecuba*), and Allan 2000 (*Andromache*).

For more on topics discussed in this chapter: ancient testimonia on Euripides' life and reputation are collected and translated in Kovacs 1994. Heath 1987a (reprinted in Mossman 2003) is a model study of one play's reception. Behler 1986 and Henrichs 1986 address Euripides' reputation in the nineteenth century. Mastronarde 2002b, 81–108, is an excellent introduction to the structure, language, and meter of tragedy, with particular attention to Euripides. For the dating of Euripides' plays using the criterion of resolution see Cropp and Fick 1985. For Euripides' lyric style see Breitenbach 1934, Barlow 1971, and Hose 1990–91. On Euripidean prologues see Erbse 1984, on *agónes* see Lloyd 1992, and on rhetoric see Collard 1975b and Buxton 1982. On stagecraft see Bain 1977 and Halleran 1985. De Romilly 1980 examines pathos in all three dramatists, and O'Connor-Visser 1987 studies Euripides' voluntary sacrificial victims. For a collection and analysis of Euripidean passages reflecting fifth-century intellectual currents see Egli 2003, and for women in Euripidean drama see Harder 1993 and Foley 2001.

CHAPTER SEVENTEEN

Lost Tragedies: A Survey

Martin Cropp

Aeschylus, Sophocles, and Euripides between them composed nearly a quarter of the plays staged at the fifth-century Dionysia, each competing nearly once in every two years of his career. A few other playwrights accounted for many of the remaining productions: Aeschylus' older contemporaries Choerilus, Phrynichus, and Pratinas; his son Euphorion and nephew Philocles; Aristarchus of Tegea, Neophron of Sicyon, Ion of Chios, Achaeus of Eretria, and Sophocles' son Iophon. Tragedy, it seems, was something of a closed shop. Its poets needed to be multitalented; only three could produce each year at the City Dionysia (and from the 430s two at the less prestigious Lenaea), and production was subject to high expectations from audiences, magistrates, and *chorégoi*, all conscious of the festival's religious and civic importance. The craft ran in families: Phrynichus, Pratinas, Aeschylus, and Sophocles all had tragedian sons (Polyphrasmon, Aristias, Euphorion, Iophon), Sophocles a tragedian grandson (Sophocles II), and Aeschylus' nephew Philocles was succeeded by two sons, a grandson, and two great-grandsons. Sons might collaborate or compete with their fathers (Iophon apparently did both), and might produce their fathers' plays posthumously, as did Aristias and Euphorion (as well as another son of Sophocles, Ariston, and Euripides' nephew Euripides). Apart from Agathon and perhaps Critias toward the end of the period, the other thirty or so fifth-century tragedians on record are now known only in a dozen play-titles and a couple of dozen lines of verse, and even for those just named the remains are pitifully small. Any account of fifth-century tragedy must inevitably be dominated by the three great trend-setters.

Evidence for lost tragedies falls loosely into five main types. First, fragmentary play-texts appear amongst the remains of ancient books, especially papyrus-texts rediscovered in modern times in the Egyptian semidesert. Secondly, since such texts were widely read and studied throughout antiquity, they figure in a great variety of other surviving texts – the parodies of Aristophanes, commentaries preserved amongst the papyri and in the margins of medieval manuscripts, quotations by literary authors such as Plutarch and Athenaeus, anthologies of well-known sayings, and a host of handbooks, encyclopedias, and grammar-books embodying hundreds of years of ancient scholarship. Thirdly, ancient summaries of the plays' narrative content (hypotheses) are preserved in some medieval manuscripts, and collections of them figure amongst the papyri and underlie some of the narratives in ancient mythological handbooks such as the *Library* of Apollodorus and the *Fabulae* of Hyginus. Fourthly, Latin tragedians of the republican period sometimes reproduced Greek models more or less closely – though the value of this now is limited as the Latin works themselves survive only in tenuous fragments. Lastly, there was a rich tradition of representing, or at least recalling, scenes from tragedy in art, especially painted pottery (durable and widespread), wall-paintings (now almost entirely lost), mosaics, and figured sculptures. (The relationship between artworks and dramatic texts and productions is now vigorously debated: see Small, chapter 7 in this volume.)

This sketch glosses over the many byways, complications, and problems that arise in assembling information about the lost works. Even in the best cases it is not possible to reconstruct a plot completely, let alone all of a play's significant detail. Many plays are known largely through isolated quotations preserved for purposes that had nothing to do with the study of the plays themselves. Sophocles' *Phaedra*, which handled the same story as Euripides' *Hippolytus* and Seneca's *Phaedra*, is known through seventeen such fragments comprising twenty-six lines, and Euripides' first *Hippolytus* is barely better served. The eighty-four fragments of Ion of Chios, more numerous than those of any other lost tragedian, include fifty-four words or phrases found in ancient reference works and twenty snippets from Athenaeus' conversational miscellany *Deipnosophistai*. The surviving information nevertheless serves to provide some context for the extant plays and broaden our understanding of tragedy as a genre.

Early Tragedy

A commemorative inscription of the third century BCE seems to have listed at most eight poets, and possibly as few as four, who won tragic victories at the Dionysia before Aeschylus, and three whose first victories fell between those of Aeschylus (484) and Sophocles (468). The latter are the virtually unknown Euetes and "—ippus" (Nothippus?), and Phrynichus' son Polyphrasmon. The lost names before Aeschylus must have included Choerilus, Phrynichus, and Pratinas. According to later tradition, tragedy was in some sense established at Athens in the late 530s, but there may have been no official competition, or records, before the first years of the democracy, and earlier recorded "facts" may be fourth-century factoids. The traditional inventor of tragedy was Thespis, who was supposed to have added a speaking part for an actor or "respondent" (*hupokritēs*) to what had previously been narrative choral performances. Aristotle's *Poetics* adds that Aeschylus introduced a second actor and Sophocles a third. These assertions probably reflect at least an underlying truth that tragedy developed out of choral performance through the successive introductions of a first, a second, and a third actor, and that one-actor tragedy was the norm until or beyond the beginning of Aeschylus' career in the early 490s. Apart from this there is little usable information about Thespis: four play-titles which might possibly be genuine (*Pelias' Funeral Games or Phorbas, Priests, Youths, Pentheus*), and five fragments probably from plays forged under his name in the late fourth century. Choerilus is hardly more substantial, with one title (*Alope*), two fragments comprising riddling phrases, and a tradition that he produced 160 plays, won thirteen prizes (possibly a record-based detail), and competed from the 520s to perhaps as late as the 460s. The first non-Athenian tragedian appears to have been Pratinas of Phlius, a versatile composer and choreographer who probably died before 467, when a production of his plays by his son Aristias, including *Perseus*, *Tantalus*, and a satyric *Wrestlers*, came second to Aeschylus' Theban tetralogy. None of his few surviving fragments is likely to be from a tragedy.

For the better-attested Phrynichus, the record shows a first victory between 511 and 508 and (more reliably) another in 476 with a production financed by the politician Themistocles. His son Polyphrasmon won his first prize in or about 471. Ten plays are known by title, and two dozen brief fragments give substance to four of them. *Alcestis* anticipated Euripides' treatment of the story, including Apollo's trading of Alcestis for Admetus and Death's appearance to claim her. *Pleuronian Women* may have concerned the suicide of Althaea after she had burned the brand on which her son Meleager's life depended. More notable than these, however, are two or three recorded tragedies that dramatized contemporary events. *Phoenician Women* was apparently the model for Aeschylus' *Persians*, and was probably part of Phrynichus' winning production in 476. The hypothesis to Aeschylus' play says that *Phoenician Women* began with a eunuch preparing for a council meeting following the news from Salamis, and this suggests a setting in the royal capital with a chorus of councilors, whereas the play's title indicates a chorus of Phoenician women and a setting in the naval base of Sidon. Perhaps the eunuch-scene belonged to a different play known as *Just Men or Persians or Councilors* (unless, as some scholars suppose, all four titles refer to a single play). At any rate, here are one or two plays about a recent event, and the earlier *Capture of Miletus* has the added distinction of being about a Greek rather than a Persian disaster, the capture and depopulation of Miletus by the Persians, which ended the Ionian revolt in 494. Our information about this tragedy comes from Herodotus (6.21), who implies that it was produced soon after the disaster and says that the Athenians were so upset by it that they fined Phrynichus "for calling to mind troubles that were their own [*oikeia kaka*]," and banned further "use" of the play (which may mean reuse of Phrynichus' material rather than reperformance: Mülke 2000). This anecdote has provoked endless speculation about Phrynichus' reasons for choosing the subject and the Athenians' reasons for condemning it, but it may be simply that the playwright's sympathetic commemoration of a terrible event proved too painful for an Athenian audience that felt strong ties with the doomed city. The episode provides a revealing insight into the emotional power of tragedy even in its early days, and it helps to explain why the tragedians generally avoided contemporary subjects. Apart from the plays about Salamis, no other such play is recorded.[1]

Any generalization about the early form and style of tragedy relies essentially on extrapolation from Aeschylus' surviving plays. Later recollections emphasized the distinction and variety of its music and choreography, and the fragments suggest that Aeschylus' elevated and abstruse poetic diction was characteristic of early tragedy. So perhaps were the dramatization of ritual forms and human interactions with the divine or supernatural, which we see in *Persians*, *Libation Bearers*, and *Eumenides* (cf. Mastronarde, chapter 20 in this volume). Later sources such as Aristotle's *Poetics* and the anonymous *Life of Aeschylus* credit Aeschylus with major advances in dramatic form, including the second actor, "reducing" tragedy's choral elements, and "giving the leading role to *logos*," that is, to the spoken word delivered by actors. Such schemata should not be pushed too far, but the broad picture is consistent and plausible. Aeschylus' *Persians, Seven against Thebes,* and *Suppliants* are two-actor plays with a simple development and a chorus closely connected with a primary character (respectively queen, king, and father), no doubt played by the first actor (who would also have played the returning king at the end of *Persians*). The chorus, or chorus and primary character together, propound and discuss the dramatic situation, and react to new events and information. *Persians* and *Suppliants*, uniquely in extant fifth-century tragedy, begin with the chorus's entrance. In *Persians* and *Seven against Thebes* the second actor (Messenger and Ghost of Darius; Scout and Messenger) merely brings new information, whereas in *Suppliants* he participates in the dramatic action (Pelasgus; Egyptian herald); but in all three plays interaction between the two actors is very limited. From such characteristics and their gradual attenuation one can plausibly posit an earlier one-actor form in which a chorus awaited the outcome of a crisis while explaining its background to the audience (*parodos* and *stasimon*), news of the outcome was brought by an actor (report-speech and perhaps question-and-answer dialogue), and its impact provoked displays of sorrow or joy, perhaps accompanying a procession or tableau. The emotional profile is anxiety and suspense, then shock (or relief), then sorrow (or joy). (On this "dynamic structure" see West 1990b, 3–25.) What one-actor drama presumably lacked was the elaboration and complication of these ingredients through debate and emotional conflict, deception and persuasion, surprise and changes of mind, conveyed largely through the discourse of individual characters. Another kind of elaboration was the linking of the plays in a production in a narratively connected tetralogy, which is particularly associated with Aeschylus. There is no evidence that his practice was at all widely imitated; in his time only Polyphrasmon's Lycurgus tetralogy is recorded, coming third behind Aeschylus' Theban tetralogy in 467.

Aeschylus

From Aeschylus we have about sixty tragedy-titles (Sommerstein 1996, 28–30), but how many comprised tetralogies remains unclear. Certain instances are the Theban tetralogy of 467, the Danaid tetralogy of (probably) the late 460s, the *Oresteia* of 458 (all surveyed by Saïd, chapter 14 in this volume), and an undated Lycurgus tetralogy (see below). The plays of 472 (*Phineus, Persians, Glaucus of Potniae, Prometheus Fire-Kindler*) appear to have been unconnected. Scholars have with more or less confidence assigned most of the other recorded titles to tetralogies concerning, for example, Prometheus, Ajax's suicide and its aftermath, Odysseus' return to Ithaca, Jason and the Argonauts in Lemnos, or the later stages of the Theban saga. The extended epic narratives that provided much of tragedy's material (see Anderson, chapter 8 in this volume) certainly invited adaptation in connected plays. Nearly two-thirds of Aeschylus' tragedies involved episodes from the Trojan War, the Returns, and the legends of Thebes, Argos, the Argonauts, Perseus, and Heracles.

The climactic events of *Iliad* 16–24 may well have been treated in a trilogy comprising *Myrmidons, Nereids,* and *Phrygians or Hector Ransomed. Myrmidons* began with a crisis conveyed in the chorus's urgent pleas to Achilles (fr. 131–32) as the Trojans invaded the Achaeans' camp and began to burn their ships. Achilles sat silently, nursing his anger against Agamemnon and ignoring entreaties to return to the battle (such "Aeschylean" silences are known largely from Aristophanes' mockery in *Frogs* 911–20), and successive scenes may have featured individual entreaties (recalling the embassy in *Iliad* 9). A papyrus fragment seems to give the moment when Achilles has finally responded to an appeal from his old tutor Phoenix – but he will relent only when Patroclus begs to fight in his place. Several more fragments come from a later scene where Antilochus has returned with Patroclus' body and Achilles laments in remorseful and notably homoerotic terms, calling for armor so that he may reenter the battle and avenge him. The story probably continued in *Nereids* (unless *Nereids* followed *Phrygians* and concerned Achilles' death, as West 2000 suggests), with Thetis and a chorus of her sister sea-nymphs bringing Achilles' new armor from Hephaestus, Achilles reentering the battle and killing Hector, and the preparations for Patroclus' burial as Hector's body lay untended. Certainly in *Phrygians* Priam visited Achilles to ransom the body; a notable fragment (fr. 266) probably comes from a speech in which Hermes admonished Achilles to respect it, and Achilles then sat silently once again as Priam arrived with a chorus of Trojans in an extensive *parodos*. Later Priam weighed out a ransom of Hector's weight in gold in a striking realization of Achilles' words to the dying Hector (*Iliad* 22.351). This trilogy may have been produced as early as the 480s, although the relevant vase-painting evidence is disputed; the textual evidence suggests a dramatization reflecting the Homeric narrative quite closely and using a fairly static two-actor technique, Achilles being the focal character throughout.

Another likely Trojan War trilogy recalls the lost epic *Aethiopis*. In *Memnon* and *Psychostasia* (*The Weighing of Souls*) the Ethiopian hero Memnon, son of the dawn-goddess Eos, arrived to aid Troy and met his death at Achilles' hands. Scarcely any text survives, but *Psychostasia* remained famous for its name-scene in which the souls of Memnon and Achilles were weighed against each other by Zeus to determine which should die (on the staging here see Mastronarde, chapter 20 in this volume). Memnon was immortalized by Zeus at his mother's request, and his transportation to heaven must have been staged in some way at the end of the play, although the mechanical crane may not have been available in the original performance. The third play might be a *Phrygian Women* (about the death of Achilles) or, preceding the other two, *Carians or Europa* which was set in Lycia and concerned the death of Sarpedon at Patroclus' hands (*Iliad* 16). A papyrus fragment probably from its prologue (fr. 99) has Sarpedon's mother Europa recalling her abduction from Sidon by Zeus in the form of a bull and the birth in Crete of her sons Minos, Rhadamanthys, and – her present concern – Sarpedon. Sarpedon's final battle must have been reported to her, and the play culminated with the spirits Sleep and Death bringing his body home to Lycia for burial. *Carians* had much in common with *Persians*: a mother awaiting news of her son's campaign, disaster reported, the vanquished or slain son returning.

Aeschylus' *Lycurgeia* treated Dionysian themes, its first and best-known play *Edonians* telling the story of Lycurgus, ruler of the region around Mount Pangaeus (an area of lively interest to Athens as a source of gold, silver, and timber). Lycurgus incurred divine punishment by trying to suppress the worship of Dionysus, and a play comparable with Euripides' *Bacchae* can be roughly reconstructed from the fragments and other evidence. It began by portraying Lycurgus' resistance to the god in the songs of the arriving chorus of elders and their dialogue with the unheeding king. Then Lycurgus faced the "captured" Dionysus (fr. 59. 61–62; West suggests a further confrontation with Dionysus' prophet Orpheus, fr. 60), and an earthquake liberated the god, manifesting his power (fr. 58). In the climax (reported from within the palace) Lycurgus was deluded by Dionysus into seeing his son Dryas ("Tree-Man") as a vine, and cut him down with an axe. Finally Lycurgus was perhaps taken away to Mount Pangaeus, to live on as a cave-oracle of Dionysus. The story of Dionysus in Thrace continued in *Bassarae*, with Orpheus killed by the god's female worshippers after turning to the worship of the sun-god Apollo; but the dramatic content must largely be guessed at (cf. West 1990b, 32–46), and there is even less evidence for the third tragedy *Neaniskoi* (*Youths*) or the satyr-play *Lycurgus*.

Plays about Dionysus at Thebes probably formed another tetralogy: *Semele or Hydrophoroi* (*Water-Bringers*) about the god's birth there; *Xantriae* (*Wool-Carders*) about the wool-working women of Thebes driven to maenadism by the arriving god; *Pentheus* or *Bacchae* (perhaps alternative titles for one play) about the destruction of the young King Pentheus, and the satyr-play *Trophoi* (*Nurses*) about the god's impact on the satyrs and nymphs who protected him as a baby. In a papyrus-fragment probably from *Semele* (fr. 158 – though it includes lines attributed by an ancient source to *Xantriae*), a choral celebration of Semele's relationship with Zeus is followed by the arrival of the jealous Hera, disguised as a wandering priestess and offering blessings from the river-nymphs of Argos, patrons of brides and childbirth. Hera will presumably persuade Semele to bring about her own destruction, and the new god's birth, by asking Zeus to visit her in his true form. In *Xantriae*, Aeschylus introduced the goddess of madness, Lyssa, as a speaking character, as Euripides later did in *Heracles*.

Divine chastisement of human transgressions was a fundamental tragic motif (discussed by Anderson and Mastronarde, chapters 8 and 20 in this volume) and the topic of several other Aeschylean plays including *Callisto*, *Toxotides* (*Archeresses*, about Actaeon), *Heliades* (*Daughters of the Sun*, about Phaethon), *Glaucus of Potniae* (devoured by his own man-eating horses), and the slightly better-known *Niobe*. In *Iliad* 24 Achilles recalls the slaughter of Niobe's children by Apollo and Artemis, offended by her disparagement of their mother Leto, and Niobe's transformation into an eternally weeping crag on Mount Sipylus in her homeland of Lydia. Aeschylus set his play after the children's deaths, and it opened with an "Aeschylean" silence as Niobe sat grieving continually by her children's tombs. In a papyrus fragment (fr. 154a) her nurse or another character describes the situation to the chorus, apparently suggesting that Tantalus will come to take her home to Lydia, and reflecting that Niobe was foolishly tempted by her own good fortune to insult the gods. Niobe probably resisted pleas to overcome her grief before finally responding to her father and leaving with him for Lydia. The book-fragments include his reflections on the transience of his wealth and fortune and the intransigence of death (fr. 158–59, 161) and Niobe's bitter recollection of her family's kinship with the gods (fr. 162). We cannot tell if Niobe became reconciled to her sorrow, nor whether the play emphasized factors that might have aggravated her offence, such as her friendship with Leto (Sappho fr. 142 Lobel and Page) or the infamous dinner offered by Tantalus to the gods. But it looks as if this play anticipated Euripides' *Trojan Women* and *Heracles* in focusing on a victim's embittered reactions to an overwhelming affliction that is just by divine standards yet at least disproportionate. Both *Trojan Women* and the conclusion of *Heracles* feature their central characters prostrate and numbed by misfortune; and in *Republic* 2 Plato counts both Niobe's punishment and the destruction of Troy as topics which the tragic poets ought not to have represented as examples of divine malevolence.

While the tragedians generally avoided contemporary subjects, they did not hesitate to reflect contemporary issues in mythical plots, as Aeschylus did in the extant *Eumenides*. *Women of Aetna* was a special case of this kind, commissioned by the Syracusan ruler Hieron I to celebrate the settlement of Aetna in 476/75 BCE (a short-lived replacement for the Ionian city of Catana, which he had depopulated). The story was probably invented to provide mythical reinforcement for Hieron's dominance over his Greek competitors and the indigenous Sicel peoples. The only significant fragment (fr. 6) features the birth of the Palici, twin local gods identified as sons of Zeus by the local nymph Thaleia (Bounty), a daughter of the volcano-god Hephaestus, who bore them beneath the gas-vented Lake of the Palici while hiding from Hera's jealousy. A papyrus hypothesis-fragment shows that the play's action moved between the regions of Mount Etna, Leontini, and Syracuse. It has therefore often been thought of as a loosely related set of mythical or historical tableaux, but it may well have been a coherent drama focusing on Thaleia's disappearance, a search by the chorus of her sister-nymphs (hence the scene changes), and the birth of her sons, all accompanied by appropriate aetiologies for the foundation of Aetna and the cults and institutions Hieron wished to appropriate.

Sophocles

Sophocles remains the most elusive of the three great tragedians. Ancient sources mention 113 or 123 plays produced in a career of over sixty years, and more than 120 titles can be listed, including perhaps a few duplicates (Radt 1991, 85–87; Lloyd-Jones 1994–96, 3: 4–9). But only about eight hundred complete lines or adjacent half-lines survive from his tragedies, and only three dozen fragments run to more than four lines. The only extensive tragic papyrus fragments, from *Eurypylus*, yield a hundred lines offering some kind of sense, but this play is otherwise almost totally unknown. The only dated lost play is *Triptolemus* (placed, by a casual remark of the elder Pliny, in 468, the year of Sophocles' first, or at least first prize-winning, Dionysia production; there is also a confusing papyrus scrap recording a production of Sophocles in the same competition as Aeschylus' Danaid tetralogy). In no case can we say which plays were produced with which. Yet Sophocles clearly played a pivotal role in developing the scope and design of tragedy, anticipating at least to some degree what may at first sight look like Euripides' innovations. As Ruth Scodel points out in this volume (chapter 15), our impression of Sophocles has been distorted by the labels "classic" and "conservative." On closer inspection his drama seems to have embraced the conservative and the innovative, the classic and the eccentric, just as his poetic style could seem elegant and Homeric to Dionysius of Halicarnassus, but extravagant and Pindaric to Longinus.

Sophocles both followed and diverged from Aeschylean subjects (Radt 1991). He relied heavily on Trojan War material (well over thirty tragedies, even without the Returns), but generally avoided simple reworking; only six plays show duplications of Aeschylus' Trojan plots (*Telephus, Iphigenia, Palamedes, Memnon/Ethiopians, Ajax,*

Philoctetes, perhaps also *Phrygians*). Many others explored episodes from the cyclic epics, some quite incidental and not obviously "tragic." On the other hand, he used a Dionysiac subject only once (one of two obscure *Athamas* plays), favored the legends of Mycenae (*Tantalus*, *Oenomaus*, *Atreus*, three *Thyestes* plays, *Clytemnestra*, *Iphigenia*, *Hermione*) and the Cretan king Minos (*Polyidus*, *Minos*, *Daedalus*, *Men of Camicus*), and helped to shape an Athenian mythology with *Triptolemus*, *Aegeus*, *Theseus*, *Ion/Creusa*, *Procris*, and *Phaedra*. Heracles appears first as a tragic figure in Sophocles' *Women of Trachis*, and his birth story may have been the subject of *Amphitryon*.

Sophoclean drama concentrated on the formation of tragic events, preparing and amplifying their impact through twists and turns of decision and action, revelations of latent truths, limitations and changes in the characters' awareness of their circumstances. Thus where Aeschylus' *Niobe* featured a static Niobe reacting to her children's deaths, Sophocles' *Niobe* (known through a fragmentary hypothesis and papyrus-fragments from its climactic scene) dramatized Niobe's initial provocation and its fatal consequences. At the outset Niobe was shown boasting about her sons' excellence while sending them off on a hunting trip – exemplifying her offence as Hippolytus does in conversation with the servant in Euripides' play. The climax came in three stages: first a messenger reported the killing of Niobe's sons by Apollo in the country, then their father Amphion wildly challenged Apollo to combat and was killed by him (also a messenger-report?), and finally the audience saw Artemis standing with Apollo on the palace-roof and shooting down Niobe's daughters in the palace-yard behind the *skênê* (fr. 441a–44), while the agonized chorus witnessed the massacre and the flight of a girl who, it seems, was to be a lone survivor.

Two Trojan War tragedies illustrate this point further. *The Gathering of the Achaeans* (probably identical with *Syndeipnoi* [*Fellow-Feasters*]) dramatized an episode from the lost epic *Cypria* in which Achilles quarreled with the Greek leaders after arriving late at their gathering on the island of Tenedos before the assault on Troy. According to Sommerstein's reconstruction, Odysseus encouraged Agamemnon to denounce Achilles and exclude him from the leaders' feast, and Achilles' violent reaction threatened to disrupt the expedition until a resolution was effected, perhaps by an intervention of Thetis. This quarrel foreshadowed the famous quarrel of the *Iliad*, dramatizing the conflicts of proud and jealous leaders and their final subordination to the will of the gods. The pattern recalls the extant *Ajax* and *Philoctetes*, and can be seen again in Euripides' *Hecuba* and *Trojan Women* and several of Euripides' lost plays. Similarly too, Sophocles' *Locrian Ajax* focused on the Greek leaders' conduct in victory, dramatizing their dispute over the punishment of the lesser Ajax for his assault on Cassandra, Ajax's denial of guilt and flight to Athena's altar, and the acquittal he secured with a false oath. In the only coherent piece (fr. 10c) of a very disjointed papyrus text, Athena addresses the Greeks with a denunciation of Ajax's crime similar to her speech at the beginning of Euripides' *Trojan Women*. The placing of this scene at the end of the play has been questioned, but since the Greeks could hardly have ignored Athena's condemnation, it must at least have followed their decision to acquit Ajax and permit him to sail for home. Thus the tragedy hinged on their ill-judged decision and the revelation "too late" of the divine punishments awaiting Ajax and those who condoned his crime.

Other plays of Sophocles developed the common tragic topic of familial and dynastic strife. Aeschylus' *Eleusinians*, *Epigoni*, and probably *Women of Argos* had dramatized episodes from the Theban saga, part of which concerned Eriphyle, who was bribed by Polynices to send her husband, the seer Amphiaraus, to a certain death in the campaign of the Seven. Their son Alcmeon led the heirs of the Seven in sacking Thebes, but like Orestes he was required by Apollo to avenge his father by killing his mother. Seeking release from persecution by the Furies, Alcmeon betrayed his wife Alphesiboea and was ultimately killed by her father. Sophocles' *Eriphyle*, *Epigoni*, *Alcmeon*, and satyric *Amphiaraus* could have been a connected tetralogy; the first two have often been considered identical, but *Eriphyle* may well have been about Eriphyle and Amphiaraus, *Epigoni* about Alcmeon's revenge, and *Alcmeon* about his madness. The few fragments of *Epigoni*, supplemented by Accius' derivative Latin *Epigoni*, suggest a large narrative scope including Alcmeon's decision to lead the campaign and accept the matricide as the price of success, and confrontations of Alcmeon with his mother before the killing and Adrastus after it.

Female revenges for male crimes of ambition, greed, or passion were a tragic theme at least from the time of Aeschylus' *Agamemnon*, and Sophocles' *Tereus* stands with Euripides' *Hecuba* and *Medea* as a lurid portrayal of such a revenge, although its chronological relationship with them is uncertain (we know only that it was produced before 414). Sophocles adapted the old myth of the origin of the swallow and the nightingale, making its two female characters Athenians and their persecutor a barbarous Thracian. Tereus, a Thracian king married to the Athenian princess Procne, rapes her sister Philomela while escorting her to Thrace for a visit, and cuts out her tongue to keep her silent. Philomela reveals the crime to her sister in a piece of weaving, and together they punish Tereus by killing his and Procne's son Itys and feeding his flesh to Tereus. As Tereus retaliates, all three become birds – the lamenting nightingale, the voiceless swallow, the reclusive hoopoe. A papyrus hypothesis suggests that in Sophocles' play Philomela was in the palace when she wove the message, not imprisoned in a rustic cabin as in Ovid's telling of the story; thus Tereus may have pretended she had died and brought her into the house disguised as a slave, so that the weaving – like the urn in Sophocles' *Electra* or the letter in Euripides' *Iphigenia among the Taurians* – served to reveal Philomela's identity as well as her mutilation. It may, then, have been Procne's belief that her sister was dead that motivated her famous complaint about married women's exile from their own families (fr. 583), and the consolation offered to her in fr. 585.

Tragedy also embraced the story pattern of the son fated to bring death to his father or ruin to his community, a pattern comprehensively fulfilled in the story of Oedipus, which was handled by Aeschylus, Euripides, Achaeus, Philocles, and others, as well as Sophocles. Sophocles probably preceded Euripides with an *Alexandros* in which Paris, exposed at birth and raised as a slave, proved his nobility in athletic games and was recognized as the son of Priam and Hecuba, and with an *Aegeus* on the story of Theseus' return to Athens, capture of the Marathonian bull, and recognition by his father (perhaps also introducing Medea's plots against Theseus into the story). Other tragedies dramatized the births of gods and heroes who narrowly survived extinction to realize their destinies, and whose mothers suffered tribulations or death (as in Aeschylus' *Semele* and *Women of Aetna*). Heracles' birth and Alcmene's rescue from her husband's wrath were probably treated in Aeschylus' *Alcmene*, Sophocles'

Amphitryon, and Ion's *Alcmene*, as well as Euripides' better-known *Alcmene*. Choerilus' *Alope* presumably anticipated Euripides' *Alope*, the heroine being killed by her father after bearing Poseidon's son Hippothoön, who survived exposure twice to become an Athenian tribal hero. Other such stories were told in Sophocles' and Euripides' *Danae* (the heroine cast out by her father after bearing Zeus' son Perseus) and Euripides' *Auge* (cast out with her son Telephus after being rescued from her father's wrath by her seducer Heracles) and *Wise Melanippe*.

Dramatic sequels reuniting such mothers with their long-lost sons seem to have been a late development and can be illustrated mainly from Euripides, but something can be said of Sophocles' first and second *Tyro*, respectively a hero-birth and a mother–sons reunion drama. The Thessalian princess Tyro's seduction by Poseidon and the birth of her sons Pelias and Neleus were well known from *Odyssey* 11 and the Hesiodic *Catalogue*, and the first *Tyro* probably elaborated this story so that the birth was discovered, the infants abandoned by Tyro in a *skaphê* (probably a basket or cradle) on the river where they had been conceived, and Tyro punished by her father. In the second *Tyro* the twins, saved and raised by a herdsman, rediscovered their mother and rescued her from the persecution of her wicked stepmother Sidero, whom Pelias killed. It was probably the second play that presented Tyro in a special mask showing the bruises on her pale complexion and her beautiful hair shorn like a slave's, and included her striking speech comparing herself with a foal whose mane has been sheared (fr. 659). Some papyrus-fragments (fr. 649 = adesp. fr. 626) probably represent an early scene, with Tyro consoled by a sympathetic chorus as she goes to fetch water to purify Sidero from an ominous dream. This errand presumably led to her meeting her sons and identifying them "by means of the *skaphê*" (*Poetics* 1454b25: one of the twins carries the *skaphê* in later depictions of their meeting at the spring).

Divine *erôs* formed the background of the tragedies just discussed and was a staple of satyr-plays, but did not in itself constitute a subject for tragic plots. *Erôs* between mortals also seems to have been rare in early tragedy, and important only as a contributing factor in the treachery or devotion of wives (Aeschylus' Clytemnestra, Phrynichus' Alcestis), or in the weightier social problems of marriage and procreation (as in Aeschylus' Danaid tetralogy). By contrast, Euripides' explorations of *erôs* are well documented and highly diverse. *Women of Trachis* gives us some sense of how Sophocles contributed to the opening up of this realm, but almost nothing is known of his treatment of Phaedra's fatal love for Hippolytus in *Phaedra*, or the marital devotion of Procris which led to her accidental killing by Cephalus in *Procris*; and while some vivid vase-paintings suggest that his *Andromeda* was produced as early as the 440s and anticipated the exoticism of Euripides' later and more celebrated treatment, the role of *erôs* in the play remains uncertain. As so often, our knowledge of Sophocles' work falls far short of its probable importance.

Euripides

Euripides is much more accessible because of his immense continuing popularity in the ancient world. He was credited with ninety-two plays, including the inauthentic *Rhesus* and the doubtful *Tennes*, *Rhadamanthys*, and *Pirithous*. Nearly a quarter of these were presumably satyr-plays, so the seventeen extant and forty-nine (or fifty-two) fragmentary tragedies now known represent nearly all of his tragic output. Ancient information and papyrus discoveries allow substantial insights into *Telephus* (produced with *Alcestis* in 438), *Phaethon* and *Erechtheus* (both from around 420), *Alexandros* (produced with *Trojan Women* in 415), *Hypsipyle* and *Antiope* (411–17), and the late *Captive Melanippe*. Papyri also supply isolated scenes from *Cretans* (430s?) and *Cresphontes* (mid-420s), and some other plays are fairly well documented, including *Stheneboea, Bellerophon, Philoctetes* (produced with *Medea* and *Dictys* in 431), *Oedipus* (after 415), *Andromeda* (a companion to *Helen* in 412), and *Archelaus* (407?). Most of these, like all the extant plays except *Alcestis*, represent the second half of Euripides' career, from 431 onwards (coincidentally the period of the Second Peloponnesian War).

Euripides' career largely coincided with Sophocles', and there are similarities in his range of tragic subjects (Jouan and Van Looy 1998–2003, 1.xxii–xxxi). He used Trojan War topics more selectively (eight extant plays, plus only *Telephus, Philoctetes, Protesilaus, Alexandros, Palamedes, Scyrians*), was equally sparing with Dionysian plots (only *Ino* and the extant *Bacchae*), treated Heracles' birth and downfall in *Alcmene* and the extant *Heracles*, and like Sophocles favored the legendary history of Mycenae (*Oenomaus, Pleisthenes, Cretan Women, Thyestes*), Crete (*Cretans, Poly-idos*), and Attica (*Alope, Aegeus, Erechtheus, Hippolytus Veiled, Theseus*, with the extant *Hippolytus, Children of Heracles, Suppliants*). About half of his tragedies shared their subjects with Aeschylus and/or Sophocles. For those shared with Sophocles (some twenty-seven) it is often uncertain who composed first. Euripides' *Philoctetes* followed Aeschylus' but preceded Sophocles' extant play (409: we know something of both lost plays from Dio Chrysostom's Orations 52 and 59). The sequence may be the same for Aeschylus' *Libation Bearers* and Euripides' and Sophocles' *Electra*, but Euripides' late *Andromeda, Antigone, Oedipus*, and *Iphigenia at Aulis* must have followed their Sophoclean counterparts, and other plays such as *Aegeus, Alexandros*, and *Ion* very probably did so. For this and other reasons it is not surprising that Euripides seems to have striven for novelty in a variety of ways – formulating new plots, reworking and recombining familiar narrative motifs and characters, modulating between high tragic, "realistic," and romantic modes, and developing stylized dramatic forms such as narrative prologue-speeches, stichomythic dialogues, rhetorical debates, "New Music" arias and choral songs, happy outcomes, and *deus ex machina* conclusions. The fragmentary plays help to illuminate these tendencies, and thus broaden and consolidate our awareness of the range, vitality, and seemingly inexhaustible diversity that gave Euripidean tragedy its lasting appeal.

Dynastic and family strife was, predictably, the basis for many of Euripides' plays, but the evidence is too limited to show whether such plays as *Alcmeon at Psophis* and *Alcmeon at Corinth* (about Amphiaraus' son, as discussed above), *Oeneus* (Diomedes restoring his grandfather to power at Calydon), or the Mycenean plays mentioned above matched the originality of the extant *Andromache, Electra, Orestes*, and *Phoenician Women*. Two other lost plays are interesting examples of tragic mythmaking with a political slant. In *Cresphontes* the Heraclid Cresphontes, rightful ruler of Messenia, had been murdered and his wife Merope stolen by a usurper Polyphontes, and his son Cresphontes, raised in exile with a price on his head, returned to gain vengeance and restoration (two papyri have supplied parts of the opening scenes establishing this situation). Cresphontes came disguised as his own killer, and this led

Merope to try to kill her own unrecognized son. In a celebrated climax she attacked him as he slept but was stayed in the nick of time by a faithful slave, and mother and son then collaborated in assassinating Polyphontes. The play was produced in the 420s when Athens was vigorously promoting resistance to Spartan domination of Messenia, and the plot was probably invented as a contribution to a new Messenian mythology; its adaptation of motifs from the story of Orestes' return is evident. Similarly *Archelaus*, supposedly produced in Macedonia shortly before Euripides' death, added substance to the mythical Greek ancestry of his patron Archelaus, the unsavory but pro-Athenian Macedonian king. It told of an earlier Archelaus, son of the Heraclid Temenus who had settled at Argos. This Archelaus was driven into exile by dynastic strife and fought for the Thracian king Cisseus after being promised his daughter's hand. Cisseus double-crossed him and tried to lure him to his death in a pit filled with burning coals, but Archelaus outwitted the king and threw him into the pit himself – a typical tragic peripeteia, which the play seems to have presented as a triumph of virtue over vice. Archelaus then moved on to Macedonia where he founded the old royal city of Aegeae and established his dynasty.

In contrast to such turbulent stories, tragedies about the "history" of Athens itself (such as Aeschylus' *Eumenides* and Euripides' *Children of Heracles* and *Suppliants*) generally presented an idealized picture. In the lost *Erechtheus*, King Erechtheus and his wife accepted an oracle's command to sacrifice their daughter so as to save their city from an attack by the Thracian king Eumolpus, a son of Poseidon (this version of the story conveniently eliminated the tradition that Eumolpus was from Eleusis and thus virtually an Athenian). The girl's sisters sacrificed themselves in her support, and during the battle Erechtheus vanished into the earth to live on as a hero. The queen's speech recommending her daughter's sacrifice (fr. 360) is quoted as a paradigm of patriotism by the fourth-century orator Lycurgus, and the extensive Sorbonne papyrus gives the ending of the play in which Athena saves her city from destruction by Poseidon's earthquake and the queen's losses are mitigated by Athena's authorization of cults on the Acropolis for Erechtheus and his daughters, now deified as the Hyacinthids (on this scene see Sourvinou-Inwood, chapter 18 in this volume).

We have noted that Aeschylus, Sophocles, and Euripides all used the Trojan War to explore paradigmatic issues of political conduct; four of the eight plots treated by all three of them were set at Troy. Amongst these Sophocles' *Philoctetes* and Euripides' *Iphigenia at Aulis* are extant, and the lost *Telephus* (438) and *Philoctetes* (431) of Euripides are fairly well known, the first especially from Aristophanes' parodies and the second from Dio Chrysostom's literary discussions. Euripides made Telephus' quest for healing from the gathering Greek leaders, in the beggar-disguise which he added to the story, the setting for a provocative debate about the justification of the war on Troy; and the exposure of Telephus led to an equally notable scene (again adapting an established motif) in which he seized the baby Orestes as a hostage and negotiated his healing by Achilles in return for piloting the Greek fleet to Troy. Odysseus here had a positive role, recognizing the sense of an oracle that indicated how the healing of Telephus could be achieved.

Philoctetes, by contrast, was remarkable for its pragmatic and ruthless Odysseus, who opened the play with his reflections on the rewards and perils facing a high-stakes political player such as himself. In this version Odysseus himself, disguised by his patroness Athena, deceived the crippled hero with a story of his own mistreatment by the Greek leaders, but then had to urge Philoctetes to remain loyal to Greece when Trojan envoys arrived seeking his defection. Ultimately Odysseus gained control of Philoctetes by stealing the bow of Heracles – there was no Neoptolemus to relent and return the bow as in Sophocles, and presumably no god to clarify Philoctetes' destiny at the end. A further play in this vein was *Palamedes*, the second play of the Trojan trilogy of 415, which concerned Odysseus' framing of Palamedes as a traitor during the siege of Troy. It featured a trial contrasting Palamedes' promotion of human culture through his many inventions (especially writing: fr. 578) with Odysseus' ruthless manipulations, but it also set Odysseus' short-lived triumph against the destruction of the returning Greek fleet, planned in revenge by Palamedes' brother and father toward the end of the play.

Hippolytus, Heracles, and *Bacchae* dramatized episodes of divine retaliation with full tragic force, throwing divine justice powerfully into question, and the lost *Bellerophon* (probably close in time to *Hippolytus*) seems to have been similar in character, treating the hero's doomed attempt to ascend to heaven on the winged horse Pegasus as a final act of despair or defiance at the end of a life dogged by unexplained ill fortune. Its many book-fragments suggest that throughout the play Bellerophon pondered his life's pattern and debated the gods' influence on it, and after his fall, crippled and close to death, remained as confident of his own righteousness as Hippolytus and Heracles in their name-plays. Still more guiltless was the young Phaethon of *Phaethon*, who was destroyed by Zeus as he tried and inevitably failed to drive his father Helios' sun-chariot across the skies. Euripides' Phaethon makes this attempt not through *hubris* but through inexperience and insecurity as he struggles to accept the assurance of his mother, the Oceanid Clymene, that his father is not her mortal husband King Merops but the sun-god. The play's exotic ambience in the land of the rising sun and its somewhat bizarre events are illustrated in two well-preserved dramatic sequences. The first includes Clymene sending her son to Helios with his fatal request at the end of the prologue-scene, then a picturesque choral *parodos* celebrating the dawn of Phaethon's wedding day, and the start of the first episode with Merops proclaiming the marriage and his ambitions for his son's future. The second gives the aftermath of Phaethon's fall from the sky, as Clymene desperately tries to conceal his smoldering remains and Merops arrives with the wedding party, only to learn of his son's destruction.

Euripides seems to have invented Clymene's marriage with Merops, her need to conceal Phaethon's paternity, and the insecurities that led him to incur his own destruction. Thus Clymene became the focal dramatic figure, speaking the prologue, persuading Phaethon to approach Helios, learning of his death, receiving the body, and facing her husband's wrath (presumably to be saved at the end by a divine intervention). This emphasis on a central female role, and on family tensions relating to sex, childbearing, wedlock, and heredity, is by no means new but is highly characteristic of Euripidean tragedies (as a rough indicator, one-third of them are named after their heroines, compared with one-fifth for Sophocles and one-seventh for Aeschylus). One of the most striking features of Euripides' *Alexandros* (produced with *Palamedes* and *Trojan Women* in 415, and now fairly well known from a papyrus hypothesis and the Strasbourg text-fragments) is the dramatic centrality of Hecuba: her grief for her lost son has moved Priam to establish the games in which Paris triumphs, her hatred for the intrusive "slave" motivates a plot against Paris' life (leading to a climactic recognition and peripeteia, as in *Cresphontes* and *Ion*), and her parental love, together with Priam's, overrides Cassandra's warnings and brings Paris into the royal family with fatal consequences for Troy. In *Oedipus*, again, Jocasta's relationship with Oedipus became more central to the drama: in the Euripidean plot, Oedipus was blinded as the killer of Laius before his incestuous marriage was discovered, but at each juncture Jocasta chose to live on with him (as we see her in *Phoenician Women*), fulfilling her obligations as a loyal wife.

Euripidean heroines are more apt to plan violence than to accomplish it, and brutal actions in the manner of Clytemnestra or Procne are rare – in the extant plays there are only the vengeful barbarians Medea and Hecuba, and Electra who suffers immediate remorse for her part in the killing of Clytemnestra. Medea appeared also in *Peliades* (455) persuading the daughters of Jason's persecutor Pelias to kill their father, and in *Aegeus* (430s?) trying to have Theseus killed by his father before his recognition. Otherwise there is only the bacchant Ino, whose complex story of maenadism and plots against Athamas' children by other wives was treated in three now obscure plays (*Ino* and the first and second *Phrixus*).

Many other heroines are cast more sympathetically – if sometimes still controversially – as victims of their own sexuality, beleaguered mothers of heroic sons, or exiles needing rescue and restoration. The extant *Hippolytus* alleviates the disgrace of Phaedra's passion for her stepson by making Aphrodite impose it in response to Hippolytus' impiety (a neat combination of the tragic motifs of destructive passion and divine retaliation), whereas the lost *Veiled Hippolytus* seems to have made her succumb to temptation more readily and attempt to seduce her stepson herself. This behavior aligns Phaedra with some other heroines in earlier plays of Euripides whose "shameless" conduct and defiantly self-justifying rhetoric became one of Aristophanes' favorite targets and were presumably received with a mixture of shock and fascination by Athens' largely male audiences. From *Cretans* a surviving page gives us most of Pasiphae's speech defending her recently discovered liaison with the bull and blaming the whole affair on her husband Minos' impiety (the outcome here is unfortunately not known). A hypothesis of *Stheneboea* shows that it dramatized the *Iliad*'s story of Stheneboea's failed seduction of Bellerophon and her plot to have him sent against the Chimaera, but enlivened it by having the hero return to Corinth and elope with Stheneboea so that he could throw her to her death from Pegasus' back. The *Odyssey*'s twelve happily intermarried sons and daughters of King Aeolus became the subjects of a tragedy of sexuality in Euripides' *Aeolus*, the incestuous marriages being promoted by the eldest son Macareus because of his love for his sister Canace. Macareus persuaded his father to authorize the marriages, only to see Canace allotted as wife to one of his brothers; this and the discovery of Canace's child by Macareus appear to have led to both their suicides.

Some of Euripides' latest tragedies, such as the extant *Iphigenia among the Taurians* and *Helen*, have sentimental features previously associated with satyr-plays or hybrids such as the prosatyric *Alcestis*. *Helen*'s companion-piece in 412 was *Andromeda*, in which the Ethiopian princess, offered to a sea-monster to appease the wrath of Poseidon, was rescued and claimed in marriage by the hero Perseus. *Andromeda* began with a mournful monody from the heroine, bound to a rock and awaiting her death, which led to sung exchanges with the nymph Echo (echoing her lament) and the chorus (her friends coming to sympathize); then Perseus flew in on the stage-crane carrying the Gorgon's head, instantly fell in love with Andromeda, and promised to kill the monster in return for her hand. The battle was reported in a messenger-speech, and the family's resistance to the marriage debated and finally overcome by an intervention of Athena, who foretold the catasterisms of Perseus, Andromeda, her parents, and the sea-monster. While the story of Andromeda was obviously suitable for this romantic treatment, Euripides' *Antigone* (known sketchily from a couple of ancient comments and some largely gnomic fragments) must have surprised by making Haemon help in the burial of Polynices' body because of his love for Antigone, and by having both of them saved from Creon's death-sentence by an intervention of Dionysus.

One of the most striking features in Euripides' heroine-centered plays was their investigation of sexuality and gender roles through dramatic conflict and rhetorical argument, as for example in the extant *Alcestis*, *Hippolytus*, and *Andromache*. Andromeda's right to promise herself to her rescuer and Haemon's determination to marry the tainted Antigone were the subjects of lively dramatic debates. In *Aeolus* Macareus made a persuasive general case for brother–sister marriage while concealing his own relationship with his sister. His speech was used in later rhetorical teaching as an example of "disguised argument," in which the speaker concealed a special motive for making his case. We have seen Odysseus doing this in *Philoctetes*, and another stock example was Melanippe's speech in *Wise Melanippe*, which is known mainly from a partial summary cited by Byzantine scholars. The remarkable heroine Melanippe, educated by her mother Hippo (daughter of the centaur Chiron) with a knowledge of the natural world and an aptitude for rational argument, was seduced or raped by Poseidon, and hid the resulting twin sons in a stable where they were discovered and threatened with destruction in the superstitious belief that a cow had produced them. A paradoxical "trial" ensued, with Melanippe maintaining that they must be the children of some poor misused girl (other than herself). The outcome of all this is uncertain, but it seems that the truth emerged and the boys' paternity was confirmed by the now deified Hippo, though not before Melanippe had been either cast out along with her sons or blinded and imprisoned while they were exposed.

Melanippe and her sons Aeolus and Boeotus were the subjects of a sequel, *Captive Melanippe*, which is one of several plays – along with Sophocles' second *Tyro*, Euripides' *Iphigenia among the Taurians* and *Helen*, and his lost *Antiope* and *Hypsipyle* – featuring complicated plots, recognitions and reunions, escapes from tribulation and danger, and ultimately happy outcomes. In *Captive Melanippe* the heroine and her sons have been transposed to southern Italy and the sons raised as potential heirs to King Metapontus (founder of the wealthy city of Metapontium) while Melanippe lives as a slave and is persecuted by the childless queen; the queen's plot against the twins leads to the deaths of her own brothers, the queen herself is killed or commits suicide, and the liberated Melanippe probably marries Metapontus while the twins migrate to Aeolia and Boeotia. Similarly in *Antiope* the heroine, mother by Zeus of the twins Amphion and Zethus, escapes from the persecution of her uncle Lycus and his wife Dirce and is by chance reunited with her sons who have been raised as peasants; they kill Dirce as she visits a nearby shrine of Dionysus, and are about to kill Lycus when Hermes intervenes and redirects them toward their destinies: they are to build the citadel of Thebes, while Dirce will become the spirit of one of Thebes' rivers. *Hypsipyle* has the most complicated of these plots: the heroine has borne twin sons to Jason during the Argonauts' visit to her home island of Lemnos, and Jason has taken the boys with him to Colchis; now living in exile and servitude as a nursemaid in the priest's household at Nemea, Hypsipyle allows the priest's son to be killed by a snake that haunts the local sanctuary, and is spared punishment only through the intervention of the seer Amphiaraus, whom she has assisted as he visits the sanctuary; Amphiaraus is marching with the Seven against Thebes, and the boy's death leads them to commemorate him by celebrating the first Nemean Games; Hypsipyle's sons, now adult, also happen to be passing through Nemea in search of their mother, and Hypsipyle learns of their identity when they compete in the games and are announced as victors.

These plays were among Euripides' latest and most popular works, and they remain relatively well documented – so much so that an adequate survey of the fragments and analysis of the plays' various dimensions is hardly possible here. Three general characteristics can however be briefly noted. First, there was an expansive mythical scope and a high degree of mythical and aetiological innovation which was to some extent ideologically motivated – for example, *Hypsipyle* linked Athens with the Nemean Games by connecting Hypsipyle with the Games' foundation myth and stressing the identification of her son Euneos as founder of an Athenian priestly family. Secondly, ethical issues and ethically reflective characters were prominent: the status of women was addressed in *Captive Melanippe* (fr. 494 has a long defense of women's dignity), *Antiope* included a debate between Amphion and Zethus (known especially through quotations in Plato's *Gorgias*) on the choice between intellectual and political lives, *Hypsipyle* presents Amphiaraus' humane defense of Hypsipyle and her piety. Thirdly, the plays were both ethically and emotionally satisfying insofar as gratuitous pain and anguish were avoided, suffering was compensated by good fortune, and a larger purpose was suggested in benevolent divine influences and constructive aetiological outcomes. A similar concern for the ethical impact of tragedy is reflected in Aristotle's *Poetics* and, to some extent, in the remnants of fourth-century tragedy.

Other Fifth-Century Figures

Several other poets made major contributions to tragic theater in the second half of the fifth century, but their contributions cannot be assessed in any detail. Some of their plays continued to be read for centuries (and there is a scattering of evidence for performances), but all were sooner or later eclipsed by the prestige of the three classic tragedians; only circumstantial facts and a handful of fragments remain. Of the hundred plays of Philocles, winner against the production of Sophocles that included *Oedipus the King*, we have eight titles and a single incomplete line. Ion of Chios is better represented, and there is interesting information about his contacts with Athenian politicians and poets and his literary versatility, but nothing that bears on his dramatic technique or his handling of myths. Some insight may come from the fragments of a *Medea* attributed to Neophron of Sicyon (a prolific contemporary of Euripides whose work is otherwise totally lost). Scholars in Aristotle's school saw similarities between this play and Euripides' *Medea*, and inferred that Neophron had anticipated Euripides in bringing Aegeus to Corinth (fr. 1), and in making Medea address her *thumos* in a monologue, torn between vengeance and love for her children (fr. 2). But the similarities are so strong that some scholars think the text in question must have been a later imitation of Euripides' play, wrongly identified as Neophron's.

Equally problematic is the work of Plato's relative Critias, who was killed in the democratic counterrevolution of 403. Critias probably composed a satyr-play *Sisyphus*, source of a much-quoted speech of Sisyphus describing the gods as a human invention (fr. 19: see Allan, chapter 5 in this volume), and this play became confused with the *Sisyphus* that Euripides produced with his Trojan trilogy in 415. There was also some confusion over the tragedies *Tennes*, *Rhadamanthys*, and *Pirithous*, commonly attributed to Euripides but flagged by the Alexandrian *Life of Euripides* as inauthentic; Athenaeus at one point attributes *Pirithous* to "either Critias or Euripides." Many scholars have accepted Wilamowitz's inference that Critias composed *Tennes*, *Rhadamanthys*, *Pirithous*, and *Sisyphus* together as a tetralogy, but the inference is not compelling (as Collard 1995 shows); the basis of the Alexandrian judgment is unknown, and only Athenaeus' ambivalent comment on *Pirithous* links Critias with any of the questioned plays. *Pirithous* dramatized the rescue of Theseus and Pirithous from the underworld by Heracles, who after conquering Cerberus negotiated Pirithous' release from the rock to which he was immovably fastened for attempting (with Theseus) to abduct Persephone. A brief ancient summary quotes a dialogue in which Heracles explains himself to the underworld official Aeacus; book-fragments give parts of a mystical hymn sung by the entering chorus (probably devotees of Persephone), and a papyrus gives parts of dialogues in which Heracles meets Pirithous and learns of his predicament, and declines Theseus' offer of help in his fight with Cerberus. The play is thus of interest for its place in the tradition of poetry about descents to the underworld (including Aristophanes' *Frogs*, which might possibly have used material from it in Dionysus' descent); but the questions of authorship and date remain undecidable.

Another late fifth-century figure, Agathon, appears in his brief career as an innovative successor of Euripides. His successful first production at the Lenaea of 416 is celebrated in Plato's *Symposium*, and remarks in the *Symposium* and Aristophanes' *Frogs* show that he left Athens for the Macedonian court in 407 or 406, where he probably died a few years later. The general character of his work can be inferred from his speech praising *Erôs* in the *Symposium*, from the opening scene of Aristophanes' *Women at the Thesmophoria* (where Euripides tries to get the effeminate Agathon to defend him against the complaints of the women of Athens), and from comments in Aristotle's *Poetics* on his use of episodic dramatic structure and choral songs unrelated to the plot (*embolima*), and on the play *Anthos* (or perhaps *Antheus*), which had a wholly fictitious plot and characters. Agathon followed Euripides in his commitment to verbal dexterity and the antithetical rhetorical style promoted by Gorgias (which several of the thirty brief fragments from his plays illustrate), and to the elaborate New Music which cultural conservatives found offensive (in *Women at the Thesmophoria* Agathon sings a slightly bizarre hymn to Apollo, Artemis, and Leto, on which Euripides' companion comments, in Jeffrey Henderson's translation [1998–2002], "What a pretty song! How feministic and tongue-gagged and deep-kissed!"). Thus Agathon appears to have progressed beyond Euripides in experimenting with an imaginative, aesthetically refined, and musically innovative form of tragedy. But beyond these generalities nothing is known about the substance of any of his plays.

The Fourth Century

Much the same must be said of the following generations, although tragedy clearly continued to be a central feature of Athenian cultural life at least until the disintegration of the democracy under Macedonian pressure in 322. In this period tragedy, which had begun to acquire cosmopolitan status as early as Aeschylus' visits to Sicily, came to be performed in theaters and courts across the Greek world, celebrated in reperformances of the classic repertoire (a contest for performances of "old" tragedies at the Dionysia was established in 386), captured in the vase-paintings of Sicily and southern Italy, and studied and imitated in higher education.

Our access to texts, however, is extremely limited; the only extant fourth-century tragedy is (probably) the *Rhesus* that appears to have replaced Euripides' own *Rhesus* in the Euripidean corpus. This play is based on *Iliad* 10, in which Odysseus and Diomedes kill first the Trojan scout Dolon and then the Thracian king Rhesus, son of a Muse and a river-god, who has recently arrived to aid Troy with his magnificent horses and chariot. It contains some lively nighttime action as Dolon's expedition is planned, Rhesus and his men arrive and are assigned quarters, the two Achaeans reach the Trojan camp after killing Dolon and are guided by Athena to the sleeping Thracians, the slaughter is reported to Hector by Rhesus' wounded charioteer, and the Muse arrives to carry her son's corpse back to Thrace where he will gain renewed life as a prophetic spirit. The unknown author had a fair though erratic grasp of tragic style, but his ability to develop action and characters was limited (the blustering Hector and Rhesus are unengaging as tragic figures), and he seems to have been preoccupied with creating a series of novel episodes which often digress into sterile debates – Hector arguing with Aeneas about strategy, with Rhesus about Rhesus' failure to show up earlier, with the charioteer about the Trojans' responsibility for Rhesus' death, and so on. It would be unfair to take this moderately competent and derivative work as representing the best that fourth-century tragedians could do.

The two decades following the deaths of Euripides and Sophocles and the fall of Athens in 404 are particularly obscure, and only from around 380 do some figures begin to emerge more distinctly through a scattering of production records, comments in Aristotle's *Poetics*, *Rhetoric*, and *Ethics*, later recollections, and an occasional papyrus or vase-painting. These include the younger Astydamas, grandson of Aeschylus' great-nephew Philocles and winner of fifteen festival victories; the younger Carcinus, son of the tragedian Xenocles, who won eleven Dionysia victories and like Plato enjoyed the patronage of the Sicilian dynast Dion; Chaeremon, for whom no exact career details are available; and Theodectas of Phaselis in Lycia, rhetorician and tragedian, who won seven Dionysia victories before his early death and delivered a eulogy of King Mausolus of Caria at the dedication of the Mausoleum in 352/51, as well as composing a tragedy, *Mausolus*. From the hundreds of plays that these four composed, some fifty titles are known (almost all denoting traditional mythical subjects), and about eighty-five short fragments.

A few plays admit some degree of speculative reconstruction (surveyed by Xanthakis-Karamanos 1980), the two most substantial cases being Astydamas' *Hector* (probably the source of a Latin *Hector Setting Forth* by Naevius) and Chaeremon's *Achilles Slayer of Thersites*. Astydamas' play dramatized Hector's final battle with Achilles from the Trojan point of view, and is probably represented by three papyri and a short book-fragment which give sixty-five lines from several scenes. The Trojans anticipate Achilles' renewed attack, his approach is reported and Hector prepares to arm himself, Hector removes his helmet to converse with Andromache and Astyanax, and a messenger reports the beginning of the fatal duel. Hector thus meets his death by leaving Troy to confront Achilles rather than lingering on the battlefield as in the *Iliad*, and the events and discourse – and the pathos – of *Iliad* 6 and 22 are combined. Chaeremon's *Achilles* is virtually unrepresented by text-fragments, but its essentials are probably depicted in a fine Apulian vase painted within a few decades of its first production (see plates 17.1 and 17.2). In the epic *Aethiopis* Achilles killed the Amazon Penthesilea in battle and insisted on treating her body honorably, Thersites accused him of acting out of love for her, Achilles retaliated by killing Thersites, and dissension ensued amongst the Achaeans until Odysseus took Achilles to Lesbos for purification. On the vase we see the decapitated corpse of Thersites lying in the foreground, Achilles sitting in conversation with his advisor Phoenix, Menelaus restraining Thersites' kinsman Diomedes, and Agamemnon hurrying to intervene. The play might be compared with those of Sophocles and Euripides that

Plate 17.1 The death of Thersites. Greek, South Italian volute-krater; style resembles the Varrese Painter. ca. 340 BCE. Boston, Museum of Fine Arts 03.804. Photograph © 2004 Museum of Fine Arts, Boston. Reproduced by permission.

Plate 17.2   Detail of plate 17.1. Photograph © 2004 Museum of Fine Arts, Boston. Reproduced by permission.

dramatized incidental episodes from the Trojan cycle and focused on conflict and debate amongst the Achaean leaders.

These two works were probably typical of the tragedy of their time in making self-presentation and self-analysis central to their characters' discourse. In *Poetics* 1450b7–8 Aristotle comments that the poets of his time made their characters speak "rhetorically" (i.e., like people reviewing and explaining their actions for an audience) rather than "politically" (like people reacting directly to real situations); Astydamas and Theodectas were both said to have studied with Isocrates (whose adopted son Aphareus was both a rhetorician and a tragedian); Theodectas was acquainted with Plato and Aristotle as well. Like some other features of fourth-century tragedy – such as the refined descriptive set-pieces which we see in a few fragments of Chaeremon – the rhetorical tendency is foreshadowed in Euripidean drama. On the other hand, a papyrus fragment of the philosopher Philodemus (first century BCE) suggests that Chaeremon, at least, avoided the gratuitous portrayals of morally inferior characters for which Euripides was criticized (cf. *Poetics* 1454a28–29). The reduction of dramatic impact and variety which these tendencies entailed may ultimately have reduced tragedy's popular appeal as it became increasingly a conventional and self-reflexive literary genre.

NOTE

1 Moschion's *Themistocles* and Lycophron's *Marathonians* were composed two centuries later. Some fourth- and third-century tragedies – Theodectas' *Mausolus*, Moschion's *Pheraeans*, Lycophron's *Cassandreans* – probably involved recent events, but their character is entirely unknown. A fifth-century vase-painting attests a tragedy on the story of the sixth-century Lydian king Croesus (adesp. fr. 5e), and a fragment from a play about his predecessor Gyges (adesp. fr. 664) is either from the fifth century or – more likely – Hellenistic; but these subjects were semimythical.

FURTHER READING

General: The standard scholarly edition of the fragments and testimonia, completely replacing Nauck 1889, is B. Snell, R. Kannicht, and S. Radt, *Tragicorum Graecorum Fragmenta* (1971–2004; for details, see Abbreviations and Editions at the front of this volume). Surveys of the lost tragedies are included in Lesky 1972 (in English, Lesky 1983), Seeck 1979b, Easterling and Knox 1985, all with full bibliographies. Kannicht and Gauly 1991 provides select testimonia and fragments from the minor tragedians, with German translations and notes. For evidence for the tragic myths and their background Gantz 1993 is often a good starting point. McHardy, Robson, and Harvey 2005 includes ten essays on various aspects of the fragments and their study.

Early tragedy: On chronological problems see Connor 1989, West 1989, Scullion 2002b, and on the question of content and form Lloyd-Jones 1990b, Schadewaldt 1974, Taplin 1977, 49–60. Phrynichus' *Capture of Miletus* is discussed at length by Rosenbloom 1993.

Aeschylus: For texts and English translations of all the substantial fragments see Smyth and Lloyd-Jones 1983, and for survey and discussion Radt 1986, Sommerstein 1996 (with bibliography). On tetralogies see Gantz 1979, 1980; on the *Lycurgeia* West 1990b, 26–50; and on the Achilles and Memnon trilogies West 2000. Michelakis 2002 discusses *Myrmidons*, and Poli-Palladini 2001a *Women of Aetna*.

Sophocles: Volume 3 of Lloyd-Jones 1994–96 includes texts and English translations of all the substantial fragments. The "General Introduction" and play introductions and notes in Pearson 1917, though old, are still of use. Sutton 1984 gives brief discussions of all the fragmentary plays, and Radt 1991 a survey of titles, mythical material, and some stylistic and dramatic features. Sommerstein 2003 includes twenty essays by various scholars on thematic features and individual plays including *Aegeus, Locrian Ajax, Nauplius, Phaedra, Syndeipnoi/ Gathering of the Achaeans, Tereus*, and the *Tyro* plays, with bibliography. See also Barrett 1964, 10–45 (*Phaedra*), Hahnemann 1999 (*Aegeus*), Fitzpatrick 2001 (*Tereus*), Dobrov 2001, 105–32 (*Tereus*).

Euripides: The Budé edition (Jouan and Van Looy 1998–2003) gives complete texts with French translations, introductions, notes, and bibliographies (the texts from papyri need to be used with caution). A Loeb edition is being prepared by C. Collard and M. Cropp. For concise editions of the more substantial plays with introductions, commentaries, and select bibliographies see Collard, Cropp, and Lee 1995 (*Telephus, Cretans, Stheneboea, Bellerophon, Cresphontes, Erechtheus, Phaethon, Wise Melanippe, Captive Melanippe*) and Collard, Cropp, and Gibert 2004 (*Philoctetes, Alexandros, Palamedes, Andromeda, Oedipus, Hypsipyle, Antiope, Archelaus*). On *Veiled Hippolytus* see Barrett 1964, 10–45, and Halleran 1995, 25–37. Fuller scholarly editions of individual plays: *Andromeda*, Klimek-Winter 1993; *Antiope*,

Kambitsis 1972; *Archelaus* and *Cresphontes*, Harder 1985; *Cretans*, Cozzoli 2001; *Hypsipyle*, Bond 1963 and Cockle 1987; *Phaethon*, Diggle 1970; *Philoctetes*, Müller 2000; *Telephus*, Preiser 2000. Webster 1967 was a ground-breaking discussion of all the lost plays (although some of his statements about their chronology are misleading: for corrections see Cropp and Fick 1985). Huys 1995 gives exhaustive discussions of the "hero-exposed-at-birth" plays (*Alexandros*, *Alope*, *Antiope*, *Auge*, *Danae*, *Ion*, *Wise Melanippe*, *Captive Melanippe*, *Oedipus*). See also Dobrov 2001, 89–104, on *Bellerophon*, and below on *Pirithous*.

Other: The literary work of Ion of Chios is surveyed by West 1985 and Dover 1986. A good starting point on Neophron's *Medea* is now Mastronarde 2002b, 57–64. On *Pirithous* see Collard 1995 (questioning attribution to Critias) and Dobrov 2001, 133–56 (on the play's content). Fourth-century tragedy is discussed at length by Xanthakis-Karamanos 1980 (and related articles), and briefly but suggestively by Easterling 1993 and 1997e; Webster 1954 gives a useful introductory survey. On the limitations of *Rhesus* see Fraenkel 1965, Kitto 1977; Burnett 1985 has argued that it is a youthful and intentionally perverse work of Euripides, Liapis 2004 that it was composed for a Macedonian production in Philip II's reign. On Astydamas' *Hector* see Xanthakis-Karamanos 1980, 162–69. Collard 1970 gives a general study of Chaeremon, and Morelli 2001 an exhaustive discussion of his *Achilles*. The very defective evidence for Hellenistic tragedy (not included in this chapter) is usefully surveyed by Xanthakis-Karamanos 1993.

CHAPTER EIGHTEEN

Tragedy and Anthropology

Christiane Sourvinou-Inwood

This chapter discusses the ways in which approaches and strategies derived from anthropology inform the study of Greek tragedy. "Anthropology" is not, of course, an unproblematic term: there are many anthropologies, and even the definition of what discourses are part of "anthropology" is fluid; for example, the term may or may not be taken to include sociology, cultural history, and the study of ideologies.[1] The approaches and strategies derived from anthropology that are deployed in the study of tragedy range from general principles based on insights that dictate certain methodological requirements to specific strategies derived from specific anthropologies – for example, the reconstruction of polarities and binary oppositions that, according to structuralists, articulate societies' conceptual universe, and so, some have argued, form the skeleton of tragedies (e.g., Segal 1981, 186).

To begin with principles, the most crucial of the insights derived from anthropology that underpin general methodological principles is that tragedy should be considered (not only, but also) as an anthropological phenomenon, as the product of a particular culture, performed in a specific Athenian festival. For tragedy was an organic part of the culture and contexts that generated it and gave meanings to each of its different elements in the eyes of the members of the culture, the ancient audiences, who shared with the tragedians their cultural assumptions, their conceptual map. This approach to the study of Greek tragedy (as a systematic enterprise based on the perception of tragedy as an organic part of a system, and involving also the reconstruction of the ancient audiences' conceptual map) was pioneered by Vernant and Vidal-Naquet (Vernant and Vidal-Naquet 1972, e.g., 9–10; 1986, e.g., 10–15).

One aspect of the Vernant/Vidal-Naquet approach was the investigation of the articulations and manipulations of rituals in the creation of tragic meanings (Zeitlin 1965, 463–508; Vidal-Naquet 1972a, 133–58; Vernant 1972a, 99–131; cf. Gould 1973, 74–103, esp. 85–90). Clearly, if, for example, a sacrificial ritual helped shape the ways in which the ancient audiences – who shared knowledge of that ritual with the tragedian – made sense of a tragic segment, not to take account of this ritual is to diverge considerably from the meanings those audiences constructed. In order to

understand how the deployment and manipulation of rituals constructed meanings
for the audiences who shared the tragedians' ritual knowledge, it is necessary first to
reconstruct as much as possible of that knowledge. Anthropology helps in such
reconstructions, by offering both comparative material and also some insight into
the various modalities that articulate rituals in other societies. Cross-cultural comparisons can function as eye-openers to show the culturally determined nature of
interpretations that seem reasonable to us, so stopping us from making sense of
rituals through our commonsense assumptions. Furthermore, cross-cultural comparisons suggest a range of possibilities for making sense of whatever element is being
considered, thus allowing us to construct methodologies that take such possibilities
into account. But care must be taken that such possibilities are not imposed (as they
sometimes were in a less anthropologically sophisticated past) as explanatory models.
Nor should they be deployed as explanatory models and subsequently tested, since
this strategy, which presents itself as more sophisticated, is equally flawed; for, instead
of attempting to minimize cultural determination, it places at the center of the
investigation assumptions that are inevitably culturally determined (about the plausi-
bility of the comparabilities between the ancient phenomenon and the anthropological comparandum), by making them into organizing centers around which the
data are arranged, and so structuring the investigation through the assumptions that
underlie the model allegedly being tested – a circular, self-validating procedure
(Sourvinou-Inwood 1995, 301–2, esp. 413–14). Finally, at the most basic level,
anthropology teaches us to recognize, for example, rituals of transition such as
initiation rituals, and so helps us consider whether certain tragedies may be structured
also with the help of manipulations of such rituals or of crystallizations associated
with ritual material, such as the figure of the "ephebe," the adolescent in transition to
adulthood (see Vidal-Naquet 1972b, 159–80; 1986b, 135–36).

As a result of the explicit deployment or implicit influence of anthropological
approaches, the place of religion in tragedy is no longer underplayed. Scholars have
studied the articulation of tragedy through rituals (Easterling 1988, 87–109; cf.
Friedrich 1996, 269–70), stressed the character of the dramatic performances as
part of a festival (Goldhill 1990, 97–129), and discussed Dionysiac aspects of tragedy
(Henrichs 1994–95, 57–58, 91–92 nn. 5–7). The importance of gender as an analytical category in the study of tragedy, and in classics in general, in the last few decades is
primarily due to contemporary preoccupations, above all to the discourse of feminism.
But (leaving aside semantic questions as to whether or not such discourses and
preoccupations are part of "anthropology") "gender" is an anthropological category,
and its study in the ancient world has also been based on anthropological insights,
including categories such as "the Other," systems of binary oppositions in which male
versus female are major articulating categories, and general cross-cultural comparisons
(des Bouvrie 1990 is a specifically anthropological study of gender in Greek tragedy).
The influence of anthropology, then, is all-pervasive in the study of tragedy, both as a
result of explicit methodological choices and through the influence of studies that
deploy principles and methods based on anthropological insights.

To return to general principles that dictate methodological requirements: the
insight that perception and judgment are culturally determined – an insight derived
not only from anthropology but also from other disciplines – further validates and
strengthens the approach that demands that tragedies be studied in their full cultural

context. As noted above, awareness of the culturally determined nature of perception and judgment has helped stop us from reading Greek tragedy implicitly through commonsense assumptions, since commonsense assumptions are culturally determined (Sourvinou-Inwood 1989a, 134–48; 1989b, 141–65).

Awareness of the culturally determined nature of perception and judgment has also, however, given rise to the opposite tendency, the more general intellectual tendency of postmodernism, to which contemporary anthropology has not been immune, and which has been pulling the study of tragedy in the opposite direction. While the anthropological approaches mentioned above have been pushing in the direction of studying tragedy as an embedded part of the culture that produced it, which involves systematic attempts to reconstruct the ancient realities and cultural assumptions that shaped the perceptual filters through which tragedies were written and made sense of by audiences who shared the tragedians' filters, postmodernism has given false methodological respectability to readings that make no attempt to reconstruct ancient realities. Postmodernism claims that we can never know anything, let alone reconstruct the ancient realities; it has thus created a presumption that attempts to reconstruct ancient realities have no validity, and therefore it is naive to embark on such attempts – the smart choice being to replace them by the commentators' feelings and personal experience explicitly set forth as such. Such at least is the theoretical postmodernist position; in practice, postmodernist critics do not always consistently present their readings as their own modern interpretations, the distinction is often blurred between these modern readings and the ancient meanings, and claims of "truth" are made, explicitly or implicitly – claims which in postmodernist eyes are somehow validated through being framed by postmodernist skepticism. For one of the masks under which such strategies are given false respectability is the tenet that there is "no right reading" – as though this absolved us of the duty to try to reconstruct, insofar as possible, the main parameters shaping the process of meaning creation by the ancient audiences in performance – the construction of complex polysemic and multivocal meanings, probably different meanings by different segments of the audience, but nevertheless meanings shaped by certain parameters determined by cultural assumptions that are different from our own. There can be no doubt that certain aspects of ancient culture, and so at least some of the parameters shaping the ancient audiences' creations of meanings, are definitely knowable, and can be enlisted in the attempt to reconstruct the ancient readings of tragedies.

Anyone who does not accept that such is the case should be prepared to accept that it was possible for the fifth-century Athenian audience, or a part of that audience, to understand Medea's chariot at the end of Euripides' *Medea* as a disguised helicopter, and Medea as an ordinary criminal making a daring escape, taking advantage of her distraught victim's traumatic confusion to tell him a lot of fantastic lies; or that Euripides' *Orestes* was a tragedy about a technologically advanced extraterrestrial called Apollo, who fooled the naive Greeks of the heroic age into worshipping him as a god and doing terrible things because he told them to. Of course no critic would accept this, because it involves concepts alien to the Greeks. In other words, even postmodernists would implicitly rely on the notion that we *can* reconstruct *some* ancient meanings if we take account of the ancient assumptions. It is, then, impossible to deny that we can reconstruct some of the parameters determining the process of meaning creation by the ancient audiences, who shared the tragedians' cultural assumptions and constructed meanings through perceptual filters shaped by those assumptions.

To minimize cultural determination we must attempt to reconstruct, as far as possible, these ancient filters, or at least reconstruct the important parameters that shaped them, and so the parameters within which the process of meaning creation by the ancient audiences took place. We may or may not be able to reconstruct the meanings created by those audiences, but we can certainly reconstruct many of the factors that blocked certain meanings and facilitated, even compelled, others. And this, I believe, should be our main aim. Though it may be legitimate, as part of a modern discourse, to reread ancient tragedies through the filters of modern assumptions (a project not unlike producing, for example, *Othello* in modern dress), in the case of Greek tragedies, which are articulated with the help of a conceptual map alien to the modern reader, this can only result in creating a reflection of modern assumptions, while the richness, complexities, and multivocalities of the ancient tragedies are obscured and lost.

I will illustrate my own version of the "anthropological" approach that studies tragedy as an organic part of fifth-century Athenian culture, a version that aims at reconstructing as much as possible the ways in which the fifth-century Athenian audience made sense of the tragedies in performance, through examples from two tragedies. These examples, I hope, will illustrate how the reconstruction of two types of assumptions helps us recover some of the meanings constructed by the ancient audiences (or at least the parameters shaping such constructions). The two types of assumptions on which I will be focusing here are, first, religious assumptions, namely rituals and religious representations, knowledge of which was shared by the tragedians and their contemporary audiences; and second, a set of assumptions that is not often considered in the reading of tragedies: the audiences' perceptions of the relationship between their world and that of the tragedies. For it is important that we do not allow ourselves to perceive, implicitly and by default, the relationship between the world of the ancient audiences and that of the tragedies on the model of such relationships in our own world. It is necessary to define this relationship, or at least reconstruct the parameters that defined it, by considering the two aspects that (cross-cultural comparisons suggest) define such relationships. First, does the world portrayed on the stage have any connection to the world of the audience? Is it part of it, or part of its past, or future? Were the two similar, or were they radically different, even alien? Second, were the two worlds kept totally separate during the performance? That is, was the world of the tragedy self-contained and insulated from the world of the audience, or did it penetrate it, and if it did, what form or forms did this penetration take?

The preferred choice for the setting of Greek tragedies was the heroic age (on this and the less common settings see Sourvinou-Inwood 2003, 15–25; also 25–66). For the fifth-century audience the relationship between their world and that of the heroic age was governed by two intertwined perspectives. On the one hand the heroic age was other, distanced from the present, a time when men could have direct contact with gods and were sometimes descended from gods, and when the most prominent and important individuals became the heroes of fifth-century cult. On the other hand the heroic age, and so the world of the tragedy, was also part of the present, in that it was a crucial part of the audience's past in which important events shaping their contemporary world had taken place; furthermore, it in some ways resembled the present. The relationship between the two worlds was not stable and inert in the course of each tragedy. I have argued – first with reference to Sophocles' *Antigone*, and most recently in great detail, and more generally (Sourvinou-Inwood 1989a, 134–48; 2003, passim, esp. 15–66; cf. Pelling 1997b, 217–18, 228–29, 233–34) – that the relationship between the world of the audience and that of the tragedy was not constant throughout each tragedy; rather, it was manipulated in the course of the performance through textual devices that operated in interaction with the assumptions the audience shared with the tragedian: "distancing devices," which had the effect of distancing the action from the world of the fifth-century Athenian polis, sharply differentiating the two; and "zooming devices," which had the effect of bringing the world of the play nearer, pushing the audience into relating their experiences and assumptions directly to the play.

One particular category of zoomings, as will become clear in the course of this discussion, is that in which the world of the audience is penetrated by the world of the play. The passages from the two tragedies that will provide the illustration of my reading methodology involve some especially strong zoomings that have important implications for the construction of meanings by the audiences.[2] They illustrate two different types of penetration. In the first, the character of the world of the tragedy as part of a ritual performance taking place in the world of the audience is activated. In the second, the superficially "other" heroic world of the tragedy is brought very near, indeed is presented as the same as, the world of the audience, especially with respect to its religious realities.

I will illustrate the first type of zooming (and to a lesser extent also the second) with an example from Aeschylus' *Eumenides*, which takes place in the heroic age. Athens is the locale for the segment I will briefly consider here. The "other," distanced from the present, nature of the world of *Eumenides* is manifested, for example, in the fact that in the play mortals have direct contact with gods; but that world was also part of the present, in that important events that shaped their audiences' world took place during that period – above all the foundation of the court of the Areopagus[3] and of the cult of the Eumenides.

The focus of my brief discussion is a ritual, the singing of a hymn by the chorus of the Erinyes. This singing takes place in a framework already charged with ritual elements. After his arrival in Athens Orestes supplicates Athena's statue, and then, after the Erinyes enter in pursuit, he describes one rite, the purification he underwent at Delphi, and then enacts another rite, another prayer to Athena (282–98). After that the chorus sings a binding-song intended to put Orestes in their power (331 = 344). Normal ritual hymns present a deity's powers, functions, and honors; here the Erinyes are doing this themselves in their own hymn; here, among other things, the Erinyes sing a hymn to themselves, about themselves. At least, they do so in the world of the tragedy, but the situation is complex. For the chorus begins their dance-song with an emphatic statement of choral self-referentiality (307–11; see Henrichs 1994–95, 60–65; also Wilson and Taplin 1993, 174), and then draw attention to their identity as performers in choral dance through their words and their actions – for example, the fact that they are stamping their feet on the *orchêstra* floor while cursing Orestes (cf. Henrichs 1994–95, 62–63, 64). This self-referentiality activated the persona of the chorus as a chorus in the present, and it resulted in the ritual's being perceived by the audience as performed not only by the Erinyes in the world of the tragedy, but also in the here and now, by the chorus of Athenian men. This double nature of the song is correlative with the oddity of the Erinyes singing a hymn to themselves, about themselves, while normally such a song would be sung by human worshippers. For the audience would not have perceived this hymn as sung only by the Erinyes in the world of the tragedy; because of the activation, through choral self-referentiality, of the persona of the chorus as a chorus in the present, they would have perceived the hymn as being sung also by the chorus of Athenian men in the present. This perception is important, because in the world of the spectators the Erinyes were indeed worshipped, and this fact was inevitably activated for them through the chorus's singing of this hymn.

The implications are significant. After the Erinyes were defeated they threatened to blight the land (780–87 = 810–17). This marked a grave danger for Athens in the world of the tragedy. But the audience was protected from feeling this danger as symbolically too close, and threatening their present, because choral self-referentiality had activated the persona of the chorus as a chorus in the present, which entailed that the audience would have perceived the hymn about the Erinyes to be sung also by the chorus of Athenian men in the here and now, which, in turn, entailed both an act of reverence to the Erinyes in the here and now, and the activation of the knowledge that in the world of the audience the Erinyes were indeed worshipped. So the threat of the Erinyes does not affect the world of the audience; it represents a danger in the past that has been overcome. Once more Athena has protected the city; in this case she eventually, after a sustained effort of persuasion (and a veiled threat at 826–29 that she may use Zeus' thunderbolt), convinces the Erinyes not to harm Athens and promises that they will receive worship by the Athenians.

The new relationship between the Erinyes and Athens is immediately enacted. At 902 the Erinyes ask Athena what blessings they should invoke upon Athens, and she gives a list which includes blessings that correspond to the curses uttered in 780–87 (907–9; see Sommerstein 1989, ad loc); then she herself gives Athens the blessing of military victory. Then the Erinyes deliver those blessings in song ("they sing a majestic hymn of benediction upon the city"; Lloyd-Jones 1971, 92), interspersed with comments from Athena, who stresses their power to curse and bless, and admonishes the Athenians to give them proper honor. Athena's comments would have zoomed the world of the tragedy to that of the audience. Her description of the powers of the Erinyes at 950–55 corresponded to the audience's own perception of the power of these goddesses, whom they worshipped in their everyday life. Above all, the statement at 993–95, that if the Athenians honor the Erinyes their city will be righteous and glorious, would have zoomed them to their religious reality, in which they did honor and worship the Erinyes – and this understanding would have brought up the expectation of the fulfillment of this promise.

The tragedy ends with a ritual, a procession establishing the cult of the Eumenides in Athens, and including torches, sacrificial victims, and the priestess and other cult-servants of Athena Polias. This procession is not a representation of the actual ritual of the cult of the *Semnai Theai*, but a construct deploying a variety of ritual elements, including elements evoking the Panathenaea (Bowie 1993, 27–28, 30); nevertheless, it would have zoomed the world of the tragedy to the cultic reality of the audience. For in the perceptions of the audience the distance between the cult they practiced and this heroic-age rite, in which both the deities being honored and the poliad deity took part, would have been correlative with, and so (in the process of meaning creation, implicitly would have) "accounted for," the differences.

To sum up. This example from Aeschylus' *Eumenides* illustrates the permeability produced by the activation of the audience's perception of the tragedy as a performance in the present. This activation, and the zoomings to the audience's religious realities, helped construct important meanings, not least the symbolic distance between the world of the audience and the Erinyes' hostility to, and curses against, Athens. This symbolic distance allowed the action of the tragedy to develop as it did, and thus was critical to the process through which the audience constructed the complex and multivocal sets of meanings pertaining to the important (interconnected) themes of the tragedy and the trilogy: revenge, matricide, killing and pollution, hierarchies and balances of power among the gods, and above all the notion of justice, both divine justice and human institutions. Importantly, the activation of the audience's awareness of the tragedy as a religious performance in the present and the zoomings to their religious realities inevitably charged the deities on stage with religious meanings and prevented the audience from perceiving them as mere theatrical devices.

Euripides' *Erechtheus* offers some especially striking instances of the type of zooming through which the superficially "other" heroic world of the tragedy is brought very near, is presented as the same as, the world of the audience, especially its religious realities. Like Aeschylus' *Eumenides*, this (fragmentary) tragedy is set in heroic-age Athens. It takes place during the reign of Erechtheus, when the Eleusinians, together with an army of Thracians led by Eumolpus, son of Poseidon, were threatening the city. Eumolpus wanted to replace Athena with his father Poseidon as the poliadic divinity of Athens. This threat is the context of fr. 351: "Raise the shrill cry, women, so that the goddess may come to help the polis wearing the golden aegis with the Gorgon." My translation makes explicit the metonymic reference to Athena's aegis. For the Athenians would have understood the expression "golden...Gorgon" through their own associations, which included their familiarity with Phidias' statue in the Parthenon of Athena Parthenos wearing a golden aegis adorned with an ivory gorgoneion (e.g., Stewart 1990, 157–58). These verses, then, evoked the goddess Athena who was the poliad divinity watching over Athens in real life; the persona of Athena protecting the city was a pervasive theme in Athenian ideology and was embodied in the statue of Athena Parthenos. The metonymic reference to the aegis would have reinforced the notion of Athena's protective power, for in myth the aegis powerfully warded off attack (cf. *Iliad* 21.400–401). *Erechtheus* was probably produced at the end of the 420s BCE or soon after (Collard, Cropp, and Lee 1995, 155). Only a few years earlier, during the Spartans' annual invasions of Attica (Thucydides 3.2, 26, 89; 4.2, 6), the audience would themselves have invoked Athena's help. This circumstance, and above all the fact that the function and iconography of Athena in the tragedy coincided with those of the goddess in Athenian cult, especially as represented in her most magnificent statue, would have zoomed the world of the tragedy very closely to that of the audience, whose past that tragedy was enacting.

To continue with the tragedy's action, the oracle told Erechtheus that he would be victorious if he sacrificed his eldest daughter to Persephone. He did so, with the consent of his wife Praxithea, and two more daughters killed themselves because of an oath they had taken. The enemy was defeated and Eumolpus was killed by Erechtheus. Erechtheus in turn was killed by Poseidon. At fr. 370.55 Poseidon, enraged at the defeat and death of his son, sends an earthquake, and Athens trembles. At this point Athena appears. She first berates Poseidon and then turns to Praxithea, to whom she gives instructions to bury her daughters, adding that she, Athena, has made them into the deified Hyacinthids whose cult she is now instituting, and giving instructions about the sacrifices and other rites that should in future be performed in their honor. The expression Athena uses to describe the fate of Erechtheus' daughters resembles closely, and thus would have recalled for the Athenian audience, the public epitaph for the men who died in the battle of Potidaea (Hansen 1983, 10.5). This would have zoomed the world of the tragedy to the world of the audience, presenting the Hyacinthids as the models for the heroization of the Athenian war dead.[4]

Athena proceeds to institute the cult of Poseidon Erechtheus. To be precise, she says that Erechtheus will take the name of his killer and be invoked in cult as Poseidon; this is one interpretation of the cult title "Poseidon Erechtheus." She orders that a sanctuary be built for this cult in the middle of the city. Obviously, the cult itself would have zoomed the world of tragedy to the world of the audience, a zooming made stronger by the fact that at that very moment a sanctuary to Poseidon Erechtheus was under construction in the middle of the city. The Erechtheum housed, in addition to minor cults and sacred spots, the cults of Poseidon Erechtheus and of Athena Polias.[5] The latter was the most important Athenian cult; it honored the very goddess who in the world of the play issues the instructions for building the Erechtheum, and who in her next words mentions her own cult; she makes Praxithea its first priestess, thus instituting the cult in the form in which it was practiced in the world of the audience. This provision zoomed the world of tragedy to the present and represented the present-day cult as symbolically anchored in the heroic world and in Athena's will. To put it differently, this tragedy was portraying events that in the audience's perceptions had taken place in their own past, very near the place in which they had occurred; it showed these events shaping the present as it is now, so that what happened on stage was de facto part of the audience's contemporary context.

But, it may be objected, how can we be sure that Athena was not perceived by the ancient audiences as a simple theatrical device, an empty gesture of closure, as some modern commentators (e.g., Dunn 1996, 32–33) believe was generally the case with Euripides' "gods on high"? I criticize such theories in more detail elsewhere (Sourvinou-Inwood 2003, 414–22; see also 459–512), but the case against this objection, and in favor of the reading offered here, is clear even when set out briefly: by the time Athena appeared on stage the audience had already identified the goddess Athena of the tragedy as a representation of the goddess they worshipped, above all in the poliadic cult, thanks to a series of zoomings of the world of the tragedy to the world of the audience; therefore, when Athena appeared she would have been perceived as a representation of the real goddess Athena, impersonated by an actor.

Representations of deities by human actors were not unknown in Greek religion. There were three basic (and very different) types of divine appearance. The first type involved straightforward epiphany; the second, impersonation of a deity by priestly personnel; the third took place in the course of festivals of advent, in which the arrival of a deity is enacted through the arrival, or the "finding," of the cult statue which had been removed from its usual place (Burkert 1988, 81–87; 1985, 134–35; 1997, 24).

"Real-life" epiphanies (on which see Pfister 1924, 277–323; Nilsson 1974, 225–27; Versnel 1990–93, 1: 190–93; Burkert 1985, 186–88; Graf 1997, 1150–51; Henrichs 1996b; Hornblower 1996, 356) took place when mortals believed that a deity had appeared to them. Though this was hardly a regular occurrence, deities were believed to appear to mortals occasionally, giving them instructions that very often resulted in the institution of a cult. These real-life epiphanies encompass two categories: dream epiphanies, in which the deity appeared when the person was asleep, and "real" real-life epiphanies, occurring when the person was awake. In fact, one of the tragedians was associated in the tradition with a dream epiphany that led to a cult foundation: Heracles was said to have appeared in a dream epiphany to Sophocles (*Life of Sophocles* 12), and informed him where to find a golden wreath that had been stolen from the Acropolis; when it was found Sophocles received a reward, which he used to found a shrine of *Heracles Mênutés* (Heracles the Informer). Sometimes the deity or hero did not make himself known but performed a miracle (e.g., Herodotus 6.61), or some other action (e.g., Herodotus 6.69). The second type of divine appearance involved the impersonation of divinities by priestly personnel in the course of ritual, and sometimes sacred drama (Burkert 1985, 186; Mylonas 1961, 261–64; Clinton 1992, 84–95). Such ritual acts may have included an "enacted" epiphany (Hägg 1986, 46–47, 60–62; Kiechle 1970, 259–71; Burkert 1997, 27–28), in which the deity was impersonated by the priest or priestess.

In *Erechtheus*, by the time Athena appeared, dense zooming in earlier parts of the play had identified the goddess Athena of the tragedy as a representation – until then a conceptual representation – of the goddess they worshipped. Therefore the audience would have perceived the deity on the stage as a representation of the real goddess, impersonated by an actor, which would have activated the ritual schema "representation of a deity in sacred drama," so that the audience made sense of the deity on stage also with the help of this ritual schema from their lived religion, especially since Athena in *Erechtheus* is presented as shaping the poliadic cult in its present form by appointing its first priestess, and ordering the foundation of, among others, another cult with which the poliadic cult is closely associated in the present. At the same time, Athena's appearance would have activated for the audience the religious schema "real-life epiphany," in which a deity appears, gives instructions, and a cult is instituted as a result. Thus, the audience would have seen Athena as a deity in epiphany to the tragic characters in the world of the tragedy, charged with religious significance through the activation of the "epiphany" schema, while at the same time this epiphany was also an impersonation of a deity by an actor, and thus would have evoked, and been perceived as partly comparable to, reenactments of cult foundations in sacred drama.

Because *Erechtheus* was located at the very center of the Athenian polis, it offers a very strong version of a penetration of the world of the audience by the world of the tragedy. In other tragedies the zooming may not be quite so strong, with zooming devices sometimes operating in terms of similarity, or closeness, to the world of the audience. Nevertheless, as I have argued elsewhere (Sourvinou-Inwood 2003, 301–458 passim, 469–500), in those tragedies too the world of the tragedy penetrated that of the audience, so that what happened in the former was perceived as part of the latter. The deities that appeared on high at the conclusion of other Euripidean tragedies had also been zoomed to the audiences' world and so had come to be perceived as representations of the deities in the audiences' lived religion; they also evoked deities in "real-life" epiphanies, so that the audience saw them as deities in epiphany to the tragic characters, giving instructions, as a result of which a cult is instituted, which zoomed the world of the play to, and had direct relevance to, the audiences' religious life. At the same time, correlatively with the penetration of the world of the tragedy into the audience's own world, the "deity on high" would also have come to be seen as an actor wearing a divine mask acting the role of a god in a mimetic performance taking place in a sanctuary during a festival, which evoked the masked impersonations of deities by cult personnel in sacred drama and so charged the deities on high with religious significance.

Thus, when these divine appearances are considered in the full context of the performance, and of the culture that produced the tragedies, it becomes clear that the modern notion that Euripidean deities on high were simply empty gestures of closure is untenable, and that to the ancient audiences the Euripidean gods were far from simple theatrical devices.

It is clear, then, that, first, the ritual schemata and other religious knowledge which the tragedians shared with the ancient audiences, and second, the zoomings and, more generally, the shifting relationships between the world of the tragedy and that of the audience, constructed through the deployment of assumptions which the tragedians shared with the spectators, helped shape the parameters within which the fifth-century audiences constructed meanings in performance. The meanings they constructed were complex, multivocal, and possibly diverse, but such constructions were shaped and defined by the parameters created through these and the other assumptions shared by the tragedian and his contemporaries.

Among the meanings constructed during the performance of *Erechtheus* within the parameters shaped by the rituals and shifting relationships discussed above was, first, the exploration (at a symbolic distance) of the notion of human sacrifice, which was problematic in the religious discourse of the present, insofar as it inevitably helped color the perceptions of the gods worshipped by the fifth-century Greeks. Second, the Hyacinthids were represented as the models for the heroization of the Athenian war dead, confirming the association between the sacrifice of a virgin and the death of men in war, an association also enshrined in the cult which associates Aglauros, another virgin who sacrificed herself to save the city, with the ephebes (Kearns 1990, 330–31, 338; 1989, 139–40, 24–27; Larson 1995, 39–41). Finally, a strong symbolic anchoring is provided for the most important Athenian cult, that of Athena Polias, and of its associated cult of Poseidon Erechtheus; these cults were symbolically reinforced through the representation of their foundation in the heroic age on the orders of Athena herself.

I have argued elsewhere (Sourvinou-Inwood 2003, e.g., 513–18) that fifth-century audiences did not perceive tragedy only as a purely "theatrical" experience, a discrete dramatic unit, simply framed by ritual, but also as a ritual performance; and that aetiologies, deities, and other religious elements were not, for them, simply theatrical devices, but were charged with religious meanings; they were, in varying degrees and ways, part of the audiences' religious realities. One of the arguments on which this conclusion was based pertains to the shifting relationships between the world of the audience and the world of the play in the different tragedies, relationships very different from those of modern theatrical performances, as has been illustrated here through the brief consideration of segments from two tragedies. Be that as it may, I hope that the two examples considered in this essay have illustrated the fact that, in order to make sense of the tragedies as nearly as possible to the ways in which the ancient audience did, it is necessary to reconstruct – among other assumptions – the ritual and other religious knowledge which the tragedians shared with their audiences, through the deployment of which meanings were constructed in performance, and also the shifting relationship between the world of the tragedy and that of the audience as perceived by the latter.

Therefore, these illustrations have also demonstrated the general methodological point that any non-anthropological approach, in the sense of any approach that does not study tragedy as an embedded part of fifth-century Athenian culture, and as a performance in the Theater of Dionysus during the Dionysia, inevitably produces meanings that are very different from those created by the ancient audiences. Our task, I have argued, is to try to make sense of the tragedies as nearly as possible to the ways the ancient audiences did.

NOTES

1 The very notion of anthropological knowledge has been problematized in postmodern discourses. The flaws of postmodernism cannot be discussed here (for a critique see, e.g., Sokal and Bricmont 1999), except insofar as they impinge directly on the study of tragedy; but in any case, I hope that the validity of the anthropological insights that are implicated in this discussion will become clear – except perhaps in the eyes of those who believe that we cannot have access to any truth whatsoever. See a discussion of the different anthropologies and their greater or lesser self-reflexivity, and the notion of anthropological knowledge, in Adam et al. 1990a, 9–17; Borel 1990, 21–69; Kilani 1990, 71–109.

2 I discuss these two tragedies more fully in Sourvinou-Inwood 2003, 25–30 (Euripides' *Erechtheus*) and Sourvinou-Inwood 2003, 234–46 (Aeschylus' *Eumenides*).

3 See on this mytheme in and before Aeschylus: Sommerstein 1989, 2–6; cf. 13–17 on the Areopagus itself.

4 On the Hyacinthids see Kearns 1989, 59–63, 201–2; Larson 1995, 20, 101–6 passim. On the heroization and immortality of the Athenian war dead and the epitaph for the men who died in the battle of Potidaea cf. Sourvinou-Inwood 1995, 194.

5 On Poseidon Erechtheus see Parker 1987, 202, 204; cf. Parker 1996, 290–93; Kearns 1989, 113–15. On the Erechtheum see now Hurwit 1999, 200–209, 316 n. 13 with bibliography. However, Ferrari (2002, 11–35) argues that the cult of Athena Polias had continued to be housed in the archaic temple which, on this argument, had continued functioning as the temple of Athena Polias, having been reconstituted as a monument in a scarred form, and had remained standing into the Roman period. This, of course, does not affect the present argument, since the Erechtheum was, in any case, being built next to the archaic temple.

FURTHER READING

On anthropology and classics see Humphreys 1978, especially 17–30. On anthropology and tragedy see the concise presentation of Goldhill 1997c. Versnel 1990–93, 2: 15–88, discusses the relationship between myth and ritual in the work of various classical scholars variously influenced by anthropology. On the religious context of tragedy and on the question of tragedy and ritual see Goldhill 1990, Sourvinou-Inwood 2003, and Easterling 1988. Henrichs 1994–95 contains a short survey of approaches to the Dionysiac aspects of tragedy (57–58, with bibliography, 91–92 nn. 5–7); see also Henrichs 1984 and 1993a, Friedrich 1996, and Seaford 1996b. On Euripides' *Erechtheus* see Collard, Cropp, and Lee 1995, 148–55.

CHAPTER NINETEEN

Values

Douglas Cairns

Tragic and Popular Ethics

Tragedy, Aristotle suggests, dramatizes the change of fortune of high-status individuals and excites the audience's pity and fear (*Poetics* 1452b28–53a39). Even in this general description lies a claim that tragedy engages the audience's ethical judgment, for pity is an emotion that typically includes an evaluation of its target's deserts (Konstan 2001). The downfall of the recipient of the audience's pity cannot be something that the audience relishes; hence one needs something like Aristotle's notion of *hamartia*, spanning a range of more or less venial conditions from mistake to moral error – another issue that will engage the audience's ethical judgment. Typically, too (as Aristotle also emphasizes, 1453b15–22; cf. Heath 1999, 138; Belfiore 2000), tragedy creates extreme conflicts of obligations, especially between family members or between the family and other imperatives; these an audience will find disturbing or horrifying precisely because ethical assumptions that are normally regarded as unproblematic are being put under strain. In these basic ways (and in many others) we can expect there to be a relation between the spectators' emotional experience of the play and their values.

But this will not be any straightforward correspondence between the values of the characters and those of the audience. One obvious reason is that the extreme situations in which tragic characters find themselves are such as the audience rarely encounters in real life. Such situations do invoke values by which the audience lives, but are contrived precisely to place those values under stress. Thus there is no necessary inference from Athenian norms to the interpretation of characters' motivations in tragedy. To take a simple example, Sourvinou-Inwood (1989a) is able to marshal arguments which "prove" that, judged by the standards normally imposed upon unmarried daughters in fifth-century Athenian society, Antigone is a problematic and deviant figure; and indeed elements of this deviance are stressed in the play itself. But this supports the conclusion that an Athenian audience will have been unsympathetic to Antigone only if we accept the premise that Athenian audiences were accustomed to view negatively any female character who departed significantly from the norms observed in their own everyday lives. That Euripides can repeatedly offer positive representations of unmarried maidens (Macaria, *Children of Heracles* 500–34; Polyxena, *Hecuba* 342–78, 546–82; Iphigenia, *Iphigenia at Aulis* 1368–1401) who heroically transcend the limitations of everyday maidenhood suggests that this premise should not be accepted.

Since the most formative earlier stage of the traditions from which the extreme conflicts of tragedy derive is heroic epic, heroic values loom large in any discussion of values in tragedy. But these heroic values are presented in a civic context that draws on the experience of the audience as participants in the social and political life of contemporary Athens; an important aspect of that social and political life is debate, both political and intellectual. Thus there is a plurality of sources of reference for the ethical dimension of tragedy, as the heroic values of epic are brought into relation with those of various elements of the contemporary political community and with the questioning of contemporary values that was such a feature of the fifth-century intellectual scene.

Much emphasis in Greek values is placed upon the possession and demonstration of prized excellences and the validation of these excellences by others. Crucial here is the concept of honor (*timê*) as a reflection of a social, public self, whose ethical dimension consists largely in the performance of the social emotions which project and protect an agent's self-esteem. Tragic dramaturgy can be seen as a pared-down version of this sort of social interaction; the issues of interpretation and evaluation of interactants' performances are not qualitatively different from those of "real life" (Easterling 1990). The values in question are not abstract, but embedded in the characterization and motivation of the dramatic characters (Heath 1999, 157). Tragedy is thus ethically polyphonic, and the dramatic context, the character's agenda, and the presentation of the character as a focus of sympathy or antipathy all matter in any interpretation of their values.

Justice and Revenge

In Aeschylus' *Eumenides* the trial of Orestes strongly suggests that the corollary of polyphony in the play is the potential for diverging interpretations in the audience. The jury of Athenian citizens pressed in service to vote in this first-ever homicide trial is equally divided, and Orestes is acquitted on the vote of Athena (734–43, 752–53). Thus the cycle of retaliation is broken, but the issue of the justice of Orestes' revenge is not resolved. *Eumenides* introduces no new, abstract conception of *dikê* as justice to contrast with the *dikê* as retaliation invoked by the characters of the previous plays of the trilogy (Goldhill 1986a, 29–31, 37–51; 1992, 26–37). It is true that each avenger of the previous two plays sees his or her vengeance as just, and a disjunction is contrived between irreconcilable claims to justice (*Libation Bearers* 461; cf. *Agamemnon* 1560–64). This disjunction is a consequence of a reciprocal conception of *dikê* that is encapsulated in the dictum that "the doer shall suffer" (*Agamemnon* 1564, *Libation Bearers* 313); the fact that all instances of offence and retribution take place within the same family creates an apparently interminable series of dilemmas in which the infliction of just retribution on the offender is simultaneously an act of injustice on the part of the avenger (see Orestes' words at *Libation Bearers* 930: "You killed whom you should not; now suffer what you should not"). But the notion of an abstract ideal of justice (*dikê*) underlying its partial or perverted implementation is as old as Hesiod's *Works and Days*, in which Dikê, the daughter of Zeus, personifies the standard by which are judged the judgments (*dikai*) of disputes between parties who each represent their own *dikê* (Cairns 1993, 153–56). Equally, in the *Oresteia*, there is no simple movement from *dikê* as revenge to *dikê* as justice; rather, acts of revenge seek to instantiate a standard of justice that is constantly invoked but never realized. The divided jury of *Eumenides* shows that the institution of the law-court does not necessarily execute perfect justice (the *dikê* by which a husband-killer is punished is still balanced by the *dikê* which demands that a matricide be punished), but it does bring the series of competing claims to an end. It does not exclude vengeance, but allows the prosecutor to pursue vengeance through the duly established institutions of the city, to enlist the citizens' anger, their desire for vengeance, in support of his own case. The anger of the Erinyes (Furies) remains embodied in the institution of the Areopagus (690–706, esp. 705), and this idea that the institutions of state punishment should be not dispassionate but irascible toward offenders is mirrored in the strategies of prosecutors in genuine fourth-century Athenian law-court speeches (Rubinstein 2004; Harris 2001, 188–90), where the regular term for what prosecutors seek and juries impose when they condemn the defendant, namely *timôria*, encompasses both punishment and revenge. Emotional attitudes remain crucial, but are now embodied in the institutions of the state. The audience of *Eumenides* is invited to conclude, therefore, that their city is fortunate in possessing a mechanism not for discerning where true justice lies, but for circumventing interminable cycles of personal vengeance (cf. Euripides, *Orestes* 507–25).

The *Oresteia* thus instantiates a major difference between the world of tragedy and that of the audience – tragic vengeance is typically extreme and bloody, but in classical Athens the pursuit of vengeance by violent means is (in most cases) outlawed. A question thus arises regarding the relation between the passion for vengeance that is so prominent in tragedy and the place of vengeance in the values of the audience. In a series of articles, Herman (1993, 1994, 1995, 1996, 1998) has argued that this relation is weak: despite the frequency of revenge in tragedy, Athenian society, with its legal mechanisms for containing vengeance, exhibits a marked tendency toward compromise and conciliation rather than retaliation. His chief evidence for this conclusion is a number of passages in fourth-century forensic oratory in which the speaker advertises his forbearance in the face of provocation and his reluctance to seek legal redress. This view may be contrasted with that of Burnett (1998), for whom Athenian society is permeated by an attachment, given artistic expression in tragedy, to a notion of *timê* in which vengeance is natural and unproblematic. Neither view can be accepted without qualification. It is significant that the Athenian state succeeded in imposing a (near-) monopoly on the punishment of offenders, and that retaliation is pursued by legal and peaceful means; it is also clear that there is mileage in representing oneself as slow to take offence and reluctant to pursue satisfaction via the law-courts (for example, Demosthenes 54.6; cf. Clytemnestra at Euripides, *Electra* 1030–31; further examples in Herman's articles; cf. Harris 2001, 184–86). As we have seen, however, the notion of vengeance is by no means excluded from the legal process: not only do angry litigants seek *timôria* by enlisting the anger of the dikasts, but there are cases in which litigants frankly admit their enmity toward their opponents (for example, pseudo-Demosthenes 53.2;

further examples in Dover 1974, 182; Cohen 1995, 61–86; Rhodes 1998), and others in which there is at least a strong suspicion that litigants are engaged in a protracted, personally or politically motivated cycle of suit and countersuit (see, for example, the ongoing feud between Demosthenes and Meidias, as discussed by MacDowell 1990, 1–13; Cohen 1995, 87–118; and Rhodes 1998). If the *dikai* of the Athenian *dikastêrion* may, in some cases at least, represent the pursuit of the vendetta by other means (Blundell 1989, 55), then the violent retaliation carried out in tragedy may strike a chord in an Athenian audience.

Burnett's view of tragic vengeance is, however, over-simple. For tragedy consistently contrives situations in which an abstract acceptance that people are entitled to retaliate when harmed will be problematic in practice. Thus, while there is extra-tragic evidence that ordinary Athenians believed that it is right to do good to those who have helped you and harm to those who have harmed you (helping one's friends and harming one's enemies is offered as a definition of *aretê*, excellence, at Plato, *Meno* 71e, and of *dikaiosunê*, justice, at *Republic* 334b; see Blundell 1989), the reality in tragedy is frequently that those whom one regards as one's enemies (*echthroi*) also have a strong claim to be regarded as one's friends (*philoi*) – as in the *Oresteia* or in Sophocles' *Antigone* – or that the logic that drives one to harm a *philos* who has become an *echthros* also leads one to harm one's dearest *philoi* – as in Euripides' *Medea*. The pursuit of revenge will be unproblematic only in a minority of cases – cases such as the murder of Aegisthus in all three tragedians, where the actions of Orestes and Electra in killing an adulterer approximate to what a cuckolded Athenian husband was, in certain circumstances, permitted to do himself (MacDowell 1978, 124–25).

Different ways of handling the clash between the drive to take revenge and other imperatives can be seen in Euripides' and Sophocles' treatments of the Orestes story. It is very unlikely that, having seen the remorse of Electra and Orestes and heard the pronouncements of Castor, the *deus ex machina*, that Clytemnestra "has her just deserts, but your [Orestes'] action is not just" (1244), and that Apollo's oracle was not wise (1245–46), the audience will not conclude that in Euripides' *Electra* the pursuit of revenge to the extent of committing matricide is presented for their condemnation. The issue is the same as in the *Oresteia*, that an act of retaliation may be just punishment for its recipient and unjust violation of the closest of obligations for its perpetrator. The same general notion is expressed in slightly different form in Euripides' *Orestes* 194, where the chorus observes that Orestes' matricide was just (*dikai men*), and Electra rejoins that it was not honorable (*kalôs d'ou*). That previous stages of the cycle of violence may be characterized in the same way is clear from the chorus-leader's comment in Euripides' *Electra* (1051) that Clytemnestra's arguments in favor of her retaliation show justice, but that her justice is shameful (*dikai' elexas, he dikê d' aischrôs echei*). A similar sentiment is given to Electra herself in Sophocles' play (558–60). In an influential study of Greek values, Adkins (1960, 156, 185–86) argued that this formulation, in which the just (*dikaion*) is opposed to the honorable (*kalon*, opposite *aischron*), as opposed to the opposition of *dikê* to *dikê* in Aeschylus, constitutes an attempted "solution" to the problem of interfamilial revenge, on the basis that to designate an action *aischron* "trumps" the claim that it is *dikaion*. This was, however, not only an odd way to think about uses of moral language, but an erroneous piece of intellectual history: Clytemnestra's murder of Agamemnon is considered *aischron* already in the *Odyssey* (11.433), and if this "solved" the problem of interfamilial revenge, no one thought to tell Aeschylus. The presentation of such revenge as a clash of competing *dikai* complements its presentation as the pursuit of the *dikaion* by means of the *aischron*: Aeschylus' Orestes firmly believes that his revenge is just; his spontaneous *aidôs* (shame) at the thought of matricide in the same scene (*Libation Bearers* 899), however, is a sign that his act of justice is also traditionally shameful (*aischron*). This clash of values is not the problem's solution, but its essence. Sophocles' Electra does indeed use the *dikaion/aischron* antithesis to condemn Clytemnestra's revenge; but a distinct parallel between mother and daughter emerges in the way that she justifies conduct which she acknowledges as shameful (605–9, 616–21) by appealing to the necessity of retaliation: "shameful deeds are taught by shameful deeds," as she claims (621). Some notice the similarity of motivation that emerges in this scene and extrapolate to the matricide which results, while others take the matricides' exultation in their action at face value. The issue, however, is much harder to judge in Sophocles than in Euripides; all we have are the arguments and reactions of the characters (and the partisan chorus) themselves; there is no *deus ex machina*, and the play ends without exploring the consequences of matricide. The varying modern interpretations of this play (straightforward celebration of justified revenge versus "ironic" undertones of its dubiety) depend less on unambiguous indicators in the text than on the suppositions that interpreters bring with them.

Honor and Shame

There is a strong self-assertive dynamic in Greek ethics that is particularly prominent in the heroic values that tragedy inherits from epic. The Homeric hero has a developed self-image that craves validation, and injury to this self-image regularly leads to a determination to restore prestige through retaliation. There is also, however, a powerful social dimension to heroic ethics – not just in the sense that popular opinion matters, that the hero's self-assertive prowess (his *aretê*) requires others' recognition, but also in a sense that the Homeric hero (here some scholars would write "*even* the Homeric hero") has reciprocal obligations to his kin, his comrades (*philoi* or *hetairoi*), and his community. The tragedy of the *Iliad* arises precisely because Agamemnon ignores established protocols for the recognition of prowess and popular opinion by taking back a prize already awarded. His failure to respect a legitimate claim provokes retaliation on the part of an Achilles who originally acted for the common good, who is outraged at breaches of protocol, but who extends his retaliation to take in not only the offender but also the *philoi* whom it was his initial impulse to protect, the ultimate result being the loss of his closest *philos*. This sort of tension between individual self-assertion and responsibility to others is also fundamental to the ethical dimension of tragedy.

In tragedy the pursuit of honor and prestige can be a straightforward and unproblematic motive. That there may be both positive and negative constructions of that motive is, however, apparent in Euripides' *Phoenician Women*, where *philotimia* (love of honor) is personified by Jocasta as the force ("the worst of divinities") which drives Eteocles to seek power above all else, regardless of his city and of the pact he had concluded with his brother (531–32); this evaluation is in response to Eteocles' own personification of Tyranny as his chosen deity at 506; to these divinities his mother opposes Equality (536, 542) in a way that draws a strong contrast between democratic values and the self-assertive pursuit of honor and power. In the same play, however, honor and reputation are prominent motives of the noble Menoeceus, who voluntarily sacrifices himself to save his city (991–1018). The presentation of *philotimia* as a force that can help or harm the community mirrors the competing positive and negative constructions of that quality in fourth-century Athenian democracy (Dover 1974, 229–34; Whitehead 1983; Wilson 2000a, 144–97).

That one aspect of the pursuit of honor that Euripides' Eteocles takes to extremes is a concern for "manliness" (it is unmanly to lose the greater share and get the smaller, he says at *Phoenician Women* 509–10) reminds us that normative concepts of gender form a major element in the self-image of the man of honor. Masculinity as a positive value underlies every appeal to the concept of *andreia* (courage, but etymologically "manliness"); thus the manifestation of *andreia* on the part of a woman can be felt as paradoxical (see Electra's vision of being praised for her *andreia* at Sophocles' *Electra* 983, and her sister's rejoinder, "You're a woman not a man," at 997; cf. the *andreia* of Artemisia at Herodotus 7.99, with Hobbs 2000, 71–74), though there are both positive and negative examples of female courage being described in other terms: *eupsuchia* is used of Macaria at *Children of Heracles* 569, 597 and of Medea at *Medea* 403; Polyxena is described as *eukardios* and "excellent in soul" at *Hecuba* 579–80 (cf. 549); and *eupsuchia* and *aretê* are applied to Iphigenia at *Iphigenia at Aulis* 1562. But the specific desire to be regarded as manly rather than womanish is also a frequent element in male characters' sense of honor. This motivation may be pathological, as in the case of Eteocles (above), of Creon in *Antigone* (484–85, 525, 678–80, 740, 746, 756), or of Pentheus in *Bacchae* (785–86; cf. perhaps Heracles at *Women of Trachis* 1071–72, Ajax at *Ajax* 651–52); but it need not be (see for example Orestes' indignation that the Argives should be ruled by "a pair of women," *Libation Bearers* 304). At *Agamemnon* 918–19 Agamemnon's desire to be honored as a man, rather than pampered like a woman, is presumably uncontroversial on first hearing, but ironic when he swiftly falls victim to his wife in a battle of the sexes (940–44).

There is also a class dimension to the self-image of the "good" (*agathos*) man: "nobility," that is, the determination to live up to the demands inherent in the prestige of one's lineage, is a major feature of tragic characters' motivation (especially Sophoclean characters: Knox 1964). But these terms referring originally to "good birth" also take on more general, morally evaluative senses (Dover 1974, 93–95), as is highlighted in the case of Electra's husband, the farmer, in Euripides' *Electra*. The farmer is of noble stock, but (as he explains, 35–39) his family's wealth has declined, hence their "*eugeneia* has perished." Orestes, unaware of the farmer's atavistic social "nobility," begs to differ, appreciative of, but also somewhat puzzled by, the moral "nobility" (*eugeneia, gennaiotês, euandria,* and *aretê*) that can be present in the low-born and absent in their betters (253, 262, 367–90). These terms, though aristocratic in origin, have by the fifth century probably become the common currency of traditional morality (Winnington-Ingram 1980, 310), but their topicalization in *Electra* also reflects contemporary interest in the issue of the heritability versus teachability of virtue that surfaces in other Euripidean contexts (e.g., *Hippolytus* 79–81, 667, 730–31; *Suppliants* 913–17; cf. Plato, *Protagoras* 323c–328d, with

Guthrie 1969, 67). This is also a theme in Sophocles' *Philoctetes*, where the cynical Odysseus warns the inexperienced Neoptolemus that he must be *gennaios* (noble, but also "true to type") in carrying out a mission that will demand deceit as well as courage (51–53). Through his association with the "noble" Philoctetes, however, the sense of honor that is part of the *phusis* (nature) Neoptolemus has inherited from his father, Achilles, reasserts itself, and he shows himself *gennaios* not in deceiving, but in supporting his new *philos* (*gennaios*: 475–76, 1068, 1402; cf. *eugenés*: 874). The potential that is his inherited nobility must be developed in an environment in which a suitable role-model is present (Nussbaum 1976, Blundell 1988; cf. Protagoras DK 3, Democritus DK 33, 182–83).

Neoptolemus has a profound attachment to ideals of honor: when Odysseus proposes a plan which, though shameless (*anaides*), will bring success (81–85), Neoptolemus declares himself willing to use force but not deceit (90–91), for he would rather behave honorably (*kalôs*) and fail than succeed basely (94–95). Though the view of Adkins (1960) – that ancient Greek society had "originally" been, and to a large extent remained, a "results culture" in which success and failure define the honorable and the shameful – is no longer as influential as it was (see Cairns 1993, 71–79, with 260–61 n. 171 on this play), there is an element of paradox in Neopto-lemus' words, for though not the only disgraceful thing there is, failure is certainly one of the things considered disgraceful in 409 BCE. But Neoptolemus is persuaded to participate in deceit, and so as the play unfolds he is forced to confront the disjunction between his desire for the honor that will accrue from successful com-pletion of his mission, and ultimately from his successful participation in the capture of Troy (112–15, 839–42; cf. 1344–47, 1381, 1421–44), and his initial sense, reactivated in the course of his interaction with Philoctetes, that it is shameful to succeed by deceit (473–79, 902–3, 906, 908–9, 929–30, 967–68, 968–74). It is the latter that wins out in the end, Neoptolemus' concerns about deceit being exacer-bated by the genuine friendship that develops between himself and Philoctetes, and he returns Philoctetes' bow, because to take it was an error (1224), a shameful deceit (1228), a shameful injustice (1234), a shameful error (1248–49). Though he then attempts to persuade Philoctetes to go to Troy of his own volition, when the latter refuses he abides by his promise to take him home (1402). Neoptolemus' sense of honor is thus at the center of the play's action; tested, and ultimately proved true to his *phusis*, he shows himself, because of this profound commitment to the honorable, able to repudiate action that he feels unworthy of himself; to evince a concern for his self-image that sets his evaluation of his conduct at variance with that of the group to which he belongs; to place his sense of himself as a just man above his concern for his reputation as warrior; and to commit his sense of honor to a friend in a way that involves respect for a friend's wishes even though he knows that this will be against both his own and his friend's best interests. The idealism manifested in this play's dramatization of the traditional ethic that it is honorable to help one's friends is not an isolated example; the commitment to friendship on the part of Theseus that persuades Heracles, in Euripides' eponymous play, that life is worth living, even after disgrace, is a striking but not isolated parallel. Plays like these remind us that Greek *philia* was not necessarily a narrowly utilitarian exchange of benefit for benefit (Konstan 1997, 57), and that tragedy can be ethically uplifting as well as unsettling.

Though Neoptolemus does not use the word *aidôs* (shame) of his emotional distress, it is clear that shame is what he is feeling: the plan he eventually repudiates is called "shameless" (*anaides*, without *aidôs*) at 83, he expresses the anxiety that he "will appear *aischros*" (in a shameful light) at 906, and he rejects his participation in deception as a "shameful error" (*hamartia aischra*, 1248–49). There are several points to note about Neoptolemus' shame. First, there is the fact that remorse and its associated desire to make good one's offence can be expressed in the traditional language of honor and shame. Such uses of this language – though not necessarily the emotions to which they refer – appear first in tragedy, and particularly in Euripides, who offers a number of new, retrospective uses of the verbs that mean "I am ashamed" (see Cairns 1993, 291–303). These uses belong with an increasing recognition of the phenomenon of the retrospective, "guilty" conscience, again especially in Euripides (Cairns 1993, 303–5). Second, though Neoptolemus does use traditional, quasi-aesthetic terminology (*aischros* basically means "ugly," and *kalos* "beautiful") and does express a concern for how things look (906), it is clear that he is not just keeping up appearances. This internalized sense of shame, based on commitment to personally endorsed standards, is a significant element in the ethical theory of the fifth-century thinker Democritus (DK 84, 244, 264; Kahn 1998, 34–36), whose injunction to "feel shame before oneself above all" is given flesh in the characterization of the Sophoclean Neoptolemus. Although ancient Greeks talk a lot about honor, reputation, and how things look, this does not mean that they lived in a "shame-culture," at least if that is taken to refer to a society in which external sanctions, rather than personal commitment to one's own values, enforce moral norms (see Cairns 1993, 27–47; Williams 1993, 88–102, 219–23; for a succinct illustration of the way that shame can promote both conformity and conviction, see *Antigone* 510–11).

The final point about Neoptolemus' sense of shame is perhaps the simplest, but possibly also the most significant: his concern for his self-image as a man of honor promotes not selfish pursuit of his own self-assertive goals, but concern for another person. The code of honor to which he subscribes is inclusive: it is disgraceful both to fail and to fail to meet one's obligations or to pursue success by excessive or improper means. This inclusivity is manifested in the semantics of the verbs that mean "to be ashamed" (*aideomai* and *aischunomai*) themselves, for though they can, in various constructions, focus on actions or states of affairs in the past, present, or future, they also take a direct object, which may refer either to the witnesses of one's actions, in whose eyes one's self-image is vulnerable, or to a person or persons toward whom one is under some obligation. In this latter sense we are driven to translate not "I feel shame," but "I respect," and it is in this sense that the verbs are at home in the contexts of *philia*, guest-friendship (*xenia*), and supplication (*hiketeia*). As this semantic inclusivity suggests, the other-regarding and self-regarding aspects of the code of honor are very closely enmeshed; thus, in Euripides' *Iphigenia among the Taurians*, Pylades can justify laying down his life for a friend with reference to his determination to avoid a reputation for "cowardice" in others' eyes (674–86); and in Sophocles' *Ajax* Tecmessa, focusing on the very sense of honor which prompts Ajax, humiliated by failed retaliation for a perceived slight, to kill himself, can remind him that it is also disgraceful for the nobleman (*eugenês*) to fail to show *aidôs* and *charis* (gratitude) toward his family and dependants (485–524). Tecmessa combines positive appeals to (other-regarding) pity, *aidós*, and gratitude (506–22) with re-minders of "what people will say" (500–504), of the damage which this will cause to Ajax's honor and that of his family (505), and of incompatibility of ingratitude with *eugeneia* (523–24). She thus appeals to a sense of *aidós* that focuses both on Ajax's own honor and on that of other people.

If *aidós* involves striking a balance between one's own *timé* and that of others, failure to strike such a balance, by over-valuing oneself and undervaluing others, can be referred to as *hubris*. As Fisher has demonstrated (1992), *hubris* is not specifically a form of overweening pride that excites the indignant retaliation (*nemesis*) of the gods, but rather a concept with (as Aristotle insists, *Rhetoric* 1378b23–30) a fundamental reference to dishonor. There is a continuity between *hubris* in tragedy and in Athen-ian law and life, where it often refers to forms of physical, sexual, or verbal assault that demonstrate the agent's contempt for his victim, but also regularly denotes ways of conducting oneself that demonstrate an inflated sense of one's own importance and a corresponding disregard for others' claims. Two general points might be made: first, the fact that *hubris*, as a way of dishonoring others, is regarded as an offence that reflects badly on the perpetrator indicates (in general) the inclusivity of the concept of honor (it is dishonorable both to fail and to go too far in the pursuit of success) and (in particular) that it is not necessarily appropriate to describe that concept in terms of a zero-sum game in which one person's loss is always another's gain. Second, *hubris* is an offence in Athenian law (Fisher 1990; 1992, 36–82), reflecting a determination to ensure that Athenian citizens have the support of the state in defending their right to honor. This notion of an entitlement to honor which it is illegitimate or illegal to infringe means that (as Aristotle recognizes at *Nicomachean Ethics* 1130b2) it is in no way misplaced to talk about a notion of justice in the distribution of honor. Given that to be an Athenian citizen is to possess a share of *timé* in theory equal to that of one's fellow citizens (loss of citizen rights being *atimia*, translated "disfranchise-ment" but etymologically "dishonor"), it is possible to see *timé* as the nearest thing that the Athenians possessed to a concept of "rights."

A proper sense of *aidós* thus forestalls *hubris*. Frequently associated with *aidós* is the virtue of *sóphrosuné*, literally "sound-mindedness" or "safe thinking," but more generally a virtue of self-control or self-restraint in the face of temptations such as food, drink, sex, power, or prestige (see North 1966); thus *sóphrosuné* can be an antonym of *hubris* (as at Sophocles, *Ajax* 1259–60; Euripides, *Electra* 257–61, *Phoenician Women* 1112). The link with *aidós* is established in such contexts as Plato's *Charmides*, where *aidós* is offered as a definition of *sóphrosuné* (160e); or in Aristotle's *Eudemian Ethics* (1234a32), where *aidós* contributes to the "natural virtue" of *sóphrosuné*. It is also apparent in Euripides' *Hippolytus*, where the associ-ation of both concepts with sex and sexuality is reflected in the *aidós* which supports Hippolytus' notion of *sóphrosuné* as an innate and total aversion to sex (78–81) and in the *aidós* which plays a more complex and ambiguous role in the *sóphrosuné* that motivates Phaedra's painful struggle to maintain both her reputation and her virtue in the face of a powerful illicit passion (244–49, 335, 375–430). Given the wide application of the term in fifth-century Greek, both Phaedra and Hippolytus could be said to exhibit at least a degree of *sóphrosuné* in the play; but there is an element of paradox in this conclusion, for in neither case does their "safe thinking" keep them safe, a paradox reflected in Hippolytus' observation that Phaedra exhibited *sóphrosuné* (by killing herself), though she was unable to be *sôphrôn* (conquer her passion), while he, who does possess *sôphrosunê*, has not used it to his own advantage (1034–35).

Gods and Men

Not only humans, but also immortals participate in a hierarchy of honor in which the *timê* that the gods possess is quantitatively but not qualitatively different from that of mortals. One indication of this is the fact that verbs meaning "honor," "respect," "revere" (*sebein* and cognates), though typically at home in the religious sphere, are also used of the response to human superiors. Gods deserve respect, however, not merely as mortals' superiors in power and honor; they can also be regarded as upholders of human morality, hence nouns and adjectives derived from *sebas* (both the awe that superiors arouse and the majesty to which such awe responds), such as *eusebês* and *eusebeia*, *dussebês* and *dussebeia*, refer not only to right and wrong ways of cultivating the divine, but to right and wrong in general (see Adkins 1960, 132–38). The varying connotations of these terms are exploited in Sophocles' *Antigone*, where Antigone's *eusebeia* in honoring her kin, the gods, and the moral laws which the gods uphold (511, 922–24, 943) is contrasted with Creon's demand for respect for the city, its laws, and himself as their upholder (166, 301, 514, 516, 730, 744). The insufficiency of each of these conceptions of *eusebeia* as aspects of the whole is encapsulated in the chorus's grudging comment to Antigone that "to show reverence [*sebein*: for the gods or for her brother?] is a sort of *eusebeia*, but power, for whomever power concerns, is in no way to be trespassed upon; it was your own willful temper that destroyed you" (872–75). In the end, however, Creon's failure to comprehend Antigone's brand of *eusebeia* is condemned (1349–50).

The gods thus function as a limitation upon human self-assertion, which, if one accepts their reality, is more effective than the limitations imposed by purely human disapproval. In theory, we can distinguish different ways in which this might be so: the gods might simply resent mortal achievement or prosperity as a threat to their own preeminence; they might see such achievement or prosperity as a form of insolent pride; they might be indignant at direct human affronts to their honor or failure to pay them due respect; or they might punish human beings for their offences against other humans out of their concern for morality in general. In tragic practice, however, these strands are difficult to disentangle.

The notion that the gods resent mortal prosperity as such is certainly not absent from tragedy. The chorus of Aeschylus' *Agamemnon* (750–56) refers to an "aged tale among mortals, uttered long ago" that great prosperity leads to disaster (though they reject that explanation in favor of one in which the *hubris* of the wealthy receives just punishment, 757–82; see Fisher 1992, 275–77, 363). Furthermore, there is a reflection of the popular superstition that good fortune attracts cosmic malevolence when Philoctetes, on granting Neoptolemus the boon of handling his marvelous bow, advises him to prostrate himself before Phthonos (Jealousy), lest this good fortune bring him pain (776–78). The notion that the universe is so ordered that human happiness cannot persist indefinitely, that the gods dispense good and bad fortune on an apparently arbitrary basis, goes back to the beginnings of Greek literature (*Iliad* 24.525–34): for Homer's Achilles, its lesson is endurance, but also a capacity for pity based on humans' shared vulnerability to vicissitude that recurs both in Aristotle's theory of the tragic and in tragic representations of pity (Sophocles, *Ajax* 121–26, *Philoctetes* 501–6, *Oedipus at Colonus* 566–68; Euripides, *Hecuba* 282–87; cf. Dover 1974, 269).

Generally, however, divine resentment in tragedy focuses on human offence. That disregard of the limitations inherent in one's human status can constitute an implicit attack on the status of the gods is demonstrated by several passages that adumbrate the gods' resentment of "big" or "more than mortal" thoughts (e.g., Aeschylus, *Persians* 820, *Seven against Thebes* 425; Sophocles, *Ajax* 760–61). A good example of the values in play in such circumstances is the presentation of the homecoming of Agamemnon in Aeschylus. Agamemnon is a returning victor, and the scene in which he is welcomed by his wife draws on the ethical framework of the victory ode for returning athletic victors, in which the poet's concern is regularly to provide appropriate praise of the victor, his achievement, and his wealth in a way that sidelines the envy of other mortals and highlights the victor's success by emphasizing the need to avoid the jealousy of the gods (see Most 2003). Clytemnestra's agenda is precisely the opposite: hence her praise is extravagant (855–913); she emphasizes the abundance of the house's wealth and its wasteful use (958–62); she persuades her husband to ignore his concerns at being honored more highly than mortals deserve (922, 925), at counting himself happy before he is dead (927–30), and, in the face of his awareness of the dangers of divine *phthonos* (921, 946–47), assures him that envy is merely a negative way of recognizing achievement (939) and that the only negative emotions he has to fear are those of inferior mortals (937). Agamemnon's *aidôs* as he takes off his shoes to mitigate his offence (944–49) is an awareness that he is pushing his claim to honor beyond the limit. Though this is an event of purely symbolic importance, that importance lies precisely in what it tells us about Agamemnon's sense of how his honor relates to that of others; Clytemnestra's perverted epinician induces him to behave in a way that affronts both gods and men, her purpose not to dispel but to attract resentment at his *hubris* (the word does not occur, but see Fisher 1992, 287–89; Cairns 1996, 19). The conviction expressed by the chorus in the previous ode (750–82), that the gods resent the *hubris* of the prosperous rather than prosperity as such, is immediately applied to the case of Agamemnon.

The pursuit of honor and over-confidence in prosperity that dishonor both god and man are also prominent in Aeschylus' *Persians*. For the Ghost of Darius (808–12 and 821–22) the Persians are guilty of *hubris*, part of which certainly (as Fisher emphasizes, 1992, 259–61) lies in their lack of *aidôs* in plundering sacred images and burning the temples of the gods (809–12); but the lesson of divine punishment for this sacrilege is that mortals "must not think excessive thoughts, for *hubris* bursts out in bloom and produces a crop of delusion/disaster [*atê*], whence it reaps a harvest of lamentation" (821–22). The reason why one should avoid "excessive thoughts" is that *hubris* leads to a harvest of lamentation, and this only makes sense if "thinking excessively" and *hubris* can be equated. This description of the Persians' acts and the dispositions from which they spring as *hubris* is (pace Gagarin 1976, 49–50) extensively prepared for in references to such typical conditions of *hubris* as youthful impetuosity (73–74, 352, 718, 744, 754, 782) and abundant wealth (3, 9, 45, 53, 79–80, 159, 163–68, 250, 252, 751, 754–56). Buoyed by their prosperity and led by their rash and youthful king, the Persians, as Darius points out, have come to believe that their prosperity will continue indefinitely (824–26), thus ignoring the unpredictability of divine favor and the gods' role in human prosperity, a theme raised by the chorus (94–115, 158, 515–16, 921), the queen (161–64, 472–77, 724), the messenger (345–47, 353–54, 362, 373, 454–55), and Xerxes himself (909–12, 942–43), as well as by the Ghost of Darius (725, 739–42). The contempt for the gods that the Persians show in their acts of sacrilege (808–12), their excessive, boastful, godless thoughts (808, 820, 825, 827–28), and their over-confident sense of themselves as masters of their destiny is also presented as an offence that threatens an entire world order: they crossed from Asia to Europe (66–71), even though it was their allotted portion (*moira*) to rule by land, not sea (101–14), and Greece and Asia constitute two distinct "lots" (186–87); once in Greece, they find the land and the elements against them (480–512, 792). Darius reacts to this disregard of natural limits in his incredulity that Xerxes closed the Bosporus (723–25), something which he and the queen agree must be the result of divinely inspired delusion (724–25); it was "youthful boldness" and "a disease of the mind" that led Xerxes, with divine assistance, to go so far as to attempt to bind the Hellespont like a slave and impose his will on the god Poseidon (742–51). The Persian attempt to enslave the free (241–42, 402–5) is also a transgression of the *timê* which Zeus granted them – that one man should rule all Asia (but not Asia and Europe together, 762–65).

For Darius, the gods' response to all this is unequivocally punishment (Zeus is a *kolastês*, punisher, of "over-boastful thoughts," 827–28). For the messenger, however, Persian defeat is due to a divine *phthonos* that Xerxes failed to foresee (362), a perspective that some (Winnington-Ingram 1983, 1–13; Fisher 1992, 261–62) have connected with apparently non-moral explanations of that defeat as the work of malicious or deceitful deities (*daimones*, etc.: 282–83, 345–47, 353–54, 454–55, 472, 513–16, 845–46, 909–12, 921, 942–43, 1005–7; for divine deceit, see 94–100, 353–63, 373, 472–73). Yet the messenger himself indicates that the reason for Xerxes' failure to suspect a divinely inspired reversal was his confidence (372–73), a phenomenon that the queen explains as a tendency blindly to believe that when things are going well (when "the *daimôn* flows fair") they will continue to do so (601–2) – the same phenomenon that Darius describes, in his warning of the consequences of *hubris*, as "despising one's current *daimôn*" (825). What the chorus and the messenger see as divine deceit or malice is what Darius and the queen recognize as the gods' guiding a human who is set on disaster (724–25, 742), and this is merely the negative counterpart of divine assistance in success. There is thus only one theological explanation of Persian defeat, although only Darius gives it full and authoritative expression.

A pietistic reading might see similar notions, in which the limits of human self-assertion are defined by the gulf between man and god, in operation in Sophocles' *Oedipus the King*: a successful and resourceful king reaches the limits of human achievement only to become a paradigm of the insignificance of man (1186–1222); his *hubris*, if there is any (873), will lie in his attempt to use human intelligence to comprehend a world that is not subject to human control. In other plays by Sophocles and Euripides, however, gods' concern for their own *timê* is more narrowly conceived: in *Ajax*, *Hippolytus*, *Trojan Women*, and *Bacchae*, for example, gods' narrow concern with their honor contrasts markedly with the more complex ethical issues raised by the conduct of the human characters; there is a particular contrast in *Ajax*, *Hippolytus*, and *Bacchae* between gods' determination to achieve satisfaction through punishment of human disrespect and humans' rejection of retaliation in their own case (*Ajax* 121–26, 1338–39; *Hippolytus* 1448–52) or deprecation of divine retaliation (*Hippolytus* 114–20, *Bacchae* 1348). In *Hippolytus* there is a possibility that the terminology employed highlights a double standard in gods' resentment of arrogance and disrespect. The servant's attempt to persuade Hippolytus to accord Aphrodite the respect she deserves involves his using the same adjective, *semnos*, pejoratively of Hippolytus and approvingly of Aphrodite (93–107): Hippolytus, he implies, is *semnos* (proud, arrogant) in refusing to honor a goddess who is herself *semnos* (august, reverend). It is a normal feature of the usage of this adjective (derived from the root *seb-* present in *sebas, sebein, eusebeia*) that it is pejorative when applied to mortals and positive when applied to gods; but the two applications are brought into very close juxtaposition here, in a scene which, after all, concludes with the servant's statement that gods should not react like mortals (120). Similar is the nurse's attempt to persuade Phaedra to give in to her passion for Hippolytus on the grounds that to resist it is "nothing but *hubris*" (474); earlier in the same speech (at 445–46) she describes Aphrodite's resentment of mortal disrespect: "Whomever she finds excessive and proud [literally "thinking big"] she takes and treats with incredible *hubris*." In straightforward cases, *hubris* is used of gratuitous affront rather than of retaliation for an affront suffered (Aristotle, *Rhetoric* 1378b25–6), though there are examples of *hubris* designating excessive revenge or, in a more descriptive sense, retaliation that replicates the original *hubris* (see *Prometheus Bound* 970, with Fisher 1992, 250). *Hippolytus* 445–46 could be one of the latter uses; but the fact that *hubris* is the word used of the goddess's retaliation for what she perceives as *hubris* at least permits the conclusion that gods behave in exactly the ways that they criticize in mortals. (The reasoning required to reach this conclusion – that one should not do oneself what one criticizes in others – is much commoner in Greek ethical discourse than is commonly realized: see Blundell 1989, 24; Cairns 2001; cf. Wattles 1996, 27–41.)

Sophocles' *Ajax*

In order to illustrate how values are embedded, manipulated, and contested in the action of a single play, I conclude with a brief discussion of Sophocles' *Ajax*. The atmosphere in this play is one of bitterness and retaliation of the sort that arises when former *philoi* feel themselves betrayed and regard each other as *echthroi*. Menelaus, Teucer, and Odysseus all trace this situation to the judgment that awarded Achilles' arms to Odysseus (1052–54, 1132–35, 1336–37); for Ajax's side, however, it was the judgment itself that constituted the betrayal, and for their opponents Ajax's reaction to that judgment. In keeping with this disagreement about "who started it," each side sees as *hubris* what the other sees as retaliation (Ajax: 153, 196, 367, 382, 454, 955–62, 966, 969–71; the Atreidae: 1061, 1081, 1087–88, 1258, cf. 1320). *Hubris* thus emerges as a term one applies polemically to the behavior of one's opponents and not to one's own, but the similarity of the conduct of both parties is underlined by Tecmessa's report (303–4) of Ajax's deluded exultation in "all the *hubris* he'd gone and paid out against them," a pregnant phrase which seems to encompass the idea that Ajax has reacted with *hubris* in retaliation for *hubris* suffered (see Garvie 1998, ad loc). The parallelism is confirmed when Menelaus justifies his own "thinking big" (*meg' au phronô*) as requital for Ajax's *hubris* at 1087–88, and the chorus-leader immediately accuses him of *hubris* in turn (1092).

This reciprocity of harm for harm is endorsed by the goddess, Athena, when she invites Odysseus to rejoice in his enemy's humiliation (79). But Odysseus does not rejoice; instead, he feels pity (121–26), because the pattern of alternation that has so reduced the once resourceful Ajax (118–19) is for him a sign of the ephemerality that he and Ajax share with all human beings. The theme of alternation permeates the play (Garvie 1998, 15). Broadly speaking, its lesson is *sôphrosunê*, yet this *sôphrosunê* is presented in multiple perspectives. For Athena, Ajax's downfall justifies human *sôphrosunê* in the face of divine power (127–33), and without this Ajax was *kakos* ("bad," i.e., without *aretê*, 132–33). For Tecmessa, changes of fortune are harsh, but must be accepted, as she has accepted her own enslavement, enforced by the superior power of the gods and Ajax himself (485–90). For Menelaus, alternation implies a balance of offence and punishment that should promote *sôphrosunê*, a sense of shame, respect for authority, and avoidance of *hubris* as the mainstay of civic and military order (1073–86), while for his brother the reduction of Ajax to a mere "shadow" means that his supporters ought to show *sôphrosunê* rather than *hubris* (1257–59). Ajax himself apparently accepts that the mutability of friendship and enmity requires a recognition of divine and human authority that he too describes as *sôphrosunê* (666–83), before confirming his implacable hatred of his enemies in the prayer to the Erinyes that precedes his suicide (835–44). In this he contrasts profoundly with Odysseus, who not only accepts (1359) but also exemplifies (1377) that mutability, intervening in an exchange of insult for insult (1320, 1324) to manifest the *sôphrosunê* called for by the chorus-leader (1264), affirming (in 1319, 1340, 1355, 1357, 1380) the *aretê* of Ajax that had been denied by Athena and Menelaus (133, 1071), and confirming, in a speech that portrays the denial of burial as dishonorably depriving a good man of the honor he deserves (1332–45), the view of Teucer and the chorus that it was *hubris* (1091, 1151, 1385, 1391–92, cf. 1306–7). Thus the *sôphrosunê* of Odysseus effects a positive alternation in the fortunes of Ajax, an alternation reflected in the way that the action is framed by Odysseus' initial pity at Ajax's fall and final affirmation of his *aretê*. Ironically, it is another's *sôphrosunê* that restores the fortunes of a man who rejected *sôphrosunê* and could not bear to live on until his fortunes might change (473–74).

The play illustrates the importance of context and presentation for our understanding of the ethical dimension of tragedy. In the abstract, Menelaus' account of the need for discipline and respect for authority (1071–86) and Agamemnon's insistence that majority decisions must be accepted (1242–49) draw on aspects of democratic ideology that an Athenian audience could be expected to endorse, yet these are contemptible characters. Equally, to think more than mortal thoughts (758–61, 777) and reject divine assistance (762–77) – that is, to manifest the *hubris* of disregarding divine *timê* (see Fisher 1992, 325, against Garvie 1998, 196) – could be represented as a grave and dangerous offence. Here it is an aspect of the genuine preeminence of an extraordinary human being, a preeminence that is consolidated in the hero-cult that begins to take shape toward the end of the play (Burian 1972, Henrichs 1993b). Most strikingly of all, Sophocles effaces the enormity of Ajax's intention to slaughter his comrades in revenge for an apparently legitimate decision: this intention is mentioned in the prologue (40–65), and Ajax never regrets it

(387–91, 447–49, 454–55), but the real emphasis is on the humiliating diversion of his revenge onto the sheep and cattle (141–53, 182–91, 214–44, 284–327, 364–67, 372–76), so that, with the sympathy of both his friends and his enemy, Odysseus, Ajax appears as a victim rather than a perpetrator, and the negative construction of his actions as *hubris* (1061) is postponed until after his death, to be advanced by a character who is himself bent on *hubris* (see Heath 1987b, 173, 200). The raw material for characterizing Ajax as a hubristic, impious criminal and the Atreidae as defenders of essential civic and military institutions is there in the play, but the poet chooses not to present it in that way.

The relation between the diverging outlooks of Ajax and Odysseus is central to the play's ethical dialectic. Odysseus' excellence (*aretê*) is confirmed by Teucer at 1381 and 1399; yet the aim of this *aretê* is to reaffirm that of Ajax (see esp. 1380), and the two forms of excellence could not be more diametrically opposed. For Ajax, the shameful is to live with the disgrace of failure (473–74), the requirement of nobility to live or die "honorably" (*kalôs*, 479–80) by showing oneself to be "not gutless" (471–72); for Odysseus, what is *kalon* is to recognize that there are limits to hatred, retaliation, and the pursuit of one's own advantage (1347, 1349), limits imposed by a concept of *dikê* (1335, 1342, 1344) that demands that one respect (*aideisthai*, 1356) the *aretê* and *timê* of others (1339–42, 1345, 1355–57). Ajax lives by the strict reciprocity that demands that you treat others as they have treated you; Odysseus extends this principle into a version of the Golden Rule, that you should treat others as you would like to be treated yourself (123–26, 1365).

Yet there are also similarities between the two men. Though their conceptions of the honorable differ, each has internalized its imperatives. While Ajax imagines his father, Telamon, as unable to look him in the eye if he returns "naked without a prize of excellence" (462–66), it is clear that he has set his father up as a standard to aspire to (434–40, 464–65, 470–72; see Williams 1993, 85). Odysseus equally uses the language of honor and shame in a context that highlights his commitment to internalized standards. He is not impartial with regard to Ajax – he was his enemy and he hated him (1347, 1355, 1357, cf. 78, 122) – so it is all the more remarkable that he overcomes his partiality to insist that Ajax receive the recognition that his *aretê* deserves. The values to which Odysseus subscribes are traditional and traditionally expressed, but his courage in acting on them in a context in which all others accept a strict polarity of friendship and enmity shows that one can be so committed to one's values that one will uphold them without consideration of personal bias or others' opinion.

If Odysseus' values endorse their opposite, the self-assertive *aretê* of Ajax, then the independent Ajax is not as independent as he thought (Winnington-Ingram 1980, 60–61); his burial, his posthumous fame, and his cult are assured only by someone who embraces the other-regarding aspects of honor to which he himself gave little consideration; Ajax's confidence that his dependants will be provided for (560–70) is justified only by the intervention of Odysseus as the embodiment of that mutability of friendship and enmity that Ajax found so intolerable. Agamemnon resembles Ajax in rejecting that mutability (1360), allowing burial out of deference toward his friend, Odysseus, while maintaining his hatred for his enemy, Ajax (1370–73). The polarity is also maintained by Teucer's rejection, as displeasing to the deceased (1393–95), of Odysseus' offer to take part, as a *philos*, in the burial of Ajax (1376–80). Odysseus is as isolated at the end of the play as Ajax was at the beginning (see Garvie 1998 on 1384). Though it may be true that the play makes a case for both Aiantean and Odyssean forms of excellence in fifth-century society (Garvie 1998, 16), it offers no easy answers as to how these are to be reconciled; it is not Ajax or Odysseus but the Atreidae whose values take account of "society." Both self-assertion and *sôphrosunê* appear in good and bad guises, and the positive form of the one not only defines, but also negates that of the other. The dialectic into which the values of this play are drawn well illustrates our inability to elucidate the ethical dimension of tragedy by applying a ready-made template of "what the Athenians believed."

FURTHER READING

Adkins 1960 still represents a good starting point for the study of Greek (and tragic) ethics, simply because it states a very strong case (that the original primacy of competitive values in Greek society created persistent problems for the development of satisfactory notions of duty and moral responsibility) on the basis of close examination of Greek value-terms. Adkins' influence is discernible in the introductions to pre-philosophical ethics in Kahn 1998 and Irwin 1989, but for an excellent, brief introduction to Greek thought that poses a radical challenge to the Adkinsian approach, see Gill 1995. The more inclusive approach to Greek ethics that Gill favors, emphasizing the role of the social emotions, of the continuity of Greek ethical thinking, and of the importance of rich, "whole-person," socially embedded values, may be traced in Blundell 1989, Fisher 1992, Cairns 1993, Williams 1993, and Gill 1996. All of these include extensive discussion of tragedy: Blundell discusses a fundamental aspect of Greek ethical thinking both in general and in Sophocles (on friendship, cf. also Konstan 1997); Cairns and Fisher look at complementary aspects of the values of honor and shame; among the other plays that they discuss, Williams focuses particularly on Sophocles' *Ajax* and Euripides' *Hippolytus*, and Gill has an extensive exploration of Euripides' *Medea*. Other emotions with major implications for tragedy are studied in Konstan 2001 (pity) and Harris 2001 (anger). Belfiore 2000 documents tragedy's recurrent focus on acts of violence between kinfolk; she, like Blundell 1989 and Harris 2001, offers a very different perspective on tragic revenge from Burnett 1998, which is, nonetheless, a challenging treatment. Ethical issues naturally loom large in many interpretative studies of tragedy. Two outstanding general approaches to interpretation that emphasize, in very different ways, the genre's ethical dimension are Goldhill 1986a and Heath 1987b. Of the many useful studies of individual tragedians that discuss the relation between tragedy and the values of Athenian society, I would single out Winnington-Ingram 1980 and 1983. Finally, any student looking for an incisive introduction to the full range and complexity of classical Greek ethical attitudes should read Dover 1974.

CHAPTER TWENTY

The Gods

Donald Mastronarde

Greek heroic myth involves the gods, both Olympian and non-Olympian, as progenitors, protectors, or antagonists of the human figures. The tradition of high-style poetry in archaic and classical Greece privileged mythic content as a form of narrative that could be more or less self-standing (as in epic, tragedy, at least some dithyrambs, and Stesichorus' great triadic lyrics) or could be incorporated within compositions that served specific purposes beyond narration (as in hymns, paeans, partheneia, epinicians). In all these situations the mythic content served the creation and transmission of cultural, political, and metaphysical values, postulating origins and exemplifying typical patterns of social and interpersonal relations and human–divine interaction. The gods in myth, as in religious practice and belief, do not have a simple and consistent role. They can at times be viewed as guarantors of order and justice and as agents who operate in a predictable manner open to straightforward explanation; at other times, however, they provide an explanation of last resort for what is uncanny, unpredictable, unseen, inexplicable, or intractable for humans. The gods of Greek tragedy feature this same diversity of function and ethical significance.

The poetic tradition also provided models for other aspects of tragedy's use of the gods. Authoritative stories of the heroic age presented negative as well as positive examples, and tragedy too features beneficent as well as malevolent, punitive, or destructive interventions of the divine. Indeed, the preponderance of the latter has led to the common assumption that disastrous misfortune is a defining criterion of the tragic genre. In traditional Greek thought (e.g., in Homer), divine and human action may be seen as operating in parallel, or human impulse and divine inspiration (or delusion) may interpenetrate or collaborate – a phenomenon often called "double motivation" or "overdetermination." Such notions of dual causation and responsibility carry over into tragedy. Even though tragedy develops a greater emphasis on human character and human responsibility, there are few if any examples of plays in which the divine plane can be entirely ignored, in which a social and psychological analysis of human action divorced from considerations of the supernatural (the kind of analysis that applies in some "realistic" drama of the nineteenth and twentieth centuries) can be considered adequate. The divine is almost always potentially present as the unseen mover, even if this aspect is sometimes concentrated in prologues, epilogue-like *deus ex machina* scenes, messengers' narrations of offstage events, or choral odes. The participation of the divine enhances the status of the represented events by adding the possibility of a higher or deeper meaning, or at minimum an exemplary force. Human action and human suffering thus become more dignified and worthy of the commemoration that tragedy offers, and the traditional system of heroic fame (*kleos*) is maintained and extended to newly invented mythic events.

The flexibility of the supernatural apparatus in tragedy is also a function of the system of polytheism and of the coexistence of individual gods with the notion of fate or destiny. As in epic, different gods can be imagined to have different favorites and different grudges and thus to be in conflict (for example, the prophetess Theonoe neatly describes a dispute between Hera and Aphrodite in Euripides' *Helen* 878–86). When it is convenient as an explanatory mechanism or as a plot device, however, a policy of non-intervention can be cited: Artemis asserts the principle that gods do not block each other's wills in Euripides' *Hippolytus* 1328–30.[1] Within this scheme, Zeus holds a special position, as the preeminent, patriarchal power. He is often cited by choruses, human characters, and other gods as the final authority who determines what must be. Unlike other deities, he was very rarely represented on the dramatic stage. There is a comparable flexibility in imagining how Zeus and the gods as a corporate body are connected to the related concepts of destiny, fate, and fortune, which are expressed by such Greek words as *moira*, *daimôn*, and *tuchê*.[2] At times, the gods are thought of as determining or at least vigorously executing what is fated and necessary. At other times, when there is a need to evoke resignation or submission, or to deflect too open resentment or disapproval, fate can be cited as a power that stands above the gods, even Zeus.

Inscrutable, Invisible Gods

Just as in the experience of gods in cult and prayer, most interaction with the gods in tragedy depends on indirect signs (oracles, dreams, omens) or on the inferences and interpretations of fallible characters and chorus. Consequently, divergent interpretations may be expressed over the course of a play or trilogy, whether by different interpreters or by the same interpreter at different times. Such inferences will normally be more authoritative toward the end of the play, when crucial events have already happened and the characters are closer to enjoying a level of knowledge equal to that of the audience. But since inscrutability is an expected feature of the supernatural, even at the end of a tragedy there may remain a residue of doubt, uncertainty, or contradictory possibilities.

Recognition that comes too late is a key device of many tragic plots, exploiting the gap between human knowledge and human judgment on the one hand and the knowledge and will of the gods on the other. Aeschylus' *Persians* reveals in successive steps the divine role in the defeat of the Persian invaders. In the entrance-song, after a moment of confidence in Persian might, the chorus reverts to anxiety in their final stanzas, pivoting on a stanza that names the "cunning-minded deception of god" as a force no mortal can elude (93–100, correctly transposed by most editors to follow 114). The queen mother soon brings ominous signs conveyed by a dream (the latest and clearest of a series) and a bird-omen, only to be followed by a messenger's

confirmation of the feared disaster, containing its own allusions to divine participation (345–47, 353–54, 362). The Ghost of Darius brings even greater clarity about
the cooperation of the gods in Xerxes' folly (724–25, 739–42) and about the further
disasters predictable from oracles (800–802). By the time Xerxes himself enters, there
is no need for him to express his own realization of his folly. In *Libation Bearers*,
Clytemnestra has a comparable warning dream and directs an abortive attempt to
avert an evil outcome, but in her final lines (928–29) she accepts the full import of
her dream, using the same keen intelligence with which she instantly comprehended
the "riddle" of Aegisthus' death (887–88) – too late, but even this late recognition
makes her death more dignified than that of Agamemnon in the preceding play. In
Seven against Thebes, whatever the precise balance of Eteocles' patriotism, accursed
ambition, and misogyny, the meaningfulness of his death is enhanced when the (self-)
entrapping process of the selection of the seven champions reaches resolution and,
recognizing the fulfillment of curse and dreams and the will of the gods, he embraces
his doom as fitting (655, 673–75, 689, 703, 709–11).

In the Aeschylean examples just cited, it is relatively easy to moralize the pattern, to
see the late-recognized divine role as punishing a transgression, whether one's own or
an ancestor's, although the notion of "cunning-minded deception" alluded to in
Persians complicates the picture. In Sophocles' *Oedipus the King*, it is true that
everything fits in the end, that the obscure and the misinterpreted have been clarified,
but equally important is the residue of the inexplicable. Here, in a single play without
the larger context of the trilogy form used in Aeschylus' treatment of the Theban
myth, Sophocles offers very little detail about the past, and the oracle given to Laius is
in an unconditional form: "You will be slain by your own child" rather than "If you
beget a child, he will kill you." It is far from obvious that one should seek an origin of
the familial disaster in a transgression (and it should go without saying that the
attempt to avoid the doom predicted by an oracle is not itself a transgression that
can explain what happens to this family) or that one should have recourse to other
versions to supply the lack of clear causation. The gulf between the immortal and the
mortal is exemplified here not only by the lateness of recognition but also by the
ultimate arbitrariness of the misfortune. More important, Oedipus thus becomes a
general example of the human condition. The situation of Heracles in *Women of
Trachis* is somewhat comparable, although there is more in that play to suggest a
"poetically just" recoil of Heracles' previous violence, against monsters and women,
upon himself, whether or not one wishes to view Zeus as offended by something
in Heracles' behavior (the interpretation that Lichas applies in the case of the
hero's servitude to Omphale as divine chastisement for the cunning murder of
Iphitus: 274–78). At the end of this play there is a notable contrast between the
fierce readiness of Heracles to die on a pyre and his son Hyllus' resentment of what is
happening as well as between an audience's traditional knowledge of Heracles'
apotheosis and the lack of an explicit pointer in the play to this compensation.

Late recognition of this kind is uncommon in Euripides, where oracular pronouncements are usually clear (as in demands for human sacrifice in *Children of
Heracles* and *Phoenician Women*) or revealed very late, almost as an afterthought (as
with Eurystheus, Polymestor, and Oedipus in the final scenes of *Children of Heracles*,
Hecuba, and *Phoenician Women*). Fuller understanding sometimes comes directly
from the mouth of a god who speaks as *deus ex machina*. In *Hippolytus*, both Theseus

and Hippolytus refer to a possible transgression by an ancestor for which they are now paying with misfortune (818–20, 831–33, 1379–84), but the point of these utterances is to demonstrate their lack of awareness of what is truly going on. The audience knows they are wrong because they have heard Aphrodite's prologue, but the characters themselves must wait to the end of the play to have their ignorance dispelled by Artemis. It is revealing to compare the Heracles of Euripides' *Heracles* with the Heracles in Sophocles' *Women of Trachis.* Euripides' hero receives no explicit or ambiguous warning of his disaster; learning of Hera's involvement does not produce resignation or acceptance, but a crisis of faith and suicidal intentions, and it is rather the process of arguing with his friend Theseus that reconciles Heracles to a mode of continuing existence. For an instance of finding meaning and encouragement in a god's unclear instruction, we must turn to a play of the "romance" type, *Iphigenia among the Taurians.* Orestes is several times close to despair and a sense of abandonment by Apollo, but once he has recognized his lost sister he becomes confident that Apollo's instruction was meant for his good and that a successful outcome is likely. He does not, however, explicitly recognize the larger purpose that an audience should see: two sisters in parallel, Artemis and Iphigenia, are being rescued and purified. Nor is a safe escape fully ensured by the realization of divine purpose. In other cases, Euripidean characters are fully absorbed in their immediate situations and it is rather the chorus that takes a long view of the action and looks back to a "beginning of evils" (for example, the birth of Paris, the judgment of Paris, or the abduction of Helen in plays related to the Trojan War and its aftermath).

The characteristic inscrutability of the gods is also evident in dramas that bring to the fore contradictions and paradoxes. The *Oresteia* provides the fullest example. Already in the entrance-song of the first play we find side by side divine support for the Argive expedition of vengeance and divine resentment and demonic wrath at the killing of innocents. Struggle as they may, neither the chorus of elders in *Agamemnon* nor modern critics can satisfactorily harmonize the contradictory involvement of divinity in the events leading to the departure for Troy. It is as paradoxical as the phrase "violent grace" (*charis biaios, Agamemnon* 182), and justice and injustice are inextricably linked in the actions of the first two plays. There seems to be no safe way for men to act in the world. En route to a solution of sorts in the third play of the trilogy, the paradox is initially sharpened: a change in the terms of the Erinyes' activity (previously they were the winged dogs of father Zeus) sets them in clear opposition to Apollo, but also to the will of Zeus as interpreted by the eventual peacemaker Athena. We cannot observe the overall development of conflict and resolution in the Danaid trilogy of Aeschylus, of which only one play, *Suppliants,* survives. Yet in that single play we can detect the paradoxical position of Zeus: on the one hand, he is progenitor of the Danaids, and they look to his gentle release of Io from her metamorphosis and subsequent wanderings as a model for their own rescue from danger; on the other hand, Zeus in Io's myth is also the model of sexually rapacious male pursuit (embodied in the sons of Aegyptus in the play) and the release he brings to Io is in fact a form of marriage and sexuality leading to offspring, a fate strongly resisted by the chorus. In a lighter vein, one may compare the contradictory features of Apollo suggested in Euripides' *Ion*: purity and sexual violence, protection and neglect, truth and deception. Such portrayals of divinity correlate with a tragic image of human existence, involving confusion and instability in human interpretations of the divine and a harsh environment for human action.

Another important aspect of divine inscrutability is the arbitrariness of action and inaction. In Sophocles' *Antigone* there are many details that support Antigone's view that she is acting on behalf of divine law, in a way that the gods would approve: the lack of tracks after the first burial, the fact that the corpse is spared attack by birds and dogs, the dust storm that conceals Antigone's arrival for the second burial, and Tiresias' authoritative interpretation of divine will. Yet Antigone herself is ultimately unsure of the gods' favor and she dies without knowing of the rumors of the populace, the support of Haemon, the advice of Tiresias, and Creon's change of mind. For critics who take a fully Hegelian view that Creon and Antigone are equally in the wrong, this lonely fate is perhaps not problematic, but most critics correctly see that by the end of the play Creon is clearly not on a par with Antigone. Another way to palliate the paradoxical mixture of divine support and divine neglect is to refer Antigone's fate to an ancestral curse and inherited delusion (*atê*), and indeed the chorus offers this interpretation in an impressive ode (582–625). Sophocles, however, has paired Antigone with Ismene in his play, both offspring of the same parents and inheritors of the same genes of destruction, and has shown their characters and fates to be completely different: this fact somewhat complicates the view that there is intelligibly consistent divine intervention in the world.

The incompleteness or arbitrary transience of divine favor is perhaps most strikingly exemplified in Euripides' *Heracles*. Despairing prayers to Zeus and outright criticism of the god's neglect are prominent in the early scenes, but the doubt and complaints are spectacularly refuted when Heracles does return from the underworld in the nick of time to save his family, leading the chorus to celebrate the justice of the world and the concern of gods for mankind. In this plot, however, the favor of Zeus only goes so far, and nothing stands in the way of Hera's final persecution of the hero. Again, some critics have tried to gloss over the arbitrariness of the divine role by pointing to a psychological origin of Heracles' madness or to some transgressiveness in his actions outside or within the play. It is better to admit that the discontinuity and arbitrariness are the tragic point of the play. A smaller example of a similar discontinuity is the role of Helios at the end of Euripides' *Medea*: although invoked by the chorus in a last desperate prayer that divine power intervene to prevent the infanticide (1251–60), Helios (and the other gods) do not answer this prayer; rather, Medea appears only fifty lines later, in a flying chariot supplied to her by Helios. The point is not that Helios is somehow an abnormal sort of god, but that he conforms to the overall unseen role of the gods in this play: answering Medea's demand for justice and helping her exact vengeance from Jason for his violation of oaths, but not concerned with the fate of the children that so strongly affects the human chorus and characters.

Visible Gods

Unseen gods are potentially important in all tragedies: their inferred, suspected, or belatedly revealed or understood interventions contribute to the dynamic of puzzlement and understanding that applies in different ways to characters, chorus, and interpreting audience. In a number of plays, however (less often in Sophocles than in Aeschylus and Euripides), divinities are represented visibly as characters of the drama.

Such visibility is one of the available conventions for distinguishing the represented world of the performance from ordinary life, and the realm of heroic myth from contemporary history. Visible gods on stage are partly analogous to the gods who appeared in contemporary sculpture and vase-painting, such as the Athena who stands by Heracles or Theseus in depictions of their labors, the Apollo who extends his arm over the battling Lapiths and Centaurs, the observing gods who witness the preparations for Pelops' chariot race, and the gods who appear on the margins of vase-painting scenes or in a higher band (and divine participants and observers must also have been shown in lost large-scale paintings). On the stage, however, the gods are not just observers or helpers, but interact more directly with humans, in the mode of epiphany, and (given the public nature of the represented space of the action) sometimes with a wider audience than would be normal for an epiphany. The example set by epic poetry and narrative elements in archaic choral poetry must also be taken into account. Whether there was also a ritual origin for the acting out of the role of a god by a masked human is hard to determine with confidence, but that origin, if any, probably had small relevance in the changed and developed context of the fifth-century Attic theater (see, however, Sourvinou-Inwood 2003).

Despite the analogies that make visible gods on stage a reasonable choice, it is clear that as the genre matured it placed limits on such portrayals. Outside of a few special cases (apparently early) to be discussed shortly, gods tend to be located at the margins of the action, in prologue and *exodos*. Tragedy's interest in human action, human decision-making, and the dramatic force of uncertainty and open-ended struggle is usually better served by keeping the gods out of sight and by revealing the disparity of knowledge and power gradually and belatedly. For this generic tendency, we may compare both Aristotle's dislike of *deus ex machina* solutions (*Poetics* 1454b1–6), his depreciation of the visual element (*opsis*: 1450b16–20, 1453b1–11), and perhaps his low ranking of plays involving Prometheus and events in Hades (1456a2–3: corrupt and obscure) and Northrop Frye's differentiation of tragedy's high mimetic mode from myth or romance (Frye 1957, 33–34). Finally, the possibility that satyr-plays more commonly featured visible gods as characters of the drama offers a relevant counterpoint to the tragic norm.

Of the tragedies that are exceptional in the use of divine characters, Aeschylus' *Eumenides* is the boldest experiment. After the dense and in part obscure or para-doxical allusions to divine will and divine favor in the first two plays of the *Oresteia*, the third play of the trilogy brings the conflict to a whole new level in order to craft a solution. The supporting and persecuting gods become separately visible on stage in Apollo (and probably Hermes) and the Erinyes, as does the reconciling goddess Athena, and in an unusual way they interact very directly and on the same physical level with the human beings – not only Orestes, but all the silent extras representing the Athenian jurors and the members of the final procession. Both the vituperative argument between Apollo and the chorus in Delphi and the trial scene in Athens reveal that a readjustment and accommodation on the divine level is required if the chain of wrongful rights (or rightful wrongs) is to be broken. Thus the presence of the divinities has the double purpose of showing the significance of the event for Zeus' regime over the other gods and over mankind and of lending solemn weight to the new aetiology of the Areopagus council that Aeschylus is creating. The Pro-metheus plays – the surviving *Prometheus Bound* and the lost *Prometheus Unbound*, about which the surviving fragments and testimonia tell us a good deal – similarly concern events of cosmic significance, with the earlier play showing Zeus as a newly installed and insecure ruler with the characteristics of a tyrant and the latter bringing a reconciliation with Prometheus. In the end, Zeus avoids indulging his lust for Thetis as he had in the case of Io, and the terms of human life under Zeus' reign have apparently improved through the world-pacifying feats of Heracles and perhaps through some greater philanthropy in Zeus himself. Unlike *Eumenides*, these two plays present locations far from human habitation, and the participation of human characters is limited to Io in one play and Heracles in the other.

Even more extraordinary may have been the dramatic portrayal of gods in Aeschylus' lost *Psychostasia*, which, in imitation of an epic motif (*Iliad* 8.69–74, 22.209–13) perhaps already used in Arctinus' epic *Aethiopis*, included a weighing of fates or souls to decide the outcome of the duel between Achilles and Memnon before Troy. Plutarch's reference to the play (*How the Young Man Should Study Poetry* 2 = *Moralia* 16F–17A) suggests that Zeus himself appeared. This would be unique for tragedy (although a disguised Zeus may have appeared in Sophocles' satyr-play *Inachus*): otherwise, as in epic, the gods who directly communicate with mankind are minor deities or Olympians other than Zeus, while Zeus sits remote, acting through agents. Plutarch's language also suggests that Thetis and Eos supplicated Zeus *while* their sons were engaged in battle.[3] The second-century CE lexicographer Pollux (*Onomasticon* 4.130) refers to the appearance of Zeus and "those with him" (this idiomatic phrase means either the two mothers or, conceivably, the mothers plus additional mute gods) on an upper level that he calls the *theologeion*, and it is reasonable to assume that he is referring to the same Aeschylean scene as Plutarch and not another play. This would then be an early use of the vertical distinction in playing level that is well established later in the fifth century: gods above on the roof or crane, mortals below on the stage and *orchêstra*. Wilamowitz imagined this scene as the prologue of the play, with no humans present, and this is the most attractive solution, since it seems less likely to posit a temporary departure of the chorus and actors in mid-play. It must be mentioned, however, that some have doubted the applicability of the late testimonia (Taplin 1977, 431–33). Such skepticism seems to me overdrawn, but one must concede that if the scene of weighing occurs in the prologue, those who are skeptical of the use of the upper level during Aeschylus' career could place the action on the stage itself, with a change of scene to the Trojan plain in the rest of the play.

Apart from these exceptional examples, visible gods in tragedy may be roughly grouped into those who punish, those who save, and those who inform. The motif of a punishing god disguised as a mortal is seen in Euripides' *Bacchae*. The audience is informed of the disguise in the prologue, and at the end Dionysus appears in open godhead in the higher position above the *skênê* and perhaps with some change of mask and costume. This motif may have figured in Aeschylus' lost *Edonoi* as well, where Lycurgus confronts a captive Dionysus with insults (Aeschylus fr. 61). Other Dionysus plays may have used the device, but the fragments provide insufficient evidence. If it is correct to combine a remark in Plato, *Republic* 381d with other clues (fr. 168), in another play by Aeschylus Hera adopted a disguise to deceive Semele into asking Zeus to appear to her in his full divinity. Divine punishment need not, however, be linked to the use of disguise. We now know from papyrus fragments an impressive scene of Sophocles' *Niobe* (fr. 441a–442) in which Artemis (on the roof of the *skênê?*) is encouraged by her brother Apollo (also on the roof?) to shoot arrows at the daughters of Niobe, first inside and then outside the *skênê*. Niobe's sons had been killed by Apollo earlier in the play, and their father Amphion had confronted Apollo in a contest of archery and lost his life (perhaps one or both of these events were reported in a narrative rather than seen on stage).

In the prologue of Sophocles' *Ajax*, Athena displays the overweening and maddened hero to his enemy Odysseus. She has simultaneously saved her favorites from Ajax's onslaught, but the goddess is shown taking more delight in Ajax's humiliation than Odysseus can muster, and there is a decided contrast between the goddess' rigid position and the human pity expressed by Odysseus, anticipating the juxtaposition in the final scenes of the play of the unattractive Atreids with the temperate and conciliatory Odysseus. Sophocles leaves implicit the same sort of objection to excessive harshness in a hostile god that is often expressed by Euripidean characters. Likewise, Athena's parting maxim, that "gods love those who are self-controlled and detest those who are bad" (132–33), has a simplicity that is out of harmony with the complex interplay and deconstruction of human values illustrated in the rest of the play – another contrast that can be paralleled in Euripides. It is also significant that the goddess does not justify her disapproval of Ajax's excess in more detail in this scene. Instead, after the pathos-generating sequence of scenes involving Ajax and his family and just before the suicide itself, crucial details of Ajax's past prideful behavior are given in the report of Calchas' advice to Teucer. Another unsettling feature is the belated revelation that Athena's wrath will pursue the hero for this day only: is this a sign of moderation in the goddess, or a cruel joke, a merely apparent choice, like Heracles' alternatives of meeting his death or being "free of toils" once a certain span of time has elapsed (*Women of Trachis* 79–81, 166–68)?

Aphrodite in Euripides' *Hippolytus* is just as determined a foe of the man who has insulted her. The young hero enacts in his dialogue-scene with the old servant (88–113) the very disrespect that Aphrodite has adduced in the prologue as her reason for punishing him, and he exhibits elsewhere some qualities that many critics take to be unattractive. Nevertheless, apart from the old servant's futile prayer that suggests the goddess is too harsh (114–20), along with the beauty of Hippolytus' devotion and integrity and the sympathy expressed later by other characters, Aphrodite's own self-presentation marks her as harsh, particularly in her indifference to Phaedra's involvement in the disaster. She may be felt to stage-manage the plot more directly than Sophocles' Athena, and her harshness is also underscored by the parallelism with Artemis, which is reinforced by details of imagery and staging[4] and evident also in Artemis' promise to destroy one of Aphrodite's favorites in turn (1420–22).

A curious variation on the punishing goddess is offered by Euripides' *Trojan Women*. Athena arrives in the middle of the divine prologue to recruit Poseidon for a planned punishment of the Greek victors that will occur after the end of the play. Here it is Poseidon rather than a human character who comments on arbitrariness and excess: "Why do you jump in this way to different behavior at different times, and hate and love so excessively whoever it happens to be?" (67–68). This privileged communication to the audience casts a somber irony over the feeling of abandonment expressed by the suffering Trojan women (whose sufferings are not, however, lessened thereby) and over the sense of control displayed by the Greeks, who dispose in turn of Polyxena, Astyanax, Andromache, and Helen. The tragic significance of such portrayal of the gods is at least twofold. First, the connection of supernatural power to morality as human beings understand it is subjected to doubt, and human values themselves appear unhappily contingent. Second, the aristocratic code of honor is queried: the gods always have the power and always feel entitled to honor, but in several tragedies they are shown to be reluctant or unable to modulate their great power with a voluntary restraint – the very restraint that is often necessary in human interactions if social structures are not to collapse into savagery.

The visible punishing god is most likely to appear in the prologue (in the case of *Heracles* the mid-play appearance begins a second half, in many respects the mirror-image of the first half of the play), while the saving god is normally a *deus ex machina*. Athena's intervention at the close of *Odyssey* 24 is a kind of epic model for such a saving intervention, and Athena has a similar function in *Eumenides*, bringing help to the troubled house of Atreus in its surviving representative Orestes and then to Athens and the Olympian dispensation by handling the angry Erinyes. It would be fascinating to know whether Aphrodite's participation in the resolution of Aeschylus' Danaid trilogy (fr. 44) was handled like Athena's in *Eumenides* or more like the typical *deus ex machina* as attested in Euripides. Some common features of the *deus ex machina* include (1) appearance on the upper level, above the human characters and chorus; (2) suddenness of arrival (sometimes the reaction of the humans and the references to the god's locomotion strongly support the use of the theater-crane, but in other cases the actor may simply have emerged onto the roof from a ladder within or behind the *skênê*); (3) stopping-function, that is, an initial command to the humans not to carry out a contemplated action, especially violence (perhaps Sophocles' *Peleus*; Euripides' *Iphigenia among the Taurians, Helen, Antiope, Orestes*; the command is to a god, Poseidon, in *Erechtheus*), but also simple intentions like Ion's insistence on asking the oracle directly about his parentage (Euripides' *Ion*), Theseus' bidding farewell to Adrastus and the Argives he has helped (Euripides' *Suppliants*), the departure of Philoctetes and Neoptolemus for home instead of Troy (Sophocles' *Philoctetes*); (4) dispositions for the future (burial, fate of the survivors, cult aetiology), sometimes accompanied by consolation (Artemis to Hippolytus, Thetis to Peleus, Dioscuri to Orestes and Electra) or blame (Artemis to Theseus, Dionysus to Cadmus and Agave). The *deus ex machina* thus partakes of the role of informing god as well. Divine epilogues often encourage acceptance or resignation in the face of terrible misfortune, both for the surviving characters and for the audience, and at the same time serve for the audience to weave the events just presented, novel though they may have been, back into the fabric of well-known stories and to relate them to monuments and cult practices surviving in the audience's world.

Sophocles appears to have made little use of the *deus ex machina*, although it must be remembered that we have very little useful knowledge about his lost plays. Apart from the possible use of Thetis in his *Peleus* to prevent further violence, there is the remarkable reversal at the end of *Philoctetes*, which serves to save the traditional outcome of the myth after the logic of the characters' behavior has led to an entirely different ending. As with other indeterminate details in this play, the ending leaves it up to the audience to decide (or remain undecided) whether to view this intervention positively as a welcome device to preserve both Philoctetes' integrity and the cure and glory that will be his in the fulfillment of Troy's destiny, or pessimistically as a subversion of human freedom and character by external forces. The examples in Euripides are of many varieties, with different motivations for arrival, different tones of interaction, and different sorts of instructions. The most extreme reversal, which many critics view as approaching the absurd, is that in *Orestes*, where Apollo brings about a shift from Orestes' holding a knife to Hermione's throat to his receiving her father's polite wishes for the pair's happy marriage. Another pattern of interest is the "patriotic" function of Athena as *deus ex machina* in plays that have connections to Attica. In Euripides, she has a saving role in *Erechtheus*, ending Poseidon's earthquake and settling an old rivalry for the good of Athens. In *Iphigenia among the Taurians* her instructions complete the Attic appropriation of elements of the Orestes and Iphigenia myths, and similarly in *Ion* her intervention not only saves Apollo the embarrassment of appearing himself (while simultaneously bringing his failings into the open), but also lays claim to Apolline glory for Attic origins and supports Attic aspirations to hegemony.

The informing function of tragedy's visible gods is found both in prologues and epilogues (and indeed in mid-play in *Heracles*). Since tragedy often exploits the discrepant awareness of audience and characters or chorus, the device of the prologue god can be very effective in facilitating certain kinds of plots. It is essential to Athena's pursuit of Ajax that the truth behind his mad attack on the flocks be made known, so her scene with Odysseus is important not only to the audience's understanding but also to the Greek army and its leaders within the play. In *Hippolytus*, by contrast, Aphrodite's revelations are aimed solely at the audience and cannot but condition how the audience receives all the following scenes. The characters are kept in the dark about her intervention, and Theseus is also kept in the dark about his wife's lie because of the oaths taken by Hippolytus and the chorus. Artemis thus assumes a parallel informing function in the final scenes, using her superior knowledge both to taunt and to console the humans. The information supplied by Apollo in the prologue of *Alcestis* is not essential in the same way (a dialogue between faithful household slaves could have supplied the same background details), but his statement of solidarity with the house of Admetus, his attempt to persuade Thanatos to spare Alcestis, and his prediction of Heracles' ultimate success in rescuing her significantly alter the way an audience will receive the scenes that follow. Hermes in *Ion*, on the other hand, is a clear precursor to the prologue gods of New Comedy, who are needed to let the audience in on the mistaken identities and misunderstandings that drive the plot. Some epilogue gods, finally, are significant not so much for revealing an unknown fact as for echoing and confirming the feelings of the characters. Thus Thetis in *Andromache*, although largely concerned with future dispositions, completes the theme of resentment toward Apollo that has been carried by the chorus, messenger, and Peleus; and Castor in *Electra* confirms the regrets and resentment of Orestes and his sister before counseling resignation and instructing them on their future (but there is one gratuitous piece of privileged information in Castor's speech, the revelation that the Trojan War was fought over an image of Helen, adding a bitter irony to all regrets about the past).

Speculation, Doubt, and Disbelief

Among the attitudes dramatized through the mythological figures of tragedy are refinements of traditional religion and theology in line with the speculations of earlier and contemporary thinkers. Euripides stands out in this regard because his characters are more analytical and articulate and inclined toward a thorough rationalism, that is to say, more reflective of the intellectual ferment of his age. This characteristic, however, is at least in part an extension of a traditional prerogative of high-style poetry: the poet's display of *sophia* lies not only in his technical expertise with words and meter or in his representation of moral values and social wisdom, but also in his appropriation of specialized knowledge, whether it be geographical (as in *Agamemnon* or *Prometheus*), medical (as in *Eumenides*), anthropological (as in the "Ode to Man" in *Antigone*), or sophistic (as in the rhetoric of the common contest of speeches or *agôn logôn*). But this appropriation and representation is not an endorsement of any particular speculation. Rather, Euripides' works dramatize crises of interpretation, faith, and intelligibility. The idealistic imposition of a human sense of decency and morality upon the gods is one reaction to such crises, as exemplified in Ion's admonition to Apollo (*Ion* 436–51), Iphigenia's criticism and then absolution of Artemis (*Iphigenia among the Taurians* 380–91), and Heracles' denial of the traditional theology that actually operates in the fictive world in which he is embedded (*Heracles* 1341–46).

Modern societies are familiar with the gap that may arise between conventional or officially regulated religious piety and instances of blasphemy, religious parody, and expressions of disbelief and doubt voiced in private contexts. What has been surprising to some scholars of Attic drama is that criticism of gods and disbelief or doubt are also depicted in a public art form of high prestige sponsored by the state and performed within a religious festival honoring a god. Some of the instances are clearly, of course, intended as negative examples: the disbelievers and blasphemers come to a bad end as the gods assert their power to punish (cf. Aeschylus, *Agamemnon* 369–72; Euripides, *Heracles* 757–59; even the remarkable speech of Sisyphus, in a fragment ascribed to Critias [fr. 19] or Euripides, claiming that morality-sanctioning gods are a human invention may have been spoken within a plot in which Sisyphus was punished by the gods). Complaints and criticisms may in fact underscore the misinterpretation or lack of understanding of the mortal speaking them: just as in Herodotus (1.91), where Croesus' complaint to Apollo about his downfall is rebutted by pointing out that Croesus himself misinterpreted the oracle, some complaints of abandonment or mistreatment by the gods in tragedy are revealed to be misinterpretations (as in *Ion* or *Iphigenia among the Taurians*). Yet there is more to the phenomenon than this. When Philoctetes says "How should I understand this, how approve it, when observing the ways of the gods I discover the gods are bad?" does an audience think he is a fool, and does the final outcome of the play cancel out such despair?[5] If Amphitryon's challenge to Zeus' morality in Euripides' *Heracles* (339–47, 498–501) is temporarily refuted by the opportune return of Heracles, that refutation is completely undermined by what happens a little later, with the arrival of Iris and Lyssa. Tragedy is an exploratory and interrogatory genre, and displays a full range of attitudes about justice, order, and virtue, and both the poets themselves and (usually) the society they lived in had the strength to confront uncertainty and the possibility of the inscrutability of the universe and the contingency of human values.

NOTES

1   While this claim is conditioned by the needs of the plot, it should not be dismissed as a one-time ad hoc feature. Compare Hera's awaiting the moment when she can act against Heracles (Euripides, *Heracles* 828–32; note too Zeus' inaction when Hera does act) and Athena's explanation of why she had not helped Odysseus return earlier (Homer, *Odyssey* 13.341–43).

2   *Tuchê* commonly refers to an event that comes upon one against one's will and is out of one's control, an event that is assumed to be caused by a supernatural power, whether specifically identified or not. Thus it is usually not a word implying disorder or random chance, although it can shade into such a meaning when there is an acute sense that a change of circumstances is arbitrary or amoral and not connected to the psychologically plausible motivation of a divine individual.

3   That is the force of the present participle *machomenôn*.

4   There are statues of the two goddesses on stage, and as characters they perhaps appear in identical positions on the *skênê*-roof. See also Frischer 1970.

5   Sophocles, *Philoctetes* 451–52: "observing" is an emendation, the manuscripts give "trying to praise," which hardly affects the point being made here.

FURTHER READING

For brief, fundamental orientation to several key issues in English, see two chapters in Easterling and Muir 1985: Gould 1985 (1–33) and Easterling 1985b (34–49); also Parker 1997 and Mastronarde 2002a (with further references). For various views suggesting that gods in tragedy may be understood largely as a literary device or may be bracketed off from "ordinary" religion, see Rosenmeyer 1982 (chapter 9), Heath 1987b, and Mikalson 1991. For a wide-ranging but in part speculative study emphasizing the importance of religion in tragedy and the continuity of tragic religion with "ordinary" religion, see Sourvinou-Inwood 2003. On the staging of the appearance of gods (with argument that more gods may have appeared on the upper level than most commentators have assumed), see Mastronarde 1990 (with further references). On the relation of religious beliefs in tragedy and in contemporary life, see Yunis 1988. For interpretation of the *deus ex machina* in terms of literary analysis of closure, see Dunn 1996. For debate on the significance of the *deus ex machina* in Euripides, see, e.g., Burnett 1971, Mastronarde 2002a, Wildberg 2002, and Sourvinou-Inwood 2003. On other aspects of religion in tragedy, see Scullion, chapter 2 in this volume.

CHAPTER TWENTY-ONE

Authority Figures

Mark Griffith

Authority comes in many forms, and goes by many names. Every human society contains several overlapping structures of political, religious, familial, and moral authority, which may or may not appear to its members (or to outside observers) to comprise a coherent system. Many of the key scenes of dilemma and confrontation in Greek tragedy arise from conflicts between different kinds of authority, whether or not the individual characters explicitly frame their concerns in such terms. Indeed, the Theater of Dionysus may be regarded as a site specifically licensed (by the terms of the festival) to confront and explore imaginary breakdowns, resistances, and abuses of authority of all kinds, and to present them in the most verbally and visually compelling manner possible. It may be helpful to begin our discussion with two well-known scenes of confrontation, which will serve both to exemplify the general point and to establish some of the most important terms and issues for the rest of our analysis.

The first scene is the encounter between Antigone and Creon in Sophocles' *Antigone* (441–525). Creon has earlier given his reasons for banning burial to the traitorous Polynices. Now, confronted by the one who has been caught defying his ban, he demands:

Creon: Tell me briefly, did you know that it had been decreed [*kéruchthenta*] not to
   do this?
Antigone: I knew; how could I not? It was clear.
Creon: And yet you dared to overstep these laws [*nomous*]?
Antigone: Yes; for it wasn't Zeus who decreed [*kéruxas*] these things,
   nor did Justice [*Diké*], co-resident of the gods below,
   define such laws [*nomous*] among human beings;
   and I didn't suppose your decrees [*kérugmata*] to have so much strength [*sthenein*]
   that they could overrun – you a mortal – the unwritten
   and infallible laws [*nomima*] of the gods...(446–55)

A little later, we find Creon commenting to the chorus:

She knew then that she was committing outrage [*hubrizein*],
when she overstepped the established laws [*nomous*];

and now that she has done the deed, this is a second outrage [*hubris*],
to exult over it and laugh about what she has done.
Truly, I am not [a] man [*anêr*], but she is [the] man [*anêr*],
if, with impunity, victory and control [*kratê*] in these things are going to be hers. (480–85)

During this brief exchange, both Antigone and Creon employ terms that explicitly
or implicitly base their respective claims on higher or more generally recognized
sources of authority. For Creon, the status of his public decree is equivalent to law,
and in the present confrontation he claims also the traditional and natural authority
of a man over a woman: his young niece's resistance to such authority amounts
therefore to transgression (449, 481) and an indefensible *hubris* (outrage). But for
Antigone, the gods' eternal laws (such as those requiring burial of her brother) are
equivalent to "justice" itself, outweighing any human decrees and therefore author-
izing her resistance to a "foolish" (*môrôi*, 470) ruler. Thus the scene is presented as
a collision between divine and human (and, as Antigone phrases it, natural and
eternal against arbitrary and temporal), as well as between male and female, claims
to authority.

In our second exemplary scene (in the first choral ode of Aeschylus' *Oresteia*), the
Argive Elders sing of the fatal events at Aulis:

> I have the authority [*kurios eimi*] to sing of the fateful power [*kratos*]
> of completely-empowered men [*andrôn ekteleôn*] on the road ...
> ... how the headlong bird-omen, king of birds to the kings of ships,
> sent the double-throned command [*kratos*] of the Achaeans,
> the like-minded lords [*tagan*] of Greece, against Troy...
> ... And the reliable army-prophet [*kednos stratomantis*] ...
> spoke thus to interpret the portent:
> "In time this road captures the city of Priam ...
> Only may no curse from god [*theothen*] darken the great bit
> fashioned into an army to muzzle Troy.
> For in pity holy Artemis resents the winged dogs of her father..."
>   (*Agamemnon* 104–35)

Here too we find multiple kinds of authority, some in direct collision with one
another, others running on separate and apparently unconnected tracks. The
human participants (the sons of Atreus) are subject to the directive of divine signs
(as interpreted by the prophet Calchas); but the signs are themselves conflicting, as
two rival forces can be discerned at work among the gods – Zeus against Artemis,
each representing a distinct set of cosmic and familial claims. Likewise among the
humans, the political-military power (*kratos*) of the Atreidae, and also that of Priam,
derives from a quite different source from the peculiar expertise and insight possessed
by Calchas, and by the chorus themselves: "I am authorized to speak ... from God"
(*kurios eimi throein ... theothen*, 104–5).

Within these two passages, we have already encountered a good number of the
Greek terms that are used most frequently to convey the notions of "authority,
author, authorize," including: *kurios* (lord, master); forms of *telos* (end, perfection,
completion, office, with such derivatives as *teleô, en telei, ektelês, teleios*); *themis* (what
is established, right) and *nomoi* (law, custom, norm); *prepon, prepei* (what is fitting,

proper, admissible) – together with several of the most common words for "rule, power, control, mastery" (*kratos/krateó, sthenos/sthenô, despotês/despozô, archê/archô, anax/anassô, basileus/basileuô*, and so forth). Each of these terms can carry – in the right circumstances and when properly invoked – the weight of legitimate authority, commanding, justifying, or forbidding certain actions, words, and behaviors. When used in combination, such terms often present conflicting demands, as different individuals make competing claims against one another, or recognize competing demands upon themselves.

Given that the sources and bases of authority can be so varied and contradictory, the theater audience may often have no reliable guarantee as to which of them should (or will) prevail in any particular case. Sometimes, to be sure, we might be aware that the authority invoked by one character may be spurious, or may not apply fully to this particular context; but we also encounter other situations in which obeying one legitimate authority seems ipso facto to involve opposing or violating another. That is the essence of a tragic *agôn*; and in such cases the very openness to dispute of the multiple claims to authority, and the strong sympathy aroused for a character's resistance to an apparently incontrovertible external force, contributes powerfully to the audience's sense of imminent and inescapable disaster.

Indeed, ever since Hegel, at least, it has been generally recognized by critics that tragedy (in the modern, narrow sense of a play with a catastrophic ending) is characteristically built around conflict, and Athenian theater audiences seem to have relished the representation of radical challenges to conventional morality and attitudes, including striking instances of resistance to authority in all its forms. This chapter focuses on the ways in which tragedy represents the various structures of human, divine, and cosmic authority operating within Athenian society and within the imaginations of its members, and considers too the ways in which the theatrical occasion itself created and imposed its own particular form of cultural "authority" for, and upon, the Athenian audience and its modern counterparts.

Four Fields of Authority

As we noted above, every society operates with a number of separate but overlapping structures, or fields, of authority, each with its own dynamics and terminologies, and its own representatives and hierarchy of values. In investigating the imaginary world of Greek tragedy, we may distinguish four broad fields and structures of authority: (1) the public, sociopolitical field, including various forms of legal and military authority exercised by and in the city (*polis*) or army (*laos, stratos*); (2) the domestic field, including relations between master and slave, and within the nuclear family, as well as most kinds of erotic and sexual interaction; (3) the religious field, including all dealings between humans and divinities, and operations and imaginings of the supernatural in general; and (4) the epistemological and literary/cultural field, including the variously authorized forms of knowledge and truth, proverb and myth, Homeric epic, and other elements of traditional wisdom.

Obviously these four fields do not in fact exist or operate separately: not only do they overlap and interpenetrate one another, but also the structures (especially) of class and gender function somewhat differently within the *oikos* and in the larger sociopolitical arena outside (as we shall see), and thus have some claim to being treated as separate fields of their own. Nor were these interlocking and competing systems of authority themselves entirely static or stable. Fifth-century Athens was a society experiencing particularly acute – and exciting – growth pains, and along with the relatively new (or newly dominant) structure of democratic and egalitarian values and political principles, we can see an older and deeply entrenched aristocratic and elitist ideology still more or less openly asserting itself. And in addition to these competing democratic and aristocratic/oligarchic ideologies, we may detect also a third: the cluster of ideas and behaviors advanced by such innovative thinkers and social-religious experimenters as the Pythagoreans and Orphics, or a little later, Socrates, Democritus, and others. In the midst of all these social, intellectual, and moral currents, the Theater of Dionysus provided a uniquely attractive and appropriate venue, a "safe place," in which Athenians could dress themselves up in extravagant clothes and disguise themselves behind masks, in order to teach a chorus (*didaskô*), make up fictions (*poiêsis*, from *poieô*), and act out stories (*hupokrinomai, prattô, drama*, from *draô*) involving the most extreme conflict imaginable, all free from serious real-life consequences or repercussions – an imitation (*mimêsis*) of life that was both highly serious and consequential (in its struggle for prizes and prestige, as well as its emotional effect), and at the same time almost completely harmless and free from danger.

Such play was both wildly fantastic and disturbingly real, for the tragedies performed in the Theater of Dionysus constructed a world that was an engaging, but inconsistent, blend of "then and there" (or "way back then") and "here and now." The Athenians themselves were conscious that in their own city constitutional power lay with the people (*plêthos, dêmos*): no monarch had ruled them since the expulsion of the sons of Pisistratus in 510 BCE. Thus the Argive, Theban, and Athenian (as well as Egyptian, Thracian, Persian, and so forth) kings, queens, and aristocratic leaders who strut through the theater are figures from a bygone era (or, in the case of Aeschylus' Xerxes, a remote location), figures whose sociopolitical roles, responsibilities, and capabilities are clearly felt to be distanced from those of the Athenian audience. Yet at the same time the personal and political dilemmas and crises faced by these heroic figures are presented in terms that often appear sharply familiar and similar to those of contemporary Athenian life, in which political and military offices continued even under the democracy to be dominated by the wealthy, especially the old aristocratic families, and brilliant dynastic display and achievement were still highly valued and contested. The result is a persistent uncertainty principle, by which the audience has to interpret and assess the status, legitimacy, and conduct of a tragic monarch or member of the nobility in the light (on the one hand) of the old traditions of Homeric epic and mythology, and (on the other hand) of the Athenian democracy itself, with its insistent suspicions of all traces of "tyrannical" aspiration and its restrictive legislation against elite privilege. Further complicating matters is the continuing phenomenon of monarchy – Spartan, Thessalian, Sicilian, and of course Persian.

With all these provisos in mind, let us now turn to investigate the four categories, which will at least provide us with a workable framework for our analysis of the multiple forms of authority – and resistance to authority – to be found in Athenian tragedy.

Forms and Figures of Political, Legal, and Military Authority

In a majority of Greek tragedies, the leading characters are members of a royal family, and one of them is usually king (*anax, basileus, tagos, koiranos, turannos*), possessed of scepter (*skêptron*), throne (*thronos*), and the other conventional accouterments of monarchical authority. The house occupied by this royal family, whose façade and front door usually dominate the acting area, is thus both a center of political authority (a palace) and a psychosocial locus of elite kin-relations. The character and style of monarchical rule can vary somewhat from play to play. In some tragedies, especially those set among "barbarian" nations (for example, Aeschylus' *Persians*; Euripides' *Iphigenia among the Taurians, Hecuba, Helen*), the king's power is more autocratic than in others (though the Theban, Argive, and Corinthian monarchs of, for example, Aeschylus' *Seven against Thebes*, Sophocles' *Antigone* and *Electra*, and Euripides' *Medea* and *Bacchae* are quite autocratic too). Not infrequently there is uncertainty expressed by one character or another as to just how much authority the king has, or should have, to act as he pleases when others disagree: so, for example, Prometheus complains in *Prometheus Bound* that Zeus, as a typical "young tyrant" (96, 148–49, 942), "keeps the law to himself" (187–88; cf. 149–50) and shows no gratitude to his former friends and allies (221–25, 304–6); and in Aeschylus' *Suppliants* the Egyptian maidens insist that Pelasgus has the authority to do whatever he likes in Argos: "You are the city, you are the people! You rule unchecked over the altars" (370–72), whereas the king himself insists that he cannot act without first putting his policy to the popular vote (397–400, 517–23).

Most kings in tragedy are hereditary, their authority deeply entrenched and recognized by all as legitimate. They are recognized as possessing the power and authority to make all executive decisions: to go to war, to give sanctuary to a visitor or suppliant, to exact punishment from disobedient individuals, to order public celebrations and sacrifices, and so forth. Thus, at the beginning of the *Oresteia*, the watchman laments the ten-year absence of his king, looking back to the good old days when things were "most excellently managed" (18–19), and looking forward to greeting Agamemnon personally on his return. The legendary Athenian king Theseus appears in several plays, and usually conducts himself admirably, as an authoritative but considerate and stylish ruler (Sophocles' *Oedipus at Colonus*, Euripides' *Heracles* – even briefly as a quasi-democrat in Euripides' *Suppliants*, 429–62); but even Theseus may behave in problematically impatient and disastrous ways on occasion (Euripides' *Hippolytus*). Two brothers may share the throne, as co-rulers (Demophon and Athamas) or may alternate as rivals (Eteocles and Polynices); and occasionally an aged monarch has ceded authority to a son or grandson, but still participates intermittently in public affairs (Cadmus in Euripides' *Bacchae*, Pheres in Euripides' *Alcestis*, Oedipus in Euripides' *Phoenician Women* and Sophocles' *Oedipus at Colonus*, Priam in *Rhesus*).

In other cases, the monarchy has been usurped by outright violence, trickery, or both: for example, Zeus in Aeschylus' *Prometheus Bound*, Clytemnestra and Aegisthus in Aeschylus' *Libation Bearers* and the *Electra* plays, Eteocles in Sophocles' *Oedipus at Colonus* and Euripides' *Phoenician Women* – though even in these cases the usurper is usually a close relative of the legitimate or previous ruler. But there are several tragic monarchs who have gained the throne through their own initiative or popular acclaim, as outsiders, a trajectory familiar from the careers of real-life tyrants such as Cypselus of Corinth, Pisistratus of Athens, and Hieron of Syracuse. Their legitimacy may or may not come into question as a result. Such is Oedipus (in Sophocles' *Oedipus the King*), apparently a Corinthian who arrived at Thebes at a moment of crisis following the death of King Laius; likewise Creon is repeatedly (in Sophocles' *Antigone*, *Oedipus the King*, and *Oedipus at Colonus*, Euripides' *Suppliants* and *Phoenician Women* – and perhaps Aeschylus' *Seven against Thebes*) represented as having risen from being regent for the two young princes to assuming sole rule after their death, in order to restore order in Thebes (similarly perhaps Danaus in the second play of Aeschylus' *Suppliants* trilogy). Of these, Oedipus is trusted and loved by his subjects (Sophocles' *Oedipus the King*) for his conscientious concern; but Creon's status (at least in Sophocles' *Antigone*) seems less secure, since the chorus's support for him is muted and circumspect, and it is stated that the townspeople also disapprove of his policies; yet at the end of the play, even though he has now lost the respect of everyone, including himself, he still retains the monarchy and the chorus's support.

In addition to, or instead of, the king himself, other significant members of the royal family may play important roles within a particular play. Most of the resultant dynastic relationships and conflicts, especially the generational conflict between father and son, will be discussed in the next section. But it is of interest to consider those contexts in which the king is absent, and someone else – a council of elders, a queen – is consequently wielding authority in his place. This is usually presented as a symptom (or cause) of dangerous instability in the structure of power, and results in catastrophe of one kind or another before normalcy (sole male rule) can be restored: thus Atossa with the council of Persian elders (Aeschylus' *Persians*), and Clytemnestra with the Argive elders (Aeschylus' *Agamemnon*) or with her blustering and cruel new husband, Aegisthus (Aeschylus' *Libation Bearers*, Sophocles' *Electra*, Euripides' *Electra*). In the "untragic" worlds of Euripides' *Helen* and *Ion*, by contrast, the royal queen/princess plays a more constructive role: in *Helen*, after King Proteus has died, his son Theoclymenus has to be outwitted and morally enlightened by his sister, Princess Theonoe, before the romantic ending can be achieved; and in *Ion* it is Creusa's determination that brings about the revelation of her son's identity and destiny. More often, we find political value residing in royal daughters because of their potential for dynastic marriage – though this may be attended by violence and disruption of its own (for example, the Danaids in Aeschylus' *Suppliants*, Hermione in Euripides' *Orestes*, and Io in Aeschylus' *Prometheus Bound*); indeed a princess's marriageability is converted into virgin sacrifice with disturbing frequency, as a means of procuring the military-political success of her father and/or the whole community (Iphigenia, Polyxena, Macaria, the daughters of Erechtheus).

In a few plays, an elite lord is visiting or residing in a polis that is not his own, or in which he does not rule: Danaus in Argos (Aeschylus' *Suppliants*); Heracles and Deianira in Trachis (Sophocles' *Women of Trachis*); Jason and Medea in Corinth (Euripides' *Medea*); Oedipus at Colonus/Athens (Sophocles' *Oedipus at Colonus*). In these cases we may or may not see the king who actually holds sway in that community; but when we do (Pelasgus of Argos, Creon of Corinth), the result is usually conflict over the issue of immigration and succession, and (in accordance with international networking protocols) the deployment of the socioreligious mechanisms of supplication, *xenia*, marriage, or burial.

Sometimes a council of elders appears to be more or less formally authorized to consult with the king (in Argos for Aeschylus' *Agamemnon*, in Susa for Aeschylus' *Persians*, and in Thebes for Sophocles' *Antigone*). In such cases, while the king usually feels obliged to consult with his "council," he may nonetheless override them if he chooses – though it is to be observed that in each of these cases the king suffers a serious setback and disgrace before the play is over. But in other contexts, a king is presented as needing to obtain permission from the people before proceeding with the policy he favors (Pelasgus in Aeschylus' *Suppliants*, Theseus in Euripides' *Suppliants*), or as deferring to the law-courts concerning the proper treatment of a homicide (Tyndareus in Euripides' *Orestes*), with results that may introduce puzzling, even disruptive, notes of anachronism into the traditional story, and thus bring that world into closer contact or collision with that of democratic Athens.

In several plays, especially those set at Troy (and thus especially influenced by the *Iliad* and other heroic traditions) we find an aristocratic council collaborating more or less successfully in a common political cause. So for example in Sophocles' *Ajax* and Euripides' *Iphigenia at Aulis*, Agamemnon is king (*anax*) and commander-in-chief, presiding over a group of military leaders who are themselves kings (*basileis*) of their respective contingents. In this context, the model may be that of kings or chieftains operating more as military co-commanders than as political leaders. The Athenians in the fifth century did in fact quite often send out multiple generals on campaign together, with results that could be effective (by providing greater breadth of expertise and distribution of responsibility) or disastrous (by undermining the unity of strategy and the loyalty of the troops). In several tragedies, tensions are shown developing between individual leaders or between the supreme commanders and the rest. Thus the near-rebellion of Neoptolemus and Philoctetes (Sophocles' *Philoctetes*) and of Achilles (Euripides' *Iphigenia at Aulis*) requires the miraculous intervention of others (Heracles, Iphigenia) to avoid disintegration of the alliance; in the case of Ajax, his individual rage (like that of Achilles in the *Iliad*) cannot be prevented, and it takes the diplomatic skills of Odysseus (again) to restore some degree of cohesion to the combined Greek leadership through the negotiations around his funeral (Sophocles' *Ajax*).

For the most part, the authority of generals on campaign to issue orders and make plans is almost absolute. Yet even a general may feel pressure to respond to the expectations and needs of his troops. Thus, faced with the prospect of sacrificing his own daughter to ensure favorable winds, Agamemnon seems to believe that he is compelled by the will of the troops, as well as the other leaders, to carry it out (Aeschylus, *Agamemnon* 212–16, 230; Euripides, *Iphigenia at Aulis* 511–18). Subordinates such as guards, scouts, and messengers are not expected to question or criticize the decisions of their commanders (indeed, it is not always clear whether these characters are free citizen soldiers or slave retainers of the royal family); but occasionally one will voice his misgivings (Aeschylus, *Agamemnon* 551–82; Sophocles, *Antigone* 388–400, 437–40; *Oedipus the King* 1149–79; Euripides, *Children of Heracles* 415–19) and thus present a momentary lower-class perspective on the action. The chorus of elders (Aeschylus' *Agamemnon*, Sophocles' *Antigone*) or the herald Talthybius (Euripides' *Trojan Women*) are higher-status subordinates who express dismay at their generals' cruel commands. In general, however, while such characters may mutter or grumble, the rank-and-file soldiers or sailors never make any concerted move to challenge their leader, and never take action on their own behalf – in marked contrast to the world of Old Comedy, and to actual Athenian political practice.

In the *Iliad* the rewards and obligations of elite leadership, and the pressures to win glory and prove oneself best in the eyes of others, are sometimes discussed with reference to "all the Achaeans," sometimes in terms of the in-group of distinguished comrades (*hetairoi*) and elders (*presbeis*). The same double focus can be observed in tragedy, though here we find less emphasis on the personal glory of the individual victor, more on the collective and on the value of victory to the army and city as a whole. In particular, whereas in the *Iliad* the amazing prowess of one god-favored individual warrior is the dominant theme, in tragedy no single warrior is credited with such military effectiveness – except in certain very peculiar (often fatal) circumstances: Philoctetes and his bow are needed for Troy to be captured (Sophocles' *Philoctetes*); Eteocles or Menoeceus, or both, must die for Thebes to prevail (Aeschylus' *Seven against Thebes*, Euripides' *Phoenician Women*); Iolaus' magical rejuvenation will win one final victory for his people (Euripides' *Children of Heracles*). Generally in tragedy it is the strategic and political authority of the war-leaders that is at issue, not their personal prowess.

At the lower end of the political spectrum, the democratic mechanisms of power and authorization make sporadic appearances in Greek tragedy. While the popular assembly (*ekklêsia*) as such, or the people as a voting, policy-making body, are rarely included in the tragic action, vaguer references to popular opinion and the dissatisfaction of the mob (*ochlos*) are widespread, as affecting the conduct of the elite. Vaguer still are the ubiquitous references to the laws (*nomoi, thesmoi*), both written and unwritten, and to the constraints of justice (*dikê, themis*), all of which are frequently cited by characters in support of their own actions or their opposition to others'. Law-courts as such are mentioned only rarely (notably in Aeschylus' *Eumenides* and Euripides' *Iphigenia among the Taurians* and *Orestes* – the latter two directly responding to the former); but we find frequent references to popular grumbling, vilification, curses, and even stoning, which might imply the existence of some kind of rudimentary judicial process. More often, however, it is the kings themselves who appear to be authorized to implement (and sometimes to invent) the laws.

Taken for themselves, as a higher (non-human) moral and institutional authority, to be cited by characters in support of their own actions or in opposition to those of others, the laws and the constraints and requirements of Justice herself are often imagined as being divine and unchallengeable. Likewise the city itself, and the collective safety and benefit of the citizens, are constantly invoked in drama, just as they were in Athenian political life. Even nature (*phusis*) and the implied cultural authority of Hellenism (as opposed to "barbarian" degeneracy or savagery) can be cited in support of a particular policy or action; and such claims will be considered later, when we turn to consider religious and moral authorities in general.

Forms and Figures of Domestic and Familial Authority

In the imaginary world of Greek tragedy, as in real-life Athenian households, economic, legal, and marital authority resided with the male head of the family, in his capacity as man or husband (*anêr*), father (*patêr*), and master (*despotês*). The formal term that most completely expresses this authority is *kurios* (lord), a term which connotes possession of the household property (including its women-folk and slaves) and entitlement to inherit or dispose of it as he chooses, subject to the provisions of the law and the rights of other *kurioi*. The authority of the Greek lord and master does not extend so far as to include the right of life and death over family members (as was reputedly the case for the *paterfamilias* in republican Rome), but is nonetheless wide-ranging and unquestionable within the province of the household and family.

In the opening pages of the *Politics*, Aristotle draws analogies between what he sees as the two most fundamental structures of power within human societies, the relationship of master to slave and that of husband to wife (and children). Aristotle shares the almost universal Greek belief that the differences in physical and mental capacity between male and female, and between free and slave, are natural and unalterable, and that the subordination of one to the other is good for both and necessary to the well-being of the *oikos* (and polis) as a whole. We can supplement Aristotle's analysis with any number of literary, medical, and philosophical texts from the eighth to the fourth century BCE, as well as other documents and visual images, confirming this strongly essentialist set of beliefs (though Plato is a rare exception, as both in the *Republic* and in the *Laws* he explores the possibility that women, if educated like men, might be capable of the same level of political and intellectual achievement); and the surviving texts of Greek tragedy not surprisingly tend to confirm these attitudes, even as they also intermittently challenge and problematize them.

In any case, Greek views on gender distinctions, slavery, and ethnicity were far from monolithic and static. So, for example, while Hesiod's *Works and Days* (dating probably to the eighth century BCE) describes the creation of the first woman, Pandora, to be a "beautiful evil" for men, and dwells on the wasteful and deceptive character of women in general, the *Homeric Hymn to Demeter* (from roughly the same period or somewhat later) describes sympathetically Demeter's outrage at Hades' seizure of her daughter, and at Zeus' – Persephone's father's – connivance at this rape, and narrates Demeter's effective resistance to male authority in obtaining Persephone's release from the underworld. Nonetheless, the strongly misogynistic currents in archaic Greek mythology and literature are obvious enough; and even such exemplary and noble female characters as Penelope (in Homer's *Odyssey*), Alcestis, and the (anonymous) wife of Xenophon's Ischomachus (in the *Oeconomicus*) all perform their noble actions within a domestic and social framework that remains resolutely patriarchal.

The supreme model of patriarchal (as well as kingly) authority is Zeus, whose familiar title in address, *Zeu pater* (Father Zeus) recurs in the Roman form *Jupiter*, and whose innumerable sexual conquests tended only to reinforce his masculine dominance and potency. This model of masculine dominance (and promiscuity) is replicated throughout the human realm; only in the topsy-turvy world of Old

Comedy is it imaginable that women should rule, or that slaves should outwit or successfully cheat their masters. There are scores of passages in Greek tragedy where one character or another expresses loyalty to the name and person of the father, husband, or master (living or dead); and many others too where obedience, submission, or silence is enjoined on a woman in the name of paternal or conjugal authority: "Woman, for a woman silence is the best adornment" (Sophocles, *Ajax* 293). Usually such reminders of female subjection are accepted without further comment. And when a female character does decide to take action on her own initiative, the result is almost always disastrous, unless she is a Greek woman seeking to escape from the clutches of a barbarian king (Euripides' *Iphigenia among the Taurians, Helen*).

But there are some striking moments at which overt criticism of fathers or husbands is ventured, even resistance attempted, not only by such outspoken and disruptive figures as Medea or Clytemnestra, but also by such quiet and dutiful ones as Eurydice (Sophocles, *Antigone* 1302–5) or Deianira (Sophocles, *Women of Trachis* 531–55, 582–87). Usually, of course, when a woman directly resists male authority it is either in retaliation for a previous wrong done to her by the man in question (Clytemnestra, Medea), or in loyalty to another male member of her family, especially her father or brother (Electra, Antigone).

In the case of fathers and sons, the picture of paternal authority in Greek tragedy is somewhat different. It is curiously rare to find a father and son on stage together at the same time; and when they are, the result is usually (as in Old Comedy) an ugly conflict. Reflecting, it seems, a social reality in which societal and familial pressures constantly drove young elite males to excel and compete against other males, relations between fathers and sons in tragedy tend to break down into bitter and incurable disputes. The positive desire to live up to and please an absent but potentially observant father may be the driving force in a son's pursuit of a violent and transgressive mission (Xerxes versus Greece, Ajax versus the Greek commanders, Orestes versus his mother); yet when the father is actually present, the result is usually rage and mutual misunderstanding (Haemon versus Creon, Admetus versus Pheres, Hippolytus versus Theseus, Polynices versus Oedipus). In such confrontations, the sympathies of the audience are typically divided, as in each case the son has a sound basis for his opposition to his father's position, even as the father articulates familiar principles of paternal authority.

Whereas gender norms and patriarchal authority, as we have seen, do get questioned and challenged from time to time in Greek tragedy – if only to be finally reinforced before the play's end – the authority of masters over slaves, and of elites over masses, never comes into serious question. Slaves are not freed (and very rarely is this even contemplated or mentioned, as at Euripides, *Children of Heracles* 788–89, 888–91); and almost never does a low-class character attempt an action that will materially affect the outcome of the play, except to carry out orders from one of the main characters. (The shepherd who disobeyed Jocasta's instructions years ago "out of pity" [Sophocles, *Oedipus the King* 1178], or the nurse who manipulates her mistress into half-authorizing an improper advance to Hippolytus [Euripides, *Hippolytus* 500–524], are only the exceptions that prove the validity of this rule through the disastrous consequences of such actions.) It is true that in Greek tragedy (unlike Japanese or Shakespearean drama) slave and low-class characters use more or less the same lexical and metrical registers as their masters and rulers: nonetheless they regularly express themselves in deferential and subordinate terms (an exception is Euripides, *Helen* 728–33; cf. 1627–41). Quite regularly, too, loyal slaves are represented in terms that seem to play strongly into every master's fantasy of the mutual benefit of this relationship. There is thus a constant reinforcement of the normalcy of slavery and of class distinction: certain characters are born to give orders, take risks, perform brilliant actions – and commit high crimes; and it is they (if anyone) who have the capacity to save the community; the rest are born to take orders, to listen and watch as the action unfolds, and (like the theater audience) to survive at the end of the day.

Apart from immediate kin, the claims of *philoi* (friends, nearest and dearest) and *xenoi* (guest-friends) represent another important layer of authority within interpersonal relations. The three prime "commandments" of traditional Greek morality (as laid down, for example, in the Hesiodic *Precepts of Chiron*) stipulated that reverence must be paid to the gods, to parents, and to *xenoi*; and if we add to these the strong bonds of sworn comradeship (*hetaireia, sunômosia*), we can recognize an elaborate system of social obligations affecting every individual's choices of action and speech. Reciprocal bonds of favors (*charis*) bound one family to another and demanded recompense over the passage of time. Likewise hatreds and grudges (*echthra*) could persist for decades and through generations: "help friends (*philoi*), harm enemies (*echthroi*)" and "do back to others as they do to you" were almost universally held maxims throughout the fifth century.

The *kleos* (name, fame, glory) of oneself and one's family (for self and family are not to be differentiated in the eyes of fifth-century Greeks) is often the chief determinant of action, stronger than any immediate practical benefit or even survival itself. Concern for praise and blame, and for the authority of posterity, sometimes outweighs the more immediate demands or threats presented by living authorities. Thus the dead come to be recognized as powerful sources of authority and obligation. Many scenes in tragedy take place at a tomb, or over the remains of a recently deceased family member: the grief and resentment of the living thus derive force and immediacy from the visual reminder of their loss and from the opportunity to address the spirit of the departed one. Laments and prayers over the dead may drive the action to a new level of intensity, or even in a new direction.

In view of these overlapping sources of familial and domestic authority, individual characters constantly find themselves trapped between competing claims and contradictory desires. Frequently gods and supernatural spirits are invoked in support of this or that set of obligations. So, for example, Artemis is patron-goddess of boys and girls under marriageable age; Demeter and Korê preside over the activities of mothers and daughters; and the Erinyes are available too as protectors of violated kin and embodiments of family curses. Functioning as a constant threat to calm and stability are those irresistible forces, Aphrodite and Eros – delightful sources of pleasure who preside over courtship and propagation, yet who all too often (especially in Greek tragedy) are agents of disastrous folly and fatal violation. Notoriously, the power of these two divinities can overwhelm even Zeus and the other gods, and can overturn cities and armies (for example, Sophocles, *Antigone* 781–806, *Women of Trachis* 407–502; Euripides, *Hippolytus* 525–64), even as the blessings they can bestow can sometimes be the key to the restoration of familial and social harmony.

But we have by now strayed into the "field" of the divine, the topic of our next section.

Forms and Figures of Religious Authority

The highest and most revered authority figures in Greek culture were, of course, the gods. Since other chapters in this volume take up the gods in tragedy (see Sourvinou-Inwood and Mastronarde, chapters 18 and 20), we need not consider all aspects of the topic here. Five main points need to be brought out, however: (1) the authority exercised by the various Olympian and chthonian gods and goddesses (*theoi, theai*), and by sundry other spirits and supernatural powers (*daimones*), tends to wax and wane during the course of a single play – that is to say, this source of authority may not be a consistent reference point, but may suddenly burst into view and as suddenly fade from consideration as other, human, perspectives come to the fore; (2) the basis and constituent elements of divine authority can be quite variable and questionable, sometimes involving a strong moral component (justice, respect for oaths and kinship-ties, concern for *xenoi* or suppliants, and so forth), but sometimes based on little more than the deity's own sense of personal status and honor; (3) individual deities, with the occasional exception of Zeus, do not usually have final authority to determine the outcome of events – there is (or so it is intermittently asserted in Greek culture) a higher, or prior, order of impersonal necessity that the Olympian and chthonian divinities alike are obliged to recognize; (4) often the agents of divine intervention and involvement in the plays are not the gods themselves but human intermediaries; (5) divine authority may often be seen less as a radically separate sphere of authority than as an extension and mystification of one or more of the human structures of authorities that we have already considered.

(1) Although modern readers of Greek tragedy often wish to analyze divine versus human causations, and to determine just how much freedom and independence of choice the human characters may have, this distinction seems rarely to have been a matter of interest to ancient playwrights or theater-goers. Divine and human motivations and causes co-exist; and we often find the focus of attention shifting back and forth, as one or other character, or the chorus, addresses a prayer, utters a curse, or narrates an explanation that may open up a new dimension on the action. And even though rival speeches in an *agón*, or in speculative choral songs, may propose contradictory views of divine concern or disregard for human affairs, divine approval or disapproval of the same event, the audience is rarely able to arrive at any clear understanding of which view, if either, is correct.

(2) Human beings generally wish their divinities to be just and honest (and even, on occasion, merciful and considerate), and gods in Greek tragedy are often represented as being committed to such standards as the basis for their actions. But at the same time it is acknowledged that gods may have many possible reasons to act, that humans cannot always expect to understand the reasons for divine action, and that gods (like other powerful persons) can be – and have the right to be – jealous, intemperate, and vindictive. So, while a few divinities (notably Themis and Diké) may by definition always act "justly," none can claim unfailing and complete moral

perfection, and most can be suspected at times of being just as selfish and limited in their goals and desires as human beings are. Thus, even as divine authority must always be respected and feared, and may (if properly invoked) be a source of individual or collective strength and salvation, nonetheless the precise degree of divine involvement and interest remains all too often dubious during the play, and even at the end a sudden divine apparition or explanation may not fully resolve questions raised earlier about the indifference and/or immorality of the powers above: so Apollo's oracle may after all have been "not wise" (Euripides, *Electra* 1246), and "there [is] nothing of these things that [is] not Zeus" (Sophocles, *Women of Trachis* 1278).

(3) The capture of Troy (by Neoptolemus and with the help of Philoctetes and his bow), the killing of Laius by his son, and other such mythological "facts" are beyond the control of individual gods – even though the gods may act purposely to bring them about (or to try to forestall or postpone them). Thus, for example, Apollo's predictions that Oedipus will kill his father, or Zeus' "sending" (Aeschylus, *Agamemnon* 59, 61, 111) of the Atreidae to recover Helen and punish Paris and his family, do not themselves "authorize" (cause, originate) those events: rather, they guarantee or confirm an already-determined outcome. Nonetheless, the distinction between events that are fated and necessary (and thus beyond the gods' control), and those that are caused by individual or collective divine decisions and actions, is rarely drawn with any clarity or consistency in Greek tragedy; and to the human participants in the tragic action, it may not make much difference. Often a character – even a god – will deflect argument about responsibility for an unpleasant outcome by stating either that it was "fated long ago" or that it was "Zeus' will" (or both), with the effect of short-circuiting any further discussion of blame and responsibility.

(4) Some of the most explosive confrontations in tragedy occur between a political/military leader and an agent of the divine, especially a priest or seer. In such scenes, the disparity between mortal aspirations and divine authority lends itself to extensive irony and demonstration of human blindness and error (*hamartia*). Sometimes the agents of the divine are represented as being entirely reliable and authoritative (for example, Theonoe in Euripides' *Helen*), but sometimes their reliability may be cast into question by another character (Tiresias in Sophocles' *Oedipus the King* and *Antigone*, and Euripides' *Bacchae*). Occasionally, too, a religious ritual may be manipulated for transparently deceptive effect (Helen and Menelaus' "purification" ceremony in Euripides' *Helen*) – a reminder that human cult practices may not always be authorized by a truly reliable divine source.

(5) As many of their names and cult epithets confirm, Greek (like most other) divinities represent to some degree personifications and mystifications of human power structures and emotions; and thus the engagement of "gods" in tragic action, so far from introducing an extraneous or additional element separate from the human players, often amounts to an extension, or projection, of the humans' personal and ideological conflicts onto an imagined higher authority.

Indeed, a fitting conclusion to this section will be a consideration of the figure of Zeus himself, the one Olympian deity never introduced on stage in Athenian tragedy, even though he often is imagined as the ultimate authority guaranteeing and, in some sense, justifying the final outcome of every play. Occasionally, such a recognition of

Zeus' authority may sound accusatory ("There is nothing in this that is not Zeus!":
Sophocles, *Women of Trachis* 1278); but usually it is resigned (for example, Euripides, *Bacchae* 1349: "My father Zeus approved all this long ago!"), or reassuring, as
if to remind the audience along with the characters that some kind of cosmic order
has now been restored, and that the suffering and danger that they have just
witnessed was not entirely pointless or random. Zeus is thus the ultimate projection
of the most deeply traditional Greek family and political structures: father (*patêr,
patrôios*), husband and lord of the household (*herkeios*), protector of strangers
(*xenios*), king (*basileus*), presider over public meetings and debates (*agoraios*) – as
well as being the one who is routinely invoked at almost every dinner and sacrifice, as
"the third, the savior" (*tritos sôtêr*), and who finally brings all things to completion
and perfection (*teleios*). All these titles for Zeus are mentioned in the course of the
Oresteia, a trilogy in which the characters and choruses ceaselessly turn to the
supreme authority for help, for understanding, and for justification of the human
conflicts and attempts at restitution that they see unfolding more or less chaotically
around them.

Knowledge, Spectatorship, and Cultural Authority

The authority of the past, and of traditional knowledge and wisdom in its various
forms (myths, names and genealogies, cults, and institutions), is another essential
ingredient in the web of structures and meanings encountered in a performance of an
Athenian tragedy (see Anderson, chapter 8 in this volume). The audience knows the
story in outline already; and as the play unfolds, all involved in its production are
constantly reminding, suggesting, confirming, and modifying bits of shared cultural
knowledge that are indispensable to the audience's understanding and enjoyment.
Of course, in drama the writer does not appear in his own persona as author, nor
does any individual character, not even the chorus, speak directly in the author's
voice. Furthermore the facts and traditions of Athenian cultural memory and expectation are far from uniform or consistent. So any presentation of reality and the
truth (*alêtheia, etuma*) in tragedy is necessarily always provisional, and more or
less indeterminate. Nonetheless, the cultural authority of *tragôidia* and of the
festival of which it is a part always brings some degree of validity – however
temporary – to the story that is being represented and to the "facts" and meanings
that are thereby being (re)established; and within the plays themselves there are
sometimes particular moments and dramatic conventions that possess a special
authority of their own.

Some Greek traditions were felt to be more authoritative than others. Thus in fifth-
century Athens the *Iliad*, while not unassailable in its details, could never be disregarded, and could usually be accepted as true, whereas the career, marriages, and
old age of Oedipus or the parentage of Odysseus were available to be told in any
number of different versions, since no single version had emerged to eclipse all others.
Certain local cults, monuments, and institutions might be unmistakably real and thus
accepted as true (the Court of the Areopagus, the cult of a local hero), but the
explanation of how they came to be named and authorized was always open to
retelling, and the authority imparted by a new or renewed tragic aetiology or
etymology might vary greatly (valid? ironic? deconstructive? paradoxical? absurd?).

Furthermore, certain particular tragic performances and texts clearly acquired a more conspicuous and enduring cultural authority than others, even after their initial production in the festival of Dionysus. Several of these have survived into the modern era – for precisely this reason (notably Aeschylus' *Oresteia*, Sophocles' *Oedipus the King* and *Electra*; Euripides' *Medea*, *Hippolytus*, and *Bacchae*); we know that others that have not survived nonetheless made an especially large impact (Aeschylus' *Niobe*, Euripides' *Telephus* and *Andromeda*). In all of these cases, the given or expected "facts" of the story were irrevocably altered by that first performance, and particular visual images or behavioral traits of major characters became fixed for all time. Doubtless there were other plays too that made significant cultural impact, though the traces are no longer detectable. In any case, the subsequent selection of the three major tragedians into the Alexandrian canon and the Hellenistic school curriculum ensured that these representatives of Athenian tragedy would permanently exercise their authority for many generations to come.

Within each play, certain modes of expression and representation, including physical enactments and speech acts, might be more authoritative than others. The lyric utterances of a chorus, for example, often carry a special authority of their own, by reason of the traditional function of choruses as performers of communal wisdom and memorialization, even though in any particular play the chorus members, qua characters, might be relatively ignorant, low-class, and unreliable. (Thus the slave women of Aeschylus' *Libation Bearers* appear at times obtuse, at other times brilliantly insightful and knowledgeable; and the Phrygian women of Euripides' *Bacchae* alternate between panic, vindictiveness, and philosophic wisdom). Messengers too, through a convention that is indebted in part to epic, may be at almost the same moment panic-stricken observers and virtually omniscient narrators of key events that nobody could in fact have so completely witnessed. Their authority as witnesses is crucial to the audience's appreciation of what has happened, even as their narrative skill is enjoyed as yet another facet of the (actual) author's dramatic skill.

One particular form of certainty and authorization of the events of the play is often provided by the familiar yet elusive Greek notions of *anankê* (necessity), *themis* (what is allowed), *dei*, *chrê*, and the like (what must be) – terms that often serve to divert inquiry or criticism concerning human or divine agency and responsibility, while leaving largely up in the air the nature of the authority that may underlie and enforce them. For the most part, such phrases merely imply that a certain outcome is inescapable (at least in the opinion of the speaker), and that some external authority has already determined that any further resistance would be futile and misguided.

One of the chief pleasures of Greek tragedy (as Aristotle first observed) is the spectators' awareness of a major character's ignorance, and their witnessing of the sequence of events through which that character eventually comes to recognize certain key pieces of information. The audience is thus placed in the position of experiencing the action from more than one perspective; that is, of both sharing the character's expectations and ambitions (identifying with her or his subject position) and at the same time looking "down" on that character (literally, from their seats in the theater; and symbolically, from their god-like level of superior knowledge). Yet at the same time, because these major characters are of such high social status, they are distinguished quite sharply from the ranks of the more ordinary members of their imagined community (guards, messengers, nurses, heralds, choruses), and from the mass of the theater audience too, with the result that we may posit yet a third angle of relationship for the spectators, one of looking "up" at these individuals with admiration and some degree of awe – even though those feelings may often be tinged also with horror or disgust at the excesses committed or attempted by those elite characters during the course of the play. That is to say, the spectators are brought to share (at least intermittently, and to some degree) the subject position of those inferior and more ordinary characters in the play who view their leaders and masters with respect, admiration, and even dependency, even as these spectators rest secure in the knowledge that, like the minor characters and choruses, they will always end the play safe and sound, while these more brilliant dynasts come crashing down to spectacular ruin and disgrace.

This mixture of responses depends crucially on the multiplicity of the kinds of "authority" that we have been exploring, and on the kinds of resistance to authority that are presented in Athenian tragedy, that most transgressive yet conservative of cultural forms. The final section of this chapter will be devoted to these issues.

Resistances to Authority

A high proportion of the surviving tragedies present one or more main characters taking an extreme or intransigent stand against some authority that appears to threaten the hero's or heroine's independence, honor, and happiness, and may also threaten that of his or her *philoi*. In some cases, the hero's resistance and self-assertion are blatantly misguided and futile (Pentheus', or Ajax's, or Clytemnestra's, or Hippolytus'): yet more often than not the attempted resistance – and the manner in which it is attempted – still command the audience's respect, admiration, and even sympathy, because the principles upon which this resistance is based have some validity, and because the energy, language, and aspirations of this hero are recognizable as being in some sense "superior." (As Aristotle puts it, they are "greater and better than us," *spoudaioteroi*.)

Within the make-believe world of the theater, as we have seen, the audience is invited to witness and judge, and also to some degree participate in, a scene of conflict and resistance that offers a large range of different subject positions for them to adopt. But almost invariably by the end of the play they find themselves experiencing a perspective closer to that of the minor characters or chorus than to that of the hero, as they all witness the main character's misery, while they themselves survive the catastrophe and prepare to resume their lives, relatively undamaged, even strengthened, by the shocking conflict that they have just witnessed. This process, even as it may often reveal the excessive ambitions, or dangerous blindness and fixation, of the protagonists, simultaneously reinforces the audience's sense of its own powerlessness, and perhaps also its sense of gratitude toward, and dependency upon, those powerful few who take the risks and suffer the consequences so that the larger community can survive and prosper. Such a dynamic (as Brecht noted with disapproval, in contrasting "Aristotelian" theater with his own "epic" theater) seems most often to result in a response of acceptance and resignation rather than any impulse toward social action or change on the part of the spectators.

This is not to deny or belittle the significance and impact of the many various representations of social and political resistance that we encounter in Greek tragedy: a considerable advance has certainly taken place from the Homeric world, in the frequency and outspokenness with which a minor character in tragedy may express disapproval, even rejection, of the policies or commands of a superior (for example, the guard in *Antigone*, the nurse in *Hippolytus* or *Medea*, the messenger in *Bacchae*); and likewise the most powerless and marginalized chorus may express thoughts of astonishing independence and insight.

Above all, the plays performed in the Theater of Dionysus gave women extraordinary prominence, and often an extraordinary moral authority as well. Such leading characters as Antigone, Deianira, and Andromache – even smaller roles such as Cassandra or Eurydice – all provide opportunities for cross-dressed male actors to articulate points of view, adopt positions of resistance, and even carry out actions that are in explicit and overt defiance of male authority. Furthermore, a high proportion of tragic choruses are female; and the combination of the authority intrinsic to choruses and the extraordinarily evocative and adventurous lyric expression that characterizes particular odes gives these female groups a biting and disturbing power to criticize the doings of a political leader or a whole army or even the gods. How do we account for this tragic license? What is the significance of such (imitations of) female resistance to male authority and such disruption of conventional gender relations? And why is it so often women, rather than men, who are allowed to utter the most vehement criticisms of political and military authority?

Recent criticism has gone back and forth over the question of whether the presence of active and articulate female heroines, and of highly sympathetic female victims, along with the recurrent presentation of direct conflict between male and female on the tragic stage, signals a positive engagement with and indirect amelioration of the repression of women in Athenian society; or whether to the contrary these plays enact a foreclosing of any such possibilities through the predictable defeat, victimization, silencing, or vilification of most of the female characters who venture too far outside the conventional.

To take just one striking example: what are we to make of the chorus of Asian bacchants, as they describe the liberating powers of Dionysus for rich and poor, high and low alike, in Euripides' *Bacchae* (417–32)? What is the force of hearing such "wisdom" emanating from a female, foreign group of exotically dressed and musically marked witnesses? On the one hand, these women appear truly liberated and empowered in ways that must have struck fifth-century Athenians as challenging and shocking; yet it is also true that this chorus is completely dependent on their male leader (Dionysus), that at the end of the play they will depart with him from Thebes and resume their travels (that is, they will not be effectively integrated into any stable political structure), and that the other females in the play who leave their homes and challenge male authority meet with an appalling fate. Unfortunately, there seems no sure way to answer the question of how the original Athenian audience reacted to such bold and transgressive scenes – though the mixed success of Euripides' plays in particular testifies to the variety of responses that tragedy could and did arouse. And modern audiences can be seen likewise to react in diametrically opposite ways to performances of the same play, depending on the style of production and the context of reception.

What is undeniable is that the continuity of tragic performance itself was never interrupted, and that legislation about the content of tragedy (in contrast to Old Comedy) seems never to have been required or proposed in Athens (outside the pages of Platonic dialogues). Tragedy was not apparently felt to be disruptive of civic order in the way that comedy could be. However shocking and disturbing any particular presentation of tragic resistance to patriarchal or divine authority might be, nobody seems either to have taken serious offence or to have attempted to bring about political or social change as a result. The festival of Dionysus permitted and encouraged recurrent resistances, even as it also foreclosed on those resistances and returned the audience to an essentially unchanged reality once the plays were over. (And it is important to remember that the tragic playwrights always concluded their sequence of plays with a satyr-play, whose emphasis on male dominance, happy endings, master–slave distinctions, and divine benevolence was relatively much more reassuring and complacent.) Tragic resistances to authority, as we have seen, come in many guises and with the support of multiple rival authorities, yet the authority, and the conclusion, of the festival itself appears to have remained unaltered from year to year.

Does this mean that nothing was changed by the plays that were performed and experienced in the theater each year? If so, their authority as forms of expression and communication would seem rather small. But this is not necessarily the case, even if the resistance depicted within the plays always seems to end in defeat, or at least in stalemate. For in truth the possibilities of resistance raised in each play, and the question of whether and where that resistance ends, lay – and still lies – with the audience. The play is never entirely over, even after the final words have been spoken. Antigone's defiant stance and uncompromising words, or the choral portrait of a warlord's mental torments as he contemplates butchering his own child to further his own political ambitions – such images and phrases (and for the original Athenian audiences, the melodies and gestures too) continue to resonate within the memories of their audiences for weeks, months, years to come. And subsequent performances and re-readings reopen still further possibilities of new authorization and interpretation, from directors, designers, actors, readers, and the audience themselves – the ultimate authorities.

FURTHER READING

On Homeric and archaic structures of political and social authority, see Donlan 1979, Latacz 1996, and Snodgrass 1980. For Greek tragedy's blending of Bronze Age or Homeric political features with contemporary Athenian institutions, see Easterling 1985a and Podlecki 1986. On the idealized figure of Theseus in fifth-century Athens, see Calame 1990, Walker 1995, and Mills 1997. On the offices and workings of the fifth-century Athenian democracy, see Sinclair 1988 and Morris and Raaflaub 1998. On class conflict in ancient Athens, see Davies 1981, Ste. Croix 1981, and Ober 1989; and on representations of class conflict in Greek literature in general, Rose 1992. For a sociology and analysis of the class relations of the characters represented in Greek tragedy, see Griffith 1995 and Hall 1997,

93–126. On the comic and/or contrastive effects of "lower-class" language or behavior in Greek tragedy, see Seidensticker 1982; also Bakhtin 1981.

On the administration of the Festival of Dionysus in Athens, see Goldhill 1990 and Wilson 2000a; on the representation of polis-ideology in tragedy see Winkler and Zeitlin 1990, Goldhill and Osborne 1999, and Seaford 1994. On the cultural authority of institutional language and ritual in general, see Bourdieu 1991. On the Athenian family, see Lacey 1968 and Just 1989; and on intra-familial dynamics, see Sourvinou-Inwood 1979, Strauss 1993, and Griffith 1998. For the conventional authority of certain types of tragic speech-act, see Mastronarde 1999, de Jong 1991, and Barrett 2002.

CHAPTER TWENTY-TWO

Women's Voices

Judith Mossman

"It is in the exercise of language that a human being is constituted as a subject" (Benveniste 1966, 259). The importance of this idea to the study of women's speech in tragedy is evident. It is perennially startling that a culture that prescribed the invisibility and silence of women produced, and indeed promoted to the highest cultural status, a genre in which women are portrayed as supremely articulate. The parts they take in the traditional stories that form the basis of the tragedies do not necessarily require much elaboration. But because they are given such an extraordinary range of voices, endowed with remarkable power and (emotional) authenticity, the female characters of tragedy resist simple relegation, and constitute a provocatively vocal and persistently eloquent Other.[1] To investigate the nature of the female subject in tragedy, it becomes vital to study the language of female characters.[2]

This all-important female speech has been studied in a variety of ways, as McClure has summarized (2001, 6–11). The most promising are a sociolinguistic approach, which seeks to relate speech to social roles and conditions, suitably adapted in the light of what is known about ancient views of language and in view of the stylization of the tragic genre, and the approach (most favored by McClure in her 1999 book) through the study of verbal genres and their manipulation by the poets. The two are not incompatible and may profitably be combined. Of course there are methodological pitfalls: what, for example, is the relationship between the speech of ancient Athenian women and female characters in Attic tragedy, if any? There does seem to have been a relationship, if a complex one, between the speech of tragic male characters and that of Athenian men: at least, some modes of speech are convincingly identified as colloquial (because they occur frequently in comedy or Platonic dialogue, in texts which do seem to aim to reproduce a recognizable diction: see Stevens 1976, for example). The iambic trimeter, the meter of the spoken parts of tragedy, is identified by Aristotle as that closest to everyday speech (*Poetics* 1449a24–27, cf. 1459a12). But if the diction of tragedy occasionally "zooms" its hearers into everyday speech (for the concept of zooming see Sourvinou-Inwood, chapter 18 in this volume), its high style cannot be said to approximate it as a general rule. The same must apply to female characters, only more so, since women's voices were intended to be rarely heard, at least outside (though see now Blok 2001, 95–116).

It is nonetheless reassuring that we have some evidence that female speech was perceived as having special linguistic characteristics of its own: for example, Plato identifies linguistic conservatism as a female tendency (*Cratylus* 418b–c), and Aristotle certainly regards some types of speech as appropriate or inappropriate to women (though this refers more to verbal genres than to linguistic features proper: see *Poetics* 1454a22–24 and 31, where he seems to be saying that Euripides' Melanippe makes inappropriate use of rhetoric). So a dramatist might have wanted in some sense to make a character sound female, even if a female tragic character did not sound much (or at all) like an Athenian woman. More importantly, there is ancient evidence for the view that language and subjectivity were linked in the minds of the Greeks: Gera, in her recent examination of ancient Greek views on the development and purpose of language, traces the important idea that "the possession of speech . . . is often thought to entail the capacity for rational thinking as well" (2003, 182). It may be possible to argue, based on this widespread ancient concept, that the articulate Greek women of tragedy, just by speaking, can be seen to lay claim to full subjectivity, even if that claim is often subsequently challenged or denied.

So although there is, clearly, a potential danger of anachronism and of cultural inappropriateness in applying some criteria to the female speech in the tragic texts, the approach still seems worth pursuing. It is very hard, and probably impossible, to identify any particular linguistic criterion that always and invariably seems to suggest a female character. One might be tempted to argue paradoxically that silence is the linguistic preserve of the tragic woman – that in Sophocles' *Oedipus the King*, for example, Jocasta leaves the stage without a word after her realization, whereas Oedipus cries out that all has become clear to him as he recognizes his fate – but there are always counterexamples. We do not know enough about Aeschylus' famous lost play *Myrmidons* to know the quality of Achilles' silence, but that he was silent for a long time was the most celebrated feature of that play and perhaps of *Phrygians* too (Aristophanes, *Frogs* 911–13, with Dover 1993a on 911–12; Taplin 1972; and now Michelakis 2002, 37–39). Sociolinguists working on modern languages, and particularly those who study "the linguistic means by which men dominate women in interaction" (Tannen 1994, 20–21), have also discovered that broad generalizations tend to fail, and have evolved methodological strategies to deal with this: as Tannen (1994, 21) has shown, "linguistic strategies are potentially ambiguous (they could 'mean' either power or solidarity) and polysemous (they could 'mean' both)." So silence (in fiction or in life) can be dominated or used as a means of control; interruption can betoken a lack of interest in what the interlocutor says, or a boundless enthusiasm for it. In an analogous way, I believe that when looking at tragedy it is necessary to take each play as a separate entity and accept that a technique used in one play to create a female character might not work in the same way in another play, with a different set of circumstances and a different linguistic atmosphere, a different word-world. This might seem rather convenient, but it is surely a necessary move: all characterization operates by placing the descriptors it uses to create a persona in a particular context and playing off the character created by those descriptors against his or her setting. The character is unintelligible out of context and the context is nothing without the character. It will be clear that while I agree with Griffith (2001,

136) that "no neatly defined portrait of 'woman' emerges (from this play [*Antigone*], or from any other – or from Greek tragedy overall)," I do believe that, despite the inevitable circularity of looking for difference in women's speech, the search can still be a fruitful exercise. But every play needs a different set of tests. There is no alternative to taking each drama individually on its own terms.

If this approach is taken, the question of whether one can discern differences in the treatment of female characters in different authors becomes more, not less, complex, especially given that so much tragedy has been lost, and that in two out of three cases the plays we have are a selection made for us by people with very different preferences and priorities from our own: Sophocles, in particular, looks a far more diverse author, and perhaps one more interested in women, when the fragments are taken into account than he does from the extant plays (one of which, *Philoctetes*, is the only extant tragedy without a female character). One could perhaps argue that in Sophocles and Euripides an ever greater desire for naturalism (a dignified and stylized naturalism, but significant and appreciable nonetheless) is in evidence where it is not in Aeschylus, and that this results in more and more subtle ways of rendering women's speech. But at this point in the argument, someone will mention Aeschylus' Clytemnestra, and the theory will collapse.

Christopher Pelling, in chapter 6 of this volume, discusses Clytemnestra's superb rhetoric, her inimitable way of misleading without ever really lying; Laura McClure (1999, 70–111) her manipulation of verbal genres; Simon Goldhill (1984, esp. 8–98) the transgressiveness of her language. I would like very briefly to discuss her short scene with Cassandra. As has often been pointed out, Cassandra is the only person not to fall under the spell of Clytemnestra's persuasion, and the only woman she encounters – hardly a coincidence, even if one does not agree entirely with McClure's characterization of Clytemnestra's persuasion as erotic (1999, 93; see also Goldhill's very interesting account of this scene [1984, 81–88], and Montiglio 2000, 213–16).

Clytemnestra tell Cassandra, "You too get yourself inside, you, Cassandra I mean; since Zeus without anger [*amênitôs*] has made you share with the house the lustral water, standing with many slaves by the household altar" (Aeschylus, *Agamemnon* 1035–38). The contrast between Clytemnestra's successful persuasion of all the other characters and Cassandra's imperviousness to her is all the more striking because Clytemnestra is at first very much in her usual flow, inserting multiple ironies into her every line: Cassandra will indeed stand by the altar for a sacrifice very soon indeed. The position of *amênitôs* ("without anger") between "Zeus" and "the house" leaves it ambiguous as to whether Clytemnestra is commenting on the impassivity of Zeus' plan or the lack of wrath in the house where she has ended up: but we know (from 155, where the chorus spoke of a "remembering, child-avenging Wrath") that a *Mênis* who shares many characteristics with Clytemnestra in fact inhabits the house. Fraenkel (1950 on 1036–38; see also Denniston and Page 1957 on 1035 ff.) comments on the inclusion of slaves in household sacrifices: "What Clytemnestra here makes appear as a special favour is in truth nothing more than the common practice of antiquity" – so the irony is the more vicious, especially as she then contrasts the kindness of masters who are *archaioploutoi* (of ancient wealth) with the unkindness of the *nouveaux riches*.

The address is "perhaps not very polite," "rather near to the limits of good manners" (Fraenkel 1950 on 1035), so there is a slightly impatient tone, but the references to the wealth of the house recall her earlier speech to Agamemnon (958–74), and Clytemnestra's use of the consolatory example of Heracles as slave in 1040–41, a rhetorical commonplace (see, for example, Sophocles, *Antigone* 944–87), perhaps recalls the method she used on Agamemnon in the tapestry-scene, introducing Priam as a (specious) example on which to model himself (935). Heracles is also a specious example in relation to Cassandra: though he did undergo sexual humiliation during his servitude to Omphale (in some versions dressing as a woman), the whole experience was always temporary, and inflicted as a punishment for misconduct (see *OCD* s.v. Omphale, and Loraux 1995, 116–39); Cassandra is innocent, not merely humiliated but violated, and would be facing a lifetime of slavery if she were not about to be murdered by Clytemnestra. But the difference in Clytemnestra's opponent is becoming apparent: Cassandra does not respond to this or any other gambit. As Clytemnestra loses her temper, she also seems to lose her grasp of the realities of language: in fact, Cassandra panics her into a linguistic Colemanball,[3] underlining her frustration at her sudden inability to communicate. Cassandra's silence, therefore, is not the silence of helplessness, but the silence of power – the power which knowledge gives her. For all that both Clytemnestra and the chorus interpret her lack of speech as making her like a wild animal (on this tendency in Greek thought see Gera 2003, 182–212), it is she who stands, paradoxically, in the position of strength. Eventually she will do as Clytemnestra says and go into the house where the sacrifice is waiting (1056–57); but when she does it will be – uniquely – on her own terms, in full knowledge of what awaits her, undeceived by Clytemnestra's double meanings. So although (as others have pointed out: see, e.g., Wohl 1998, 113) she is figured in many ways very like Iphigenia (each, for example, is hauntingly compared to a picture: *Agamemnon* 242, 1328–29), there is a contrast between them too. Iphigenia, gagged and so deprived of speech, can only communicate silently, as a picture does; Cassandra, initially silent, becomes wonderfully eloquent, giving the house a voice, narrating story after story – until she exits and her picture is wiped out. She is never referred to after the end of the play, and her death is not mentioned as being avenged by Orestes. So Cassandra's silence, and her speech, both acquire meaning from the text which surrounds them.

A useful comparison may be made with another prisoner of war: Tecmessa in Sophocles' *Ajax*. Tecmessa comes out of Ajax's tent to describe the horror of Ajax's madness (significantly, she does so after asking, "how shall I tell the unspeakable tale?" – which sets the tone for the concentration on speech acts which will follow) and the "double sorrow" of his realization of it. As she relates the beginning of his insanity (284–87), her ready and detailed narration recalls the way in which Deianira in *Women of Trachis* inclines to narrative and story-telling (on which see Kraus 1991). Her description of Ajax's brusque and stereotypically masculine response (so Segal 1981, 109, 133–38; and see Aristophanes, *Lysistrata* 507–20) when she queries his departure in the middle of the night is ironic in the light of her function in the play so far, which has been, and will continue to be, one of reporting and verbal interpretation, as well as those very female verbal genres, consolation and lamentation. His proverbial rebuke of her speech, enjoining silence onto her, applies only to the immediate context; indeed, by 312 he is threatening her if she does not speak to him and tell him what has happened. It is in fact primarily in terms of his speech acts that Tecmessa reports his madness and recovery from it, moving from his crazed volubility in his madness (represented both directly in 91–117 and in Tecmessa's description at 301–6) to silence (311), to threats (312), to groaning, which he previously regarded as unworthy of a hero (instead of his usual inarticulate animal cries – 322), and back to quieter lamentation (325). Segal (1981, 133–38) has noted Ajax's progression from these reported generic expressions of grief and pain to the double-edged eloquence of the Deception Speech. From our point of view it is particularly interesting that Tecmessa concentrates so carefully on the noises Ajax makes: she, unlike Clytemnestra in the presence of Cassandra, really wants to be able to interpret Ajax, to understand and communicate with him, but is hampered in constructing interpretations of Ajax by the limited material he gives her.

This contrasts with the opening scene and the first choral ode, where there is more concentration on what Ajax does than on what he says, and it is the voices of his enemies that are foregrounded: Odysseus addresses Athena as a voice (14); she tells him to proclaim Ajax's madness (67), and later warns him to control his speech (127–30). The chorus then concentrates on the malignant force of rumor (142, 148, 155–56, 166, 167–68) and calls upon Ajax to appear to inflict silence on his enemies (169–71). They address and personify the rumor at 173–74; beg Zeus and Apollo to avert it at 187; and return to it again at 188–92 and 198–99. Tecmessa's purpose in her explanatory narrative is ultimately to allow the chorus's words to do their utmost in helping him (330), but not even her own words will ultimately do much good. But her attempts at interpretation do not only characterize Ajax as inaccessible and delineate the violence of his moods, they also characterize her as a gentle mediator and as one who, despite everything, genuinely cares for Ajax and is affected by what will happen to him. One might dare to say that it also makes her sound very female as she continually struggles to find the best possible response to her focus of care, Ajax. At the same time, her interaction with the male chorus, a cooperative and mutually respectful relationship, must characterize Ajax as representing an extreme of masculinity.

In the following scene it is not only the text in which Ajax and Tecmessa operate that endows their speech with meaning, but also the Homeric text against which they are written. As Segal points out (1981, 134): "Homer's Hector and Andromache ...can hear and move one another; Ajax and Tecmessa, like Heracles and Deianira, speak different languages." It is most important that in this version of the scene between Hector and Andromache in the *Iliad* (6.390–502) Tecmessa is forced into playing both characters: she echoes both the speech in which the loving Hector foreshadows Andromache's fate and Andromache's words in which she reminds Hector that he is all she has left (*Iliad* 6.447–65 and *Ajax* 496–505; *Iliad* 6.429–32 and *Ajax* 514–17; see Bers 1997, 50–51, and de Jong 1987). Tecmessa's performance at least provokes pity from the chorus, if not from Ajax, but when Ajax comes to play Hector in the scene with Eurysaces, it proves a travesty. The Homeric scene ends with premature lamentation for Hector: Ajax closes the Sophoclean version down by brusquely rejecting lamentation with another masculine generalization (580, cf. 586). But like his last such comment, this one fails in its effect, this time even in its immediate context. His final metaphor ("The wise physician does not chant incantations over a wound that calls for surgery," 581–82) is complicated, not least because it is so concisely expressed. On the surface it contrasts magical chanting (used to stop bleeding at *Odyssey* 19.457 and elsewhere) with surgery. But because the word he uses for incantation is also commonly applied to erotic magic and hence to a particular type of (usually female) persuasion, and because the audience will inevitably see his reference to cutting as pointing to his suicide, it also contrasts Tecmessa's words with his own impulse to action. But his effort to have the last word is temporarily frustrated by the chorus's and Tecmessa's forcing him into stichomythia (one-line exchanges) and then into *antilabê* (part-line exchanges).

When Ajax reemerges and speaks the Deception Speech, he describes his new attitude by saying (in a literal translation), "I was made female in respect of my mouth at this woman's hands" (651–52). Zeitlin (1990a, 82, also 72–73) has said of this: "[Ajax] in his madness has not acted the part of the hero.... Thus the deceptive speech makes sense as a feminine strategy enlisted in the service of restoring an unequivocal manliness he can only achieve... by dying the manly death – heroically and publically onstage – yet in the woman's way." The phrasing suggests that it is *only* in words that Ajax has changed, that his mode of outward communication rather than his attitude is different. But it is the gentler tone of these lines rather than their deceptive aspect that Ajax might see as feminized: in *Ajax* deception is in fact most associated with Odysseus rather than with women. Some would also dispute Zeitlin's contention that suicide is a feminine death, and indeed one that Greek society condemned (see de Romilly 2003). The rhetoric of this speech is off-key in a number of ways, as Pelling has shown (see chapter 6 in this volume).

We might conversely ask whether there are any implications for Tecmessa in the fact that she is forced to adopt two Homeric roles, one male, one female. Tecmessa is not a transgressive female character like Clytemnestra, who adopts male language in order to get her way;[4] she may not keep quiet for very long despite Ajax's orders, but she does go inside when he tells her to, she laments for him and covers up his corpse, and in every respect her behavior is aimed at securing what is best for him. Rather, her adoption of a dual role in this scene is forced on her by (and of course simultaneously serves to delineate) the comparative unconcern of Ajax. This is underlined by the fact that when she plays Andromache and describes the ruin of her home and family at 515–17, it becomes clear that where Andromache speaks of Achilles killing her father and brothers, it was actually Ajax who ravaged Tecmessa's home (though her parents were killed in some other way, like Andromache's mother). It fits well that Tecmessa the interpreter of Ajax should also have to supply her own sympathy and interest. Tecmessa thus emerges as a strong focus of the important theme of language in this play, whose own language conveys a character defined by its relation to Ajax as distinctively female, and contributes a voice against which to judge Ajax's.

Yet more prisoners of war will help us make some further points. In Euripides' *Trojan Women*, we find perhaps the greatest variety of female characters in any single play. *Trojan Women* is rarely treated as a problem play, and yet in many respects it is remarkably difficult to fit into many schemas that seek to formulate a definition for tragedy. So, for example, Rivier says of it (1944, 175): "There is nothing tragic about this play, even though it abounds in bloodshed and tears, since tragedy stems from reflections on the origin of misfortune, not on the mere perception of its physical effects." Its structure encourages the reader (or audience) to compare the succession of women with whom Hecuba interacts to one another; and as the action of the play happens mostly off-stage (or indeed before the play begins), the criteria for comparison are very largely conveyed by their contrasting modes of speech. The male characters of the play, apart from Astyanax, are Greek, not Trojan, and this intensifies the feeling that the women exist in a rather separate world from men. Talthybius goes to and fro; Menelaus judges the *agón*; but neither of them has much at stake, since neither is aware of the doom hanging over the Greeks which is determined in the prologue. It is hard indeed to feel that, compared with the onstage direct presentation of the women and their concerns, "the self that is really at stake is to be identified with the male" (Zeitlin 1990a, 68) – either the Greeks or even Astyanax, so much more important for his potential and for his symbolic value than for his present persona. The important things are said by women in this play, because they are felt by them. And Euripides is careful to make what they say appropriate to female characters and a female chorus, avoiding showing people in an extreme situation all sounding the same (a phenomenon discussed by Silk 1996b and Mossman 2001, 376). This play is about the death of a city, and the city is usually primarily a male concern; but in this play the city is shown through the minds of the Trojan women as the frame for the *oikos* (household), conceived of less as a state than as a collection of families (see 198–206, for example). Although Astyanax becomes almost symbolic of the future of the city, he is simultaneously (perhaps primarily) a vulnerable family member for Hecuba. Of course cities and *oikoi* have a common characteristic: when there are no men in them they are conceived of as empty (see Thucydides 7.77.7 and Lysias 7.41), and of course the women's feelings about the fall of the city overlap with what those of male non-combatants might be (had the Greeks left any of them alive). It is a question of emphasis, but the emphasis is on that which an Athenian audience might expect to be of most importance to women: the family.

How then does Euripides differentiate this multiplicity of female voices? It is not hard in *Ajax* to discern a contrast between the male voice of Ajax and the female voice of Tecmessa; but how are Cassandra and Andromache and Helen and Hecuba individualized? I think it is possible to see that each of the major female characters has her own peculiar voice; it is also possible to see each voice as connecting with and relating to the others and performing an intellectual function within the play. It has been rightly pointed out (e.g., by Croally 1994, 84–97, esp. 86–90; see also Scodel 1998, esp. 145–54) that each of the characters is profoundly concerned with marriage in one way or another: Cassandra sings a perverted marriage-hymn; Hecuba reflects bitterly on the marriages which should have been made for her daughters but which will never be; Andromache is troubled by the new "marriage" she must contract and what her conduct in it should be; Helen's ruptured marriage to Menelaus is to be resumed, and her perverted marriage to Paris has caused all the trouble. This is important, and obviously contributes to the female atmosphere of the play. As important for their individuality, though, is the way in which the characters express this concern.

Hecuba is the focus around which the action revolves; as one might expect of a character who bears the weight of the tragedy, it is she who is the great poet and orator of the play. This would surely be true of a male protagonist as well; but it might still be legitimate to look for ways in which her gender is expressed as part of her individuality. First, solo and antiphonal lamentation, the most obvious female speech genre (since it was, and is, perceived as a function of women in life as well as in fiction: see McClure 1999, 40–47; Alexiou 1974; and on this play, Gregory 1991, esp. 160–62 and 176–78), marks her as the non-combatant female survivor of the sack of a city. But in her other utterances a distinctive view of what has happened to her emerges. For one thing, she is the character in the play who most consistently questions the gods and the accepted order of the universe: not surprisingly, this tends to make her the character who uses the most abstract language. She also, though, has the widest range of different tones and roles: mother, mother-in-law, grandmother, captive, queen, victim, accuser. Hecuba is the only character (apart from the chorus) to report conversations with others: she renders in direct speech conversations she had with Helen and recalls how Astyanax would chatter away to her (see Bers 1997, 100–101). More fundamentally, she has been described as inconsistent, especially with regard to advising Andromache to buckle down and carry on as a concubine and telling Helen she should have killed herself if her position was genuinely that of a captive bride (see Waterfield 1982). It could be argued that this multiplicity of voice is most characteristic of a female protagonist (changeability being a female characteristic from early Greek poetry on: see Semonides fr. 7.27–42 West, where he compares one of his female character types to the sea). Clytemnestra and Medea are obvious examples of sinister multivocal female protagonists. Although some female leads are not (or not in the same way: Deianira, for example), it is hard to think of a male protagonist who is: Ajax, for example, maintains his own voice even in the Deception Speech. Even Odysseus (in *Ajax* and other plays) is less changeable.

If Hecuba sounds slightly different in every scene, as I believe she does, that must be at least partly to do with the differing nature of her interlocutors. I have noted elsewhere (Mossman 2001) that women may argue differently in the presence of men from the way they do when in a single-sex group: in *Trojan Women*, however, this cannot be argued, as I did for *Electra*, by studying the numbers of general reflections, as there are remarkably few of those in the play as a whole, and there does not seem to be much, or indeed any, correlation between the presence of men and the predominance of sententiousness, as there was in *Electra*. This is an example of what I said above about every play constituting its own word-world. The general principle, however, does seem to me to hold good in the scene between Hecuba and Helen in the presence of Menelaus, in that both attempt to manipulate him; but the presence of Talthybius makes much less difference to them: he is the go-between with the male world of the Greeks and as such is accepted and does not modify their speech as Menelaus can be seen to do.

What of the female characters? It might have been expected that Cassandra, not Hecuba, should have been the one most given to abstract thought and expressions, but in fact the most disconcerting thing about Cassandra is her determination to take literally what most would see as metaphors and act out the logical consequences of them, to insist that her future liaison with Agamemnon is a marriage and to celebrate it accordingly; to take what she knows about the future and see herself as literally sacking Agamemnon's house in return (359), and to view the disaster which will befall the Greeks as a victory for the Trojans, which should therefore be celebrated. This is, of course, in stark contrast to the Aeschylean Cassandra, whose metaphors cluster densely, but whose conduct remains consonant with the nature of her situation and the world around her; and it has the effect of making her even more disconcerting to the other characters, and even to the audience, who might be taken aback by her extreme application of logic even though they know she is right. (Croally 1994, 230, has a different comparison with the Aeschylean Clytemnestra.)

The effect is heightened by minimizing the number of actually metaphorical expressions she uses: in all of 353–405 the only metaphors which could be described as "live" are *antiporthêsô* ("I shall sack [Agamemnon's house] in turn," 359), which she turns out to mean literally, and her use of *stephanos*, "crown," at 401, a term suggested by the comparison (almost a competition) she is drawing between the Greeks and Troy. In her response to Talthybius she introduces one figurative comparison which cannot be connected to her obsessions, marriage and victory, when she says that Odysseus will one day think the Trojans' troubles like gold when compared with his own (432). At 444 she calls her description of his wanderings "hurling words like javelins," which, again, does not connect with her literalized metaphors; but when in the next line she says her marriage to Agamemnon will take place in the house of Hades she may almost mean this literally (445). The same may be true when she calls herself one of the three Furies (457) and when she envisages herself victorious in Hades and claims again that she will sack the house of Atreus (460–61). For the audience these expressions both emphasize the strangeness of Cassandra (especially in the light of the intertextuality with Aeschylus) and simultaneously invest what she says with a very strong air of plain truth; for Hecuba and Talthybius they make her seem demented. It is important that Hecuba responds to Cassandra's marriage-hymn with a reproachful address to Hephaestus (343–45); this will contrast with Hecuba's later, less conventional addresses to the gods (see Croally 1994, 79–81).

When Cassandra has left the stage, Hecuba's speech highlights how little she has been able to inspire belief: the keynote of this speech is the contrast of present woe and future uncertainty with past happiness, underlined linguistically by Hecuba's persistent use of *polyptoton*, as she uses the same verb in different tenses and voices (see 468, 487–88, 499; she also uses different parts of the same adjective at 496). Intentionally simple though the diction of this great speech is, Hecuba is more inclined to "live" metaphors than Cassandra (cf. 469, 496–97, and 508–9). At 489 the imagery of the cornerstone metaphor seems especially appropriate since Hecuba is relating the troubles of her house.

The scene with Andromache is particularly interesting in this context. For one thing, there is a surprising amount of tension between Hecuba and Andromache, which emerges after the antiphonal lament they share. Hecuba has been totally supportive and protective of her daughter, and there were some indications in Cassandra's madness of concern for Hecuba, notably her eagerness to show that Hecuba would not after all be a slave to Odysseus (427–30). But the dynamic is different with Andromache. She quite abruptly insists that Polyxena is better off dead, and specifically better off than herself, rejecting Hecuba's "while there's life, there's hope." A scholion on 634 is so wrong-headed it actually says something very interesting: "he is not aiming at the underlying characters. For now Andromache philosophizes along the same lines as Cassandra did before." But the two characters are in fact totally different. Cassandra, as we have seen, didn't really philosophize at all; Andromache's first speech, though, is full of moral reflection, albeit of a different type from Hecuba's.

Here, rather than in relation to the male characters, it may be interesting to consider the proportion of general reflection in the speeches of the three female characters we have encountered so far. Cassandra has 3 lines of general reflection in

353–405 (3/50, omitting 383–85, or 6 percent) and 2.5 lines in 424–61 as we have it, though there is a lacuna after 434 (2.5/38, or 6.57 percent; this includes the lines in trochaic tetrameters). Andromache in 634–83 gives by far the most sententious speech in this play: she has 11.5 lines out of 48 (deleting 634–35), or 23.9 percent. This is evidently because she is struggling to work out a moral position for herself in the midst of chaos: she speaks no generalizations at all in 740–79 in her response to Talthybius' announcement that the Greeks have decided to kill Astyanax. That would seem to hold the key to why using the same criteria for interpreting speech characteristics does not necessarily work in different plays: here the women are in such extreme circumstances that the kind of social constraints which dictate Electra's use of general reflections are no longer valid: why should Andromache now care what Talthybius thinks or modify her speech in any way? Ironically, as she describes her attitude to her first marriage (643–58), she does so insistently in terms of speech and speech acts (compare Tecmessa), and the control over her speech which she exerted is the essence of her virtue: "I aimed at *high repute*," she explains [*toxeusasa* in 643 is a common metaphor for speaking as well as aiming at something: see Aeschylus, *Suppliants* 446; Euripides, *Hecuba* 603]; "whether *blame* already attaches to women or not...I put aside my longing for the very thing that brings the most *scandal*, namely staying outside, and I stayed in the house. [Contrast Andromache in *Iliad* 6, who is, of course, not in the house at all, and see Croally 1994, 90 n. 43.] I didn't let into my house the *clever talk of women* but I was content with having in my own mind a sound teacher from my own resources. I kept before my husband *a quiet tongue* and a tranquil look.... *Report* of this reached the Greek camp" (trans. Barlow 1986; my italics). In keeping with this is her comparison of herself and Hector to yokemates who have been parted (669–72): if a dumb animal is unhappy in such circumstances, how much more so will be an articulate human being, who has taken so much care over her speech? (See Gera 2003, 182–212.) The total despair and frustration which makes her tell Talthybius to take Astyanax away and eat his flesh if he likes is very different from her earlier "philosophizing."

A similar point could be made about Hecuba's speeches (taking only the long speeches for reasons of space): Hecuba's first speech (for which no men are present) has a generalization ratio of 4.5/45, or 10 percent. At 686–708 (again, no men are present unless you count Astyanax) she speaks none as such (686–94 are an extended metaphor rather than a general reflection). Interestingly, in the *agôn*, where one often finds general reflections clustering and Menelaus is judging the contest, Helen (on the attack) speaks none, and Hecuba, attacking back, in all of 969–1032 speaks only 2 generalizing lines out of 64 (3.125 percent), though she has an impressive and ominous general remark at 1051. Burying Astyanax at 1156–1206, again, with no men present, she reverts to a similar proportion as in her first speech: 5.5/50, or 11 percent; but when she tries to rush toward the fire that is consuming Troy, generalization is obviously going to be lacking: her own specific suffering is naturally what she cries aloud, Talthybius or no Talthybius (1272–83).

Andromache is seeking the best line of conduct for herself in this new, chaotic universe; as such she speculates more than Cassandra, who is sure even of the new order and her place in it. Andromache indeed also uses more metaphors; but she does not query its nature, as Hecuba does. Andromache in cursing Helen makes use of abstractions, calling her the daughter not of Zeus, but of Avenging Curse, of Envy, of Murder and Death (766–71); but Hecuba questions the nature of Zeus himself, in a famous and arresting passage before the *agôn* with Helen (884–88). Only Hecuba, the character who most consistently speculates about the gods (Croally 1994, 70–84), could meaningfully have said this (in this play), and only she could take on Helen directly and on her own terms. The *agôn* has been much studied (see, e.g., Lee 1976, Barlow 1986 ad loc, Lloyd 1984 and 1992, and Meridor 2000), and space will not permit a full analysis here; but a few brief points should be made.

This passage, as is characteristic of any *agôn*, is highly rhetorical, and in keeping with this Hecuba's speech takes on a new and different aspect, as has often been said. This is the voice she uses that stands out most clearly from the others, and that it does so must be partly due to Helen. It is interesting to contrast Helen, the wicked wife, with Andromache, the good one: where Andromache's speech acts were the essence of her virtue, Helen's are rhetorical markers in an oration. Indeed, even when she is just asking Menelaus why she has been brought outside she uses a word which is also a rhetorical technical term (*phroimion*, "beginning," 895).[5] Her speech of 49 lines (deleting 918, 959–60) has a four-line preamble followed by a formal tricolon ("first ... second ... then ... "). There are two more rhetorical narration-dividers (931, 945), and two examples of *hypophora* (938 and 951; *hypophora* is the anticipation of one's opponents' objections). Helen thus lays tremendous stress on the act of argument and the present speech (as opposed to the control of speech in the past). Hecuba's speech is quite different in this regard (though of course nonetheless rhetorical for all that). In 64 lines we have a two-line preamble (969–70: "First of all I shall become an ally for the goddesses and show that this one does not speak justly"), whose phrasing actually points not to Hecuba's speech but to the falsity of Helen's, and then no formal rhetorical marker (that is, no reference to this speech *as* a speech) until 1029. Hecuba does use the retrospective equivalent of *hypophora* in that she constantly interrogates what Helen has said (and indeed what she has *not* said: see Lloyd 1984 and also Croally 1994, 120–62; Hecuba refers to Helen's speech at 981–83, 998, and 1010); but she does so with much more apparent naturalism. In general Hecuba's speech gives the impression of tumbling out of her in a tirade: note, for example, the way that Helen uses the interjection *eihen*, "well now," outside the meter, creating a very strong break between 944 and 945 as she moves from one argument to another; whereas Hecuba incorporates it into her line, making only a small pause, at 998. Not all of Hecuba's arguments are reasonable; but her anger is sincere, and shines through her rhetoric, whereas Helen's sterile logic, as ruthless as Cassandra's but self-serving where hers was not, is also conveyed through the conventions of language.

Why do all this? Why write a play where almost all the characters are women, indeed women in the process of suffering the most brutal type of objectifying exchange transaction possible (to borrow the type of terminology used by Wohl 1998, 59–117), being transformed from free women into slaves? Can there be any reason other than that the poet wished to demonstrate that subjectivity and identity can transcend even the most dire circumstances if it can still speak? True, the poet is male (as are the actors). But just as the male actor must wear a female mask and perhaps modify his voice to sound female (see Pickard-Cambridge 1988, 167–71), so the poet can be seen to modify his voice and allow his characters to sound, if not like women, at least like tragic women, and to sound like individuals at that. And if they sound like individuals, it becomes much easier to see them as moral agents, as subjects, as thinking beings, much harder for the contemporary audience simply to dismiss, and much more rewarding for later audiences and readers. What would tragedy be if its women were as silent as the (unnamed, dumb) girl in Menander's *Dyskolos*? In one sense the action revolves around her; but only in the sense that the action of a Hitchcock film revolves around the MacGuffin, the indeterminate object that serves only to advance the plot or motivate the main characters; this might be tolerable in a comedy, but would make for very impoverished tragedy. The silent Iole in Sophocles' *Women of Trachis* is the exception that proves the rule: it is, after all, Deianira's reaction to her that dictates the movement of the tragedy as much as Heracles'. But in any case, because her silence is characterized and conjectured about by others, just as Cassandra's is, it ceases to be dumb and takes on a communicative value, even if it is open to multiple interpretation. As Wohl puts it (1998, 56): "in the silent *parthenos* lies tragedy's preservation of a fantasied space . . . of a female other beyond the control of the male self."

As it is, the interrelation of male and female speech in tragedy, in all its diversity and poetic elaboration, so problematizes the male/female self/other polarity that women become, as Croally has said (1994, 97), "the other inside." In this problematization lies the greatness of the Athenian dramatists' achievement.

NOTES

1   Zeitlin 1990a coined the powerful phrase "playing the other" to describe women's role in Greek tragedy. Subsequent work has built on her important study and sought to describe the function of this "other" further, but most have broadly concluded that, as Foley succinctly puts it (2001, 12–13), "Greek tragedies . . . provide poetic justification for the subordination of women, foreigners, and slaves. The voices and freedom to act with which drama endows women may in fact . . . largely serve this same end despite appearances to the contrary." Female characters, in the end, are the tools of the male poets in reasserting masculine identity and supremacy. The overall thrust of this consensus must be right, since the alternative is to suppose that the Athenian dramatists were campaigners for women's rights (or indeed the abolition of slavery), which is obviously wrong. But the central premise of much of this work is highly, and perhaps anachronistically, political: it strongly implies that tragedy is all about the city and women's place in it. Important though tragedy may have been for the Athenian polis, and vice versa, tragedy is not only about Athenian political thought (or we would have stopped reading it long ago). Perhaps there should be more emphasis on the emotional response of audiences to these highly elaborate portrayals of women. After all, one can see the tendency to represent female perspectives in ways which differentiate, but do not devalue them, as early as the *Iliad* and *Odyssey*.

2   Wohl 1998, xxix–xxx, is well aware of the importance of language to subjectivity: she quotes Lévi-Strauss: "[the woman] could never become just a sign and nothing more, since even in a man's world she is still a person, and since in so far as she is defined as a sign she must be recognised as a generator of signs" (1969, 496), but herself thinks, "On the one hand, the woman is not as obvious or secure a subject as the man; on the other, she is not a complete object," and argues that the female characters "try to define a subjectivity for themselves, in the process exposing the components and modalities of the tragic

subject." The attempt to define this subjectivity, like the fact of subjectivity itself, must be determined and shaped by language.

3   The text of 1052 is extremely problematic: *esô phrenôn legousa peithô nin logôi*, lit. "speaking inside the/her mind I persuade her with my words." Is Clytemnestra proposing to use telepathy or can the phrase represent the Homeric phrase *tou (tôi) thumon eni stêthessin epeithen*, "s(he) persuaded him in his mind"? In any case, Clytemnestra sets up a clash between Cassandra's supposed voice and her own, even though Cassandra is not saying anything in any language, and surely what we expect to be at stake is her understanding, not her utterance. The lines seem then to suggest that Clytemnestra will manage almost miraculously to persuade her as long as she utters (utters, *not* understands) Greek, as long as she can get her to participate in a verbal struggle such as she has just had with Agamemnon; but in this she fails.

"Colemanball" is a term coined by the British satirical magazine *Private Eye* in honor of a particularly accident-prone sports commentator, David Coleman. The most famous example of the genre was part of a TV snooker commentary by Ted Lowe: "Griffiths is snookered on the brown, which, for those of you watching in black and white, is the ball just behind the pink." Actually closer to Clytemnestra's remark is one of Coleman's own: "and for those of you watching who haven't television sets, live commentary is on Radio 2." Attempts such as that of Denniston and Page 1957 to mitigate this (deliberate, important) absurdity are not a success.

4   See *Agamemnon* 351 and Goldhill 1984, 39, for one definition of what component of her speech is masculine – "the power of conceptualisation in language." See also McClure 1999, 74, who takes both rationality and persuasiveness as masculine (though persuasion is very often associated with female speakers and I doubt whether it can really be gendered). Sociolinguistic studies often show modern women consciously adopting male language strategies in public: see, e.g., Tannen 1994, 195–221, which interestingly links this and other phenomena to do with conversation at work to Goffman's argument that the relationship between language and gender is a matter of display rather than identity (1979).

5   The scholiast thought Helen addressing Menelaus by name and not as "husband" indicated boldness. However that may be, Helen's naming of her husband certainly contrasts with Menelaus, who doesn't like saying Helen's name at 869–70, and relates to Helen's elaborate use of both Paris' names at 941–42 (perhaps with some resonance with the earlier part of the trilogy, but perhaps also distancing herself from him). Hecuba uses names in a sophisticated manner in the *agôn* scene: she plays a variation on a regular pun on Helen's name at 891 (see also *Agamemnon* 689–90) and on Aphrodite's at 989–90, thus creating a verbal link between them just as she is arguing that the Cypris who accompanied Paris was Helen's own mind. Compare the way that Sophocles' Ajax continues the persistent concentration on words and speaking shown in his lament with Tecmessa and the chorus (see 354, 362, 368, 386, 392–93, 410–11, 423–24, 428–29) into his speech at 430–80 by means of his pun on his name at 430–33.

FURTHER READING

The bibliography on the portrayal of women in Greek tragedy is vast and ever increasing, especially when contributions on individual plays are taken into account. Classic treatments of the subject in general include Foley 1981, des Bouvrie 1990, Zeitlin 1990a, and Seidensticker 1995. For a very useful survey of recent views and approaches see Foley 2001, 6–18. There is much less written specifically on the portrayal of their language, but see McClure

1995 and 1999, Griffith 2001, and Mossman 2001. On the speech of real Athenian women see most recently Sommerstein 1995, who mostly uses evidence from comedy. He identifies a number of differences from male speech and concludes: "Certain of these differences clearly reflect the subordinate status of women in society" (84). On silence in Athenian culture in general see Montiglio 2000. On female costumes and masks, supposedly invented by Phrynichus, an older contemporary of Aeschylus, see Pickard-Cambridge 1988, 190 and n. 4. On acting styles and the limited evidence for differentiation in voice and manner between male and female roles see now Easterling and Hall 2002, especially the essays by Edith Hall (2002; 3–38), Eric Csapo (2002; 127–47), and Ismene Lada-Richards (2002; 395–418).

CHAPTER TWENTY-THREE

Marginal Figures

Mary Ebbott

The term "marginal" assumes a center against which the margins are defined. For any group of people, those belonging to the center can be considered "insiders," while those who are excluded are "outsiders." Outsiders are defined by not being insiders, but insiders would not be insiders without outsiders to define them as such. The boundary between them may at times be emphasized to reinforce the distinction, but at other times it may be open for crossing in either direction. In this sense the boundary can be imagined as a space, a liminal area that divides but also links inside and outside. The margin, then, can be considered the point or zone of interaction between insiders and outsiders. Tragedy creates an opportunity for such an interaction in its performance generally, and especially in its portrayal of marginal figures.

In fifth-century BCE Athens, the center of the polis was the body of free, legitimate, adult, Athenian male citizens, and these same men were the intended audience for tragedy. In fact, these qualifications are somewhat redundant, since by definition one could not be a citizen of Athens without being Athenian by birth (with very few exceptions), free, adult, legitimate, and male. Conceptual oppositions existed between categories such as Athenian and foreign, adult and non-adult, male and female, free and slave, legitimate and illegitimate, citizen and non-citizen, and created a notional margin that separated and defined insiders and outsiders. Greek tragedy includes many types of marginal figures, characters who are outsiders from the perspective of the Athenian center: foreigners, slaves, women, and others excluded from citizenship in Athens, such as pre-adult boys and bastards. These categories differ from one another in significant ways, but they can all be marginalized when opposed to the center.

The act of defining through opposition works in both directions: Athenian citizens are also defined by what they are not. Such a phenomenon is found in many cultures: "It is a commonplace both of sociological theory and of everyday experience that a human group often perceives and defines itself partly in terms of that which it is not – the Other" (Browning 2002, 257). But the boundary that defines both insider and outsider allows for an interaction that calls these distinctions into question. Tragedy is indeed often described in terms of this interaction: it is said to involve an exploration of the Self *through* the Other.

Through this exploration, tragedy as a genre also stages the interaction occurring on the margin. Seeing the Self through the portrayal of the Other necessarily involves crossing what seems in other times and places to be a clear-cut boundary between the two. As Charles Segal has said, "Both tragic hero and tragic performance partake of the freedom of marginality" (1981, 48). The "freedom of marginality" refers to the power of tragedy to explore and question these definitions of the center while remaining a civic institution, oscillating between oppositions, at the boundary we may call marginal or liminal.

Tragedy is neither wholly civic nor wholly subversive in its nature; it is simultaneously inside and outside, or, rather, somewhere in between. Michelle Gellrich has noted that tragedy is as powerful as it is because it does not lie on either side of these oppositions, but rather occupies the margin, the place in between: "the vitality of tragedy as I am describing it would have to be linked with a place neither totally within nor totally without the *polis*; it would be neither simply ideological or purely nonideological, but a performance opening up some space in between" (1995, 48; see also Segal 1981, 47–51; and Croally 1994, 11, 43–45). The dynamic of tragedy is to be neither/nor as well as both/and when it comes to common cultural oppositions and definitions: tragedy may resist the categories it appropriates and explores, but it does not obliterate them entirely. Arguing for the nonpolitical or even antipolitical nature of tragedy, Nicole Loraux identifies the significant role of oxymoron in tragedy: "tragedy, using oxymoron to play on the contradictions presented by civic discourse, defines its specificity by combining elements usually contrasted in political discourse" (2002, 66–67). The contrast is still present, however, as it must be if the combination is to have any effect.

Marginal figures in tragedy operate within this context of opposition and combination taking place on the margin. Other genres may maintain the strict oppositions that I have enumerated between insiders and outsiders, but in tragedy these outsiders break down difference even as they create, mark, and signify it. The boundaries they define they also cross, and these seemingly contradictory actions co-exist, as we will see in the tragedies examined below. The Self is explored through the Other, but is not subsumed by the Other. Instead, a dynamic interaction occurs between the two.

One of the paradoxes of tragedy is that marginal figures can take center stage. A great deal of scholarship has focused on women as the predominant Other in Greek tragedy (see, among others, Zeitlin 1996, Foley 2001, and Griffith and Mossman, chapters 21 and 22 in this volume). In my examination of the significance of marginal figures I will focus on such categories as foreigners, slaves, and bastards, each of which exemplifies in diverse ways the interaction on the margins that plays out in tragedy.

One type of interaction is an overlapping of or equation between outsider categories. Such an overlapping is not surprising even outside of tragedy: foreignness and slavery, for example, could be associated, because many slaves were also foreigners. In tragedy, however, the definitions of marginal categories can be confused and exploited to the point where they are exposed as arbitrary. Similarly, the distinction between categories may be blurred, because the space outside is not further defined or delineated. Once defined as any kind of outsider, a marginal figure can then be associated with all other outsiders as well.

An example of this lack of distinction between marginal categories is found in the character of Teucer in Sophocles' *Ajax*. Teucer is known to us, and would also be known to the ancient audience, from the *Iliad*, in which he figures as an archer and the illegitimate brother of Ajax, son of Telamon (see Ebbott 2003, 37–44, for more on the Homeric Teucer). His illegitimacy arises from his mother's status as a captive, foreign woman awarded as a prize to Telamon, but in the *Iliad* it is no impediment to Teucer's participation in the Greek warrior community. In *Ajax* Teucer's illegitimacy is underscored once he becomes suspect in the eyes of the Greek leader Agamemnon because of the actions of his brother. Agamemnon insultingly calls Teucer the son of a spear-captive woman (*Ajax* 1228), a slave (*doulos*, 1235), and a speaker of barbarian language (1263), and treats him as less than a free man (1260–61). Earlier Teucer had imagined that his father Telamon, blaming Teucer for Ajax's death, would also insult him and turn him out of his home, calling him a bastard (*nothos*, 1013), attacking his manhood (cf. *kakandria*, cowardice, 1014), and making him appear more like a slave (*doulos*, 1020) than a free man. One form of marginality is combined with others, and as Teucer's situation worsens, the marginality of his illegitimacy is amplified to classify him as a foreigner, a slave, and less than a man. In tragedy (unlike epic), Teucer's borderline status slips ever further into the margins and is there linked with other forms of marginality.

That Teucer, who is undeniably a free man, worries about being called a slave should caution us against interpreting these marginal categories too literally. The categories seem too easily combined with one another to be understood as strictly applied; moreover, they do not present us with a picture of social reality. In fact, the category of slave seems to function most often as an exploration of what it means to be free. Both Teucer's imagined encounter with Telamon and his real one with Agamemnon involve the term *doulos*, but there is never any actual threat that Teucer will be enslaved. Instead, the term becomes a means of imagining a reduced state of existence, reinforcing the difference between free and slave even as a free man is equated to a slave.

When we do see ordinary household slave characters in tragedy (a category that excludes newly enslaved captive women, whose situation is a vast topic I must leave aside), they in fact often speak or enact cultural ideals, especially when free characters pose challenges to prevailing norms. When, for example, mothers are portrayed as dangerous to the family, female slaves are presented as maternal, taking on the culturally approved role for free women. In Euripides' *Medea*, Medea's nurse affirms her gender solidarity with Medea, but she also expresses concern for the well-being of the children (89–95, 98–105, 116–18), substituting as a maternal figure while their mother becomes a threat to them. An elaborate example comes from Aeschylus' *Libation Bearers*, when Orestes pretends to be a messenger bringing news of the death of Orestes to his mother, Clytemnestra, and her lover, Aegisthus. Although Orestes' nurse plays an extremely small part in moving the plot along, she is given a long speech about how the news of Orestes' death has affected her and her masters. Clytemnestra, she says, "in front of the servants put on grief with sad eyes, concealing her laughter that matters have turned out well for her" (737–40). In contrast to Clytemnestra's barely hidden joy at the news, the nurse proclaims that she has never yet suffered such pain as the report of the death of Orestes brings to her (747). Her detailed account of her intimate familiarity with the body of Orestes in his infancy through nursing and cleaning him calls to mind a mother's lament for a dead child, and it heightens the contrast again when Clytemnestra, facing death at the hands of her own son, claims the same bodily intimacy by bidding Orestes to have respect for her breast at which he nursed (896–98). These maternal female slaves are foils for the threatening mothers.

Slaves are thus presented on stage as embodying cultural ideals of how slaves should think and act. That is, slaves are portrayed not as distinct persons but simply in their function as slaves and as reflections of the attitudes and ideology of their masters or of the dominant culture. In Euripides' *Andromache*, Hermione's nurse directs Hermione to act in a manner appropriate for a free woman, instructing her to "cover up" (832) and "go inside" before she is disgraced (877). She expresses cultural ideals for high-status wives even though she herself is not one. As we have seen with Orestes' nurse, slaves in tragedy also often express their emotional connection to their masters. Medea's nurse similarly says to her fellow-slave, the tutor: "For good slaves, the misfortunes of our masters fall on us heavily and reach our hearts" (*Medea* 54–55). In Euripides' *Helen*, two different slaves, one belonging to Menelaus, a Greek, and one belonging to the Egyptians Theoclymenus and Theonoe, express sentiments that would be very welcome to the slave owners in the audience. Menelaus' slave reacts to the discovery of the real Helen by saying, "He is a bad slave who does not revere the affairs of his masters, both feeling joy along with them and feeling shared pain in their troubles" (726–27). Theoclymenus' slave takes loyalty even further by proclaiming, "To die on behalf of their masters brings the greatest glory for noble slaves" (1640–41). These slaves express an identification with their masters' situations and emotions and a willingness to put themselves in their masters' place. The slaves do not seem so Other in these cases, as they articulate the same ideals, feel the same feelings, and identify their own well-being with that of their masters.

These ordinary slave characters and the words they speak reinforce social norms, so much so that Nancy Sorkin Rabinowitz, in her study of women and class in Euripidean tragedy, concludes, "The slaves in tragedy do not represent a real class but rather respond to the desires and anxieties of the author and *his* audience" (1998, 66). That is, slave characters do not represent real-life slaves or present a challenge to the ideology or practice of slavery as such. Pierre Vidal-Naquet has pointed out that there is no myth explaining the origins of slavery similar to those that account for the subjugation of women, and he argues that this absence suggests that slavery as an institution is not troubling enough to prompt a justification as such in myth or a deep examination in tragedy (1986a, 218). The marginal slave characters themselves, then, speak with the center, and it is the idea of the change from freedom to slavery that is explored from the perspective of the insiders. Slavery is contemplated as the opposite of freedom, and this contemplation uses other types of marginal characters, as we saw with the illegitimate Teucer, to imagine slipping into slavery. The interaction on the margin denies the slave characters a separate identity while maintaining the category as a fearful alternative for the center, the free men.

The association of Teucer in *Ajax* with foreigners, slaves, and a lack of manhood suggests that once defined against the center, one could acquire any marginal status, or all of them at once. The emphasis on his illegitimacy also reveals the arbitrary nature of marginal status. As we have already seen, Teucer's illegitimacy is emphasized and elaborated in that drama. Ajax's son, Eurysaces, is in the same position, since his mother is also a foreign, captive woman, and yet he is broadly treated as legitimate. It will fall to Teucer, in fact, to present Eurysaces to Telamon as Ajax's legitimate son (*Ajax* 562–70). The disjunction between the situations of Teucer and Eurysaces highlights the permeability of the boundary between legitimate and illegitimate. Similarly, Hippolytus in Euripides' *Hippolytus* is marked as a bastard in part because his mother is not Athenian, while Theseus' children with the non-Athenian Phaedra are considered legitimate.

Tragedy can play with current standards in this way by applying them to the heroic past. Anachronism complicates the status of these so-called bastards (*nothoi*, singular *nothos*), and underscores the arbitrary boundary between legitimate and illegitimate. Both Hippolytus and Ion are portrayed as *nothoi* in Euripides' tragedies, although in other genres they could be considered legitimate and very closely tied to Athens. Hippolytus is the son of Theseus, the foremost hero of Athens, and Ion is the son of the god Apollo and Creusa, the descendant of founding heroes of Athens. Not only could the two young men be central in the heroic world, they are also sons of Athenian rulers, who occupy the very center of the polis. These illegitimate sons are outsiders who could easily be insiders. Their situations challenge the boundary line, asking where the distinctions truly lie and whether they are worthwhile to maintain.

Let us consider the case of Ion in Euripides' *Ion*. The son of Apollo and originating namesake of the Ionian Greeks, Ion would be a hero in a genre such as epic. For the Athenians he is an important link back to their autochthonous origins. As the son of Creusa, Ion is the last of the line of the Athenian autochthon or "earth-born" Erechthonius, who sprang from the earth (the mythical and plot background emerges via stichomythia at *Ion* 260–304). The ideal behind the myth is that the Athenians are strictly native to their city: they did not come from elsewhere to settle it, but were born from the very soil of their land. As the direct descendant of the autochthonous hero and king of Athens and of an Olympian god, Ion should possess the ultimate Athenian identity and legitimacy.

As the play begins, however, he is not only illegitimate but completely without identity. As we hear in the prologue (14–52), Ion was born in the royal house of Athens to Creusa, the daughter of the king, but in secret. He was exposed as a newborn and left to die in a cave on the outskirts of the city, but he was saved by Apollo and Hermes and brought to Apollo's temple in Delphi, where the priestess took him in as a foundling. He now inhabits a sacred space, the temple of Apollo (315), rather than a civic one in Athens. He does not know who either of his parents is (109, 313); his lack of identity is so complete that as the drama begins he has no name: Creusa asks him his name and his reply is, "I am called 'slave of the god,' and I am" (309). Ion is as marginal as possible: a slave lacking parents, a city, and a name.

As the drama progresses, Ion will take on several permutations of identity, all variations on the marginal. Creusa and her husband Xuthus, who is not Athenian himself, have come to Delphi to inquire about a solution to their childlessness (302–5). Ion is first claimed as son by Xuthus, who has been told by the oracle that he fathered a son many years ago as a result of an anonymous one-night stand in Delphi and will encounter that son when he leaves the temple (517–62). This encounter is in fact what gives Ion his name: Xuthus names him Ion – which can mean "coming" or "going" – since he came upon him as he left the temple (660–62). Ion's name has precisely the opposite connotations to the Athenian ideal of autochthony, of having never come from somewhere else. Even his new name marks him as an outsider.

Ion recognizes that this marginal identity as the bastard son of a foreigner, albeit the current king, will cause difficulties for him at Athens. He knows that there is a strict definition of native or insider at Athens, and he has two strikes against him: "They say that famous, autochthonous Athens is not an alien people, so that I will find myself possessing two ailments, having an imported father and being born a bastard" (589–92). Ion imagines that he will encounter difficulties from wealthy and poor Athenians alike, regardless of whether he aspires to a prominent life or is content with an obscure one (592–606). Xuthus' solution is to deny even this marginal status and introduce Ion at first as a guest (*xenos*) and visitor (*theatês*) and not his son. Once again we see an instability of marginal categories as Ion slips from bastard to foreigner.

The hostile Athenian reaction to outsiders that Ion envisions is subsequently realized: told that Ion is Xuthus' bastard son, Creusa tries to kill him. Just as Ion attempts to kill her in return, however, the priestess brings out the tokens that Creusa left with Ion when she exposed him, tokens of his true identity as Creusa's son and as an Athenian. Thus Ion is placed in another marginal situation, as he goes from bastard son of Xuthus to bastard son of Creusa (upon discovering that he is Creusa's son, Ion again laments his illegitimate status: 1473, 1523–27).

Ion does not return to Athens on these terms either, however. Athena commands Creusa not to make known that Ion is her son and to allow Xuthus the pleasure of believing that Ion is his (1601–2). Ion goes to Athens with a private, secret identity of the son of a god and the autochthonous Creusa, but with a public identity as the bastard son of the foreigner Xuthus. Through the events of the drama, the slave Ion has become free, the illegitimate foundling discovers he is a member of the autochthons who represent ultimate legitimacy at Athens, and the youth without a name returns home to achieve manhood. His movement from margin to center challenges the distinction between the two, and the movement is only accomplished with a crossing of the two: the son of the autochthon becomes king as the supposed son of the outsider Xuthus. The ideal of autochthony takes pride in sameness and connected origins, but only through a *nothos* posing additionally as a foreigner are the native, autochthonous origins of the Athenians continued and, in turn, linked to contemporary institutions of the audience (see Ebbott 2003, 80).

Ion passes back and forth through many identities, and in the end he has no one story of who he is. These complications defy the notion of a fixed line between the center and the margins, since Ion seems to oscillate from one identity to another without achieving any final sense of self. His drama, like that of Hippolytus, plays with the definition of outsider in cases of those who are so close to being insiders that the distinction between insider and outsider is questioned. But it is not only the marginal figures who are very close to insiders who cross boundaries in tragedy; such an interaction also happens with more pronounced Others, such as foreigners, or, to use the Greek term, barbarians.

Barbarians in tragedy elude easy stereotyping. We might expect that the Taurians of Euripides' *Iphigenia among the Taurians*, who practice human sacrifice, would be portrayed as savage barbarians who engage in a taboo ritual; in fact, their human sacrifices are specifically linked to the Greek Agamemnon's attempt to sacrifice his daughter Iphigenia (*Iphigenia among the Taurians* 336–39). Moreover, it is their respect for Greek religious ritual that provides the means for Iphigenia, Orestes, and Pylades to escape: the Taurian king Thoas allows Iphigenia to take the statue of Artemis along with two "captives" to the sea to be purified. The irony is thick when the supposed barbarian Thoas, hearing that purification is necessary because the would-be victims are polluted by matricide, exclaims in shock: "By Apollo, not even among the barbarians would anyone dare to do that!" (1176).

Similarly, the Phrygian in Euripides' *Orestes* is strongly marked as the Greek stereotype of the Asian barbarian, but the stereotype is pushed so far as to render it ridiculous. The fact that it is the Phrygian himself who calls his clothing, actions, and attitudes "barbarian" (1369–70, 1374, 1385, 1395–96, 1507) exposes the stereotype for what it is, and all told, the Phrygian "is never anything but a grotesque caricature of Orestes" himself (Saïd 2002a, 83). In these examples and many others, the context in which barbarian characters appear or in which statements about barbarians are made undercuts the stereotype or the opposition of the Greek and barbarian created by these markers of difference, smudging the boundary drawn by the characters or their statements.

Aeschylus' *Persians* offers perhaps the most complex example of foreigners as marginal characters. Complicating interpretation of this play is the fact that *Persians* is the earliest extant Athenian tragedy, first performed in 472 BCE. It is also the only surviving Athenian tragedy that centers on historical events rather than those we consider mythical – and recent historical events at that: the battle of Salamis between the Athenians and the Persians in 480 BCE. The characters in the drama are all Persians, including the historical king Xerxes, and the setting is the Persian royal court in Susa. Critics have argued over how to interpret this tragedy, which presents a Greek victory over their deadliest enemies, who had devastated Athens during this, their second invasion of Greece. Should we understand the tragedy as celebrating the Athenian victory over their enemies, showing that Xerxes got what he deserved for his hubristic acts in the course of the invasion? Or should we instead point to the mythical qualities of the historical event within the tragedy and understand the portrayal of the enemy to be sympathetic in some way? (See Loraux 2002, 45, for an example of one critic who has, over time, changed her opinion about the basic tenor of the play.)

Edith Hall sums up her discussion of *Persians* by emphasizing the polarity created in the play: "Aeschylus presents Persian characteristics as vices exactly correlative to the cardinal democratic Athenian virtues. Portrayal of the enemy has thus become self-definition and self-praise" (Hall 1989, 100). The Athenian self-definition and self-praise that Hall argues for, however, must arise from a self-contemplation encouraged by the play, and in this contemplation, connection as well as distinction emerges. Both Nicole Loraux (2002, 50) and Christopher Pelling (1997a, 13–17) have emphasized that the audience's reaction would be mixed and multiple, and *Persians* in particular reveals how opposition and identification can co-exist in tragedy. The resolution to the question of interpretation may lie in seeing the tragic application of barbarian stereotypes familiar to us from other genres, such as history, ethnography, and oratory, as necessarily distorted by a genre that blurs as many distinctions as it sets up. The portrayal of the barbarian in Greek tragedy is complicated and warped in various ways by the generic context. This is not to say that the opposition between Greek and barbarian is not present or is somehow "corrected" in tragedy. But the ideology behind the stereotype does not operate in tragedy as elsewhere. As Michelle Gellrich points out about tragedy's relationship to ideology in general: "The problem with readings of tragedy that seek to demonstrate its ideological character is that they are impervious to the ways in which performance eludes ideological constraints. In other words, such readings overestimate the role of social substructure in producing the meaning of texts" (1995, 50). As we will see, it is indeed in the performative context that *Persians* transcends the strict opposition of Greek and barbarian.

Let us consider in greater detail how the Persians are portrayed and also how the story of their defeat by the Athenians could be constructed as a tragedy before an Athenian audience. In so doing, we can see how differences are created but also collapsed by the genre and performance of tragedy. The defeat of the Persians is narrated on stage from the Persian point of view. As the play opens, the chorus, whose character is Persian elders, and the queen await news about the war. Through a series of arrivals – a herald, an apparition of the dead former king Darius, and Xerxes himself – the defeat of the Persians by the Athenians is first reported, then explained, and finally lamented.

The Persians are contrasted with the Athenians explicitly and symbolically through-out the drama. The Persians' wealth, especially in gold, and their love of luxury; their excessive emotions, especially fear, panic, and despair; and their distinct language, dress, weapons, and political structure have all been pointed out as differences that Aeschylus establishes and exploits within the tragedy (Hall 1989, 79–100). The cumulative effect of these differences is to cast the Persians in some way as the opposite of the Athenians themselves. If, however, tragedy is an exploration of the Self through the Other, how do these theatrical Persians allow the Athenians to think about themselves beyond the opposition?

One aspect of the drama to notice is that the tragedy of the Persians is conceived in Greek terms. Greek ritual and speech forms are integrated into the Persian milieu (see Ebbott 2000 for an example), and the Persians give voice to a very Greek understand-ing of the events. As Pelling points out with reference to the portrayal of Darius in the play, "even a Persian character can articulate responses and insights which the Greek audience can share, he can serve as their 'focus,' and those responses and insights can be seen as transcending national boundaries" (1997a, 15–16). Much of the drama would be familiar as well as foreign, a blending of the two that would call attention to the supposed differences and might also introduce elements of commonality.

It is particularly performance, the presentation of Persian characters on stage, that produces the breakdown of difference. Tragedy as a genre calls for a different state of mind and set of reactions from the other contexts in which we find portrayals of Persians and other foreigners. Nicole Loraux, in her recent argument against an overly political interpretation of tragedy as a whole (she concedes that the chorus of male advisors to the king in *Persians* sets it up as a more political play than most [2002, 46]), maintains that we should not expect the same response to Xerxes and the Persians in the theater as we would in a political context:

> We miss any sense of tragedy's specificity if we think that the Athenians heard in *The Persians* only a eulogy for their city. If, however, as I believe, every tragedy deals with the

staging of mourning, then we can imagine that the citizens of Athens, invited in their capacity as hearers of a tragedy to take part in a production of a drama that resembled a long lamentation, were able to respond to the latter in the appropriate manner. In other words, they were able to resist the immediate pleasure of being the cause of the suffering represented on the stage, because, in the cries of the defeated enemy, tragedy taught them to recognize something that touched them above and beyond their identity as Athenians. (Loraux 2002, 48)

I will return to the idea of tragedy as "the staging of mourning," but the point I wish to stress here is that tragedy is meant to engage certain emotions and to move beyond rigid oppositions and definitions of identity. The very fact that *Persians* is a tragedy changes the interpretative framework for the Persians who are lamented on stage, and we can see an opportunity for moving beyond difference.

The audience witnesses only Persian characters on stage, as I have noted, but the physical staging itself also blurs boundaries, especially between actor and character. The actor wears the mask, and in the case of *Persians* may wear a markedly foreign costume, but the Greek identity of the actor would not entirely vanish. Claude Calame (1995, 97–115) has shown that, linguistically and physically, the tragic performance and its use of masks blend the two identities rather than substituting one for the other. In a narrative, the narrator is linguistically first-person "I" while the subject of the narrative is third-person "s/he." In drama, Calame explains, the actor is the narrator, but the subject is represented by the mask that he wears, blending the two identities in a process he describes as shiftings-in and shiftings-out (1995, 99). The early masks in tragedy, Calame points out, were made of cloth, and so the wearer of the mask is veiled, but still visible. The mask itself is used "for cults that define and guarantee the various limits of the concept of civilization, cults of the periphery, of the passage from interior to exterior, from the self to different – and vice versa!" (1995, 106). Thus the mask itself is involved in marginality and acts as the margin as the Self plays the Other represented by the mask. For the spectators, the Other on stage is portrayed by a Greek male, and his identity as such is not entirely obscured but is in constant play with the identity of the mask he wears.

As the Greeks play Persians, then, the losses and sufferings of the war recalled in the tragedy are not only those of the Persians, but of the Greeks as well, who although victorious nevertheless suffered greatly during the war. The contemplation of such suffering in the theater requires distance (Loraux 2002, 52). That is, the staging of mourning that Loraux sees as the core of tragedy cannot be too direct, but must be mediated through the suffering of the Other. This distance, an emotional cushion for the spectators, is usually accomplished in tragedy through the use of stories from the distant (mythical) past. In this case, the distance is created by the foreign setting and characters, producing a spatial and conceptual rather than temporal distance (Vernant and Vidal-Naquet 1988, 245; Calame 1995, 113). But the emotions provoked by *Persians* are for the Self as much as the Other: the Athenians' own losses are contemplated through the losses of the Persians, showing a common connection while maintaining the distance and the difference that the barbarian portrayal creates and allows. (See Ferrari 2000 for another example of how the Athenians could contemplate their losses in the Persian wars by means of identification with foreigners – in that case, the Trojans.) Recalling Gellrich's description of tragic performance opening a space in between, we can see in *Persians* that the momentous events of the war are contemplated within that space: neither too close to the center, nor so far as to be entirely foreign. The opposition between the Persians and the Athenians is not lost or replaced but is also not so rigid as to preclude interaction along the margins.

The significance of marginal figures in tragedy is embodied in Dionysus, the very god at whose festival tragedy is performed. Like the foreigners and *nothoi* we have discussed, Dionysus is on the margins of the polis. He is an insider who appears to be an outsider, a god who, we know from archaeological evidence, has a long history of worship by the Greeks but is portrayed as recently introduced (Nagy 1990, 297). He is a native god whose myth presents him as foreign: "As the myth of Dionysus evolves through the ages, it keeps attracting features that characterize what is perceived as foreign to each passing age of Hellenism; what remains as a constant is simply the foreignness of the figure, and it is this foreignness that is paradoxically native to him. Moreover, it is an old theme that he is always new: the structure keeps asserting that it is very new, when it is in reality very old" (Nagy 1990, 297). At any particular point in time, whatever feature is considered foreign, new, and exterior to Greek culture is associated with the myth of Dionysus.

In Euripides' *Bacchae* this aspect of his myth is played out when Dionysus comes to Thebes, the native city of his mother Semele, to claim his place there and be recognized as a god. Arriving, as he says in the prologue, from Asia, Dionysus appears as a foreigner, sharing some characteristics with the then-current Asian stereotype: he has long hair, pale skin, an air of sensual luxuriousness, and a gender-bending appearance (455–58, 493–94). That is, the contemporary construct of "foreignness" is applied to this Dionysus. In Pentheus' view he is a dangerous outsider who disturbs the order in Thebes by introducing the worship of the supposedly new god. In reality Dionysus is very much an insider in Thebes: his mother Semele is the daughter of Cadmus, the city's founder, and sister of Pentheus' own mother Agave. He is neither foreign nor an outsider, and for the spectators in the Theater of Dionysus, he is no new god. The discovery of his true identity entails the destruction of those who at first denied it: the ultimate understanding of "the paradox that whatever is alien is also native" (Nagy 1990, 295) comes at a terrible price for the characters in the tragedy, but can be experienced by the audience with the safety of the distance provided by performance.

Tragedy may portray itself as foreign (Loraux 2002, 61) even as it is distinctively Athenian. Dionysus, the god of tragedy, eludes categorization using binary oppositions, but as Michelle Gellrich persuasively argues, it is not that Dionysus simply breaks down categories and oppositions but that he precedes or exists apart from them: "Dionysus appears to signify not a discrete being with a definable identity but a condition prior to or other than 'identity.' He does not so much destroy or confuse distinctions as configure the nondifferentiation out of which such distinctions eventually arise – notably, the foundational ones of female/male and nature/culture" (1995, 53). In the Theater of Dionysus tragic performance has the capacity to break down differences and oppositions or even move entirely beyond them, as it takes place on the boundary between these distinctions. Tragedy has the power to defy the difference between the center and the marginal or to reinforce it, and in fact, it does both. The marginal figures in tragedy, outsider roles performed by and for insiders, can also be paradoxically central in this dynamic theatrical experience.

FURTHER READING

For more on the idea of exploring the Self through the Other in tragedy, see Zeitlin 1996 and
    Loraux 2002. For a detailed study of the construction of the Other in historical genres and
    the spatial concept of frontiers in thinking about the Self and Other, see Hartog 1988. For
    more on slaves in tragedy, see the introduction in Joshel and Murnaghan 1998, setting out
    their interpretative framework for the intersection of representations of slaves and women.
    For tragedy's social criticism of slavery, see Gregory 2002. For more on bastards in Greek
    tragedy, see Ebbott 2003, which treats metaphors of illegitimacy in classical Greek literature
    with attention to tragedies like Euripides' *Hippolytus* and *Ion* and Sophocles' *Ajax*. For a
    historical account of Greek bastardy, including some discussion of the bastards in tragedy and
    other genres, see Ogden 1996. For more on the portrayal of barbarians in tragedy, Hall 1989
    is the starting point for recent interpretation. Her groundbreaking study has been and
    remains influential, although later work, such as Vidal-Naquet 1997 and some of the essays
    in Harrison 2002, aims to temper her findings. For the view that the representation of
    barbarians in tragedy changes over the fifth century, see Saïd 2002a, who argues that
    Aeschylus' portrayal is stereotypical and Euripides' nuanced; but see Nippel 2002 for the
    view that Aeschylus' portrayal is sympathetic to a degree, while Euripides' is the more
    stereotypical. For intersections between the barbarian Other and the female Other, see
    Segal 1990. For recent work on the marginality of tragic choruses, see Foley 2003. For
    connections between Dionysus and the performance of tragedy, see Segal 1982, Henrichs
    1984, and Vernant and Vidal-Naquet 1988 (especially "The God of Tragic Fiction,"
    181–88).

PART IV

Reception

CHAPTER TWENTY-FOUR

Text and Transmission

David Kovacs

Thirty-two tragedies and one satyr-play have come down to us under the names of Aeschylus, Sophocles, and Euripides. These thirty-three plays (seven tragedies each of Aeschylus and Sophocles, eighteen tragedies and one satyr-play of Euripides) are all we have left of roughly three hundred plays by these playwrights. Their lesser-known rivals also wrote plays, and the total number of plays produced by tragic poets over the whole of the fifth century was around twelve hundred. How is it that we have the thirty-three plays we have, and how reliable is their text? In between the author's autograph copy in the fifth century BCE and the earliest complete copies *we* possess, made in the tenth to fourteenth centuries CE, what happened to the texts? To what corruptions were they exposed, and can these be detected and if possible corrected? These questions are the subject of this chapter.

Tragedy Scripts in the Fifth Century

The history of the text of a play by Aeschylus, Sophocles, or Euripides begins when it was first written down by the dramatist. These texts were scripts for performance, and they were not intended in the first instance for any other readership than the actors and chorus who were to realize the play under the guidance of the poet himself. In the latter half of the fifth century Sophocles and Euripides may have envisaged secondarily a reading public, particularly toward the end of the century. But Aeschylus did not (see Steidle 1968, 11).

Up until the end of the fifth century, Athenians and other Greeks made their acquaintance with literature principally by hearing and seeing it performed rather than through reading. Copies of Homer could be acquired, but most people would know the *Iliad* and *Odyssey* by hearing them recited at the Panathenaea. They encountered the work of comic and tragic poets at the festivals of Dionysus, the Lenaea in late winter and the City Dionysia in early spring, and would know the lyric poets from hearing their works sung at drinking parties or at celebrations of athletic victories. Not only were books expensive, but reading was a laborious process. Literary texts were written on papyrus rolls, which were cumbersome to use, and the text was written without spaces between words or punctuation. We have no evidence for books being widely disseminated until the last decade of the fifth century. Our earliest evidence for a member of the public *reading* a tragedy comes from Aristophanes' *Frogs* (52–54; see also 1005–18), which was produced in 405. There is evidence of a different kind, however, for the writing down of parts of a tragic text – a choral ode, say, or a *rhêsis* (speech) – possibly as an aid to memory. At *Frogs* 151, one figure in a comic list of sinners being punished in Hades is "anyone who has had a copy made of a *rhêsis* by Morsimus," which implies that having copies made of bits of tragedy, presumably for later recitation, was a recognized activity. We hear of such a recitation at *Clouds* 1369–72 and Ephippus fr. 16.3 *PCG*. Though reading plays was not a common activity and papyrus rolls containing an entire tragedy did not enjoy wide circulation, it would seem that it was not difficult to get access to a copy of a play one admired.

Our earliest papyrus fragments of dramatic texts give us an idea of what these autograph copies must have looked like (see Turner 1987, 60–61 and 74–77). Since they were scripts meant to be realized under the poet's own direction, the poet did not feel the need to provide anything more than the words that were to be spoken. There were no stage directions since these would be supplied orally in rehearsal. There were probably not even speaker indications, merely a horizontal line, called a *paragraphos*, under the first word of a speech and extending into the left margin, to show that there was a change of speaker, with a colon-like mark, if needed, to mark change of speaker mid-line. There was a tendency already in Aeschylus for significant stage action to be alluded to in the words spoken, so that if a significant prop or gesture is used, the characters refer to it. As a result, the absence of stage directions does not seem to be as much of a hindrance as it would be for someone trying to produce a modern play from a copy that gave only the characters' words. The medieval manuscripts all have speaker indications, and these, although not derived from the author's autograph, are correct in the vast majority of cases, being based on inference from the text or on the tradition of performance.

It is often assumed that each fifth-century tragedy was written in principle only for a single performance. That is not the case, and there were many other venues, both in Attica and in the larger Greek world, where plays were performed and a particular play could receive a repeat performance (see Csapo and Slater 1995, 121–38). There was, however, a restriction against putting on work at the City Dionysia that had already been produced there.

The single exception to this in the fifth century was a law, passed shortly after Aeschylus' death, that provided for the revival of his plays. A poet, wishing to produce his own play, had to ask the official in charge of the festival to "grant him a chorus," that is, give him permission to compete and the requisite state funding. But by the terms of this law anyone who wanted to produce Aeschylus was automatically "granted a chorus." We are told by Quintilian in the Roman period that "revised plays of his" (*correctas eius fabulas*) were entered in the competition and that many received the first prize (*Institutio Oratoria* 10.1.66). It is alarming to hear that later producers so cavalierly set about to "revise" Aeschylus, adjusting him to the taste of their own day. We do not know the source of Quintilian's information or whether it is accurate, but it is worth noting that Aeschylus' *Seven against Thebes* was at some point given a new and updated ending, designed to allude to the edict forbidding the burial of Polynices and Antigone's disobedience of that edict as dramatized in Sophocles' *Antigone*. It is at least possible that this ending is the result of a fifth-century revival.

The Athenians were inveterate record keepers, and the archon who "granted a chorus" to the tragic poets to compete in the City Dionysia probably kept a record of the names of the plays each poet entered in the contest, how the poets fared in the awarding of the prizes, and, after 447, who the winner of the actors' competition was. At any rate, this is the information that Aristotle, who was interested in the history of tragic poetry, gathered together in two works, which were then the source for the production information in our medieval manuscripts and elsewhere. (The authors and plays whose production dates are known to us are summarized in Snell 1971, 3–52.) There is also the possibility that the archon kept a copy of the plays themselves. This has been doubted (Griffith 1977, 232; Mastronarde 1994, 40 n. 1). We know that an official copy of the works of Aeschylus, Sophocles, and Euripides was made for a specific purpose in the second half of the fourth century (see below), but there might also have been archival copies of all the competing plays. This would explain how later authors could quote from so many of the lesser figures of the fifth century (e.g., Choerilus, Phrynichus, Aristias) whose plays were not popular in the intervening centuries. But even if these archival copies existed, most of the copies that circulated in the fourth century and later probably derived from other sources: actors might have lent their copies to interested persons or even participated in the mass production of copies by reciting their lines to a whole group of copyists.

The Fate of Fifth-Century Tragedy in the Fourth Century

In the fourth century BCE, from 386 onward, it was provided that in addition to the three new tetralogies offered every year at the City Dionysia there was to be the performance of one "old" tragedy. Our records of these performances are not as full as we could wish, but we can see that in the fourth and third centuries this provision was mostly used to put on plays of Euripides. (See Snell 1971, 13–16, under the years 341, 340, 339, 308, s. III[a]. There is some evidence for revivals of Sophocles but none for revivals of Aeschylus, to say nothing of lesser fifth-century figures.) We know that one of Euripides' *Iphigenia* plays was put on in 341 and his *Orestes* in 340 and again sometime in the third century.

The fourth century was, much more than the fifth, the age of the actor. Aristotle says that "the actors are more important now than the poets," meaning that the contest was now one of delivery rather than of the words themselves (*Rhetoric* 1403b31). This preeminence extended also beyond the festival. Actors were highly paid, enjoyed international fame, and were even employed as emissaries by powerful princes such as Philip II of Macedon. The tragic actors Aristodemus and Neoptolemus, for example, were lavishly entertained by Philip, given huge gifts, and sent to Athens as his messengers.

The scholia (notes written in the margins of our medieval manuscripts) several times express the suspicion that actors have tampered with the original text. Modern scholars, following up these hints, have cast their suspicious gaze on other passages not mentioned in the scholia and have identified numerous places where a later hand can be detected with virtual certainty, where there are clear differences from the rest of the author's work in vocabulary, style, or dramatic usage, or where lines are intrusive and interrupt and weaken the surrounding argument. The actors also occasionally altered the words to give greater scope to their vocal abilities, for instance omitting a negative in order to make a plain statement sarcastically ironic. I cannot here give an exhaustive typology of these interventions but six widely recognized categories may be named. (1) Dramatically arresting lines that are at home in one place in the play are repeated at another where they are less at home; for example, *Medea* 1324 (genuine) is repeated at 468, and *Orestes* 625–26 (genuine) is repeated at 536–37. (2) The same thing often happens between plays; for example, *Phoenician Women* 972 (genuine) is repeated at *Helen* 780. (3) Brief passages, such as *Medea* 1233–35 or *Hippolytus* 871–73, are inserted to heighten pathos. (4) Longer passages are added to bring the play into mythical agreement with another well-known play; for example, *Seven against Thebes* 1005–78, added to allow for the plot of Sophocles' *Antigone* (still decades in the future in 467 when *Seven against Thebes* was first put on), and *Phoenician Women* 1625–1757, added to reflect the events both of *Antigone* and *Oedipus at Colonus* (the latter put on a decade after *Phoenician Women*). (5) Longer passages of general reflection are added by way of allusion to contemporary politics; for example, *Orestes* 907–13, a clearly un-Euripidean passage on demagogues. (6) Longer passages are added to extend the argument or narration; for example, *Andromache* 668–77, *Phoenician Women* 1104–40, and (I have argued) *Andromache* 334–51.

Actors doubtless felt that it was reasonable for them to revise and update the repertoire, and on the evidence of plays such as *Seven against Thebes*, *Phoenician Women*, and *Iphigenia at Aulis* they gave themselves a high degree of latitude. But not everyone thought this interference was proper, and at some point in the fourth century an Athenian politician tried to put a stop to it. Pseudo-Plutarch tells us (*Lives of the Ten Orators* 841) that Lycurgus, the statesman who was in charge of reforming the Athenian financial system from 338 to 326, not only rebuilt in stone the wooden Theater of Dionysus on the south slope of the Acropolis and erected bronze statues of the three great fifth-century tragic poets, but also arranged for the creation of an official state copy of their plays, establishing by law that actors should henceforth not deviate from this text in their performances. Lycurgus' one surviving oration contains a 55-line quotation from Euripides' *Erechtheus*, probably to be delivered from memory. Clearly Lycurgus loved his city's poetic patrimony and was trying to preserve it. Clearly also he thought that this patrimony was being threatened by the interference of actors,[1] and he must have thought that his law would safeguard it by creating official texts.

Where did Lycurgus get these official texts? The possibility was mentioned above that the archon in charge of the festival could have kept official copies of the year's tragic offerings (see Reynolds and Wilson 1991, 5). This has been doubted on the basis of the wording of Pseudo-Plutarch (*Lives of the Ten Orators* 841), which seems to imply that Lycurgus' innovation consisted in putting copies of these plays in the public archive. This would mean that no one had done so before (thus Battezzato 2003, 10). In reality, the translation of Pseudo-Plutarch's *tas tragóidias autón en koinói grapsamenous phulattein* as "that their tragedies be written out and kept in a public depository" is probably wrong,[2] and it probably means "that a combined copy of their plays be made and preserved." We therefore need not conclude that no official copies were kept before that date.

But even if we take this more optimistic view of the sources of Lycurgus' copy, corrupt and interpolated copies of plays would have circulated from the fourth century onward, with considerable capacity to influence the text in later centuries. And well-intentioned though Lycurgus' measure was, it is obvious that it would have been only temporarily effective, if at all, against actors' interpolations.

Scholars and the Text of Tragedy

Aristotle and his associates at the Lyceum were engaged in investigating all branches of human knowledge, and they were the first to make the literary creations of the past an object of scientific study. Aristotle's *Poetics* not only treats such "philosophical" questions as the way *mimêsis* (imitation, artistic representation) contributes to knowledge and what kind of plots are necessary for a successful epic, tragedy, or comedy but also attempts (in part, speculatively) to trace the history of tragedy and comedy. He or his pupils also collected the information on dramatic productions – who produced what plays in which year. We have no evidence that they were specifically concerned with restoring and handing on the original text or producing commentaries. That was left to the scholars of Alexandria, men whom the Ptolemies, the Macedonian rulers of Egypt, brought to their new cultural center in the Nile delta for the purpose of collecting and preserving the best of Greek literary culture.

The institution that housed and fed these scholars and gave them the leisure to pursue their researches was the Museum, organized as a religious association in honor of the Muses and financed heavily by the Ptolemies. These men, whose squabbles among themselves are described in a contemporary satirical squib (see Fraser 1972, 1: 317), collected works of literature wherever they could find them and treated the whole literary patrimony of Greece as an object of intense study. One of the most famous of their number, Callimachus, produced in 120 books (papyrus rolls) a work called *Pinakes* or *Tables of persons eminent in every branch of learning and of their works*. This included a brief biography of each writer as well as a list of his works and an indication of their length. Questions of the authenticity and genre of particular works probably had a place here. This listing, which probably also included the titles of works that did not survive to Alexandria, is to be distinguished from the catalogue of the Alexandrian Library.

Just how these scholars proceeded is clear in a few details. We are told that any ship putting into Alexandria with books in its cargo was required to surrender these for copying. The scholars of the Museum must also have traveled or sent agents to those parts of Greece and the wider Greek-speaking world where they thought copies of literary texts were to be found, especially the two main book markets of Athens and Rhodes. We know that when a book was added to the library, a careful note was made of its geographical provenance, its previous owner, or the name of the person who had corrected its text if these were known. Multiple copies of the same work were thereby distinguished. One index of the success of their collecting efforts is that later authors such as Athenaeus are able to quote from a considerable number of both tragedies and comedies from the fifth and fourth centuries.

A story told by the physician Galen (translated in Csapo and Slater 1995, 11) in the second century CE gives some idea of the lengths to which the Ptolemies' support of scholarship was prepared to go. We are told that Ptolemy III Euergetes paid a deposit of fifteen talents (90,000 drachmas) to take away the collected works of Aeschylus, Sophocles, and Euripides (presumably the official, Lycurgan copy), on the understanding that he was going to have a copy made and return the original. Then he made a lavish copy of it on the best-quality papyrus and sent *this* back to Athens, retaining the original and inviting the Athenians to keep the fifteen-talent deposit. It should be noted that there appears to be something else at stake for Ptolemy than getting the purest text, for a carefully made copy of the manuscript would have served just as well for that purpose. Rather, the Lycurgan exemplar itself was retained probably because it was a material link with the poets' own city and thereby conferred cultural prestige on the newly founded city of Alexandria, much the way that today the library of a university trying to rise in the world might buy a large archive of original letters and manuscripts.

In addition to the task of collection there was also that of producing editions of, and commentaries on, the texts collected. An "edition" in this sense, called either an *ekdosis* or a *diorthôsis* (on the distinction see Fraser 1972, 2: 647 n. 3), was a single copy of a work whose text had been examined and corrected by a scholar such as Aristarchus, and also usually equipped with a special set of critical signs to indicate that the editor considered a particular line spurious or had some other comment to make about it. Under the ancient conditions of book distribution this single copy would have been made available, perhaps in the Library, for further copying and in this way could reach a wider audience. If the editor of a text wrote a commentary, it was contained in a separate papyrus roll. It is necessary to discuss the evidence for Alexandrian editions and commentaries on the tragic poets separately.

Our knowledge of what Alexandrian scholarship did for tragedy comes to us largely in the scholia to the three tragic poets. Since, however, this material is limited in scope, a more comprehensive view of those activities must necessarily rely on analogies with these same scholars' treatment of Homer, where the evidence is more plentiful. In the earliest period, under Ptolemy Philadelphus (286–47), we are told that Alexander of Aetolia and Lycophron of Chalcis produced critical editions of (*diôrthôsan*) the dramatic poets, with the former editing the tragedies and satyr-plays and the latter the comedies, and that Zenodotus did the same for epic and lyric. Of Alexander's and Lycophron's editions not a single reading or comment has come down to us, and it is not clear that their editorial ministrations were very extensive or that they wrote commentaries. Zenodotus, it seems, did not write a commentary on Homer, and later scholars, when considering a Zenodotean variant reading or athetesis (a deletion of lines as spurious), seemingly could only guess at his reasoning. He did, however, mark individual lines with critical signs, a practice that was further developed by Aristophanes of Byzantium and Aristarchus of Samos.

Aristophanes of Byzantium and Aristarchus of Samos were the most important names in the next generation, the great age of Alexandrian scholarship. The former devoted his attentions to tragedy, and various material from his hand has come down to us in the scholia to Euripides, sometimes at one or two removes. Aristophanes is the source for the more scholarly kind of hypothesis copied as a preface to some of our tragedies in the medieval manuscripts. These hypotheses give the very briefest summary of the plot, usually a single sentence; they indicate whether the story was treated by other dramatists, and give the geographical location of the action, the identity of the chorus, the speaker of the prologue, and the date of the production together with the names of the poet's other plays of that year, the names of his competitors, and whether the play received a first, second, or third prize. Whether this was intended to be prefixed to the plays in his edition or to stand in the commentary volume is unclear.

When considering the nature of the Alexandrian editions of the tragic poets we must again argue largely by analogy from the case of Homer. Scholarly Homeric texts probably included all the lines transmitted by the tradition, even where the editor thought that some of them were spurious. Any doubts were expressed by marginal signs and argued for in the commentary, if there was one. Variant readings, too, must have had a place only in the commentary. If tragic editions followed the same pattern, we should expect that the text would include everything or almost everything transmitted. The signs indicating athetesis might not make their way into all or even most copies of the text, and the commentary arguing for it would likewise tend not to be transmitted. Only the variant readings approved by the editor would make it into the descendants of these copies, and if unapproved variant readings appeared later in the tradition, as we have reason to believe they did, they might well have come from another source than the learned tradition of Alexandria; that is, from an ordinary manuscript of which there must have been an abundance in the Greek-speaking world. A famous Homeric example is the proem of the *Iliad*. At 1.4–5 all our manuscripts read *helôria teuche kunessin / oiônoisi te pasi*, "made them a prey for dogs and for *all* birds," but allusions in Aeschylus, Sophocles, and Euripides make it plain that the fifth century knew a reading *daita* for *pasi*, "a prey for dogs and a *feast* for birds." This reading was rejected by Aristarchus on the (inadequate) grounds that *dais* is used in Homer only of human meals, not those of animals. Aristarchus' edition thus apparently caused this reading to virtually disappear, and it survives only in a quotation in Athenaeus. (It may well be what Homer wrote or recited: see Pfeiffer 1968, 111–13, and Latacz 2000 ad loc.) It is reasonable to suppose that in tragedy as in Homer the Alexandrian edition must at times have driven genuine readings from the field, though at other times a variant may have survived by another route.

One other feature of Aristophanes' text must be described, its colometry (the layout of lyric verse on the page). To judge from our earliest papyri, in fifth-century books lyric verse was written out as if it were prose. (Contrast iambic trimeter or dactylic hexameter, where every line has the same metrical pattern and it is written one verse to a line.) We have evidence that Aristophanes devoted attention in his editions of Pindar and other lyric poets to dividing their verse into its constituent metrical cola, and it is reasonable to suppose that he did the same with tragic lyric. It is often confidently stated that from the (varied) colometry of our medieval manuscripts it is possible in principle to reconstruct the colometry employed by Aristophanes, and that this should be treated with respect even where it is at variance with modern theories. But it is by no means certain that Aristophanes' tragic colometry, if he produced such, was the only attempt made in antiquity to divide by metrical cola. First, at least one papyrus, the Lille Stesichorus, shows division into cola and appears to antedate the career of Aristophanes (see Turner 1987, 124–25). Second, while the medieval manuscripts show a fair degree of unanimity in easier meters such as anapests and dochmiacs, with their differences being chiefly that some manuscripts divide a single word between two cola and others avoid this, in more difficult meters the variations are so great (see, for example, *Hecuba* 444–54 and 455–65 in the apparatus colometricus of Daitz 1973, 92–93) that the hypothesis that they go back to different colometries altogether cannot be dismissed.

Aristophanes also wrote commentaries on at least some of the plays he edited.[3] Comments of his are transmitted in the scholia to Euripides, and we know that he discussed variant readings and indicated his preferences at *Orestes* 713, 1038, and 1287, brought *Trojan Women* 47 into discussions of Homeric athetesis, and alleged (mistakenly) that the *ekkuklêma* was used for Phaedra's entrance at *Hippolytus* 171. This last comment shows interest in questions of staging, as does a discussion of the opening scene in *Orestes* preserved as part (apparently) of the hypothesis ascribed to Aristophanes. So it is not unlikely that, living as he did in an age when the plays were still enjoying widespread revival, he thought about matters of staging in the light of current practice. Perhaps some of the comments on actors' interference and other matters of production may go back to him.[4] Since he produced editions of Homer, Hesiod, and the lyric poets, it is not likely that he had time to write commentaries on more than a small selection of the tragedies, presumably ones in which the public or the scholars of Alexandria were most interested.

As will be apparent from the above, Aristophanes' work comes down to us piece-meal. It is only later scholars, excerpting his work, who preserve his comments for us. The *subscriptiones* or ending-notes to Euripides' *Medea* and *Orestes* mention two scholars who appear to be the immediate source for the scholia on these plays, Dionysius and Didymus. About the former we know next to nothing. Didymus of Alexandria, by contrast, was a prodigiously productive scholar of the second half of the first century BCE. His nickname was Chalkenteros, "with guts of bronze," because of his industry in reading all of Greek literature and writing some 3,500 or 4,000 books (papyrus rolls) of scholarship: he had, as we would say, a cast-iron stomach. In some cases there were further intermediaries, as when at *Orestes* 1038 a textual preference of Aristophanes is reported at second hand from his pupil Callistratus. The comments ascribed to Didymus himself are not notable for their acuteness.

The Alexandrian *ekdosis* of the tragic poets consisted of all the plays the scholars were able to unearth. In addition, Callimachus' *Pinakes* would have listed those works whose titles were known but which did not survive to Alexandria. We are told that the Alexandrians possessed two plays that were labeled "Aeschylus' *Women of Aetna*," and that they called one of them spurious, so the possibility of forged or falsely ascribed works reaching Alexandria cannot be ruled out, a point of some importance, as we will see. For all three poets our sources give inconsistent figures for the number of plays they wrote. Aeschylus is credited in one source with seventy "dramas" (tragedies), and "around five" satyr-plays, and in another source with ninety plays. The latter figure is the more plausible. Aristophanes of Byzantium credited Sophocles with 130 plays, whereas the *Suda* says "he produced 123 plays, or, as others maintain, rather more." Euripides, we are told in one source, produced plays on twenty-two occasions, thus presumably producing eighty-eight plays, with three other tragedies and one satyr-play being of disputed authorship. The figure of ninety-two plays is confirmed in other sources, which disagree, however, on how many plays survived (see Kannicht 1996). There is evidence in the form of an inscribed stone advertising volumes of Euripides that plays were sometimes sold grouped in rough alphabetical order, perhaps five to six plays to a papyrus roll. This may have been the arrangement adopted by one or another of the Alexandrian editors.

The Corpus is Narrowed Down

Until the middle of the third century CE writers are able to quote from a large number of these roughly three hundred plays, as well as from plays by less esteemed tragic poets. But from about 250 onward, quotation seems to be confined to seven plays each of Aeschylus and Sophocles (the seven that have come down to us) and ten of Euripides (those with scholia – *Hecuba, Orestes, Phoenician Women, Hippolytus, Medea, Alcestis, Andromache, Rhesus,* and *Trojan Women* – plus *Bacchae*). It is possible that this represents some kind of deliberate selection, perhaps motivated by pedagogy, though in the absence of any uniform system of education in the Greek world it is hard to see how such a decision could have had wide influence in determining what was available. It could equally well have been a chance result brought about by the popularity of these plays or (what may come to the same thing) the availability of commentaries. At about the same time occurred the change from the papyrus roll to the papyrus codex (the ancestor of our modern book, a sheaf of pages bound along one edge) and it has been suggested that the formation of collections of seven or ten plays to bind together in a book might have encouraged the process of selection. Whatever the cause, henceforth only these plays were widely copied, and it was these that reached Byzantium. There, as part of the revival of learning in the ninth century, the tragic patrimony was recopied, still in codices but this time in the newer minuscule hand. It is to be noted that among these plays are two, *Prometheus Bound* and *Rhesus*, that are now widely believed to be by persons other than their nominal authors.

The Byzantine scholars distilled the commentary on these plays until it would fit into the margins: the text itself was copied in a larger hand, and the commentary was written in tiny letters around it. These *scholia vetera*, as they are called, remnants of ancient scholarship, are to be distinguished from the *scholia recentiora*, comments intended to smooth the way for readers of medieval date, for whom the language of tragedy was becoming increasingly difficult. For a time all twenty-four of these plays were copied and commented on, but at some point in the thirteenth century a further selection was made, again possibly on pedagogical grounds. For each of the poets three plays were chosen, the "Byzantine triad," and henceforth the majority of tragic texts copied were of these nine plays. There are far more copies of these available to the modern editor than of the others.

But a happy accident provided a source for further plays of Euripides. Nine plays beginning with the letters epsilon, eta, iota, and kappa (*Helen, Electra, Heracles, Children of Heracles, Suppliants, Ion, Iphigenia among the Taurians, Iphigenia at Aulis,* and *Cyclops*) somehow survived from the end of antiquity to be recopied in the Middle Ages. These plays have no scholia, and it is thought that they are the remnant of an Alexandrian edition arranged in rough alphabetical order. These "alphabetic" plays survive only in a fourteenth-century manuscript in Florence. So for these nine plays (plus *Bacchae*, which survives only in this manuscript and a copy of it) nearly nineteen centuries separate Euripides' autograph from our earliest witness. For centuries on end, therefore, the text of these plays was subjected to corruption from the fallible eyes and fallible fingers of countless scribes and also to the interference of actors, scholars, and ordinary readers, some of whom may have thought they were making the plays better even as they corrupted them.

The Long Road Back: Textual Scholarship since the
Fifteenth Century

The first printed editions of tragedy belong to the end of the fifteenth century. It has been well said that the age of the printed book dawned just in time to secure the survival of the genre of tragedy. From now on the inevitable process of corruption could be not only halted but also turned back. From the fifth century BCE to the fifteenth century CE the text of the tragic poets underwent, as we have seen, a progressive deterioration. Some scholars, of course, such as Aristophanes of Byzantium, were aware of corruption and tried to correct it. But in the absence of printing their work could have little effect on the majority of copies. It was in any case, as far as we can tell, unsystematic and focused on particular cases, without any attempt to formulate a general plan of attack. With the Renaissance begins a new era in the history of the text, an era when improvements once made could be transmitted to future generations and piecemeal and scattershot methods were gradually replaced with a systematic and scientific attempt to view problems whole. Like the natural sciences, which made impressive progress in the same period, classical scholarship now tried increasingly to discover the regularities of its subject and use them to explain or correct the primary evidence presented to our senses, the text given in our manuscripts. It is an impressive achievement of the human spirit, and to it we owe the fact that our texts of the tragic poets, like those of all classical authors, are now intelligible in so many places where they were previously obscure. It is impossible in this brief treatment to touch on all the kinds of investigation that have contributed to this effort, and we will have to be content with illustrative synecdoche.

To collect all the variant readings for a given text and make them available for the reader was a big step, one already taken unsystematically in Alexandria. But it became gradually clear that textual witnesses, like witnesses in a court of law, had to be evaluated, not merely cited. By the nineteenth century scholars learned to eliminate manuscripts that were merely copies of other existing manuscripts (*codices descripti*): such derivative witnesses will contain no new truth. Then they learned to sift through what was left, trying to arrive in each case at the earliest state of the text attested to by our manuscripts. This in turn they learned to subject to examination: is this what the author wrote, and if not can we make a guess, based on the regularities of the genre and the author's style, as to what he did write? The principles on which this *recensio* or sifting of the evidence is based are commonsensical once stated, but it took a while for them to be formulated.

Our principal means of testing transmitted readings to see if they are genuine has to do with the observed regularities of Greek grammar, Greek meter, and tragic convention. The relationship between a "rule" of grammar, meter, or convention and the manuscripts is often paradoxical, for to almost every rule the manuscripts give exceptions, and often the critic finds himself deriving a rule from the witness of the manuscripts but then turning around and correcting the exceptions. This is paradoxical but is not as irrational as it sounds. Take, for example, the metrical example of Porson's Law, which says that when in a tragic trimeter there is a word break before the third syllable from the end, the syllable before that word break, which could theoretically be long or short, must be short. How do we deal with the exceptions (for there are some)? Some of the exceptions, scholars have decided, require us to refine the rule: thus examination of a large category of exceptions leads to the conclusion that if the syllable before the word break is a monosyllabic word, then it need not be short. But in other cases we decide that a line that violates this rule cannot have been written as it stands by a tragic poet in the classical period: at *Iphigenia at Aulis* 1578–1614, where Porson's Law, together with many other rules of tragic meter, is repeatedly broken, scholars diagnose later interpolation, whereas in *Ion* 1 they emend to produce regular meter. In the case of all such rules and apparent exceptions we must decide whether there is some good reason for the exception (in which case it may be allowed to stand) or whether, on the contrary, we can see other features that show the passage in question to have been interpolated or corrupted. By studying the regularities of tragic style and the typical ways the tragic poets dealt with recurring dramatic situations, or by paying attention to the habits of scribes or studying the habits of interpolators where interpolation has been convincingly diagnosed, other scholars have given their successors a body of evidence with which to judge the soundness of our texts.

The idea is occasionally expressed by scholars who should know better that after five centuries of assiduous effort by scholars in nearly all the countries of Europe and North America all the corruptions in our tragic texts are either healed or incurable. The truth is that students of tragedy who know Greek well, are willing to take the trouble to acquire the technical knowledge and the familiarity with the tragic texts possessed by their predecessors, and have some measure of their predecessors' knack of seeing just where a text is ailing and what might set it right, need not despair of improving the text.

I end with two examples of textual argument chosen because they can be made intelligible to a Greekless reader. There are some technical points at issue in each of them, but they also show that it is at times useful to be conscious of one's own literary presuppositions and those of one's predecessors. For literary presuppositions play an important role in the decisions editors make, and it is much better if editors are conscious of these presuppositions and aware that there may be evidence against them (an argument made at greater length in Kovacs 1987). To put this another way, when examining any particular passage in a play it is a good idea to have the entire play in view.

My first example demonstrates that not even well-established conjectures should be taken on authority: all must be scrutinized again from time to time. At the end of Euripides' *Electra*, when Electra and Orestes, having killed Clytemnestra, have fallen into despair, Castor and Polydeuces arrive by the stage crane (*méchanê*) and announce the future for the two siblings: both must leave Argos, Electra to marry Pylades and Orestes to be pursued by the Erinyes until, having finally been acquitted in Athens, his troubles are ended and he lives happily ever after. Immediately after Castor's speech, there is the following interchange:

Orestes: Sons of Zeus, may we have speech with you?
Castor: Yes, you may, for you are not polluted [masculine adj.] by this bloodshed.
Electra: May I too speak to you?
Castor: You too may do so: for it is Apollo I blame for this murderous affair.

The first printed edition of the play, edited by Petrus Victorius (Pietro Vettori), appeared in 1545. (*Electra* was somehow overlooked in the first printed edition of the extant plays of Euripides, the 1503 Aldine.) Feeling that Orestes was indeed "polluted by this bloodshed" Victorius gave Orestes' line to the leader of the chorus of Argive women, which means Castor used that phrase of her. As previously noted, speaker indications do not go back to the author's autograph, so changing them with good cause is a sensible thing to do. In this case, however, Victorius also had to change the masculine adjective for "polluted" to feminine. Two slight changes, therefore, that seemed to give better sense.

In fact, however, the sense was decidedly worse. (1) When a *deus ex machina* appears at the end of a play, he comes to address the principals of the drama, and it is without parallel in tragedy for a chorus to push themselves forward to meddle in a conversation that does not directly concern them. (2) Castor, as his preceding speech has made clear, has come to console his kinsman, not to chastise him, but with Victorius' emendation Castor's speech makes a gratuitous jab at Orestes: "Yes, you may, for you (unlike Orestes) are not polluted by this bloodshed." (3) After such a comment to the chorus-leader there is no reason for Electra to ask, "May I too speak?": Castor has allowed the chorus-leader to speak only because she is innocent of Clytemnestra's murder, and Electra is not. (4) Castor's reply to Electra makes no sense either since his leniency toward her because of the command of Apollo applies no less to Orestes than to her, and if she is free to address the gods, so should he be. By contrast, if we take the parallelism of the two answers at face value and assign the two questions to the two siblings, this suggests that both address Castor and both are excused by him. In effect he says to both, "I do not regard you as polluted by this bloodshed since it is Apollo I blame for this murderous affair," this single statement being parceled out between his two interlocutors. There is a parallel for Castor's view of pollution (if your actions were not morally blameworthy you are not polluted) at *Orestes* 75–76. In my view, the transmitted assignments are correct, and every editor from Victorius in 1545 until Basta Donzelli's Teubner fascicle of 1995 has got the thing wrong, exactly 450 years of error. (It must be noted, however, that some had argued against Victorius: see Stoessl 1956, 82–85; Kovacs 1985, 310–14.) The persistence of such an error owes much, in my judgment, to the belief that Euripides' *deus ex machina* scenes are not really intended to resolve anything and are not to be taken seriously. By contrast, an editor who is willing to look independently at the tone of the final scene and is not ready to believe on very little evidence that Euripides' dialogue will be incoherent can restore Euripides' meaning.

My second example shows the converse duty of skepticism toward what is transmitted. Immediately after the *parodos* of Euripides' *Bacchae*, the prophet Tiresias comes to Cadmus' house to take him to the mountains to worship Dionysus. Their dialogue at 195–203 runs as follows:

Cadmus: Shall we alone dance in the god's honor?
Tiresias: Yes, we alone have sense, the others none.
Cadmus: The wait is long. But take hold of my hand.
Tiresias: There, clasp my hand and pair it with your own.
Cadmus: I do not despise the gods, mortal that I am.
Tiresias: In no way do we play the sophist to the powers above.

the traditions of our fathers, which we possess coeval with time,
no argument shall overthrow them,
no matter what subtleties have been invented by deep thinkers.

There are problems here that many editors have chosen to ignore. (1) The dative *toisi daimosi*, "*to* the powers above," has no obvious construction in Greek. It could be accommodated by redividing *ouden sophizomestha* as *oud' ensophizomestha*, "nor do I play the sophist among," as suggested by Musgrave. (2) In a continuous argument it is customary to connect each sentence with the previous one by means of a connecting particle, just as it is in English to start it with an uppercase letter. Only when the second sentence is explicative of the first (and we would punctuate at the end of the first with a colon) is it usual to leave out the connective. Between 200 and 201 there is no connective, an effect I have approximated by printing 201 without its initial capital. (3) In 202 the superfluous "them" is as clumsy in Greek as in my English translation, indeed more so since it does not agree in gender with "traditions." (4) The appeal to traditions coeval with time seems an odd way to promote the new god Dionysus. The previous Oxford editor, Gilbert Murray, was untroubled by these problems and printed the text as it is transmitted. The latest Oxford editor, James Diggle, rightly thinks they cannot be ignored. His way of fixing them is to bracket 199–203 (an earlier scholar had already proposed bracketing 201–2).

Now the absence of a connective and the inept pronoun might be thought to point to a clumsy writer of a later age, but no diagnosis of interpolation is fully plausible unless we can see some motive for it. What could have motivated an interpolator here? In particular what person of any age could have thought of the idea of describing the worship of the new god Dionysus as "coeval with time"?

Once we ask this question, it answers itself: this is precisely what Euripides does elsewhere in the play, and the paradoxical idea of connecting the worship of Dionysus with age-old sanctities could only be his. In 96–97 he has his chorus say, "I shall hymn the god with songs that have ever been in use," and at 890–96 the chorus, urging piety toward Dionysus, praise as sovereign "what through long ages has ever been lawful and upheld by nature." It is in this same vein that Euripides gives Dionysus' cult many of the trappings of the ancient religion of Cybele, the Great Mother Goddess. Why he does this can be briefly put: Pentheus in this play is to be a fighter not merely against novel divinities but against divinity in general. (On this point see Kovacs 1994–2004, 6: 6–8.) Once we realize that this idea is central to the whole play, our duty is plain: we must emend, not delete. The absence of a connective could be a sign that a line has dropped out (as suggested by Kirchhoff: there are other such lacunae [gaps] at 652, 843, and 1036). The lost line could have had a verb to govern "traditions," and then we could repunctuate before "no argument" with a perfectly idiomatic colon (in Greek a raised period) and put the offending pronoun in a different sentence. Here is a restoration (with the second speaker change moved down a line and Musgrave's redivision of *ouden sophizomestha* as *oud' ensophizomestha* adopted):

Cadmus: I do not despise the gods, mortal that I am,
  nor do I play the sophist among the powers above.
Tiresias: <No, it is not the part of a wise man to look down on>

the traditions of our fathers, which we possess coeval with time:
no argument shall overthrow them,
no matter what subtleties have been invented by deep thinkers.

Progress is indeed possible. Neither the scribes who copied our manuscripts nor their many predecessors in the chain of transmission deserve our uncritical faith; likewise even the most well-established conjectures of our scholarly predecessors can sometimes be reexamined with profit. We can judge for ourselves the regularities of the Greek language and tragic convention and the practice of the individual playwrights. What is needed is knowledge of the requisite technicalities joined with a sense for the work as a whole.

NOTES

1 In 341 BCE, three years before Lycurgus took office, there was a revival of one of Euripides' *Iphigenia* plays. It is tempting to think (though we cannot prove) that it was *Iphigenia at Aulis*, by far the most heavily interpolated of the plays of Euripides we possess, that much of this interpolation belongs to the performance of 341, and that the clearly non-Euripidean character of much of the dialogue provided a large impetus to Lycurgus to safeguard the text by law. For a recent discussion of *Iphigenia at Aulis* and a new hypothesis regarding its interpolations, see Kovacs 2003.
2 This is the translation of H. N. Fowler (1936) in the Loeb. Similar translations in Csapo and Slater 1995, 10, and, alas, Kovacs 1994, 117. The word order suggests taking *en koinôi* with *grapsamenous* rather than *phulattein*. More important, *anarthrous en koinôi* is implausible as the equivalent of *en tôi dêmosiôi* or *tois dêmosiois*, and furthermore where *en koinôi* occurs elsewhere it is adverbial or adjectival in meaning. The meaning is that they made *one single* written collection of the three poets' plays: there was no need to go searching for them in more than one place.
3 Another early commentator to be mentioned is Crates of Mallos, a leading figure of the school founded by the Attalids of Pergamum in western Asia Minor.
4 Good candidates are found in the scholia to *Orestes* 57 (actors now wrongly put on a silent entrance of Helen with the spoils of Troy), 176 (technical comment on music), 268 (actors playing Orestes nowadays use no bow but mime the shooting), 643 (nowadays the actor playing Menelaus acts as if he thinks Orestes is asking for the return of money), 1366 (actors interpolated 1366–68 in order to avoid the dangers of entering by a leap from the top of the *skênê*), *Medea* 96 (wrongly positing use of *ekkuklêma*), 1320 (Medea's chariot pulled by dragons).

FURTHER READING

For a clear and readable discussion of the way ancient texts come down to us and the dangers to which they are exposed see Reynolds and Wilson 1991. Readers interested in the principles of textual criticism as applied to Greek and Latin texts are well provided for in West 1973. Paul Maas's earlier treatment of this same subject (Maas 1958) discusses in greater detail how to draw up a family tree of manuscripts or *stemma codicum*, and how to use it to eliminate readings as secondary. For other histories of the transmission of Greek tragic texts see Barrett 1964, 45–90, and Mastronarde 1994, 39–52.

The subject of books and their readers in the ancient Greek world is discussed in Easterling and Knox 1985, 1–41. Samples of ancient papyrus fragments from antiquity are reproduced in Turner 1987. Specimens of Greek bookhands from later antiquity through the Middle Ages can be seen in Barbour 1981. Antiquity's great "information technology" breakthrough, the invention of the codex, is the subject of Roberts and Skeat 1983. The work of the scholars of the Museum in Alexandria is discussed in Pfeiffer 1968, Fraser 1972, chapter 8, and Griffith 1977, 225–45. Canfora 1989 examines the vicissitudes of the library at Alexandria. Scholarship under the Byzantine Empire and the revival of Greek learning in Renaissance Italy are described in N. G. Wilson 1983 and 1992. Important work on the manuscript tradition of Aeschylus is in Dawe 1964, on that of Sophocles in Dawe 1973–78, and on that of Euripides in Zuntz 1965. This last includes an intriguing bit of detective work (a presumed mark of punctuation turned out to be a piece of straw) that proved once and for all the exact relationship between two manuscripts of Euripides, something with large consequences for the constitution of the text. (The straw is preserved in the Laurentian Library in Florence for future scholars to consult.)

Countless scholars, writing in most of the modern languages of Europe and in Latin, have identified corruptions in Greek tragedy and tried to fix them by conjecture. For examples of this activity carried out with style and panache see Jackson 1955 and Housman 1972, 181–208, the latter a bit acid for some tastes. For an eloquent refutation of the view that further progress in this field is impossible, see West 1990b, 369–72.

CHAPTER TWENTY-FIVE

Learning from Suffering: Ancient Responses to Tragedy

Stephen Halliwell

Classical Athenian tragedy not only inaugurated one of the major traditions of Western drama and poetry, it also motivated a history of critical reflection and theorizing that has continued almost unbroken to this day. Theories of tragedy have always, however, found it hard to escape paradox. Central to the concerns of tragic drama (and of other tragic art forms) is a confrontation with extremes of action and experience that stretch comprehension to its limits. One abiding puzzle, trenchantly formulated by Augustine (*Confessions* 3.2.2) – a pagan devotee of tragedy who later turned into a Christian denouncer of it – is why human beings should want to contemplate images of "the worst" in this way at all. What is the purpose and value of tragedy? Can its audiences really learn something, or somehow benefit, from watching the sufferings of characters who often go to the edge of what it is possible even to imagine? If tragic drama is itself inherently paradoxical in striving to give articulate form and voice to realms of consciousness that resist the resources of coherent expression, critical readings and theories of tragedy heighten the paradox by taking it upon themselves to make sense, at one further remove, of what arguably lies beyond the reach of explanation. Whatever may ultimately be made of individual tragic works, the Western tradition has been preoccupied with the *idea* of tragedy. This chapter will address some of the most important versions of that idea to have taken shape in antiquity.

Classical Responses to Tragedy: Echoes of Lost Voices

In Timocles' comedy *Women Celebrating the Dionysia*, probably written in the third quarter of the fourth century BCE, an unknown character delivers a speech arguing that tragic drama can provide its audience with "consolation" (*parapsuchai*) and a means of coping with life's inevitable sufferings. While watching a tragedy performed,

> ... the mind forgets its own problems
> And finds itself engrossed in others' afflictions,
> Then goes home edified as well as pleased.
> (Timocles fr. 6.5–7 *PCG*)

Tragedy shows us, on this account, that heroes suffer greater misfortunes than ourselves; Niobe's story, the speaker suggests, will comfort anyone who has lost a child, while Philoctetes' will have the same effect on the lame. By the date of Timocles' play, Attic comedy had an established convention of casting sidelong glances at its sister-genre tragedy. Such material, as we shall see with Aristophanes' *Frogs*, always needs interpreting circumspectly. But the juxtaposition of life and theater in Timocles' fragment, though not without a humorous slant, provides an illuminating glimpse of some possible attitudes to tragedy in the late classical period. Building on the folk wisdom that life is hard, the speaker construes tragic myth as a magnified reflection of the scope of human suffering, a reflection that affords spectators a perspective on their own lives and makes their troubles seem more endurable. But Timocles' speaker also identifies a double element in the immediate theatrical experience of tragedy: first, an imaginative-cum-emotional enthrallment, *psuchagôgia* (6; literally, "soul-conjuring"), that is presumably related to the pleasure, *hêdonê*, of line 7; secondly, a process of edification or enlightenment. This last point looks, at first sight, synonymous with the "benefit" (*ôphelein*, 9) that the speaker goes on to illustrate through a series of exempla. But there is reason to suppose it extends further. The spectator *leaves* the theater having been edified or "educated" (*paideutheis*, 7), which ought to imply that the watching of plays is itself instructive. Moreover, the spectator departs, literally, "with pleasure and having been educated at the same time," as though pleasure and understanding are somehow interwoven in the viewing of tragic drama.

All the themes just touched on exhibit links with more discursive classical sources. Coping better with one's sorrows by contemplating the greater woes of others is an idea found in Democritus: one should aim at tranquility of mind, the goal of Atomist ethics, by "contemplating (*theôreein*) the lives of the wretched and dwelling on their sufferings" (DK 191). Democritus is not known to have applied this principle to tragedy as such, but Timocles' fragment intimates that others may have done so (as too, with a new twist, some Stoics would later do). The notion of *psuchagôgia*, metaphorically extended from ritual conjuring of souls (as at *Odyssey* 11.24–50), was employed earlier than Timocles to denote the spellbinding effects of tragedy and other art forms. Aristotle unselfconsciously uses such terminology twice in the *Poetics*, attaching it to the components of "complex" plots (1450a33) and also to the gripping potential of spectacle (1450b16–17). "Soul-conjuring" could clearly encompass various aspects of tragedy's capacity to compel the minds and imaginations of its audiences. The idea distilled a culture of emotionalism (scrutinized, with an ironic eye, at Isocrates 4.168 and Andocides 4.23) that undoubtedly surrounded tragedy in classical Athens and was rooted in the psychological intensity of the plays themselves.

Of related importance is Timocles' reference to the tragic audience's emotional absorption in the "suffering of others," *pros allotriôi ... pathei* (6). (The well-known story at Herodotus 6.21 exemplifies how a tragedy could fail if it openly reminded the city of its *own* sufferings.) This phrasing resembles a passage of Gorgias' *Encomium of Helen* where poetry's hearers are said to experience fearful shudders, tears of pity, a longing for grief, and a personal passion that responds to "the affairs of others" (*allotriôn pragmatôn*, DK 11.9); it also has affinities with Socrates' account of what the tragic spectator's soul undergoes at Plato, *Republic* 606b, a text itself probably influenced by Gorgias' *Helen*. Gorgias and Plato concur that tragedy's audience is exposed to a concentrated, soul-transforming experience. Beyond that, however, their viewpoints diverge: Plato's text emphasizes the dangerously irrational consequences of such emotional expenditure, while Gorgias considers the experience a paradoxical medium of insight. Gorgias anticipates the line taken by Timocles' character, whose contention that the tragic spectator is "educated" matches a wider classical conception of poets as "teachers" of their communities.

If Timocles' fragment opens a comically oblique window on ideas of tragedy current in classical Athens, it is to Gorgias we must turn for the earliest critical model of tragedy we can directly identify. Gorgias' views must be reconstructed principally from two pieces of evidence: first, the passage of his *Encomium of Helen*, noted above, that describes the pity, fear, and other passions the soul undergoes or "suffers" (*paschein*) when listening to poetry; secondly, his riddling remark, specifically on tragedy, that "the one [that is, the poet] who deceives is more just than the non-deceiver, and the deceived [spectator] is wiser than the undeceived" (DK 23). It is one thing to assume these elements belonged to a coherent conception of tragedy; quite another to translate the conception into full-blown theory. The strands of Gorgias' argument are intricate. At the outset (1–2) he affirms that the excellence of all *logos* (speech, argument) – including, therefore, his own – consists in truth, and implies that (some) poets propagate falsehood (*pseudesthai*) about Helen. In section 7 he states that if Helen was the victim of force she deserves to be *pitied*, not blamed, for what she suffered (*paschein*). In section 8, immediately before his reference to the emotive power of poetry, he couples the notions of *logos* as persuasion and as deception, a combination which illustrates the twin powers of discourse to arouse and control emotion ("to stop fear... and augment pity"). In section 10, immediately after the reference to poetry, Gorgias speaks of "inspired incantations" (a phrase evocative of poetry itself) which can induce pleasure, reduce sorrow, and by bewitchment and magic (traditional Greek metaphors for the potency of poetry) persuasively transform the listener's soul; magic, he adds, involves "deceptions of belief" (*doxēs apatēmata*). Finally, in section 14 Gorgias draws an analogy between words and drugs, reiterating the former's emotional efficacy (grief, joy, fear, courage are mentioned this time) and equating the force of persuasion with soul-medicine and soul-magic.

These elements of the *Encomium of Helen* leave a teasingly self-referential impression. Discourse (*logos*) can equally speak the truth or conjure deception; either way, it can manipulate the emotions of audiences. Gorgias himself uses *logos* to persuade his hearers that the power of persuasion is a dangerous "drug," yet he poses a conundrum by describing his own speech, in its very last word, as a *paignion* (a game or jeu d'esprit). But his accumulated images of passionate emotional persuasion remain plausible, not least when applied to poetry, which he presents as an irresistible verbal art. Moreover, while *Helen* treats deception, poetic or otherwise, as potentially blameworthy, it also links the motif, through metaphors of soul-magic and soul-medicine, with the traditionally acknowledged delight of poetic "bewitchment" (*thelgein*). This leaves enough room to infer that poetic "deception" may have either a positive or a negative force: negative, if it simply distorts belief, but positive if it arouses rewarding emotions and induces hearers to grasp an underlying insight beneath the surface of stories. In this light, the riddlingly commended deception of fr. 23 (paralleled in the anonymous, near-contemporary *Dissoi Logoi*, 3.10), can legitimately be taken to frame á serious tragic paradox, the acquisition of wisdom through an emotionally psychotropic experience. Furthermore, by his separate suggestions that Helen, if the victim of erotic violence, would constitute a suitable object of pity, but equally, if the subject herself of erotic desire (*erós*), could count as the sufferer of an affliction or misfortune (*atuchêma*), Gorgias seems to be sketching out scenarios in which Helen might, on his own terms, be made into a tragic figure – one whose story might absorb us in deep emotions that mediate insights into the human condition.

It is frustrating that we cannot do more to reconstruct Gorgias' approach to tragedy. Scholars have surmised that his thoughts on the subject proved influential (even on Plato and Aristotle), but the evidence is incomplete. However, Gorgias demonstrates that in the mid- and late fifth century the importance of Attic tragedy had generated conceptual reflections on the nature of the genre. So too, in a very different vein, does the famous contest of tragedians in the second half of Aristophanes' *Frogs* (405). Aristophanic comedy in general sets up an almost ceaseless counterpoint to tragic drama, frequently parodying it and playing metatheatrically with its conventions (as in Dicaeopolis' visit to Euripides at *Acharnians* 393–488, Trygaeus' ride on the "machine" at *Peace* 82–179, and throughout *Women at the Thesmophoria*). Comic references disclose, albeit through a distorting lens, diverse contemporary perceptions of tragedy: its status within Dionysiac festivity (*Peace* 530–38), the importance of masks and costumes for its performance (*Acharnians* 412–44, *Birds* 100–101, 512, *Wealth* 423–24), the provocative prominence of females in tragic myth (*Lysistrata* 138), or the controversial relationship of Euripidean drama to traditional religious convictions (*Women at the Thesmophoria* 449–52). But it is above all in *Frogs* that the versatility of Aristophanic humor prompts us to discern echoes of ways in which classical Athenians may have thought (and argued) about tragedy.

Attempts to use *Frogs* as evidence for contemporary ideas are, nonetheless, fraught with uncertainty. We should be satisfied if we can trace some plausible clues to the spectrum of late fifth-century attitudes, but we should avoid the temptation to *reduce* the play's significance to transparent sense. *Frogs*, like all Aristophanes' work, is multilayered fantasy: an exercise in inter-generic rivalry (making comedy out of tragedy), a satire on sophistic/intellectual techniques of disputation, a parody of contemporary traits of poetic criticism, including "close reading" of texts, and a multifarious assortment of imagery for poets and their creations. Comic complication is pervasive, not least a tension between the *familiarity* of judging poetry (all Athenian drama is staged competitively) and the potential *absurdity* of trying to validate such judgments by "objective" standards: when Xanthias hears that "*mousikê* [musico-poetic art] will be measured on scales," his expostulation, "What! They'll weigh tragedy like sheep for sacrifice?" (798), strikes a programmatically ironic note. Moreover, most of the Aeschylus–Euripides contest relates to tragedy as a species of poetic art, *technê*, in general (though without ruling out the "madness" of inspiration, 816) and to its place in musico-poetic culture (*mousikê*) as a whole. Hence the mélange of criteria – technical, formal, stylistic, mythological, psychological, educational, and moral – introduced by the two sides. The safest inference we can draw from the second half of the play is that when Athenians argued about the merits of tragedies, there was an ample (and conflicting) choice of standards they could invoke.

Through *Frogs'* fantasized dialectic of critical voices, however, it may be feasible to discover a set of tragedy-specific issues. These issues cluster around a (schematic) sense of tragedy's evolution from an older, "Aeschylean" to a modern, "Euripidean" phase – the former supposedly marked by inflated dramaturgy, portentously obscure meaning, and audience-effects that were "deceptive" (910), frightening (962), yet inducive of noble, militaristic impulses (1013–42; compare 1021 with Gorgias DK 24 for a possible, but contentious, influence); Euripides' work, by contrast, allegedly encouraging spectators to speak democratically and *think* critically (948–58), while debasing the genre by confusing it with ordinary life (959), making its characters overtly *pitiful* (1063–66; cf. *Acharnians* 413), and peddling immorality of various kinds (especially vis-à-vis female characters, 1043–54, 1079–82). For our purposes, blatant comic exaggerations and distortions matter less than the critical templates that may have shaped them. Most interesting of all is the contrast between tragedy as fear-arousing yet courage-inducing and, on the other hand, as a genre that *softens* its audience (as well as its characters) through pity. Part of what seems to lie behind this contrast (which later influenced Nietzsche's *Birth of Tragedy*) is a distinction between heroically uplifting and pessimistically life-denying types of tragedy. This dichotomy never crystallizes into a lucid framework of judgment (Dionysus' final verdict is a comically sentimental piece of cultural nostalgia), but there are enough hints to make it plausible that these divergent construals of tragedy's relationship to overarching life-values had some salience within contemporary reactions to the genre (Konstan 1999).

We can draw tentative lines of connection between *Frogs* and our other evidence for classical responses to tragedy. Might, for example, Euripides' gibe that Aeschylus' pompous nonsense "deceived" (*exapatan*) his gullible audiences (910) reflect the Gorgianic concept of tragic deception we have already considered? Alternatively, we might wonder whether Gorgias himself was reworking into a deliberate paradox (we can *learn* from tragic "deception") an existing slur against theatrical illusionism. There are also interesting parallels between motifs found in *Frogs* and some fourth-century sources on tragedy: a resemblance, for instance, between Aeschylus' standard of heroically more-than-human grandeur (esp. *Frogs* 1058–61) and Aristotle's for-mulation in the *Poetics* of tragic characters as generically "better than people of the present." Equally, the critique of tragic pity in book 10 of Plato's *Republic* (as an emotion with "depressing" consequences for the spectators' own lives) perhaps encapsulates one version of the Aeschylean case against Euripides in *Frogs* (and a version diametrically opposed to the idea of tragedy as "consolation" found in Timocles fr. 6 *PCG*). Such suggestions can assimilate the comic schematizations of *Frogs* while still detecting in the play some echoes of ongoing arguments about tragedy in Athenian culture. But those arguments must have had ramifications that Aristophanes has no incentive to render faithfully. Where *Frogs* appears to pit tragic fear against tragic pity (a standpoint we will reencounter in Longinus), Gorgias, Plato, and Aristotle all took their possible combination for granted; where *Frogs* presents pity as an emotion of weakness, Timocles' character, as we saw, could claim that it fortified tragic audiences in their own endurance of suffering. The relationship between tragic emotions and tragic pleasure is another psychological complexity on which *Frogs* makes no clear-cut sense, though it does occasionally edge toward the issue, notably when Dionysus describes the thrill he derived from the grief-laden atmosphere of Aeschylus' *Persians* (1028–29). *Frogs* yields no secure evidence for individual theories of tragedy, but it offers intermittent pointers to some of the disagreements by which Athenian discussion of tragedy was animated. It was against that cultural background, in the following century, that two key philosophical accounts of tragedy formed themselves.

Philosophical Interpretations of Tragedy

Plato's Athenian upbringing steeped him in the traditions of tragic theater. Yet his relationship to those traditions became both unsettling and complex: unsettling, because his own work developed a conspicuously anti-tragic perspective on life; but complex, because the anti-tragic voices heard in his dialogues are articulated through disparate elements (quotations, references, criticisms, allusions, borrowings, and metaphors) which afford no definitive authorial judgment on the genre. The idea of tragedy formed a constant presence in the shadows of Plato's thinking. That presence must have been incited in part by the experience of Socrates' death and, equally importantly, Socrates' own attitude to his death. Toward the end of *Phaedo* (115a) Plato makes Socrates speak with gentle irony of how a "tragic man," *anêr tragikos*, might solemnly approach his death as a "destiny" (*heimarmenê*), while Socrates himself proceeds to strip the event down to the practicalities of washing himself and drinking the poison (Halliwell 1984b, 55–58). Equally revealing, though differently nuanced, is a passage of *Laws* (book 7) where the Athenian pictures an ideal city's rulers telling a troupe of tragic actors: "we ourselves aspire to be poets of the finest, best tragedy; our whole political organization [*politeia*] is a representation [*mimêsis*] of the finest, best life – which is what *we* count as the truest tragedy" (817b). The philosophical law-givers conceive of themselves as rival "poets," or makers, of the best tragedy/life. They symbolically gesture toward a thought also conveyed by Socrates in the *Phaedo*: what counts as "tragedy" is a question that presupposes a valuation of existence itself. If there is a core to the many uses of tragedy found in Plato's oeuvre, it lies in this idea of "the tragic" as the forging of a (re)valuation of life on the anvil of extreme suffering (Halliwell 2002, 98–117).

If Plato was haunted by the metaphysics of tragedy, he nonetheless kept in view the material and cultural conditions of tragic theater. In the *Republic*, the vocal behavior of theater audiences is included in a vignette of public opinion at work in civic settings (492b–c); in the *Laws* this phenomenon is dubbed "theatrocracy" (*theatrokratia*, 701a), a sort of democracy in theatrical guise. On a different level, a passage of *Phaedrus* indicates that Plato was aware that tragic emotion was not a merely raw experience but was causally related to the narrative structure of dramatic works. Socrates and Phaedrus agree that it would be absurd to reduce tragic playwriting to techniques for making pity- or fear-arousing speeches, rather than understanding it as an art for fitting such things together harmoniously into a unified whole (268c–9a, an exemplification of Socrates' earlier principle of the "organic" unity required for all effective discourse, 264c). So when in *Laws* 7 the rulers express "rivalry" with the poets and players of tragedy, they are admitting the genre's real power. Tragic drama was a highly organized, sophisticated medium that could grip the imaginations and emotions of a city by tapping into a whole worldview: the law-givers want their own values, embodied in social and political institutions, to wield the same psychological potency within a carefully designed structure of life.

The passages just noted attest an idea of tragedy as a public art form preeminently capable of swaying the minds of audiences and thereby exercising major cultural influence. This model of tragedy's status – simultaneously political, ethical, and psychological – appears elsewhere in Plato: it crops up, for instance, in the classification of tragedy as a prime type of poetic "rhetoric," an agency of mass persuasion (*Gorgias* 502b–d). Most importantly, it underpins the critique of the genre in the *Republic*'s two discussions of poetry. In books 2–3 (376e–392c), where Socrates outlines the education of the future Guardians of the ideal city, the spotlight falls chiefly on epic, but tragedy is cited alongside it and there is no doubt that the critique of a mythology of malevolently destructive gods (esp. 380a–b) and self-pitying, life-craving heroes (386a–388d) has clear implications for tragedy too. Such a mythology is attacked for presenting a perspective that finds the world (and its masters, the gods) inhospitable to human hopes of justice and happiness (esp. 392a–b). That what is under scrutiny here is an irredeemably pessimistic mentality receives confirmation from the second discussion of poetry, in book 10, where tragedy is referred to prominently and its conjunction with epic is tightened by the view that Homer himself is "first" of the tragedians, their "teacher and leader" (595c, 607a; cf. 605c10). The central target here is an emergent concept of "the tragic" that embraces but extends beyond Attic drama, though the peculiar mass psychology of theatrical performance remains in view, not least in the image of throngs addicted to plays about unstable characters (604e). Tragedy is configured here as poetry that condenses a whole evaluation of life into scenes of convulsive human grief and failure. By doing so it allegedly draws out, but also reinforces, deep grief-directed instincts within the psyche: tragedy is rooted, the argument suggests, in the conflicting propensities of the human mind itself.

This conception of tragedy comes to a climax at 605c–6d, where Socrates brings what he calls "the greatest charge" against poetry, its capacity to "maim" the souls even of "the best of us" by exploiting the tension between the biddings of reason (which tells us that "no human affairs are worth real seriousness," 604b10–c1) and the lower soul's craving for emotional immersion in the sufferings of the characters displayed. The "better" the tragedy, the greater its ability to command the audience's emotional "surrender" to pity (605d3). Released from social pressures to temper *self-pity* for their own misfortunes, spectators of tragedy enjoy becoming vessels for a pity that wells up at the sight and sound of heroic characters (like Priam or Achilles – both earlier cited in book 3) who lament compulsively over their own psychic wounds. This strong bond of imaginatively shared emotion (*sumpaschein*, 605d3–4), Socrates submits, turns tragedy into the expression of an irremediably despairing view of human existence – one with the power to "infect" and corrode the feelings of "even the best." To purchase theatrical pleasure at the price of the underlying pessimism that feeds tragic emotion is, he claims, to destabilize the soul's true harmony and its only reliable basis for happiness.

Plato may have been the first Greek, apart from the tragedians themselves, to articulate a sense of tragedy as the vehicle of a whole *Weltgefühl* or life-sense. He was certainly the first to do so for the purposes of resisting and indeed repudiating tragedy as a culturally imposing "falsehood." If Plato was familiar with Gorgias' model of tragic "deception" as an emotional conduit of insight, he has inverted it: tragedy, his arguments suggest, pulls the mind down from higher truth to lower falsehood. The Platonic tendency to think of tragedy, even "the tragic," in such terms is reflected further in passages that expand the concept in a boldly metaphorical manner. Only two of these can be mentioned briefly here. The first is *Cratylus* 408, where in the midst of some semi-playful etymologizing Socrates introduces an image of Pan as a hybrid being whose top half epitomizes the "smooth, divine" nature of truth, while his lower half remains "harsh and tragic" (*trachu kai tragikon*, with a pun on *tragikos* as "goatlike"), an embodiment of the falsehood of human existence: "for it is in this world that many myths and falsehoods about the tragic life [*peri ton tragikon bion*] belong" (408c7–8). Although the passage touches on tragic drama only allusively, it clearly posits (like *Laws* 817b, cited earlier) the phenomenon of a "tragic" (conception of) life, a false conception/life trapped within crudely human limitations, including misleading myths, and blind to divine truth. The superimposition of generic categories onto life itself is taken one step further in the analysis of the mixed pleasure-and-pain of tragedy in *Philebus*, where Socrates speaks of the experience of grief "not only in stage-plays but in the entire tragedy and comedy of life" (50b, the first known occurrence of the "all the world's a stage" topos). Beyond its obvious evocation of mixed fortunes, the idea of life as tragicomic subtly insinuates that "tragedy," the genre of supposedly supreme seriousness, purports yet fails to give an authoritative view of life's significance, since it is so readily collapsible, where the human scene as a whole is concerned, into its opposite. (The argument is, of course, reversible for comedy.) To transcend "tragedy," whether in art or life, what is needed is a philosophical wisdom that sees beyond the attachments expressed in human emotions.

Plato was obsessed with tragedy yet constantly seeking an escape from it. Aristotle, by contrast, strove to introduce philosophical order into its interpretation. Even at this late stage in the history of theories of tragedy, the *Poetics* remains the most commonly cited reference-point in the field. Its ideas have suffered, however, from their very longevity: if they have often functioned as a stimulus to debate, they have also become encrusted with inherited assumptions and prejudices (both pro and contra). It is right, therefore, to take little for granted here; we should build up from the basic to the complex. Aristotle's primary experience of tragedy belonged to the years he spent at Athens, first from 367 to 347 (as a member of Plato's Academy) and later as head of his own philosophical school in the Lyceum (335–23). Because the *Poetics* is equivocal about theatrical production, claiming that the essential effect of tragedy is available through reading (meaning, probably, expressive recitation) as well as in performance (1450b16–20, 1453b1–11, 1462a11–18), it is frequently supposed that Aristotle had scant knowledge of tragedy in the theater. The inference is mistaken. At *Rhetoric* 1404b21–24, Aristotle praises the brilliant artistry of Theodorus, the most successful tragic actor of the 370s and 360s (cf. *Politics* 1336b28); his comparative formulation (Theodorus' voice always "seems to belong to the character speaking," while those of other actors sound artificially "alien" to them) demonstrates that he drew on extensive theatrical experience. Aperçus in the *Poetics* itself reinforce this point: the famous reference to Euripides as "most tragic" of the poets (1453a29–30), for instance, is couched in language that implies direct observation of theater audiences. Aristotle's conception of tragedy was shaped by a combination of watching and reading plays – in what proportion, we will never know. Outside the *Poetics* he quotes or cites tragedy on dozens of occasions: Euripides most of all (reflecting, no doubt, his fourth-century popularity in the theater); Sophocles more than Aeschylus; and plays by over half-a-dozen other tragedians.

If the personal background to Aristotle's treatment of tragedy was broad, the conceptual apparatus he applies to the genre is methodical. His approach to tragedy is not freestanding but embedded in a treatise on poetic art. We accordingly find a dynamic interplay, as in the poetic *agôn* of *Frogs*, between ideas on poetry in general and tragedy in particular. The first five chapters of the treatise erect a framework for both the synchronic and diachronic investigation of poetry: the first (chs. 1–3) in terms of the mimetic (i.e., representational/expressive) configurations of media, objects, and (narrative/dramatic) "modes" available to it; the second (chs. 4–5) in terms of cultural evolution from "primitive" poetic experiments (driven partly by ethical impulses to celebrate or castigate human behavior) to the elaborate generic conventions of epic and drama. Within this framework, tragedy is elucidated through common principles of poetic art: Aristotle notes its use of all the media of poetry (ch. 1), its representation of characters "better than people of the present" (ch. 2), its disputed historical origins (ch. 3), its layered "genetic" relationship to Homeric epic and to dithyramb (chs. 4–5), and its theatrical development over several generations (ch. 4). What emerges from these early pages of the *Poetics* is a conviction that tragedy was anticipated by Homeric epic (an idea we have already met in Plato) but has in turn largely replaced its ancestor as the archetypal poetry of serious or elevated (*spoudaios*) themes – "replaced" it generically, that is, since Aristotle yields to no one in his admiration for the genius of Homer.

Tragedy is for Aristotle, then, a major manifestation of poetic art at the service of a quasi-philosophical human instinct to understand the world (see *Poetics* 1448b4–17). A combination of analytical and historical perspectives enables him to encapsulate tragedy's essence in a working definition: "tragedy is a representation of action that is elevated, complete, and of magnitude, in language embellished by distinct forms in its various parts, employing the mode of enactment rather than narrative, and through pity and fear accomplishing the *katharsis* of such emotions" (1449b24–28). The definition displays a synthesis of formal, linguistic, and psychological factors. Like Plato's *Phaedrus*, it correlates the "internal" requirements of dramatic construction with the emotional effects of plays on audiences. But, unlike Plato, Aristotle shows no inclination to convert tragedy into an existential worldview in its own right.

The *Poetics'* account of tragedy forms an interlocking, hierarchical argument. Aristotle insists that plot-structure is "the first principle (*archê*) and, as it were, soul (*psuchê*) of tragedy" (1450a38–39); everything else is, one way or another, for the sake of plot, which constitutes the formally designed and emotionally efficacious significance of a drama. While accessible to criticism on a technical level (by reference to length, proportion, unity), plot-structure also requires interpretation through the vocabulary of ethics and psychology. Aristotle regards poetic *mimêsis* (representation/expression) as manifesting a human capacity to model and imaginatively enact the possibilities of experience (Halliwell 2002, 151–206). Tragedy is a *mimêsis* "not of individual people but of action(s) and life" (1450a16–17), a selectively enlarged image of coherently conceivable events, revolving around major changes of fortune

(1451a3–15) and raising issues of grave importance for human success or failure, happiness or unhappiness. Although tragedy, like all poetry, depicts "the kinds of things that might occur, according to necessity or probability" (1451a37–38), it is not straightforwardly realistic. Tragic characters, for one thing, should be "better than people of the present": not idealized prototypes of humanity but (mythically) magnified figures whose "great renown and prosperity" (1453a10) makes them especially vulnerable to acute shifts of fortune. Aristotle's comparative reference to "people of the present" echoes passages such as *Iliad* 5.304 and 12.383 where the grandeur of the heroic past is contrasted with the human present. Yet his model of tragedy welds this sense of heroic elevation to a requirement that tragic characters should be sufficiently "like ourselves" (1453a4–6, cf. 1454a24–25), in psychological and ethical make-up, to engage fully our understanding and emotional sympathy: Aristotle's position instructively seeks to hold a delicate balance between ideals akin to the "Aeschylean" and "Euripidean" types of tragedy caricatured in *Frogs*. Moreover, its principles of characterization blend ethical and status-related considerations in a manner influenced by a person like the Oedipus of *Oedipus the King*. Oedipus has achieved outstanding things for his city, saving it from extinction by the Sphinx and becoming a father-figure beloved by his people; yet he is also, like all Greek heroes, an all-too-human character, capable of irrationality, irascibility, and even injustice. Such a figure, on Aristotle's reading, can focus a heroically intensified image of life, while still allowing a vital bond of rapport between audience and character.

Part of the Platonic case against tragedy had been that the genre displays extreme afflictions overcoming supposedly exceptional figures (esp. *Republic* 387d–88c). Such plots imply a pessimistic view of the world: even the best can suffer the worst; goodness and happiness are dislocated from one another. Aristotle actually concedes part of this case: to show the worst happening to the best is, he believes, morally "disgusting" (*Poetics* 1452b34–36). But he aims to protect tragedy from outright pessimism by making its best plots paradigmatic of a pity-and-fear-arousing mutability whose human subjects are something other than victims of arbitrary impingements of fate, misfortune, or divine malice. A nodal point in this theory is the concept of *hamartia*. The ideal tragic protagonist should suffer a shift into great adversity "not through evil and wickedness . . . but through some *hamartia*," indeed "through a great *hamartia*" (*Poetics* 1453a8–16). The causal force of *hamartia* is explicitly set against that of sheer human evil (which is not the same as excluding evil characters from tragedy altogether). The modern critical consensus has moved away from an older view of *hamartia* as an essential "tragic flaw" of character to the judgment that it centers on possibilities of error and ignorance, not least the ignorance of identity exemplified by several of the plays cited in *Poetics* 14. But the compression of Aristotle's wording in *Poetics* 13, together with the range of mistakes and shortcomings he classifies with similar terminology in the *Ethics*, entitles us to treat *hamartia* as less of a rigidly specified template of tragic causation than a loose grouping of suitable plot-types (and appropriate protagonists). Furthermore, *hamartia* contributes to an essentially secularized understanding of tragedy. Though Aristotle leaves room for the occasional involvement of divine characters, his core conception of the genre, in keeping with his own ethical philosophy as a whole, detaches the conditions of human existence, and the ways in which it can go badly wrong, from theological premises.

Whether, in this respect, the *Poetics* successfully answers, or simply sidesteps, Platonic concerns, remains disputable.

The formula of "a great *hamartia*" will encompass various kinds of scenario in which the limitations of human agency – limitations of knowledge or ethical judgment – lead, by compelling dramatic logic ("by probability or necessity"), to pitifully far-reaching consequences. *Hamartia* is the hinge of tragedy's concentrated exposure of human fallibility. This appraisal of tragedy's essence, contrary to what has often been claimed for or against it, is no version of moralism. Aristotle shows no signs of believing that tragedy has any overt lessons to teach, beyond, at any rate, the impossibility that human agency can ever be entirely autonomous. For him, tragedy, like other forms of mimetic art, is no simple "mirror" to life (a metaphor we know he disliked: *Rhetoric* 1406b12–13). It represents "action(s) and life," for sure, but it does so with crafted selectiveness; there can be no easy transference from art back to life. Hence *Poetics* 8's important indication that "real life" mostly lacks the integrally ordered unity of well-made dramatic plots – an indication that leads directly into chapter 9's striking distinction between poetry's hypothetical yet "universal" and history's actual events.

Aristotle is emphatic that the finest kind of tragic action is the so-called "complex" plot, whose definition (ch. 10) is anticipated by his remark that pity and fear are best induced "when things happen contrary to expectation but because of one another" (1452a1–4). Ruptures of dramatic expectation are here paradoxically fused with the intelligibility that an audience can find in the well-constructed tragedy. By following the tightly coiled action of a complex plot, we recognize how and where things go tragically wrong, at the same time as being drawn, through imaginative sympathy (with characters to some degree "like ourselves"), into a profound emotional absorption in the events of the play. To understand how actions and characters fit together is to grasp the "universals" that Aristotle believes poetry (comedy as much as tragedy, we must remember) somehow communicates (1451b5–11). Those universals, however, are not didactic messages but something more like a rich subtext of meaning that underlies the integrated depiction of "action(s) and life." The unified tragedy rewards its audience with an insight that simultaneously flows through the emotions – a point on which Aristotle and Gorgias, it seems, would have agreed (Lada 1996). But such insight discerns connections in the complex web of human agency and fallibility that cannot easily be reduced to self-contained statement.

Where, finally, does this leave *katharsis*, the most vexed of all issues in the *Poetics*? We lack enough evidence to answer this question confidently, but our best hope is to combine *Politics* 8.5, 1341a21–42a15, which applies the term to certain musico-poetic experiences, with the general tenets of Aristotle's moral psychology of the emotions as expounded in the *Ethics* and *Rhetoric*. Until recently, a consensus built on the nineteenth-century work of Jacob Bernays (uncle by marriage of Sigmund Freud) favored a purely "medical" view of *katharsis* as a vent for pathological excesses of pity and fear – a strange notion to incorporate in a definition of tragedy's essence. Now, though, many scholars prefer an interpretation that preserves an ethical dimension for the concept. *Politics* 8, despite some difficulties, establishes that Aristotle regards the arousal of emotion by music (and, equivalently, by poetry) as fundamentally ethical; that is, capable of shaping the character, *êthos*, of its hearers (1340a5–12).

The *Politics* also suggests that (musico-poetic) *katharsis* is available in some degree to *everyone* (1342a5–6) and is an experience associated, though not necessarily equatable, with both pleasure and psychological "alleviation" (1342a14–15; for "alleviation" cf. Timocles fr. 6.14 *PCG*). This points to a close relationship between tragic *katharsis* and the transformation of pity and fear (normally, for Aristotle, "painful" emotions) into essentially pleasurable emotions in the theater (*Poetics* 1453b10–14), a transformation in which a tragic audience's cognitive understanding interacts with its highly charged emotional response. *Katharsis*, on this reading, will denote the overall ethical benefit that accrues from such an intense yet fulfillingly integrated experience. Exempt from the stresses that accompany pity and fear in social life, the audience of tragedy can allow these emotions an uninhibited flow that, contra Plato, is satisfyingly attuned to its contemplation of the rich human significance of a well-plotted play. A *katharsis* of this kind is not reducible to *either* "purgation" *or* "purification." But it would aptly embody Aristotle's alignment with an old Greek tradition (glimpsed earlier in the overlapping testimonies of Gorgias, Plato, and Timocles) of deep sensitivity to the soul-changing powers of poetry and music.

Postclassical Revaluations

After the end of the classical period, the performance of tragic drama continued to take place in numerous parts of the Greek and Greco-Roman worlds for many centuries. Classical tragedies were also widely read, in the course of their education and beyond, by the cultural elite. At the rudimentary level of classification, later reflected in marginal notes (scholia) to texts of the tragedians (Meijering 1987, 209–20), the genre was standardly assumed to focus on the exhibition of great suffering, *pathos*, and to aim above all at the arousal of pity. But beyond that basic generic characterization the Hellenistic and Imperial periods saw a number of important developments in attitudes to tragic drama and/or life. One new factor, though picking up from *Poetics* chapter 9, was a debate about the relationship between tragedy and history. Some Hellenistic historians foregrounded deliberately theatrical, pity-inducing scenes in their writing, a tendency which could be criticized, as at Polybius 2.56, for confusing historiography with tragedy (and thus dubbed "tragic history" by modern scholars). Yet Polybius, a forthright opponent of tragic history, himself believed that historiography could function as an instruction in the human condition, showing its readers how to learn from the misfortunes of others (1.35) – in other words, appropriating for itself one conception of tragedy's own purpose, as Polybius acknowledges by tragic references and vocabulary in this context. These issues have ramifications which cannot be pursued here, but they illustrate how ideas of tragedy continued to find their way into intellectual controversies that reached far beyond the theater itself.

From the full range of postclassical responses to tragedy, I have selected just two, one philosophical and one "literary," for concentrated attention in this final section. I start with Stoic attitudes to tragedy, which grew from an attempt to answer the challenge thrown down to "lovers of poetry" by Plato (*Republic* 608d) to show that poetry "is a source not only of pleasure but also of benefit to communities and to human life." The Stoic answer was unreservedly didactic. It propounded the thesis that poetry could and should vividly epitomize moral paradigms and their consequences. Poetry, on this view, is a type of popular philosophy, a means of bringing home certain truths to the minds of those who might lack the ability to contemplate them in more abstract form (De Lacy 1948). Tragedy is an important test case for this Stoic thesis, since its subject matter highlights the starkest examples of how disastrously the lives of human beings can go wrong. Weaker forms of didacticism had some currency in the classical period itself. Timocles' comic character, we recall, claims that tragedy "benefits" (*ôphelein*) spectators by helping them see certain things about the world and thereby influencing their broader outlook on life. But the Stoics give tragic didacticism a special twist. They do not so much extend earlier thinking about tragedy as stand it on its head. In the process, and under the pressure of their larger enterprise of reforming human emotions (Sorabji 2000), they change the very idea of what constitutes the tragic. We can trace one remarkable case of this in the recorded thoughts of the Stoic ex-slave Epictetus.

"What are tragedies," asks Epictetus bluntly, "other than the sufferings [*pathê*], displayed in verse, of people who have admired external things?" (*Discourses* 1.4.26). We should notice at once that the term *pathê* refers at least as much to the psychological trauma, the anguished "passions," of the characters in question as to their physical adversity. Just before asking his question Epictetus has described the goal of achieving virtuous independence from "externals" (i.e., material circumstances) as the removal of "griefs and lamentations" from one's life (1.4.23). He has contrasted Socrates' tranquility in the face of death with the self-pitying exclamations of tragic figures like Priam and Oedipus, indeed "kings in general" (1.4.24–25). By definition Epictetus cannot be citing Priam and Oedipus solely as great instances of the impingement of misfortune; he must mean them as examples of the *psychic* depths of possible human misery. Such misery is measured by the tragic subject's own tortured reaction to the loss of external prosperity (symbolized by the possession of monarchical power). Tragic "suffering," *pathos*, is truly in the mind, like all Stoic virtue and vice. But this opens up a potentially puzzling space between the subjectivity of the tragic character and the viewpoint of the spectators whose goal is to remove "griefs and lamentations" from their own lives.

The argument presented by Socrates in *Republic* 10 insisted that the tragic spectator "sympathizes" (*sumpaschein*) or "suffers with" the tragic character and is therefore infected emotionally by the latter's values (i.e., attachment to externals, including one's own kith and kin). The Stoic Epictetus seems to imply that the properly attuned spectator of tragedy will observe the character's *pathê* (sufferings) with detachment, recognizing how the latter's unhappiness is really self-inflicted, since the result of false judgments of value. But there is a problem. The genuine Stoic might be capable of watching tragedy in that state of mind, but he or she would have no need to do so; whereas anyone *not* already convinced of the truth of Stoicism might have difficulty achieving such detachment at all. So the status of Epictetus' conception of tragedy seems unclear. If meant normatively, it is far from obvious why tragedy should have any role in the life of the (would-be) Stoic, especially given the danger of the soul's "surrender," in Platonic terms, to the dramatic characters' emotions; if descriptively, it seems simply false – that just isn't the way tragic audiences are known to react. What, we wonder, has happened to pity (and fear), or, more generally, to tragic *psuchagôgia* (imaginative/emotional enthrallment)?

One possibility is that Epictetus means to preserve something like a traditional notion of *psuchagôgia*, but thinks this can ultimately operate in support of Stoic principles. On this view, the arousal of the passions in the theater will (later) assist us in extirpating them from our own lives. This possibility, which was certainly endorsed by another Stoic, Marcus Aurelius (*Meditations* 11.6), is opened up by Epictetus' statement, immediately after his "What are tragedies...?" question, that even being "deceived" (*exapatan*) is a price worth paying in order to learn (*man-thanein*) the irrelevance of externals (1.4.27). Could Epictetus here be echoing the old Gorgianic notion that in tragedy "the one who deceives is more just than the non-deceiver, and the deceived is wiser than the undeceived"? If so, his position would amount to a two-stage response to the Platonic charge of *Republic* 10: first, an admission that even the ethically mature tragic spectator might be drawn into the imaginative world of the play, "deceived" into taking its characters seriously; but, secondly, an unplatonic claim that such a spectator could nonetheless emerge from the experience with a better grasp of true (Stoic) priorities, all the more convinced of the irrelevance of externals for having been vicariously absorbed in the passions of those who erroneously attach great importance to them. We might think of this hypothesis as a sort of ethical aversion therapy.

A consideration which obstructs this reading, however, is that at 1.4.24, just before the reference to tragedy, Epictetus speaks of the need to "learn" (*mantha-nein*) in real life "what death, exile, prison, and hemlock are," in order to emulate the equanimity of Plato's Socrates in the dialogue *Crito*. This characteristically Platonic-Stoic conception of philosophy as a rehearsal for death suggests that the normal hold of bodily suffering over the mind can be actively defeated. On this premise, we would expect the experience of tragedy to furnish opportunities to practice active *resistance*, even imperviousness, to emotions such as pity and fear. With both the alternatives I have set out, Epictetus' view of tragedy would ironically amount to a variant on the (tragic) principle of *pathei mathos*, "learning from suffering." What is at issue here, however, as regards the psychological health of the (would-be) Stoic spectator, is whether tragedy is to function as an enactment of ethical anti-models to be watched with outright revulsion (see Plato, *Republic* 605e5 for this idea in a counterfactual form), or, as for Marcus Aurelius, a medium of emotional exposure which is only a step on the road to knowing what is misplaced about the values of tragic characters. On the first reading, not only does one lose the Gorgianic interpretation of "deception" at 1.4.27; it is also hard to see why one would want to attend the tragic theater, or read tragic texts, at all, given the over-whelming cultural presumption that what is on offer is profoundly emotional in nature. On the second reading, it remains unclear exactly how Stoics are supposed to *survive* and benefit from exposure to pity and fear (or other tragic emotions), rather than being thereby made more susceptible to such emotion in their own lives, as Socrates had maintained at *Republic* 606a–b. The likeliest answer to this last problem – and one which gained adherents among neo-Stoic theorists of tragedy in the Renaissance – would be that the sheer intensity of emotion experienced in the theater leads to subsequent repudiation of the false life-values that generated the unhappiness displayed in tragedy.

Can Epictetus' other references to tragedy help to clarify the puzzle, seemingly posed by 1.4.25–27, of how far the Stoic should temporarily "live through" the miseries of tragic characters, as opposed to observing their calamities with dispassionate detachment? At 1.24.15–18 Epictetus reinforces the point, already made at 1.4.25, that it is "among the rich, kings, and tyrants" that tragedies (in reality as much as on the stage) "have their place," not in the lives of the poor. He cites Oedipus' cry, "O Cithaeron, why did you accept me?" from Sophocles' *Oedipus the King* (1390; a cry that chimes with the paradigmatic pessimism of "better never to have been born") as a microcosm of how blighted a *whole life* can be by a mistaken estimation of external circumstances. Stoics are actually advised to see "tragedy" in the world around them: "when you approach one of those people [i.e., kings, etc.], remember you are approaching a tragic performer [*tragôdos*] – but not the actor, rather Oedipus himself." (See the reference to the tyrant at Plato, *Republic* 577b1 for an antecedent to this motif of tragedy played out within the show of public life.) There is no suggestion here that the Stoic should feel sympathy for such people, merely that he should inspect their predicament and realize afresh the unenviable delusions of their social status.

At 1.28.31–33 Epictetus derives all tragedies from the source of misguidedly following sense-impressions or appearances (*phainomena*) without proper consideration. He cites four tragedies, including Euripides' *Atreus*, Sophocles' *Oedipus the King*, and Euripides' *Hippolytus*, as emblematic of this point; in each case he seems to have in mind the disastrous consequences of a mistaken belief (such as Theseus' certainty of his son's guilt in *Hippolytus*). This way of adducing plays is most compatible, once again, with the idea that the ideal Stoic spectator would observe the errors of tragic agents with enlightened impassivity, not become emotionally engrossed in their stories. At 2.16.31 Epictetus' conception of tragedy reaches an extreme of vehemence which makes it even harder to see how he could find much value in the genre. After mocking the childish dependence of many people on material circumstances, he produces a parodic tragic trimeter on the subject of baths and water-supply, then exclaims: "See how tragedy comes about when chance events befall fools!" If the characters of tragedy are nothing better than "fools" (*môroi*), how can the Stoic spectator sympathize in any way with them? Similarly, the injunction at 4.7.15, "do not turn death into a tragedy" (*mê tragôdei to pragma*), harks back to Platonic gibes at the "so-called seriousness" of tragedy: the implication is that tragic characters make big mistakes about the significance of death (and therefore the value of life). From this perspective, to understand and learn from tragedy will be to grasp the nature of such mistakes, not to be emotionally moved by their perpetrators.

What emerges most clearly from the passages cited above is an idea of tragedy as grounded in far-reaching misjudgments about the nature of ethical value, and therefore as something that happens both inside and outside the theater. Less stable is Epictetus' view of the usefulness of beholding the psychological trauma of tragic agents. At one extreme (tragedy befalls "fools"), he seems to leave little room for anything like a traditional version of tragic emotionalism, but at 1.4.25–27 there is a glimmer of a suggestion that, for some people at least, exposure to the "deception" of tragedy, and therefore perhaps its emotional power, may serve to bring home by counter-example the truth of Stoicism's own worldview. However precariously, Epictetus manages to avoid a wholesale rejection of tragedy. The tone of contempt conveyed by some of his references to it is not contempt for tragic theater or plays *tout court* but for the human errors which, in principle, tragedy can help us to understand and avoid.

It was not only Stoics who could find themselves ambivalently disposed toward the importance of tragedy. The general status of tragedy in the Imperial period was ambiguous. Greek thinkers were influenced by culturally elitist, and in part philosophical, attitudes (anticipated in the classical period: Aristotle, *Poetics* 1461b26–62a11) that regarded the theater with some disdain as a populist institution and sometimes perceived tragedy itself as a hyperbolic, overblown art form (again, an old complaint). On the other hand, tragic texts retained a substantial, even prestigious, role in the literate culture that defined the self-images of Greek intellectuals and writers in this period. The resulting ambivalence can be traced, for example, in the prolific work of Plutarch, who regularly associates tragedy with falsehood and pretence, yet also manifests the influence of tragic story-patterns in his own writing (Mossman 1988). But I have space here to present only one case-study, that of the treatise *On the Sublime* (whose author I shall follow custom in calling Longinus). The rationale of "the sublime" as a literary category is unequivocally positive; it tethers the potential of the human mind and imagination to the greatness of nature and the cosmos. It is therefore unsurprising that Longinus should harbor reservations about tragedy. We know, on the other hand, that some versions of tragedy could be deemed life-affirming, expressive of heroically aspirational ideals, or edifying in other ways. What kind of accommodation did Longinus reach between sublimity and tragedy?

Early in *On the Sublime* (3.1) Longinus uses a quotation of what he takes to be overwrought tragic rhetoric (Aeschylus fr. 281, but author uncertain) to illustrate how easily a writer can slip from true sublimity into mere bombast. In doing so, however, he acknowledges production of "the fearful" (*to phoberon*) and stylistic grandeur as a pair of quintessential tragic features that are, by implication, compatible with the sublime. Yet such features carry, in his eyes, a heightened risk of crossing the dividing line between the acceptably "tragic" (*tragikos*) and an effect of inadvertent self-parody or counterfeit tragedy (*paratragôdos*). This risk exemplifies Longinus' larger concern with the relationship between the authentically sublime and the pseudo-sublime. What is at stake here, as throughout the treatise, is not purely stylistic; it involves a complex interplay between style and substance, between language and a vision of human existence. Tragedy, with its generic tendency toward extremes of experience and a concomitantly expansive style, accordingly becomes an important challenge for Longinus' theory.

The ways in which tragedy threatens to fail the test of sublimity amount to more than bombast. The sublime stems in part from ambitiously soaring thoughts and strongly "inspired" emotion (8.1); but there are also "low" (*tapeinos*, 9.10), that is, unheroic, emotions which block sublimity (Innes 1995): Longinus (8.2), at least indirectly influenced by Stoicism in this respect, denominates some types of "pity, grief, and fear" (*oiktoi, lupai, phoboi*) in this class. Now, if *to phoberon* (3.1) is compatible with sublimity, while various kinds of *phoboi* are not, clearly Longinus assumes a distinction between different emotional effects relating to fear. The legitimately "fearful," 3.1 indicates, requires impressively imposing, forceful (*deinos*) imagination; in such cases *to phoberon* will be (or cause) a kind of awe in the hearer's or reader's mind (cf. 34.4), whereas at 8.2 Longinus appears to deprecate the depiction of unmitigated states of fearfulness and grief. Consistent with this is the fact that at 9.7 he praises the Iliadic description of cosmic upheaval during the battle of the gods as *phobera* (though also – a separate point – verging on the irreligious). Consistent too, if more subtly, is 22.2, where Longinus admires the Herodotean depiction of a character who voices instinctive fear but does so (we notice) in a speech exhorting his audience with rousing fervor to risk everything in defense of their homeland. Both these cases harness "the fearful" to sublime ends.

What, though, of pity? At 11.2 the possibility of successfully creating pitiful effects (*oiktoi*) is expressly dissociated from the sphere of the sublime. It makes sense, then, that this should be part of the repertoire of Hyperides (34.2), an author Longinus thinks multi-talented but lacking in grandeur. Also revealing is that lamentations and expressions of (self-)pity (*oiktoi* again) are picked out as characteristic of the "ebbing" genius of Homer in the *Odyssey* (9.12), in contrast to the supposedly more dramatic heroism of the *Iliad*. It is not that Longinus has a poor opinion of the *Odyssey*; he has shrewdly registered the work's penchant for scenes where characters' recollections reduce them (and others) to tears. But he finds it a less sublime epic than the *Iliad* because he takes the latter's heroes (typified by the Ajax of book 17 who cries to Zeus, "Kill us if you want, but do so in the daylight, not in darkness") to be energized by bold aspirations that transcend an attachment to mere survival. The implications of this contrast for Longinus' estimation of tragedy are corroborated at 15.5, where he compares the "heroically" daring imagination of Aeschylus to the warriors of *Seven against Thebes*, warriors whose lack of (self-)pity (*oiktos*) Longinus specifically recalls. True heroism, whether that of the fighting warrior or of the heroic writer himself (who faces his own "dangers," 15.4–5, and must be fearless, 14.3), strives courageously into zones which lie beyond pity (as well as beyond the kind of fear that merely incapacitates). Longinus occupies a critical position which commits him to rejecting tragedy qua pessimistic, life-denying genre, and (re)conceiving it as a vehicle for the expression of soaringly heroic ambitions. The sublime – which is a creatively *joyous* state of mind (7.2), capable of embracing a vision of the entire cosmos (ch. 35) – demands this of him.

On the Sublime does not follow through this logic by formulating an explicit theory of tragedy. But it unmistakably associates the traditionally canonical tragic emotion of pity with emotional states below that of the sublime, while concomitantly distinguishing the awesome "fearfulness" attaching to (some dimensions of) the sublime from the "low" emotion of ordinary, inhibiting fear. This leaves Longinus free to find sublimity selectively in individual passages of tragedy (though he can also admire a whole play: see 33.5 on *Oedipus the King*). Chapter 15, in particular, praises all three of the major fifth-century tragedians for their sublime powers of vivid visualization (*phantasia*). Most interesting here is the praise of Euripides, a poet Longinus takes not to be naturally sublime, for "forcing" his imagination to depict emotions such as madness and love with an intensity that transports the hearer into each character's state of mind. Although the characters in question may be tragically doomed, Longinus' critical framework redeems them for sublimity by identifying an exhilarating, mind-transforming experience (a form of *ekplêxis*, "amazement," 15.2) in our exposure to their passionate consciousness.

One further Euripidean example, if carefully interpreted, confirms this complex stance. At 40.3 Longinus praises a single line of *Heracles* (1245: "I am fully loaded with sufferings – no room for more") for its phrasing of ordinary words into a magnificent whole. On one level the point looks like a formally rhetorical comment on word arrangement; but there is more to it. If we ask how Longinus would square his admiration of the passage with his earlier disapproval of (tragic) pity, we might notice that Euripides' Heracles thinks of himself as somehow *beyond pity* (1237), as well as beyond the limits of suffering, and that he exhibits a scornful defiance toward the gods that makes him not unlike the Iliadic Ajax, whose appeal to Longinus' sensibility has already been mentioned. If Longinus can discover sublimity in a scene that might strike other eyes as a paradigm of the tragically (even nihilistically) pitiful, this is because he discerns an enduring assertion of Heracles' own will in the face of "the worst" that the gods and the world can throw at him. Euripides' Heracles, on this (partial) reading, transcends pity and leaves a sense of greatness that befits the sublime's perspective on eternity (35.2). True tragedy, for Longinus, escapes any pessimism over the loss of material fortune (which in quasi-Stoic fashion he glosses as "that which is externally trumped up à la tragedy," *to exóthen prostragódoumenon*), including the loss of life itself. Revaluated in the light of the sublime, tragedy becomes a statement of a force that can rise heroically above such loss to affirm an inner human nobility – even, symbolically at least, a kind of immortality.

Longinus corroborates one of the principal claims of this chapter, that ancient responses to tragedy were not just codifications of a highly elaborate art form (interested though Greek critics often were in the genre's general poetic and drama-turgical components) but entailed attempts to locate meaning and value in, or beyond, existence itself. Ideas of tragedy are built around the relationship, and the intersection, of drama and life. That helps to explain why the last notable ancient response to tragedy, though one which lies outside the scope of my treatment, was that of Christianity, which reacted to, and against, tragedy as a central phenomenon of the whole mentality of paganism. By late antiquity ideas of tragedy in the Greco-Roman world, both pagan and Christian, formed an arena of diverse possibilities whose legacy was to be reworked in the Middle Ages (Kelly 1993) and, subsequently, in both the dramatic practice and the critical doctrines of the Renaissance, Neoclas-sicism, Romanticism, and modern literary theory. The history of ancient responses to tragedy – a history that has never been fully written – is of importance in its own right but also for its long-lasting repercussions within the cultural categories of Western thought.

FURTHER READING

On classical Athenian responses to tragedy, Stanford 1983 correlates the emotionalism of audiences with the nature of the plays (but see Konstan 1999 for more nuanced consider-ations); Heath 1987b, 5–89, maintains that the pleasure of emotions carried greater weight than intellectual or moral benefits; Lada 1996 (citing earlier articles) argues that Athenians regarded emotion and understanding as complementary in the experience of tragedy. Gor-gias' ideas are explored by Segal 1962. On Aristophanes' *Frogs* see Herington 1985, 105–11, and Holzhausen 2000, 33–52. For Plato and tragedy see Halliwell 1996 (revised: Halliwell 2002, 98–117), with Dalfen 1972 on Plato's vocabulary of "the tragic," and Nussbaum 1986, 122–35, on the anti-tragic cast of Plato's own writing. Aristotle's model of tragedy is analyzed in Halliwell 1986, 168–237, and Halliwell 2002, 177–233. On Hellenistic "tragic history" see Fornara 1983, 124–34; on Plutarch, Mossman 1988 and Duff 1999, 41–42, 123–26. De Lacy 1948 surveys Stoic attitudes to poetry; Nussbaum 1993, 97–145, presents a more probing argument; on Epictetus, consult the commentary in Dobbin 1998. Longinus' view of "low" emotions is discussed by Innes 1995. Most 2000b, 15–35, relates ancient to modern theories of tragedy (with some over-simplifications); Judet de La Combe 2000 ponders how philosophical concepts of the tragic impinge on criticism of Greek tragedy.

CHAPTER TWENTY-SIX

Polis and Empire: Greek Tragedy in Rome

Vassiliki Panoussi

Greek tragedy had a profound influence on Roman theater and on Roman literature in its entirety. Establishing the history of Greek tragedy's early reception in Rome is a daunting task, however, given that no tragedy written or performed in Rome before the time of Seneca has come down to us. Livy (7.2) tells us that Livius Andronicus presented the first drama in Rome in 240 BCE, yet we are not certain of the process that led to the performance of this first tragedy. To be sure, contact with Greece was a crucial factor: the expansion associated with the Punic Wars brought commerce and arts from the Greek world to Rome and exposed the Romans to the more sophisticated art form of theater (Beacham 1992, 15). Roman playwrights based their dramas on the famed Greek plays of the classical period, but the impact of Hellenistic theater (especially of that of southern Italy) on the Roman stage was just as crucial. Here too our ability to draw conclusions regarding the relationship of Hellenistic and Roman drama is impaired by the fragmentary nature of our evidence for Hellenistic tragedy.[1] As a result, we need to develop alternative strategies in order to assess the dynamics of Greek tragedy's reception in Rome.

In the last two decades scholars have illuminated the important role of religion and politics for an understanding of Greek tragedy. Religion, and ritual in particular, is key for an appreciation of the tragic context and content. I concur with scholars such as Richard Seaford who maintain that drama, as an institution sponsored by political authorities, inevitably served political ends: it helped cement a sense of civic identity and belonging in the Athenian consciousness (Seaford 1994; for the controversy on this issue see Croally, chapter 4 in this volume). In what follows, I argue that religion and politics, identity and ideology, are critical for an understanding of Roman tragedy as well. I go on to suggest that themes, motifs, and techniques used in Greek and Roman tragedy for the exploration of such issues are also manipulated by authors of other genres in Roman literature, who thus find a fresh avenue for exploring the political and social crises of their times. Finally, I consider the continuity of Seneca's *Trojan Women* with both its tragic Greek predecessors and the Roman literary tradition.

In Rome as well as in Greece, theatrical performances occur within the context of religious festivals. Though the particular contours of the relationship between Roman religion and theater during the earlier years of the Roman republic cannot be accurately reconstructed, religious festivals and holidays set the stage for Roman drama (Conte 1994, 30). Livius' first tragedy was performed at the Ludi Romani in honor of Jupiter Optimus Maximus. Furthermore, ritual, by its formulaic nature, its repetition of gestures, and its rich symbolism, is a type of proto-theater (Beacham 1992, 2). Scholars have not identified any direct relationship between Roman religious rituals and specific plays (Beacham 1992, 21); nevertheless, the deeply theatrical nature of ritual provides a connecting thread. A revealing example of the close relationship between ritual and theatrical performance in Rome can be seen in the practice of "instauration": if the performance was interrupted, or if there was an omission or other mistake, it had to be repeated from the beginning in the manner of religious ceremonies (Beacham 1992, 21). As is the case in Greece, Roman drama finds in the appropriation of ritual motifs a fruitful way to encode rich symbolic meaning.[2] One can therefore argue for the existence of a general framework, a certain symbolic vocabulary accessible to all that the theater audience would instinctively recognize and interpret.

The second important link between Athenian tragedy of the fifth century BCE and the Roman stage is found in their connection with political authority. The Athenian model, with its institutionalized citizen participation, does not recur in ancient Rome; but in organizing theatrical performances (as well as games and other spectacles), Rome's aristocratic elite found a powerful way to win the favor of the public at large. It is no coincidence that Roman drama is born at the end of the Punic wars, at a time when the plebs becomes politically important. Scholars of Roman theater believe that politicians exercised pressure on the playwrights but deny that the authorities sponsoring the plays considered them as a means for direct political debate. The audience, on the other hand, looked forward to these events for their entertainment value (Beacham 1992, 16–17; Goldberg 1996, 269–70). Yet even if the aim of the authorities was to provide escapist fare for the masses, it does not necessarily follow that the playwrights shared the same goals or that the audience would be incapable of relating what went on on stage to contemporary reality. Critics have shown that the so-called escapist literature of the Hellenistic period in fact relates to important sociopolitical issues (see, for instance, Hunter 1993, 152–69). Similarly, it has been shown that Roman comedy reflects as well as manipulates concerns and anxieties vis-à-vis social hierarchies and personal identity (McCarthy 2000). No literary genre stands apart from the reality that generated it; one can therefore safely extend this argument to encompass Roman tragedy as well. Varius Rufus' *Thyestes*, a play staged at the games celebrating the victory at Actium in 29 BCE, may be a case in point. The legendary events depicted in the play may have also served as a commentary on Rome's recent civil wars (Hardie 1997, 319).

Even if a religious and political approach is helpful for an appreciation of the relationship between Greek and Roman tragedy, the paucity of evidence for early Roman tragedy remains a stumbling block. As an alternative strategy, we may turn to other literary genres, especially epic. Although Roman drama flourished in the early years of the republic, at the time of the late republic there was a decline in the production of new plays (Goldberg 1996, 270). We still hear of prominent figures composing tragedies, such as Julius Caesar, Asinius Pollio, Varius Rufus, Ovid, even Octavian. These plays were not produced but probably circulated among a small number of elite friends (Goldberg 1996, 271–72). Goldberg (1996, 273) posits the existence of "literary drama" in the late republic and early principate, a type of theater heavily influenced by rhetoric and declamation, which survives in Seneca's plays. Stage drama appears to have been replaced by literary drama. But such an exchange may also imply the opposite phenomenon: the appropriation of specifically tragic elements by other literary genres, as has long been noted, for instance, in the case of Vergil's *Aeneid* (Hardie 1997).

Rome's sociopolitical reality at the time of the late republic and early principate also contributed to the suitability of this type of appropriation. Both fifth-century Athens and first-century Rome were periods of important sociopolitical change (Hardie 1997, 314–15). Athens was in the process of developing a democratic political system, while republican Rome, devastated by a series of civil wars, gradually turned into a monarchy after Augustus' victory at Actium in 31 BCE. Greek tragedy, as a religious and political institution, served as a vehicle for negotiating and defining civic identity and ideology. In Rome, poets who were closely associated with the new emperor also engaged with issues of identity and ideology generated by the new political order. I argue that authors writing under Augustus inaugurate a practice of appropriating tragedy's religio-political symbolism in order to problematize ideological issues, a practice that continues well into the first century CE.

More specifically, this study identifies a handful of tragic patterns and motifs characteristic of Greek tragedy that are employed by Roman authors. My analysis focuses on two areas where tragedy's import seems paramount: the prominence of female figures as a means through which sociopolitical conflicts are explored, and the use of ritual representations to articulate problems of identity and ideology. There are many instances in Roman literature, as in Greek tragedy, where women play an especially important role in the performance of rituals. Often these rituals go awry, thereby drawing attention to the crisis operative in the plot as well as a more general crisis of Roman religious, social, and political institutions. Thus Greek tragedy's ways of exploring issues of civic identity and ideology are put to work at the dawn of monarchy in Rome. In the interest of space, I limit my inquiry to a handful of examples of tragic themes in Vergil, Ovid, and Seneca as suggestive of an approach that could prove fruitful for our understanding of the reception of Greek tragedy in Rome.

Alcestis and Dido: Substitution and Exchange

No other Roman heroine resembles more clearly a protagonist of tragedy than does the Dido of the *Aeneid*. Since the time of Servius her tragic pedigree has been acknowledged and analyzed. She is at once a Medea, an Ajax, a Phaedra, and a Deianira. Book 4 has been examined in terms of dramatic structure (Quinn 1968) or Aristotelian notions of tragic characterization (Moles 1984); it has also been viewed as a lens for focusing the construction of a Roman civic identity (Panoussi 2002). Here I shall consider Dido's actions and ultimate death in light of Euripides' *Alcestis*, and in particular the notions of substitution and exchange operative therein. After briefly discussing the textual links between Euripides' *Alcestis* and the Dido episode in the *Aeneid*, I argue that the connection of the two tragic heroines legitimizes Dido's claim to be a wife to Aeneas and underscores the fact that her death occurs in exchange, as it were, for Aeneas' (and Rome's) ultimate survival and prosperity. At the same time, Dido's public persona, like that of Alcestis, depicts woman as subject and agent. Both Dido and Alcestis, however, ultimately control only their own death and both make a "return" that silences and objectifies them. Yet despite their objectification they also represent a model of superior moral behavior, whose loss is not without consequences for the patriarchal order that required their death.

The connection of Euripides' Alcestis and Dido is forged in the very last scene of book 4, when Iris, at the request of Juno, descends from Olympus to collect a lock of hair from the dying queen:

> Then almighty Juno, taking pity on her long suffering
> and her difficult death, sent Iris from Olympus
> to release her struggling spirit from the bondage of her limbs;
> for since she was dying neither a death deserved by fate nor natural,
> but wretched before her time and burning by sudden rage,
> Proserpina had not yet cut the blond lock from her
> head and had not sent her to Stygian Orcus.
> Therefore dewy Iris flew down with her saffron wings,
> trailing through the sky a thousand different colors
> against the light of the sun, and stood over her head. "I was bid
> to take to Dis this sacred lock and release you from this body."
> Thus she spoke and cut the lock, and at once all warmth
> melted away and her life vanished in the winds.
> (693–705; except where noted, all translations are my own)

Both Servius (on *Aeneid* 3.46) and Macrobius (*Saturnalia* 5.19.2) note that these lines look back to the words of Thanatos in Euripides' *Alcestis*, who explains that he has come to take Alcestis' life:[3]

> The woman is going down in any case to the house of Hades. I go to her to take the first sacrificial cutting of her hair. For when this sword has consecrated the hair of someone's head, he is the sacred property of the gods below. (73–76; trans. Kovacs 1994–2004)

The Vergilian text appropriates Thanatos' sacrificial vocabulary and thus links the two heroines at the moment of their death. There is a certain antithetical symmetry in their connection: whereas Thanatos appears at the beginning of the Greek play, Iris cuts Dido's lock of hair at the very end of *Aeneid* 4. Both scenes carry connotations of ritual sacrifice (although Dido's death is a suicide that occurs as the climax of a magic ritual). There are also obvious differences: Alcestis is the paradigm of the loyal wife, while Dido's "marriage" to Aeneas is a subject of debate; Alcestis dies to save her husband's life, while Dido repeatedly curses Aeneas and openly wishes for his death (612–20).

Yet on closer scrutiny, the linking of Dido to Alcestis at the end of book 4 may prove not all that coincidental. As we reflect on the portrayal of the Carthaginian queen in light of her shared final moment with Alcestis, other connections become possible, connections that may illuminate Dido as a subject and a model leader. Both women emerge as powerful matriarchs, whose domestic affairs affect the prosperity of their city. As they face their death, they both address their marriage bed and revisit their life-choices. In both cases, their final moments reveal that they view their public and private lives as inextricably linked.

Alcestis' farewell to her marriage bed has parallels to Deianira's similar scene in Sophocles' *Women of Trachis* (900–935). Yet Alcestis differs from Deianira in that, as she bids her children farewell, she moves from the private to the public realm and establishes her authority as a matriarch and head of her household. In a perceptive analysis of the drama, Wohl demonstrates that Alcestis transforms her private bed-chamber into the administrative center of the *oikos* (Wohl 1998, 133–42). After privately bidding farewell to her marital bed (177–86), Alcestis gradually expands the domestic space to encompass first her children (189–91) and then her slaves (192–95). Alcestis' last exchange with Admetus establishes her authority and sub-jectivity, as she is the one to set the terms for the *oikos* even after her death. Admetus' ready acceptance of these terms confirms not only that Alcestis saves the *oikos* but also that the *oikos* that survives is hers rather than Admetus' (Wohl 1998, 137). As a result, her domestic and maternal authority are linked with political authority (Wohl 1998, 142). Her final words suggest her separateness from Admetus and self-determination in her choice to die. Admetus' helplessness in the face of her death implies that she is a model of authority that he cannot hope to match (Wohl 1998, 138–44).

At the moment of Dido's death, we witness the same conflation of domestic and public space:

> there, when she saw the Trojan clothes and the familiar
> bed, a little hesitant by tears and thoughts, she
> fell upon her bed and spoke words most strange:
> "sweet remains, while fate and god allowed,
> accept my soul and release me from these cares.
> I have lived and finished the course that fortune had given me
> and now a great image of what I was will go to the earth below.
> I have founded a glorious city, I have seen my own walls,
> I have taken revenge for my husband from my brother who's my foe." (4.648–56)

The interiority of Dido's chambers does not stop her from making public statements. Her final words are of her accomplishments as a leader and a queen, a founder of a glorious city (655) and an avenger of wrongs (656). Although her suicide takes place inside the palace, its effects quickly ripple through the city, prefiguring its eventual destruction (669–71, 682–83). As in the case of Alcestis, Dido's domestic and political authority are inextricably linked: her failure to preserve her marriage is also a failure to save her city.

The connection of Dido with Alcestis, the loyal wife par excellence, prompts a new look at Dido's marital status. The narrative makes clear that the supernatural wedding scene in the cave leaves each participant with a different perception of their bond. Dido considers herself married, while Aeneas explicitly denies it (338–39). Yet throughout book 4 he has shared her kingdom (259–61) as well as her bed (648). The link between Dido and Alcestis may lead readers to reevaluate the bond between Aeneas and Dido. Since Alcestis is the ideal wife whose defining characteristic is loyalty to her husband, her juxtaposition with Dido also sheds light on the problem of her identity as Aeneas' wife. To be sure, Dido is akin to a number of other tragic wives, such as Medea. Yet in that case, the point is to highlight Dido's persona as a dangerous foreigner. Through her association with Alcestis, Dido is cast as the loving and loyal wife and is thus implicitly justified in her perception of herself as married to Aeneas.

The tragic notions of substitution and exchange that define the plot of *Alcestis* are also operative in the *Aeneid*. Although Dido's death may doom her city, it ensures the birth of another. Through her death she saves, as it were, Aeneas for Rome. The notions of substitution and exchange at work may also help explain the ritual, and more specifically, the sacrificial elements that figure in the description of Dido's death.[4] Iris' cutting of Dido's hair replicates the cutting of the victim's hair before a sacrifice. As noted above, Dido's death also symbolically stands for the death of Carthage, the city that threatened the very existence of Rome. The text renders this symbolic link explicit when at the moment of Dido's death the women's lamentations are compared to those that would accompany the fall of Carthage (669–71). Yet Dido, like Alcestis, resists the objectification that this exchange imposes on her. By taking their fate into their own hands, both women assert their subjectivity. Both highly successful matriarchs, they face their death with determination and bravery, and present a model of leadership for the men. At the same time, their loss, with its devastating consequences for the people around them, serves as an implicit critique of the order that dictated their destruction.

Both Dido and Alcestis return after their death, but they no longer speak. Whereas Alcestis is literally brought back from Hades by Heracles, Dido "returns" in the narrative when Aeneas encounters her in the underworld (*Aeneid* 6.450–76). To be sure, Dido's silence most obviously mirrors Ajax's angry reaction to Odysseus' presence in the underworld in *Odyssey* 11.543–67. The scene ends with Dido turning her back on Aeneas to follow her first husband, Sychaeus, thus implying her complete severance from the Trojan hero. Although she died a leader of a city, she returns as a wife, an *imago* of her former self (654). In Euripides' *Alcestis* too the final exchange replaces Alcestis with herself, but this new woman does not quite possess Alcestis' original subjectivity (Wohl 1998, 174). Both women are thus ultimately objectified, their silence signifying an otherness that both tragedy and the *Aeneid* finally suppress. At the same time, however, this otherness, expressed with stark poignancy, constitutes a form of both resistance and reproach. In the *Aeneid*, as in Euripides, the dead woman returns incorporated within the new order the poem celebrates. Dido's ultimate silence evokes another silent heroine, Lavinia. In a symbolic way, when it comes to model wives, Dido is exchanged with Lavinia, whose silence throughout the epic is emblematic of neutralized otherness.

Ovid's Procne: Bacchic Madness and the Killing of Kin

Descriptions of bacchic frenzy abound in Greek and Roman literature and are usually read as a metaphor for uncontrollable female madness. Recent work on the Dionysian elements of Greek tragedy has demonstrated that descriptions of bacchic madness, whether within the context of an actual bacchic ritual or as metaphor, are closely related to the central issues of Greek drama; many plays focus on the destruction of a household. The annihilation of the *oikos* is usually divinely inspired and eventually brings salvation to the polis in the form of cult (Seaford 1994, 354). Maenadism is closely associated with this theme. While in ritual practice maenadism is a benign communal negation of female adherence to the household, in tragedy it is represented as an uncontrollable force, causing the collapse of the structures that preserve the integrity of the house (Seaford 1994, 352).

Though tragic maenadism is brought about by divinely inspired frenzy, frenzy is never the sole reason behind maenadic behavior. It is occasioned by other features such as resistance to the male (Seaford 1994, 357). Indeed the theme of female transgression into the male sphere is a pivotal component of the thematic structure of most tragedies. Women who participate in this transgression are frequently portrayed as maenads, actual or metaphorical. Thus in tragedy the image of bacchic frenzy followed by the maenadic departure from home is associated with the negation of marriage ritual, the destruction of the household (Seaford 1994, 355–57), and the killing of offspring (Schlesier 1993).

Roman authors, such as Catullus and Vergil, display a sure understanding of these themes, which they manipulate for their own poetic purposes (Panoussi 1998, 2003). In his account of the story of Procne and Philomela, Ovid puts the Dionysian motif to work to illustrate the processes of the destruction of Tereus' family, which begins with the empowerment of his wife Procne and sister-in-law Philomela and culminates in the cooking and eating of his son, Itys.

Side by side with the Dionysian motifs, Ovid manipulates the motifs of perverted rituals of marriage and perverted sacrifice. Greek tragedy regularly depicts marriage rituals gone awry or imagines death rituals as weddings (Rehm 1994). Rites that belong to the realm of the family are used in order to explore issues pertaining to the social and political realms. In Roman thought familial ties are the cornerstone of social structures: the relationships among men of the state are regularly depicted as bonds of kinship, and political alliances are often cemented through marriage. At the same time, the leader of the state and his relationship to his people is typically cast in the image of the *paterfamilias* ruling over his family. Given this ideological framework, it is no surprise that Roman authors choose to appropriate motifs of marriage, maenadism, and sacrifice to explore problems in the Roman sociopolitical realm.

Distorted rites of marriage, maenadism, and sacrifice frame Ovid's story of Philomela, drawing attention to the perversion of family relations in the Thracian royal household. These motifs signify the empowerment of the women in this household and trace their transformation from victims to aggressors. The narrative puts in sharp relief the vicious retribution that abusive power may generate, thus perpetuating a cycle of violence that can destroy the most fundamental social (and by extension political) structures.

Ritual perversion figures prominently in the opening scene of the episode, which features a detailed description of the wedding ceremony of Tereus and Procne:

> Juno was not present in the marriage as *pronuba* [matron of honor],
> nor Hymenaeus, nor the Graces:
> Furies held torches snatched from a funeral,
> the Furies made the bed, and an ominous owl settled in
> their house and sat on the roof of their bedroom. (6.428–32)

The deities that regularly sanction marriage are replaced by Furies holding funeral torches, a disturbing exchange that sets the tone for the narrative that follows. Here Ovid deploys the motif of marriage to death differently from Greek tragedy: death awaits not the bride but the groom. The perverted nature of Procne's and Tereus' marriage ceremony indicates the perversion of the family bonds that it creates: *hac ave coniuncti Procne Tereusque, parentes/hac ave sunt facti* [with such an omen Procne and Tereus were united, they were made parents with such an omen] (433–34). In the narrative, Tereus' lust for his wife's sister Philomela is described primarily as confusing and distorting family ties. This outcome is foreshadowed in the description of Tereus' sexual fantasies (*quotiens amplectitur illa parentem,/esse parens vellet: neque enim minus inpius esset* [whenever she embraces her father, he wants to be her father: nor would he be less sinful]; 481–82) and made explicit by Philomela in her powerful speech to Tereus after her rape: *omnia turbasti: paelex ego facta sororis,/ tu geminus coniunx* [you've confused everything: I have become the rival of my sister, you a husband to two women] (537–38; Pavlock 1991, 38–39; Raval 1998, 118, 120–21). Elements of defiled wedding rites also appear in the scene where Pandion entrusts Philomela to Tereus by joining their right hands (506–7), thus evoking the *dextrarum iunctio* of the marriage ceremony. This gesture, normally expressing *fides* (loyalty) between husband and wife (Pavlock 1991, 35), ironically underscores Tereus' violation of the sanctity of his marriage to Procne and of Philomela's virginal body.

Family relations in the episode also function as a metonymy for political relations. The hand of Procne comes as a reward for Tereus' military aid to Athens (424–25) and fixes the alliance between the two men and their two kingdoms. Pandion thus neutralizes the barbarian threat (*barbara ... agmina*, 424) by aligning himself with the barbarian Tereus. The antagonism between Athens and Thrace, Greek and barbarian, however, surfaces in Tereus' jealousy of Pandion as Philomela embraces him, which may be thus taken to symbolize Tereus' desire to control Athens (Joplin 1984, 32–33). As a result, the perversion in ritual expresses the perversion of family relations, which in turn stand for the perversion of political relations and institutions.

The turning point of the narrative, the empowerment of Procne with its fatal consequences for her household, occurs within the context of bacchic ritual. Procne, under the pretext of participating in an all-female bacchic cult, goes to the cabin where Tereus has hidden her raped sister, breaks open the door, seizes Philomela, dresses her in bacchic clothing, and brings her home (587–600). The narrative lingers at the moment of Procne's assumption of the bacchic ritual attire, indicating that her dress is commensurate with a negation of civilized values. To be sure, the narrator explicitly states that Procne's participation in the rites is a sham and that the motive for her actions is frenzy and anger (595–96; see Joplin 1984, 44; Pavlock 1991, 43). Yet these emotions are precisely the effects of bacchic possession. When Procne dons the bacchic accouterments she is invested with the power that allows her to negate her marriage to Tereus. In dressing Philomela in bacchic dress and hiding her secretly inside her house, Procne transfers her loyalties from her husband and son back to her natal family. Both women move from enclosure to wilderness and back to the domestic interior (Segal 1994, 271). But their return to the house via the forest signals a renewal of their bond that necessitates aggression against Tereus. Since bacchic ritual frenzy is also synonymous with the killing of kin, the sisters' disguise prefigures the subsequent murder of Itys (see also Segal 1994, 270–71). Their collusion is made possible through the performance of a rite that aids and abets the ultimate destruction of Tereus' household. A similar development can be seen in Euripides' *Bacchae*, where the removal of women of the household to Mount Cithaeron under the spell of bacchic frenzy sets in train the killing of Pentheus, the exile of Cadmus and Agave, and the destruction of the Theban royal family. The episode also appropriates elements from other texts: the bacchic ritual conducted by Amata in *Aeneid 7* and the brutality of Hecuba's revenge on Polymestor in Euripides' *Hecuba*. (See further Segal 1994, 270–71, 274, 277.)

The killing of Itys is presented as a result of the confusion of family relations that Tereus' rape brought about. Bacchic activity facilitates Procne's alignment with her sister, and Itys becomes a target because he is perceived as belonging to his father (622). When the boy speaks to his mother, she contrasts his ability to speak with her sister's muteness (631–32). Procne is presented as considering who merits her loyalty: *cui sis nupta, vide, Pandione nata, marito/degeneras! scelus est pietas in coniuge Tereo* [watch that you may not disgrace your husband, daughter of Pandion! But loyalty to my husband Tereus is a crime] (634–35). But when she considers her options, it becomes obvious that she has already made her choice: even as she asserts her status as Tereus' wife, she addresses herself as daughter of Pandion, an identification registered in the text with the juxtaposition of *nata* and *marito*.

Critics have long noted that Agave's killing of Pentheus in Euripides' *Bacchae* bears the marks of a sacrifice (Seaford 1994, 311–18). In Ovid too the description of Itys' killing resembles the preparation for a sacrificial meal (640–46). Philomela's cutting of the boy's neck looks back to the cutting of her tongue by Tereus (553), which is rife with sacrificial symbolism (Pavlock 1991, 39, 44). The boy's killing also implies bacchic *sparagmos* (rending), since his limbs are taken apart and roasted while he is still alive (Pavlock 1991, 44). Procne serves Tereus his son's flesh, an act that constitutes a horrific reversal of the fertility ritual she purports to be offering (*patrii moris sacrum mentita* [lying about a ritual meal for fathers], 648; Pavlock 1991, 44). The killing of Itys in the deep recesses of the house (*penetralia*, 646) indicates the destruction of Tereus' *domus* from within. The innermost corners of Tereus' house, where the atrocious sacrifice of Itys takes place, look back to the darkness of the night that hosted the bacchic rites and Philomela's liberation (588–90, where *nox* is repeated three times), as well as to the "dark earth" on which Philomela's severed tongue quivered like a snake (558; see Richlin 1992, 164).

Woman, darkness, and the earth are all linked with the presence of Furies (Richlin 1992, 164), who thus frame the story with the theme of crime and retribution: Furies presided over the wedding of Tereus and Procne, while Philomela resembles a Fury with her hair spattered with gore as she hurls the bloody head of Itys to Tereus (*sparsis furiali caede capillis*, 657). Procne too was Fury-like when she hastened to her sister's rescue dressed as a bacchant (*terribilis Procne furiisque agitata*, 595; Segal 1994, 275). Furies are evoked by Tereus to avenge the death of his son (661–62). Tereus abuses his power over the women, thus bringing about the killing of his son and the destruction of his household (see also Pavlock 1991, 45). Bacchic ritual lends strength to the wronged woman, who nevertheless exacts her revenge by forfeiting her role as mother and wife. The ritual perversion framing both the beginning of the episode (the wedding of Procne and Tereus) and the end (the sacrifice of Itys) draws attention to the distortion of family relations, while maenadism is the catalyst that propels the women to destructive action.

In Roman literature the problematization of family relations often expresses anxieties about the stability of the state. Tereus, described as *tyrannus* in the narrative (549, 581), abuses his power as *paterfamilias* and defiles family bonds and loyalties. In the *Metamorphoses*, the term *tyrannus* is synonymous with authoritarianism and ruthlessness (Pavlock 1991, 34). Ovid stresses the political nature of Tereus' and Procne's union as an exchange for military assistance in times of war (426–28). The portrayal of Tereus as a tyrant with utter disregard for social institutions also suggests that abusive authority may lead to the breakdown of the very values on which society rests (Pavlock 1991, 45). The empowerment of Procne and Philomela and their ultimate revenge poignantly dramatize the distortion of social (and by extension political) relations as well as the destruction of the social and political fabric.

Seneca's *Trojan Women*: Marriage to Death and the Triumph of the Victim

Seneca's plays offer the unique opportunity to evaluate the import of Greek tragedy on Roman tragedies. Often characterized as adaptations of Greek originals, Seneca's dramas have long been considered inferior to the tragedies of the classical period (see, for instance, Calder 1970). Recent work, however, has shown that Seneca's methods of intertextual appropriation are highly sophisticated and complex, involving a radical reworking of the Greek tragedies, as well as elements from other genres, such as Hellenistic comedy and Augustan epic (Tarrant 1978, 1995). More specifically, Seneca's *Trojan Women* is based on Euripides' *Trojan Women*, *Hecuba*, and *Andromache* (Calder 1970; Fantham 1982, 71–75). But Seneca's play is very different from those of Euripides, due to the mobilization of a number of other intertextual layers: Catullus 64, *Aeneid* 2 and 3, and Ovid's *Metamorphoses* 12 and 13 (see M. Wilson 1983, 28–29; Boyle 1994, 27–28). As a result, in addition to an examination of the specific intertextual contact between Seneca's *Trojan Women* and its Greek models, it may also be fruitful to explore the deployment of patterns and motifs more generally characteristic of tragedy. An examination of the tragic motif of marriage to death offers a lens through which we may reach a new appreciation of the play's relationship with Greek tragedy.

The motif of marriage to death permeates Seneca's *Trojan Women*, since the play's climax is Polyxena's sacrifice at the tomb of the dead Achilles. The perversion of marriage ritual is closely linked to the play's major themes: the disintegration of a civilization, that is, of social, political, familial relations; the recycling of perverted rituals through time; and the continual process of dissolution extending over past, present, and future. The play also explores the callousness of those in power and the arbitrariness of the divine, both of which collude to implement barbarism (Boyle 1994, 21). Finally, it poignantly dramatizes the triumph of the victim and the defeated who find freedom and moral transcendence in death.

Polyxena's "marriage" to the dead Achilles is not simply a private drama of a young virgin who dies prematurely, but the focal point of a play dramatizing the horrors of war and the callousness of those in power. The destruction of Troy is not only denoted by the destruction of its buildings, the killing of its men, and the enslavement of its women; it is also articulated through the disintegration of religious and social institutions. Marriage, a ceremony that is supposed to promote life, is shown to cause destruction and death. The devastation of the city is equated with the institution of marriage. Andromache eloquently ties the death of Polyxena to the destruction of Troy:

> This one evil was lacking to the ruined Trojans,
> to rejoice. Troy's ruins lie blazing all around:
> great time for a wedding! Would anyone dare
> refuse? Would anyone hesitate to enter a marriage
> that Helen proposes? You plague, destruction, pest
> of both peoples, do you see these tombs of leaders
> and the bare bones of so many lying all over the plain
> unburied? These your wedding [*hymen*] has scattered.
> . . .
> Who needs the marriage brands or the ritual torch?
> Who needs fire? Troy provides the light for this strange marriage.
> Celebrate Pyrrhus' wedding, Trojan women,
> Celebrate properly: let blows and groans resound. (888–902)

Andromache uses irony and paradox to underscore the link between marriage and war. Helen's "marriage" to Paris caused the destruction of Troy. The term *hymen*, with its ritual implications, highlights the irony of Polyxena's proposed union with Pyrrhus. At the same time, we see a reversal of the emotions appropriate to rituals, as Polyxena's marriage becomes an occasion for lamentation (901–2).

Such ritual reversals and perversions create paradoxical familial relations: when Helen relates the advantages of a marriage between Polyxena and Pyrrhus, she effects a "drastic reordering of kinship" (M. Wilson 1983, 38) naming Tethys, Thetis, Peleus, and Nereus as Polyxena's family (879–82). As a result, Pyrrhus will be the son-in-law of his victim Priam and of Hecuba, before whose eyes he murdered her husband: *leuiora mala sunt cuncta, quam Priami gener/Hecubaeque Pyrrhus* [all evils are lesser than that Pyrrhus should be the son-in-law to Priam and Hecuba] (934–35).

Paradoxical family relations in times of conflict are common in narratives of war, and civil war in particular, and reflect crisis in social and political institutions. In Seneca's play, the private and familial are linked with the public and the political (Lawall 1982, 252; Bishop 1972, 334, 336). The figure of Hecuba is a case in point: when Hecuba opens the prologue of the play, she speaks as a wife and a queen; the destruction of Troy is also the destruction of her family (M. Wilson 1983, 48). The Trojan War is not simply a metaphor for war in general but for a social and political reality in crisis.

Polyxena's "marriage to death" serves to underscore not only the crisis itself but the lack of any resolution or restoration of the disrupted social, religious, and political order within which the play unfolds. Throughout the play, Polyxena's death evokes two prior examples of perverted sacrifice: that of Iphigenia (248–49) and Priam's murder at his own household altar (44–56, 310–13). These instances have also a rich literary pedigree: the former from Greek tragedy and the latter in a succession of Roman texts, the most celebrated of which is Vergil's *Aeneid* (2.501–2). This linkage of perverted rituals past and present is part of a rhetorical topos that sheds light on Pyrrhus' character (M. Wilson 1983, 37). But it also suggests a process that repeats itself without any hope of end or restoration. The textual repetition and continuation achieved through an amalgam of literary topoi is thus manipulated to demonstrate the permanence of ritual perversion and, by extension, the ceaseless disintegration of civilized life. (On repetition throughout the play see Boyle 1994, 147–48.)

The recycling of perverted rituals is partly due to the callousness of those in power and the cruel arbitrariness of the divine. The *agôn* (debate) between Pyrrhus and Agamemnon is an eloquent demonstration of the cynicism of the powerful victor (M. Wilson 1983, 37–38). Agamemnon, whose past experience and mistakes seem to have made him more compassionate, argues against human sacrifice (330, 334). Pyrrhus, on the other hand, is a cynic who dismisses the moral principles of compassion and mercy (329, 333, 335) and is quick to point out the irony of Agamemnon's defense of Polyxena when he sacrificed his own daughter, Iphigenia (*Iamne immolari uirgines credis nefas?* [So now you consider it a sin to sacrifice virgins?]; 331). While Agamemnon attempts to disassociate himself from his image as a father who slaughtered his daughter by offering the dubious excuse that he was acting for the benefit of his country (332), Pyrrhus dwells on Agamemnon's past behavior in order to legitimize his proposed course of action. As a result, Pyrrhus and Agamemnon emerge as mirror images of each other, two leaders who have put their power to base ends.

Their *agôn* reaches a moral impasse that is resolved by the prophecy of Calchas. The seer represents a higher authority, a *deus ex machina* of sorts, who unlike his Euripidean counterparts lays down a savage law and licenses the powerful Greeks to commit further atrocities:

> Dant fata Danais quo *solent* pretio uiam:
> mactanda uirgo est Thessali busto ducis;
> sed quo iugari Thessalae cultu *solent*
> Ionidesue uel Mycenaeae nurus,
> Pyrrhus parenti coniugem tradat suo:
> sic rite dabitur. . .
>
> Fate grants the Greeks passage at the usual price:
> a virgin must be sacrificed at the tomb of the Thessalian chief;
> but in the usual dress of brides
> from Thessaly, Ionia, or Mycenae,
> let Pyrrhus hand the wife to his father:
> thus she will be wed according to ritual custom . . . (360–65)

The use of *solent* (360) to describe fate's role in times of war and crisis casts both the divine and the Greeks in the role of permanent aggressor. The reiterated *solent* (362), now referring to ritual custom, links the Greeks' renewed aggression with ritual repetition. The violence of the divine causes ritual perversion and perpetuates a cycle of destruction that is not destined to end.

Calchas sides with Pyrrhus in dictating the barbarous sacrifice of Polyxena and Agamemnon does not challenge him. The arbitrary cruelty of the divine matches that of Pyrrhus. As a result, ritual acts, usually thought of as ensuring communication and exchange with the divine and providing hope and comfort in an uncertain world, have now lost their meaning. Their distortion reflects not only the disintegration of a society but also the callous nature of its gods.

Polyxena's marriage to death (942–44) thus dramatizes both the problematic nature of a society on the verge of a breakdown and an extraordinary individual's response to the ethical challenges placed before her. Polyxena goes to her death with a nobility and courage that contrast sharply with the passivity of those watching her end (M. Wilson 1983, 54–55):

> The bold virgin did not step back.
> Facing the stroke she stands fierce with a grim look.
> Such a brave spirit strikes everyone's heart
> and, a strange portent, Pyrrhus is slow to kill.
> When his hand buried the sword thrust deep,
> a sudden gush of blood streamed from the huge wound
> as she embraced death. Not even in death
> does she lose her courage. To make the earth
> heavy on Achilles, she fell forward with angry force. (1151–59)

Polyxena's self-control at the time of death and her last act of defiance, her angry fall, render her triumphant in this final moment of the play.[5] Just as Hecuba in the opening of the play claimed control of her victimhood when she asserted that the fall of Troy is her responsibility (36–40; see M. Wilson 1983, 49–51), so Polyxena now controls her fate. The moral transcendence gained with death endows the individual with a secure sense of self and contrasts with the perverted nature of the ritual that takes her life. The description of Polyxena's death concludes with an emphasis on ritual correctness (*hic ordo sacri* [this was the rite's sequence]; 1162) paradoxically underscoring the fact that, despite the victor's assertion to the contrary, these rites have been defiled and stripped of their meaning (Boyle 1994, 232).

Resolution or restoration are wholly absent from the play, which ends with the messenger's order to the captive women *repetite…maria* [make for the sea once again] (1178). The idea of repetition points to the Trojan women's previous journeys in other renditions of the story (Boyle 1994, 233), as well as to the repetition of the perverted sacrifices therein. In a world where the powerful are free to do as they please, the victim's brave defiance of death is the only stance that offers stable moral ground.

Since Troy is a prototype for Rome, the resonances of the play for the Rome of the time of Nero are plain to see. As was the case in Vergil and Ovid, the victims of authority are women, who nevertheless find ways to resist or transcend the constraints imposed on them. Even in their final defeat, they exemplify an alternative attitude, which, ultimately futile though it may be, points to the flaws of the order that demands their demise.

The examples offered above may serve only as a point of departure for exploring the impact of Greek tragedy in Rome. We can find other instances where women and ritual acts serve as a site onto which ideological issues are mapped out in the *Aeneid* (Helen and Amata conduct bacchic orgies), the *Metamorphoses* (the story of Polyxena or of Orpheus and Eurydice), and other Senecan plays (*Medea, Phaedra*). Ritual representations are regularly employed by other Roman poets for a variety of poetic purposes. Lucan uses the vocabulary of sacrifice to mark the destruction of civil war, and Statius at the end of the *Thebaid* blends the women's lamentations with his own poetic voice (Fantham 1999, 231). Epic, with its large scope, offered Roman authors fertile ground for the use of these tragic elements. Yet similar practices can be identified in other genres, such as elegy and the novel. When applied to Roman texts, the insights of recent criticism on Greek tragedy prove that the Romans found creative ways to incorporate a wealth of tragic material in their works in order to express the problems, anxieties, and ambiguities of their own times.

NOTES

I would like to express my warm thanks to the editor for inviting me to be a part of this volume and for her perceptive suggestions. This essay is dedicated to the memory of my dear friend and colleague Shilpa Raval.

1   The importance of Etruscan influence should also be noted. See Beacham 1992, 10–13.
2   Even in some of the fragments of Roman drama we can see the workings of this process, though we may be limited in our ability to interpret it: for instance, the description of Priam's death at the altar in Ennius' *Andromacha* (*TRF* 86–88), or the simile comparing Hesione to a bacchant conducting an orgy in Pacuvius' *Teucer* (*TRF* 422–23).
3   Austin 1955, 200: "In a sacrifice the hair of a victim was first removed and offered as a first-fruit; and when men die at the appointed time, Proserpina herself cuts off a lock of hair as a like first-fruit.... [B]ut she could not do this for the untimely dead, and so Iris is sent to do it, out of special compassion for Dido."
4   Hardie 1993, 32: "Sacrifice operates through substitution and exchange; the victim is offered in exchange for benefits or in payment of a negative balance incurred through earlier crimes. The victim itself has a symbolic value, standing in as a surrogate for those who offer it." Alcestis' death in Euripides' *Alcestis* is also brimming with sacrificial symbolism and vocabulary (Gregory 1979; Rabinowitz 1993, 67–99).
5   *Trojan Women* 1154, Pyrrhus' hesitation before he goes on to kill Polyxena, looks back to Euripides' *Hecuba* 566. But Euripides describes Polyxena facing her death in erotic terms from the perspective of the male gaze: see Segal 1990, 111–13. For a summary of the various readings of the passage, see Gregory 1999, 112–13. In Seneca, Pyrrhus' hesitation is due to a consciousness of Polyxena's moral superiority.

FURTHER READING

For a good introduction on the Roman stage, Roman tragedy, and their Greek models, see Conte 1994, 29–38. Beacham 1992 is an excellent guide to Roman theater. Goldberg 1996 and Tarrant 1995 are particularly helpful for an understanding of late republican and Augustan tragedy, respectively. Hardie 1997 offers an illuminating discussion on Vergil and Greek tragedy, with useful bibliography. For a different example of Ovid's use of Greek tragedy, see Gildenhard and Zissos 2000. On the appropriation of Greek tragedies in Seneca's other plays, see Segal 1986, 202–14, and Schiesaro 2003, 221–51. Herington 1966 remains an excellent introduction to Senecan drama. For those with an interest in Seneca's *Troades* (*Trojan Women*), there are now three commentaries available: Fantham 1982, Boyle 1994, and Keulen 2001. On the uses of ritual in Roman literature, see Feeney 1998.

CHAPTER TWENTY-SEVEN

Italian Reception of Greek Tragedy

Salvatore Di Maria

In the Middle Ages and early Renaissance, Italian theater consisted mainly of farcical representations and religious dramatizations of Bible stories and lives of saints. In the fifteenth century Italian humanists launched the Latin comedy on the example of Plautus and Terence, and a few wrote modest tragedies in Latin following Seneca's model. Though comedy flourished by adapting and imitating the Roman playwrights, tragedy received its impetus from the discovery of the great tragedians of ancient Greece, Aeschylus, Sophocles, and Euripides. In a brief sketch of tragedy's long journey appended to his *Ifigenia* (1560), the prolific playwright Lodovico Dolce writes that Lady Tragedy, after her glorious days in Greece, refused to live in Rome and moved to Florence where she was received with great enthusiasm and honored by accomplished dramatists such as Trissino, Alamanni, Rucellai, Aretino, Giraldi, Speroni, and, of course, himself.

The noble genre, as tragedy was called, made its way into modern civilization between the end of the fifteenth and the beginning of the sixteenth centuries, mainly through the efforts of dedicated Italian scholars. Italian fascination with the classics was already running high in the quattrocento, when manuscript hunters were scouring libraries throughout Europe looking for ancient texts. Greek texts were very difficult to find, given almost two millennia of neglect and obscurity, and difficult also to have translated, as there were very few Greek scholars living in Italy at the time. But the challenge had its rewards, and humanists ventured throughout Greece and its islands in search of ancient texts. The Sicilian Giovanni Aurispa was in Greece in 1413 and again in 1421, purchasing manuscripts of Sophocles and Euripides and other ancient works. When he returned to Italy, he brought with him a library of 238 Greek manuscripts (Garin 1995, 32).

It was not enough merely to own an ancient text. Scholars were eager to learn and discuss its contents, especially in cases where the works were known only through short selections or anecdotes. Theoretical tracts, such as Aristotle's *Poetics*, were generally translated and circulated within the academic community. Works aimed at a wider audience, such as tragedies, tended to be discussed or read aloud in courtly settings. At first, tragedies were appreciated mainly as literary texts. As men of letters learned about the formal aspects of the genre, they discovered that the notion of tragedy handed down to them through the Middle Ages was not consistent with Aristotle's definition or with the practice of Aeschylus, Sophocles, Euripides, and the Roman Seneca.

In the Middle Ages, scholars had known of Greek and Roman tragedy mostly through excerpts and vague references. They thought of tragedy as a poem dealing with bloody deeds, often instigated by women, such as Helen of Troy or Cleopatra. Early in the fourth century, Donatus conceived of tragedy as a literary composition dealing with noble characters and great horrors, with a sorrowful conclusion. In the sixth century Isidore of Seville considered it a mournful poem dealing with the bloody crimes of wicked rulers (Kelly 1993, 31, 76–77 passim). In the thirteenth century Dante, expanding this view to include Lucan's understanding of the genre as involving "mastery of grand style," concluded that tragedy consisted of a serious subject treated in sublime style and having a horrible conclusion. He expressed this view of tragedy in the *Divine Comedy*, where Vergil refers to his *Aeneid* as "my high tragedy [written] in lofty verses" (*Inferno* 20.113; cf. 26.82).[1] Significantly, in this evolving notion of the genre there was no mention of tragedy as a theatrical representation other than incidental references to its being recited or mimed in public.

It was not long before Italian dramatists tried their hands at composing their own tragedies. At the outset these tragedies were intended for a reading audience and were viewed primarily as occasions for verbal rhetoric. In 1524, Alessandro Pazzi de' Medici was still referring to his tragedies as poems to be *lecte et recitate* (read and recited; Pazzi 1524, 141). Trissino's *Sofonisba* (1515) was reprinted six times and translated into French before it was performed for the first time in 1562; and Rucellai's *Rosmunda* (around 1515), though reprinted at least five times in the course of the century, was never performed. Yet the growing interest in tragedy, even as mere reading text, not only fueled the ongoing search for Greek tragedies, but also led to a flurry of translations and reworkings appropriately called *volgarizzamenti*. Renaissance playwrights were inspired to draw on the values and aesthetic principles of the past to give dramatic expression to their own culture, thus revitalizing classical tragedy.

The process was facilitated by the diffusion of Aristotle's *Poetics*, which, together with Horace's *Ars poetica*, provided guidance and formal authority. The notion of the three unities, in particular, imposed coherence on the newly discovered genre. Differences of opinion about various elements of tragedy led to lively debates ranging from whether it was better to follow the example of the Greeks or the Romans to whether plots should be based on historical or fictional events. There were also questions about the form: what type of verse was suitable to tragedy, how long should a representation last, how many characters might there be in a scene. The question of how a play should be divided was never resolved; some playwrights followed the Senecan model with its division into acts and scenes, while others, such as Trissino, Rucellai, Pazzi, and Martelli, remained faithful to the episodic Greek tradition and accordingly became known as the Grecians (Herrick 1965, 43–71). With regard to other issues of theatrical poetics, playwrights enjoyed plenty of freedom, since they could appeal to the authority of Horace whenever they departed from Aristotelian precepts, and vice versa.

If the debates failed to reach general consensus on several important issues, they succeeded in generating wide interest in the genre and in promoting the notion that tragedy belonged not in the "closet" as a poem to be read (see Barish 1994), but on the stage. The honor of restoring tragedy to the stage belongs to Giambattista Giraldi Cinthio, perhaps the most important theater theorist and playwright of the sixteenth century. Following the great success of Giraldi's *Orbecche* (1541), stage performances became more and more frequent as artists and patrons sought to quench an increasing thirst for dramatic representations set in ancient times. The first theater, the Teatro Olimpico di Vicenza (plate 27.1), was inaugurated in 1585. But even before that, patrons wishing to exploit the political advantage of being associated with a glorious tradition commissioned plays and sponsored performances that were put on either at court or in private residences before large but select groups of spectators. When Lodovico Dolce's *Marianna* was performed in Ferrara in 1565, the author wrote to a friend that the large audience actually hindered the first performance, and the play was performed more successfully a second time (Dolce 1565, 745). For the 1568 performance of Gabriele Bombace's *Alidoro* in honor of Queen Barbara of Austria, so many nobles traveled to Reggio Emilia that, in order to accommodate the visitors, local gentry were not allowed to attend opening night (Ariani 1977, 985).

Despite this popularity, tragedies were never represented as frequently as comedies, partly because the high style of tragedy and the gravity of its subject matter appealed only to the educated few. A more pragmatic consideration, however, was the prohibitive cost associated with stage productions. Unlike comedy, tragedy required the construction of majestic sets and the use of elaborate costumes for its royal characters and their large retinues. It was not unusual for Renaissance performances to feature casts of more than eighty characters and supernumeraries, all sumptuously dressed with fine cloth embroidered in gold and other precious metals.

Performances of tragedy became the occasion for ostentatious displays of political authority. Spectators came from miles around and the noisy streets were thronged with people and carriages. The ubiquitous presence of armed honor guards in colorful uniforms contributed to the cheerful mood of pomp and pageantry and served as a reminder of the sponsor's power.[2] In most cases, the ruling prince attended the performance in full regalia. Surrounded by nobles and dignitaries ranged according to rank and influence, the prince vied with the performers for the public's attention and approval.

Although the rhetoric of power expressed itself in pageantry and spilled into the auditorium through seating arrangements, the stage spectacle itself remained largely an artistic representation of a fictional world. One must resist the temptation to assume that playwrights, by virtue of their education, were de facto members of the nobility or bourgeoisie and tended, therefore, to promote the preservation of the sociopolitical system in which they had a vested interest. In fact, not all playwrights were nobles: Aretino, for instance, was the son of a shoemaker, Lodovico Dolce made a living as a teacher and a printer, and the self-taught Luigi Groto found sporadic employment as a tutor and as a spokesman for various causes. It is difficult to see what interest these playwrights could have in promoting a system that essentially excluded them. Admittedly, the search for patronage was a driving force behind the artists' work, but it was the urge to surpass their rivals that inspired them to their greatest achievements. They aimed to go beyond the mere imitation of the classics and to

Plate 27.1 Teatro Olimpico, Vicenza. Interior view. Photograph © Alinari/Art Resource, NY.

bring on stage a world that drew meaningful parallels to their own, even as it retained its ancient allure. Not surprisingly, they gave their plays such names as *Antigone*, *Edippo*, *Hecuba*, *Ifigenia*, *Medea*, *Oreste*, *Didone*, *Orazia*, *Sofonisba*, and *Tullia*. Though audiences cherished the prestige of the Greek and Roman traditions, it was the plays' formal and thematic innovations as well as their novel stagecraft that helped to narrow the gap between the fiction of the stage and the real world of the auditorium.

In order to close this gap and make their works appealing, playwrights knew that their theater had to address current sociopolitical issues as well as meet prevailing aesthetic expectations. A political topic of obvious relevance to the times that dominates many a Renaissance tragedy is the notion of kingship that Machiavellian theory had brought to the forefront of political discourse. The ideology informing the role of most stage rulers clearly mirrored the ongoing debate on royal prerogatives and princely virtues. The rulers tended to dismiss their counselors' advice to govern with justice and magnanimity – an attitude that dramatized Machiavelli's rejection of humanist notions of princeship as too idealistic and incompatible with current real-politik. However, the violent deaths of those same rulers pointed to a rejection of Machiavellian amoralism and the emergence of a political philosophy based on the moral and religious values of Counter-Reformation Italy. On the social plane, the plays challenge the traditionally misogynist view of womanhood – an issue with profound cultural implications. The issue is highlighted by the conflicting perspectives that articulate the tragic role of the stage queen or princess. On the one hand, she is characterized as subservient, of limited intellect, and prone to emotionalism. On the other hand, she is portrayed as an intelligent and strong individual demanding the right to live with human dignity. In most dramas, the debate ended with the heroine's tragic demise; however, the composure and resolve with which victims such as Dido and Sofonisba faced death elevated them to the dignity of their male counterparts.

Length, Language, and Politics

Stage representations had to bear a strong resemblance to reality in order to get around the audience's instinctive reluctance to be drawn into the fictional world of the stage and in order to establish theater as a viable cultural force. Invoking the poetics of verisimilitude, dramatists argued against the slavish imitation of long-dead traditions and insisted that plays represent current, living customs. Dolce offered a simple but suggestive insight into this principle of poetics when, in the prologue to his *Medea* (1558), he described the play as a "new tragedy" because it had been "dressed in new clothes." The novelties included language, length, spatial settings, courtly ambiance, religion, dramaturgical techniques, and stagecraft.

Most Renaissance dramas are nearly twice as long as a typical Greek or Roman tragedy. Dolce's *Medea*, for example, has approximately 2,350 lines, more than double the 1,000 lines of its Senecan prototype; Anguillara's *Edippo* (1565) is 3,180 lines long, or twice as long as its source, Sophocles' *Oedipus the King*; and Groto's *Adriana* (1578), perhaps the longest of all Italian Renaissance tragedies, is about 4,420 lines. This unusual length was culturally warranted. Greek tragedy was one of several entertainments offered at the City Dionysia (see Seidensticker, chapter 3 in this volume), but Renaissance dramatic representations were unique sociopolitical events. In some instances, the sponsors demanded that a play be long enough to provide a full day's entertainment. When Duke Ercole d'Este of Ferrara commissioned *Didone* from Giraldi, he requested that it be at least six hours long (Giraldi 1543, 485). The length of the representation included *intermezzi* or self-contained spectacles meant to provide a light distraction from the seriousness of the staged drama. With time allowed for honored guests to arrive and take their seats according to protocol, the whole event could conceivably last into the wee hours of the morning. Filippo Pigafetta, who attended the 1585 performance of Giustiniani's *Edippo*, noted that the representation lasted over twelve hours. Spectators began arriving at four in the afternoon; the performance started at one-thirty and was over at little after five o'clock in the morning (Pigafetta 1585, 55–56). Giacomo Dolfin, another eyewitness, reported that the representation began with the sound of trumpets, the roll of drums, and the rumbling of artillery rounds, and it was so gratifying that it was worth the wait (Dolfin 1585, 34).

Faced with the sponsor's demands, playwrights tended to stretch the length of their texts by elaborating selected scenes, spinning subplots, adding characters with speaking parts, and appending other dramatic features, such as long, argumentative epilogues. Their task was facilitated by the prevailing humanist predilection for rhetoric. Italian tragedy's preference for telling over showing would have found little favor with a popular audience such as that of Renaissance England, but it had a receptive public in the well-educated guests who normally attended the performances.

The emphasis on rhetoric encouraged long-drawn-out elaborations of the original text. Luigi Alamanni's *Antigone* (1533), for example, though a faithful translation of Sophocles' play, is about three hundred lines longer than the original and features innovations that call attention to the translator's culture. This intent is especially evident in Alamanni's treatment of the chorus. In the Greek version, soon after Tiresias predicts ruin for Thebes, the chorus sings that the whole city is in the grip of disease and begs Dionysus to "come with cleansing step over Parnassus' slope" (1140–44). In the Italian translation, this prayer gives way to a secular protest against the capriciousness of powerful and "fallacious" Fortuna, which the chorus characterizes in typically Renaissance terms as *fragil, senza fede/instabil, varia, e leve/lubrica et inconstante* [fragile, untrustworthy, unstable, shifting, and volatile, slippery and inconstant] (p. 197). The protest is rendered in lyrical Petrarchan style, reflecting both the taste of the times and the author's determination to display his poetic virtuosity.

In adaptations, too, lengthy scenes contrast sharply with the relative brevity and simplicity of the original version. The description of the capture scene in Rucellai's *Oreste* (1520–25), for example, is much longer and more elaborate than in its source, Euripides' *Iphigenia among the Taurians*. In the Greek original, a messenger recounts in about eighty lines how Taurian herdsmen captured Orestes and his boyhood friend Pylades (260–339); in the Italian version the same episode is 129 lines long (1.429–558). The expansion details the epic resistance put up by the protagonists whose *gesta* (deeds) are reminiscent of Ariosto's chivalric heroes. The messenger reports that the two friends retreated like lions facing their hunters, and fought with the ferocity of tigers protecting their cubs. He also likens them to stinging hornets fighting against a cloud of bees or an army of ground ants. The narrative abounds in rhetorical devices, especially hyperbole, a figure of speech typical of chivalric literature. Thus, the youths throw the boat on the water as easily as if it were a hive of bees; on Pilade's shield lands a forest of enemy arrows; a thousand lances and swords fall on Oreste; Oreste's breathing becomes so heavy that it turns into black, thick vapor. Unfortunately, this epic scene, while extolling the young men's superhuman strength, is largely inconsequential to the development of the plot, since both men are ultimately overpowered and taken prisoner, just as in Euripides.

Courtly Ambiance

In their attempt to involve the audience in the dramatic action, dramatists tended to place ancient myths in modern settings, often referring to mythological characters as knights and barons and setting the dramatic events in castles or fortresses. The imposing structure dominating the scenic space in Rucellai's *Oreste*, for instance, looks more like a Renaissance fortress than a Greek temple. In the Italian adaptation, Artemis' shrine takes on the appearance of a fortress with high walls, immense turrets, a deep moat, iron doors, and a drawbridge suspended by huge chains (1.93–94, 113–18).

This attempt to transpose myth into a familiar spatial setting is also apparent even when the castle is not part of the visible scene. In Anguillara's *Edippo*, a messenger tells how Polynices sent one of his captains to take over the castle where Oedipus was being held prisoner. He describes the castle as having five heavily defended ramparts, each guarded by valiant knights faithful to the castellan, who refused to surrender the fortress to anyone other than the lawful king of Thebes (4.2, p. 103). The castellan, the fortress, the ramparts, Polynices' intent to force the day (*tentar la Fortuna*) with four hundred men in order to take control of the fortress (*insignorirsi del castello*) convey a strong sense of Renaissance reality. The modernization is especially apparent when one sets the scene against the simplicity of Euripides' *Phoenician Women*, where Oedipus is held "behind the locked doors" of the stage-building (64). For contemporary audiences the realistic description of the castle cut across the barrier of time and myth, enlivening the representation with a sense of cultural immediacy. They could easily place in the context of their own times the castellan's refusal to surrender the stronghold to Polynices' forces, for Renaissance history abounds in episodes of loyal or disloyal castellans. In 1499, for example, Caterina Sforza's faithful castellan Dionigi Naldi refused to surrender the castle, declaring that he was not afraid to die by the enemy's sword (Breisach 1967, 212–18).

The aura of contemporary realism included the presence of barons and knights or *cavalieri*. In Rucellai's *Oreste*, King Toante goes about the city accompanied by his *baroni* (3.5); in Dolce's *Medea*, Creon and Medea refer to Jason as *cavaliere*, and a messenger reports that Jason's royal wedding was attended by the most distinguished *baroni* in Corinth (Act 4). In Anguillara's *Edippo*, *cavalieri* of great virtue are said to be everywhere in the kingdom. The male chorus refers to Creon as a knight of honor, and Oedipus remembers that he once fought and killed four honorable knights (3.2). These knights and men of honor are more than mere mythological figures with modern appellations, for they often exhibit qualities reminiscent of knights from the courtly love tradition. Dolce's Medea speaks of Jason and his deeds as if he were a villainous knight of King Arthur's court when she accuses him of having taken her "virginity and honor" (2, p. 17). After she appeals to his sense of *cortesia*, Jason, who describes himself as a knight of noble lineage, offers her his protection *per bontà, per amor, e per pietade* [out of kindness, love, and compassion] (2, pp. 18–19), qualities reminiscent of the knights that populate the chivalric world of King Arthur and Ariosto's *Orlando Furioso*.

The sense of cultural proximity was perhaps more immediate when barons were actually seen on stage, as in *Oreste*. Though their contribution to the development of the plot is insignificant, their role as courtiers satisfied the requirements of Renaissance courtly realism. In the 1585 performance of Giustiniani's *Edippo*, Oedipus appeared on stage with an escort of twenty-four soldiers, all in exotic Turkish uniforms (Pigafetta 1585, 56), which, incidentally, was equal in number to Duke Ercole's armed guard (Gundersheimer 1973, 184). Angelo Ingegneri, who directed the performance, noted that between actors, chorus, escorts, and other extras, there were 108 participants. They were all so beautifully and expensively dressed, he observed, that after the performance many spectators approached the players to ascertain that the costumes were as sumptuous as they appeared from afar (Ingegneri 1598, 303). Such opulence was in sharp contrast to the simplicity of Sophocles' play, where Oedipus presumably enters alone.

The notion of princely decorum and the ostentation on which it was predicated had the specific, if unspoken, purpose of projecting the ruler's reputation for power. Machiavelli underscored the importance of princely reputation, noting that a ruler's failure or success in preserving his state often depended on how weak or how strong he was perceived to be. It is not at all surprising, then, that honor and reputation often inform the thought and deeds of mythological characters represented on the Renaissance stage. In Anguillara's rendition of the Oedipus myth, for example, the young princes prevent their father from leaving the city because they fear that news of the patricide, the incest, and the eye-gouging would spread from court to court and forever tarnish the reputation of the royal family (*Edippo* 4.1). Renaissance audiences surely understood the importance that the two mythological brothers place on reputation. Undoubtedly, many were reminded of the bloody episode that at the turn of the century had brought shame to the court of Ferrara. Duke Alphonse went out of his way to protect the honor of the Este family, following the gruesome quarrel between his younger brothers Giulio and Ippolito, in which Giulio lost an eye and was severely disfigured. In a note to his sister Isabel, the duke expressed his apprehension about the negative impact on the Este reputation should the truth become known. Such was his anxiety that he asked her to destroy the note and proceeded to mount an all-out diplomatic effort to control the damage. The official version practically exonerated cardinal Ippolito, but the Este were widely censured for their cruelty, just like the two Greek brothers.

Religion

The issue of religion presented Renaissance playwrights with the challenge of drawing a Christian audience into the pagan world of ancient theater. Undoubtedly, audiences would tend to withhold their sympathy from characters who placed their faith in multiple and often petty and promiscuous deities. Even the most sophisticated and tolerant spectators would understandably, and perhaps unwittingly, persist in regarding the stage action as the representation of a distant world bearing little resemblance to their own. Most dramatists opted to endow pagan gods with Christian attributes, thus preserving the ancient atmosphere while dramatizing a notion of deity closer to their own. Mythological characters populating Renaissance tragedies naturally appeal to immortal beings such as Apollo, Artemis, and Zeus; however, these appeals are in a different key from the religious sentiments expressed by the source characters. In Sophocles' *Oedipus the King*, for example, Oedipus does not implore divine help; he simply laments the gods' cruelty and lack of compassion. He blames Apollo for bringing "my evil sufferings to completion" (1330), sees himself as "the most cursed, and furthermore the most hateful of mortals to the gods" (1345–46), and feels "detested by the gods" (1519). This view of an unpropitious and even hostile deity contrasts sharply with the reverential tone in which Anguillara's Edippo mentions the name of God. He is happy and thankful that "by the grace of God" his sons have been model children, and exhorts them to harbor in their hearts "the fear of God," to follow the example of their "saintly" mother, and to perform virtuous deeds that are "pleasing to God" (1.2). And finally, with exquisite dramatic irony, he prays: "May God send His ire, His vengeance/ against those who with their own flesh and blood/seek to satisfy their incestuous lust" (1.2, p. 19).

Lest these pious allusions be seen as isolated instances peculiar to individual characters, let us consider the religious beliefs professed by various choruses, keeping in mind that the chorus tends to reflect the concerns and the ethos of the stage audience and often the author's point of view. In Anguillara's *Edippo*, both male and female choruses articulate through their prayers a notion of the divine that is fundamentally Christian. They invoke the "Holy Spirits" in Heaven, appeal to the "Father of Heaven...God Omnipotent" to manifest his "Holy Will" (2.3), and believe that "only those who rely on God" may count on a propitious outcome (3.5). On the eve of the battle between Eteocles and Polynices, the people of Thebes beg God to intercede, and vow to fast until sundown. At the same time, men and women from various choruses plead with the King of Heaven on their knees and kiss the ground as a sign of humility and helplessness (4.3). Expressions of religious ardor, such as fasting, genuflecting, and kissing the ground, are clear markers of Christian worship.

While such conventions suggest that the deity informing the world of cinquecento tragedy was basically Christian, they should not be seen as evidence that Renaissance dramatists attempted to convert the mythological world to Christianity. They simply sought to "clothe" the old with the new, without ever intending for the modern to blot out the ancient from which they drew both inspiration and prestige. They aimed for a theatrical representation in which the new existed alongside the old, a representation that would speak to their contemporaries with the authority of the ancients. One is not surprised to find Christian and pagan terms used interchangeably, and often in the same sentence. In Anguillara's *Edippo*, where references to *Dio* and *Giove* appear side by side, the chorus refers to the high priests as *i santi servi di Giove* [the holy servants of Jupiter] (4, p. 108). And while Rucellai's Oreste professes beliefs that could easily be considered Christian both in tone and substance, his sister Ifigenia identifies herself as the daughter of a direct descendant of Jupiter, "King of humans and father of the Gods" (*Oreste* 1.261–62), and swears by "that Goddess I so much adore" (2.169).

The two religions never merge into a single notion of the divine and are generally associated with specific dramatic roles. Usually the chorus and helpless victims tend to invoke a deity that is essentially Christian; villains and fearsome tyrants, in contrast, appeal to the more earthly gods of mythology. Thus, in Dolce's *Thieste* (1543), the ferocious Atreus calls on the gods of revenge, while the grieving Thieste pleads with a compassionate deity (*celeste pietate*, p. 28) to end his suffering. Spectators must have instinctively feared and rejected the world of violence that Atreus and his vengeful gods represent. Conversely, they must have sympathized with Thieste, since they believed in the same caring and just deity. They also shared the chorus's belief that God's justice, though late in coming, will not leave unpunished Atreus' unspeakable crime: "The High Maker of the world/just and loving God,/shall never let go/ without just revenge/this evil sin" (5.5). The religious essence of this conviction is particularly relevant when compared with the notion of the divine prevailing in the Senecan source, where the gods have vanished and Thyestes is left to experience his tragedy all alone. His heartrending plea to the gods is more a cry of despair than a true act of faith in divine assistance: "You too, you gods, wherever you have fled, hear what a deed is done!" (*Thyestes* 5.1069–70).

What was the essence of the deity invoked by the Renaissance mythological characters, since the *Dio* or the *Giove* they worship may refer to the Christian God as well as to a pagan deity? In the literary tradition, it was not unusual for Christian authors to invoke the powers of the gods or refer to the Christian Godhead as Jove without ever implying belief in the ancient deities. Petrarchist poetry in particular is awash with references to mythological divinities, such as Apollo, Diana, Juno, Mars, Minerva, and Venus. The practice was so common that some modern scholars have viewed it as yet another pagan element of the age. In reality, the poets invoked the gods not as divine beings but as literary topoi meant to evoke the prestige of the ancients. Suffice it to recall that Dante in the *Divine Comedy*, the most Christian of poems, did not hesitate to invoke the gods of Homer and Vergil or refer to Christ as "Highest Jove" (*Purgatory* 6.118).

Dramaturgical Innovations and Dramatic Space

Though many Renaissance tragedies were rightly labeled "closet dramas" for their excessive reliance on verbal rhetoric, many more were perfectly suited for the stage. By and large, dramatists sought to enliven tragic representations. For example, they reduced lengthy narratives and presented the background to the dramatic action in dialogue form, with one character telling the story and the other interrupting with exclamations and leading questions. They also enlivened the stage by increasing to five or more the number of speaking characters in a scene. This was indeed a novelty, considering that ancient tragedy does not allow more than three characters with speaking roles on the stage at the same time (see Halleran, chapter 11 in this volume). Playwrights also opted for a more visual representation of the action. One such technique was the *hic et nunc* expedient, whereby a character observes and describes, as they happen, dramatic events too gruesome or too cumbersome to show on stage (see Di Maria 1995a). In Giraldi's *Orbecche*, for example, Orbecche kills her father King

Sulmone and hacks his body to pieces just inside the palace doors. The bloody deed is reminiscent of Clytemnestra's murder of Agamemnon in Aeschylus' *Agamemnon*, where the audience hears the cries of the dying king without ever seeing the actual killing. But, whereas in the Greek play there is no contemporaneous eyewitness account of the murder, in *Orbecche* a horrified female semichorus witnesses and describes the slaying while it is happening. The frightful facial expression, the stammering speech, and the shrill tone of voice informing the description raise the spectators' level of anxiety and receptiveness, drawing them ever so close to the unrepresentable misdeed.

Innovations were also changing the physical structure of the stage in response to the rising aesthetic expectations of contemporary audiences. Famous artists and architects, such as Peruzzi, Aristotile da Sangallo, and Vasari, were often called upon to design costumes, build elaborate scenes, and create special stage effects. With regard to the stage set, the Italians did not follow the ancient model, partly because by the time they began to emulate classical theater they had already acquired a new notion of theatrical space. The fifteenth-century architect Leon Battista Alberti, undoubtedly inspired by Vitruvius' *De Re Architectura*, was one of the first authors to suggest that the stage set should include the pictorial representation of residences of private citizens. This inclusion of urban spaces and other novel ideas proposed by other Vitruvian commentators formed the basis of Renaissance stage architecture. Chiefly responsible for propagating the new concept of scenic space was the sixteenth-century author Sebastiano Serlio, who discussed and sketched dramatic scenes for the four theatrical genres: comic, tragic, pastoral, and satyr-play or burlesque. The most important feature of Renaissance theater was its use of perspective, which allowed for the pictorial representation of streets and various types of buildings, depending on the type of scene. The tragic scene consisted of temples, palaces, and stately private residences, adorned with arches, columns, and other architectural decorations. The buildings flanked a wide street that vanished into the city projected on the backdrop (plate 27.2).

The stage set of Aretino's *Orazia* (1546), for instance, consists of the city of Rome depicted on the backdrop and a major street that vanishes into the city's houses and rooftops. At the top of the street (on stage), there is the temple of Minerva on one side and the Oratii's house on the other. The entrances to the two buildings serve as functional exits. It may help to conceive of the scenic space as a magnified section of the city that allows the spectator to zoom in, so to speak, and behold urban spaces characteristic of the whole city. Minerva's temple, then, may be seen as the concrete representation of several other shrines alluded to throughout the play, and the Oratii's residence is a physical representation of all the houses painted on the backcloth. The buildings' appearance, the activities taking place inside, and the constant entering and exiting lend a realistic dimension. Spectators cannot but assume that similar human activities enliven the houses and the temples they see depicted on the set. In their theatrical experience, the rooftops, suggested by the set's pictorial images and mentioned by several characters throughout the play, are more than a mere abstraction. They denote areas where some of the play's events take place and where many characters are said to work and live with their families. The whole city may be seen as an extension of the stage. Indeed, it was increasingly assumed that

Plate 27.2 *Scena tragica*. Sebastiano Serlio. Bibliothèque de l'Arsenal, Paris. Photograph © Giraudon/Art Resource, NY.

dramatic space included any area where events relevant to the plot are perceived as taking place at the time of the action (see Di Maria 1995b).

The Language of Stagecraft: Sounds and Movements

This notion of dramatic space allowed for the virtual representation of visibly inaccessible or unrepresentable events through the *hic et nunc* expedient and, more often, through the use of sensorial signs, such as sounds and lighting. In Aretino's *Orazia*, both the stage and the theater public are startled by the sounds of trumpets and cries of joy coming from afar. In an instinctive attempt to see what is happening, they all turn in the direction of the racket. And though neither the characters on the stage nor the spectators can see what is going on, they can all hear and appreciate the euphoria of the Roman people celebrating Horace's victory over the Curiatius brothers. In this way, noise extends the space of the dramatic action to the streets of Rome, the stage, as it were, of the events signified by the commotion. Thus Rome, visible only in scenic perspective, comes to life as the staging ground of events that converge through street noises on the actual stage, where they are verbally explained and placed in the context of the main action.

The increasing tendency to signify space and events through sensorial signs points to an evolving notion of theater as a mimetic vehicle of reality. This encouraged the introduction and use of mechanical devices meant to *show*, rather than tell, the occurrence of specific sensorial phenomena. Thus, instead of verbally informing the audience of the action's time frame, a luminous contraption representing the sun or the moon moving slowly across the fictional skies of the stage showed the time of day and its passing (Vasari 1568, 442). Prismatic devices, called *periatti*, facilitated the change of scenes by rotating their painted surfaces to form new perspectives. And the rolling of a large stone on the floor above the stage produced the sound of thunder, while flashes of burning powder created the illusion of lightning. Serlio even suggested ways to simulate thunderbolts. He insisted on the use of mechanical devices largely because he believed that sensory effects such as lightning, the sounds of trumpets, human voices, footsteps, and horses' hoofbeats delighted the spectators and excited their fancy (Serlio 1545, 205). Perhaps most amusing was the realistic reproduction of certain natural phenomena, which in the past had usually been suggested through verbal constructs. But, whereas words could only evoke the idea of, say, thunder, the noise simulating its sound appealed to the spectators' senses, intensifying their theatrical experience and drawing them further into the illusion of theater.

The language of loud noises, motions, and movements played a fundamental role in the dramaturgical development of Renaissance theater. To be sure, dramatists did not set out to revolutionize ancient drama, which continued to be a source of authority and imitation. They simply introduced changes that reflected their enlarged concept of theatrical communication. The capture scene in Rucellai's *Oreste*, mentioned earlier, is a good example of how Renaissance playwrights enlivened the representation through the use of sensory signs. In Euripides, the episode is mostly narrated and presented as far removed from the audience both in time and space. A messenger reports that local herdsmen have apprehended two strangers hiding by the rocks on the seashore. The spectators gather that the captives are the two youths who, at the beginning of the play, faced with the difficult task of breaking into the temple, decided to hide on the shore until nightfall and attempt the break-in under the cover of darkness (*Iphigenia among the Taurians* 106–12). In the adaptation, however, the youths are forced to abort their plan and go into hiding because of the sudden sounds of a horn and loud human voices. Pilade succeeds in convincing Oreste to get away from the temple only after pointing out that a noisy crowd is coming toward the temple: "Can you not *see* [*non vedi*] all those people gathering?" he asks rhetorically, "Can you not *hear* [*non senti*] the shrill voices and the sound of the horn?" (1.174–75).

These loud noises tend to free the action from the verbal constraints of the original version and thrust it more toward a theatrical realization. In the Greek source, the young men discuss the danger of scaling the temple's high walls or of forcing the "brazen locks" (99) in plain daylight, and come to the logical conclusion that the best strategy is to hide until dark. The sequence develops entirely on the discursive plane. In Rucellai, by contrast, the youths' decision to withdraw is occasioned not by verbal arguments but by the alarming sound of the horn and the excitement it has generated among the gathering crowd. The commotion (not found in Euripides) indicates clearly that dramatic events relevant to the plot are taking place in areas beyond the scenic space, promoting the illusion that the whole town is a stage and that all its citizens are on it. The noises also foster in the audience the sensation of being close to the developing action, for noises tend to bridge the distance between the "somewhere" of the action and the spectators. This sense of proximity is also achieved through the eyes of Pilade as he notices people gathering in the distance and points them out to Oreste (*vedi...senti*). We would expect the exhortation to rouse Oreste's anxiety as well as the curiosity of the spectators who, like the young protagonists, turn their heads in the direction of the noise. As the spectators cannot see beyond the physical limits of the stage, Pilade's eyes become the visual medium through which they may behold, in the mind's eye of course, the unseen space and the action associated with it. Thus, they watch and wait with anticipation for the crowd to converge in front of the temple, on stage, and shed light on the meaning of the tumult.

Unlike noise, movement often does not create suspense because it is visually perceptible and is generally observed in association with its referent, thus communicating directly and immediately with the audience. But movement too contributes to a lively representation and, in some instances, may even help to shed light on the personality of a character. Consider the flurry in the scene following Artemis' alleged displeasure with the sacrificial victims, Orestes and Pylades. In *Iphigenia among the Taurians*, the rapid stichomythia of Iphigenia's dialogue with King Thoas connotes agitation and urgency. The conversation turns on the need to keep all citizens off the streets, while the young priestess goes to the shore to purify Artemis' statue and her two prisoners (1157–1221). But there is hardly any action on stage; there is only the idea of movement verbally created. In Rucellai, on the other hand, this same scene is characterized by both emotional excitement and hasty physical movement, as suggested in part by the use of *reduplicatio* or repetition. Here is King Toante shouting orders, following Ifigenia's warning to keep everybody inside:

> Andiam via tosto, andiam via tosto, andiamo,
> Andiam via, fuggiam via, entriam là dentro,
> E voi, Olimpia, prendete le chiavi,
> Ch'in la più scura parte io vo' serrarmi.

> Let's go away quickly, let's go away quickly, let's go,
> let's go away, let's flee, let's enter there,
> and you, Olimpia, get the keys,
> for I want to lock myself in the safest corner. (5.145–48)

This speech prompts one to visualize a stage in total disarray, with frightened people running in all directions. Most terrified of all is Toante, who runs around looking for a secure place to hide, and screaming over and over the only command his fear-gripped mind is capable of articulating. This unexpected terror shatters in an instant the carefully fashioned image of Toante as a cruel tyrant and externalizes his true nature: the savage king is actually a wretched coward. This trait is in stark contrast with the kingly demeanor of his Greek counterpart, and accounts for the different conclusions of the two plays. In *Iphigenia among the Taurians*, a wise Thoas follows

Athena's admonition and, swallowing his pride, calls off the pursuit of the fleeing Greeks in the belief that there is nothing admirable in challenging a god (1478–79). Order is thus reestablished in the Taurian kingdom. *Oreste*, instead, ends with Toante frantically cursing the gods and inciting his subjects to pursue the fugitives and avenge their king. The kingdom plunges deeper into chaos, as the cowardly king tries recklessly to reassert his old, tyrannical image.

Although thematic novelty, contemporary sociopolitical issues, formal innovations, and new dramaturgical techniques point to the rise of a typically Italian theater, Renaissance Italy never fully broke away from the great tragedians of ancient Athens and classical Rome. Indeed, without ever losing enthusiasm for the *auctoritas* of the past, cinquecento playwrights made tragedy a mirror of their own culture. On the stage, audiences saw their own customs, recognized their own religious beliefs, experienced their own fears, witnessed debates on social prejudice and political ideology, heard the language of Dante and Petrarch, and marveled at the ingenuity of famed stage "architects." They saw their living world cast in the prestigious and revered traditions of Aeschylus, Sophocles, Euripides, and Seneca. Dramatists were proud to emulate the giants of the Greek and Roman stage, wealthy patrons eagerly sought the honor of sponsorship, and audiences cherished their reputation as people of culture and sophistication.

Because of its deep admiration for the classics, Renaissance Italy tolerated anachronistic situations in an otherwise realistic theater, finding it acceptable that pagan characters should pray to a Christian deity or that mythological kings should dress like Renaissance princes and live in modern castles with their barons and knights. These contradictions notwithstanding, the tragic theater of the Renaissance became an important legacy in Italy and in all of Europe. As Kyd's Hieronimo remarks, the Italian Renaissance example inspired "stately-written tragedies...[for] the Italian tragedians were so sharp of wit" (*The Spanish Tragedy* 4.1.155, 160). The Italians' most important legacy lies in having discovered classical tragedy, given it a modern identity, and guaranteed its survival in Western culture.

NOTES

This chapter is largely based on material from my *The Italian Tragedy in the Renaissance* (2002). Unless otherwise indicated, all translations are my own. Citations from Renaissance plays are by act, scene, and line (e.g., *Orbecche* 5.3.2906), or, if the edition is not divided into scenes, by act and line (e.g., *Marianna* 5.2870), and by the line number only if there are no other divisions (e.g., *Rosmunda* 520). Where the lines are not numbered, I give the page number (e.g., *Didone* 5, p. 125).

1   In explaining the title of his poem to Can Grande della Scala, Dante points out that, contrary to comedy, tragedy at the beginning is admirable and serene; at the end, its conclusion is foul and horrible (*Epistola* 13.29). In *De vulgari eloquentia*, having noted that, contrary to the ordinary style of comedy, tragedy uses the higher style, Dante also observes that the tragic style is clearly to be used whenever both the magnificence of the verses and the lofty excellence of construction and vocabulary accord with the gravity of the subject matter (2.4.7).

2   Filippo Pigafetta, who attended the 1585 representation of Orsato Giustiniani's *Edippo il tiranno* at the Teatro Olimpico in Vicenza, reported that of the three thousand spectators in attendance more than two thousand were from out of town. One did not see in the streets anything but noblemen, noblewomen, carriages, horses, and visitors who had come for the representation. In addition, he continues, soldiers were stationed at every door both for reasons of security and for any other good purpose (Pigafetta 1585, 55–56).

FURTHER READING

For a comprehensive introduction to Italian Renaissance tragedy, including poetics, biographical and bibliographical data, and summaries and analyses of plays, see Herrick 1965. Italian readers interested in data and critical analysis may wish to consult Neri 1904 and Musumarra 1972. For details on the various notions of tragedy in the Middle Ages, see Kelly 1993. For Renaissance theories on theater and stagecraft, see Attolini 1988; on the Renaissance view of tragedy as a "closet" drama, see Barish 1994. On the hunt for ancient manuscripts, their popularity, and their availability, see Pertusi 1966. On the negative reaction to stage extravagance in the Renaissance, especially with regard to the 1585 performance of Giustiniani's *Edippo*, see A. Riccoboni's letter, 39–51, and S. Speroni's "Proposte," 31, both in Gallo 1973. For a close, critical analysis of Giambattista Giraldi Cinthio's tragedies and his critical work on theater, see Horne 1962. On Dolce's adaptations and translations of Greek and Roman tragedies, see Terpening 1997. On Seneca's influence on the development of the Italian Renaissance tragedy, see Charleton 1946. For an overall view of theater poetics in the Italian Renaissance, see Carlson 1993, 37–56. For basic notions of stage setting and representations, see Kernodle 1970.

CHAPTER TWENTY-EIGHT

Nietzsche on Greek Tragedy and the Tragic

Albert Henrichs

Friedrich Wilhelm Nietzsche is far better known as a cultural critic and thinker than as a Hellenist, but no matter which hat he was wearing at any given moment or how deeply he was tormented by ill health, lack of recognition, and his own inner demons, Greece and the Greeks were never far from his mind, and neither was Greek tragedy. Exposed to the plays of the three tragedians at an early age, he thought and wrote about them throughout the lucid phases of his life. In their suffering and destruction rather than their triumphs, the principal characters of Aeschylus and Sophocles appealed to him as paradigms of human existence in the face of extreme adversity. When lecturing to his students ex cathedra he was surprisingly conventional in his quasi-Aristotelian emphasis on plot and character and on the nuts and bolts of the dramatic art. But in his nonacademic essays for the educated public, most prominently in *The Birth of Tragedy Out of the Spirit of Music* (henceforth *BT*), he spoke with a prophetic voice as a *praeceptor Germaniae* (teacher of Germany) to convey his unorthodox and daring vision of the "tragic worldview" and its relevance to contemporary German culture. It is this duplexity in Nietzsche's approach to Greek tragedy, as well as its inherent duplicity, that will be the focus of this chapter.

Between "Philology" and "Philosophy"

A pastor's son, Nietzsche learned Greek and Latin at an early age and was an accomplished classicist long before he became a philosopher (Reibnitz 1992, 9–35). Like his nemesis Ulrich von Wilamowitz-Moellendorff, he was an alumnus of Germany's foremost humanistic boarding school, the Royal State School at Pforte in Saxony, from which he graduated in 1864 with a Latin thesis on Theognis. Greek tragedy was an integral part of the curriculum at Schulpforte, and the twin concepts of "the tragic" and of a tragic or "Dionysian" philosophy of life remained central concerns for Nietzsche long after his career as a classicist had come to an early and unhappy end.

   During his two semesters at Bonn as a student of theology (1864/65), Nietzsche was preoccupied with the study of classical philology and archaeology, apart from his active participation in the Bonn music scene. Preliminary drafts on the poetry of Theognis, on Simonides' Danae poem, and on Longinus' *On the Sublime* survive. In the fall of 1865 he transferred to the University of Leipzig, where he enrolled as a student of philology for four semesters. After a year of military service in the cavalry he returned to Leipzig in search of a dissertation topic. While still a student there, in 1867/68, he published four innovative and meticulously researched articles on the Theognidea, on Simonides' "Lament of Danae," and on the sources of Diogenes Laertius (*KGW* II 1, 1–245; Reibnitz 1992, 15–24, 347). In addition, he worked extensively on Democritus and on Greek tragedy and laid the foundation for his two groundbreaking articles on the treatise titled *About the Lineage of, and Contest between, Homer and Hesiod*, the core of which he traced back to the late fifth-century Sophist Alcidamas (*KGW* II 1, 271–337).

Nietzsche was never to learn that his conclusions about Alcidamas as the ultimate source of the *Contest* were corroborated decades later by the discovery of two new texts on papyrus (Vogt 1962; Lloyd-Jones 1979, 6–7; Reibnitz 1992, 127–28). Nietzsche's studies of the *Contest* reinforced his notion of archaic and classical Greece as an "agonistic culture," a concept shared by his Basel colleague, the eminent cultural historian Jacob Burckhardt. Nietzsche was well aware, of course, that Attic tragedy was an essential part of that culture. After all, the annual dramatic performances in Athens were organized as a competition (*agôn*) among several playwrights under the aegis of Dionysus (see Scullion and Seidensticker, chapters 2 and 3 in this volume), a competitive pattern that is comically dramatized in the *Frogs* of Aristophanes (405 BCE).

In March 1869 the University of Leipzig awarded Nietzsche a doctoral degree solely on the basis of his published work without his having written a dissertation, a procedure that was unusual but not unprecedented (Gutzwiller 1951, 150–51). Six weeks earlier, in a surprise move, the University of Basel, Switzerland, had offered him the position of professor extraordinarius. In his letter of recommendation, his Leipzig teacher Friedrich Ritschl said of Nietzsche's promise as a scholar: "Indeed, he will be able to do anything he wants" (Stroux 1925, 36). Ritschl's judgment turned out to be right, in ways he could have never imagined. By waiving the usual requirements for the doctorate, the Leipzig faculty tried belatedly to normalize the circumstances of Nietzsche's Basel appointment, which had raised many eyebrows in Germany's academic circles and made Nietzsche at the age of twenty-four one of the youngest classics professors on record.

Nietzsche's tenure as a professional classicist at the university level came none too soon. Tormented by chronic self-doubts and deep disenchantment with Germany's classical establishment, he was toying with the idea of abandoning classics to study chemistry as late as January 1869 (Cancik 1995, 20). Nevertheless, in April 1869 the Prussian subject gave up his nationality, moved to Switzerland, and took up residence in Basel as a stateless alien, a status he retained until his death. In May he visited Richard Wagner in Tribschen near Lucern for the first time. His visit marked the beginning of an intellectual friendship that ended acrimoniously in 1878.

Also in May, he gave his inaugural lecture, "Homer and Classical Philology" (*KGW* II 1, 247–69), which revisits the Homeric Question and culminates in the quintessentially Nietzschean paradox that "what used to be philology has become philosophy." Most classicists of Nietzsche's time, including his mentor Ritschl, were adamantly opposed to any contamination of philology, a discipline sworn to rigorous method and objectivity, with philosophical speculation. Not so Nietzsche, whose philosophical calling would ultimately prevail over the philologist in him. Even his views on tragedy are characterized by a distinct philosophical dimension: both the figure of Socrates and the tenets of Arthur Schopenhauer play a pivotal role in *BT*.

In April 1870, one year after his arrival in Basel, Nietzsche was promoted to full professor. But due to health problems, inner turmoil, and a latent disdain for his profession, he never settled fully into a happy and productive academic life as a classicist. In January 1871 he tried to escape from it by applying unsuccessfully for the vacant chair of philosophy at his own university (Stroux 1925, 72–80). He declares in his application that he is better suited for philosophy than philology. Two months later, in a letter to the Hellenist Erwin Rohde, a close friend, he mentions his "exuberant alienation from philology." As he became more disillusioned with the "philistine" nature of the German educational system and with the classical profession that embodied it, he gradually transformed himself into a cultural critic and a philosopher, a process that took ten long years and brought him repeatedly to the brink of physical and mental breakdown (Cancik 1995, 1999). As far as Nietzsche was concerned, the classical philologists entrenched in the German *gymnasiums* and universities of his time were incapable of understanding themselves, let alone the Greeks (*KGW* IV 1, 203; Henrichs 1995, 433–36). As he saw it, philology as an academic discipline was very much part of the problem, one of the principal causes of the cultural malaise, whereas the Greeks were the solution. For Nietzsche, the "physician of culture" (*KGW* III 4, 141; *KGB* II 3, 132 and 136), the ancient Greeks provided the antidote against many of the ailments that beset modern society: "Greek antiquity... offers a way to understand ourselves, to pass judgment on our own time, and thereby to overcome it" (*KGW* IV 1, 173, an aphorism from *We Philologists*).

Plagued by chronic illness, Nietzsche had to cancel his courses in March 1879, one week before the official end of the term. Less than three months later, he took early retirement and left Basel for good, thus effectively ending his academic career. A professor emeritus at the age of thirty-four, he spent the next decade of his life homeless, an itinerant intellectual and solitary philosopher, constantly traveling, writing, and convalescing while in a perennial state of ill health and inner restlessness. His entire philosophical oeuvre, from *Human, All Too Human* (1878/79) to *Twilight of the Idols* and *Ecce Homo* (1889), dates from this period. Recognition, fame, and material wealth all eluded him – his books did not sell until after his death. On 3 January 1889 he collapsed in the streets of Turin, apparently after embracing a horse. He gradually lapsed into irreversible insanity and spent the rest of his life in the care of doctors, nurses, and family members, largely detached from his surroundings and oblivious of his own past. Almost until the end, however, he remembered that he had written "nice books," whose titles he could still recite but which he would now hold upside down, as if to mark the distance that separated him from his former self (Benders and Oettermann 2000, 802–3).

The Three Tragedians

Only the first of Nietzsche's books, *BT*, deals with Greek drama. Its long and complex genesis begins in the years between 1858 and 1864, when he was a schoolboy at Schulpforte (Janz 1981, 1: 65–132). Not only were the seeds of his abiding interest in Greek tragedy planted there, but his teachers also instilled in him a lifelong aversion to Euripides. Invented by Aristophanes, Euripides-bashing had been elevated to an art form by August Wilhelm Schlegel in his 1808 Vienna lectures on dramatic art and literature (Behler 1986), which went through four editions between 1809 and 1846. In Schlegel's words, Euripides "not only destroyed the external order of tragedy, but missed its entire meaning." Nietzsche inherited Schlegel's negative view of Euripides and appropriated it with a vengeance. His debt to Schlegel explains why he privileged Aeschylus and Sophocles over Euripides, whom he ignored in his lectures and seminars and whose plays he did not know at all well (Henrichs 1986). In his autobiographical sketch from 1864 he reminisces about his "first impressions of Sophocles, of Aeschylus, of Plato" (in Janz 1981, 1: 121) – the omission of Euripides is ominous. Ironically, it was Wilamowitz who rehabilitated Euripides in numerous publications between 1875 and 1926 and restored his reputation as a serious and superior playwright (Calder 1986).

The tragedies to which Nietzsche returned most often in the course of his active life are Sophocles' *Oedipus the King*, Aeschylus' *Libation Bearers*, and the Aeschylean *Prometheus*, whose authenticity he took for granted. He lectured on all three plays during his Basel years, but they preoccupied him long before he became a professor there. At fourteen, in his first year at Pforte, he researched the figure of Prometheus (Janz 1981, 1: 87–88). When *BT* was finally published thirteen years later, the Aeschylean Prometheus loomed large in its argument (Reibnitz 1992, 238–52, 273–74). More conspicuously, the title page of the first edition carried a vignette with the classicistic image of a Prometheus unbound. On it the defiant Titan is sitting comfortably on the rock to which he was once chained; the fetters are dangling from his hands, and his right foot is trampling the dead bird of prey that used to feed on his liver (Brandt 1991).

In the spring of 1864, shortly before his graduation from Pforte, Nietzsche wrote an ambitious term paper in Latin, German, and ancient Greek on the first chorus of *Oedipus the King* (*HKGW* 2, 364–99). The tragedians, he argues, were not only poets but also composers who set the music for the dances of the chorus (*HKGW* 2, 376). He owed this point to Rudolf Westphal, then the leading expert on Greek music (Latacz 1994, 38). In a deliberate departure from Aristotle, Nietzsche insists on the pivotal role of choral performance and its emotional effect on the audience (cf. Silk 1998). His paper thus anticipates his future argument in *BT*, which derives tragedy "from the spirit of music." Thanks to his emphasis on tragedy as theater and on its performative function as reflected in the singing and dancing of the chorus, Nietzsche emerges as one of the precursors of dominant trends in the current criticism of tragedy (see Wilson, chapter 12 in this volume).

On the larger question of the meaning of the Oedipus myth and of *Oedipus the King* (Burkert 1991), Nietzsche complains that the criticism of his day is excessively concerned with the guilt of Oedipus. In his eyes, categories such as guilt and punishment do not apply to Oedipus. Oedipus cannot be guilty because he did not commit his crimes intentionally, and he cannot be punished because he is not guilty. Destined to suffer, his suffering serves the divine world order. Like the majority of more recent critics, Nietzsche assumes a close conceptual connection between Sophocles' two Oedipus plays and adopts the Hegelian and Schlegelian view according to which *Oedipus at Colonus* finally furnishes the necessary "conclusion and reconciliation" (*HKGW* 2, 369) that the first Oedipus play fails to provide (Seidensticker 1972; Bernard 2001, 12–17, 58–83). On this reading, the Oedipus figure of the earlier play is revalidated by its sequel, in which culpability is converted into heroic status through human suffering and divine intervention (Reibnitz 1992, 228–32). By rejecting the moral calculus of retributive justice conventionally applied to Oedipus, Nietzsche seeks to liberate him from Christianizing distortions and to restore that hero's Greek identity as he sees it – that is, his suffering and his status as a cult hero. The "most sorrowful figure of the Greek stage, the unfortunate Oedipus" (*BT* 9: 61.24–25),[1] would occupy Nietzsche for years to come. In the first of his 1870 lectures on *Oedipus the King*, which compares ancient and modern definitions of the tragic, he returns to the issue of Oedipus' crime and punishment and reasserts his earlier view:

> The tragic worldview is found only in Sophocles. He saw the undeserved fate as tragic: the enigma of human existence and the truly terrible constituted his tragic muse. *Katharsis* occurs as a necessary feeling of consonance in a world of dissonance. The suffering, the origin of tragedy, achieves a transfiguration in his work: it is understood as something that sanctifies. The mystical, beneficial translation of Oedipus at Colonus is a case in point. (*KGW* II 3, 40, cf. 415; echoed at *KGW* III 5/1, 167 and *BT* 9: 62.9)

At first glance, Nietzsche's insistence on the "sanctity" of the suffering hero appears to be supported by a passage in *Oedipus at Colonus*: "I come as someone sacred and reverent [*hieros eusebés te*], a benefit to the citizens here" (287–88). But the similarity is superficial. Sophocles does not present Oedipus' heroization as a reward for his suffering. Ironically, despite Nietzsche's deep-rooted disdain for all things Christian, the implied causal connection between suffering and sanctity reflects Christian rather than Greek sentiment. Two years later, in *BT*, Nietzsche revisits Oedipus, "the noble human being [who] does not sin" (9: 61.29–30), and drastically reconceptualizes the concept of heroic suffering by recasting the suffering heroes of tragedy as human surrogates of the "suffering god" Dionysus. Here Nietzsche's recourse to Christian concepts is even more palpable.

As a student at Leipzig, in 1866/67 and again in 1868, Nietzsche immersed himself in Greek tragedy, thus setting the stage for his early Basel lectures on the subject and ultimately for *BT* (Reibnitz 1992, 17–19). To judge by his notebooks, he worked extensively on textual problems in all three tragedians, contemplated a future lecture course on Aeschylus' *Libation Bearers*, and planned articles on such tragic topics as "guilt and aesthetics in antiquity," "fate and tragedy," and "optimism and pessimism of the Greeks." With the exception of the lectures on *Libation Bearers*, none of these projects ever materialized.

Nietzsche started his tenure in Basel as the newly installed Professor of Greek in the summer of 1869, and he taught there for ten years (Meister 1948). His duties included not only giving lectures and seminars at the university, but also teaching six hours per week in the highest grade of the senior high school, the Pädagogium, where he offered courses on the tragedians, Euripides included, on a regular basis between 1869 and 1876 (Gutzwiller 1951, 177–83; Janz 1981). Decades later several of his students recalled that he set very high standards and challenged them to think hard and creatively. In his annual report for 1870/71, for instance, Nietzsche states that he had them write an essay about "their impression of the *Bacchae* of Euripides and about the nature of the cult of Dionysos" while they were translating the play (quoted by Gutzwiller 1951, 182 and 204–5; Henrichs 1986, 378). In a note from the summer of 1870 Nietzsche adds: "According to the statements of my pupils [the play] made a strong impression and aroused their interest" (*KGW* III 3, 93). Unfortunately we will never know whether Nietzsche discussed the issues that would make Dionysus, Euripides, and *Bacchae* such central concerns in *BT* when he introduced his young audience to the most Dionysiac of all extant tragedies.

In the larger picture of Nietzsche's academic teaching as a whole, the course on *Bacchae* remains an anomaly. Nietzsche's prejudice against Euripides was so great that he never made him the subject of any of his lecture courses or seminars at the university, where he invariably treated him as a mere foil for Aeschylus and Sophocles. His university lectures covered a lot of ground, from Greek literature, philosophy, and religion to meter, rhetoric, and Latin epigraphy (Janz 1974). Invariably, Nietzsche was meticulously prepared, as his extensive lecture notes attest. In preparing his lectures, he relied heavily on the work of other scholars, but with few exceptions he does not acknowledge his sources, nor was he expected to do so. The surviving autographs of his lectures are among the least researched texts in the entire Nietz-schean corpus; they are only now beginning to be recognized as important documents in their own right from which valuable information can be gleaned about Nietzsche's scholarship and about the dissemination of knowledge during one of the most formative periods of the nineteenth century (Most 2000a; Porter 2000b).

In his first semester Nietzsche gave two lecture courses, on Aeschylus' *Libation Bearers* (*KGW* II 2, 3–104) and Greek lyric poetry (*KGW* II 2, 107–82), respectively. The combination of these topics reflected his vision of the evolution of lyric poetry and tragedy as closely related products of the Dionysian spirit (*BT* 5–6). In his eyes, the primitive "folk-poetry of the masses" performed at the festivals of Dionysus is the matrix from which tragedy originates: "It is an awesome fact that tragedy was born from the musical lyrics of the Dionysia" (*KGW* II 3, 14–15). This is not a reference to the twenty dithyrambs performed each year at the City Dionysia, but to the more ecstatic Dionysiac cult songs of the archaic period: "Originally the expression of a wine-induced state of pleasure, an intoxicated optimism, with dancing, mimicry and improvisation. Its core [was] a mime in which figures from the entourage of Dionysus frolicked: (hi)story of the god: exuberant music of the pipes" (*KGW* II 2, 146). According to Nietzsche, the oldest and most authentic form of the dithyramb reenacted the "suffering of Dionysus"; its plots and its music provided the model of "solemnity, sorrow, and passion" that inspired the tragedians (*KGW* II 2, 158–59). By contrast, the dithyrambs of "the official polis cult" were, in Nietzsche's eyes, more subdued and less expressive of the Dionysian mood (*KGW* II 2, 146–47), a view that is echoed in the 1870 lectures on Sophocles (*KGW* II 3, 14–17, see below) and developed further in *BT* 2 (Reibnitz 1992, 119–22). Nietzsche's construct of the alleged antecedents of the dithyramb is characteristic of the recourse to evolutionist models and of the preoccupation with imaginary "origins" that he shared with much of the scholarship of his time (Wessels 2003) and that is reflected in the very concept of "the *birth* of tragedy."

After the Platonic dialogues, tragedy was the one genre to which he would return most often in his teaching. In the short span of five years, he lectured three times on *Libation Bearers* and once on *Oedipus the King*. In addition, he three times gave a seminar on *Libation Bearers*. His interest in "the artistic problem of the [play's] middle position" within the trilogy (*KGW* II 2, 36) and his fascination with its chthonian ambience (*KGW* II 2, 36, 47–50) may explain his preferential treatment of *Libation Bearers*. But one can only wonder why he lectured on Sophocles only once and failed to offer any other course on that playwright except for a seminar on "The Life of Sophocles" in the winter of 1873/74 (cf. *KGW* II 3, 45–56).

Meticulous and technical, Nietzsche's lectures on *Libation Bearers* combine a line-by-line philological commentary with more general introductory material in which Nietzsche, playfully posing as a latter-day Aristophanes of Byzantium, reconstructs the lost hypothesis of the play by discussing the structure of the plot, the treatment of the Orestes myth before and after Aeschylus, Aeschylean stagecraft, choral performance, and the history of the Aeschylean text. Interesting mini-essays embedded in the commentary deal with central issues such as the trilogic form, the strophic arrangements of the choral odes, and the cult of the dead. One of the more memorable moments of Nietzsche's engagement with the play is this tantalizingly aphoristic comment on its "theatrical effect": "The scenes rigorously symmetrical. The drama lacks perspective. Scene after scene is treated in the same way. *All the scenes are equally near and detailed*" (*KGW* II 2, 36, trans. Porter 2000c, 414–15). Similarly on music: "The musicality. The music of the language. All is music, there are no spoken and sung parts, everything sung. The song-dance too never ceases" (*KGW* II 2, 35). Nietzsche's interest in the performative dimension of tragedy and his insistence on the preeminent role of music and choral dance in *Libation Bearers* are the principal links between these lectures and *BT*.

On the whole, Nietzsche's Basel lectures, whether on tragedy or on other subjects, are admirably clear, systematic, and informative, but they are hardly riveting. Unremarkable in tone and conventional in conception as well as content, they rarely reveal their author's true genius. Still, they make fascinating reading today, precisely because they illustrate a side of Nietzsche that is fundamentally different from his essays, his letters, and his philosophical works. The lectures on *Libation Bearers* are a case in point. Their attention to detail and lack of imaginative insight set them apart from the flights of fancy found in *BT*.

The exact opposite is true for his lectures on Sophocles. Delivered in the summer of 1870, less than two years before the publication of *BT*, as an introduction to Nietzsche's interpretation of *Oedipus the King*, they anticipate major themes of his first book. Outlines of fifteen lectures survive in his handwriting (*KGW* II 3, 1–57). The lectures open with a comparison of ancient and modern drama in which Nietzsche differentiates the "pessimism" of Greek tragedy and the inexplicable suffering of its heroes (cf. *BT* 9–10) from the moralistic nexus of guilt and punishment that preoccupied playwrights like Schiller and Grillparzer. The next five lectures deal with fundamental aspects of Greek tragedy and bear a distinctly Nietzschean stamp: the origin of tragedy in the "ecstatic state" and transformative power of the primitive spring festivals of Dionysus (*BT* 1–2, 4); the antagonistic and yet complementary art forms of the Apollinian, which represents order and restraint, and the Dionysian, which stands for abandon and dissolution (*KGW* II 3, 11, the first occurrence of this influential concept; cf. *BT* 1–6, 9, 16, 21); the cultic setting and "democratic" audience of the tragic performances, which aimed at producing emotions (*pathos*) rather than action (*dran*) – both positions considerably modified in *BT* 7 and 12; the chorus as an ideal poetic construct that transcends and transforms reality (*BT* 7–8); and, finally, tragic plots as a sublimation of their epic antecedents (*BT* 3–4, 10). The general part concludes with a section titled "Ancient Tragedy and Opera," in which Nietzsche discusses the modern reception of Greek drama and acknowledges Gluck and Wagner as representatives of "this ancient union of composer and poet" (*KGW* II 3, 32; cf. *BT* 19–25). Lectures 8–15 deal directly with Sophocles and compare him with Aeschylus and Euripides. Nietzsche sees the succession of the three tragedians as an evolution from the primitive "artistic instinct" to cogitation and reasoning; that is, as a pattern of progressive rationalization that culminated in the Socratic rationalism of Euripides: "Reformation of the [tragic] art according to Socratic principles: everything must be sensible so that everything makes sense" (*KGW* II 3, 44). In Euripides, "reason destroys instinct" (*KGW* II 3, 37). By contrast, Sophocles, the most tragic of the tragedians, preserves the true tragic spirit and "purifies dramatic poetry by separating reflection from the action of the characters" and "relegating it to the chorus" (*KGW* II 3, 39, and 44). One wonders how Nietzsche managed to reach such an implausible conclusion. It is remarkable that while critical of Euripides in these lectures, Nietzsche does not come down on him quite as hard as he does later in *BT*. In 1870, Euripides is not yet held responsible for "the death of tragedy" (*BT* 11: 71.23–24; cf. Steiner 1961).

In the posted announcement the lectures on Sophocles were billed as an "Introduction to Sophoclean Tragedy," but Nietzsche's actual autograph offers a more telling title: "ΑΞΙΕ ΤΑΥΡΕ. On the History of Greek Tragedy" (*KGW* II 3, 1). The Greek quotation, "worthy bull," is taken from an Elian cult song in honor of Dionysus, whom the women of Elis invoked in one of his tauromorphic manifestations (*PMG* 871; cf. Scullion 2001). Is it mere accident that the "worthy bull" of Elis caught the attention of two devoted "disciples" of Dionysus, Jane Harrison and Walter F. Otto (Harrison 1903, 438; Otto 1965, 80 and 193)? This remarkable motto puts a distinct Dionysiac imprint on the entire lecture course, in which the tragic is defined with a Schopenhauerian twist (and in anticipation of *BT* 2–3) as follows: "The tragic idea is that of the cult of Dionysus: the dissolution of individuation into another world order: guidance toward the belief in transcendence through the horrible terrors of existence" (*KGW* II 3, 12; for additional affinities with *BT* see Reibnitz 1992, 28–35).

A later and more conventional discussion of tragedy and the tragedians including Euripides can be found in Nietzsche's lectures on the history of Greek literature (*KGW* II 5, 79–146), which were delivered in two sequels, in winter 1874/75 and summer 1875, when the controversy over the publication of *BT* had already hurt

Nietzsche's reputation as a classicist. Not surprisingly, *BT* is never mentioned in these lectures, and the account of the origins of tragedy that opens the section on the tragedians is remarkably different from *BT* and refrains from reiterating the extreme positions of the earlier book. To give but one example, Nietzsche maintains in these lectures, as he does in *BT*, that the earliest form of tragedy dramatized the sufferings of Dionysus (*KGW* II 5, 80–81). In *BT* he goes on to argue that the divine suffering is reenacted on the tragic stage by each suffering hero, whom he considers "mere masks" of the suffering Dionysus (*BT* 10). In his lectures of less than three years later, however, he toned down his earlier claim considerably. Instead of postulating an identity between Dionysus and the tragic heroes as suffering protagonists, he merely juxtaposed the "sufferings" (*pathea*, cf. Herodotus 5.67.5) of Dionysus with those of "other heroes" as two successive stages in the evolution of tragedy (*KGW* II 5, 80). It looks as if Nietzsche had decided to mitigate his earlier view in order to avoid further controversy.

The Birth of Tragedy: Origins, Dionysus, Suffering

During his ten years as a university teacher Nietzsche attracted between two and nineteen students per course, or eight on average (Stroux 1925). This figure is not untypical for a small provincial university like Basel, which had a student body of 116 in 1870. He reached considerably larger audiences through two ambitiously conceived and exquisitely worded lectures for the educated public (Reibnitz 1992, 36–40). Not long after his arrival in Basel, in January 1870, he lectured on Greek tragedy as "music drama" of the Wagnerian type – a concept so outlandish that even Wagner protested (*KGW* III 5/1, 22). In another public lecture two weeks later, he presented Socrates as the paragon of rationality whose bad influence on Euripides caused the decline of tragedy as an art form: "Euripides is the poet of Socratic rationalism" (*KGW* III 2, 32; Landfester 1994, 57). Nietzsche goes on to argue that Socratic dialectic is by definition optimistic. As such it contrasts sharply with the tragic worldview: "Originating from the deep spring of shared suffering, tragedy is by nature pessimistic" (*KGW* III 2, 38; Landfester 1994, 63). The respective titles of these lectures, "The Greek Music Drama" and "Socrates and Tragedy," were deliberately provocative, even irritating, and the reception was mixed.

Nietzsche's indictment of Socrates and Euripides as the destroyers of tragedy and the nexus of drama, music, and suffering anticipate major themes of *BT*, the work that would soon immerse its young author in a national controversy. Published in Leipzig in January 1872 and dedicated to Richard Wagner, *BT* is a literary masterpiece that reads as if it was conceived and written as a seamless, continuous whole. But it was not. Its accomplished form conceals a very complex textual history whose successive stages have not yet been fully elucidated (Vogel 1966, 108–13, 150; Silk and Stern 1981, 31–61; Reibnitz 1992, 36–53; *KGW* III 5/1, 209–302; Landfester 1994, 446–55). However, this much is certain: *BT* is an artful collage based on a series of preexistent essays and drafts. Yet no preliminary drafts for the Wagnerian part of *BT* seem to exist; it appears to have been written during the final phase, presumably later than April 1871 (Vogel 1966, 150; Silk and Stern 1981, 59–60). What started as a book on the Greeks – his "Griechenbuch," as Nietzsche called it – metamorphosed into a study of Wagner as the German reviver of Greek tragedy.

As a work of aesthetic criticism and cultural psychology, *BT* is a conceptual tour de force. It argues that Greek culture of the archaic and classical period, tragedy included, is the product of the interaction of two "art forms" symbolically named after two antithetical and yet complementary divinities, Apollo and Dionysus (1–6); that tragedy originated in the intense emotional states and in the singing and dancing associated with the cult of Dionysus (7–10); that Greek tragedy "died by suicide" when its innate Dionysian spirit was destroyed by the rationalism of Socrates and Euripides (11–15); and that a rebirth of that tragic spirit has taken place in Germany thanks to Richard Wagner's "music drama" (16–25). The Greek part of *BT* and its Wagnerian counterpart are two sides of the same coin – an urgent call for the renewal of contemporary German culture through recourse to the musical and choral culture of pre-Hellenistic ancient Greece.

Nietzsche thought that he was not primarily writing about antiquity, but about his own time. The Greeks were merely role models. *BT* is by its own declaration first and foremost a work of cultural criticism. Bringing Wagner into the picture was not an anachronism designed to make the ancient Greeks look more relevant. To the contrary, intellectually and culturally, Wagner remains Nietzsche's true point of departure, at least for the final version of *BT*. Nietzsche's affinity with Wagner had three roots: love of the Greeks, especially of the archaic period; a creative commitment to musical culture; and a missionary zeal to save the German culture of their time from the perils of the industrial revolution (cf. Bremer 1987). Intimately familiar with Greek tragedy, albeit mainly through translations, Wagner saw eye to eye with Nietzsche on the tragedians and anticipated the latter's value judgments by more than two decades: "Birth out of music: Aeschylus. Decadence: Euripides" (Wagner in 1849, quoted by Vogel 1966, 99). Like the Greek tragedians, Wagner was both a poet and a composer who drew on myth for the subject matter of his operas. He admired and imitated the trilogic/tetralogic form of Aeschylean tragedy and confessed that he entered into an ongoing "state of rapture" when he read the *Oresteia* for the first time (Bremer 1987, 42–43 and 54–58). But the similarities between Wagner and Greek tragedy end here.

Nietzsche was a gifted pianist and music critic, and his initial admiration for Wagner was based on his profound musical connoisseurship as well as the intellectual kinship between the two. But to interpret the origins of tragedy with recourse to Wagner and his music was an approach that was singularly unfortunate and bound to fail. It forced Nietzsche to privilege music as the key element of tragedy to the exclusion of almost everything else, and to talk about the nature of tragic music with an inner certainty that belies the fact that the musical dimension of tragedy is almost entirely lost. In his "Attempt at a Self-Criticism" of 1886, some eight years after his break with Wagner, Nietzsche declared Wagnerian music "the most un-Greek of all possible art forms" (*KGW* III 1, 14, 23–24) and regretted having conceived the Wagnerian part of *BT* in the first place. Many readers of *BT* would agree with Nietzsche's second thoughts, and few will complain that Reibnitz (1992) omitted sections 16–25 from her magisterial commentary.

Wagner is not the only modern intruder who works havoc in the pages of *BT*. A more profound influence on Nietzsche's interpretation of the Apollinian/Dionysian duality and its alleged influence on Greek tragedy was Arthur Schopenhauer. In the fall of 1865, Nietzsche discovered Schopenhauer's principal work, *The World as Will and Representation* (1818, 1844), in an antiquarian bookstore, bought it, and became an instant convert to this peculiar philosophy. Wagner too was an admirer of Schopenhauer, in whose aesthetics music ranked as the highest form of art because, unlike the other arts, it transcends appearances and represents the "world will" itself. Schopenhauer's "principle of individuation," his doctrine of universal suffering with its innate pessimism, and the privileged role he assigned to music made a lasting impression on Nietzsche and determined his understanding of Dionysus, Greek art, and Greek tragedy. Schopenhauer's name and concepts loom large at the beginning and end of *BT* (especially secs. 1–2, 4, 16, and 21–22). According to Schopenhauer, the driving force behind every activity on the human and cosmic level is a primordial and irrational "will" which expresses itself in the world of phenomena, a dream world based on illusion as the "will to life." Individually this force is experienced through one's awareness of one's own self as will. This process of the objectivation of the universal will in individual bodies, urges, and life-experiences – the *principium individuationis*, which is invoked in eleven of the twenty-five sections of *BT* – is an ongoing, never-ending effort because the eternal striving of the will cannot be satisfied. Dissatisfaction with the insatiability of the will is the cause for endless suffering in the world. The only escape from suffering is the complete surrender of one's own individuality, which is tantamount to a renunciation of the individual will to life.

Although Schopenhauer's principal tenets are evidently indebted to Indian philosophy and have no immediate parallels in Greek thought, Nietzsche miraculously found a Greek comparandum in the myth of Dionysus Zagreus. Attested mainly in Neoplatonic sources, the myth relates "that as a boy [Dionysus] was torn to pieces by the Titans" and restored to a new life through reconstitution of his dismembered body. By calling it Dionysus' "rebirth" (*BT* 10: 68.26), Nietzsche adopts a late antique detail of the Zagreus myth that may or may not have been present in the classical period (Henrichs 2004, 126). According to Nietzsche, Dionysus Zagreus is "the suffering Dionysus of the Mysteries, the god experiencing in himself the agonies of individuation" (*BT* 10: 68.11–13), whose fate is reenacted in the suffering heroes of tragedy, who "are mere masks of this original hero, Dionysus" (*BT* 10: 67.23–24; cf. Henrichs 1993a, 36–39). In an even bolder move, Nietzsche suggests that his Schopenhauerian reading of the Zagreus myth captures the essence of tragedy, which he defines as follows: "the fundamental knowledge of the oneness of everything existent, the conception of individuation as the primal cause of evil, and of art as the joyous hope that the spell of individuation may be broken in augury of a restored oneness" (*BT* 10: 69.3–7).

Needless to say, Nietzsche's notion of an archetypal tragedy dramatizing the suffering of Dionysus is not supported by any Greek evidence. Even if the Zagreus myth is as old as the late archaic or classical period (Parker 1995, 494–96), it is unthinkable that the tragedians and their audience would have understood it as the foundation myth of Attic tragedy. Nor could they possibly have seen the tragic heroes as human surrogates of the suffering Dionysus. The known versions of the Zagreus myth do not emphasize the suffering of the god, but his return to life. In the final analysis, Nietzsche's "suffering Dionysus" who is reincarnated in tragic heroes like

Oedipus and Prometheus must be exposed as a Christian construct in pagan disguise, modeled on the figure of *Christus patiens* and superimposed on Greek tragedy by a pro-pagan and anti-Christian pastor's son.

Nietzsche inherited the polarity of Apollo and Dionysus from the Romantic scholarship of the early nineteenth century but drastically reinterpreted and problematized the conventional definition of the two divinities (Vogel 1966, Reibnitz 1992). His innovation was to turn the two gods into the dual concept of the Apollinian and Dionysian, thereby transforming a minimalist approach to Greek polytheism into a grand aesthetic theory (Henrichs 2004, 125–28). The shift from religion to art explains why in the course of *BT* the two "art deities" give way to the two "art forms" that are named after them (Henrichs 1993a, 23–26). Again appropriating Schopenhauerian concepts and terminology, Nietzsche associates the Apollinian with "dreams" and "illusions"; that is, with the clearly delineated and demarcated world of natural phenomena which is tantamount to the "principle of individuation" (*BT* 1). The Dionysian corresponds to "intoxication" (*BT* 1), to the primeval "oneness" of things (*BT* 2–3, 5, 10), and ultimately to Schopenhauer's "will." Tragedy is the product of the interaction between the two principles: "What we call 'tragic' is precisely this Apollinian elucidation of the Dionysian" (*KGW* III 3, 200, from 1870/71). Nietzsche makes his case with visionary certainty; no proofs are adduced, and none is available. His argument that Greek tragedy constitutes a mirror image of the universal scenario of cosmic struggle and human suffering has had a tremendous impact on classicists and non-classicists alike; it is almost irresistible, and yet it must be resisted because it is refuted by the very different roles that Apollo and Dionysus play in Greek culture and in the Greek tragedies that survive.

In retrospect Nietzsche described *BT* as his sacrifice to Dionysus (*Beyond Good and Evil*, sec. 295), but his ideas on "the birth of tragedy" are a far cry from current theories, which tend to interpret *tragôidia* as a song having to do with the sacrifice of a goat. The origins of tragedy are lost to us and cannot be recovered, and speculation is no substitute for hard evidence, which is unavailable. Nietzsche derives tragedy with Aristotle from the cult of Dionysus, and the majority of scholars would agree that he has a point, even though the idea that the original Dionysian chorus of proto-tragedy consisted of satyrs is sheer fantasy. The importance of Dionysus for Greek tragedy, as far as both its origins and his role in the extant plays are concerned, remains controversial. In the current debate the minimalists are contesting the progress that has been made in recent years thanks to more holistic interpretations (Friedrich 1996 and Scullion, chapter 2 in this volume versus Bierl 1991 and Henrichs 1995). Ironically, Nietzsche has been invoked by both sides.

The Immediate Aftermath, and Beyond

Contemporary reaction to *BT* was divided, but on the whole it was overwhelmingly negative – a mixture of condemnation and indifference (Howald 1920, 22–30; Gründer 1969; Silk and Stern 1981, 90–107; Calder 1983). To Nietzsche's surprise, the initial blow came in May 1872 from a fellow Schulpforte alumnus and potential ally. Wilamowitz was twenty-three years old at the time and ready for action. Unlike Nietzsche, he had earned his Berlin doctorate the hard way, by writing a dissertation. Irked by what he saw as Nietzsche's preferential treatment by the Leipzig faculty and his disdain for historical truth and scholarly method, two of the "untouchable" and "sacred" values fostered at Schulpforte, he wasted no time and responded with a vitriolic pamphlet that tore *BT* to shreds, castigated its author for his lack of competence and frivolous manipulation of the truth, and catalogued a host of factual errors with merciless glee (Wilamowitz-Moellendorff 1872, published less than five months after *BT*). Furthermore, he rejected as un-Hellenic Nietzsche's vision of an archaic Greek culture awash in Dionysiac ecstasy, mysticism, and irrationalism. And finally, he ridiculed Nietzsche's enthusiasm for Wagner's music and sarcastically parodied the anti-Wagnerian slogan "Zukunftsmusik" ("music of the future") in the title of his pamphlet, *Zukunftsphilologie!* ("philology of the future"). Led by Erwin Rohde, a scholar whom Wilamowitz later learned to admire, Nietzsche's friends came to his rescue, only to elicit another barrage of criticism from Wilamowitz (Rohde 1872, Wilamowitz-Moellendorff 1873).

Within a matter of months, *BT* became a cause célèbre as well as a source of acute embarrassment. Ritschl, once Nietzsche's staunchest supporter, dismissed it as a youthful "flight of fancy," and Hermann Usener (1834–1904), who thought highly of Nietzsche's early work in Greek doxography, regarded *BT* as "sheer nonsense" and pronounced its author "dead in the eyes of scholarship" (in Benders and Oettermann 2000, 199 and 282). The acrimony of the debate took its toll on Nietzsche; it alienated him even further from classics as an academic discipline and effectively prevented him from writing another book on the Greeks. On the positive side, "it accelerated in Nietzsche the process of obtaining clarity about himself" (Landfester 1994, 521). The most immediate victim of the controversy over *BT* was the book itself, not its author. In 1886, Nietzsche republished his "impossible book" with the new subtitle "Hellenism and Pessimism" and prefaced it with "An Attempt at a Self-Criticism" in which he distanced himself from the tone and tenor of *BT* with disarming self-irony and with a host of unanswered, and largely unanswerable, questions. Nietzsche's second thoughts did nothing to improve the fortune of his book. For more than a century after its publication, *BT* was ostracized by the mainstream of the classical profession, which was loath to acknowledge its existence.

From a strictly historicist perspective, that is in terms of attested historical fact, Wilamowitz was for the most part right in his criticism of Nietzsche. As far as the history of tragedy is concerned, a more mature Wilamowitz set the record straight once and for all in his monumental *Introduction to Greek Tragedy* (= Wilamowitz-Moellendorff 1959, vol. 1), in which *BT* is nowhere mentioned and the meaning of tragedy and the tragic is not addressed. Half a century after the confrontation with Nietzsche, Wilamowitz looked back to the episode, admitting that his juvenile attack had been misguided (Mansfeld 1986). Still, he saw "no reason for remorse" and even took credit for making Nietzsche abandon philology and embrace philosophy (Wilamowitz-Moellendorff 1928, 129–30). In 1928, the vast majority of classicists still rallied around Wilamowitz, but in hindsight, telltale signs of a gradual paradigm shift toward Nietzsche and a more dynamic and differentiated view of Greek culture and its ambivalences were already visible or soon to appear inside and outside the profession.

Shortly after Nietzsche's death in 1900, avant-garde German writers, artists, and intellectuals in search of a "new life" rediscovered Nietzsche's Dionysus with the help of *BT* and initiated a Dionysian renaissance that culminated in Walter F. Otto's *Dionysos* of 1933 (Vogel 1966, 247–80; Cancik 1986; Landfester 1994, 521–26). In England it was Jane Harrison who became a convert to Nietzsche and his idea of the polarity of Apollo and Dionysus as a cultural force (Henrichs 1984, 229–34). An eminent interpreter of Dionysus in her own right, she declared herself a "disciple" of Nietzsche and acknowledged her debt to him in two groundbreaking and influential books (Harrison 1903, 1912; Schlesier 1994, 123–92).

During and after Wilamowitz's lifetime several of his own pupils, most prominently Paul Friedländer and Karl Reinhardt, did not disguise their admiration for Nietzsche, and their work shows how much they were influenced by him (Lloyd-Jones 1979 and 1983, 247–49; Calder 1983; Henrichs 1995). Yet the same Reinhardt could still declare in 1942 that "the history of philology has no place for Nietzsche." He should have known better. In a collection of essays on the status of classical studies during the Weimar Republic (Flashar 1995), the names of Wilamowitz, Nietzsche, and Werner Jaeger stand out and are mentioned more often than those of any other classicists.

Fifteen years after Wilamowitz's death, Thomas Mann expressed surprise that Wilamowitz had "dared to as much as open his mouth after his attack on Nietzsche" and pronounced that "he was of no account as an intellect" (in a letter to Karl Kerényi dated 15 July 1936; see Calder 1977, 281). In several of his works, Mann adopted the wild and ecstatic images of Dionysus propagated in Nietzsche's *BT* and Rohde's *Psyche*. Mann's creative engagement with *BT* was not an isolated case. For more than a hundred years, Nietzsche's first book has found a huge and receptive audience among poets, critics, and intellectuals. Apart from Mann, readers of *BT* intrigued by Nietzsche's two "art forms" of the Apollinian and Dionysian, his construct of "madness" as a positive cultural force, and his reflections on Greek tragedy include William Butler Yeats, Ruth Benedict, Eugene O'Neill, Walter Benjamin, Michel Foucault, and Peter Szondi, to mention only a few.

The Wilamowitz–Nietzsche struggle, as it has been dubbed, was not merely a row among extremely young and immature scholars (Lenson 1987, 14) but a paradigmatic clash of two giants over seemingly conflicting principles – historical truth and imagination, scholarship and art, or academia and life (Henrichs 1995) – on which neither side could compromise. The issues are still before us, but positions are less hardened today. Wilamowitz may have won the battle, but he lost the war. His pamphlet has been largely ignored, whereas Nietzsche's *BT* enjoys unrivaled success today, and current notions of pre-Hellenistic Greek culture are closer in spirit to Nietzsche than they are to Wilamowitz. Depending on one's criteria, *BT* can be read in multiple ways – as a paradigm of inspired cultural criticism (the prevalent reading), as a continuation of the author's philological work that contains the seeds of his later philosophy (Porter 2000a), or as a splendid piece of historical fiction – a "historical novel" (Howald 1920, 19) that has a plot, divine and human protagonists, a victim, and a not so happy ending; in short, all the trappings of a Greek tragedy (Henrichs 2004). Apart from its sublime prose, the very fictionality of *BT* and the powerful imagination that produced it are, I believe, among its most enduring assets. If *BT* had been based on hard facts, it would have long since been replaced by more recent attempts to reshuffle the known data. Nietzsche's daring vision and its impact on generations of readers must be one of the reasons why Richard Rorty chose to include *BT* in his list of "brilliantly iconoclastic books" that inaugurated "paradigm-shifts in disciplines such as classics, philosophy or comparative literature" (Rorty 2004, 4).

NOTES

I am grateful to Professor Marian Demos and Dr. Sarah Nolan for their beneficial comments.

1   I refer to Nietzsche's *BT* by section number as well as the page and line numbers of the standard German text in *KGW* III 1 (1972) 21–152 = *KSA* 1 (1980) 25–156. Quotations are from Walter Kaufmann's English translation (Nietzsche 1967).

FURTHER READING

An exhaustive day-by-day documentation of Nietzsche's life from the cradle to the grave has been assembled by Benders and Oettermann 2000. A documented chronicle of his life from April 1869 to the end of 1874 can be found in *KGW* III 5/1, 3–108. For an eminently informative and readable Nietzsche biography see Janz 1981. Most of Nietzsche's Basel lectures survive as autographs; they are published in *KGW* II 2, 3, 4, and 5. An indispensable research tool for the scholarly study of *BT* is the line-by-line commentary on the non-Wagnerian sections 1–12 by Reibnitz 1992, 54–342. Silk and Stern 1981 remains the standard English analysis of the argument and historical background of *BT.* Lenson 1987 is the only English commentary on *BT,* but it barely meets the most rudimentary needs and is in any case more concerned with Nietzsche's overall philosophical thought than his views on Greek tragedy.

On the polarity of Apollo and Dionysus and on Nietzsche's concept of Dionysus and the Dionysian see Vogel 1966, Silk and Stern 1981, and Henrichs 1984, 1986, and 1993a. Porter 2000a is a penetrating study of Nietzsche's multifaceted Dionysus, the interplay of philology and philosophy in *BT,* and *BT*'s pivotal place in Nietzsche's oeuvre as a whole. Henrichs 2004 explores the Dionysian scenarios of *BT* and its idiosyncratic configuration of Greek polytheism.

Informed comments on Nietzsche's accomplishments as a philologist, his contribution to the modern understanding of the Greeks, and his provocative concept of antiquity can be found in Lloyd-Jones 1979, Pöschl 1979, Silk and Stern 1981, Reibnitz 1992, Cancik 1995, Porter 2000b, and several of the articles in Bishop 2004, especially Hamilton 2004, 54–69, and Porter 2004, 7–26. On the reception or rejection of Nietzsche's vision of the ancient world and his standing among classicists past and present see Howald 1920, Lloyd-Jones 1979, and Cancik 1999. The basic documentation on the so-called Wilamowitz–Nietzsche struggle, including the three notorious pamphlets that sealed the rift (Wilamo-witz-Moellendorff 1872 and 1873, Rohde 1872), is reproduced in Gründer 1969; additional documents and background in Calder 1983. Representative treatments of Nietzsche's views on Greek tragedy include Silk and Stern 1981, Arnott 1984, Reibnitz 1992, and Latacz 1994.

CHAPTER TWENTY-NINE

Greek Tragedy and Western Perceptions of Actors and Acting

Ismene Lada-Richards

This chapter focuses on Greek tragedy's self-reflexive conceptualization of the actor's art in relation to selected landmarks in European performative discourse: the period of puritan anti-theatricality; Diderot's seminal discussions of acting; Stanislavsky's "method"; Brecht's "Epic" theater; and the "avant-garde" theater movement of the twentieth century, as exemplified by Antonin Artaud and Jerzy Grotowski. Although they are not theoretical documents, the tragic texts themselves explore acting and actors in manifold and subtle ways, rivaling in their complexity that high-water mark of artistic self-consciousness, the drama of the English Renaissance.

It cannot be stressed too strongly that identifying and discussing points of contact between fifth-century tragic plays and modern theorizations of the actor's self and art is not an attempt to force Greek drama into alien molds. The artistic problems probed self-reflexively by Greek tragedy manifest themselves with renewed force in later European drama and European theatrical discourse. Broadening our scope to encompass later Western perceptions of actors and acting is simply another way to apprehend the vibrancy, versatility, and enduring relevance of Greek tragedy.

Tears from the Heart or Tears from the Brain?

At the core of all considerations of the art of acting lies the question of the actor's emotional experience *in* performance: Does he *really* feel with the feelings of his characters, weep with *their* agony, tremble with *their* terror, rage with *their* anger? Or does he only borrow and skillfully display the signs of each passion, while he himself remains cool and uninvolved?

Such questions have been vaulted center-stage by the treatise that has been most influential in shaping modern perceptions of the art of acting, namely, the *Paradoxe sur le Comédien*, written by the eighteenth-century French philosopher, art critic, novelist, and playwright Denis Diderot. The controversy it provoked still resonates in such landmark publications of Western performance theory as William Archer's *Masks or Faces?* (1888), a survey of the performance experience of hundreds of living actors, and continues to reverberate in the polarity between the "involved" acting style most famously associated with Konstantin Sergeievich Stanislavsky, the seminal theoretician of the modern stage, and the "estranged" manner of acting advocated by Bertolt Brecht.

To see how the Greek tragic texts afford their own insights on actors and acting, I turn first to Euripides' *Helen*. Trapped in Egypt with her husband Menelaus, Helen sees their only hope of salvation in outright fraud: "together we must frame a plan (*mêchanên*) for our escape" (1033–34). The plot she hatches – wrought around the fabricated narrative of Menelaus' death – is inherently "theatrical," as it depends not only on the manipulation of appearances (1087–89) and the sensational effect of props and costume (1079–80, 1204), but also on the assumption of different identities: Helen must pretend to be the newly widowed wife, with the black dress, shorn hair, and torn cheeks that go with the part, while her rag-dressed husband Menelaus is cast in the role of a shipwrecked sailor, sole eyewitness to his master's dismal death. Playwright, *didaskalos* (instructor), and actor in her own drama, Helen has conceived what Diderot would call the "ideal model" of her assumed character and executes it to perfection. Her performance in front of Theoclymenus is an excellent illustration of Diderot's artistic paradox, emotional intensity being the outcome of "pure mimicry" (Diderot 1883, 16) and calculated reflection, tears coming from the brain rather than the actor's heart (Diderot 1883, 17). If Helen is a figure for the stage actor, her histrionic talent resides not in "feeling" but in "rendering so exactly the outward signs of feeling" that the audience (in her case Theoclymenus) "fall[s] into the trap" (Diderot 1883, 16); "knowing well" and imitating well "the outward symptoms of the soul" she borrows (Diderot 1883, 74), she enshrines a view of acting as co-extensive with the art of simulated, rather than felt, emotion.

Nevertheless, the modern analogue of the "Diderodian" performer is by no means the sole way of conceptualizing the actor in Greek theatrical discourse. Perhaps the most widely known example of the dazzling histrionic possibilities Greek tragedy afforded to its actors for the display of sincerely felt emotion on the stage is the anecdote (which may or may not be true) related by the second century CE sophist Aulus Gellius about Polus, the celebrated tragic actor of the fourth century BCE. In this rare insight into artistic subjectivity in the ancient world we read that when playing the role of Electra in Sophocles' tragedy, Polus took from the tomb of his deceased son the urn containing his ashes and used them as a prop in his performance, embracing them "as if they were those of Orestes" (*quasi Oresti amplexus*); as a result, he

> filled the whole place, not with the appearance and imitation of sorrow, but with genuine grief and unfeigned lamentation. Therefore, while it seemed that a play was being acted, it was in fact real grief that was enacted. (*Attic Nights* 6.5.7–8; trans. Rolfe 1927)

Flying in the face of Aristotle's author-and-text-based approach to Greek tragedy, this story demonstrates that Greek tragedy becomes alive *in* and *through* performance, acquiring its fullest meaning at the intersection of dramatic role and actor, embodied stage-character and addressees/spectators. By highlighting artistic *technê*, the anecdote dovetails with other evidence suggesting the increased prominence of actors over dramatists in the postclassical period. Even more significantly, it implies a view of tragedy as the performance medium that empowers, enables, celebrates, and liberates the actor's inner self. If the actor can imbue his role with his lifeblood, acting is neither a mechanical nor a derivative task but an all-consuming experience, during which the playwright's "role" and the actor's "self" are inextricably welded together. Central to Gellius' story is a conception of acting whereby the performer demonstrates "that he is no sham, no puppet, no simulacrum, but in real earnest all that he pretends to be; that Othello, Hamlet, and Samson are not merely aped by him, but live and suffer in his person" (Shaw 1962 [1889], 15, on the Italian sensation of the nineteenth-century tragic stage Tommaseo Salvini).

In fact, Polus' acting, vehemently repudiated as "barbaric" by Brecht (1964, 270), bears a striking affinity to the foundational technique of Stanislavskian acting, namely, "affective" or "emotion" memory (the recall and exploitation in performance of feelings and situations belonging to the actor's own past), itself anticipated by several actors and theorists of acting on the Victorian stage. Lady Pollock, for example, records that each time William Charles Macready, the famous nineteenth-century tragedian, was called upon to act Hamlet, he "summoned up" the "extraordinary emotion" of a dream he once had as a young man, when he "saw and heard definitely and distinctly a friend lately dead, who came to address to him words of admonition" (1884, 11). And George Henry Lewes, whose collection *On Actors and the Art of Acting* (1875) was hailed by some contemporaries as a veritable "science" of the actor's craft, foregrounded genuine emotion, imaginative sympathy, and the memory of past feelings as the most sublime means by which the performer could transmit his passion to the audience (see Roach 1980).

Also foregrounded in Gellius' narrative is a concept of the actor as an integral aspect of the work of art, the dramatist's fellow artist and creative equal. What the spectators saw in the performance Gellius describes was not Sophocles' Electra pure and simple, but Electra as mediated, made present, recreated, and "reborn" in *Polus'* body, clothed in *Polus'* emotional reserves. It is precisely this irreducibility and ineradicable presence of the actor's self in the theatrical event that constitutes Polus' performative legacy: the "making" of stage-characters does not require the complete "un-making" and disintegration of the actor's real self, the divesting of his own personality, as claimed by Western opponents of the stage. Whether the "self" is seen and used as a repository of emotional experiences that can be reawakened in search of what is most congenial to the fictive character's stage-life (Stanislavsky) or as a social self that must be distanced from the role so as to criticize or contradict it (Brecht), no actor can escape "his own material" (Coquelin 1915 [1880], 40), his own psychosomatic entity. Even when merging with his part like Polus, it is his own nature that provides the building blocks for the creation of his "character." Gellius' tale rests on a perception of the tragic impact as grounded in the actor's self and in the actor's feelings (cf. Auslander 1997, 28–38). For, in the words of the nineteenth-century French actor Constant Coquelin, "It is with this individual *self* that [the actor] makes you by turns shiver, weep, or smile, the noblest shudders, the most melting tears, the humanest smiles" (Coquelin 1915 [1880], 83).

The juxtaposition of metatheatrical material in Euripides' *Helen* and Gellius' anecdote about Polus underscores the fragmentary state of our evidence. The ability to make the audience weep seems to have been the constant measure of performative success from Plato to St. Augustine, yet we will never know the strategies deployed by individual actors in order to move the audience's collective *psuché* (soul). With respect to Greek tragic acting or even ancient *perceptions* of such acting, the dilemma of head or heart, tears from the heart or brain, defies resolution. It is nevertheless possible to affirm that both Athenian tragedy and Greco-Roman discourse about tragedy antici-pate modern acting theory in viewing the question of emotional involvement as inextricably interwoven with the actor's art.

"Double" the Actor: Messenger Scenes and "Brechtian" Performance

Diderot has often been seen as a precursor of Brecht, though it is doubtful whether Brecht actually knew the *Paradoxe sur le Comédien*. Diderot's belief that the actor has, or should have, a double nature, being at all times both him/herself and the character, at the same time "the little Clairon and . . . the great Agrippina" (Diderot 1883, 11), resurfaces even more urgently in Brecht's demand that the actor detach and dissociate himself as much as possible from the dramatis persona he is called upon to incarnate. Rather than fusing himself with his part in an emotionalist and Stani-slavskian way, he is required to "estrange" himself from it (the much discussed notion of *Verfremdung*), stand aside and criticize it. Actor and character "are not merged into one," for the actor "never forgets, nor does he allow it to be forgotten, that he is not the subject but the demonstrator" (Brecht 1964, 125). Both "character" and "actor" are simultaneously laid bare to the spectator's view:

> The actor does not allow himself to become completely transformed on the stage into the character he is portraying. He is not Lear, Harpagon, Schweik; he shows them. He reproduces their remarks as authentically as he can; he puts forward their way of behaving to the best of his abilities and knowledge of men; but he never tries to persuade himself (and thereby others) that this amounts to a complete transformation. (Brecht 1964, 137)

In the manner of Dicaeopolis disguised as the Euripidean Telephus in Aristophanes' *Acharnians*, the Greek tragic actor does not set out to display or draw attention to his own awareness of *not being* the character but merely the character's imperson-ator/demonstrator. Keen to encourage the spectator to surrender, to suspend disbe-lief, and to lose sight of the very process of artistic transformation, the actor chooses to offer his audience a unified vision, the image of a thorough merging with his part. In Dicaeopolis' words, a tragic actor will aim to "seem to be a beggar" (*doxai ptôchon einai*), retaining his individual identity (*einai men hosper eimi*) but rendering it virtually invisible (*phainesthai de mê*) (Aristophanes, *Acharnians* 440–41). The same idea of leading the spectator to imagine the presence of the "character" itself, while eliding the actor's intrusive physical identity, underlies a scholiast's comment on Timotheus of Zacynthus in the role of the Sophoclean Ajax: when he was falling on the sword, the audience was able to bring to mind the *pathos* of the hero himself:

> It must be conjectured that he falls on his sword, and the actor must be strongly built so as to bring the audience to the point of visualizing Ajax, as is said of Timotheus

of Acanthus, whose acting carried along and enthralled the spectators so much that he
acquired the "tag" Sphageus [the Slayer]. (Scholion on Sophocles' *Ajax* 864)

Even though the balance that the typical Greek tragic actor aims to strike between
character and actor is clearly un-Brechtian, the complexities of a Diderodian and
Brechtian double vision can be found glimpsed elsewhere, namely in the convention
of the messenger speech. Viewed from a metatheatrical perspective, the tragic messenger is a good figure for the actor insofar as he doubles and divides himself: he is *the
part* and *not the part*, he is *himself* (a shepherd, a servant) and *not himself*, appropriating an alien voice and an "I" (e.g., of Oedipus or Pentheus) which is not his own.
There is a vital difference between this "internalized" actor and the rest of his co-
players. While the other tragic actors present the audience with one single dimension
wherein performer and character are merged, the messenger, like the Brechtian
"showman," "must not suppress the '*he* did that, *he* said that' element in his
performance" and "must not go so far as to be wholly transformed into the person
demonstrated" (Brecht 1964, 125).[1]

Canceling, Losing, and Finding the "Self" in Acting

For many theorists and theater practitioners in the Western theatrical tradition
successful acting consists in "nullifying all . . . personal characteristics, in order to let
those of the character flower" (Boal 1992, 44). Exercises and training routines, such
as those devised by the Brazilian theater director, writer, and theorist Augusto Boal,
are put in place to teach the actor to "abolish" his own personality in order to induce
the "birth" of his dramatic character (Boal 1992, 44). As performance theorist Bert
States (1994, 27–28) puts it, "theater is unique among the arts . . . because it is made
of real human beings who have 'annihilated' themselves in order to become unreal
human beings for our pleasure and instruction." In Greek theater, where role-
doubling is the norm, and where an actor frequently faces the need to step onto
the stage "in one guise" after having "killed himself in another guise" (see Damen
1989, 328–29; Pavlovskis 1977, 119), this notion of self-annihilation before the
"character" is born is always tacitly present. At certain moments, however, the actor's
renunciation of his own identity is self-reflexively foregrounded by performative or
textual means, as when the actor playing Agave is shown to peer into the blood-
stained *prosôpon* of the dismembered Pentheus, the now redundant, empty mask of
his abandoned previous "self" (see *Bacchae* 1277–84; cf. 1139–42, 1200–1215), or
when Helen's husband Menelaus is cast into the role of a shipwrecked sailor, whose
task is to announce Menelaus', that is his own, offstage death: "Are you willing to be
reported dead in word, although you haven't died?" Helen asks, in her attempt to
mount a "play-within-the-play" in order to deceive her suitor Theoclymenus. "I am
willing to accept that I have died in word, though (in reality) I haven't," replies
Menelaus (*Helen* 1050–52). By means of such interchanges Greek theater self-
consciously explores the performative truth that a character is "born" when the
real-life agent who embodies it recedes to the background, becoming virtually invisible
and metaphorically "dead." Like the famous Shakespearean actor Richard Burbage,
who was reportedly able to divest his "self" together with "his Cloathes" and "never
(not so much as in the Tyring-house) assum'd himself again until the Play was done"

(see Chambers 1923, 4: 370), King Menelaus, who plays at being a mere sailor, is required to blot out his own identity and therefore "die in word."

At the same time, however, sloughing off one's personality in order to assume the one required by the role is a regularly maligned aspect of the actor's art. Caught in the dizzying display of multiple, protean selves and false identities, the actor becomes "a daily counterfeit," "a shifting companion" who "lives effectually by putting on and putting off" (see J. Cocke in Chambers 1923, 4: 255 and 257 [*A common Player*]); by feeding parasitically on his own character, the actor's roles erode his innermost essence and imperil his personal integrity. Classicists are familiar with this attitude primarily through Plato's prohibition against the imitation of things "shameful" and things "unbecoming the free man," lest "as a result of the imitation (*ek tês mimêseôs*) they [sc. the imitators] become infected with the reality (*tou einai apolausôsin*)" of what they represent (*Republic* 395c). As Constant Coquelin (1915 [1880], 81–82) puts it, anti-histrionic prejudice is predicated on the false presumption that "the renunciation by the actor of his own personality, to assume the character of one, ten, or twenty other people, is . . . a renunciation of his own dignity, and a denial of the dignity of mankind . . . in ceasing to be himself, you feel that he ceases to be a man."

Linked as it is to role-playing in the service of deception, Menelaus' temporary eradication of himself highlights the risk that, as Jean-Jacques Rousseau (1948 [1758], 108) has put it, an actor "obliterates himself, so to speak, canceling himself out with his hero." Even for a man of the theater, like Eugene Ionesco, the kind of self-effacement Menelaus lightheartedly accepts casts the shadow of shame on the acting profession as a whole. Recalling his early experiences as a theater-goer, Ionesco confesses his displeasure:

> It was beyond me how anyone could dream of being an actor. It seemed to me that actors were doing something unacceptable and reprehensible. They gave up their own person-alities, repudiated themselves, changed their own skins. How *could* they consent to being someone else and take on a character different from their own? For me it was a kind of vulgar trick, transparent, inconceivable. (Ionesco 1964, 13)

Vulnerable though the actor's self may be to the multitude of masks besieging it, it runs an even greater risk of being subsumed by a single dramatic character. Theater often reflects upon its own almost magical ability to change one person into another, as is the case in Euripides' *Heracles* and, more specifically, in the "inset" drama (822–1015) designed by Hera, directed by Lyssa (Madness), and "staged" on the audience's behalf by a messenger speech (922–1015), whose extraordinary viv-idness (*enargeia*) is almost unparalleled in Athenian drama.[2] The space where loss of the self during performance is enacted is the Theban palace's interior, invisible behind the closed doors of the *skênê* yet mapped out in words by the messenger's narrative. What turns this mental space into a theatrical stage, inhabited by actors (Amphitryon, Megara, the servants, and Heracles himself) and a chorus (Heracles' children) and complete with stage-properties (Heracles' bow, club, and imaginary attributes) and set (the palace), is above all its transformative potential. Displaying all the dynamism and versatility of stage signs (see, e.g., Elam 1980, 12–16; Honzl 1976), the Theban palace is able to mutate, representing now the city of Nisus (954), now the wooded plains of the Isthmus (958), and now Heracles' final destination (943), Mycenae itself (963). The inner drama climaxes when the palace doors as parts of stage architecture fade in order to transform themselves under the internalized actor's gaze – a theatrical vision of sorts – into "the very walls the Cyclopes have built" (998); dug out and wrested from their frames, they expose to Heracles' murderous frenzy the last of his victims.

But all is not well, all is not as it should be in the theater, in Lyssa's inset drama. For a start, although "the adoption of otherness *while remaining oneself* is an essential and highly dynamic attribute of the actor's art" (Harrop 1992, 5; my italics), Amphitryon's voice, as replicated in the messenger's narration, indicates that Heracles has suffered a massive alienation from his normal self: "What is the matter, my son? What is the nature of this aberration?" (965–66; cf. 931: "suddenly, he was no longer himself"). Heracles, the acting agent, has lost the binocular vision that enables an actor to hold the imaginary and the material constituents of a performance simultaneously in view. In Heracles' distorted vision, only the symbolic, referential dimension of stage signs seems real. Moreover, he has lost a stage actor's multiple consciousness, the faculty that makes it possible for him to be aware of himself *and* the part, his fellow-actors *and* their roles, as separate entities, and in such a way that neither awareness risks canceling the other out: for Heracles, his children and Eurystheus' children, his father and Eurystheus' father have fused and merged (967–71). While they, as unwilling actors in the inset drama, pay the price for the wrongdoings of characters superimposed upon their own selves (see 982–83), the play enacts one of the greatest prejudices against theatrical fictionality, namely, the view that actors are personally responsible for the villainy of their dramatic characters; in Ferdinand's words in John Webster's *The Duchess of Malfi* (1614), it is the way of the tragic stage ("as we observe in tragedies") "That a good actor many times is cursed/For playing a villain's part" (4.2.281–83).

In relation to his own actions, too, Heracles has lost his bearings. A stage actor remains conscious of his own attempt to work on our "imaginary forces" (Shakespeare, *King Henry V*, Prologue 18), so that we can "see" the figments of the dramatist's imagination, whether these are Furies (cf. Longinus 15.2) or "the vasty fields of France" crammed in an "unworthy scaffold"(*King Henry V*, Prologue 10–12). But such self-consciousness is lacking in Heracles. The invisible and non-existent and all manner of "conceit[s] deceitful" (Shakespeare, *The Rape of Lucrece* 1423) he treats as materially present. And while theatrical vision registers much more than can be seen with physical eyesight *without* failing to remember that the "eye of mind" is at work (*The Rape of Lucrece* 1426), Heracles literally (mis)takes "airy nothing" (*A Midsummer Night's Dream* 5.1.16) for solid, three-dimensional forms: he mounts a fictitious chariot (947–48), strikes imaginary horses with his whip (949), eats an insubstantial banquet (956–57), wrestles in unreal games at the Isthmus, and proclaims himself a victor over no opponent in front of an imagined crowd (959–62).

The bystanders respond to Heracles' actions with sheer bewilderment. Like Gertrude asking Hamlet "Alas, how is't with you,/That you do bend your eye on vacancy,/And with th' incorporal air do hold discourse?" (*Hamlet* 3.4.115–17), the palace servants find their master's behavior indecipherable. As reported by the messenger, their comments not only accentuate the sheer uncanniness of Heracles' actions but most importantly effect a *mise en abyme* of the very nature of "acting": is acting a harmless, playful reconstruction of our world along the lines of "symbolic" vision or is it meaningless, pointless, and disorienting action bordering on clinical insanity?

"Is the master playing a joke on us or is he in the grip of madness?" wonder the attendants (*Heracles* 952). The polarity their bafflement constructs between the states of "playing" (*paizein*) and "being mad" (*mainesthai*) qualifies dramatic space as ambiguous, uncertain ground. Its one end is adjacent to theatrical *il*-lusion, where the dead can only "bleed in sport" (Shakespeare, *Julius Caesar* 3.1.114) and where tragedy is "played in jest by counterfeiting actors" (Shakespeare, *Henry VI Part 3*, 2.3.27–28).[3] Its other end verges on *de*-lusion, the distorted vision that elides the gap between sign-vehicles and what they represent. Embedded in Euripides' tragedy, Lyssa's playlet is self-reflexive drama, forcing us to plunge into the vertiginous depths of mimetic representation, where the distinction between reality and the pretence of reality is blurred and where "playing" the Other and "being" the Other are disturbingly intermeshed. For the unsettling truth conveyed metatheatrically in Lyssa's playlet is that "Heracles" both *paizei* (as the professional actor impersonating the hero of Euripides' tragedy on the Athenian stage) and *mainetai* (as a dramatic character embarking on a "secondary" impersonation) at once, aligning thus the stage-player and the madman in a manner reminiscent of European puritan anti-theatricality. As William Prynne complains,

> He who shall seriously survay the ridiculous, childish, inconsiderate, yea, mad and beastly actions, gestures, speeches, habits, prankes and fooleries of Actors on the stage (if he be not childish, foolish, or frentique himselfe), must needs deeme all Stage-players children, fooles, or Bedlams; since they act such parts, such pranks, yea, use such gestures, speeches, rayment, complements, and behaviour in Iest, which none but children, fooles, or mad-men, do act, or use in earnest. (Prynne 1974 [1633], 174, Z3v)

Furthermore, seen from a slightly different perspective, the inset drama opens up a vista on the figure of the actor that could activate the most haunting fears of theatrophobes from Plato onwards. The gradual conversion of the triumphant (*kallinikos*) Heracles, the player in the Euripidean plot, into a polluted killer of kin, his role in the enfolded play (Lyssa's plot), rehearses the intense anti-theatrical anxiety that the "I" of the actor may be totally subsumed into the "I" of his part or, to put it differently, that a stage-player may be shaped and conditioned by his role, reconstituted and refashioned *as* his dramatis persona.

The fear that illusion may lapse into delusion and that symbolic vision may unseat or cloud our physical eyesight is rehearsed by Greek tragedy itself at self-reflexive moments. Interestingly, Elizabethan drama also replicates the anxieties of its opponents. The elision of the gap between reality and role, Heracles *ho tekōn* (the father) and Heracles *ho ktanōn* (the killer) in Lyssa's inset plot (cf. Kraus 1998, 155), is a good analogue of the ultimate fusion of actor and part metatheatrically implanted in Thomas Kyd's *The Spanish Tragedy* (ca. 1587). Enacted before an internal audience, the embedded playlet of *Soliman and Perseda* (Act 4) stages the disintegration of all that is "fabulously counterfeit" (4.4.77) into sinister reality, transmuting feigned deaths into irrevocably real corpses and transforming the fiction's pretend-murderer into a real-life killer. Greek theater differs from that of the Elizabethans in its clear branding of the "actor-*as*-character" amalgam as an aberration that only takes shape when theater space is infected by divinely inflicted madness. Yet Greek as well as Renaissance tragedy creates spectacle out of its own heightened awareness that the stage and all that it encompasses are precariously poised between imaginative pretense and the mistaking of imagination for reality; between, for example, Richard Burbage's "so lively" stage-deaths and his "amazed" co-players' fear that he had died in actual fact:

> Oft have I seen him play this part in jest
> So lively that spectators, and the rest
> Of his sad crew, whilst he but seem'd to bleed,
> Amazed, thought even then he died in deed.
> (Anonymous funeral elegy for the Shakespearean actor Richard Burbage, 1619;
> text in Wickham, Berry, and Ingram 2000, 181–83)

If the determining act of public theater is the preservation of the balance between likeness as representation (this is *like* that) and likeness as reality (this *is* that), Greek and Renaissance tragedy share an awareness of the actor's catalytic role in preserving as well as unsettling that balance.

Acting can be more than a site of self-negation or loss of self; in a world where the person within is threatened more seriously by social than by theatrical masks, it can be seen as offering the possibility for authentic rather than purloined expression. The Polish director and producer Jerzy Grotowski, for example, treats the actor's "getting out of himself" as the beginning of a journey of self-discovery and self-realization, leading to a clearer, deeper, and more truthful understanding of the inner self. In Grotowski's "poor theater" every role (conceived now much more broadly as a social function rather than a text-specific dramatis persona) is a means of self-exploration, provided the actor learns to use it

> as if it were a surgeon's scalpel, to dissect himself. It is not a question of portraying himself under certain given circumstances, or of "living" a part.... The important thing is to use the role as a trampoline, an instrument with which to study what is hidden behind our everyday mask – the innermost core of our personality – in order to *sacrifice* it, expose it. (Grotowski 1968, 37; my italics)

For Grotowski, the quintessence of the theater event is the actor's "self-sacrifice," the actor's making a gift of himself, "opening up" instead of "closing in" on himself: "It is all a question of giving oneself" (Grotowski 1968, 38).

This very notion of role-playing as sacrifice, as a complete and unconditional offering of the actor's self, seems to be metatheatrically conveyed by the famous robing-scene of Pentheus in Euripides' *Bacchae* (912–76). An initially unwilling actor in a play-within-the-play, which, as Foley points out, is "replete with set, costume and spectators" (Foley 1980, 110), Pentheus gradually relinquishes his stubborn hold on his identity, and culminates the process by dedicating himself (see Dodds 1960 and Seaford 1996a on *Bacchae* 934) to Dionysus/the Stranger, the director of the inner drama designed and staged for his undoing. In anticipation of the sacrificial manner of Pentheus' death on Mount Cithaeron (see esp. Seidensticker 1979a and Seaford

1994, 281–93), the language used in the robing-scene has clear ritual and sacrificial overtones. Like a sacrificial animal brought into the realm of the divine prior to its ritualized slaughter, Pentheus delivers himself up to Dionysus, who will turn him into a comic as well as a gruesome spectacle (see esp. *Bacchae* 823, 854–56, 914, 1075, 1095, 1200–1203, 1279–82) for the edification of the Theban polis (*Bacchae* 39–40): "I am dedicating myself [literally, giving myself up as an offering] to you" (*soi . . . anakeimestha*, 934).[4]

In Grotowski's theater the actor's everyday self is relentlessly confronted with its own "deep roots and hidden motives" (Grotowski 1968, 52); when successfully performed, the role leads to the unveiling of powers that lie dormant in "the most intimate layers of his being and his instinct" (Grotowski 1968, 16). In Euripides' *Bacchae*, it is precisely the "gear of a woman, a maenad, a bacchant" (915), the role of a Dionysiac devotee, that functions as the catalyst that ultimately unleashes the secret tides of Dionysianism concealed in Pentheus' own heart. Even though against his own will, and prompted by the skillful enticements of the Stranger who plays to Pentheus' most secret longings,[5] the actor finally drops what Grotowski would have called his psychic blocks and social inhibitions and indulges in "the act of laying oneself bare, of tearing off the mask of daily life" (Grotowski 1968, 210): disguised as a woman and exchanging his Theban seat of power for a hiding place in the wilds of Mount Cithaeron, the obstinately male and overbearingly royal Pentheus allows his Dionysiac part to work through and in collusion with his own natural impulses. Like Dionysus Lusios and Luaios, "the Deliverer" and "Liberator" who, according to Aelius Aristides, "releases from everything" (2.331 Keil 1898; see Lada-Richards 1999, 317), Grotowskian role-playing too releases the flood of repressed matter in the actor's own psyche, strips away the accumulated layers of pretense and falsehood, exposes the very core of his existence and in so doing produces "an excess of truth" (Grotowski 1968, 53). In Pentheus' case, his prior metaphysical confusion, best reflected in Dionysus/the Stranger's taunt, "You know not what your life is nor what your actions mean nor who you are" (506), gives way to a newly acquired vision ("now you see what you should see," 924) and a different mentality ("I praise you for having changed your mind," *Bacchae* 944). But, whereas for the Grotowskian actor the enactment of a part engages the "total act" of his "psycho-physical resources from the most instinctive to the most rational" (Grotowski 1968, 209), Pentheus embarks on the journey to self-realization when deprived of his reason (*exó d' elaunôn tou phronein*, 853). For Euripides' metadramatic "actor," the moment of Grotowskian "illumination" or "translumination" (see 1120–21) is co-extensive with his own death. The sacrificial metaphor of the theatrical experience gives way to real sacrifice when role-playing takes place in the ritual realm.

Finally, Pentheus' performance affords interesting links with essential concepts in Antonin Artaud's immensely influential "Theater of Cruelty." Like Grotowski, Artaud envisages a theater that integrates actors and spectators in a single "living" organism, bringing them into direct communion. When the maenads encircle and uproot the fir-tree in whose branches Pentheus is perched (1106–13), thus initiating his final move from the safe position of a *theatês* (spectator) to the violent center of the action, the inset play's imaginary space not only replicates the actual, theatrical space, where a semicircular auditorium surrounds the performer on the acting floor, but also seems to realize Artaud's elemental vision of a spectator "seated in the center of the action," "encircled and furrowed by it" (1974, 73–74). Artaud envisaged a theatrical experience so intense and all-consuming as to instigate traumas in the audience's psyche. Yet the wounds are such as to be clinically invisible. Acting "physically" upon his viewers without leaving any physical marks upon their bodies, the Artaudian actor turns the theater into the conceptual analogue of the plague: in one of Artaud's best-known metaphors, just as the body of the plague victim shows no organic lesions, so actor and spectator are shattered by the eruption of extreme emotions while their bodies are unharmed (see Artaud 1974, 7–21).

Sophocles' *Philoctetes* can also be interpreted in Artaudian terms. In desperate need of Philoctetes and his bow for the success of the Greek cause at Troy, Odysseus devises a plot (a play-within-the-play, which we could name "The Capture of Philoctetes") whose execution requires the services of Neoptolemus as an actor. An actor in Odysseus' plot, Neoptolemus is also an internalized audience for Philoctetes' outbursts of pain and despair. It would be difficult to find a performative moment more expressive of emotional and physical agony purging the actor's self internally without deforming it externally than Neoptolemus' reaction to the enfolded spectacle of the diseased Philoctetes. Neoptolemus' privileged metatheatrical position as both actor and spectator simultaneously illustrates the link Artaud aspired to forge between the two constituents of the theatrical event. And if Artaud's ideal spectator is so deeply shocked and scarred by the performer's anguish as to feel his whole frame shaken into a near physical involvement, Neoptolemus participates in Philoctetes' torment through an almost bodily ordeal of pure, unmitigated suffering: his anguished cry *algô*, "I am in pain" (806), gives voice to his affliction by appropriating the language of physical anguish. The fatal fusion of actor, spectator, and spectacle in Euripides' *Bacchae* and Neoptolemus' direct exposure to Philoctetes' disease without the protective screen of an aesthetic frame give form to Artaud's conception of theater as an "immediate stage experience that comprehends the audience's reality in the heightened reality of the performance itself" (Worthen 1984, 158). For Pentheus and Neoptolemus acting is a means of "finding" the self, but only through an overwhelming envelopment in "sensory violence" (Sontag 1983, 34), in the middle of a theater where actors and spectators feel caught "as if in a vortex of higher forces" (Artaud 1974, 63).

Being and Not-Being: Euripides' Helen and the Paradox of Acting

I close by returning to Euripides' *Helen*. Our idea of "Helen" wavers constantly between what seems to us a "real," visible, somatic presence on the stage (the Helen who dwells in Egypt, Menelaus' chaste wife wooed unlawfully by an Egyptian king) and what we experience as an unreal, invisible, ethereal absence (the phantom-Helen that went to Troy, the adulterous wife of Menelaus). In the eyes of phenomenologically oriented critics of the stage, this "new Helen" (cf. Aristophanes, *Women at the Thesmophoria* 850) of Euripides exemplifies the "ontological double status" of the actor on the stage, the paradox of being both real and unreal at once (States 1994, 26).

The question of reality and unreality is further probed through the striking disparity between Helen's and other characters' perspectives. Helen knows herself, her staged body, to be the real thing, the prototype, while "Helen of Troy," the phantom fashioned by Hera, is merely an *eidôlon*, a simulacrum of her real self (33–34). The *eidôlon* as a *mimêma* of Helen inverts the natural relationship between the actor and the character within the role: it is the actor who is judged as a truthful and persuasive or a false and ineffectual imitation of the character that he or she is called upon to incarnate. Indeed, Helen does seem to think of the *eidôlon* as a dramatic mask the gods inflicted upon her, a role which stains and destroys her reputation with the enormous weight of *duskleia* and *aischunê* (ill-repute and shame) that is permanently attached to it (*Helen* 66–67, 270–72). Yet, in both Teucer's perspective and in the eyes of Menelaus prior to the play's "recognition," it is the phantom-Helen who constitutes the real body, while the stage-Helen living in Proteus' palace is merely her copy and resemblance (*mimêma*, 74; *homoian*, 563; *eoikas*, 579; *prospherês*, 591), an altogether hateful, "lethal likeness" (*echthistên . . . eikô phonion*, 72–73). Though unjustified by the play's plot, Teucer's and Menelaus' perspective restores the normal balance between character and actor: it is the actor's "staged" body that resembles or demonstrates or even "lives" a bodiless shape, an absent character, an empty *onoma* (name). But in a play where all manner of certainty is thrown into confusion, irreconcilable perspectives have an unsettling effect on *our* vision: how can we tell the real from the counterfeit, the prototype from its lookalike? who should we ultimately believe to be the real Helen, if such a thing exists? The *sôma* or the *onoma*, the visible or the invisible, the actor or the part?

More intensely than any other classical tragedy, Euripides' *Helen* casts light on the perceptual problems associated with stage-acting. Yet no pat answers are provided. In the mirror of this play, as in all Athenian tragedy, modern performance theories will be able to discern parts of their own image. No single reflection will amount to more than a glimmer, yet all the images taken together demonstrate tragedy's dynamism and versatility as a generic form that ceaselessly turns itself and its performance into an object of inquiry. The ancient actor, as configured by the tragic texts, has multiple resonances in Western performance history, in theory as well as in practice.

NOTES

1   For further discussion of Brechtian and non-Brechtian elements in the tragic convention of messenger speeches, see Lada-Richards 1997, 87–90; for an insightful discussion of the "spectating," as opposed to the "acting," aspect of the messenger convention, see Barrett 2002 (esp. 102–31 on messengers in *Bacchae*), who ascribes to messengers a "privileged spectatorship" (124), sometimes "marked by a virtual invisibility and disembodiment" (118).

2   The following discussion should be read in parallel with Kraus 1998, 151–56, the most incisive recent discussion of the play's messenger speech.

3   In a theatrical context *paizein* is a highly self-conscious term, taking us to the heart of theater's artistic nature; see, e.g., Aristophanes *Frogs* 522–23, where the quintessential theatrical act of an actor's dressing up for his part is the stuff of jesting, *paizein* (Lada-Richards 1999, 319–20); in Renaissance treatises, too, performing an action "in jest" or "in sport" is synonymous with performing it in the course of a dramatic play (see, e.g., Prynne 1974 [1633], 174; cf. the elegy for Richard Burbage, in the text). Lionel Trilling (1967, 360) aptly emphasizes the derivation of the word "illusion" from the Latin *illudere* (mock), itself deriving from *ludere* (play).

4   For the idea of "handing oneself over" as linked with initiation into mystic cults in ancient Greece, see Lada-Richards 1998, 3–4.

5   See Dodds 1960, 172, on Dionysus' tempting of Pentheus: "In the maddening of Pentheus...the poet shows us the supernatural attacking the victim's personality at its weakest point – working upon and through nature, not against it. The god wins because he has an ally in the enemy's camp: the persecutor is betrayed by what he would persecute – the Dionysiac longing in himself." On Pentheus' repressed Dionysianism, see Winnington-Ingram 1997, 159–60; Segal 1997, 21–22.

FURTHER READING

The first port of call for anyone interested in the conditions of theatrical production (including actors and acting) in fifth-century Athens is still Pickard-Cambridge 1988, supplemented by Csapo and Slater 1995, several chapters of which are devoted to the actor's art throughout antiquity (all ancient sources are cited in translation). Supremely illuminating is also J. R. Green 1994, who takes into account depictions of actors on a wide variety of Greek and Roman artifacts. For a meticulous collection of testimonia on individual theatrical performers in antiquity, see Stephanis 1988 (in Greek, but one can still follow the ancient sources). Those who read French can still benefit from Ghiron-Bistagne 1976, a sociological analysis (pioneering in its time) of the actor's calling in ancient Greece, while for a new and fascinating exploration of several aspects of the acting profession in antiquity, see the collection of essays by Easterling and Hall 2002.

On Stanislavsky's and Brecht's theatrical practices there is, as can well be expected, a vast literature. My personal selection on Stanislavsky includes: Wiles 1980, 13–36; Jones 1986, 15–77; and Leiter 1991, 1–43; see also the very interesting contributions of Rapoport, Sudakov, Vakhtangov, and Giatsintova in Cole 1955. The best summary of the *System* can be found in Moore 1966; very informative is also Magarshack 1961. For Brecht's "Epic" theater, the starting point of all preliminary reading should be Brecht 1964 and 1965; excellent discussions can be found in Willet 1977; Ben Chaim 1984, 25–38; Brooker 1988 and 1994; and Eddershaw 1982 and 1994. On Artaud and Grotowski there are excellent introductions in Wiles 1980 and Innes 1993; more advanced discussions may be found in Esslin 1976, Worthen 1984, and Wolford and Schechner 1997. English texts from the period of puritan anti-theatricality can be found in Chambers 1923, vol. 4, and now Wickham, Berry, and Ingram 2000.

CHAPTER THIRTY

The Theater of Innumerable Faces

Herman Altena

Greek tragedy has never been performed so frequently and on such a worldwide scale as during the last fifteen years. Helmut Flashar has noted the marked increase in productions of Greek drama, both translations and adaptations, that began in the 1950s and 1960s. From the 1970s on the number of productions grew at an even faster pace. Directors no longer restricted themselves to the canon of well-known plays, such as Sophocles' *Oedipus the King*, *Antigone*, and *Electra*, or Euripides' *Medea*, but began to explore the whole corpus of ancient drama (Flashar 1991, 199–302). Recent figures from the Archive of Performances of Greek and Roman Drama in Oxford show a further acceleration of productions during the 1990s and the first years of our century. In December 2003, the Archive's database registered 4,246 productions of Greek drama worldwide, performed between 1951 and December 2003, of which almost 1,200 were mounted during the 1990s. As I write, there is no sign that the popularity of ancient drama among modern theater artists is waning, given the 454 productions between 2001 and December 2003 worldwide.

This spectacular increase in absolute numbers raises the question "why?" Why do a growing number of modern directors all over the world gravitate so strongly to this genre that they are willing to confront all the strange elements that, while organic to Greek tragedy, reveal an enormous gap between their own culture and the remote fifth-century Athenian society? These are elements that even scholars sometimes have difficulty apprehending: mythical figures whose hybrid social structure encompasses both the old aristocratic codes and the democratic innovations of fifth-century Athens; gods from an unfamiliar pantheon, who appear on stage and communicate directly with human beings; formal elements – lengthy monologues, high poetry, a paucity of onstage action, and the continuous presence of the chorus – that run counter to every dictate of modern entertainment. Why do some theater artists go to the trouble of toning down or even eliminating such distinctive elements in order to retain little more than the basic story? Why do others feel the need to rework these basic stories and to create adaptations that sometimes seem to have forfeited almost all connection with the original plays? And why do spectators feel impelled to watch such productions?

In order to answer the question "why?" we need a representative collection of data. Not only do we need to know what ancient tragedies were performed where, when, and by whom, we also need descriptions of how they were staged, for what audience, and under what historical and cultural conditions. The sheer volume of productions and their global and temporal spread make it difficult to gain full access to all relevant data. Happily, data collections registering the reception of ancient drama are growing rapidly. In the United Kingdom the Open University maintains an online database to register productions of ancient drama. Individual countries, such as the Czech Republic and Greece, have developed similar national databases. The Oxford Archive, which is the most comprehensive because of its international scope, has already proved an invaluable tool for many scholars. Its potential will increase still further if it can be linked to databases with other specializations (such as the reception of Shakespearean drama or the theater history of individual countries).

At the present state of research, the available international data provide information about the who, what, where, and when, but a more thorough analysis of the performances themselves, and how they affected their audiences, is still lacking. A small canon of international productions has received much critical attention. However, a general picture of the global reception of ancient drama requires that we focus more systematically on local differences. If research into the global perform-ance history of ancient drama is to pass from the descriptive to the analytical phase, both supranational and interdisciplinary collaboration will be indispensable. A full assessment of past and present manifestations of ancient drama requires not only specialists in the discipline of classics, but also in theater history and theoretical and empirical theater research. The European Network of Research and Documentation of Ancient Greek Drama, situated in Athens, represents a first step in this direction.

Since a comprehensive answer to the question "why?" cannot be furnished at the present state of academic research, in this chapter I will present some partial answers that have been offered by scholars and theater artists and that command a certain degree of universality. I will discuss the attractions Greek tragedy exerts and the obstacles modern directors and actors have to overcome in staging Greek tragedy. I will focus mainly on Greek tragedy in translation, because a key feature of the revivals of the last century, in my view, is the unprecedented attraction exerted by the original texts in translation, as opposed to adaptations. This development had its start in nineteenth-century Germany, Britain, and France, and spread rapidly over Europe and the United States from the 1880s on. In the last decade of the twentieth century more directors than ever turned to Greek tragedy in translation and faced the challenge of appropriating and reinterpreting its unfamiliar formal elements. This is not to say that performances of translations outnumber the adaptations. On the contrary, research I recently conducted on the reception of ancient Greek themes in the Dutch professional theater between 1951 and 2003 shows that out of 250 productions related to ancient Greek mythological themes, only 65 concerned Greek tragedy in translation (against 113 adaptations and 72 new versions based on themes not treated in extant Greek tragedy). The figures of the Oxford database show a comparable proportion. Those of the Czech Republic, however – and this illustrates the limited value of generalizations – show a clear preference for translations. I will return to the Czech case later.

Partial answers to the question "why?" (and "how?") have been formulated from different angles and with varying degrees of sophistication. Answers from the perspective of cultural philosophy take a broad view and concentrate on the fundamental existential struggle of Western man in periods of severe crisis throughout Western history (Decreus 2002 and 2003). More circumscribed answers originate in the context of contemporary and global sociopolitical criticism (Rehm 2003). Others are determined by historical and local sociopolitical conditions, or emerge in the context of performance aesthetics (Taplin 1999a, Hall, Macintosh, and Wrigley 2004). Specialized publications on the performance history of specific works, such as the *Oresteia* (Bierl 1997), *Medea* (Hall, Macintosh, and Taplin 2000), *Agamemnon* (Macintosh et al. forthcoming), or in individual countries, provide many partial answers that have a potentially broader significance. Finally, numerous responses from theater artists all over the world have been offered in interviews and printed in performance programs (although practically speaking, these are the most difficult to get hold of). The status of all these answers varies: some reflect private truths, others claim universal validity; some are descriptive, others normative.

Cultural philosophers have tried to define the social and cultural conditions and the mental climate in which tragedy, both ancient and modern, and more specifically the tragic feeling, the consciousness of humanity's finiteness, can prosper. According to Freddy Decreus, the tragic feeling

> mainly depends on a Western and originally Greek vision of the world and presents a fundamental idea of life and death which is not Christian and neither chthonic nor matriarchal.... The tragic feeling discusses the finiteness of the human being, the constant threat of losing a presumed security.... Therefore, the tragic condition and the endeavour it inspires to undertake actions, to make choices and thus to assume responsibility (and to become guilty), leads necessarily to "acting" in a fundamental way, away from nature. (Decreus 2003, 62)

This tragic feeling emerges with special force in periods of severe crisis, whether political, cultural, or both, and it is reflected in performances of tragedy. "The literary history of the West is characterized by a long chain of literary and aesthetic products called tragedies, which commented on man's existential, political, philosophical and economic situation during important moments of (r)evolution" (Decreus 2002, 325). These plays either promise the possibility of a solution, or display man acting heroically in the face of his tragic condition, or expose the tragic awareness that in this bleak world there is no exit, no meaningful action, no communication, and no shared emotion. These visions of the tragic Decreus terms respectively the proto-tragic, the absolute-tragic, and the post-tragic (Decreus 2003, 73–74). The first category is exemplified by Aeschylus' *Oresteia*, with its promise of a better future; the second by Sophocles' *Oedipus the King*, Euripides' *Bacchae*, or Shakespeare's *King Lear*; the third by modern rewritings such as Sarah Kane's *Phaedra's Love* (based on Euripides' *Hippolytus*), or performances such as Romeo Castelucci's *Oresteia*, with its "shocking images of desolated human bodies" (Decreus 2003, 73–76). The last example illustrates an important extension of the categorization, for it shows that modern performances of a proto-tragic work like the *Oresteia* do not necessarily subscribe to the proto-tragic vision. In fact, the performance history of the *Oresteia* shows that many modern directors question rather than endorse its promise of a better future (Bierl 1997). This clash of interpretations incidentally reflects a comparable debate among classical scholars (Glau 1998).

Decreus' broad cultural-philosophical analysis of the tragic and of tragedy performances in the theater of the past and present provides a model for anyone who tries to understand the vast diversity of modern productions in what may be called the theater of innumerable faces. However, it is a model based on and particularly relevant to the work of the most prominent theater directors and authors. Although their engagement with ancient drama has gained much critical attention, the revival of Greek tragedy is not limited to a few high-profile productions. This revival manifests itself no less strongly in thousands of other more modest productions that attract an even larger number of theater-goers. These productions neither lay claim to nor are credited with epoch-making new world-visions – which is not to say that they lack vision or skirt the question "why." On the contrary, they are representative of the more localized, more circumscribed answers to this question. These answers involve three characteristics that uniquely define Greek tragedy, and that will concern me in the next part of this chapter: the myths that provided the stories, the universal themes and ideas adumbrated by these stories, and the specific form of Greek tragedy.

"Myth is the attempt to understand the world through art," the German dramaturge Helmut Schäfer has remarked (Schäfer 1998, 439). To that end, Greek myth offers a rich source of powerful stories that belong to the public domain, are not linked with any major religion, and can thus be freely appropriated (Foley 1999, 6). In an era that has lost its grand narratives, the longing for explanation through storytelling motivates numerous modern directors to turn to Greek tragedy. Even if the modern audience is secularized and the cultic-mythical horizon alien to them, the basic stories that provide the material for many Greek tragedies are still widely known. Yet the broader mythical context from which the plots are taken, and to which they often allude, has become less familiar as modern education has marginalized the classics. The desire to "tell the whole story," to disclose the long chain of cause and effect that extends beyond the plot of a single play, underlies the various productions that involve double bills (for example, Sophocles' *Oedipus the King* followed by *Oedipus at Colonus*), adaptations that extend the plot of a single tragedy and incorporate previous events (for example, *Mamma Medea* by the Flemish author Tom Lanoye, based on Apollonius' *Argonautica* and Euripides' *Medea*), and vast mythical narratives such as John Barton's *Tantalus*. For many theater artists it suffices to retell these horrifying stories and treat their audiences to an evening of intense aesthetic pleasure. For others, it is essential that the disturbing elements reflect upon and be relevant to contemporary social issues.

The mythical stories that underlie Greek tragedy deal with universal themes and issues central to human life. Greek tragedy considers the universals of warfare and its consequences, and the conflicting obligations of leadership. It has to do with conflicts between nations but also, as Ariane Mnouchkine has emphasized, with "internal wars, civil wars. They are wars in the family, but cruel wars" (Mnouchkine 1996, 181). Greek tragedy deals with universal emotions, universal fears, and the acts of capricious powers beyond human control. It brings on stage moderation and responsibility, and their counterparts excess and recklessness. It exhibits the sacrifice of children, cruel murders, suicides, horrible acts of revenge, and the fatal consequences of ignorance. And it does so in a straightforward manner that leaves little room for evasion or compromise.

It is a consensus of recent scholarship that Greek tragedy in its own time not only aimed at aesthetic pleasure, but that the performances were charged with political if not ideological significance. The definition of that ideological significance remains in dispute (see Croally, chapter 4 in this volume), but the topics of many of these plays suggest that Greek tragedy used the realm of myth to give voice to the other side of contemporary male-dominated Athenian society. Rehm has recently questioned some current assumptions about the ideological thrust of Greek tragedy. "As a product of the society from which it sprang, tragedy reflected Athenian imperialism, sexism, hypocrisy, intolerance, and a host of other ills. And yet time and again the plays confront and expose these failings, challenging the audience to think them through" (Rehm 2003, 34). The notion that tragedy reinforces patriarchy and male domination is called into question by the fact that the plays feature so many outstanding female characters as well as female choruses, female captives, and female slaves. The ideologies of warfare and militarism are challenged by plays like *Hecuba* and *Trojan Women*. The ideology of democracy is challenged by plays attacking "politicians and public speakers who manipulate crowds in their own interest" (Rehm 2003, 106 – this is an issue with no lack of analogies in the modern world).

Myth offered a secure framework for these sociopolitical concerns of Greek tragedy. The dramatic action, set in the mythical world, provided various models for examining historical events without becoming overtly topical or dangerously subversive. The mythical framework allowed the Greek tragedians to explore the human condition and the consequences of every kind of human behavior at its most extreme and horrifying. At the same time it created critical distance, because it constantly allowed the spectators to shift between mythical story and contemporary life. At any moment, each member of the audience could appropriate the weighty issues as relevant to his own experiences, or dismiss them as belonging to the mythical story and refuse to see the staged events as a matter of personal concern. This, in short, is what Kevin Lee has called a comfort zone (Lee 2001, 82–85).

This distancing quality of the mythical stories has also played an important role in the modern theater's reception of ancient drama. It made Greek tragedy a powerful instrument for registering dissident opinions in many countries during periods of severe censorship when modern plays were blacklisted, but classical tragedies were still permitted – and welcomed by the audience as tokens of a lost humanism or shining examples of indomitability. Such was the case in Europe during World War II (for example, Sartre's *Les Mouches*, performed in 1943 in Nazi-occupied Paris); it was also the case in Eastern European and other countries living under repressive regimes. In the former Czechoslovakia the freedom to perform Greek tragedy became a barometer for the political climate: during the severest periods total prohibition was the rule, whereas veiled topical interpretations were permitted in times of relaxation (Stehlíková 2000). I surmise that the issue of the comfort zone explains the Czech preference for translations over freer and more dangerous adaptations. The contradictory interpretations of Heiner Müller's adaptation of Sophocles' *Philoctetes* (the play was published in 1965, premiered in 1968 in Munich, and had its first professional production in East Germany only in 1977) either as an anti-war play that criticized pre-socialist societies, or as a veiled criticism of the actual socialist ideology that governed the former German Democratic Republic (Lefèvre 2000, 429–30), neatly exemplify the working of the comfort zone Müller had created. Even directors in the modern Western theater value the distancing quality of mythical stories. For Peter Sellars, who views the theater as centrally concerned with contemporary social issues, performing the classics, whether the ancients or Shakespeare, offers a welcome alternative to literal-mindedness. "The reason we apply poetry to these questions is because in the end it's more interesting than journalism. Shakespeare can go further than *Newsweek*. Shakespeare's equipment is better calibrated to deal with what we are actually facing as a society" (Sellars 1996, 226).

When the comfort zone offered by Greek myth and the more traditional performances of Greek tragedy is undermined or removed altogether, the audience may experience the staged events as such an intrusion that they respond with fierce rejection, even if the performance's subject matter is of great concern. This response became painfully clear when a radical adaptation of Aeschylus' *Oresteia* was presented at the Holland Festival in 2000. The Belgian company Het Toneelhuis mounted *Aars!* (*Ass!*), written by Peter Verhelst and directed by Luk Perceval (now one of the artistic directors of the Berlin Schaubühne). The authors called their play "an anatomical study of the *Oresteia*" which tried to probe beneath the surface of so much male and female violence. Man's major vital instinct, according to the authors, is sexual fulfillment, and in their version of the *Oresteia*, the relations between the four members of the family (Agamemnon, Clytemnestra, Electra, and Orestes) are fundamentally incestuous. In the course of the play, all except Electra are killed. Electra refuses further procreation by sewing shut her sexual organs. The performance represented a fundamentally post-tragic vision. Relations between male and female were described in terms of food and digestion, or in terms of war. Descriptions of war carried strong sexual overtones. This introverted world, where life is sex and sex is life, was staged as an inferno: a round basin filled with water, one rectangular table and four chairs, strong spotlights from all sides, stroboscopes dazzling the eyes, and the dominant music by DJ Eavesdropper (Yves De Mey) assaulting the ears (plate 30.1). The action unfurled with a strong dynamic thrust: slowness and softness, seemingly gentle, built up to a sometimes devastating and cruel tempo. Many spectators walked out during the performance and the press condemned the production. I must confess that I experienced negative reactions myself, but a subsequent published interview with the author and director made me revise my ideas and reevaluate this performance. The authors were deeply disappointed that no one in the audience dared to face the reality that their own society was so deeply rotten within: at this time Belgium was rocked by a traumatic scandal involving the sexual abuse of children.

Many people were also shocked by the fact that this production was explicitly linked to the *Oresteia*, although the original story had been dropped almost completely. Why did the authors not compose a new play about the scandal instead of distorting the *Oresteia*? But to write a new play directly exploiting such a delicate social issue would have invited spectators and critics to assess the work in terms of its historical accuracy, not in terms of essential truths of the human condition. By breaking the myth open the artists forced their audiences to revise their worldview. After all, the traditional story of Agamemnon is part of the spectators' cultural memory, and may even ground their fundamental thinking on such issues as justice or the blessings of democracy; so a radical break with that tradition makes their world

Plate 30.1 Agamemnon, Clytemnestra, Orestes, and Electra in the production of *Aars!* by Het Toneelhuis (co-production with Holland Festival), directed by Luk Perceval, Amsterdam, 2000. Photograph © Phile Duprez. Used by permission.

tremble on its foundations. This new version was not just about Belgium on the eve of the twenty-first century. It went beyond recent history and beyond Greek tragedy. It dealt with the foundations of humanity itself and presented an utterly bleak, monolithic worldview to which one might or might not subscribe, but which left no one in the audience unaffected. The performance was probably one of the strongest acts of sociopolitical and cultural resistance the Dutch stage had experienced for many years, but the absence of a comfort zone rendered it unbearable for many spectators.

The mythical stories dramatized by the Greek tragedians recognize time and again that individual human beings are responsible for the world they create, even if irrational forces may at any moment undermine their efforts. Many modern theater artists feel that this emphasis on personal responsibility in a world of imponderable forces is particularly relevant as an alternative model to a modern Western entertainment culture that shuns complexity and fosters indifference. It offers an alternative to the fable of total individual freedom and the suggestion that we can fully master our lives; an alternative to the promise of a world of free nations that believes in progress and that considers the past not a guide but a restraint that impedes the present and the future; an alternative to social and political utopias and to religious values that have proved deficient in the face of ongoing violations of humanity; and, finally, an alternative to the self-interest that governs national and global policies (Sellars 1996, Raddatz 2002, Rehm 2003, passim). For many modern directors, staging Greek tragedy is an act of sociopolitical and cultural resistance, less hazardous than under the repressive regimes mentioned above, but driven by the same impulses. Peter Sellars' productions of Sophocles' *Ajax*, Aeschylus' *Persians*, and (most recently) Euripides' *Children of Heracles* (plate 30.2) are telling examples. "For me the appeal of Greek drama is this insistence of those three playwrights to ask questions that our society rejects before you even ask. And yet they asked them anyway, and they asked them at length" (Sellars in McDonald 1992, 93). Greek tragedy is especially appealing because, as Helene Foley has observed, "Greek plots . . . provide a more complex notion of motivation than can be projected by reduced, modern characters in the present" (Foley 1999, 5).

The reason why Greek tragedy proves such a timeless source of aesthetic pleasure and such a powerful instrument for various political and cultural aims lies not only in its powerful stories and the universality of its themes and ideas, but also in the manner these are presented in the plays. Greek tragedy is compact and avoids the anecdotal. "The ancient texts . . . are almost free of history and allow one to face the essential issues directly" (Schäfer 1998, 430). The conflicts are presented in an extremely lucid way, and the arguments and underlying dilemmas often possess an internal logic that makes both positions understandable. Hence many of these plays accommodate shifts of sympathy over time, and are able to corroborate competing models. In productions of Euripides' *Bacchae* from the 1960s Dionysus was welcomed as the liberating god, for example in Richard Schechner's *Dionysus in 69* (Zeitlin 2004), whereas more recent performances emphasize his cruel, threatening aspect (for example the Dutch theater company ZT Hollandia's *Bacchanten*, to which I will return). In 1936, in the context of the Olympics in Berlin, the German director Lothar Müthel mounted a version of the *Oresteia* that glorified the Nazi regime – the only instance of a Greek tragedy being used for this aim (Flashar 1991, 164–65). During World War II, the

Plate 30.2 Iolaus, guard, immigrant children, and chorus in the production of Euripides' *Children of Heracles* by the American Repertory Theater (co-production with Ruhr-Triennale), directed by Peter Sellars, Botrop, 2002. Translation by Peter Gladstone. Photograph © Richard Feldman. Used by permission.

humanistic values of Greek tragedies became a source of moral support for dissidents living under repressive regimes, and after the war performances of ancient drama were mounted on the German stage to reestablish the humanistic perspective that had been befouled by the Nazis. Helmut Flashar points to the increase in productions of *Oedipus the King* after the war, the subject matter of the play being related to the issue of German war-guilt (Flashar 1991, 181–84).

The third feature that commends Greek tragedy to modern directors is its formal diversity. The combination of theater and music, soloists and chorus, speech and song, movement and dance, text and rhythm, lower and higher poetry, monologues, stichomythia, and formal debates – elements that characterize all Greek tragedies – is a rich source of inspiration, and in part explains the preference of many modern theater artists for staging Greek tragedy in translation. This return to the basic form of the Western theater is sometimes occasioned by situations of artistic and social crisis when, as Rush Rehm puts it, "We must grapple with unfamiliar cultural assumptions and the peculiarities of foreign dramatic conventions, in order to see our own society and its artifices from a new perspective" (Rehm 2003, 38). Max Reinhardt's experiments with his Theater of Five Thousand, in which different social strata merged into one theatrical experience (he produced *Oedipus the King* in 1910 at the Circus Schumann in Berlin, and the *Oresteia* in 1911 in the Musikfesthalle in Munich, with other productions taking place in venues throughout Europe), are one of the early and famous twentieth-century examples; here Greek tragedy and its original performance characteristics were used to break with traditions in the current theater. Reinhardt experimented with massive choruses and an acting style unprecedented in productions of Greek tragedy; this style gave precedence to the actors' bodies and movements and accentuated their sensuousness, vitality, and energy, instead of elevating the words of the play in the manner characteristic of the insipid contemporary theater (Fischer-Lichte 1999, 5–11).

The formal qualities of Greek tragedy, however, are equally attractive in periods when the theater is flourishing. It may be an exaggeration to say that Greek tragedy is one great challenge to experiment, but its performance history shows that it can accommodate a broad range of formal experiments. It invites artists – directors, actors, and set designers, young and old, novice and experienced – to plumb their creative faculties in order to master these plays, and to sort out the elements essential to their concept of what theater is or should be. Every time the decision is made to stage a Greek tragedy, the artists are forced to rediscover and reinterpret the raw form. Some consciously reject all formal characteristics as outdated impediments to a modern vision of the play. They prefer to tell the bare story, to try to locate the dramatic and theatrical energy in the psychology of the characters. This seems an easy way out, but it is not. Since the dramatic figures of Greek tragedy are not colored by much explicit psychology (Euripidean tragedy is the most explicitly psychological of the three), this approach is extremely demanding and the result often falls flat.

Other artists welcome the formal characteristics and consider them essential to the staging of ancient drama, and a potential enrichment of their theatrical know-how. They are eager to glean any information scholarship can offer about the ancient conditions of performance. This information was vital to the reconstructionist approaches that characterized most performances until the 1950s. For modern theater artists, however, it is more often the case "that the aspects that most interest [scholars] are not necessarily those that are going to interest or inspire the theatrical interpreters" (Taplin 2002, 21). For modern artists it is the gap rather than the connections between ancient and modern performance that releases the artistic energy they need to mold tragedy's raw material into a compelling new form.

Experiments with the form of Greek tragedy confront modern directors and actors with serious paradoxes. When, for example, a director decides to use a translation that is faithful to the metrical shape of the original text, the actors face the curious situation that the expression of emotions is strictly bound to modes of delivery. At the moments of greatest emotion the protagonists in the ancient performance had recourse to song and to a more elevated poetic register. That is, unrestrained emotion is expressed in high poetry, under the supreme control of the singing voice, and through the controlled movements of the dancing body. This convention creates a paradoxical situation for modern actors and spectators, who are familiar with a naturalistic display of emotions. If the director and the actors decide to sing and dance, the challenge is to find a key that turns this alien convention into a credible emotional moment. Those who succeed often discover that stylization in Greek tragedy has an extremely powerful effect on the audience. Those who decide to ignore the convention have to face another paradox, that of reuniting an elevated poetic register with a naturalistic display of emotions. Both decisions demand a high level of craftsmanship from the actors.

Another paradox is presented by the iambic trimeter that characterizes the orderly, eloquent monologues, the messenger speeches that conjure up such powerful images of offstage action, and the contentious dialogues in which words are forged into weapons. On the one hand verse is a valuable tool for the actors, because the iambic trimeter regulates the tempo of delivery. Yet it is a hazardous tool as well, because the easy-going verses tend to slacken the concentration both of the actors and the audience. Only the greatest actors make the best of this paradox by exploring and exploiting the trimeter's possibilities. They master these texts by constantly searching for the right tempo; they have the courage to slow down and take the time to gain full control over the emotional dynamic. They make the words do the work by breaking up the rhythm of the verses, thus emphasizing the significant. They succeed in feeling true to the text and true to themselves, and they are immediately rewarded for it. For them, these difficult texts open themselves up to be interpreted afresh each performance by means of shifting emphases. Skillful actors and actresses can make texts speak in ways that readers only seldom experience.

Not only do actors face the challenge of making themselves familiar with the formalities of the language and the fierce emotions of Greek tragedy; they may also be required to dance and sing, or to use masks, which require a different attitude to body language. With masks, the body must take over some of the expressive functions of the face – although we should never forget how expressive the mask can be on the face of the greatest performers (on the use of masks in modern productions, see Wiles 2004). Actors and actresses may be obliged to impersonate such alien figures as gods or seers, or perform unfamiliar formal actions involving, for example, prayer or sacrificial rituals. To retain one's credibility in such unfamiliar situations is a continuous challenge. For actors the religious dimension is probably the most difficult to grasp. The Greek concept of divinity differs from the Christian one: the Greek gods are not omnipotent and omniscient, but exert power over limited domains. They sometimes display the worst human traits, but they still remain gods. A tragedy may incorporate rituals and prayers that were central to Greek culture, but for which our modern society has no counterparts. One cannot simply replace ancient Greek religious rituals in performance with modern ones, unless one acknowledges that these bring a totally different set of connotations into play. There is no modern religion and no set of religious rituals that are shared by a majority of modern spectators. Whether to devise and perform rituals that are neither exotic and alien, not tainted by Christian overtones yet cogent in performance, or to adopt current rituals is another dilemma that every production has to sort out anew.

In other respects as well Greek tragedy is a treasure-trove for theater artists. As Helene Foley and others have observed, the plays offer "dramatic opportunities for actors of all ages," as well as an "extraordinary repertoire of powerful and subtle female roles" (Foley 1999, 4). She has recently shown how the gender politics of Greek tragedy inspired many contemporary female theater artists, especially in Japan, the United States, and Ireland (Foley 2004). A recent production of Euripides' *Hecuba* and *Trojan Women* (called *De Trojaansen*) by the Dutch theater company Onafhankelijk Toneel moved one step beyond the attractiveness of female roles, and mounted these plays with an all-female cast (plate 30.3). The director, Mirjam Koen, took this step because she and her cast were sincerely interested in how women would react to assuming the role of men at war, how it would feel to play the conquerors as well as the victims. She wanted to show that women can be brutes like men and that they are as guilty as men. The production grew out of a deep concern with the female victims of war. In several interviews Koen made explicit reference to the women of Srebrenica, whose husbands and sons were deported by the Bosnian Serbs during the summer of 1995 in front of a powerless Dutch UN battalion. Koen chose Euripides' plays because the central themes, especially the mechanisms of power, are universal. Hecuba, one of the great female parts of Greek tragedy, was interpreted as a powerful mother, protective, comforting and also vengeful, determined not to be broken by the unending cruelties that assault her. Ria Eimers, the actress who played Hecuba, received the most prestigious annual theater prize for her role.

The formal density of Greek tragedy also allows for large cooperative projects – otherwise offered only by musical theater – involving live music, composers, and choreographers. Performances of Greek tragedy, to be distinguished from operatic versions, have always attracted famous composers and musicians, from Felix Mendelssohn-Bartholdy in Ludwig Tieck's *Antigone* (1841) to Harrison Birtwistle in Peter Hall's *Bacchae* (National Theatre, 2002). In the Netherlands the world-famous Amsterdam Concertgebouw Orchestra participated in performances of Sophocles' *Electra* in the 1920s and 1930s, and today well-known Dutch composers are still eager to involve themselves with Greek tragedy.

The last formal element that will occupy me, one that is both a tremendous challenge and unequivocally the greatest stumbling-block in modern productions, is the chorus. Theater artists in general are convinced that the chorus is such an important constitutive element of Greek tragedy that a performance without a chorus cannot stand. Therefore, they are obliged to find an artistic answer to the function of the chorus in the play, whether in modern or in ancient performance – a subject that has occupied scholars ever since Aristotle. Scholars are fortunate because they can make tentative or qualified judgments. Theater artists, however, have to take

Plate 30.3 Cassandra, Hecuba, seated chorus member, and Talthybius in the production of *De Trojaansen* by Onafhankelijk Toneel, directed by Mirjam Koen, Rotterdam, 2001. Translation by Gerard Koolschijn (adaptation: Mirjam Koen). Photograph © Ben van Duin. Used by permission.

decisions that allow the chorus to fit organically into the overall performance concept. Dealing with the chorus is not just a matter of interpreting its dramatic role. It is also a matter of the size and quality of the cast; budgetary considerations will determine whether a director can choose a large chorus of professional dancers and singers or must limit the choral presence to one or two individual actors. The theatrical possibilities of the chorus in performance also depend on the status of the choral texts. As long as a chorus reacts directly in its songs to the situations it is experiencing, it is relatively easy to give it a dramatic function in the performance. However, when the songs deal with gods and mythical figures that are only names for actors and audience alike, the choral songs, and in extreme cases the entire presence of the chorus, become a fundamental problem. There is no all-purpose formula for solving this problem, because the chorus of each tragedy is different and the conditions and artistic aims of each production are different. The best solutions, however, are found when the chorus (especially a chorus that is only marginally involved in the plot) is treated as the starting point rather than the tail-end of the production process. Many directors will probably want to drop the chorus from a production of Euripides' *Iphigenia at Aulis* because it seems so detached from the action. In Ariane Mnouch-kine's *Les Atrides*, which incorporates the Iphigenia story as the first part, to be followed by the *Oresteia*, the choral presence was more organically involved in the action than in many performances of Greek tragedy that feature less problematic choruses. When artists do not succeed in giving the chorus a meaningful role within the overall concept, the performance will lose its edge. In such cases (indeed, the same holds for all formal elements that over the course of the rehearsal process turn out to be impracticable), it is often better to drop the chorus entirely, rather than to attempt forced solutions that can never lead to an organic whole. For such is the strange power of Greek tragedy that although the aesthetic experience will be less profound when its formal features are ignored, the absence of these features does not necessarily destroy the emotional impact of the basic story and the central themes. The reason lies in the dual character of the tragedies, which are "always written both in an aesthetic (literary) language and in an existential one" (Decreus 2002, 325).

The combination of powerful mythical stories, a wide range of universal themes deeply experienced on a human level, and a wealth of formal theatrical elements constitutes the unique character of Greek tragedy and explains the great attraction the genre exerts even across the boundaries of Western culture. Japanese directors like Tadashi Suzuki (Suzuki 1986) and Yukio Ninagawa (Smethurst 2000) turned to ancient Greek tragedy in the 1970s and afterwards, even though their own theater tradition offered them powerful stories of a comparable mythical grandeur and a mode of acting as formalized as (presumably) the ancient Greek theater's. For the Japanese these tragedies counted as "the fountainhead of the Western humanist tradition, in their search for the values of freedom and democracy (tinged with Marx and Weber) that had eluded their own culture" (Macintosh 1997, 312).

In return, several Western directors turned to Eastern theater traditions to find what the Western theater tradition could not give them: a way to experience the formal elements characteristic of the ancient Greek theater: the power of formalized acting and dancing, of masks and rituals, and the emancipation of the actor over the text (Foley 1999, 2–3). "I think we have the writers.... They invented the actors. They discovered the art of acting. And I think when you succeed in having both the

Western dimension and the Oriental, then you have the theatre I aspire to"
(Mnouchkine 1996, 188–89). Cross-cultural application, however, whether Oriental
or African, requires a journey to the heart of the other culture. Otherwise, cross-
cultural borrowing becomes cross-cultural shopping: superficial, lacking theatrical,
artistic, and aesthetic truth, and finally meaningless.

One recent example illustrating the cross-cultural power of Greek tragedy is the
large international festival production of Euripides' *Bacchae* mounted by ZT Hollandia in 2002. The directors, Johan Simons and Paul Koek, invited the Syrian composer
Nouri Iskandar to write music for the choruses on the basis of an Arabic translation.
Iskandar is a well-known specialist in the tradition of Syrian-orthodox music, which
he believes has close connections with ancient Greek music. A large group of professional Syrian musicians and singers came over to the Netherlands and worked for two
months with Dutch actors and musicians well trained in the vocabulary of contemporary Western music. The performance became an encounter between cultures,
fostered by opposite opinions about the role of the god Dionysus. For Iskandar,
Dionysus represented the freedom of religion, which he emphatically expressed in his
celebratory music for soloists and a large mixed chorus. For Simons and Koek,
Dionysus personified the dangers of Western and Eastern religious fundamentalism.

The encounter took place on two artistic levels moving in opposite directions. On
the level of the dramatic events, the production was staged as a terrible nightmare in
which Pentheus' resistance to the god was hopeless from the outset, and Dionysus
lived up to his reputation of being gentle to those who fear him, and cruel to those
who reject him. The final scene was staged as an outcome without winners: although
Dionysus had proven his divine status, in so doing he destroyed his only human roots,
the Theban royal family; and although Agave was broken by the loss of her son, she
persevered even more strongly in her rejection of the god: here was an absolute-tragic
ending that showed both visions of Dionysus as irreconcilable. Simultaneously, an
opposite movement took place on the musical level. In the first part of the performance the acoustic Syrian instruments took the lead, but as Pentheus decides to dress
himself up to spy on the Bacchants, Western electronics entered. What began as a
fierce confrontation developed over the second half of the play into an entirely new
musical idiom in which the two fundamentally different musical traditions harmon-
ized. Where the confrontation of religious and political powers ended up in stubborn
resentment, the confrontation of artists led to mutual understanding and harmonious
cooperation, a proto-tragic vision. Here the cross-cultural power of Greek tragedy
was at its strongest: the performance was a shared act of cultural resistance in a world
of increasing polarization (plate 30.4)

Many are the attractions of ancient Greek tragedy, many the challenges and many
the obstacles. Amy Green's discussion of modern recreations of classical drama makes
one thing very clear: there is no such thing as an ideal formula allowing modern
directors to create a successful production of ancient drama. "The director must craft
a rigorous and disciplined performance format to withstand the forces these plays
exert on the stage, both as monumental works of art and as cultural monuments. . . .
Successful concepts fly in the face of traditional styles, settings, and interpretations,
but the new production aesthetic and its execution must have equally high aspirations
or risk reductionism or, worse, parody" (A. S. Green 1994, 43). The styles we
encounter on the modern stage are manifold, ranging from realist to modernist and

Plate 30.4 Syrian chorus and musicians in the production of *Bacchanten* by ZT Hollandia (co-production with Ruhr-Triennale, KunstenFESTI-VALdesArts, and others), directed by Johan Simons and Paul Koek, Brussels, 2002. Translation by Herman Altena. Photograph © Ben van Duin. Used by permission.

postmodernist, from reconstructionist to experimental, and the possibilities for modern directors are virtually infinite. Whether a production will be good or not does not depend on the style chosen. A reconstructionist approach is not a surer guarantee for a successful production than a postmodernist one, nor is an adaptation in comparison with a translation. What gives a production of Greek tragedy the best chance of success is the artistic sureness that allows theater artists to choose and interpret a play in the context of their own sociopolitical and cultural context; to separate the relevant from the irrelevant; to have the artistic courage, even the artistic hunger, to face all the elements that are inherent in the genre and in each individual play and to make a selection by conscious choice, while remaining fully aware of the consequences of omissions. The artists must have the artistic sureness to devise a performance concept – in terms of performance location, cast, acting style, set design, use of electronics, and so forth – that organically absorbs all the elements selected, even if the performance celebrates postmodern fragmentation. Finally, they must know their audience; know how to involve the spectators both rationally and emotionally, and know how to shock in order to please them.

NOTE

I would like to thank Amanda Wrigley and Eva Stehlíková for sending data about modern performances, Maria van Erp Taalman Kip and Oliver Taplin for commenting on a draft of this essay, Justina Gregory for her suggestions, patience, and for improving my English, and Mary Bellino for her editorial assistance.

FURTHER READING

Taplin's chapter on round plays in square theaters (Taplin 1978) introduces a number of problems related to modern productions (and see Walton 1987). A theoretically based analysis of the classics on the modern stage and a short history of the development of the director's theater is given by A. S. Green 1994. More recent developments are analyzed by Decreus 2003, whose article contains an extensive bibliography. Rehm 2003 is a thought-provoking plea for staging the classics in our modern world.

There are many surveys of the modern reception of ancient drama. McDonald 2003 is a good start for exploring the field. Flashar 1991 surveys the reception of ancient drama in the world theater, with special focus on German-speaking countries and a small chapter on foreign productions. McDonald 1992 offers a more in-depth treatment of a limited number of important productions and directors. Hall, Macintosh, and Wrigley 2004 focuses on the last decades of the twentieth century. Other article collections covering international productions are Flashar 1997, Mercouris 1998, Patsalidis and Sakellaridou 1999, Hardwick et al. 2000. On reception studies in general see Hardwick 2003b.

On global reception: Africa (Wetmore 2002), Canada (Day 1999), Czech Republic (Stehlíková 2000, 2001), Germany (Flashar 1991), Ireland (McDonald and Walton 2002), Netherlands (Haak 1977, Altena 1999), Poland (Axer and Borowska 1999), Portugal (Fátima Sousa e Silva 1998, 1999), Rhodesia/Zimbabwe (Maritz 2002), Scotland (Hardwick 2003a), South

Africa (Mezzabotta 2000), Taiwan (Williams 1999), UK (Hall 1999b, Hazel 1999, Hall and Macintosh 2004), United States (Hartigan 1995). On the reception of individual plays: Aeschylus' *Oresteia* (Chioles 1993, Bierl 1997), *Agamemnon* (Macintosh et al. forthcoming), Sophocles' *Oedipus the King* (Macintosh, forthcoming), Euripides' *Medea* (Hall, Macintosh, and Taplin 2000).

Several institutions maintain websites devoted to the modern reception: the Archive of Performances of Greek and Roman Drama at Oxford University (www.apgrd.ox.ac.uk/), the European Network of Research and Documentation of Ancient Greek Drama in Athens (www.cc.uoa.gr/drama/network/index.html), and the Reception of Texts and Images of Ancient Greece in Late Twentieth-Century Drama and Poetry in English research project at the Open University in Milton Keynes (www2.open.ac.uk/ClassicalStudies/GreekPlays/). This website also hosts the electronic journal *Didaskalia* (didaskalia.open.ac.uk/), with special issues on reception, reviews, and listings of performances. Journals and periodicals devoted to the reception of ancient Greek drama are listed in Hazel 2001 (also available on the Open University's website). The German periodical *Drama: Beiträge zum antiken Drama und seiner Rezeption* features a large number of special issues devoted to the reception of Greek and Roman drama. A journal that appeared as this volume was in press, *Arion* 11.1 (2003), contains contributions by leading contemporary theater directors and scholars to the 2002 Symposium on Ancient Drama at the J. Paul Getty Museum.

CHAPTER THIRTY-ONE

Justice in Translation: Rendering Ancient Greek Tragedy

Paul Woodruff

Like the art of living, the art of translation is about making wise choices in order to produce an admirable and coherent whole. None of us can do all of the good things possible in life. We can't help all the people near us who are in need; we can't write all the books that are in us to write or love all the beautiful people we encounter. The art of living is creative and independent; it follows its own vision of loving and caring. But the art of translation puts creativity in the service of someone else's vision. Translators express, in the medium of a new language, as much as they can of what they believe the first artist expressed.

A translation from ancient Greek is a lifeboat for a work of art that would otherwise sink into obscurity. Translation carries the work of art from a dead language across to one that is living. Translators cannot bring across all of the virtues and beauties of their originals. In a shipwreck, passengers transfer themselves and their most treasured belongings from a foundering ocean liner into a lifeboat. Their lifeboat will not hold all the lovely things they had in their staterooms. Good passengers know the value of their possessions, and they save what they think is best to save, but even good passengers may have different priorities – one chooses to save his diamonds, another her precious books, a third his fine clothes, and a fourth tucks in a supply of food.

So it is with translation; good translators know the many values in an original, so that they are able to make wise choices about what to put into the lifeboat of translation. But they may have different priorities. After my imaginary shipwreck, the passengers may need to pool what they have saved, so that they will all have what they need. Keep this in mind if you depend on translations, and look at different ones for the same play. The second translation you read may have picked up something wonderful that the first one left behind.

Keep in mind, also, that translators may supply things they did not find in the original text. Here the lifeboat analogy breaks down. Suppose a translator wishes to make sure that readers appreciate the lyricism of a passage, and therefore adds rhyme to the ends of lines. Ancient Greek lyric never uses end rhyme as lyrics in English do. So the translator has added one thing (rhyme) in order to bring another thing (lyricism) across to the living language. This is a good choice in some cases, but an intrusive one. Readers need to be on the lookout for translators' insertions. Tragic choruses often use internal rhyme (that is, repeating vowel or consonant sounds in assonance or alliteration), and a translator may reproduce this in English – although perhaps in a different place from the original.

Good choices in translation flow from a deep and thorough understanding of a text. To understand a text thoroughly enough to translate it well, you must know much more than a beginning Greek student would know – more than word meanings and syntax. You must be able to appreciate fine points of style – poetic figures, characterization by level of diction, word music, and so forth. To appreciate such points you must see what each contributes to the effect of the play.

Take any few lines from the chorus of a tragic play. Here is a passage from the *parodos* (entry-song) of Sophocles' *Antigone* (134–40):

> He crashed to the ground
> Like a weight slung down, in an arc of fire,
> This man who had swooped like a dancer in ecstasy,
> Breathing hurricanes of hatred.
> But his threats came to nothing:
> The mighty war-god, fighting beside us,
> Swept them aside.
>
> (Woodruff 2001, 6–7)

List in your mind the factors that give these lines value. Looking at the original, I would include emotional intensity, concision or brevity, juxtaposition of images, emphasis created by word order, metrical structure, and internal rhyme. In the larger context I would look also at the character of the speakers, their ethical views or arguments, and the tonal level of their language. By "tonal level" I mean the answer to questions such as these: whether the lines are high-toned like a mock epic, or whether they have the lilt of a love-lyric or the reverence of a hymn. Low on my list of the lines' beauties would be the grammatical structure in Greek – translating a word in subject position as a subject, or a word in predicate position as a predicate.

Already my list of beauties is too long. No translation can carry all of these to a new life in the host language. If you choose to carry Greek lyric metrical structure into English, for example, you will labor so hard on this task that you will lose most of the other values of the lines. Which of these lines' many beauties and strengths are most important? To answer this you must understand very well both the play and the technique of the artist who created it. But two translators may understand the play equally well and still choose to rescue different elements. That is why prudent readers should consult several translations, unless they know the original language well enough to make their own choices wisely.

There are other kinds of choices to make. Translators must decide where to put their translations on the spectrum from foreign to familiar. You could make a version of *Antigone* so familiar that an audience would take it for a contemporary play. Or you could make the play so foreign that you would remind the audience at every line that this comes from an era long dead and far away. Anouilh's marvelous *Antigone* translates Sophocles' play into contemporary French existentialist terms. By contrast, many English versions have been so faithful that they use odd and awkward English, in order to bring across the play's antiquity.

Then there is the choice of audience. High school students in a literature course need a translation they can read and understand without straining. Actors in a production need lines they can speak. Beginning Greek students need an aid to understanding the Greek text. Literary critics need to be informed about any literary feature of the text that might be important to them. Philosophers need to be able to see how an argument works. More advanced Greek scholars simply need a reminder of a text they know well but do not perfectly remember. All of these choices produce translations that are worthy of respect, although none of them can do full justice to the originals.

Philosophy of Translation

To translate is to betray, according to an Italian proverb, and indeed no translation can do justice to its original. Justice requires that the version in the host language reproduce in the host language all of the effects that the play has in the original language, so that a reader of the translation could have the same experience as would readers of the original, if they were at home in the language of the original.

Justice in translation could be realized if three conditions were met: if words had fixed meanings, if the meanings of words were all that texts were meant to convey, and if some two languages corresponded in the structure of meanings (that is, if for every word in one language, there is a word with the same meaning in the other). The translator would simply ascertain the meanings of the words in the original language, find words in the host language with the same meanings, and write those down. But none of these conditions holds.

First, words do not have fixed meanings. Dictionaries list multiple meanings, and any skilled user of language knows how words work differently in different contexts; even a change in tone of voice can alter meaning. The American dialect answer "Yeah, sure" can be said as a positive or as a negative, depending on whether the speaker's voice has a rising or falling intonation. Speakers and writers often deliberately choose words that pull in two different ways; such choices are especially common in jokes such as puns, but they serve also in poetry, which often works important effects through dissonance or harmony of secondary meanings. Figurative uses of language such as metaphor are endemic to poetry, and the sensitive reader of a living metaphor hears two meanings at once. Irony is often at the core of dramatic dialogue, and irony can bring contrary meanings into play at the same time, pulling the moment into a delicious tension. So a translator must not stop at one meaning per word.

Second, the meanings of words are not all that texts are meant to convey. Words are often assembled as much for their sound as for their sense, and the music of poetry is sometimes as pure as that of an instrumental composition. But the same musical effects are not available in all languages. The tonal patterns of classical Chinese *shih* poetry, for example, totally defy translation into European languages, and the gorgeous soft consonants of Russian poetry, such as *shch*, have no equivalents in English. Rhyme flows more naturally in Italian than in English poetry, and in ancient Greek poetry it hardly flows at all.

Third, two languages rarely have the same system of meanings, so that you can't just match a word in the first language with a word in the second. A famous choral ode in Sophocles' *Antigone* begins with *polla ta deina*, "many are the things that are *deinos*" (332). English has equivalents for the first two words, "many" and "the," but not for the third: *deinos* has a complex meaning that hovers over connotations of wonder and terror, admiration and contempt. In such a case, one translator might choose the English word closest to the meaning of the Greek in this context, perhaps adding a footnote to explain the broader reach of the word. Or another might use more than one word – the strategy I prefer in cases such as this, in which the whole range of the word is in play: "Many wonders, many terrors," begins the choral ode in my version. Either way, we must admit that translation does not do justice to the original.

So far I have been writing of "the original" as if we all knew what that is. But we can't possibly know this, for reasons both historical and philosophical. The manuscripts we have were copied many hundreds of years after the plays were written, and they often disagree in cases in which we have more than one manuscript for the same text. Scribes erred in copying, mistaking one letter or word for another, sometimes transposing lines that began in similar ways. Some scribes, on encountering a passage they did not understand, would change the text to make what they considered a better meaning. Some translators depend on editors who have sifted the manuscript alternatives and made educated choices for publishing a text; other translators make their own judgments.

What is it, however, that scholars are trying to recover? If the artist revised the play, there may have been alternative versions even in antiquity. The original intention of the author is lost, if there ever was such a thing. But even living writers are uncertain about their intentions. This philosophical problem grows on deep uncertainties about self-understanding and creativity. Some living writers will revise a work as it undergoes translation, and they do so not in order to recover an original vision, but to make their creation better or more translatable. Justice in translation ought to be doing justice to something, but we cannot easily say what that something is.

In short, perfect justice is beyond our reach in translation, as in life. This has given translation a bad name, especially among poets. Wallace Stevens writes: "The writer who is content to destroy is on a plane with the writer who is content to translate. Both are parasites" (Stevens 1989, 192). And yet many notable poets have been translators. Great translators are not parasites; they do not drink the blood of other artists. They try, instead, to drink from the same spring as the first artists and so to find the strength to give new life to aging works of art. A translator is a second artist.

The translator of Greek tragedy must bridge a number of gaps between English-language conventions and those of ancient Greece. These gaps are quite different from the ones that divide us from prose authors, such as Plato or Thucydides, and somewhat different from those that divide us from Homer or Sappho.

Emotional Intensity

English and American cultures are stiff-upper-lippish in the expression of emotion, but are tolerant of emotion as part of human life. Ancient Greek culture alternately wallows in emotion (as in any play by Sophocles) and seeks to control it (as in the philosophical tradition that begins with Socrates and culminates in Stoicism). The last third of *Oedipus the King* consists largely of lamentation. English theater has no parallels to this. Shakespeare's King Lear has as great a cause as Oedipus to lament at the end of his play, but his lamentation is soon over. Attempts to reproduce Greek-style intensity in English are usually laughable, but no translator wants an audience to burst out laughing when the main character breaks down in grief.

Idiomatic translation of tragic laments is impossible. *Oimoi, talain' egô* (O me, miserable me!) repeats again and again, along with a great range of expressions of grief that are not so readily taken into English. But straight translation is never equal in affect to the Greek. "O me" and "O my" and "Oh dear" are all too weak for the power of feeling in these Greek passages. "Oh no!" is better, but a translator should consider other options, including stage directions such as "Electra gives a grief-stricken cry." The Greek tragic poets can sustain high levels of honest emotional intensity far longer than any English-language playwright, and this is important enough to the plays that translators should try to preserve it.

Differentiation of Speakers

Modern playwrights, from Shakespeare on, have often given different kinds of language to different kinds of speakers. British writers, in particular, have indicated social class or place of origin by the use of dialect. Such differentiation is not entirely absent in ancient Greek theater, but tragic poets tend to give all of their characters the same fairly formal and poetic diction. Characters are differentiated in more subtle ways than in English. For example, Antigone's lines are more heavily enjambed than Ismene's; that is, Antigone spills over at the end of one line and plunges into the beginning of the next more often than her sister does. This is a formal way of marking the emotional difference between the two sisters.

Some differences show in the content of speeches. In the same play, Haemon's and Creon's arguments are equally platitudinous, full of generalizing clichés, and this differentiates both men from the passionate and peculiar reasoning of Antigone. These subtleties are hard to translate; a Greek platitude may seem brilliantly original in English, and spillover lines hardly catch our attention at all.

As for social class, keep in mind that tragic poets are ardent supporters of democracy, and they are writing for an audience that does not believe that people are better if they come from a higher or wealthier social class. The watchman in *Antigone* is brilliant, well educated, and every inch a common man. He does not speak like a yokel, and yet some translations make him do so. His style, in fact, is mock-heroic, and he uses it to dance verbal rings around the ponderous mind of the king. The *paidagôgos* (tutor) in Sophocles' *Electra* is either a slave or a servant, yet he has educated Orestes, and he speaks in the language of someone who is highly educated, even, sometimes, pedantic.

Some speakers in ancient tragedy seem to have no character at all. Messengers, when they speak as messengers, rarely have any individual character or personality. They speak like epic poets (see Halleran, chapter 11 in this volume), but they do not do this in mockery (as the watchman does when he banters with Creon). Somewhere in the ancestry of Greek tragedy lies the narrative poetry of epic, and this legacy is clear in the messenger speeches. These are gripping narratives, with the emphasis usually on the story being told, rather than on the quality of the teller.

Choruses are usually supposed to represent some group that is affected by the action of the play, but they are rarely consistently written in character. They may represent the opinions of the people of Athens, even when the play is set somewhere else. The chorus in *Bacchae* represents foreign women from Asia, but they speak for the sentiments of democratic Athens. Sometimes a chorus seems to speak directly for the playwright during one ode, like the *Antigone* passage that begins "Many wonders, many terrors" (332). Where a play in English would try to create a definite character for the chorus, for the benefit of the actors, a faithful translator of the Greek must usually be content with the faceless beauty of poetry.

Hyperbaton

The opening lines of Sophocles' *Electra* are impossible. Orestes' tutor is addressing the young man he has cared for and trained since childhood:

> O, of commanding the army at Troy, once,
> Of Agamemnon, son!

Orestes knows who his father is and what he did. Why is the tutor telling him these familiar truths? And why is he doing it in such a contorted way? Different readers may come to different conclusions, but here are mine.

The explanation for the content of the opener is easy to grasp. The tutor is identifying the young man to the audience, so the lines have a role in exposition. But this is not the full explanation. Sophocles has an eye on dramatic context, as well as on the audience, and in the context of this scene the tutor is reminding Orestes of his duty as a son of the murdered Agamemnon, a duty sharpened by his father's legacy of greatness.

The contortion is beautiful and suggests an additional meaning. Ancient Greek allows a structure that is nonsense in English. The participle "commanding" would be a noun phrase in English, "the man who commanded." And because each word has an ending that shows its role in the sentence, Greek readers can see that "O" belongs to "son" and that this one phrase, "O son," is cut open in order to embrace a reference to the boy's father. And the reference to the boy's father is also split open: "Of commanding the army, Agamemnon" is opened to make room for "at Troy, once." This device of opening one phrase to accept another is common in both Greek and Latin poetry; it is known as *hyperbaton* – overleaping. The meaning leaps from "O" at the beginning of the sentence to "son" at the end. Greek makes this overleaping easy to follow by marking these two words with the same grammatical case, the vocative (used only for addressing someone). But English does not mark cases so clearly. A translation that preserved the order of ideas in good English would look like this:

> My boy, your father commanded the army at Troy;
> You are Agamemnon's son.

To do this, I have had to alter the syntax and make explicit that the speaker is reminding Orestes of his father's importance – not because the boy could forget, but because the tutor wants to motivate him to do great deeds. I have also had to add the word "father," which is not explicit in the Greek, and to drop the word "once" which we would not use in this context, and which would mar the concision of the lines. The following would be closer to the grammar (or syntax) of the original:

> O son of Agamemnon, who once commanded the army at Troy!

But I cannot imagine anyone saying this in English, especially on stage in a play. Worse, it loses the beautiful embracing of the original, the surrounding of the father by the son. The word order matters because it represents in the first two lines one of the main themes of the play, that the status of the dead father is now entirely in the hands of the son. Had the poet reversed the order, we would have these lines, which suggest a different deeper meaning:

> O of Agamemnon the son, of him who once commanded the army at Troy!

Here the son is obscured, and not ennobled, by the presence of a reference to his father. Sophocles could have done it either way. He is not showing off his verbal technique here; he is doing something brilliant with the tools he has. Greek offers the poet many elegant tools that a translator into English cannot use. But, at a small cost to grammar, a translator may preserve the beauty of word order. Often, as here, word order is the most important feature of a passage.

Set-Piece Speeches and Debates

Greek audiences adored debate, as they adored every kind of contest, and playwrights obliged by writing formal debates into many plays. These are usually about equal in length, as fair play in a debate demands, and they often employ popular tools of rhetoric that sound too studied and contrived for a modern audience to accept as dialogue in a play. Often, also, to the distress of modern readers, they do not directly advance the action of the play.

By contrast, Henry V in Shakespeare's play delivers a number of highly rhetorical set-piece speeches, but we do not hear them that way, because the rhetorical devices are cleverly hidden, and because he is not opposed (as a Greek tragic king would be) by equal speeches from the opposite side. Henry's stage audiences miss the rhetorical cleverness also; they are simply moved to surrender, or to fight, or (as in the case of the conquered princess) to consent to marriage.

A translator of Greek plays may choose between making the lines of a speech actable on the modern stage and bringing across the exercise it contains in formal rhetorical technique. Or the translator can try to make the rhetoric seem plausible in context. Sophocles makes this easy in *Antigone*, where Creon and his son debate in equal speeches and using arguments that balance one another. There, the debate represents an initial stage in the quarrel between the two men, in which they both try to be respectful and decorous, their passions held back by the formality of the debate. This changes in the line-on-line debate that follows, a more flexible form that allows respect to modulate quickly into rage.

Such exchanges of one-liners (stichomythia) are ubiquitous in Greek plays. These too are a kind of contest, a sort of verbal tennis, in which each speaker seizes on a word the other had just used, and turns it against him. A translator whose eye is on the character of the speakers or on the precise content of the lines would have to leave this behind, if the same word calls for different renderings in different lines. The challenge to the translator is to make the exchanges seem plausible while conveying the meaning of the original and bringing out the elements of verbal contest in the scene.

Polysemy and Etymology

One word can have two or more meanings, as I have already shown, and the line-on-line contests often exploit the power of language to keep alternative meanings in the air simultaneously. English words don't carry the same ambiguities as Greek ones, with the result that a translator may have to use more than one word to render a single Greek one, or else explain the matter in a note. Even words that seem to mean only one thing have complex associations or etymological baggage that is registered by ordinary speakers. No translator, therefore, can bring across the entire complex meaning of even a simple phrase.

One of the worst faults of novice translators is etymological translation. A colleague once proposed to translate *pleonexia* as "having more." That is indeed the etymology, but the actual usage of the word is better captured by "avarice." It means "getting or trying to get more than your share," and is by implication always in violation of justice. Good translators are aware of the usage of a word in a variety of texts. The sin of etymological translation is pardonable, however. Etymologies are beautiful, and even false ones are felt in the cloud of nuanced meanings that surrounds a word. But the translator must sometimes leave beautiful things behind. Etymology rarely comes across from one language to another.

Translating for Performance

Private reading was rare in the ancient world, and most texts, whether poetry or prose, were written to be presented aloud. All translators of ancient languages need to be aware of this, and translators of plays need to consider whether their translations could be used for staged performance or for out-loud reading in class. (To start a classroom discussion, I recommend having students take parts and read a scene.) To translate a performance text as a performance text requires an understanding of performance conventions in both cultures, and places additional demands on the translator, demands that cannot be met by word-for-word translation. Therefore, performance translations do not suit the needs of students who want to know just how the Greek text was constructed. Performance versions can, however, follow the original closely in spirit.

First, a performance text must be clear enough that an audience can follow it just by listening. Sentence structures must not be as complicated as they often are in Greek, because English uses simpler structures than ancient Greek did, and because modern English-speaking audiences are not prepared to decode long complex sentences. So a performance version will alter the punctuation of the original, making sentences shorter and more immediately clear than they would otherwise be.

Second, a performance text must be friendly to performers. Actors must be able to speak the lines effectively. Speakable lines cannot deviate too far from the idiom of the language – from the way people commonly speak. Good translators try to avoid the use of "translatorese," by which they mean a dialect of English used mainly by translators of Greek. "This being so," is a good example; it translates what grammarians call an absolute expression, something we do not use in idiomatic English. You should not assign such an expression to actors unless you want them to play the part of someone who is formal and pedantic. Speakable lines also need to meet certain conditions of sound. I once used "shipshape" in a translation; it was a good word for the meaning, but a very hard word for an actor to say on stage.

Performance-friendly translation gives the actors and director plenty of clues about the motivations of speakers, and therefore such translations may be more deeply affected by the interpretation of the translator than translations made for other purposes.

Translating Poetry

What marks poetry as poetry? Different features of language make poetry what it is in different cultures, though in traditional cultures all features of poetry serve at least this purpose – to make a text memorable. For translators of poetry into English, the degree of difficulty rises from French (fairly easy, with identical verse forms) to Chinese (fiendishly hard, with verse forms that cannot be replicated in non-tonal languages). Greek is somewhere in between.

If you asked contemporaries of Sophocles about the difference between poetry and prose, they would probably have spoken first of rhythm – of the use of complex repeatable metrical structures. This is the most prominent formal feature of lyric poetry from the period. But modern readers should notice the powerful use of juxtaposed concrete images that runs through the entire tradition, from Homer to Callimachus.

Verse in English traditionally marks line breaks with capital letters at the beginning of each line. Ancient Greek needed no such convention, owing to the clarity of its metrical forms. Old-fashioned translators followed the English convention; most recent ones have not done so. But well-placed line breaks are an essential part of ancient Greek poetry, and it is wise to mark these well in a translation that aims at saving the poetry of the original. Words at the beginnings or ends of lines have special emphasis owing to their positions. Enjambment, moreover, is part of the poetry, and not merely a convenience. Sometimes this puts an important word in a prominent position, sometimes it helps bring across the breathless enthusiasm of the speaker.

Verse in English is usually marked by rhyme, and this has been true from Chaucer to the latest rap lyrics. If you want your readers to recognize your text as verse, therefore, you will be tempted to use rhyme. Some translators have carried this off with success. Richard Wilbur's translations of Molière are wonderfully like the original, and Gilbert Murray's rhyming versions of Greek plays (see below) had a great success in the early years of the twentieth century. But the Greeks did not use rhyme at the ends of lines, and so the impression this gives has seemed false to most purists. Internal rhyming, however – repeating the sounds of vowels or consonants – is an important feature of Greek tragic poetry, and this is easily translated.

Meter is essential to ancient Greek poetry, and it is tempting to try to reproduce this in English, or at least to use comparable metrical forms. Greek meter is based on quantities, however; that requires attention to the length of each vowel sound and syllable. English meter, which is based on emphasis, is oblivious to quantity. Fair approximations of Greek meters can be achieved in English for the iambics of the speeches, and for certain other meters (such as anapests) that occur in tragedy. But complex lyric meters, such as those used in the choral odes, are almost impossible to render.

Translators who serve either rhyme or meter will have a hard time serving other beauties of the text. To make the rhymes come out right, or to fill in the meter to perfection, translators usually have to alter meanings or introduce language that is not required for translating the meaning of the text. Even if the new language leaves the old meaning unscathed, the new verbosity kills one beauty of the original – concision. The choral odes of tragic plays are splendidly concise, in the works of all three playwrights, and this concision allows them to juxtapose images with startling direct- ness and simplicity:

> To dance the long night!
> Shall I ever set my white foot
> so, to worship Bacchus?
> Toss my neck to the dewy skies
> as a young fawn frisks
> in green delight of pasture?
> (Euripides, *Bacchae* 863–67; Woodruff 1998, 35)

Anything the translator did to separate these images with excess verbiage would weaken the peculiar poetry of these lines, the play of white against green, the evocative leap from human dance to an animal frisking, the transfer of the epithet "green" from "pasture" to "delight." Gilbert Murray's version has a different loveliness, a kind of word music aided by repetitions:

> Will they ever come to me, ever again,
>   The long long dances,
> On through the dark till the dawn-stars wane?
> Shall I feel the dew on my throat, and the stream

> Of wind in my hair? Shall our white feet gleam
>   In the dim expanses?
> Oh, feet of a fawn to the greenwood fled,
>   Alone in the grass and the loveliness.
>   (Murray 1904, 51)

Most readers would find the Murray version more poetic, because it conforms to the rules of traditional English poetry. Murray was writing in 1904, and his translations made Greek plays accessible to a generation of ordinary readers and playgoers. But the style seems antique to a reader of twenty-first-century poetry, and Euripides was anything but antique. His style was fresh, even startlingly new. In our time, now, we see that the last few generations of poets have given us examples of lyricism that may be closer to that of the ancient Greeks. Consider this famous poem:

> so much depends
> upon
>
> a red wheel
> barrow
>
> glazed with rain
> water
>
> beside the white
> chickens.
> (Williams 1985, 36)

If this is great poetry, as many critics agree it is, it opens new ways for other poets and translators alike to follow their art. A translator who wishes to save as much of the poetry of the original as possible needs to be well read in English and American poetry. Murray knew the poetry of his day very well, and his knowledge shows in the gracious verse that he turns. Times change, however, and call for new translators. Poetry in 2004 looks very different from poetry in 1904.

Monuments of Translation

William Arrowsmith was the pioneer of idiomatic translations into American English. The first choral ode of *Bacchae* (64–169) probably comes from an ancient liturgy of Dionysus worship. Here is Arrowsmith, bringing the liturgical element front and center, with strong intimations of Christianity (the long dashes are meant to divide the lines among members of the chorus):

> – Blessèd, blessèd are those who know the mysteries of god.
> – Blessèd is he who hallows his life in the worship of god,
>   he whom the spirit of god possesseth, who is one
>   with those who belong to the holy body of god.
> – Blessèd are the dancers and those who are purified,
>   who dance on the hill in the holy dance of god.
> – Blessèd are they who keep the rite of Cybele the Mother.
> – Blessèd are the thyrsus-bearers, those who wield in their hands

the holy wand of god.
– Blessèd are those who wear the crown of the ivy of god.
– Blessèd, blessèd are they: Dionysus is their god!
(72–87; Arrowsmith in Grene and Lattimore 1959, 4: 546)

Here is Gilbert Murray's version for comparison, written in a less liturgical style:

All the maidens:
Oh, blessèd he in all wise,
    Who hath drunk the Living Fountain,
    Whose life no folly staineth,
        And his soul is near to God;
Whose sins are lifted, pall-wise,
    As he worships on the Mountain,
    And where Cybele ordaineth,
        Our Mother, he has trod.

His head with ivy laden
    And his thyrsus tossing high,
    For our God he lifts his cry...
        (Murray 1904, 10–11)

Unlike Arrowsmith, he has seen no reason to repeat the word "Blessèd," the original of which occurs only once in the Greek. Murray becomes more biblical, however, in translating the hymn to reverence (370–85), which comes later in the same play:

Some maidens:
Thou Immaculate on high;
Thou Recording Purity;
Thou that stoopest, Golden Wing,
Earthward, manward, pitying.
Hearest thou this angry King?
Hearest thou the rage and scorn
    'Gainst the Lord of Many Voices,
Him of mortal mother born,
    Him in whom man's heart rejoices,
Girt with garlands and with glee,
First in Heaven's sovranty?
    For his kingdom, it is there,
    In the dancing and the prayer,
In the music and the laughter,
    In the vanishing of care,
And of all before and after;
In the Gods' high banquet, when
    Gleams the grape-blood, flashed to heaven;
Yea, and in the feasts of men
Comes his crownèd slumber; then
    Pain is dead and hate forgiven.
        (Murray 1904, 22–23)

While Arrowsmith chooses a plainer style for this hymn:

> Holiness, queen of heaven,
> Holiness on golden wing
> who hover over earth,
> do you hear what Pentheus says?
> Do you hear his blasphemy
> against the prince of the blessèd,
> the god of garlands and banquets,
> Bromius, Semele's son?
> These blessings he gave:
> laughter to the flute
> and the loosing of cares
> when the shining wine is spilled
> at the feast of the gods,
> and the wine-bowl casts its sleep
> on feasters crowned with ivy.
> (Arrowsmith in Grene and Lattimore 1959, 4: 557–58)

The magnificent opening choral ode of Aeschylus' Agamemnon contains some of the most challenging Greek for a translator. I have chosen to look at the passage containing the famous words *pathei mathos*, "learning by suffering" (160–83), in the work of two poet-translators, Robert Fagles and Richmond Lattimore.

Here is Fagles, who achieves a powerful effect from rhythm and repetition:

> Zeus, great nameless all in all,
> if that name will gain his favor,
>   I will call him Zeus.
> I have no words to do him justice,
>   weighing all in the balance,
>   all I have is Zeus, Zeus –
> cast this weight, this torment from my spirit,
>   cast it once for all.
>
>   He who was so mighty once,
> storming for the wars of heaven,
>   he has had his day.
> And then his son who came to power
>   met his match in the third fall
>   and he is gone. Zeus, Zeus –
> raise your songs and call him Zeus the Victor!
>   You will reach the truth:
>
>   Zeus has led us on to know,
>   the Helmsman lays it down as law
> that we must suffer, suffer into truth.
> We cannot sleep, and drop by drop at the heart
>   the pain of pain remembered comes again,
>   and we resist, but ripeness comes as well.
> From the gods enthroned on the awesome rowing-bench
>   there comes a violent love.
> (Fagles 1975, 98)

And Lattimore, in chiseled monumental lines:

> Zeus: whatever he may be, if this name
> pleases him in invocation,
> thus I call upon him.
> I have pondered everything
> yet I cannot find a way,
> only Zeus, to cast this dead weight of ignorance
> finally from out my brain.
>
> He who in time long ago was great,
> throbbing with gigantic strength,
> shall be as if he never were, unspoken.
> He who followed him has found
> his master, and is gone.
> Cry aloud without fear the victory of Zeus,
> you will not have failed the truth:
>
> Zeus who guided men to think,
> who has laid it down that wisdom
> comes alone through suffering.
> Still there drips in sleep against the heart
> grief of memory; against
> our pleasure we are temperate.
> From the gods who sit in grandeur
> grace comes somehow violent.
>   (Lattimore in Grene and Lattimore 1959, 1: 39–40)

How should the Greekless reader respond to such broad differences in translation? Is it *torment* or *ignorance* that the speakers pray to cast off in the chorus of *Agamemnon*? Is the gods' gift to be violent *love* or violent *grace*? *Must* we suffer into truth? Or does Zeus allow those who do not suffer to continue in undamaged ignorance? The translators have seen the evidence and made their choices. Readers must learn Greek if they wish to make their own choices. Otherwise, they may read a variety of versions, if they have a good tolerance for being bewildered. For most readers, the best course is to find, and to trust, a gifted translator.

NOTE

Grateful acknowledgment is made for permission to reprint "The Red Wheelbarrow" by William Carlos Williams, from *Collected Poems: 1909–1913, Volume 1*, copyright © 1938 · by New Directions Publishing Corporation.

FURTHER READING

There are many translations of ancient Greek tragedy, none of which has achieved canonical status. In addition to the literary versions I have mentioned above, readers should be aware of three series of scholarly editions that are highly reliable. The series edited by Grene and Lattimore for the University of Chicago Press (1959) is especially well suited to classroom use and is, on the whole, quite close to the Greek. Grene's translations are noteworthy for clarity and closeness to the original. The new Focus Classical Library editions, such as that of Blondell (2002b), are based on fine scholarship and contain much useful material for beginning and advanced scholars alike. The recent Loeb editions are far better than the older ones. Lloyd-Jones's Sophocles (1994–96) is based on a lifetime of study, and Kovacs' Euripides (1994–2004) is also the work of a serious scholar. Both are about as accurate as translations can be. The new Hackett series, in which my translations appear (Woodruff 1998 and 2001), aims for literary and performance qualities without sacrifice of accuracy. Fagles' fine translation of Sophocles' Theban plays has the same virtues as his version of the *Oresteia*, from which I quoted above.

Bibliography

Journal Abbreviations

A&A	Antike und Abendland
AC	Acta Classica
AHB	Ancient History Bulletin
AJA	American Journal of Archaeology
AJAH	American Journal of Ancient History
AJP	American Journal of Philology
AthMit	Athenische Mitteilungen
BICS	Bulletin of the Institute of Classical Studies of the University of London
BMCR	Bryn Mawr Classical Review
CA	Classical Antiquity
CB	Classical Bulletin
CJ	Classical Journal
CM	Classica et Mediaevalia
CP	Classical Philology
CQ	Classical Quarterly
CR	Classical Review
CW	Classical World
G&R	Greece and Rome
GRBS	Greek, Roman and Byzantine Studies
HSCP	Harvard Studies in Classical Philology
ICS	Illinois Classical Studies
IJCT	International Journal of the Classical Tradition
JHS	Journal of Hellenic Studies
MD	Materiali e discussioni
MHR	Mediterranean Historical Review
MLN	Modern Language Notes
MPhL	Museum Philologum Londiniense
MusHelv	Museum Helveticum
NNS	New Nietzsche Studies
NS	Nietzsche-Studien

PCPS	*Proceedings of the Cambridge Philological Society*
QUCC	*Quaderni Urbinati di Cultura Classica*
REG	*Revue des études grecques*
RhM	*Rheinisches Museum für Philologie*
RivFil	*Rivista di filologia e d'istruzione classica*
RSC	*Rivista di Studi Classici*
SemRom	*Seminari Romani di Cultura Greca*
SIFC	*Studi italiani di filologia classica*
SyllClass	*Syllecta Classica*
TAPA	*Transactions of the American Philological Association*
TJ	*Theatre Journal*
YCS	*Yale Classical Studies*
ZPE	*Zeitschrift für Papyrologie und Epigraphik*

Adam, J.-M., M.-J. Borel, C. Calame, and M. Kilani. 1990a. Anthropologie, épistémologie, sémiologie. In J.-M. Adam et al. 1990b. 9–17.

Adam, J.-M., M.-J. Borel, C. Calame, and M. Kilani. 1990b. *Le discours anthropologique*. Paris.

Adams, S. M. 1952. Salamis symphony: the *Persae* of Aeschylus. In M. E. White, ed., *Studies in Honour of Gilbert Norwood*. Toronto. 46–54. Repr. in E. Segal, ed., *Oxford Readings in Greek Tragedy*. Oxford. 34–41, 409–10.

Adkins, A. W. H. 1960. *Merit and Responsibility: A Study in Greek Values*. Oxford.

Aichele, K. 1971. Das Epeisodion. In Jens 1971. 47–83.

Alexiou, M. 1974. *The Ritual Lament in Greek Tradition*. Cambridge.

Allan, W. 1999–2000. Euripides and the Sophists: society and the theatre of war. In Cropp, Lee, and Sansone 1999–2000. 145–56.

Allan, W. 2000. *The Andromache and Euripidean Tragedy*. Oxford.

Allan, W. 2001a. Euripides in Megale Hellas: some aspects of the early reception of tragedy. *G&R* 48: 67–86.

Allan, W., ed. and trans. 2001b. *Euripides: The Children of Heracles*. Warminster.

Allan, W. 2002. *Euripides: Medea*. London.

Altena, H. 1999. Greek tragedy in the Netherlands: from Mendes da Costa to Simons and Koek. In Mavromoustakos 1999. 131–56.

Anderson, M. J. 1997. *The Fall of Troy in Early Greek Poetry and Art*. Oxford.

Anguillara, G. A. dell'. 1565. *Edippo*. In Poggiali 1808–12. 8: 3–132.

Archer, W. 1888. *Masks or Faces? A Study in the Psychology of Acting*. London.

Ariani, M., ed. 1977. *Il teatro italiano: la tragedia del Cinquecento*. Vol. 2. Turin.

Arnott, P. 1962. *Greek Scenic Conventions in the Fifth Century B.C.* Oxford.

Arnott, P. 1989. *Public and Performance in the Greek Theatre*. London.

Arnott, W. G. 1973. Euripides and the unexpected. *G&R* 20: 49–64.

Arnott, W. G. 1978. Red herrings and other baits: a study in Euripidean techniques. *MPhL* 3: 1–24.

Arnott, W. G. 1982. Off-stage cries and the choral presence: some challenges to theatrical convention in Euripides. *Antichthon* 16: 35–43.

Arnott, W. G. 1984. Nietzsche's view of Greek tragedy. *Arethusa* 17: 135–49.

Arrowsmith, W. 1963. A Greek theater of ideas. *Arion* 2.3: 32–56.

Artaud, A. 1974. The theatre and its double. Trans. Victor Corti. *Collected Works*. London. 4: 1–110.

Ashby, C. 1999. *Classical Greek Theatre: New Views of an Old Subject*. Iowa City.

Assael, J. 1993. *Intellectualité et théâtralité dans l'œuvre d'Euripide*. Nice.

Assael, J. 2001. *Euripide, philosophe et poète tragique*. Louvain.

Attolini, G. 1988. *Teatro e spettacolo nel Rinascimento*. Bari.

Auslander, P. 1997. *From Acting to Performance: Essays in Modernism and Postmodernism.* London.

Austin, R. G., ed. 1955. *P. Vergili Maronis Aeneidos Liber Quartus.* Oxford.

Axer, J., and M. Borowska. 1999. The tradition of the ancient Greek theatre in Poland. In Mavromoustakos 1999. 69–74.

Badian, E. 1993a. *From Plataea to Potidaea.* Baltimore.

Badian, E. 1993b. The Peace of Callias. In Badian 1993a. 1–72.

Badian, E. 1993c. Towards a chronology of the Pentecontaetia down to the renewal of the Peace of Callias. In Badian 1993a. 73–107.

Bain, D. M. 1977. *Actors and Audience: A Study of Asides and Related Conventions in Greek Drama.* Oxford.

Bakhtin, M. 1981. *The Dialogic Imagination.* Ed. M. Holquist, trans. C. Emerson and M. Holquist. Austin, Tex.

Bakker, E. J. 1997. *Poetry in Speech: Orality and Homeric Discourse.* Ithaca, NY.

Bakker, E. J., I. J. F. de Jong, and H. Van Wees, eds. 2002. *Brill's Companion to Herodotus.* Leiden.

Barbour, R. 1981. *Greek Literary Hands, A.D. 400–1600.* Oxford.

Barish, J. 1994. The problem with closet drama in the Italian Renaissance. *Italica* 71: 4–30.

Barker, A. D., ed. 1984–89. *Greek Musical Writings.* 2 vols. Cambridge.

Barlow, S. A. 1971. *The Imagery of Euripides.* London.

Barlow, S. A., ed. and trans. 1986. *Euripides: Trojan Women.* Warminster.

Barner, W. 1971. Die Monodie. In Jens 1971. 277–320.

Barnes, J. 1982. *The Presocratic Philosophers.* London.

Barrett, J. 2002. *Staged Narrative: Poetics and the Messenger in Greek Tragedy.* Berkeley.

Barrett, W. S., ed. 1964. *Euripides: Hippolytos.* Oxford.

Barsby, J., ed. 2002. *Greek and Roman Drama: Translation and Performance.* Stuttgart.

Battezzato, L. 1995. *Il monologo nel teatro di Euripide.* Pisa.

Battezzato, L. 2001. *Enjambement*, iati e stile di recitazione nella tragedia greca. *SemRom* 4: 1–38.

Battezzato, L. 2003. I viaggi dei testi. In L. Battezzato, ed., *Tradizione testuale e ricezione letteraria antica della tragedia greca.* Amsterdam. 7–31.

Beacham, R. C. 1992. *The Roman Theatre and Its Audience.* Cambridge, Mass.

Bees, R. 1993. *Zur Datierung des Prometheus Desmotes.* Stuttgart.

Behler, E. 1986. A. W. Schlegel and the nineteenth-century *damnatio* of Euripides. *GRBS* 27: 335–67.

Belfiore, E. S. 1992. *Tragic Pleasures: Aristotle on Plot and Emotion.* Princeton.

Belfiore, E. S. 2000. *Murder among Friends: Violation of Philia in Greek Tragedy.* Oxford.

Ben Chaim, D. 1984. *Distance in the Theatre: The Aesthetics of Audience Response.* Epping.

Benders, R. J., and S. Oettermann. 2000. *Friedrich Nietzsche: Chronik in Bildern und Texten.* Munich.

Benveniste, E. 1966. *Problèmes de linguistique générale.* Paris.

Bernard, W. 2001. *Das Ende des Ödipus bei Sophokles. Untersuchung zur Interpretation des "Ödipus auf Kolonos."* Munich.

Bers, V. 1985. Dikastic *thorubos.* In P. A. Cartledge and F. D. Harvey, eds., *Crux: Essays presented to G. E. M. de Ste. Croix on his 75th Birthday.* London. 1–15.

Bers, V. 1994. Tragedy and rhetoric. In I. Worthington, ed., *Persuasion: Greek Rhetoric in Action.* London. 176–95.

Bers, V. 1997. *Speech in Speech: Studies in Incorporated Oratio Recta in Attic Drama and Oratory.* Lanham, Md.

Bierl, A. 1991. *Dionysos und die griechische Tragödie: politische und "metatheatrische" Aspekte im Text.* Tübingen.

Bierl, A. 1997. *Die Orestie des Aischylos auf der modernen Bühne: Theoretische Konzeptionen und ihre szenische Realisierung.* Stuttgart.

Bishop, J. D. 1972. Seneca's *Troades*: dissolution of a way of life. *RhM* 115: 329–37.

Bishop, P., ed. 2004. *Nietzsche and Antiquity: His Reaction and Response to the Classical Tradition.* Rochester, NY.

Blok, J. H. 2001. Virtual voices: towards a choreography of women's speech in classical Athens. In Lardinois and McClure 2001. 95–116.

Blom, E., ed. 1954. *Grove's Dictionary of Music and Musicians.* Fifth edition. 9 vols. London. Supplementary volume 1961.

Blondell, R. [previously M. W. Blundell]. 2002a. *The Play of Character in Plato's Dialogues.* Cambridge.

Blondell, R., trans. 2002b. *Sophocles: The Theban Plays.* Cambridge, Mass.

Blundell, M. W. 1988. The *phusis* of Neoptolemus in Sophocles' *Philoctetes. G&R* 35: 137–48.

Blundell, M. W. 1989. *Helping Friends and Harming Enemies: A Study in Sophocles and Greek Ethics.* Cambridge.

Blundell, M. W. 1993. The ideal of Athens in the *Oedipus at Colonus.* In Sommerstein et al. 1993. 287–306.

Boal, A. 1992. *Games for Actors and Non-Actors.* Trans. A. Jackson. London.

Boedeker, D. 2001. Heroic historiography: Simonides and Herodotus on Plataea. In D. Boedeker and D. Sider, eds., *The New Simonides: Contexts of Praise and Desire.* Oxford. 120–34.

Boedeker, D. 2002. Epic heritage and mythical patterns in Herodotus. In Bakker, de Jong, and Van Wees 2002. 97–116.

Boedeker, D., and K. A. Raaflaub, eds. 1998. *Democracy, Empire, and the Arts in Fifth-Century Athens.* Cambridge, Mass.

Boegehold, A. L., and A. C. Scafuro, eds. 1994. *Athenian Identity and Civic Ideology.* Baltimore.

Bond, G. W., ed. 1963. *Euripides: Hypsipyle.* Oxford.

Booth, W. C. 1961. *The Rhetoric of Fiction.* Chicago.

Borel, M.-J. 1990. Le discours descriptif, le savoir et ses signes. In J.-M. Adam et al. 1990b. 21–69.

Bourdieu, P. 1991. *Language and Symbolic Power.* Ed. J. B. Thompson, trans. G. Raymond and M. Adamson. Cambridge, Mass.

Bowie, A. M. 1993. Religion and politics in Aeschylus' *Oresteia. CQ* 43: 10–31.

Bowie, A. M. 1997. Tragic filters for history: Euripides' *Supplices* and Sophocles' *Philoctetes.* In Pelling 1997c. 39–62.

Bowra, C. M. 1944. *Sophoclean Tragedy.* Oxford.

Boyle, A. J., ed. and trans. 1994. *Seneca's Troades.* Leeds.

Brandt, R. 1991. Die Titelvignette von Nietzsches *Geburt der Tragödie aus dem Geiste der Musik. NS* 20: 314–28.

Brecht, B. 1964. *Brecht on Theatre: The Development of an Aesthetic.* Ed. and trans. J. Willett. London.

Brecht, B. 1965. *The Messingkauf Dialogues.* Trans. J. Willet. London.

Breisach, E. 1967. *Caterina Sforza: A Renaissance Virago.* Chicago.

Breitenbach, W. 1934. *Untersuchungen zur Sprache der euripideischen Lyrik.* Stuttgart.

Bremer, D. 1987. Vom Mythos zum Musikdrama: Wagner, Nietzsche und die griechische Tragödie. In D. Borchmeyer, ed., *Wege des Mythos in die Moderne: Richard Wagner, "Der Ring des Nibelungen."* Munich. 41–63.

Bremmer, J., ed. 1987. *Interpretations of Greek Mythology.* London.

Broadhead, H. D., ed. 1960. *The Persae of Aeschylus.* Cambridge.

Brockmann, C. 2003. *Aristophanes und die Freiheit der Komödie.* Munich.

Brommer, F. 1959. *Satyrspiele. Bilder griechischer Vasen.* Second edition. Berlin.

Brommer, F. 1982. *Theseus: die Taten des griechischen Helden in der antiken Kunst und Literatur.* Darmstadt.

Brooker, P. 1988. *Bertolt Brecht: Dialectics, Poetry, Politics.* London.

Brooker, P. 1994. Key words in Brecht's theory and practice of theatre. In Thomson and Sacks 1994. 185–200.

Brown, A. L. 1983. The Erinyes in the *Oresteia*: real life, the supernatural, and the stage. *JHS* 103: 13–34.

Browning, R. 2002. Greeks and others: from antiquity to the Renaissance. In Harrison 2002. 257–77.

Budelmann, F. 2000. *The Language of Sophocles: Communality, Communication and Involvement.* Cambridge.

Burian, P. 1972. Supplication and hero cult in Sophocles' *Ajax. GRBS* 13: 151–56.

Burian, P. 1974. Suppliant and saviour: Oedipus at Colonus. *Phoenix* 28: 408–29.

Burian, P., ed. 1985. *Directions in Euripidean Criticism.* Durham, NC.

Burian, P. 1997. Myth into *muthos*: the shaping of tragic plot. In Easterling 1997a. 178–208.

Burkert, W. 1966. Greek tragedy and sacrificial ritual. *GRBS* 7: 87–121.

Burkert, W. 1985. *Greek Religion: Archaic and Classical.* Trans. J. Raffan. Oxford.

Burkert, W. 1988. *Katagógia-Anagógia* and the goddess of Knossos. In R. Hägg, N. Marinatos, and G. C. Nordquist, eds., *Early Greek Cult Practice.* Stockholm. 81–88.

Burkert, W. 1991. *Oedipus, Oracles, and Meaning: From Sophocles to Umberto Eco.* Toronto.

Burkert, W. 1997. From epiphany to cult statue: early Greek *theos.* In A. B. Lloyd, ed., *What Is a God? Studies in the Nature of Greek Divinity.* London. 15–34.

Burkert, W. 1999. The logic of cosmogony. In Buxton 1999. 87–106.

Burnett, A. P. 1971. *Catastrophe Survived: Euripides' Plays of Mixed Reversal.* Oxford.

Burnett, A. P. 1985. *Rhesus*: are smiles allowed? In Burian 1985. 13–51, 177–88.

Burnett, A. P. 1998. *Revenge in Attic and Later Tragedy.* Berkeley.

Burton, R. W. B. 1980. *The Chorus in Sophocles' Tragedies.* Oxford.

Buxton, R. G. A. 1982. *Persuasion in Greek Tragedy: A Study of Peitho.* Cambridge.

Buxton, R. G. A. 1994. *Imaginary Greece: The Contexts of Mythology.* Cambridge.

Buxton, R. G. A., ed. 1999. *From Myth to Reason? Studies in the Development of Greek Thought.* Oxford.

Buxton, R. G. A. 2002. Time, space and ideology: tragic myths and the Athenian *polis.* In López Férez 2002. 175–89.

Cairns, D. L. 1993. *Aidôs: The Psychology and Ethics of Honour and Shame in Ancient Greek Literature.* Oxford.

Cairns, D. L. 1996. *Hybris,* dishonour, and thinking big. *JHS* 116: 1–32.

Cairns, D. L. 2001. Affronts and quarrels in the *Iliad.* In D. L. Cairns, ed., *Oxford Readings in Homer's Iliad.* Oxford. 203–19.

Calame, C. 1990. *Thésée et l'imaginaire Athénien: Légende et culte en Grèce antique.* Lausanne.

Calame, C. 1995. *The Craft of Poetic Speech in Ancient Greece.* Trans. J. Orion. Ithaca, NY.

Calame, C. 1999. Performative aspects of the choral voice in Greek tragedy: civic identity in performance. Trans. R. Osborne. In Goldhill and Osborne 1999. 125–53.

Calder, W. M. 1970. Originality in Seneca's *Troades. CP* 65: 75–82.

Calder, W. M. 1971. Sophoclean apologia: *Philoctetes. GRBS* 12: 153–74.

Calder, W. M. 1977. Seventeen letters of Ulrich von Wilamowitz-Moellendorff to Eduard Fraenkel. *HSCP* 81: 275–97.

Calder, W. M. 1983. The Wilamowitz–Nietzsche struggle: new documents and a reappraisal. *NS* 12: 214–54. Repr. in W. M. Calder, *Studies in the Modern History of Classical Scholarship.* Naples: 1984. 183–223.

Calder, W. M. 1986. Ulrich von Wilamowitz-Moellendorff: *Sospitator Euripidis. GRBS* 27: 409–30.

Cancik, H. 1986. Dionysos 1933: W. F. Otto, ein Religionswissenschaftler und Theologe am Ende der Weimarer Republik. In R. Faber and R. Schlesier, eds., *Die Restauration der Götter. Antike Religion und Neo-Paganismus.* Würzburg. 105–23. Repr. in H. Cancik, *Antik – Modern. Beiträge zur römischen und deutschen Kulturgeschichte.* Ed. R. Faber, B. von Reibnitz, and J. Rüpke. Stuttgart: 1998. 165–86.

Cancik, H. 1995. *Nietzsches Antike: Vorlesung.* Stuttgart.

Cancik, H. 1999. Der Einfluss Friedrich Nietzsches auf klassische Philologen in Deutschland bis 1945. Philologen am Nietzsche-Archiv. In H. Cancik and H. Cancik-Lindemaier, eds., *Philolog und Kultfigur: Friedrich Nietzsche und seine Antike in Deutschland.* Stuttgart. 231–49.

Canfora, L. 1989. *The Vanished Library.* Trans. M. Ryle. London.

Carey, C. 2000. Old comedy and the sophists. In D. Harvey and J. Wilkins, eds., *The Rivals of Aristophanes.* London. 419–36.

Carlson, M. 1993. *Theories of the Theatre.* Ithaca, NY.

Carpenter, T. H. 1991. *Art and Myth in Ancient Greece: A Handbook.* London.

Carpenter, T. H., and C. Faraone, eds. 1993. *Masks of Dionysus.* Ithaca, NY.

Cartledge, P. 1997. "Deep plays": theatre as process in Greek civic life. In Easterling 1997a. 3–35.

Cassio, A., D. Musti, and L. Rossi, eds. 2000. *Synaulia: cultura musicale in Grecia e contatti Mediterranei.* Naples.

Chambers, E. K. 1923. *The Elizabethan Stage.* 4 vols. Oxford.

Charleton, H. B. 1946. *The Senecan Tradition in Renaissance Tragedy.* Manchester.

Chioles, J. 1993. The *Oresteia* and the avant-garde: three decades of discourse. *Performing Arts Journal* 45 (15.3): 1–28.

Christ, M. R. 1990. Liturgy avoidance and *antidosis* in classical Athens. *TAPA* 120: 147–69.

Clinton, K. 1992. *Myth and Cult: The Iconography of the Eleusinian Mysteries.* Stockholm.

Cockle, W. E. H., ed. 1987. *Euripides: Hypsipyle.* Rome.

Cohen, D. 1995. *Law, Violence, and Community in Classical Athens.* Cambridge.

Cole, T[oby], ed. 1955. *Acting: A Handbook of the Stanislavski Method.* New York.

Cole, T[homas]. 1990. *Democritus and the Sources of Greek Anthropology.* Atlanta.

Cole, T[homas]. 1991. *The Origins of Rhetoric in Ancient Greece.* Baltimore.

Collard, C. 1970. On the tragedian Chaeremon. *JHS* 90: 22–34.

Collard, C., ed. 1975a. *Euripides: Supplices.* 2 vols. Groningen.

Collard, C. 1975b. Formal debates in Euripides' drama. *G&R* 22: 58–71. Repr. in Mossman 2003. 64–80.

Collard, C. 1995. The Pirithous fragments. In J. A. López Férez, ed., *De Homero a Libanio: Estudios actuales sobre textos griegos 2.* Madrid. 183–93.

Collard, C., M. J. Cropp, and K. H. Lee, eds. and trans. 1995. *Euripides: Selected Fragmentary Plays.* Vol. 1. Warminster.

Collard, C., M. J. Cropp, and J. Gibert, eds. and trans. 2004. *Euripides. Selected Fragmentary Plays.* Vol. 2. Oxford.

Conacher, D. J. 1967. *Euripidean Drama: Myth, Theme and Structure.* Toronto.

Conacher, D. J. 1981. Rhetoric and relevance in Euripidean drama. *AJP* 102: 3–25. Repr. in Mossman 2003. 81–101.

Conacher, D. J. 1998. *Euripides and the Sophists.* London.

Connor, W. R. 1989. City Dionysia and Athenian democracy. *CM* 40: 7–32.

Connor, W. R. 1994. The problem of Athenian civic identity. In Boegehold and Scafuro 1994. 34–44.

Conraidie, R. J. 1981. Contemporary politics in Greek tragedy: a critical discussion of different approaches. *AC* 24: 23–35.

Conte, G. B. 1994. *Latin Literature: A History.* Trans. J. B. Solodow, Rev. D. Fowler and G. W. Most. Baltimore.

Coquelin, C. 1915. *Papers on Acting II: Art and the Actor* (1880). Trans. A. L. Alger. Intro. H. James. New York.

Cozzoli, A.-T., ed. and trans. 2001. *Euripide: Cretesi.* Pisa.

Crane, G. 1989. Creon and the "Ode to Man" in Sophocles' *Antigone. HSCP* 92: 103–16.

Cremante, R. 1988. *Teatro del Cinquecento: La tragedia.* Milan.

Croally, N. T. 1994. *Euripidean Polemic: The Trojan Women and the Function of Tragedy.* Cambridge.

Cropp, M. J., ed. and trans. 1988. *Euripides: Electra.* Warminster.

Cropp, M. J., ed. and trans. 2000. *Euripides: Iphigenia in Tauris.* Warminster.

Cropp, M. J., and G. Fick. 1985. *Resolutions and Chronology in Euripides: The Fragmentary Tragedies.* London.

Cropp, M. J., K. H. Lee, and D. Sansone, eds. 1999–2000. *Euripides and Tragic Theatre in the Late Fifth Century.* Champaign, Ill. (*ICS* 24–25.)

Csapo, E. 1999–2000. Later Euripidean music. In Cropp, Lee, and Sansone 1999–2000. 399–426.

Csapo, E. 2002. Kallippides on the floor-sweepings: the limits of realism in classical acting and performance styles. In Easterling and Hall 2002. 127–47.

Csapo, E. 2004. The politics of the New Music. In Murray and Wilson 2004. 207–48.

Csapo, E., and W. J. Slater. 1995. *The Context of Ancient Drama.* Ann Arbor, Mich.

Curd, P. 2002. The presocratics as philosophers. In A. Laks and C. Louguet, eds., *Qu'est-ce que la philosophie présocratique?* Villeneuve-d'Ascq. 115–38.

Currie, B. 2004. Reperformance scenarios for Pindar's odes. In Mackie 2004. 49–69.

D'Alessio, G. B. 2004. Past future and present past: temporal deixis in Greek archaic lyric. *Arethusa* 37: 267–94.

Daitz, S. G. 1973. *Euripides: Hecuba.* Leipzig.

Dale, A. M., ed. 1954. *Euripides: Alcestis.* Oxford.

Dale, A. M. 1968. *The Lyric Metres of Greek Drama.* Second edition. Cambridge.

Dale, A. M. 1969. *Collected Papers.* Ed. T. B. L. Webster and E. G. Turner. Cambridge.

Dale, A. M. 1971–83. *Metrical Analyses of Tragic Choruses.* 3 vols. London.

Dalfen, J. 1972. Übertragener Gebrauch von τραγικός und τραγῳδεῖν bei Platon und anderen Autoren des 5. und 4. Jahrhunderts. *Philologus* 116: 76–92.

Damen, M. 1989. Actor and character in Greek tragedy. *TJ* 41: 316–40.

Davies, J. K. 1981. *Wealth and the Power of Wealth in Classical Athens.* New York.

Dawe, R. D. 1964. *The Collation and Investigation of Manuscripts of Aeschylus.* Cambridge.

Dawe, R. D. 1973–78. *Studies on the Text of Sophocles.* 3 vols. Leiden.

Dawe, R. D., ed. 1982. *Sophocles: Oedipus Rex.* Cambridge.

Day, M. 1999. "A new Athens rising near the pole": Canada and the Greek exemplum 1606–1954. *SyllClass* 10: 235–58.

Debnar, P. 2001. *Speaking the Same Language: Speech and Audience in Thucydides' Spartan Debates.* Ann Arbor, Mich.

Decreus, F. 2002. Some aspects of methodological blindness in interpreting Sophocles' *Oedipus. Euphrosyne* 30: 325–33.

Decreus, F. 2003. About Western man and the "gap" that is constantly threatening him: or how to deal with the tragic when staging Greek tragedies today? *Euphrosyne* 31: 61–82.

de Jong, I. J. F. 1987. The voice of anonymity: tis-speeches in the *Iliad. Eranos* 85: 69–84.

de Jong, I. J. F. 1991. *Narrative in Drama: The Art of the Euripidean Messenger-Speech.* Leiden.

De Lacy, P. 1948. Stoic views of poetry. *AJP* 69: 241–71.

Delgado, M. M., and P. Heritage, eds. 1996. *In Contact with the Gods? Directors Talk Theatre*. Manchester.

Del Grande, C. 1947. *Hybris. Colpa e castigato nell' espressione poetica e letteraria degli scrittori della Grecia antica da Omero a Cleante*. Naples.

De Martino, F., and A. H. Sommerstein, eds. 1995. *Lo Spettacolo delle Voci*. Bari.

Denniston, J. D., ed. 1939. *Euripides: Electra*. Oxford.

Denniston, J. D. 1954. *The Greek Particles*. Second edition. Rev. K. J. Dover. Oxford.

Denniston, J. D., and D. L. Page, eds. 1957. *Aeschylus: Agamemnon*. Oxford.

de Romilly, J. 1968. *Time in Greek Tragedy*. Ithaca, NY.

de Romilly, J. 1975. *Magic and Rhetoric in Ancient Greece*. Cambridge, Mass.

de Romilly, J. 1980. *L'évolution du pathétique d'Eschyle à Euripide*. Paris.

de Romilly, J. 1992. *The Great Sophists in Periclean Athens*. Trans. J. Lloyd. Oxford.

de Romilly, J. 2003. The rejection of suicide in the *Heracles* of Euripides. Trans. D. Mossman and J. M. Mossman. In Mossman 2003. 285–94.

des Bouvrie, S. 1990. *Women in Greek Tragedy: An Anthropological Approach*. Oslo.

Detienne, M. 1965. En Grèce archaïque: géométrie, politique et société. *Annales: Économies, Sociétés, Civilisations* 20: 425–41.

Detienne, M. 1996. *The Masters of Truth in Ancient Greece*. Trans. J. Lloyd. New York.

Di Benedetto, V. 1978. *L'ideologia del potere e la tragedia greca: ricerche su Eschilo*. Turin.

Di Benedetto, V., and E. Medda. 1997. *La tragedia sulla scena: la tragedia greca in quanto spettacolo teatrale*. Turin.

Diderot, D. 1883. *The Paradox of Acting: Translated with Annotations from Diderot's "Paradoxe sur le Comédien."* Trans. W. H. Pollock. London.

Diggle, J., ed. 1970. *Euripides: Phaethon*. Cambridge.

Diggle, J., ed. 1984–94. *Euripidis Fabulae*. 3 vols. Oxford.

Dilke, O. A. W. 1985. *Greek and Roman Maps*. London.

Di Maria, S. 1995a. The dramatic *hic et nunc* in the tragedy of Renaissance Italy. *Italica* 72: 275–97.

Di Maria, S. 1995b. Spazio e tematica nell' *Orazia* di Pietro Aretino. In M. Lettieri, S. Bancheri, and R. Buranello, eds., *Pietro Aretino e la cultura del Rinascimento*. 2: 803–28. Rome.

Di Maria, S. 1996. Towards an Italian theater: Rucellai's *Oreste*. *MLN* 111: 123–48.

Di Maria, S. 2002. *The Italian Tragedy in the Renaissance: Cultural Realities and Theatrical Innovations*. Lewisburg, Penn.

Dobbin, R., ed. and trans. 1998. *Epictetus: Discourses Book I*. Oxford.

Dobrov, G. W. 2001. *Figures of Play: Greek Drama and Metafictional Poetics*. New York.

Dodds, E. R., ed. 1960. *Euripides: Bacchae*. Second edition. Oxford.

Doherty, L. 2001. *Gender and the Interpretation of Classical Myth*. London.

Dolce, L. 1549. *Giocasta*. In Poggiali 1808–12. 6: 5–118.

Dolce, L. 1560. *Tragedie di M. Lodovico Dolce, cioè, Giocasta, Didone, Thieste, Medea, Ifigenia, Hecuba, di nuovo ricorrette e ristampate*. Venice.

Dolce, L. 1565. *Marianna*. In Cremante 1988. 741–877.

Dolfin, G. 1585. Lettera di Giacomo Dolfin. In Gallo 1973. 33–37.

Donlan, W. 1979. The structure of authority in the *Iliad*. *Arethusa* 12: 51–70.

Dover, K. J. 1974. *Greek Popular Morality in the Time of Plato and Aristotle*. Oxford.

Dover, K. J. 1986. Ion of Chios: his place in the history of Greek literature. In J. Boardman and C. E. Vaphopoulou-Richardson, eds., *Chios*. Oxford. 27–37. Repr. in K. J. Dover, *The Greeks and Their Legacy*. Oxford: 1988. 1–12.

Dover, K. J., ed. 1993a. *Aristophanes: Frogs*. Oxford.

Dover, K. 1993b. The contest in Aristophanes' *Frogs*: the points at issue. In Sommerstein et al. 1993. 445–60.

Drew-Bear, T. 1968. The trochaic tetrameter in Greek tragedy. *AJP* 89: 385–405.

DuBois, P. 1982. *Centaurs and Amazons: Women and the Pre-History of the Great Chain of Being*. Ann Arbor, Mich.

Duchemin, J. 1968. *L'agôn dans la tragédie grecque*. Second edition. Paris.

Ducrey, P. 1968. *Le traitement des prisonniers de guerre dans la Grèce antique*. Paris.

Duff, T. 1999. *Plutarch's Lives: Exploring Virtue and Vice*. Oxford.

Dunn, F. M. 1992. Introduction: Beginning at Colonus. In Dunn and Cole 1992. 1–12.

Dunn, F. M. 1996. *Tragedy's End: Closure and Innovation in Euripidean Drama*. New York.

Dunn, F. M. 2000. Euripidean aetiologies. *CB* 76: 3–27.

Dunn, F. M., and T. Cole, eds. 1992. *Beginnings in Classical Literature*. Cambridge. (*YCS* 29.)

Easterling, P. E. 1967. Oedipus and Polynices. *PCPS* 13: 1–13.

Easterling, P. E. 1973. Presentation of character in Aeschylus. *G&R* 20: 3–19.

Easterling, P. E. 1977. Character in Sophocles. *G&R* 24: 121–29.

Easterling, P. E. 1984. Kings in Greek tragedy. In J. Coy and J. de Hoz, eds., *Estudios sobre los géneros literarios, II*. Salamanca. 33–45.

Easterling, P. E. 1985a. Anachronism in Greek tragedy. *JHS* 105: 1–10.

Easterling, P. E. 1985b. Greek poetry and Greek religion. In Easterling and Muir 1985. 34–49.

Easterling, P. E. 1988. Tragedy and ritual: "Cry 'Woe, woe', but may the good prevail." *Métis* 3: 87–109.

Easterling, P. E. 1990. Constructing character in Greek tragedy. In Pelling 1990. 83–99.

Easterling, P. E. 1991. Euripides in the theatre. *Pallas* 37: 49–59.

Easterling, P. E. 1993. The end of an era? Tragedy in the early fourth century. In Sommerstein et al. 1993. 559–69.

Easterling, P. E. 1994. Euripides outside Athens: a speculative note. *ICS* 19: 73–80.

Easterling, P. E., ed. 1997a. *The Cambridge Companion to Greek Tragedy*. Cambridge.

Easterling, P. E. 1997b. Constructing the heroic. In Pelling 1997c. 21–37.

Easterling, P. E. 1997c. Gilbert Murray's reading of Euripides. *Colby Quarterly* 33.2: 113–27.

Easterling, P. E. 1997d. Form and performance. In Easterling 1997a. 151–77.

Easterling, P. E. 1997e. From repertoire to canon. In Easterling 1997a. 211–27.

Easterling, P. E. 1997f. A show for Dionysus. In Easterling 1997a. 36–53.

Easterling, P. E. 1999. Actors and voices: reading between the lines in Aeschines and Demosthenes. In Goldhill and Osborne 1999. 154–66.

Easterling, P. E. 2002. Actor as icon. In Easterling and Hall 2002. 327–41.

Easterling, P. E., and E. Hall, eds. 2002. *Greek and Roman Actors: Aspects of an Ancient Profession*. Cambridge.

Easterling, P. E., and B. M. W. Knox, eds. 1985. *The Cambridge History of Classical Literature I: Greek Literature*. Cambridge.

Easterling, P. E., and J. V. Muir, eds. 1985. *Greek Religion and Society*. Cambridge.

Ebbott, M. 2000. The list of the war dead in Aeschylus' *Persians*. *HSCP* 100: 83–96.

Ebbott, M. 2003. *Imagining Illegitimacy in Classical Greek Literature*. Lanham, Md.

Eco, Umberto. 1979. *The Role of the Reader*. Bloomington, Ind.

Eder, W. 1998. Aristocrats and the coming of Athenian democracy. In Morris and Raaflaub 1998. 105–40.

Eddershaw, M. 1982. Acting methods: Brecht and Stanislavsky. In G. Bartram and A. E. Waine, eds., *Brecht in Perspective*. London. 128–44.

Eddershaw, M. 1994. Actors on Brecht. In Thomson and Sacks 1994. 254–72.

Edmunds, L., ed. 1990. *Approaches to Greek Myth*. Baltimore.

Egli, F. 2003. *Euripides im Kontext zeitgenössischer intellektueller Strömungen*. Munich.

Elam, K. 1980. *The Semiotics of Theatre and Drama*. London.

Else, G. F. 1957. *Aristotle's Poetics: The Argument*. Cambridge, Mass.

Else, G. F. 1965. *The Origin and Early Form of Greek Tragedy*. Cambridge, Mass.

Erbse, H. 1984. *Studien zum Prolog der euripideischen Tragödie*. Berlin.

Esslin, M. 1976. *Artaud*. London.

Euben, J. P., ed. 1986. *Greek Tragedy and Political Theory*. Berkeley.

Fagles, R., trans. 1975. *Aeschylus: The Oresteia*. Intro. and notes by W. B. Stanford. New York.

Fagles, R., trans. 1982. *Sophocles: The Three Theban Plays*. Intro. and notes by B. M. W. Knox. New York.

Fantham, E. 1982. *Seneca's Troades*. Princeton.

Fantham, E. 1999. The role of lament in the growth and eclipse of Roman epic. In M. Beissinger, J. Tylus, and S. Wofford, eds., *Epic Traditions in the Contemporary World*. Berkeley. 221–35.

Fantuzzi, M. 1993. Preistoria di un genere letterario: a proposito degli Inni V e VI di Callimaco. In R. Pretagostini, ed., *Tradizione e innovazione nella cultura greca da Omero all'età ellenistica: scritti in onore di Bruno Gentili*. Rome. 3: 927–46.

Fátima Sousa e Silva, M. de, ed. 1998. *Representações de Teatro Clássico no Portugal Contemporâneo*. Lisbon.

Fátima Sousa e Silva, M. de. 1999. Le Portugal de nos jours et les représentations de théâtre grec. In Mavromoustakos 1999. 105–9.

Feeney, D. C. 1998. *Literature and Religion at Rome*. Cambridge.

Ferrari, G. 2000. The Ilioupersis in Athens. *HSCP* 100: 119–50.

Ferrari, G. 2002. The ancient temple on the Acropolis at Athens. *AJA* 106: 11–35.

Fischer-Lichte, E. 1999. Between text and cultural performance: staging Greek tragedies in Germany. *Theatre Survey* 40.1: 1–30.

Fisher, N. R. E. 1990. The law of *hubris* in Athens. In P. Cartledge, P. Millett, and S. Todd, eds., *Nomos: Essays in Athenian Law, Politics and Society*. Cambridge. 123–38.

Fisher, N. R. E. 1992. *Hybris: A Study in the Values of Honour and Shame in Ancient Greece*. Warminster.

Fitzpatrick, D. 2001. Sophocles' *Tereus*. *CQ* 51: 90–101.

Flashar, H. 1991. *Inszenierung der Antike: das griechische Drama auf der Bühne der Neuzeit 1585–1990*. Munich.

Flashar, H., ed. 1995. *Altertumswissenschaft in den 20er Jahren. Neue Fragen und Impulse*. Stuttgart.

Flashar, H., ed. 1997. *Tragödie: Idee und Transformation*. Stuttgart.

Fleming, T. 1999. The survival of Greek dramatic music from the fifth century to the Roman period. In B. Gentili and F. Perusino, eds., *La colometria antica dei testi poetici Greci*. Pisa. 17–29.

Flory, S. 1978. Medea's right hand: promises and revenge. *TAPA* 108: 69–74.

Foley, H. P. 1980. The masque of Dionysus. *TAPA* 110: 107–33.

Foley, H. P. 1981. The conception of women in Athenian drama. In H. P. Foley, ed., *Reflections of Women in Antiquity*. New York. 127–68.

Foley, H. P. 1985. *Ritual Irony: Poetry and Sacrifice in Euripides*. Ithaca, NY.

Foley, H. P. 1993. The politics of tragic lamentation. In Sommerstein et al. 1993. 101–43.

Foley, H. P. 1999. Modern performance and adaptation of Greek tragedy. *TAPA* 129: 1–12.

Foley, H. P. 2001. *Female Acts in Greek Tragedy*. Princeton.

Foley, H. P. 2003. Choral identity in Greek tragedy. *CP* 98: 1–30.

Foley, H. P. 2004. Bad women: gender politics in late twentieth-century performance and revision of Greek tragedy. In Hall, Macintosh, and Wrigley 2004. 77–111.

Fornara, C. W. 1971. Evidence for the date of Herodotus' publication. *JHS* 91: 25–34.

Fornara, C. W. 1983. *The Nature of History in Ancient Greece and Rome*. Berkeley.

Foucault, M. 1979. What is an author? In J. V. Harari, ed., *Textual Strategies: Perspectives in Post-Structuralist Criticism*. Ithaca, NY. 141–60.

Fowler, D. 1989. First thoughts on closure: problems and prospects. *MD* 22: 75–122. Repr. in Fowler 2000. 239–83.

Fowler, D. 1997. Second thoughts on closure. In Roberts, Dunn, and Fowler 1997. 3–22. Repr. in Fowler 2000. 284–307.

Fowler, D. 2000. *Roman Constructions: Readings in Postmodern Latin*. Oxford.

Fowler, H. N., ed. and trans. 1936. *Plutarch: Moralia*. Vol. 10. Cambridge, Mass. LCL.

Fowler, R. L. 1987. The rhetoric of desperation. *HSCP* 91: 5–38.

Fraenkel, E., ed. 1950. *Aeschylus: Agamemnon*. 3 vols. Oxford.

Fraenkel, E. 1961. Eine Anfangsformel attischer Reden. *Glotta* 39: 1–5.

Fraenkel, E. 1965. Review of W. Ritchie, *The Authenticity of the Rhesus of Euripides*. *Gnomon* 37: 228–41.

Fraenkel, E. 1967. Zwei Aias-Szenen hinter der Bühne. *MusHelv* 24: 79–86.

Fraenkel, E. 1977. *Due seminari romani di Eduard Fraenkel: Aiace e Filottete di Sofocle*. Rome.

Fraser, P. M. 1972. *Ptolemaic Alexandria*. 3 vols. Oxford.

Frazer, J. G., ed. and trans. 1921. *Apollodorus: The Library*. 2 vols. Cambridge, Mass. LCL.

Frede, M. 1996. Introduction. In M. Frede and G. Striker, eds., *Rationality in Greek Thought*. Oxford. 1–28.

Friedrich, R. 1996. Everything to do with Dionysos? Ritualism, the Dionysiac, and the tragic. In Silk 1996a. 257–83.

Friis Johansen, H. 1959. *General Reflections in Tragic Rhesis*. Copenhagen.

Friis Johansen, H., and E. Whittle, eds. 1980. *Aeschylus: The Suppliants*. 3 vols. Copenhagen.

Frischer, B. D. 1970. *Concordia discors* and characterization in Euripides' *Hippolytos*. *GRBS* 11: 85–100.

Frye, N. 1957. *Anatomy of Criticism: Four Essays*. Princeton.

Gagarin, M. 1976. *Aeschylean Drama*. Berkeley.

Gallo, A., ed. 1973. *La prima rappresentazione al teatro Olimpico con i progetti e le relazioni dei contemporanei*. Milan.

Gantz, T. 1979. The Aischylean tetralogy: prolegomena. *CJ* 74: 289–304.

Gantz, T. 1980. The Aischylean tetralogy: attested and conjectured groups. *AJP* 101: 133–64.

Gantz, T. 1993. *Early Greek Myth: A Guide to Literary and Artistic Sources*. Baltimore.

Garin, E. 1995. *La cultura del Rinascimento*. Milan.

Garner, R. 1990. *From Homer to Tragedy: The Art of Allusion in Greek Poetry*. London.

Garvie, A. F. 1969. *Aeschylus' Supplices: Play and Trilogy*. Cambridge.

Garvie, A. F., ed. 1986. *Aeschylus: Choephori*. Oxford.

Garvie, A. F., ed. and trans. 1998. *Sophocles: Ajax*. Warminster.

Gellrich, M. 1995. Interpreting Greek tragedy: history, theory, and the new philology. In Goff 1995a. 38–58.

Gentili, B. 1988. *Poetry and Its Public in Ancient Greece*. Baltimore.

Gentili, B., and L. Lomiento. 2003. *Metrica e ritmica: storia delle forme poetiche nella Grecia antica*. Milan.

Gera, D. L. 2003. *Ancient Greek Ideas on Speech, Language, and Civilization*. Oxford.

Ghiron-Bistagne, P. 1976. *Recherches sur les acteurs dans la Grèce antique*. Paris.

Gibert, J. 1995. *Change of Mind in Greek Tragedy*. Göttingen.

Gildenhard, I., and A. Zissos. 2000. Ovid's Narcissus (*Met.* 3.339–510): echoes of Oedipus. *AJP* 121: 129–47.

Gill, C. 1995. *Greek Thought*. Greece and Rome New Surveys in the Classics 25. Oxford.

Gill, C. 1996. *Personality in Greek Epic, Tragedy, and Philosophy*. Oxford.

Giraldi, G. C. 1541. *Orbecche*. In Cremante 1988. 281–448.

Giraldi, G. C. 1543. Lettera sulla tragedia. In Bernard Weinberg, ed., *Trattati di poetica e retorica del Cinquecento*. 1: 471–86. Bari: 1970.

Glau, K. 1998. Zur Diskussion um die Deutung des Schlusses der Aischyleischen *Eumeniden*. *Poetica* 30: 291–315.

Gödde, S., and T. Heinze, eds. 2000. *Skenika: Beiträge zum antiken Theater und seiner Rezeption*. Darmstadt.

Goff, B. 1990. *The Noose of Words: Readings of Desire, Violence, and Language in Euripides' Hippolytos*. Cambridge.

Goff, B., ed. 1995a. *History, Tragedy, Theory: Dialogues on Athenian Drama*. Austin, Tex.

Goff, B. 1995b. Introduction. In Goff 1995a. 1–37.

Goff, B. 1999–2000. Try to make it real compared to what? Euripides' *Electra* and the play of genres. In Cropp, Lee, and Sansone 1999–2000. 93–105.

Goffman, E. 1979. *Gender Advertisements*. Cambridge, Mass.

Goldberg, S. M. 1996. The fall and rise of Roman tragedy. *TAPA* 126: 265–86.

Goldhill, S. 1984. *Language, Sexuality, Narrative: The Oresteia*. Cambridge.

Goldhill, S. 1986a. *Reading Greek Tragedy*. Cambridge.

Goldhill, S. 1986b. Rhetoric and relevance: interpolation at Euripides *Electra* 367–400. *GRBS* 27: 157–71.

Goldhill, S. 1990. The Great Dionysia and civic ideology. In Winkler and Zeitlin 1990. 97–129.

Goldhill, S. 1991. *The Poet's Voice: Essays on Poetics and Greek Literature*. Cambridge.

Goldhill, S. 1992. *Aeschylus: The Oresteia*. Cambridge.

Goldhill, S. 1994. Representing democracy: women at the Great Dionysia. In Osborne and Hornblower 1994. 347–69.

Goldhill, S. 1996. Collectivity and otherness – the authority of the tragic chorus: response to Gould. In Silk 1996a. 244–56.

Goldhill, S. 1997a. The audience of Greek tragedy. In Easterling 1997a. 54–68.

Goldhill, S. 1997b. The language of tragedy: rhetoric and communication. In Easterling 1997a. 127–50.

Goldhill, S. 1997c. Modern critical approaches to Greek tragedy. In Easterling 1997a. 324–47.

Goldhill, S. 1999. Programme notes. In Goldhill and Osborne 1999. 1–29.

Goldhill, S. 2000. Civic ideology and the problem of difference: the politics of Aeschylean tragedy, once again. *JHS* 120: 34–56.

Goldhill, S., and R. Osborne, eds. 1999. *Performance Culture and Athenian Democracy*. Cambridge.

Gomme, A. W. 1938. Aristophanes and politics. *CR* 52: 97–109.

Gomme, A. W. 1945–56. *A Historical Commentary on Thucydides*. Vols. 1–3. Oxford.

Gould, J. 1973. Hiketeia. *JHS* 93: 74–103. Repr. in Gould 2001. 22–74.

Gould, J. 1978. Dramatic character and "human intelligibility" in Greek tragedy. *PCPS* 24: 43–67. Repr. in Gould 2001. 78–111.

Gould, J. 1985. On making sense of Greek religion. In Easterling and Muir 1985. 1–33. Repr. in Gould 2001. 203–34.

Gould, J. 1996. Tragedy and collective experience. In Silk 1996a. 217–43. Repr. in Gould 2001. 378–404.

Gould, J. 1999. Myth, memory, and the chorus: "Tragic rationality." In Buxton 1999. 107–16. Repr. in Gould 2001. 405–14.

Gould, J. 2001. *Myth, Ritual, Memory, and Exchange: Essays in Greek Literature and Culture*. Oxford.

Graf, F. 1993. *Greek Mythology: An Introduction*. Trans. T. Marier. Baltimore.

Graf, F. 1997. Epiphanie. *Der Neue Pauly*. Stuttgart. 1150–51.

Green, A. S. 1994. *The Revisionist Stage: American Directors Reinvent the Classics*. Cambridge.

Green, J. R. 1990. Carcinus and the temple: a lesson in the staging of tragedy. *GRBS* 31: 281–85.

Green, J. R. 1991. On seeing and depicting the theatre in classical Athens. *GRBS* 32: 15–50.

Green, J. R. 1994. *Theatre in Ancient Greek Society*. London.

Green, J. R. 1995. Theatre production: 1987–1995. *Lustrum* 37: 7–202, 309–318.

Green, J. R., and E. Handley. 1995. *Images of the Greek Theatre*. Austin, Tex.

Green, P. 1999. War and morality in fifth-century Athens: the case of Euripides' *Trojan Women*. *AHB* 13.3: 97–110.

Gregory, J. 1979. Euripides' *Alcestis*. *Hermes* 107: 259–70.

Gregory, J. 1991. *Euripides and the Instruction of the Athenians*. Ann Arbor, Mich.

Gregory, J. 1995. Genealogy and intertextuality in *Hecuba*. *AJP* 116: 389–97.

Gregory, J., ed. 1999. *Euripides: Hecuba*. Atlanta.

Gregory, J. 1999–2000. Comic elements in Euripides. In Cropp, Lee, and Sansone 1999–2000. 59–74.

Gregory, J. 2002. Euripides as social critic. *G&R* 49: 145–62.

Grene, D., and R. Lattimore, eds., 1959. *The Complete Greek Tragedies*. 4 vols. Chicago.

Griffin, J. 1990. Characterization in Euripides: *Hippolytus* and *Iphigeneia in Aulis*. In Pelling 1990. 128–49.

Griffin, J. 1998. The social function of Attic tragedy. *CQ* 48: 3–61.

Griffin, J. 1999a. Sophocles and the democratic city. In Griffin 1999b. 73–94.

Griffin, J., ed. 1999b. *Sophocles Revisited: Essays Presented to Sir Hugh Lloyd-Jones*. Oxford.

Griffith, M. 1977. *The Authenticity of Prometheus Bound*. Cambridge.

Griffith, M., ed. 1983. *Aeschylus: Prometheus Bound*. Cambridge.

Griffith, M. 1995. Brilliant dynasts: power and politics in the *Oresteia*. *CA* 14: 62–129.

Griffith, M. 1998. The king and eye: the rule of the father in Greek tragedy. *PCPS* 44: 20–84.

Griffith, M. 2001. Antigone and her sister(s): embodying women in Greek tragedy. In Lardinois and McClure 2001. 117–36.

Grotowski, J. 1968. *Towards a Poor Theatre*. New York.

Gründer, K., ed. 1969. *Der Streit um Nietzsches "Geburt der Tragödie": Die Schriften von E. Rohde, R. Wagner, U. v. Wilamowitz-Möllendorff*. Hildesheim.

Gudeman, A., ed. 1934. *Aristoteles: Peri Poiêtikês*. Berlin.

Gundersheimer, W. L. 1973. *Ferrara: The Style of Renaissance Despotism*. Princeton.

Guthrie, W. K. C. 1969. *A History of Greek Philosophy*. Vol. 3: *The Fifth-Century Enlightenment*. Cambridge.

Gutzwiller, H. 1951. Friedrich Nietzsches Lehrtätigkeit am Basler Pädagogium 1869–1876. *Basler Zeitschrift für Geschichte und Altertumskunde* 50: 147–224. Repr. in D. M. Hoffmann, ed., *Beiträge zu Friedrich Nietzsche*. Vol. 5. Basel: 2001. 147–224.

Haak, A. C. 1977. Melpomene en het Nederlands toneel. With a German survey. Diss. Utrecht.

Hägg, R. 1986. Die göttliche Epiphanie im minoischen Ritual. *AthMit* 101: 41–62.

Hahnemann, C. 1999. Zur Rekonstruktion und Interpretation von Sophokles' "Aigeus." *Hermes* 127: 385–96.

Hall, E. 1989. *Inventing the Barbarian: Greek Self-Definition through Tragedy*. Oxford.

Hall, E. 1993. Political and cosmic turbulence in Euripides' *Orestes*. In Sommerstein et al. 1993. 263–85.

Hall, E. 1995. Lawcourt dramas: the power of performance in Greek forensic oratory. *BICS* 40: 39–58.

Hall, E., ed and trans. 1996a. *Aeschylus: Persians*. Warminster.

Hall, E. 1996b. Is there a *polis* in Aristotle's *Poetics*? In Silk 1996a. 295–309.

Hall, E. 1997. The sociology of Athenian tragedy. In Easterling 1997a. 93–126.

Hall, E. 1999a. Actor's song in tragedy. In Goldhill and Osborne 1999. 96–122.

Hall, E. 1999b. Greek tragedy and the British stage, 1566–1997. *Cahiers du GITA* 12: 113–33.

Hall, E. 2002. The singing actors of antiquity. In Easterling and Hall 2002. 3–38.

Hall, E., and F. Macintosh. 2004. *Greek Tragedy and the British Theatre 1660–1914*. Oxford.

Hall, E., F. Macintosh, and O. Taplin, eds. 2000. *Medea in Performance: 1500–2000*. Oxford.

Hall, E., F. Macintosh, and A. Wrigley, eds. 2004. *Dionysus Since 69: Greek Tragedy at the Dawn of the Third Millennium*. Oxford.

Haller, R. S., ed. and trans. 1973. *Literary Criticism of Dante Alighieri*. Lincoln, Nebr.

Halleran, M. 1985. *Stagecraft in Euripides*. London.

Halleran, M., ed. and trans. 1995. *Euripides: Hippolytus*. Warminster.

Halliwell, S. 1984a. Aristophanic satire. *The Yearbook of English Studies* 14: 6–20.

Halliwell, S. 1984b. Plato and Aristotle on the denial of tragedy. *PCPS* 30: 49–71. Rev. repr. in A. Laird, ed., *Oxford Readings in Ancient Literary Criticism*. Oxford: Forthcoming.

Halliwell, S. 1986. *Aristotle's Poetics*. London. Second edition with a new introduction, Chicago: 1998.

Halliwell, S., ed and trans. 1987. *The Poetics of Aristotle*. London.

Halliwell, S. 1996. Plato's repudiation of the tragic. In Silk 1996a. 332–49.

Halliwell, S. 1997. Between public and private: tragedy and Athenian experience of rhetoric. In Pelling 1997c. 121–41.

Halliwell, S. 2002. *The Aesthetics of Mimesis: Ancient Texts and Modern Problems*. Princeton.

Halliwell, S. 2003. Nietzsche's "Daimonic force" of tragedy and its ancient traces. *Arion* 11.1: 103–23.

Hamilton, J. 2004. Ecce Philologus: Nietzsche and Pindar's Second Pythian Ode. In Bishop 2004. 54–69.

Hamilton, R. 1978. Prologue, prophecy and plot in four plays of Euripides. *AJP* 99: 277–302.

Hammond, N. G. L. 1972. The conditions of dramatic production to the death of Aeschylus. *GRBS* 13: 387–450.

Hammond, N. G. L. 1984. Spectacle and parody in Euripides' *Electra*. *GRBS* 25: 373–87.

Hansen, M. 1976. How many Athenians attended the *Ecclesia*? *GRBS* 17: 115–34.

Hansen, M. H. 2003. 95 theses about the Greek *polis* in the archaic and classical periods. *Historia* 52: 257–82.

Hansen, P. A., ed. 1983. *Carmina epigraphica graeca: saeculorum VIII–V a. Chr. n.* Berlin.

Harder, A., ed. 1985. *Euripides' Kresphontes and Archelaus*. Leiden.

Harder, R. E. 1993. *Die Frauenrollen bei Euripides*. Stuttgart.

Hardie, P. 1993. *The Epic Successors of Virgil: A Study in the Dynamics of a Tradition*. Cambridge.

Hardie, P. 1997. Virgil and tragedy. In C. Martindale, ed., *The Cambridge Companion to Virgil*. Cambridge. 312–26.

Hardwick, L. 2003a. Classical theatre in modern Scotland – a democratic stage? In L. Hardwick and C. Gillespie, eds., *The Role of Greek Drama and Poetry in Crossing and Redefining Cultural Boundaries*. Milton Keynes. Also available online. www2.open.ac.uk/ClassicalStudies/GreekPlays/Seminar02/LHFinal.htm.

Hardwick, L. 2003b. *Reception Studies. Greece and Rome New Surveys in the Classics* 33. Oxford.

Hardwick, L., P. E. Easterling, S. Ireland, N. Lowe, and F. Macintosh, eds. 2000. *Selected Proceedings of the January Conference 1999: Theatre Ancient and Modern*. Milton Keynes. Also available online. www.open.ac.uk/Arts/CC99/.

Harris, W. V. 2001. *Restraining Rage: The Ideology of Anger Control in Classical Antiquity*. Cambridge, Mass.

Harrison, J. 1903. *Prolegomena to the Study of Greek Religion*. Cambridge.

Harrison, J. 1912. *Themis: A Study of the Social Origins of Greek Religion*. Cambridge.

Harrison, T., ed. 2002. *Greeks and Barbarians*. New York.

Harrop, J. 1992. *Acting*. London.

Hartigan, K. V. 1995. *Greek Tragedy on the American Stage: Ancient Drama in the Commercial Theater, 1882–1994*. Westport, Conn.

Hartog, F. 1988. *The Mirror of Herodotus: The Representation of the Other in the Writing of History*. Trans. J. Lloyd. Berkeley.

Harvey, A. E. 1955. The classification of Greek lyric poetry. *CQ* 5: 157–75.

Hazel, R. 1999. Unsuitable for women and children? Greek tragedies in modern British theatres. *SyllClass* 10: 259–77.

Hazel, R. 2001. *Bibliography of Theatre Journals, Periodicals and Other Resources*. Milton Keynes. Also available online. www2.open.ac.uk/ClassicalStudies/GreekPlays/Projectsite/Bibintro.htm.

Heath, M. 1987a. "Jure principem locum tenet": Euripides' *Hecuba*. *BICS* 34: 40–68. Repr. in Mossman 2003. 218–60.

Heath, M. 1987b. *The Poetics of Greek Tragedy*. London.

Heath, M. 1987c. *Political Comedy in Aristophanes*. Göttingen.

Heath, M. 1989. *Unity in Greek Poetics*. Oxford.

Heath, M. 1999. Sophocles' *Philoctetes*: a problem play? In Griffin 1999b. 137–60.

Hedreen, G. 1992. *Silens in Attic Black-Figure Vase-Painting: Myth and Performance*. Ann Arbor, Mich.

Heidel, W. A. 1937. *The Frame of the Ancient Greek Maps*. New York.

Heiden, B. 1991. Tragedy and comedy in *The Frogs* of Aristophanes. *Ramus* 20: 95–111.

Henderson, J. 1990. The *démos* and the comic competition. In Winkler and Zeitlin 1990. 271–313.

Henderson, J. 1991. Women and the Athenian dramatic festivals. *TAPA* 121: 133–47.

Henderson. J., ed. and trans. 1998–2002. *Aristophanes*. 4 vols. Cambridge, Mass. LCL.

Henrichs, A. 1975. Two doxographical notes: Democritus and Prodicus on religion. *HSCP* 79: 93–123.

Henrichs, A. 1984. Loss of self, suffering, violence: the modern view of Dionysus from Nietzsche to Girard. *HSCP* 88: 205–40.

Henrichs, A. 1986. The last of the detractors: Friedrich Nietzsche's condemnation of Euripides. *GRBS* 27: 369–97.

Henrichs, A. 1993a. "He has a god in him": human and divine in the modern perception of Dionysus. In Carpenter and Faraone 1993. 13–43.

Henrichs, A. 1993b. The tomb of Aias and the prospect of hero cult in Sophokles. *CA* 12: 165–80.

Henrichs, A. 1994–95. "Why should I dance?": choral self-referentiality in Greek tragedy. *Arion* 3.1: 56–111.

Henrichs, A. 1995. Philologie und Wissenschaftsgeschichte: Zur Krise eines Selbstverständnisses. In H. Flashar, ed., *Altertumswissenschaft in den 20er Jahren*. Stuttgart. 423–57.

Henrichs, A. 1996a. Dancing in Athens, dancing on Delos: some patterns of choral projection in Euripides. *Philologus* 140: 48–62.

Henrichs, A. 1996b. Epiphany. *OCD* 546.

Henrichs, A. 1996c. *"Warum soll ich denn tanzen?": Dionysisches im Chor der griechischen Tragödie*. Stuttgart.

Henrichs, A. 2004. "Full of gods": Nietzsche on Greek polytheism and culture. In Bishop 2004. 114–37.

Herington, C. J. 1963. The influence of old comedy on Aeschylus' later trilogies. *TAPA* 94: 113–25.

Herington, C. J. 1966. Senecan tragedy. *Arion* 5: 422–71.

Herington, C. J. 1970. *The Author of the Prometheus Bound*. Austin, Tex.

Herington, C. J. 1985. *Poetry into Drama: Early Tragedy and the Greek Poetic Tradition*. Berkeley.

Herington, C. J. 1986. *Aeschylus*. New Haven.

Herman, G. 1993. Tribal and civic codes of behaviour in Lysias 1. *CQ* 43: 406–19.

Herman, G. 1994. How violent was Athenian society? In Osborne and Hornblower 1994. 99–117.

Herman, G. 1995. Honour, revenge, and the state in fourth-century Athens. In W. Eder, ed., *Die athenische Demokratie im 4. Jahrhundert v. Chr.: Vollendung oder Verfall einer Verfassungsform?* Stuttgart. 43–66.

Herman, G. 1996. Ancient Athens and the values of Mediterranean society. *MHR* 11.1: 5–36.

Herman, G. 1998. Reciprocity, altruism, and the prisoner's dilemma: the special case of classical Athens. In C. Gill, N. Postlethwaite, and R. Seaford, eds., *Reciprocity in Ancient Greece*. Oxford. 199–225.

Hermann, G. 1799. *Aeschyli Eumenides*. Leipzig.

Herrick, M. 1965. *Italian Tragedy in the Renaissance*. Urbana, Ill.

Hesk, J. 1999. The rhetoric of anti-rhetoric in oratory. In Goldhill and Osborne 1999. 201–30.

Hesk, J. 2000. *Deception and Democracy in Classical Athens*. Cambridge.

Hesk, J. 2003. *Sophocles: Ajax*. London.

Hobbs, A. 2000. *Plato and the Hero: Courage, Manliness and the Impersonal Good*. Cambridge.

Hoffmann, D. M., ed. 1994. *Nietzsche und die Schweiz*. Zürich.

Holzhausen, J. 2000. *Paideía oder Paidiá: Aristoteles und Aristophanes zur Wirkung der griechischen Tragödie*. Stuttgart.

Honzl, J. 1976. The dynamics of the sign in the theater. Trans. I. R. Titunik. In L. Matejka and I. Titunik, eds., *Semiotics of Art: Prague School Contributions*. Cambridge, Mass. 74–93.

Hoppin, M. C. 1990. Metrical effects, dramatic illusion, and the two endings of Sophocles' *Philoctetes*. *Arethusa* 23: 141–82.

Hornblower, S. 1996. *A Commentary on Thucydides*. Vol 2. Oxford.

Horne, P. R. 1962. *The Tragedies of Giambattista Cinthio Giraldi*. Oxford.

Hose, M. 1990–91. *Studien zum Chor bei Euripides*. 2 vols. Stuttgart.

Housman, A. E. 1972. *The Classical Papers of A. E. Housman*. Vol 1. Ed. J. Diggle and F. R. D. Goodyear. Cambridge.

Howald, E. 1920. *Friedrich Nietzsche und die klassische Philologie*. Gotha.

Humphreys, S. C. 1978. *Anthropology and the Greeks*. London.

Hunter, R. L. 1979. The comic chorus in the fourth century. *ZPE* 36: 23–38.

Hunter, R. L. 1993. *The Argonautica of Apollonius*. Cambridge.

Hurley, S. L. 2003. *Justice, Luck, and Knowledge*. Cambridge, Mass.

Hurwit, J. M. 1999. *The Athenian Acropolis: History, Mythology, and Archaeology from the Neolithic Era to the Present*. Cambridge.

Hussey, E. 1972. *The Presocratics*. London.

Hutchinson, G. O., ed. 1985. *Aeschylus: Septem contra Thebas*. Oxford.

Hutton, J., trans. 1982. *Aristotle's Poetics*. New York.

Huys, M. 1995. *The Tale of the Hero Who Was Exposed at Birth in Euripidean Tragedy*. Leuven.

Ieranò, G. 1997. *Il ditirambo di Dioniso: le testimonianze antiche*. Pisa.

Ingegneri, A. 1598. *Della poesia rappresentativa e del modo di rappresentare le favole sceniche*. In F. Marotti, ed., *Storia documentaria del teatro italiano: Lo spettacolo dall'Umanesimo al Manierismo*. Milan: 1974. 271–308.

Innes, C. 1993. *Avant Garde Theatre, 1892–1992*. London.

Innes, D. 1995. Longinus, sublimity, and the low emotions. In D. Innes, H. Hine, and C. Pelling, eds., *Ethics and Rhetoric: Classical Essays for Donald Russell on his Seventy-Fifth Birthday*. Oxford. 323–33.

Ionesco, E. 1964. *Notes and Counter-Notes*. Trans. D. Watson. London.

Irwin, T. 1983. Euripides and Socrates. *CP* 78: 183–97.

Irwin, T. 1989. *Classical Thought.* Oxford.

Jackson, J. 1955. *Marginalia Scaenica.* Oxford.

Jacob, C. 1988. Inscrire la terre habitée dans une tablette. Réflexions sur la fonction de la carte géographique en Grèce antique. In M. Detienne, ed., *Les savoirs de l'écriture: en Grèce ancienne.* Lille. 273–304.

Jameson, M. H. 1956. Politics and the *Philoctetes. CP* 51: 217–27.

Janz, C. P. 1974. Friedrich Nietzsches akademische Lehrtätigkeit in Basel 1869–1879. *NS* 3: 192–203.

Janz, C. P. 1981. *Friedrich Nietzsche: Biographie.* 3 vols. Munich.

Jebb, R. C., ed. and trans. 1892–1912. *Sophocles: Plays and Fragments.* Cambridge.

Jens, W., ed. 1971. *Die Bauformen der griechischen Tragödie.* Munich.

Jones, D. R. 1986. *Great Directors at Work: Stanislavsky, Brecht, Kazan, Brook.* Berkeley.

Jones, W. H. S. 1935. *Pausanius.* Vol. 4. Cambridge, Mass. LCL.

Joplin, P. K. 1984. The voice of the shuttle is ours. *Stanford Literature Review* 1: 25–53.

Joshel, S. R., and S. Murnaghan, eds. 1998. *Women and Slaves in Greco-Roman Culture: Differential Equations.* London.

Jouan, F., and H. Van Looy, eds. and trans. 1998–2003. *Euripide. Tome VIII. Fragments. 1e–4e parties.* Paris.

Judet de La Combe, P. 2000. Entre philosophie et philologie: définitions et refus du tragique. In C. Morenilla and B. Zimmermann, eds., *Das Tragische.* Stuttgart. 97–107.

Just, R. 1989. *Women in Athenian Law and Life.* London.

Kahn, C. H. 1981. The origins of social contract theory. In G. B. Kerferd, ed., *The Sophists and Their Legacy.* Wiesbaden. 92–108.

Kahn, C. H. 1998. Pre-Platonic ethics. In S. Everson, ed., *Ethics.* Cambridge. 27–48.

Kaimio, M., et al. 2001. Metatheatricality in the Greek satyr-play. *Arctos* 35: 35–78.

Kambitsis, J., ed. 1972. *L'Antiope d'Euripide.* Athens.

Kannicht, R. 1996. Zum Corpus Euripideum. In C. Mueller-Goldingen and K. Sier, eds., *Lênaika: Festschrift für Carl Werner Müller zum 65. Geburtstag.* Stuttgart. 21–31.

Kannicht, R. 2004. *Tragicorum Graecorum Fragmenta.* Vol. 5: *Euripides.* Göttingen.

Kannicht, R., and B. Gauly, eds. and trans. 1991. *Musa Tragica: die griechische Tragödie von Thespis bis Ezekiel.* Göttingen.

Kannicht, R., and B. Snell, eds. 1981. *Tragicorum Graecorum Fragmenta.* Vol. 2: *Fragmenta Adespota.* Göttingen.

Käppel, L. 1992. *Paian. Studien zur Geschichte einer Gattung.* Berlin.

Kassel, R. 1955. Bemerkungen zum Kyklops des Euripides. *RhM* 98: 279–86.

Kearns, E. 1989. *The Heroes of Attica.* London.

Kearns, E. 1990. Saving the city. In O. Murray and S. Price, eds., *The Greek City: From Homer to Alexander.* Oxford. 323–44.

Keil, B. 1898. *Aelii Aristidis Smyrnaei quae supersunt omnia.* Vol. 2. Berlin.

Kelly, H. 1993. *Ideas and Forms of Tragedy from Aristotle to the Middle Ages.* Cambridge.

Kermode, F. 1967. *The Sense of an Ending: Studies in the Theory of Fiction.* Oxford. Second edition, Oxford: 2000.

Kernodle, G. R. 1970. *From Art to Theater.* Chicago.

Keulen, A. J., ed. 2001. *L. Annaeus Seneca: Troades.* Leiden.

Kiechle, F. K. 1970. Götterdarstellung durch Menschen in den altmediterranen Religionen. *Historia* 19: 259–71.

Kilani, M. 1990. Les anthropologues et leur savoir: du terrain au texte. In Adam et al. 1990b. 71–109.

Kingsley, P. 1995. *Ancient Philosophy, Mystery, and Magic: Empedocles and Pythagorean Tradition.* Oxford.

Kirkwood, G. M. 1958. *A Study of Sophoclean Drama.* Ithaca, NY.

Kirkwood, G. M. 1986. From Melos to Colonus: τίνας χώρους ἀφίγμεθ'...; *TAPA* 116: 99–117.

Kitto, H. D. F. 1961. *Greek Tragedy.* Third edition. London.

Kitto, H. D. F. 1977. The *Rhesus* and related matters. *YCS* 25: 317–50.

Kitzinger, R. 1993. What do you know? The end of Oedipus. In Rosen and Farrell 1993. 539–56.

Klimek-Winter, R., ed. 1993. *Andromedatragödien: Sophokles, Euripides, Livius Andronikos, Ennius, Accius.* Stuttgart.

Knox, B. M. W. 1952a. The *Hippolytus* of Euripides. *YCS* 13: 3–31. Repr. in Knox 1979b. 205–30.

Knox, B. M. W. 1952b. The lion in the house (*Agamemnon* 717–36 [Murray]). *CP* 47: 17–25. Repr. in Knox 1979b. 27–38.

Knox, B. M. W. 1957. *Oedipus at Thebes.* New Haven.

Knox, B. M. W. 1961. The *Ajax* of Sophocles. *HSCP* 65: 1–37. Repr. in Knox 1979b. 125–60.

Knox, B. M. W. 1964. *The Heroic Temper: Studies in Sophoclean Tragedy.* Berkeley.

Knox, B. M. W. 1966. Second thoughts in Greek tragedy. *GRBS* 7: 213–32. Repr. in Knox 1979b. 231–49.

Knox, B. M. W. 1979a. Euripidean comedy. In Knox 1979b. 250–74.

Knox, B. M. W. 1979b. *Word and Action: Essays on the Ancient Theater.* Baltimore.

Kolb, F. 1979. Polis und Theater. In Seeck 1979a. 504–45.

Konstan, D. 1997. *Friendship in the Classical World.* Cambridge.

Konstan, D. 1999. The tragic emotions. *Comparative Drama* 33: 1–21.

Konstan, D. 2001. *Pity Transformed.* London.

Kovacs, D. 1985. Castor in Euripides' *Electra* (*El.* 307–13 and 1292–1307). *CQ* 35: 306–14.

Kovacs, D. 1987. Treading the circle warily: literary criticism and the text of Euripides. *TAPA* 117: 257–70.

Kovacs, D. 1994. *Euripidea.* Leiden.

Kovacs, D. ed. and trans. 1994–2004. *Euripides.* 6 vols. Cambridge, Mass. LCL.

Kovacs, D. 2003. Toward a reconstruction of *Iphigenia Aulidensis. JHS* 123: 77–103.

Kranz, W. 1933. *Stasimon. Untersuchungen zu Form und Gehalt der griechischen Tragödie.* Berlin.

Kraus, C. S. 1991. "Λόγος μέν ἐστ' ἀρχαῖος": stories and story-telling in Sophocles' *Trachiniae. TAPA* 121: 75–98.

Kraus, C. S. 1992. Thessalian Orestes. *MD* 29: 157–63.

Kraus, C. S. 1998. Dangerous supplements: etymology and genealogy in Euripides' *Heracles. PCPS* 44: 137–57.

Krumeich, R. 1999. Archäologische Einleitung. In Krumeich, Pechstein, and Seidensticker 1999. 41–73.

Krumeich, R., N. Pechstein, and B. Seidensticker, eds. 1999. *Das griechische Satyrspiel.* Darmstadt.

Krummen, E. 1990. *Pyrsos Hymnon: Festliche Gegenwart und mythisch-rituelle Tradition als Voraussetzung einer Pindarinterpretation (Isthmie 4, Pythie 5, Olympie 1 und 3).* Berlin.

Kubo, M. 1967. The norm of myth: Euripides' *Electra. HSCP* 71: 15–31.

Lacey, W. K. 1968. *The Family in Classical Greece.* London.

Lada, I. 1993. "Empathic understanding": emotion and cognition in classical dramatic audience-response. *PCPS* 39: 94–140.

Lada, I. 1996. Emotion and meaning in tragic performance. In Silk 1996a. 397–413.

Lada-Richards, I. 1997. "Estrangement" or "reincarnation"? Performers and performance on the classical Athenian stage. *Arion* 5.2: 66–107.

Lada-Richards, I. 1998. Staging the *Ephebeia*: theatrical role-playing and ritual transition in Sophocles' *Philoctetes*. *Ramus* 27: 1–26.

Lada-Richards, I. 1999. *Initiating Dionysus: Ritual and Theatre in Aristophanes' Frogs*. Oxford.

Lada-Richards, I. 2002. The subjectivity of Greek performance. In Easterling and Hall 2002. 395–418.

Lain Entralgo, P. 1970. *The Therapy of the Word in Classical Antiquity*. Ed. and trans. L. J. Rather and J. M. Sharp. New Haven.

Landels, J. 1999. *Music in Ancient Greece and Rome*. London.

Landfester, M. 1979. Geschichte der griechischen Komödie. In Seeck 1979a. 354–400.

Landfester, M. 1994. *Friedrich Nietzsche, Die Geburt der Tragödie. Schriften zu Literatur und Philosophie der Griechen herausgegeben und erläutert von Manfred Landfester*. Frankfurt am Main.

Lanza, D. 1963. NOMOS e ISON in Euripide. *RivFil* 91: 416–39.

Lardinois, A., and L. McClure, eds. 2001. *Making Silence Speak: Women's Voices in Greek Literature and Society*. Princeton.

Larson, J. 1995. *Greek Heroine Cults*. Madison, Wis.

Lasserre, F. 1973. Le drame satyrique. *RivFil* 101: 273–301.

Latacz, J. 1994. Fruchtbares Ärgernis: Nietzsches "Geburt der Tragödie" und die gräzistische Tragödienforschung. In Hoffmann 1994. 30–45.

Latacz, J. 1996. *Homer, His Art and His World*. Trans. J. Holoka. Ann Arbor, Mich.

Latacz, J., ed. 2000. *Homers Ilias: Gesamtkommentar*. Band I. 2. Munich.

Latte, K. 1957. ΑΣΚΩΛΙΑΣΜΟΣ. *Hermes* 85: 385–91.

Lawall, G. 1982. Death and perspective in Seneca's *Troades*. *CJ* 77: 244–52.

Lear, J. 1988. Katharsis. *Phronesis* 33: 297–326.

Lebeck, A. 1971. *The Oresteia: A Study in Language and Structure*. Cambridge, Mass.

Lee, K. H., ed. 1976. *Euripides: Troades*. Basingstoke.

Lee, K. H., ed. and trans. 1997. *Euripides: Ion*. Warminster.

Lee, K. H. 2001. The Dionysia: instrument of control or platform for critique? In D. Papenfuss and V. M. Strocka, eds., *Gab es das griechische Wunder? Griechenland zwischen dem Ende des 6. und der Mitte des 5. Jahrhunderts v. Chr.* Mainz. 77–89.

Lefèvre, E. 2000. Sophokles' und Heiner Müllers *Philoktet*. In Gödde and Heinze 2000. 419–38.

Lefkowitz, M. R. 1979. The Euripides *Vita. GRBS* 20: 187–210.

Le Guen, B. 1995. Théâtre et cités à l'époque hellénistique. "Mort de la cité" – "Mort du théâtre"? *REG* 108: 59–90.

Leiter, S. L. 1991. *From Stanislavsky to Barrault: Representative Directors of the European Stage*. New York.

Lenson, D. 1987. *The Birth of Tragedy: A Commentary*. Boston.

Lesky, A. 1966. Decision and responsibility in the tragedies of Aeschylus. *JHS* 86: 78–85.

Lesky, A. 1972. *Die tragische Dichtung der Hellenen*. Third edition. Göttingen.

Lesky, A. 1983. *Greek Tragic Poetry*. Trans. M. Dillon. New Haven.

Lévêque, P., and P. Vidal-Naquet. 1996. *Cleisthenes the Athenian*. Ed. and trans. D. A. Curtis. Atlantic Highlands, NJ.

Levine, D. B. 1985. Symposium and the *polis*. In T. Figueira and G. Nagy, eds., *Theognis of Megara: Poetry and the Polis*. Baltimore. 176–96.

Lévi-Strauss, C. 1969. *The Elementary Structures of Kinship*. Revised edition. Trans. J. H. Bell and J. R. von Sturmer, ed. R. Needham. Boston.

Lewes, G. H. 1875. *On Actors and the Art of Acting*. London.

Lewis, D. M. 1992a. Mainland Greece, 479–451 B.C. *CAH* 5. 96–120.

Lewis, D. M. 1992b. The Thirty Years' Peace. *CAH* 5. 121–46.

Liapis, V. 2004. They do it with mirrors: the mystery of the two *Rhesus* plays. In D. I. Jacob and E. Papazoglou, eds., *Ekkyklema: Theatrical Studies in Honour of Professor N. C. Hourmouziades*. Heraklion. 159–88.

Ling, R. 1991. *Roman Painting*. Cambridge.

Lissarrague, F. 1990. Why satyrs are good to represent. Trans. A. Szegedy-Maszak. In Winkler and Zeitlin 1990. 228–36.

Liuzzi, T. 1992. Il significato filosofico della tragedia sofoclea. In *Studi di filosofia greca e tardo-antica*. Bari. 13–33.

Lloyd, A. B., ed. 1997. *What is a God? Studies in the Nature of Greek Divinity*. London.

Lloyd, G. E. R. 1966. *Polarity and Analogy*. Cambridge.

Lloyd, M. 1984. The Helen scene in Euripides' *Troades*. *CQ* 34: 303–13.

Lloyd, M. 1992. *The Agon in Euripides*. Oxford.

Lloyd-Jones, H. 1962. The guilt of Agamemnon. *CQ* 12: 187–99.

Lloyd-Jones, H., ed. and trans. 1970. *Aeschylus: Agamemnon*. Englewood Cliffs, NJ.

Lloyd-Jones, H. 1971. *The Justice of Zeus*. Berkeley.

Lloyd-Jones, H. 1979. Nietzsche and the study of the ancient world. In J. C. O'Flaherty, T. F. Sellner, and R. M. Helm, eds., *Studies in Nietzsche and the Classical Tradition*. Second edition. Chapel Hill, NC. 1–15. Repr. in Lloyd-Jones 1983. 165–81.

Lloyd-Jones, H. 1983. *Blood for the Ghosts*. Baltimore.

Lloyd-Jones, H. 1990a. *Greek Epic, Lyric, and Tragedy*. Oxford.

Lloyd-Jones, H. 1990b. Problems of early Greek tragedy: Pratinas and Phrynichus. In Lloyd-Jones 1990a. 225–37.

Lloyd-Jones, H. 1990c. Tycho von Wilamowitz-Moellendorff on the dramatic technique of Sophocles. In Lloyd-Jones 1990a. 401–18.

Lloyd-Jones, H., ed. and trans. 1994–96. *Sophocles*. 3 vols. Cambridge, Mass. LCL.

Lloyd-Jones, H., and N. G. Wilson. 1990. *Sophoclea: Studies on the Text of Sophocles*. Oxford.

Long, A. A. 1968. *Language and Thought in Sophocles: A Study of Abstract Nouns and Poetic Technique*. London.

Long, A. A., ed. 1999. *The Cambridge Companion to Early Greek Philosophy*. Cambridge.

López Férez, J. A., ed. 2002. *Mitos en la literatura griega arcaica y clásica*. Madrid.

Loraux, N. 1995. *The Experiences of Tiresias: The Feminine and the Greek Man*. Trans. P. Wissing. Princeton.

Loraux, N. 2002. *The Mourning Voice: An Essay on Greek Tragedy*. Trans. E. T. Rawlings. Ithaca, NY.

Lupaş, L., and Z. Petre, eds. 1981. *Commentaire aux "Sept contre Thèbes" d'Eschyle*. Bucharest.

Maas, P. 1958. *Textual Criticism*. Trans. B. Flower. Oxford.

Maas, P. 1962. *Greek Metre*. Trans. H. Lloyd-Jones. Oxford.

McCarthy, K. 2000. *Slaves, Masters, and the Art of Authority in Plautine Comedy*. Princeton.

McClure, L. 1995. Female speech and characterization in Euripides. In De Martino and Sommerstein 1995. Part 2, 35–60.

McClure, L. 1999. *Spoken Like a Woman: Speech and Gender in Athenian Drama*. Princeton.

McClure, L. 2001. Introduction. In Lardinois and McClure 2001. 3–16.

McDonald, M. 1992. *Ancient Sun, Modern Light*. New York.

McDonald, M. 2003. *The Living Art of Greek Tragedy*. Bloomington, Ind.

McDonald, M., and J. Walton, eds. 2002. *Amid Our Troubles: Irish Versions of Greek Tragedy*. London.

MacDowell, D. M., ed. 1962. *Andokides: On the Mysteries*. Oxford.

MacDowell, D. M. 1978. *The Law in Classical Athens*. London.

MacDowell, D. M., ed. 1990. *Demosthenes against Meidias (Oration 21)*. Oxford.

McHardy, F., J. Robson, and D. Harvey, eds. 2005. *Lost Dramas of Classical Athens: Greek Tragic Fragments*. Exeter.

Macintosh, F. 1997. Tragedy in performance: nineteenth- and twentieth-century productions. In Easterling 1997a. 284–323.

Macintosh, F. Forthcoming. *Sophocles' Oedipus Tyrannus: A Production History.* Cambridge.

Macintosh, F., P. Michelakis, E. Hall, and O. Taplin, eds. Forthcoming. *Agamemnon in Performance: 458 BC–2004 AD.* Oxford.

Mackie, C. J., ed. 2004. *Oral Performance and its Context.* Leiden.

Macleod, C. W. 1982. Politics and the *Oresteia. JHS* 102: 124–44. Repr. in Macleod 1983. 20–40.

Macleod, C. W. 1983. *Collected Essays.* Oxford.

Magarshack, D. 1961. Introduction. In K. Stanislavksy, *Stanislavsky on the Art of the Stage.* Trans. D. Magarshack. London. 11–87.

Mansfeld, J. 1986. The Wilamowitz–Nietzsche struggle: another new document and some further comments. *NS* 15: 41–58.

Maritz, J. 2002. Greek drama in Rhodesia/Zimbabwe. In Barsby 2002. 197–215.

Marshall, C. W. 1995. Review of N. T. Croally, *Euripidean Polemic: The Trojan Women and the Function of Tragedy. Didaskalia* 2.3: n.p. Online. didaskalia.open.ac.uk/issues/vol2no3/croally.html.

Marshall, C. W. 1999–2000. Theatrical references in Euripides' *Electra.* In Cropp, Lee, and Sansone 1999–2000. 325–41.

Martin, R. P. 1989. *The Language of Heroes: Speech and Performance in the Iliad.* Ithaca, NY.

Martinelli, M. C. 1997. *Gli strumenti del poeta: elementi di metrica greca.* Second edition. Bologna.

Mastronarde, D. J. 1979. *Contact and Discontinuity: Some Conventions of Speech and Action on the Greek Tragic Stage.* Berkeley.

Mastronarde, D. J. 1990. Actors on high: the skene roof, the crane, and the gods in Attic drama. *CA* 9: 247–94.

Mastronarde, D. J., ed. 1994. *Euripides: Phoenissae.* Cambridge.

Mastronarde, D. J. 1998. Il coro euripideo: autorità e integrazione. *QUCC* n.s. 60: 55–80.

Mastronarde, D. J. 1999. Knowledge and authority in the choral voice of Euripidean tragedy. *SyllClass* 10: 87–104.

Mastronarde, D. J. 1999–2000. Euripidean tragedy and genre: the terminology and its problems. In Cropp, Lee, and Sansone 1999–2000. 23–39.

Mastronarde, D. J. 2002a. Euripidean tragedy and theology. *SemRom* 5: 17–49.

Mastronarde, D. J., ed. 2002b. *Euripides: Medea.* Cambridge.

Mavromoustakos, P., ed. 1999. *Productions of Ancient Greek Drama in Europe during Modern Times.* Athens.

Meier, C. 1993. *The Political Art of Greek Tragedy.* Trans. A. Webber. Baltimore.

Meiggs, R. 1972. *The Athenian Empire.* Oxford.

Meijering, R. 1987. *Literary and Rhetorical Theories in Greek Scholia.* Groningen.

Meister, R. 1948. Nietzsches Lehrtätigkeit in Basel 1869–1879. *Anzeiger der Österreichischen Akademie der Wissenschaften. Philosophisch-historische Klasse* 7: 103–21.

Melchinger, S. 1974. *Das Theater der Tragödie. Aischylos, Sophokles, Euripides auf der Bühne ihrer Zeit.* Munich.

Mendelsohn, D. 2002. *Gender and the City in Euripides' Political Plays.* Oxford.

Mercouris, S. 1998. *A Stage for Dionysus: Theatrical Space and Ancient Drama.* Athens.

Meridor, R. 2000. Creative rhetoric in Euripides' *Troades*: some notes on Hecuba's speech. *CQ* 50: 16–29.

Mezzabotta, M. 2000. Ancient drama in the new South Africa. In Hardwick et al. 2000. 246–68. Also available online. www.open.ac.uk/Arts/CC99/mezza.htm.

Michelakis, P. 2002. *Achilles in Greek Tragedy.* Cambridge.

Michelini, A. N. 1982. *Tradition and Dramatic Form in the Persians of Aeschylus.* Leiden.

Michelini, A. N. 1987. *Euripides and the Tragic Tradition.* Madison, Wis.

Michelini, A. N. 1999–2000. The expansion of myth in late Euripides: *Iphigenia at Aulis.* In Cropp, Lee, and Sansone 1999–2000. 41–57.

Mikalson, J. D. 1991. *Honor Thy Gods: Popular Religion in Greek Tragedy.* Chapel Hill, NC.

Miller, M. C. 1997. *Athens and Persia in the Fifth Century BC: A Study in Cultural Receptivity.* Cambridge.

Mills, S. 1997. *Theseus, Tragedy and the Athenian Empire.* Oxford.

Mills, S. 2002. *Euripides: Hippolytus.* London.

Mitchell-Boyask, R., ed. 2002. *Approaches to Teaching the Dramas of Euripides.* New York.

Mnouchkine, A. 1996. Conversation with Maria M. Delgado, 14.10.1995. In Delgado and Heritage 1996. 179–90.

Moles, J. L. 1984. Aristotle and Dido's *hamartia.* *G&R* 31: 48–54.

Moles, J. L. 2002. Herodotus and Athens. In Bakker, de Jong, and Van Wees 2002. 33–52.

Montiglio, S. 2000. *Silence in the Land of Logos.* Princeton.

Moore, S. 1966. *The Stanislavksi System: The Professional Training of an Actor.* London.

Morelli, G. 2001. *Teatro attico e pittura vascolare: una tragedia di Cheremone nella ceramica italiota.* Hildesheim.

Moret, J.-M. 1975. *L'Ilioupersis dans la céramique italiote. Les mythes et leur expression figurée au IVᵉ siècle.* 2 vols. Geneva.

Moretti, J.-C. 1999–2000. The theater of the sanctuary of Dionysus Eleuthereus in late fifth-century Athens. Trans. E. Csapo. In Cropp, Lee, and Sansone 1999–2000. 377–98.

Morgan, K. A. 2000. *Myth and Philosophy from the Presocratics to Plato.* Cambridge.

Morgan, T. 1998. *Literate Education in the Hellenistic and Roman Worlds.* Cambridge.

Morris, I., and K. Raaflaub, eds. 1998. *Democracy 2500? Questions and Challenges.* Dubuque, Iowa.

Mossman, J. M. 1988. Tragedy and epic in Plutarch's *Alexander. JHS* 108: 83–93.

Mossman, J. M. 1995. *Wild Justice: A Study of Euripides' Hecuba.* Oxford.

Mossman, J. M. 2001. Women's speech in Greek tragedy: the case of Electra and Clytemnestra in Euripides' *Electra. CQ* 51: 374–84.

Mossman, J. M., ed. 2003. *Oxford Readings in Classical Studies: Euripides.* Oxford.

Most, G. W. 2000a. Between philosophy and philology. *NNS* 4: 163–70.

Most, G. W. 2000b. Generating genres: the idea of the tragic. In M. Depew and D. Obbink, eds., *Matrices of Genre: Authors, Canons, and Society.* Cambridge, Mass. 15–35.

Most, G. W. 2003. Epinician envies. In D. Konstan and N. K. Rutter, eds., *Envy, Spite, and Jealousy: The Rivalrous Emotions in Ancient Greece.* Edinburgh. 123–42.

Mülke, M. 2000. Phrynichos und Athen: der Beschluss über die Miletu Halosis (Herodot 6, 21, 2). In Gödde and Heinze 2000. 233–46.

Müller, C. W., ed. and trans. 2000. *Euripides: Philoktet. Testimonien und Fragmente.* Berlin.

Müller, K. O., ed. 1833. *Aischylos: Eumeniden.* Göttingen.

Münscher, K. 1927. Zur mesodischen Liedform. *Hermes* 62: 154–78.

Murray, G., ed. and trans. 1904. *Euripides: The Bacchae.* London.

Murray, G. 1940. *Aeschylus, the Creator of Tragedy.* Oxford.

Murray, G. 1946. *Euripides and His Age.* Second edition. London.

Murray, P., and P. Wilson, eds. 2004. *Music and the Muses: The Culture of Mousikê in the Classical Athenian City.* Oxford.

Musumarra, C. 1972. *La poesia tragica italiana nel Rinascimento.* Florence.

Mylonas, G. E. 1961. *Eleusis and the Eleusinian Mysteries.* Princeton.

Nagy, G. 1990. *Pindar's Homer: The Lyric Possession of an Epic Past.* Baltimore.

Neri, F. 1904. *La tragedia italiana nel cinquecento.* Florence.

Nestle, W. 1901. *Euripides: Der Dichter der griechischen Aufklärung.* Stuttgart.

Nestle, W. 1940. *Vom Mythos zum Logos.* Stuttgart.

Neustadt, E. 1929. Wort und Geschehen in Aischylos' Agamemnon. *Hermes* 64: 243–65.

Nietzsche, F. 1967. *The Birth of Tragedy and The Case against Wagner.* Trans. W. Kaufmann. New York.

Nightingale, A. W. 1995. *Genres in Dialogue: Plato and the Construct of Philosophy.* Cambridge.

Nilsson, M. P. 1974. *Geschichte der griechischen Religion II: Die hellenistische und römische Zeit.* Third edition. Munich.

Nippel, W. 2002. The construction of the "Other." Trans. A. Nevill. In Harrison 2002. 278–310.

North, H. 1966. *Sophrosyne: Self-Knowledge and Self-Restraint in Greek Literature.* Ithaca, NY.

Nussbaum, M. C. 1976. Consequences and character in Sophocles' *Philoctetes. Philosophy and Literature* 1: 25–53.

Nussbaum, M. C. 1986. *The Fragility of Goodness: Luck and Ethics in Greek Tragedy and Philosophy.* Cambridge.

Nussbaum, M. C. 1993. Poetry and the passions: two Stoic views. In J. Brunschwig and M. C. Nussbaum, eds., *Passions and Perceptions: Studies in Hellenic Philosophy of Mind.* Cambridge. 97–149.

Nuttall, A. D. 1996. *Why Does Tragedy Give Pleasure?* Oxford.

Ober, J. 1989. *Mass and Elite in Democratic Athens: Rhetoric, Ideology, and the Power of the People.* Princeton.

Ober, J. 1994. Civic ideology and counterhegemonic discourse: Thucydides on the Sicilian debate. In Boegehold and Scafuro 1994. 102–26.

Ober, J. 1998. *Political Dissent in Democratic Athens: Intellectual Critics of Popular Rule.* Princeton.

Ober, J., and B. Strauss. 1990. Drama, political rhetoric, and the discourse of Athenian democracy. In Winkler and Zeitlin 1990. 237–70.

O'Connor, J. B. 1908. *Chapters in the History of Actors and Acting in Ancient Greece.* (Diss. Princeton.) Chicago.

O'Connor-Visser, E. A. M. E. 1987. *Aspects of Human Sacrifice in the Tragedies of Euripides.* Amsterdam.

Oehler, R. 1925. *Mythologische Exempla in der älteren griechischen Dichtung.* (Diss. Basel.) Aarau.

Ogden, D. 1996. *Greek Bastardy: In the Classical and Hellenistic Periods.* Oxford.

Ormand, K. 1999. *Exchange and the Maiden: Marriage in Sophoclean Tragedy.* Austin, Tex.

Osborne, R. 1985. *Demos: The Discovery of Classical Attika.* Cambridge.

Osborne, R., and S. Hornblower, eds. 1994. *Ritual, Finance, Politics: Athenian Democratic Accounts presented to David Lewis.* Oxford.

Ostwald, M. 1992. Athens as a cultural centre. *CAH* 5. 306–69.

Otto, W. F. 1965. *Dionysus: Myth and Cult.* Trans. R. B. Palmer. Bloomington, Ind.

Padel, R. 1974. "Imagery of the elsewhere": two choral odes of Euripides. *CQ* 24: 227–41.

Panagl, O. 1971. *Die "dithyrambischen Stasima" des Euripides.* Vienna.

Panoussi, V. 1998. Epic transfigured: tragic allusiveness in Vergil's *Aeneid.* Diss. Brown University.

Panoussi, V. 2002. Vergil's Ajax: allusion, tragedy, and heroic identity in the *Aeneid. CA* 21: 95–134.

Panoussi, V. 2003. *Ego Maenas*: maenadism, marriage, and the construction of female identity in Catullus 63 and 64. *Helios* 30: 101–26.

Parker, R. 1987. Myths of early Athens. In Bremmer 1987. 187–214.

Parker, R. 1995. Early orphism. In A. Powell, ed., *The Greek World.* London. 483–510.

Parker, R. 1996. *Athenian Religion: A History.* Oxford.

Parker, R. 1997. Gods cruel and kind: tragic and civic theology. In Pelling 1997c. 143–60.

Patinella, V. 1986. *Logos e dran: Parmenide, Eraclito, Eschilo*. Palermo.

Patsalidis, S., and E. Sakellaridou, eds. 1999. *(Dis)Placing Classical Greek Theatre*. Thessaloniki.

Pattoni, M. P. 1987. *L'autenticità del Prometeo Incatenato di Eschilo*. Pisa.

Patzer, H. 1962. *Die Anfänge der griechischen Tragödie*. Wiesbaden.

Pavlock, B. 1991. The tyrant and boundary violations in Ovid's Tereus episode. *Helios* 18: 34–48.

Pavlovskis, Z. 1977. The voice of the actor in Greek tragedy. *CW* 71: 113–23.

Pazzi (Paccio) de' Medici, A. 1524. Prefactione della tragedia Cyclope. In A. Solerti, ed., *Le tragedie metriche di Alessandro Pazzi de' Medici*. Bologna: 1969. 43–53.

Pearson, A. C. 1917. *The Fragments of Sophocles*. 3 vols. Cambridge.

Pechstein, N. 1999. Kritias. In Krumeich, Pechstein, and Seidensticker 1999. 552–61.

Pelling, C. B. R., ed. 1990. *Characterization and Individuality in Greek Literature*. Oxford.

Pelling, C. B. R. 1997a. Aeschylus' *Persae* and history. In Pelling 1997c. 1–19.

Pelling, C. B. R. 1997b. Conclusion. In Pelling 1997c. 213–35.

Pelling, C. B. R., ed. 1997c. *Greek Tragedy and the Historian*. Oxford.

Pelling, C. B. R. 2000. *Literary Texts and the Greek Historian*. London.

Pendrick, G. J., ed. and trans. 2002. *Antiphon the Sophist: The Fragments*. Cambridge.

Pertusi, A. 1966. Il ritorno alle fonti del teatro greco classico: Euripide nell'Umanesimo e nel Rinascimento. In A. Pertusi, ed., *Venezia e l'Oriente fra tardo Medioevo e Rinascimento*. Florence. 205–24.

Perusino, F., ed. and trans. 1993. *La Tragedia Greca: Anonimo (Michele Psello?)*. Urbino.

Petrounias, E. 1976. *Funktion und Thematik der Bilder bei Aischylos*. Göttingen.

Pfeiffer, R. 1968. *History of Classical Scholarship: From the Beginnings to the End of the Hellenistic Age*. Oxford.

Pfeijffer, I. L. 1999. *First Person Futures in Pindar*. Stuttgart.

Pfister, F. 1924. Epiphanie. *RE* Suppl. 4: 277–323.

Philippo, S. 2003. *Silent Witness: Racine's Non-Verbal Annotations of Euripides*. Oxford.

Phillips, K. M., Jr. 1968. Perseus and Andromeda. *AJA* 72: 1–23.

Pickard-Cambridge, A. W. 1927. *Dithyramb, Tragedy and Comedy*. Oxford.

Pickard-Cambridge, A. W. 1962. *Dithyramb, Tragedy and Comedy*. Second edition. Rev. T. B. L. Webster. Oxford.

Pickard-Cambridge, A. W. 1988. *The Dramatic Festivals of Athens*. Second edition. Rev. J. Gould and D. Lewis. Oxford.

Pigafetta, F. 1585. Lettera di Filippo Pigafetta. In Gallo 1973. 53–58.

Podlecki, A. J. 1966a. *The Political Background of Aeschylean Tragedy*. Ann Arbor, Mich.

Podlecki, A. J. 1966b. The power of the word in Sophocles' *Philoctetes*. *GRBS* 7: 233–50.

Podlecki, A. J. 1986. *Polis* and monarch in early Attic tragedy. In Euben 1986. 76–100.

Podlecki, A. J., ed. and trans. 1989. *Aeschylus: Eumenides*. Warminster.

Podlecki, A. J., trans. 1991. *Aeschylus: The Persians*. Second edition. Bristol.

Poggiali, G., ed. 1808–12. *Teatro italiano antico*. 10 vols. Milan.

Pohlenz, M. 1965. Das Satyrspiel und Pratinas von Phleius. In M. Pohlenz, *Kleine Schriften II*. Ed. H. Dörrie. Hildesheim. 473–96.

Pöhlmann, E. 1986. Bühne und Handlung im Aias des Sophokles. *A&A* 32: 20–32.

Pöhlmann, E., and M. L. West. 2001. *Documents of Ancient Greek Music: The Extant Melodies and Fragments*. Oxford.

Polignac, F. de 1984. *La naissance de la cité grecque: cultes, espace et société VIIIe–VIIe siècles avant J.-C.* Paris.

Poli-Palladini, L. 2001a. Some reflections on Aeschylus' *Aetnae(ae)*. *RhM* 144: 287–325.

Poli-Palladini, L. 2001b. Traces of "intellectualism" in Aeschylus. *Hermes* 129: 441–58.

Pollock, Lady Juliet Creed. 1884. *Macready as I Knew Him*. London.

Poole, W. 1994. Euripides and Sparta. In A. Powell and S. Hodkinson, eds., *The Shadow of Sparta*. London. 1–33.

Popp, H. 1971. Das Amoibaion. In Jens 1971. 221–75.

Porter, J. I. 2000a. *The Invention of Dionysus: An Essay on The Birth of Tragedy.* Stanford.

Porter, J. I. 2000b. *Nietzsche and the Philology of the Future.* Stanford.

Porter, J. I. 2000c. "Rare impressions": Nietzsche's *Philologica*: A review of the Colli–Montinari critical edition. *IJCT* 6: 409–31.

Porter, J. I. 2004. Nietzsche, Homer, and the classical tradition. In Bishop 2004. 7–26.

Porter, J. R. 1994. *Studies in Euripides' Orestes.* Leiden.

Porter, J. R. 1999–2000. Euripides and Menander: *Epitrepontes*, Act IV. In Cropp, Lee, and Sansone 1999–2000. 157–73.

Pöschl, V. 1979. Nietzsche und die klassische Philologie. In H. Flashar, K. Gründer, and A. Horstmann, eds., *Philologie und Hermeneutik im 19. Jahrhundert*. Göttingen. 141–55.

Preiser, C., ed. 2000. *Euripides: Telephos.* Hildesheim.

Pretagostini, R. 1995. L'esametro nel dramma antico del V secolo: problemi di "resa" e di "riconoscimento." In M. Fantuzzi and R. Pretagostini, eds., *Struttura e storia dell'esametro greco*. 2 vols. Rome. 2: 163–91.

Privitera, G. A. 1970. *Dioniso in Omero e nella poesia greca arcaica.* Rome.

Prynne, W. 1974. *Histrio-mastix: The Player's Scourge or Actor's Tragedy* (1633). Preface A. Freeman. New York.

Quinn, K. 1968. *Virgil's Aeneid: A Critical Description.* Ann Arbor, Mich.

Raaflaub, K. A. 1998. The transformation of Athens in the fifth century. In Boedeker and Raaflaub 1998. 15–41.

Raaflaub, K. A. 2004. *The Discovery of Freedom in Ancient Greece.* Trans. R. Franciscono. Chicago.

Rabe, H. 1908. Aus Rhetoren-Handschriften. *RhM* 63: 127–51.

Rabinowitz, N. S. 1993. *Anxiety Veiled: Euripides and the Traffic in Women.* Ithaca, NY.

Rabinowitz, N. S. 1998. Slaves with slaves: women and class in Euripidean tragedy. In Joshel and Murnaghan 1998. 56–68.

Rabinowitz, P. J. 1995. Other reader-oriented theories. In R. Selden, ed., *The Cambridge History of Literary Criticism*. Vol. 8: *From Formalism to Poststructuralism*. Cambridge. 375–403.

Raddatz, F. M. 2002. Athen, Rom, Washington D.C. Über die erneute Popularität des Tragischen der Antike. *Theater der Zeit* Heft 3: 54–55.

Radt, S. L. 1977. *Tragicorum Graecorum Fragmenta*. Vol. 4: *Sophocles*. Göttingen.

Radt, S. L. 1985. *Tragicorum Graecorum Fragmenta*. Vol. 3: *Aeschylus*. Göttingen.

Radt, S. L. 1986. Der unbekanntere Aischylos. *Prometheus* 12: 1–13.

Radt, S. L. 1991. Sophokles in seinen Fragmenten. In H. Hofmann and A. Harder, eds., *Fragmenta Dramatica: Beiträge zur Interpretation der griechischen Tragikerfragmente und ihrer Wirkungsgeschichte*. Göttingen. 79–110.

Rau, P. 1967. *Paratragodia: Untersuchungen einer komischen Form des Aristophanes.* Munich.

Raval, S. 1998. *Pudibunda Ora*: Gender, Sexuality, and Language in Ovid's *Metamorphoses*. Diss. Brown University.

Rehm, R. 1988. The staging of suppliant plays. *GRBS* 29: 263–307.

Rehm, R. 1992. *Greek Tragic Theatre.* London.

Rehm, R. 1994. *Marriage to Death: The Conflation of Wedding and Funeral Rituals in Greek Tragedy.* Princeton.

Rehm, R. 2002. *The Play of Space: Spatial Transformation in Greek Tragedy.* Princeton.

Rehm, R. 2003. *Radical Theatre: Greek Tragedy and the Modern World.* London.

Reibnitz, B. von. 1992. *Ein Kommentar zu Friedrich Nietzsche "Die Geburt der Tragödie aus dem Geiste der Musik" (Kapitel 1–12).* Stuttgart.

Reinhardt, K. 1938. Aristophanes und Athen. *Europäische Revue* 14: 754–68. Repr. in K. Reinhardt, *Tradition und Geist*. Göttingen: 1960. 227–56.

Reinhardt, K. 1949. *Aischylos als Regisseur und Theologe*. Bern.

Reinhardt, K. 1960. Die Sinneskrise bei Euripides. In *Tradition und Geist*. Göttingen. 227–56. Repr. as "The intellectual crisis in Euripides," trans. J. Mossman and J. M. Mossman, in Mossman 2003. 16–46.

Reinhardt, K. 1979. *Sophocles*. Trans. H. and D. Harvey. Oxford.

Reynolds, L. D., and N. G. Wilson. 1991. *Scribes and Scholars: A Guide to the Transmission of Greek and Latin Literature*. Third edition. Oxford.

Rhodes, P. J. 1985. *The Athenian Empire. Greece and Rome New Surveys in the Classics* 17. Oxford.

Rhodes, P. J. 1992a. The Athenian revolution. *CAH* 5. 62–95.

Rhodes, P. J. 1992b. The Delian League to 449 B.C. *CAH* 5. 34–61.

Rhodes, P. J. 1998. Enmity in fourth-century Athens. In P. Cartledge, P. Millett, and S. von Reden, eds., *Kosmos: Essays in Order, Conflict and Community in Classical Athens*. Cambridge. 144–61.

Rhodes, P. J. 2003. Nothing to do with democracy: Athenian drama and the *polis*. *JHS* 123: 104–19.

Richardson, B., ed. 2002. *Narrative Dynamics: Essays on Time, Plot, Closure, and Frames*. Columbus, Ohio.

Richlin, A. 1992. Reading Ovid's rapes. In A. Richlin, ed., *Pornography and Representation in Greece and Rome*. Oxford. 158–79.

Rivier, A. 1944. *Essai sur le tragique d'Euripide*. Lausanne.

Rivier, A. 1968. Remarques sur le "nécessaire" et la "nécessité" chez Eschyle. *REG* 81: 5–39.

Roach, J., Jr. 1980. G. H. Lewes and performance theory: towards a "science of acting." *TJ* 32.3: 312–28.

Roberts, C. H., and T. C. Skeat. 1983. *The Birth of the Codex*. London.

Roberts, D. H. 1987. Parting words: final lines in Sophocles and Euripides. *CQ* 37: 51–64.

Roberts, D. H. 1988. Sophoclean endings: another story. *Arethusa* 21: 177–96.

Roberts, D. H. 1989. Different stories: Sophoclean narrative(s) in the *Philoctetes*. *TAPA* 119: 161–76.

Roberts, D. H. 1993. The frustrated mourner: strategies of closure in Greek tragedy. In Rosen and Farrell 1993. 573–89.

Roberts, D. H., F. M. Dunn, and D. Fowler, eds. 1997. *Classical Closure: Reading the End in Greek and Latin Literature*. Princeton.

Robertson, N. D. 1980. The true nature of the "Delian League," 478–461 B.C. *AJAH* 5: 64–96, 110–33.

Rode, J. 1971. Das Chorlied. In Jens 1971. 85–115.

Rohde, E. 1872. *Afterphilologie. Zur Beleuchtung des von dem Dr. phil. Ulrich von Wilamowitz-Möllendorff herausgegebenen Pamphlets: "Zukunftsphilologie!"* Leipzig. Repr. in Gründer 1969. 65–111.

Roisman, J. 1988. On Phrynichos' *Sack of Miletos* and *Phoinissai*. *Eranos* 86: 15–23.

Roisman, J. 1997. Contemporary allusions in Euripides' *Trojan Women*. *SIFC* 15: 38–47.

Rolfe, J. C., ed. and trans. 1927. *The Attic Nights of Aulus Gellius*. 3 vols. Cambridge, Mass. LCL.

Rorty, R. 2004. Looking back at "literary theory." Online. Website of the American Comparative Literature Association. www.stanford.edu/~saussy/acla/rorty-essay.pdf.

Rose, P. W. 1976. Sophocles' *Philoctetes* and the teaching of the Sophists. *HSCP* 80: 49–105.

Rose, P. W. 1992. *Sons of the Gods, Children of Earth: Ideology and Literary Form in Ancient Greece*. Ithaca, NY.

Rose, P. W. 1995. Historicizing Sophocles' *Ajax*. In Goff 1995a. 59–90.

Rosen, R. M., and J. Farrell, eds. 1993. *Nomodeiktes: Greek Studies in Honor of Martin Ostwald*. Ann Arbor, Mich.

Rosenbloom, D. 1993. Shouting "fire" in a crowded theater: Phrynichos's *Capture of Miletos* and the politics of fear in early Attic tragedy. *Philologus* 137: 159–96.

Rosenbloom, D. 1995. Myth, history, and hegemony in Aeschylus. In Goff 1995a. 91–130.

Rosenmeyer, T. G. 1982. *The Art of Aeschylus*. Berkeley.

Rösler, W. 1970. *Reflexe vorsokratischen Denkens bei Aischylos*. Meisenheim am Glan.

Rossi, L. E. 1971a. Il Ciclope di Euripides come κῶμος "mancato." *Maia* 23: 10–38.

Rossi, L. E. 1971b. I generi letterari e le loro leggi scritte e non scritte nelle letterature classiche. *BICS* 18: 69–94.

Rousseau, J.-J. 1948. *Lettre à Mr. D'Alembert sur les Spectacles* (1758). Ed. M. Fuchs. Lille.

Rozik, E. 2002. *The Roots of Theatre: Rethinking Ritual and Other Theories of Origin*. Iowa City.

Rubinstein, L. 2004. Stirring up dikastic anger. In D. L. Cairns and R. A. Knox, eds., *Law, Rhetoric, and Comedy in Classical Athens: Essays in Honour of Douglas M. MacDowell*. Swansea. 187–203.

Rucellai, G. 1520–25. *Oreste*. In G. Mazzoni, ed., *Le opere di Giovanni Rucellai*. Bologna: 1887. 107–229.

Russell, D. A. 1981. *Criticism in Antiquity*. London.

Rutherford, I. 1994–95. Apollo in ivy: the tragic paean. *Arion* 3.1: 112–35.

Rutherford, I. 2001. *Pindar's Paeans*. Oxford.

Said, E. 1975. *Beginnings: Intention and Method*. New York.

Saïd, S. 1985. *Sophiste et Tyran ou le problème du Prométhée enchaîné*. Paris.

Saïd, S. 1998. Tragedy and politics. In Boedeker and Raaflaub 1998. 275–95, 410–15.

Saïd, S. 2002a. Greeks and barbarians in Euripides' tragedies: the end of differences? Trans. A. Nevill. In Harrison 2002. 62–100.

Saïd, S. 2002b. Herodotus and tragedy. In Bakker, de Jong, and Van Wees 2002. 117–47.

Ste. Croix, G. E. M. de. 1972. *The Origins of the Peloponnesian War*. London.

Ste. Croix, G. E. M. de. 1981. *The Class Struggle in the Ancient Greek World*. Ithaca, NY.

Sansone, D. 1995. Review of N. T. Croally, *Euripidean Polemic: The Trojan Women and the Function of Tragedy*. *BMCR* 95.07.04. Online. ccat.sas.upenn.edu/bmcr/1995/ 95.07.04.html.

Sansone, D. 1996. Plato and Euripides. *ICS* 21: 35–61.

Schadewaldt, W. 1926. *Monolog und Selbstgespräch: Untersuchungen zur Formgeschichte der griechischen Tragödie*. Berlin.

Schadewaldt, W. 1974. Ursprung und frühe Entwicklung der attischen Tragödie. In H. Hommel, ed., *Wege zu Aischylos. Erster Band: Zugang, Aspekte der Forschung, Nachleben*. Darmstadt. 104–47.

Schäfer, H. 1998. Interview with Helmut Schäfer. In Gerhard Binder and Bernd Effe, eds., *Das Antike Theater: Aspekte seiner Geschichte, Rezeption und Aktualität*. Trier. 425–43.

Schein, S. 2001. Heracles and the ending of Sophocles' *Philoctetes*. *SIFC* 19: 38–52.

Schiesaro, A. 2003. *The Passions in Play: Thyestes and the Dynamics of Senecan Drama*. Cambridge.

Schlegel, A. 1966. *Kritische Schriften und Briefe V: Vorlesungen über dramatische Kunst und Literatur, Erster Teil*. Ed. E. Lohner. Stuttgart.

Schlegel, F. 1979. *Kritische Friedrich-Schlegel-Ausgabe. Erster Band*. Ed. E. Behler. Paderborn.

Schlesier, R. 1993. Mixtures of masks: maenads as tragic models. In Carpenter and Faraone 1993. 89–114.

Schlesier, R. 1994. *Kulte, Mythen und Gelehrte. Anthropologie der Antike seit 1800*. Frankfurt am Main.

Schmid, W. 1929. *Untersuchungen zum gefesselten Prometheus*. Stuttgart.

Schmidt, D. J. 2001. *On Germans and Other Greeks: Tragedy and Ethical Life*. Bloomington, Ind.

Scodel, R. 1980. *The Trojan Trilogy of Euripides*. Göttingen.

Scodel, R. 1998. The captive's dilemma: sexual acquiescence in Euripides' *Hecuba* and *Troades*. *HSCP* 98: 137–54.

Scodel, R. 1999–2000. Verbal performance and Euripidean rhetoric. In Cropp, Lee, and Sansone 1999–2000. 129–44.

Scott, W. C. 1984. *Musical Design in Aeschylean Theater*. Hanover, NH.

Scott, W. C. 1996. *Musical Design in Sophoclean Theater*. Hanover, NH.

Scullion, S. 1994. *Three Studies in Athenian Dramaturgy*. Stuttgart.

Scullion, S. 1999–2000. Tradition and invention in Euripidean aitiology. In Cropp, Lee, and Sansone 1999–2000. 217–34.

Scullion, S. 2001. Dionysos at Elis. *Philologus* 145: 203–18.

Scullion, S. 2002a. "Nothing to do with Dionysus": tragedy misconceived as ritual. *CQ* 52: 102–37.

Scullion, S. 2002b. Tragic dates. *CQ* 52: 81–101.

Seaford, R., ed. 1984. *Euripides: Cyclops*. Oxford.

Seaford, R. 1990. The imprisonment of women in Greek tragedy. *JHS* 110: 76–90.

Seaford, R. 1994. *Reciprocity and Ritual: Homer and Tragedy in the Developing City-State*. Oxford.

Seaford, R. 1995. Historicizing tragic ambivalence: the vote of Athena. In Goff 1995a. 202–21.

Seaford, R., ed. and trans. 1996a. *Euripides: Bacchae*. Warminster.

Seaford, R. 1996b. Something to do with Dionysos – tragedy and the Dionysiac: response to Friedrich. In Silk 1996a. 284–94.

Seaford, R. 2000. The social function of Attic tragedy: a response to Jasper Griffin. *CQ* 50: 30–44.

Seale, D. 1982. *Vision and Stagecraft in Sophocles*. London.

Sealey, R. 1976. *A History of the Greek City States 700–338 B.C.* Berkeley.

Seeck, G. A., ed. 1979a. *Das griechische Drama*. Darmstadt.

Seeck, G. A. 1979b. Geschichte der griechischen Tragödie. In Seeck 1979a. 155–203.

Segal, C. 1962. Gorgias and the psychology of the logos. *HSCP* 66: 99–155.

Segal, C. 1981. *Tragedy and Civilization: An Interpretation of Sophocles*. Cambridge, Mass.

Segal, C. 1982. *Dionysiac Poetics and Euripides' Bacchae*. Princeton.

Segal, C. 1986. *Language and Desire in Seneca's Phaedra*. Princeton.

Segal, C. 1990. Violence and the other: Greek, female, and barbarian in Euripides' *Hecuba*. *TAPA* 120: 109–31.

Segal, C. 1992. Tragic beginnings: narration, voice, and authority in the prologues of Greek drama. In Dunn and Cole 1992. 85–112.

Segal, C. 1993. *Euripides and the Poetics of Sorrow: Art, Gender, and Commemoration in Alcestis, Hippolytus, and Hecuba*. Durham, NC.

Segal, C. 1994. Philomela's web and the pleasures of the text: reader and violence in the *Metamorphoses* of Ovid. In I. J. F. de Jong and J. P. Sullivan, eds., *Modern Critical Theory and Classical Literature*. Leiden. 257–80.

Segal, C. 1997. *Dionysiac Poetics and Euripides' Bacchae*. Princeton.

Segal, C. 2003. Introduction. In R. Gibbons and C. Segal, trans., *Sophocles: Antigone*. Oxford. 3–35.

Seidensticker, B. 1972. Beziehungen zwischen den beiden Oidipusdramen des Sophokles. *Hermes* 100: 255–74.

Seidensticker, B. 1979a. Sacrificial ritual in the *Bacchae*. In G. W. Bowersock, W. Burkert, and M. C. J. Putnam, eds., *Arktouros: Hellenic Studies Presented to Bernard M. W. Knox on the Occasion of his 65th Birthday*. Berlin. 181–90.

Seidensticker, B. 1979b. Das Satyrspiel. In Seeck 1979a. 204–57.

Seidensticker, B. 1982. *Palintonos Harmonia: Studien zu den komischen Elementen der griechischen Tragödie*. Göttingen.

Seidensticker, B. 1995. Women on the tragic stage. In Goff 1995a. 151–73.

Seidensticker, B. 1999. Philologisch-literarische Einleitung. In Krumeich, Pechstein, and Seidensticker 1999. 1–40.

Seidensticker, B. 2002. Myth and satyrplay. In López Férez 2002. 387–404.

Seidensticker, B. 2003. The chorus of Greek satyrplay. In E. Csapo and M. Miller, eds., *Poetry, Theory, Praxis*. Oxford. 100–21.

Sellars, P. 1996. Conversation with Michael Billington, 18.11.1994. In Delgado and Heritage 1996. 224–38.

Serlio, S. 1545. *Il secondo libro di prospettiva*. In F. Marotti, ed., *Storia documentaria del teatro italiano*. Milan: 1974. 190–205.

Shapiro, H. A. 1994. *Myth into Art: Poet and Painter in Classical Greece*. London.

Shaw, B. 1962. Acting, by one who does not believe in it (1889). In D. H. Lawrence, ed., *Platform and Pulpit*. London. 12–23.

Sifakis, G. M. 1979. Children in Greek tragedy. *BICS* 26: 67–80.

Sifakis, G. M. 2001. *Aristotle on the Function of Tragic Poetry*. Herakleion.

Silk, M. S., ed. 1996a. *Tragedy and the Tragic: Greek Theatre and Beyond*. Oxford.

Silk, M. S. 1996b. Tragic language: the Greek tragedians and Shakespeare. In Silk 1996a. 458–96.

Silk, M. S. 1998. "Das Urproblem der Tragödie": notions of the chorus in the nineteenth century. In P. Riemer and B. Zimmermann, eds., *Der Chor im antiken und modernen Drama*. Stuttgart. 195–226.

Silk, M. S. 2000. *Aristophanes and the Definition of Comedy*. Oxford.

Silk, M. S., and J. P. Stern. 1981. *Nietzsche on Tragedy*. Cambridge.

Simon, E. 1982. *The Ancient Theatre*. Trans. C. E. Vafopoulou-Richardson. London.

Sinclair, R. K. 1988. *Democracy and Participation in Athens*. Cambridge.

Slatkin, L. 1986. Oedipus at Colonus: exile and integration. In Euben 1986. 210–21.

Small, J. P. 2003. *The Parallel Worlds of Classical Art and Text*. Cambridge.

Smethurst, M. 2000. The Japanese presence in Ninagawa's *Medea*. In Hall, Macintosh, and Taplin 2000. 191–216.

Smith, B. H. 1968. *Poetic Closure: A Study of How Poems End*. Chicago.

Smyth, H. W., and H. Lloyd-Jones, eds. and trans. 1983. *Aeschylus*. Vol. 2: *Agamemnon, Libation-Bearers, Eumenides, Fragments*. Cambridge, Mass. LCL.

Snell, B. 1928. *Aischylos und das Handeln im Drama*. Leipzig.

Snell, B. 1953. *The Discovery of the Mind: The Greek Origins of European Thought*. Trans. T. G. Rosenmeyer. Cambridge, Mass.

Snell, B. 1971. *Tragicorum Graecorum Fragmenta*. Vol. 1: *Didascaliae Tragicae, Catalogi Tragicorum et Tragoediarum, Testimonia et Fragmenta Tragicorum Minorum*. Göttingen.

Snodgrass, A. 1980. *Archaic Greece: The Age of Experiment*. Berkeley.

Sokal, A. D., and J. Bricmont. 1999. *Intellectual Impostures: Postmodern Philosophers' Abuse of Science*. Second edition. London.

Solmsen, F. 1949. *Hesiod and Aeschylus*. Ithaca, NY.

Sommerstein, A. H., ed. 1989. *Aeschylus: Eumenides*. Cambridge.

Sommerstein, A. H. 1993. Kleophon and the restaging of the *Frogs*. In Sommerstein et al. 1993. 461–76.

Sommerstein, A. H. 1995. The language of Athenian women. In De Martino and Sommerstein 1995. Part 2, 61–85.

Sommerstein, A. H. 1996. *Aeschylean Tragedy.* Bari.

Sommerstein, A. H. 1997. The theatre audience, the *demos*, and the *Suppliants* of Aeschylus. In Pelling 1997c. 63–79.

Sommerstein, A. H., ed. 2003. *Shards from Kolonos: Studies in Sophoclean Fragments.* Bari.

Sommerstein, A. H., S. Halliwell, J. Henderson, and B. Zimmermann, eds. 1993. *Tragedy, Comedy and the Polis.* Bari.

Sontag, S. 1980. *Under the Sign of Saturn.* London.

Sorabji, R. 2000. *Emotion and Peace of Mind: From Stoic Agitation to Christian Temptation.* Oxford.

Sourvinou-Inwood, C. 1979. *Theseus as Son and Stepson: A Tentative Illustration of the Greek Mythological Mentality.* London.

Sourvinou-Inwood, C. 1989a. Assumptions and the creation of meaning: reading Sophocles' *Antigone. JHS* 109: 134–48.

Sourvinou-Inwood, C. 1989b. The fourth stasimon of Sophocles' *Antigone. BICS* 36: 141–65.

Sourvinou-Inwood, C. 1994. Something to do with Athens: tragedy and ritual. In Osborne and Hornblower 1994. 269–90.

Sourvinou-Inwood, C. 1995. *"Reading" Greek Death: To the End of the Classical Period.* Oxford.

Sourvinou-Inwood, C. 2003. *Tragedy and Athenian Religion.* Lanham, Md.

Stanford, W. B. 1942. *Aeschylus in his Style.* Dublin.

Stanford, W. B. 1983. *Greek Tragedy and the Emotions.* London.

States, B. O. 1994. *The Pleasure of the Play.* Ithaca, NY.

Stehle, E. 1997. *Performance and Gender in Ancient Greece: Nondramatic Poetry in its Setting.* Princeton.

Stehle, E. 2004. Choral prayer in Greek tragedy: euphemia or aischrologia? In Murray and Wilson 2004. 121–55.

Stehlíková, E. 2000. *Antigone* and its Czech audience. In Gödde and Heinze 2000. 403–8.

Stehlíková, E. 2001. Productions of Greek and Roman drama on the Czech stage. *Eirene* 37: 71–160.

Steidle, W. 1968. *Studien zum antiken Drama.* Munich.

Steiner, D. T. 1994. *The Tyrant's Writ: Myths and Images of Writing in Ancient Greece.* Princeton.

Steiner, G. 1961. *The Death of Tragedy.* New York.

Stephanis, I. 1988. ΔΙΟΝΥΣΙΑΚΟΙ ΤΕΧΝΙΤΑΙ. Herakleion.

Stevens, P. T. 1956. Euripides and the Athenians. *JHS* 76: 87–94.

Stevens, P. T. 1976. *Colloquial Expressions in Euripides.* Wiesbaden.

Stevens, W. 1989. *Opus Posthumous.* Ed. Milton J. Bates. New York.

Stewart, A. 1990. *Greek Sculpture.* New Haven.

Stinton, T. C. W. 1986. The scope and limits of allusion in Greek tragedy. In M. Cropp, E. Fantham, and S. E. Scully, eds., *Greek Tragedy and Its Legacy: Essays Presented to D. J. Conacher.* Calgary. 67–102.

Stoessl, F. 1956. Die Elektra des Euripides. *RhM* 99: 47–92.

Storey, I. C. 2002. Cutting comedies. In Barsby 2002. 146–67.

Strauss, B. 1993. *Fathers and Sons in Athens: Ideology and Society in the Era of the Peloponnesian War.* Princeton.

Stroux, J. 1925. *Nietzsches Professur in Basel.* Jena.

Sutton, D. F. 1973. Satyric elements in the *Alcestis. RSC* 21: 384–91.

Sutton, D. F. 1980. *The Greek Satyr Play.* Meisenheim am Glan.

Sutton, D. F. 1984. *The Lost Sophocles*. Lanham, Md.

Sutton, D. F. 1989. *Dithyrambographi Graeci*. Hildesheim.

Suzuki, T. 1986. *The Way of Acting: The Theatre Writings of Tadashi Suzuki*. Trans. J. T. Rimer. New York.

Szlezák, T. 1994. Sophokles oder die Freiheit eines Klassikers. In E. Pöhlmann and W. Gauer, eds., *Griechische Klassik*. Nuremberg. 65–92.

Szondi, P. 1987. *Theory of the Modern Drama*. Ed. and trans. M. Hays. Cambridge.

Szondi, P. 2002. *An Essay on the Tragic*. Trans. P. Flemming. Stanford.

Tannen, D. 1994. *Gender and Discourse*. New York.

Taplin, O. 1971. Significant actions in Sophocles' *Philoctetes*. *GRBS* 12: 25–44.

Taplin, O. 1972. Aeschylean silences and silences in Aeschylus. *HSCP* 76: 57–97.

Taplin, O. 1977. *The Stagecraft of Aeschylus: The Dramatic Use of Exits and Entrances in Greek Tragedy*. Oxford.

Taplin, O. 1978. *Greek Tragedy in Action*. London.

Taplin, O. 1983a. Sophocles in his theatre. In J. de Romilly, ed., *Sophocle, Sept exposés suivis de discussions. Entretiens Hardt* 29. Geneva. 155–83.

Taplin, O. 1983b. Tragedy and trugedy. *CQ* 33: 331–33.

Taplin, O. 1986. Fifth-century tragedy and comedy: a *synkrisis*. *JHS* 106: 163–74.

Taplin, O. 1993. *Comic Angels: And Other Approaches to Greek Drama through Vase-Painting*. Oxford.

Taplin, O. 1996. Comedy and the tragic. In Silk 1996a. 188–202.

Taplin, O. 1999a. Greek with consequence: the rebirth of ancient tragedy. In Mavromoustakos 1999. 37–42.

Taplin, O. 1999b. Spreading the word through performance. In Goldhill and Osborne 1999. 33–57.

Taplin, O. 2002. An academic in the rehearsal room. In Barsby 2002. 7–22.

Taplin, O., and P. Wilson. 1993. The "aetiology" of tragedy in the *Oresteia*. *PCPS* 39: 169–80.

Tarrant, R. J. 1978. Senecan drama and its antecedents. *HSCP* 82: 213–63.

Tarrant, R. J. 1995. Greek and Roman in Seneca's tragedies. *HSCP* 97: 215–30.

Terpening, R. H. 1997. *Lodovico Dolce: Renaissance Man of Letters*. Toronto.

Thalmann, W. G. 1978. *Dramatic Art in Aeschylus's Seven against Thebes*. New Haven.

Thalmann, W. G. 1985. Speech and silence in the *Oresteia* 2. *Phoenix* 39: 220–37.

Thomson, P., and G. Sacks, eds. 1994. *The Cambridge Companion to Brecht*. Cambridge.

Trendall, A. D., and T. B. L. Webster. 1971. *Illustrations of Greek Drama*. London.

Trilling, L. 1967. *The Experience of Literature*. Garden City, NY.

Turner, E. G. 1987. *Greek Manuscripts of the Ancient World*. Second edition. Ed. P. J. Parsons. London.

Unz, R. K. 1986. Chronology of the Pentekontaetia. *CQ* 36: 68–85.

van Erp Taalman Kip, A. M. 1987. Euripides and Melos. *Mnemosyne* 40: 414–19.

Vasari, G. 1568. *Le vite de' più eccellenti pittori, scultori ed architettori scritte da Giorgio Vasari pittore aretino*. Vol. 6. Ed. G. Milanesi. Florence: 1906.

Vernant, J.-P. 1972a. Ambiguïté et renversement: sur la structure énigmatique d'*Œdipe-Roi*. In Vernant and Vidal-Naquet 1972. 99–131.

Vernant, J.-P. 1972b. Ebauches de la volonté dans la tragédie grecque. In Vernant and Vidal-Naquet 1972. 41–74.

Vernant, J.-P. 1980. *Myth and Society in Ancient Greece*. Trans. J. Lloyd. Brighton.

Vernant, J.-P. 1982. *The Origins of Greek Thought*. Ithaca, NY.

Vernant, J.-P. 1983. *Myth and Thought among the Greeks*. London.

Vernant, J.-P. 1988a. The historical moment of tragedy in Greece: some of the social and psychological conditions. In Vernant and Vidal-Naquet 1988. 23–28.

Vernant, J.-P. 1988b. Tensions and ambiguities in Greek tragedy. In Vernant and Vidal-Naquet 1988. 29–48.

Vernant, J.-P., and P. Vidal-Naquet. 1972. *Mythe et tragédie en Grèce ancienne*. Paris.

Vernant, J.-P., and P. Vidal-Naquet. 1986. *Mythe et tragédie en Grèce ancienne Deux*. Paris.

Vernant, J.-P., and P. Vidal-Naquet. 1988. *Myth and Tragedy in Ancient Greece*. Trans. J. Lloyd. New York. Translation of Vernant and Vidal-Naquet 1972 and 1986.

Versnel, H. S. 1990–93. *Inconsistencies in Greek and Roman Religion*. 2 vols. Leiden.

Vidal-Naquet, P. 1972a. Chasse et sacrifice dans l'*Orestie* d'Eschyle. In Vernant and Vidal-Naquet 1972. 133–58.

Vidal-Naquet, P. 1972b. Le *Philoctète* de Sophocle et l'éphébie. In Vernant and Vidal-Naquet 1972. 159–84.

Vidal-Naquet, P. 1986a. *The Black Hunter: Forms of Thought and Forms of Society in the Greek World*. Trans. A. Szegedy-Maszak. Baltimore.

Vidal-Naquet, P. 1986b. The black hunter revisited. *PCPS* 32: 126–44.

Vidal-Naquet, P. 1988. Sophocles' *Philoctetes* and the ephebeia. In Vernant and Vidal-Naquet 1988. 161–79.

Vidal-Naquet, P. 1997. The place and status of foreigners in Athenian tragedy. In Pelling 1997c. 109–19.

Vlastos, G. 1995. Theology and philosophy in early Greek thought. In D. W. Graham, ed., *Studies in Greek Philosophy I: The Presocratics*. Princeton. 3–31.

Vogel, M. 1966. *Apollinisch und Dionysisch. Geschichte eines genialen Irrtums*. Regensburg.

Vogt, E. 1962. Nietzsche und der Wettkampf Homers. *A&A* 11: 103–13.

von Reden, S., and S. Goldhill. 1999. Plato and the performance of dialogue. In Goldhill and Osborne 1999. 257–89.

Walker, H. J. 1995. *Theseus and Athens*. New York.

Wallace, R. 2004. Damon of Oa: a music theorist ostracized? In Murray and Wilson 2004. 249–67.

Wallinga, H. T. 1987. The ancient Persian navy and its predecessors. In H. Sancisi-Weerdenberg, ed., *Achaemenid History I: Sources, Structures, and Synthesis*. Leiden. 47–77.

Wallinga, H. T. 1993. *Ships and Sea-Power before the Great Persian War: The Ancestry of the Ancient Trireme*. Leiden.

Walsh, G. B. 1984. *The Varieties of Enchantment: Early Greek Views of the Nature and Function of Poetry*. Chapel Hill, NC.

Walton, J. M. 1980. *Greek Theatre Practice*. Westport, Conn.

Walton, J. M. 1984. *The Greek Sense of Theatre: Tragedy Reviewed*. London.

Walton, J. M. 1987. *Living Greek Theatre: A Handbook of Classical Performance and Modern Production*. New York.

Waterfield, R. A. H. 1982. Double standards in Euripides' *Troades*. *Maia* 34: 139–42.

Wattles, J. 1996. *The Golden Rule*. Oxford.

Webster, T. B. L. 1954. Fourth-century tragedy and the *Poetics*. *Hermes* 82: 294–308.

Webster, T. B. L. 1967. *The Tragedies of Euripides*. London.

Webster, T. B. L. 1970a. *Greek Theatre Production*. Second edition. London.

Webster, T. B. L., ed. 1970b. *Sophocles: Philoctetes*. Cambridge.

Welcker, F. G. 1826. *Nachtrag zu der Schrift ueber die Aeschylische Trilogie nebst einer Abhandlung ueber das Satyrspiel*. Frankfurt am Main.

Wessels, A. 2003. *Ursprungszauber: Zur Rezeption von Hermann Useners Lehre von der religiösen Begriffsbildung*. Berlin.

Wessner, P., ed. 1902–5. *Aeli Donati quod fertur "Commentum Terenti."* 2 vols. Leipzig.

West, M. L. 1973. *Textual Criticism and Editorial Technique*. Stuttgart.

West, M. L. 1974. *Studies in Greek Elegy and Iambus*. Berlin.

West, M. L. 1979. The Prometheus trilogy. *JHS* 99: 130–48.

West, M. L. 1982. *Greek Metre*. Oxford.

West, M. L. 1985. Ion of Chios. *BICS* 32: 71–78.

West, M. L., ed. and trans. 1987. *Euripides: Orestes*. Warminster.

West, M. L. 1989. The early chronology of Attic tragedy. *CQ* 39: 251–54.

West, M. L., ed. 1990a. *Aeschyli Tragodiae cum incerti poetae Prometheo*. Stuttgart.

West, M. L. 1990b. *Studies in Aeschylus*. Stuttgart.

West, M. L. 1992. *Ancient Greek Music*. Oxford.

West, M. L. 1997. *The East Face of Helicon: West Asiatic Elements in Greek Poetry and Myth*. Oxford.

West, M. L. 2000. *Iliad* and *Aethiopis* on the stage: Aeschylus and son. *CQ* 50: 338–52.

West, M. L., ed. and trans. 2003. *Greek Epic Fragments from the Seventh to the Fifth Centuries BC*. Cambridge, Mass. LCL.

Wetmore, K. J., Jr. 2002. *The Athenian Sun in an African Sky: Modern African Adaptations of Classical Greek Tragedy*. Jefferson, NC.

White, S. A. 1992. Aristotle's favorite tragedies. In A. O. Rorty, ed., *Essays on Aristotle's Poetics*. Princeton. 221–40.

Whitehead, D. 1983. Competitive outlay and community profit: φιλοτιμία in democratic Athens. *CM* 34: 55–74.

Whitman, C. H. 1951. *Sophocles: A Study of Heroic Humanism*. Cambridge, Mass.

Whitman, C. H. 1974. *Euripides and the Full Circle of Myth*. Cambridge, Mass.

Wickham, G., H. Berry, and W. Ingram, eds. 2000. *English Professional Theatre, 1530–1660*. Cambridge.

Wilamowitz-Moellendorff, T. von. 1996. *Die dramatische Technik des Sophokles* (1917). Ed. E. Knapp. Fourth edition. Hildeshiem.

Wilamowitz-Moellendorff, U. von. 1872. *Zukunftsphilologie! Eine Erwidrung auf Friedrich Nietzsches, ord. Professors der classischen Philologie zu Basel, "Geburt der Tragödie."* Berlin. Repr. in Gründer 1969. 27–55. English trans. G. Postl in *NNS* 4 (2000): 1–32.

Wilamowitz-Moellendorff, U. von. 1873. *Zukunftsphilologie! Zweites Stück. Eine Erwidrung auf die Rettungsversuche für Fr. Nietzsches "Geburt der Tragödie."* Berlin. Repr. in Gründer 1969. 113–35.

Wilamowitz-Moellendorff, U. von. 1928. *Erinnerungen 1848–1914*. Leipzig.

Wilamowitz-Moellendorff, U. von. 1959. *Euripides: Herakles*. 3 vols. Darmstadt.

Wildberg, C. 2002. *Hyperesie und Epiphanie: Ein Versuch über die Bedeutung der Götter in den Dramen des Euripides*. Munich.

Wiles, D. 1997. *Tragedy in Athens: Performance Space and Theatrical Meaning*. Cambridge.

Wiles, D. 2000. *An Introduction to Greek Theatre*. Cambridge.

Wiles, D. 2004. The use of masks in modern performances of Greek drama. In Hall, Macintosh, and Wrigley 2004. 245–63.

Wiles, T. J. 1980. *The Theater Event: Modern Theories of Performance*. Chicago.

Willet, J. 1977. *The Theatre of Bertolt Brecht: A Study from Eight Aspects*. London.

Willi, A. 2002. Aischylos als Kriegsprofiteur: Zum Sieg des Aischylos in den "Fröschen" des Aristophanes. *Hermes* 130: 13–27.

Williams, B. 1993. *Shame and Necessity*. Berkeley.

Williams, B. 2002. *Truth and Truthfulness: An Essay in Genealogy*. Princeton.

Williams, D. 1999. Greek drama in Taiwan: persistent and prophetic paradigms. In Patsalidis and Sakellaridou 1999. 210–20.

Williams, R. 1979. *Modern Tragedy*. London.

Williams, W. C. 1985. *Selected Poems*. New York.

Willink, C. W., ed. 1986. *Euripides: Orestes*. Oxford.

Wilson, J. B. 1979. *Pylos 425 B.C.: Historical and Topographical Study of Thucydides' Account of the Campaign*. Warminster.

Wilson, M. 1983. The tragic mode of Seneca's *Troades*. In A. J. Boyle, ed., *Seneca Tragicus: Ramus Essays on Senecan Drama*. Victoria. 27–60.

Wilson, N. G. 1983. *Scholars of Byzantium*. Baltimore.

Wilson, N. G. 1992. *From Byzantium to Italy: Greek Studies in the Italian Renaissance.* Baltimore.

Wilson, P. J. 1991. Demosthenes 21 (*Against Meidias*): democratic abuse. *PCPS* 37: 164–95.

Wilson, P. J. 1996. Tragic rhetoric: the use of tragedy and the tragic in the fourth century. In Silk 1996a. 310–31.

Wilson, P. J. 1997. Leading the tragic *khoros*: tragic prestige in the democratic city. In Pelling 1997c. 81–108.

Wilson, P. J. 1999. The *aulos* in Athens. In Goldhill and Osborne 1999. 58–95.

Wilson, P. J. 1999–2000. Euripides' tragic muse. In Cropp, Lee, and Sansone 1999–2000. 427–49.

Wilson, P. J. 2000a. *The Athenian Institution of the Khoregia: The Chorus, the City and the Stage*. Cambridge.

Wilson, P. J. 2000b. Powers of horror and laughter: the great age of drama. In O. Taplin, ed., *Literature in the Greek World*. Oxford. 70–114.

Wilson, P. J. 2002. The musicians among the actors. In Easterling and Hall 2002. 39–68.

Wilson, P. J., and O. Taplin. 1993. The "aetiology" of tragedy in the *Oresteia*. *PCPS* 39: 169–80.

Winkler, J. J., and F. I. Zeitlin, eds. 1990. *Nothing to do with Dionysos? Athenian Drama in its Social Context*. Princeton.

Winnington-Ingram, R. P. 1961. The Danaid trilogy of Aeschylus. *JHS* 81: 141–52. Rev. repr. as "The Danaid trilogy," in Winnington-Ingram 1983. 55–72.

Winnington-Ingram, R. P. 1968. *Mode in Ancient Greek Music*. Cambridge.

Winnington-Ingram, R. P. 1969. Euripides: *poiētēs sophos*. *Arethusa* 2: 127–42. Repr. in Mossman 2003. 47–63.

Winnington-Ingram, R. P. 1977. *Septem contra Thebas*. *YCS* 25: 1–45. Rev. repr. in Winnington-Ingram 1983. 16–54.

Winnington-Ingram, R. P. 1980. *Sophocles: An Interpretation*. Cambridge.

Winnington-Ingram, R. P. 1983. *Studies in Aeschylus*. Cambridge.

Winnington-Ingram, R. P. 1997. *Euripides and Dionysus: An Interpretation of the Bacchae*. Second edition. Bristol.

Wohl, V. 1998. *Intimate Commerce: Exchange, Gender, and Subjectivity in Greek Tragedy.* Austin, Tex.

Wolff, C. 1968. *Orestes*. In E. Segal, ed., *Euripides: A Collection of Critical Essays*. Englewood Cliffs, NJ. 132–49.

Wolford, L., and R. Schechner, eds. 1997. *The Grotowski Sourcebook*. London.

Woodford, S. 2003. *Images of Myths in Classical Antiquity.* Cambridge.

Woodruff, P., trans. 1998. *Euripides: Bacchae*. Indianapolis.

Woodruff, P., trans. 2001. *Sophocles: Antigone*. Indianapolis.

Worthen, W. B. 1984. *The Idea of the Actor: Drama and the Ethics of Performance*. Princeton.

Wright, D. H. 1993. *The Vatican Vergil: A Masterpiece of Late Antique Art*. Berkeley.

Xanthakis-Karamanos, G. 1980. *Studies in Fourth-Century Tragedy.* Athens.

Xanthakis-Karamanos, G. 1993. Hellenistic drama: developments in form and performance. *Platon* 45: 117–33.

Yunis, H. 1988. *A New Creed: Fundamental Religious Beliefs in the Athenian Polis and Euripidean Drama*. Göttingen.

Yunis, H. 1996. *Taming Democracy: Models of Political Rhetoric in Classical Athens*. Ithaca, NY.

Zeitlin, F. I. 1965. The motif of the corrupted sacrifice in Aeschylus' *Oresteia*. *TAPA* 96: 463–508.

Zeitlin, F. I. 1970. The Argive festival of Hera and Euripides' *Electra*. *TAPA* 101: 645–69. Repr. in Mossman 2003. 261–84.

Zeitlin, F. I. 1980. The closet of masks: role-playing and myth-making in the *Orestes* of Euripides. *Ramus* 9: 51–77. Repr. in Mossman 2003. 309–41.

Zeitlin, F. I. 1982. *Under the Sign of the Shield: Semiotics and Aeschylus' Seven against Thebes.* Rome.

Zeitlin, F. I. 1985. The power of Aphrodite: Eros and the boundaries of the self in Euripides' *Hippolytus*. In Burian 1985. 52–111, 189–208. Repr. in Zeitlin 1996. 219–84.

Zeitlin, F. I. 1990a. Playing the other: theater, theatricality, and the feminine in Greek drama. In Winkler and Zeitlin 1990. 63–96.

Zeitlin, F. I. 1990b. Thebes: theater of self and society in Athenian drama. In Winkler and Zeitlin 1990. 130–67.

Zeitlin, F. I. 1996. *Playing the Other: Gender and Society in Classical Greek Literature*. Chicago.

Zeitlin, F. I. 2004. Dionysus in 69. In Hall, Macintosh, and Wrigley 2004. 49–75.

Zimmermann, B. 1989. Gattungsmischung, Manierismus, Archaismus: Tendenzen des griechischen Dramas und Dithyrambos am Ende des 5. Jahrhunderts v. Chr. *Lexis* 3: 25–36.

Zimmermann, B. 1992. *Dithyrambos. Geschichte einer Gattung*. Göttingen.

Zuntz, G. 1955. *The Political Plays of Euripides*. Manchester.

Zuntz, G. 1965. *An Inquiry into the Transmission of the Plays of Euripides*. Cambridge.

Index

on number of actors, 203
on *opsis*, 184, 326
on origins of tragedy, 23–26, 34–36,
   159–60
on pity and fear, 305, 402, 404
on "political" and "rhetorical" characters,
   290
on primacy of plots, 109, 184, 402
on probability and necessity, 42–43
and production records, 381
on psychology and rhetoric, 100
on the ridiculous, 43
schematization in, 24–26, 72
Aristoxenus, 184
Arrowsmith, W., 500–502
art, relationship to tragic texts, 103–17, 195,
   197, 272, 289
Artaud, A., 468–69
askólia, etymology of, 31
ate, 315, 325
Athens
   and appropriation of myth, 123–24, 330
   and autochthony, 370–71
   as center, 61, 73
   as city of words, 59, 83–84, 175
   and conflicting ideologies, 336
   cult of Athena Polias, 300
   and Delian League, 7, 11
   and democracy, 9–12, 21
   Egyptian expedition, 10, 217
   and empire, 7–12
   and First Peloponnesian War, 9–11
   and insider/outsider antithesis, 366
   long walls of, 10, 18
   and naval power, 5–8
   and oligarchic revolution, 17, 19
   and Peloponnesian War, 3, 11–17 passim
   political and legal institutions, 64, 307–8
   and political factions, 19–20
   as portrayed in tragedy, 4, 21, 73, 129,
      278, 282
   and treatment of conquered, 13, 15–16
   see also democracy: Athenian
audience, 208–9, 348–50
   as collective, 64
   composition of, 62–64
   construction of meaning by, 293–94,
      296–303
   detachment of, 407
   emotional responses of, 43, 60, 396, 398,
      406, 461–62

expectations of, 55, 143–44
identification with protagonists, 42, 347
superior knowledge of, 94–95, 246–47,
   328–29, 347–48
suspicion of rhetoric, 84
Augustine, 394
aulos, 38, 150–51, 185, 190, 197
Aulus Gellius, 460
Aurispa, G., 428
authorial intention, 493
authority
   resistance to, 342, 348–50, 479, 486
   structures of, 333–50

Bacchylides, 27, 39, 49, 122, 234
Barton, J., 475
bastard(s), 368–71
beginnings of plays, 136–42, 151, 169, 330
Boal, A., 463
Bowie, A. M., 15–16
Brasidas, 15
Brecht, B., 348, 460–63
Burbage, R., 463, 467
Burckhardt, J., 445
Burnett, A. P., 307–8
Byzantine triad, 255, 387

Calame, C., 374
Callimachus, 383
Carcinus, 210
Carthage, 418
causation, 344–45
center/margin antithesis, 61, 366–75
Chaeremon, 288–90
Choerilus, 272–73
chorégos, 62, 196
choreography, 46, 205
chorus, 150, 154–56, 188
   authority of, 155, 165, 347
   codas of, 146–47
   as collective, 155, 188
   gender, 155, 349
   in modern productions, 483, 485
   movements, 171, 183, 207–8
   prominence, 183–84, 219
   relationship with characters, 157–58, 240,
      356
   of satyr-play, 45–46
   self-referentiality, 149–50, 165, 267,
      297–98
   status, 154–56, 495

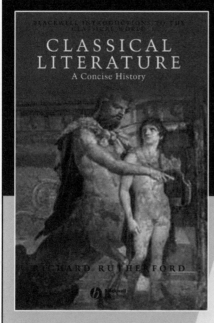